American Reference Books Annual

Volume 50

2019 Edition

American Reference Books Annual
Advisory Board

2019
EDITION

AMERICAN REFERENCE BOOKS ANNUAL

Volume 50

Juneal M. Chenoweth, Associate Editor

LIBRARIES UNLIMITED™

An Imprint of ABC-CLIO, LLC

Santa Barbara, California • Denver, Colorado

LIBRARIES UNLIMITED
An Imprint of ABC-CLIO, LLC
147 Castilian Drive
P.O. Box 1911
Santa Barbara, California 93116-1911
www.abc-clio.com

Library of Congress Cataloging-in-Publication Data
American reference books annual, 1970-
Santa Barbara, CA, Libraries Unlimited.
v. 19x26 cm.
Indexes:
1970-74. 1v.
1975-79. 1v.
1980-84. 1v.
1985-89. 1v.
1990-94. 1v.
1995-99. 1v.
2000-04. 1v.
2005-09. 1v.
2010-14. 1v.
I. Reference books--Bibliography--Periodicals.
Z1035.1.A55 011'.02
ISBN 978-1-4408-6913-6 (2019 edition)
ISSN 0065-9959

Contents

Preface

Here is the interesting and challenging landscape for reference resources today. On the one hand, we clearly see the reference book diminished in the work of students, and the priorities of libraries. Going or gone are the vast collections of bound volumes in designated reference reading rooms. The disruptive element of course is technology: instantaneous access to online information. And reference seems to be the loser.

On the other hand, technology makes reference activity a winner too, but so seamlessly that the connection to old-fashioned reference work can be overlooked. All of us enjoy and use online tools to find airline ticket prices and flight schedules, weather forecasts and current conditions, currency exchange rates, stock prices, hotel and restaurant reviews, street maps, and foreign language translators. In the past we turned to print tools to meet these needs, with less convenience and less currency. Thanks to technology, we now have alternatives that match, and often surpass, yesterday's print reference works: timetables, weather almanacs, financial reports, tourist guidebooks, atlases, and bilingual dictionaries. So if reference is alive and well, but living under another name, where is the crisis? Which is to say, where is the change taking place?

Scholars have defined reference works in administrative, descriptive, and functional terms. The administration definition was something like this: "a reference book is a book located in a non-circulating reference collection." Today, we no longer focus on printed books (though we may work with their e-book descendants), and resource access is no longer confined to a specific place. The descriptive definition has been more durable: a reference work incorporates elements of organization and presentation that reflect and promote its intended use ... consultation as quickly and easily as possible. Hence subject indexes, alphabetical order for entries, or numerical coding, as well as newer features like cross-reference hot links. The functional definition perhaps has held up the best: while many sources can conceivably be used to answer a "reference question," a reference work is created for that purpose, and its form (those elements in the descriptive definition) follows that function. As long as readers seek information, that function has value.

Nor have the characteristics of "good" reference tools changed: when we want information, we want information that is accurate, objective, authoritative, current, and complete, as well as reliably accessible, clearly presented, and easily understood. Online reference sources meet these requirements just as thoroughly as do print-format classics like the *OED*, the *World Book*, the *National Geographic World Atlas*, or the *Statistical Abstract of the United States* (all of which have expanded to online versions).

One final element makes modern life tough for reference: the general discounting of authority. Reference tools rely on the notion that important information is stable and therefore can be discovered, described, and evaluated. Behind the pursuit of "facts" to answer a reference query is an assumption that "facts" exist, that one answer is true and "best," that the "right" answer is available to us, and that reasonable people will agree about the "correct" answer when they see it. We may expect to argue about the best 10 American novels, but we expect to agree about the melting temperature of copper. In a world of relativism, conspiracy theories and Heisenberg's uncertainty principle, not only are authorities in doubt, but even the facts themselves. And without the concept of correct facts, reference has no leg to stand on.

It is encouraging to see this aphorism widely quoted: "Everyone is entitled to his own opinion, but not to his own facts." When most of us can agree about facts, reference can thrive. Incidentally, this quotation itself illustrates the reference value of truth-seeking and fact-checking. Generally attributed to Daniel Patrick Moynihan, the *Dictionary of Modern Proverbs* (Yale, 2012) also documents similar statements extending back to Bernard Baruch in 1946.

If there are four participants in the ecology of reference–readers, authors, publishers, and librarians–then perhaps it is fair to say that two are leading and two are catching up. Readers still have plenty of questions to answer, and authors still eagerly turn out resources to meet that need. The challenges seem greatest for publishers and librarians, as value-added contributions shift from presentation in print to presentation in online form.

–**Steven Sowards**

Introduction

We are pleased to provide you with volume 50 of *American Reference Books Annual* (ARBA), a far-reaching review service for reference books and electronic resources. As Steven Sowards points out in the preface, the reference landscape has changed considerably since the publication of ARBA's first volume in 1970. Reference users no longer need to spend hours in a library consulting bound volumes, microfiche, or microfilm when much sought-after information is available online. As the preface also highlights, this easy accessibility does not eliminate the need for well-curated, professionally produced reference material and the guidance of trained librarians.

ARBA strives to provide comprehensive coverage of English-language reference resources, both digital and print, published in the United States and Canada during a single year. We review both subscription-based and free websites, as well as dictionaries, encyclopedias, indexes, directories, bibliographies, guides, concordances, atlases, gazetteers, and other types of ready-reference tools. Generally, encyclopedias that are updated annually, yearbooks, almanacs, indexing and abstracting services, and other annuals or serials are reviewed at editorially determined intervals. Reviews of updated publications attempt to point out changes in scope or editorial policy and comparisons to older editions.

Certain categories of reference sources are usually not reviewed in ARBA: foreign-language titles, books of fewer than 48 pages that are not part of a larger set, those produced by vanity presses or by the author as publisher, and those generated by library staff for internal use. Highly specialized reference works printed in a limited number of copies and that do not appeal to the general library audience ARBA serves may also be omitted.

For nearly two decades, ARBA has also been a go-to source for reviews of new literature written specifically for the library professional; this year's ARBA features approximately 90 reviews of professional development titles. These include monographs and handbooks that address the concerns of library and information specialists and can be found in chapter 11, titled "Library and Information Science and Publishing and Bookselling."

In 2002, Libraries Unlimited launched ARBAonline, an authoritative database designed to provide access to all reviews published in the print version of ARBA since 1997. The editorial staff updates ARBAonline monthly, giving librarians evaluations of the most up-to-date materials along with depth of coverage as they make purchasing decisions.

Reviewing Policy

To ensure well-written, balanced reviews of high quality, the ARBA staff maintains a roster of more than 400 scholars, practitioners, and library educators in all subject specialties at libraries and universities throughout the United States and Canada. Because ARBA seeks to be a comprehensive reviewing source, the reviews are generally longer and more critical than other review publications to detail the strengths and weaknesses of important reference works. Reviewers are asked to examine books and electronic resources and provide well-documented critical comments, both positive and negative. Coverage usually includes the usefulness of a given work; organization, execution, and pertinence of contents; prose style; format; availability of supplementary materials (e.g., indexes, appendixes); and similarity to other works and previous editions. Reviewers are encouraged to address the intended audience but not necessarily to give specific recommendations for purchase.

Arrangement

This year's ARBA consists of 37 chapters, an author/title index, and a subject index. It is divided into four alphabetically arranged parts: "General Reference Works," "Social Sciences," "Humanities," and "Science and Technology." "General Reference Works" is subdivided by form: almanacs, bibliography, biography, and so on. Within the remaining three parts, chapters are organized by topic. Thus, under "Social Sciences" the reader will find chapters titled "Economics and Business," "Education," "History," "Law," "Sociology," and so on.

Each chapter is subdivided to reflect the arrangement strategy of the entire volume. There is a section on general works followed by a topical breakdown. For example, in the chapter titled "Literature," "General Works" is followed by "National Literature." Subsections are based on the amount of material available on a given topic and vary from year to year.

Users should keep in mind that many materials may fall under several different chapter topics. The comprehensive author/title and subject indexes found at the end of the volume will assist users in finding specific works that could fall under several different chapters. Additionally, readers seeking out reviews of digital resources can find these quickly using the Website and Database Review Locator (p. xxiii).

Acknowledgments

In closing, we wish to express our gratitude to the many talented contributors without whose support this volume of ARBA could not have been compiled. Many thanks also go out to our distinguished Advisory Board members whose contributions greatly enhance ARBA and ARBAonline. We would also like to thank the members of our staff who were instrumental in its preparation.

Contributors

Heather Freas Adair, Research & Instruction Librarian, Assistant Professor, Sam Houston State University, Newton Gresham Library, Huntsville, Tex.

Anthony J. Adam, Senior Training Consultant, Strategic Planning Online, Brenham, Tex.

January Adams, Asst. Director/Head of Adult Services, Franklin Township Public Library, Somerset, N.J.

Maria Agee, Indiana University Bloomington, Hays, Kans.

James W. Agee, Independent Scholar, Hays, Kans.

Karen Alexander, Library Media Specialist, Lake Fenton High School, Linden, Mich.

Delilah R. Alexander, Online Services Librarian and Adjunct Instructor, Southwestern College, Winfield, Kans.

Donald Altschiller, Librarian, Mugar Memorial Library, Boston University.

Adrienne Antink, Medical Group Management Association, Lakewood, Colo.

Thomas E. Baker, Assoc. Professor, Department of Criminal Justice, University of Scranton, Pa.

Laurie Balderson, LA/History Teacher, St. Mark Catholic School, Wilmington, N.C.

Stephanie Bange, Director, Educational Resource Center, Wright State University, Dayton, Ohio.

Joshua Barton, Head of Cataloging and Metadata Services, Assistant Head of Technical Services, Michigan State University Libraries, East Lansing.

Augie E. Beasley, Retired Media Specialist, Charlotte, N.C.

Joshua Becker, Information Literacy and Assessment Librarian, Assistant Professor, Southern New Hampshire University.

Lucas P. Berrini, Holds, Recalls, and Missing Items Manager, Joyner Library, East Carolina University, Greenville, N.C.

Barbara M. Bibel, Reference Librarian, Science/Business/Sociology Dept., Main Library, Oakland Public Library, Calif.

Peg Billing, District Librarian, Tomahawk School District, Wis.

Daniel K. Blewett, Reference Librarian, College of DuPage Library, Glen Ellyn, Ill.

Michelle Bridges, Media Specialist, Sugar Creek Elementary School, Fort Mill, S.C.

Alicia Brillon, Head of Technical Services and Acquisitions, James E. Faust Law Library, University of Utah.

Georgia Briscoe, Assoc. Director and Head of Technical Services, Law Library, University of Colorado, Boulder.

John R. Burch Jr., Library Director, University of Tennessee at Martin.

Joanna M. Burkhardt, Head Librarian, College of Continuing Education Library, University of Rhode Island, Providence.

Diane M. Calabrese, Freelance Writer and Contributor, Silver Springs, Md.

Bert Chapman, Government Publications Coordinator, Purdue University, West Lafayette, Ind.

Boyd Childress, Reference Librarian, Ralph B. Draughon Library, Auburn University, Ala.

Brian Clark, Professor & Librarian, Western Illinois University, Macomb.

Kristin Elizabeth Cole, Assistant Professor/Assessment and Special Projects Librarian, Otterbein University, Westerville, Ohio.

Rosanne M. Cordell, (formerly) Head of Reference Services, Franklin D. Schurz Library, Indiana University, South Bend.

Gregory Curtis, Regional Federal Depository Librarian for Maine, New Hampshire, and Vermont, Fogler Library, University of Maine, Presque Isle.

Cathy DeCampli, Emerging Technology Librarian, Haddonfield Public Library, Haddonfield, N.J.

Scott R. DiMarco, Director of Library Services and Information Resources, Mansfield University, Mansfield, Pa.

Lucy Duhon, Scholarly Communications Librarian, University of Toledo, Ohio.

Joe P. Dunn, Charles A. Dana Professor of History and Politics, Converse College, Spartanburg, S.C.

Bradford Lee Eden, Dean of Library Services, Valparaiso University, Valparaiso, Ind.

Sheri Edwards, Assistant University Librarian, Florida Atlantic University, Boca Raton.

Susan Elkins, Digital Resources Librarian, Sam Houston State University, Newton Gresham Library, Huntsville, Tex.

Autumn Faulkner, Asst Head of Cataloging and Metadata Services, Michigan State University Libraries, East Lansing.

Josh Eugene Finnell, Reference Librarian, Ohio.

Brian T. Gallagher, Access Services Librarian, Head of Access Services, University of Rhode Island, Kingston.

Zev Garber, Professor and Chair, Jewish Studies, Los Angeles Valley College, Calif.

Denise A. Garofalo, Systems and Catalog Services Librarian, Curtin Memorial Library, Mount Saint Mary College, Newburgh, N.Y.

Kasey Garrison, Lecturer & Children's Specialization Coordinator, Charles Sturt University, Sydney, NSW, Australia.

John T. Gillespie, College Professor and Writer, New York, N.Y.

Caroline L. Gilson, Coordinator, Prevo Science Library, DePauw University, Greencastle, Ind.

Michelle Glatt, Librarian, Chiddix and Evans Junior High Schools, Bloomington-Normal, Ill.

Cynthia Goode, Lone Star College System, Houston, Tex.

Anitra Gordon, Educational Reviewer, Ann Arbor, Mich.

Carin Graves, Social Science Librarian, Michigan State University Libraries, East Lansing.

Linda W. Hacker, Reference Librarian, SUNY Brockport, Brockport, N.Y.

Muhammed Hassanali, Independent Consultant, Shaker Heights, Ohio.

Alexandra Hauser, Business Librarian, Michigan State University Libraries, East Lansing.

Lucy Heckman, Reference Librarian (Business-Economics), St. John's University Library, Jamaica, N.Y.

Mark Y. Herring, Dean of Library Services, Winthrop University, Dacus Library, Rock Hill, S.C.

Ladyjane Hickey, Reference Librarian, Austin College, Tex.

Anne L. Hoffman, Library Media Specialist, Regis Catholic Schools, Eau Claire, Wis.

Shanna Hollich, Collections Management Librarian, Wilson College, Chambersburg, Pa.

Michelle Hudiburg, School Library Science and Ed Tech Instructor, Pittsburg State University, Pittsburg, Kans.

Jennifer Brooks Huffman, Serials/ILL Librarian, University of Wisconsin-Stevens Point.

Jonathan F. Husband, Program Chair of the Library/Reader Services Librarian, Henry Whittemore Library, Framingham State College, Mass.

Amanda Izenstark, Asst. Professor, Reference and Instructional Design Librarian, University of Rhode Island, Kingston.

Valerie Jankowski, Library Media Specialist, Washington Middle School, Washington, Mo.

Jeffrey A. Jensen, Lead Librarian, Independence University, Salt Lake City, Utah.

Kyla M. Johnson, NBCT Librarian, Farmington High School, N. Mex.

Melissa M. Johnson, Reference Services, NOVA Southeastern University, Alvin Sherman Library, Ft. Lauderdale, Fla.

MaryAnn Karre, Retired Librarian, Vestal, N.Y.

Craig Mury Keeney, Cataloging Librarian, South Caroliniana Library, University of South Carolina, Columbia.

Andrea C Kepsel, Health Sciences Educational Technology Librarian, Michigan State University Libraries, East Lansing.

Dianna L. Kim, Assistant Professor/Research and Instruction Librarian, Sam Houston State University, Newton Gresham Library, Huntsville, Tex.

Cynthia Knight, retired reference librarian.

Amy Koehler, Distance Learning Librarian, University of Chicago, Chicago, Ill.

Chana Kraus-Friedberg, Librarian 1, Michigan State University Libraries, East Lansing.

Robert V. Labaree, Reference/Public Services Librarian, Von KleinSmid Library, University of Southern California, Los Angeles.

Peter Larsen, Physical Sciences and Engineering Librarian, University of Rhode Island Libraries, Kingston.

Martha Lawler, Assoc. Librarian, Louisiana State University, Shreveport.

Shelly Lee, National Board Certified Library Media Specialist, Central Junior High, Moore, Oklahoma.

Richard Nathan Leigh, Metadata & Digital Resources Developer, Ball State University Libraries, Muncie, Ind.

Robert M. Lindsey, Instruction and Reference Librarian, Pittsburg State University, Pittsburg, Kans.

Jessica Graves Louque, General Reference Librarian Assistant Professor, University of Louisiana at Monroe.

Megan W. Lowe, Reference/Instruction Librarian, University of Louisiana at Monroe.

Tyler Manolovitz, Digital Resources Coordinator, Sam Houston State University, Newton Gresham Library, Huntsville, Tex.

Kathleen McBroom, Coordinator, Compensatory Education and School Improvement, Dearborn Public Schools, Dearborn, Mich.

Peter H. McCracken, Library Technical Services, Cornell University, Ithaca, N.Y.

Kevin McDonough, Reference and Electronic Resources Librarian, Northern Michigan University, Olson Library, Marquette.

Jessica Crossfield McIntosh, Reference Services Coordinator, Asst. Professor, Otterbein University, Westerville, Ohio.

Lawrence Joseph Mello, Asst. Reference and Instruction Librarian, Florida Atlantic University, Boca Raton.

Melinda W. Miller, PK-12 Library Media Specialist, Colton-Pierrepont Central School, Colton, N.Y.

Rachel Meredith Minkin, Head of Reference Services, Michigan State University Libraries, East Lansing.

Lisa Morgan, Regional Branch Manager, Hudson Library, Pasco County Library System, Hudson, Fla.

Emily Lauren Mross, Business and Public Administration Librarian, Penn State University, University Park.

Kat Landry Mueller, Electronic Resources Librarian, Sam Houston State University, Newton Gresham Library, Huntsville, Tex.

Theresa Muraski, Associate Professor, University of Wisconsin-Stevens Point.

Paul M. Murphy III, Director of Marketing, PMX Medical, Denver, Colo.

Madeleine Nash, Reference/Instruction Librarian, Molloy College, Rockville Center, N.Y.

Mary Northrup, Reference Librarian, Metropolitan Community College-Maple Woods, Kansas City, Mo.

Thomas O'Brien, Librarian, Florida Atlantic University, Boca Raton.

Cynthia Ortiz, School Librarian, Hackensack High School.

Amy B. Parsons, Catalog Librarian/Assistant Professor, Columbus State University , Columbus, Ga.

Rares G. Piloiu, Information Literacy Librarian, Otterbein University, Westerville, Ohio.

Erik Ponder, African and Ethnic Studies Librarian, Michigan State University Libraries, East Lansing.

Allen Reichert, Electronic Access Librarian, Otterbein University, Westerville, Ohio.

Richard Salvucci, Professor, Economics, Trinity University, San Antonio, Tex.

Bruce Sarjeant, Reference, Documents & Maps Librarian, Northern Michigan University, Marquette.

Mark Schumacher, Art and Humanities Librarian, University of North Carolina, Greensboro.

Colleen Seale, Humanities and Social Sciences Services, George A. Smathers Libraries, University of Florida, Gainesville.

Ravindra Nath Sharma, Dean of Library, Monmouth University Library, West Long Branch, N.J.

Stephen J. Shaw, Graduate Research Librarian, Antioch University, Yellow Springs, Ohio.

Trent Shotwell, Special Collections Librarian, Sam Houston State University, Newton Gresham Library, Huntsville, Tex.

Darshell Silva, Librarian and Technology Integration Specialist, Rocky Hill School, East Greenwich, R.I.

Breezy Silver, Collection Coordinator and Business Reference Librarian, Michigan State University Libraries, East Lansing.

Pamela K. Simmons, Librarian, Penn Yan Middle School, Penn Yan, N.Y.

Todd Simpson, Assistant Professor/Reference Librarian, York College Library, CUNY, Jamaica, N.Y.

Kay Stebbins Slattery, Coordinator Librarian, Louisiana State University, Shreveport.

Steven W. Sowards, Asst. Director for Collections, Michigan State University Libraries, East Lansing.

John P. Stierman, Reference Librarian, Western Illinois University, Macomb.

Eric Tans, Environmental Sciences Librarian, Michigan State University Libraries, East Lansing.

Elizabeth Webster, Teaching & Learning Librarian, Michigan State University Libraries, East Lansing.

Holly Weimar, Associate Professor, Department of Library Science, Sam Houston State University, Huntsville, Tex.

Holly Whitt, Librarian, Walnut Grove Elementary, New Market, Ala.

W. Cole Williamson, Instruction Librarian, University of Arkansas, Little Rock.

Angela Wojtecki, District Library Media Specialist, Nordonia Hills City Schools, Macedonia, Ohio.

Julienne L. Wood, Head, Research Services, Noel Memorial Library, Louisiana State University, Shreveport.

Mary Rebecca Yantis, Assistant Professor/General Reference Librarian, University of Louisiana at Monroe.

Laura Younkin, Librarian, Ballard High School, Louisville, Ky.

Susan Yutzey, School Library Media Specialist, Upper Arlington High School, Columbus, Ohio.

Website and Database Review Locator

Reference is to entry number.

Part I

GENERAL
REFERENCE
WORKS

1 General Reference Works

Acronyms and Abbreviations

1. **A Guide to Federal Terms and Acronyms.** 2d ed. Don Philpott, ed. Lanham, Md., Bernan Press, 2017. 938p. $199.00; $189.00 (e-book). ISBN 13: 978-1-59888-929-1; 978-1-59888-930-7 (e-book).

At more than nine hundred pages, this second edition symbolizes in book form the complex and often opaque layers of American government bureaucracy that exist today. This, however, is why this work remains a useful resource. The book provides a comprehensive reference guide to the most common specialized jargon and terminology of government and spells out the thousands of acronyms and abbreviations used as shorthand by many federal agencies. Obtaining concise definitions of specialized terminology contributes to understanding the unique culture of bureaucratic functions, rules, operations, and hierarchy of authority within government. The second edition includes new sections on AIDS, long-term health care, Alzheimer's and dementia, the federal budget, and the U.S. legal system. Contents are arranged by subject matter (e.g., Contracts and Contracting) or by federal organization (e.g., Coast Guard). Each section consists of concise definitions of terms used within these areas of government, followed by a list of abbreviations, all of which is arranged alphabetically. Definitions cover common words or phrases that have specific contextual meaning within the work of an agency, such as, "accuracy" in relation to the Census Bureau. Agency programs, personnel titles, and specialized words or concepts are also defined. *See* references are used to guide readers to alternative usages. Most definitions are brief but some are lengthier depending on the complexity of the term. As noted by the editor, the book does not include all federal department glossaries because it would require multiple volumes. For example, there is no section devoted to defining terms or spelling out acronyms and abbreviations associated with the consumer protection responsibilities of various government agencies, nor is the domain of antitrust law (e.g., TRR, Trade Regulation Rule) covered in the section on Justice. Nevertheless, the work provides definitions for the core jargon of most levels of government and remains a useful quick reference guide for students and professionals.— **Robert V. Labaree**

Almanacs

2.   **Canadian Almanac & Directory 2018.** 171st ed. Toronto, Grey House Publishing Canada, 2018. 2275p. illus. maps. index. $439.00. ISBN 13: 978-1-68217-470-8; 978-1-68217-470-8 (e-book).

3.   **Canadian Almanac & Directory 2019.** 172d ed. Toronto, Grey House Publishing Canada, 2018. 2254p. illus. maps. index. $449.00. ISBN 13: 978-1-68217-822-5; 978-1-68217-823-2 (e-book).

In each year of this almanac and directory, users will find more than 50,000 entries. Information is conveyed in 17 sections that are arranged according to subject. Articles, color maps, photographs, charts, and tables supplement the first section, Almanac, comprised of 10 parts: History of Canada; Vital Statistics; Geography; Science; Economics & Finance; Exhibitions, Shows & Events; Awards & Honours; Government; Regulations & Abbreviations; and Weights & Measures. The other sections are: Arts & Culture; Associations; Broadcasting; Business & Finance; Education; Federal/Provisional Government; Municipal Government; Judicial Government; Hospitals & Health Care Facilities; Law Firms; Libraries; Publishing; Religion; Transportation; and Utilities. An entry name index facilitates navigation. This comprehensive, accurate source is recommended for academic and public libraries.—**ARBA Staff Reviewer**

4.   **The World Almanac and Book of Facts 2019.** New York, World Almanac Books, 2019. 1008p. illus. maps. index. $36.95. ISBN 13: 978-1-60057-220-3.

The latest edition of this essential reference work includes the 2018 year in review, with the top ten news topics, statistical spotlight, specifics on the 2018 elections, a chronology of the year's events, U.S. Supreme Court decisions, and historical anniversaries, along with two large sections of color pictures of the important events and people of 2018. The major sections of this tome have been brought up to date related to recent facts, figures, and statistics; these sections include Economy, Business, & Energy; Crime; Military Affairs; Health & Vital Statistics; Personalities, Arts, & Media; Science & Technology; Consumer Information; U.S. Facts & History; World Maps & Flags; U.S. Government; U.S. Cities, States, & Population; World History & Culture; Nations of the World; and Sports. Packed full of important statistics and facts, this is a must-have book for any reference collection.—**Bradford Lee Eden**

Bibliographies

5.   **Iberian Books Bibliography https://iberian.ied.ie/.** [Website] Free. Date reviewed: 2019.

This site catalogs thousands of books published between 1472 and 1700 in Spain, Portugal, and the Iberian New World. Gathered from over two thousand international repositories, Iberian Books offers a centralized listing of thousands of pages of diverse materials including religious texts, poetry, histories, ordinances, medical texts, and much more, with added focus on women publishers, authors, and litigants. The project is based at the School of History, University College Dublin. Users can find detailed bibliographical information for these materials, some including links to digitized versions. The homepage allows users to conduct an Advanced Search by inputting Title/Keyword, Author, Printer, Place of Printing, Year, or other identifying information, which can be filtered by Country, Topic, Language, and Format. Alternatively, users can conduct a Basic Search or Browse titles (in the Spanish or Portuguese language) in the database. Items in the database may be sorted by relevance, title, or date. Users can access a bibliographical record by clicking on the title—the record may include a Physical Description, Citation/Reference, Place of Origin (with map), Subject, or a listing of known Exemplars, among other data. A selection of Similar Items runs down the left side of the page for each selected title. If an item has been digitized, the database will include a thumbnail photograph which may link to the item's original source collection. Aside from the database, users can find generous information under the Visualizations tab. An interactive map of the Iberian Peninsula examines how publishing in Spain, Portugal, and the New World evolved before 1701. Another map notes specific publishers by city or year. Other visualizations highlight the geography of printing in Madrid before 1701, provide location information for the rarest Iberian books, and more. Much more than a simple bibliography, Iberian Books shines a spotlight on the publishing world at a time when Spain and Portugal extended their rich influence throughout the western hemisphere.—**ARBA Staff Reviewer**

Biography

6.   **Canadian Who's Who 2018: Volume L.** Toronto, Grey House Publishing Canada, 2018. 1149p. $299.00. ISBN 13: 978-1-68217-532-3.

Canadian Who's Who is a biographical directory of the "country's most noteworthy citizens, researching and presenting the details of their lives and careers." The 50th edition of this resource features entries for 10,000 noted individuals and information presented includes: date and place of birth, education, family (names of parents and children), educational background, career information, honors, publications, and memberships plus contact information and social media and websites, where applicable. Biographies are listed in alphabetical order and, in addition, there is a separate directory "In Memoriam" of recently deceased individuals. An abbreviations listing is provided and includes those relating to academic degrees, honors and awards, job titles, and associations. Among those included are heads of state, lawyers, politicians, actors, athletes, scientists, and musicians. Among notables featured are: Prime Minister Justin Trudeau, William Shatner, Christopher Plummer, Celine Dion, Anna Paquin, Bobby Orr, Wayne Gretzky, Arthur B. McDonald, Alice Munro, Margaret Atwood, and Bryan Adams. Editors also "invite prominent individuals to complete questionnaires from which new biographies are created." Information is based on "reliable sources of information" from government, business, academia, associations, and media outlets. *Canadian Who's Who* is highly recommended to academic and larger public and research libraries. It is a both a source for quick reference and a place to begin research on a specific person.—**Lucy Heckman**

7.   Jones, Barry. **Dictionary of World Biography.** 5th ed. Acton, Australia, Australian National University Press, 2018. 932p. $90.00pa.; Free (e-book). ISBN 13: 978-1-7604-

6218-5; 978-1-7604-6219-2 (e-book)

Barry Jones, Australian politician, writer, and lawyer painstakingly compiled this dictionary of world biography, now in its 5th edition. Available in print, the electronic version is freely available. The title includes information on thousands of people worldwide (far more of them are men). In the front matter, users will find a list of abbreviations and an introduction. Entries vary in length. There are short entries (2-3 lines of text) for such people as Sir Sonny Ramphal (1928-), Guyanan lawyer and administrator; Australian painter Lloyd Frederick Rees (1895-1988); American film critic Pauline Kael (1919-2001); and Japanese Liberal Democratic politician Takeshita Noburu (1921-2000). People like German composer Wagner and Queen Elizabeth I get far longer entries. Some entries are followed by source references, and the dictionary makes good use of *see* references (e.g., El Greco see Greco, El). This is a reliable resource that is recommended, particularly in light of the fact that the electronic version is available at no cost.—**ARBA Staff Reviewer**

8.   **Nobel Prize Winners: 2002-2018 Supplement.** Bronx, N.Y., H. W. Wilson, 2019. 576p. illus. index. $175.00. ISBN 13: 978-1-68217-878-2.

Nobel Prize Winners: 2002-2018 Supplement is exactly as it describes itself—a collection of biographies of all the Nobel laureates from 2002 through 2018 with descriptions of the works or achievements that won the laureates their prize. Laureates are listed alphabetically. Most entries contain pictures of the winners. All entries contain which Nobel Prize the individual won; when and where they were born; and the aforementioned biography which usually contains a narrative of the individual's relevant professional career. Entries contain the sections Early Life and Education, Career, and Impact, followed by a bibliography of resources by the winner or which can provide more information about the winner. The entries are very direct and well written, with the average length of entries being about 2-3 pages (pages are formatted with content in 2 columns). While this is certainly a convenient resource for obtaining vetted information on laureates, similar information is available for free on the Nobel Prize organization's website. That this information is freely available through other legitimate websites is key, especially given the $175 price tag and no e-book option. Content-wise, the title is certainly recommended for any library, but there are more affordable and easier-accessed resources that can provide the same information.—**Megan W. Lowe**

Dictionaries & Encyclopedias

9.   **The Canadian Encyclopedia https://www.thecanadianencyclopedia.ca/en.** [Website] Free. Date reviewed: 2019.

This freely accessible online resource provides users with more than 19,500 articles on Canada by more than 5,000 contributors. Approximately 60 articles are added or revised each month. Under the About tab, users can find information about the editorial team, funding sources, and partnerships. The homepage will draw researchers in with its featured collections and education guides along with an almanac and list of most recently added articles (the most recent article at the time of this review was added 3/8/19). The encyclopedia is easy to navigate, and information is discoverable in a variety of ways— via a basic search screen, by a search of people, places, or things under a Browse tab, by clicking on Collections or Timelines, and by choosing from among the many curriculum resources available under the Educators tab. The timelines are organized by topic as are the collections (e.g., First Nations, Women in Canada, Acadian Heritage). The encyclopedia itself offers articles that vary in length depending on subject. The entry for Indigenous Peoples of Canada is quite substantial, for example, while the article for Alaska Highway is a few paragraphs. Entries are signed and many also provide information about the contributors. Entries can also include photographs, tables, further reading suggestions, external links, and more.—**ARBA Staff Reviewer**

10.   Sorgatz, Rex. Illustrated by Lorenzo Petrantoni. **The Encyclopedia of Misinformation: A Compendium of Imitations, Spoofs, Delusions, Simulations, Counterfeits, Imposters, Illusions, Confabulations, Conspiracies & Miscellaneous Fakery.** New York, Abrams, 2018. 233p. illus. $19.99pa. ISBN 13: 978-1-4197-2911-9; 978-1-68335-234-1 (e-book).

This fun-filled tour through decades of misinformation (broadly defined) is not designed as a comprehensive, scholarly reference book. Rather, it includes nearly 300 instances of imitations, spoofs, delusions, simulations, counterfeits, imposters, illusions, confabulations, conspiracies, and miscellaneous fakery, as the subtitle indicates. The entries are arranged in an A-to-Z format, and most entries run from half a page to just over a page. The book does not contain an index or a works cited, but it does make good use of *see also* references after each entry. A number of illustrations also add to the work. The writing style is informal, and, in many cases, the opinion of the author comes through clearly. Here readers will find explanations, definitions, and the history of such things as astroturfing (the term for impersonating a grassroots movement for political gain); catfish (a person who creates a fake online identity for romantic purposes); Rachel Dolezal (a white woman who posed as a black woman); exploding pop rocks (child star Mikey of Life Cereal fame did not die from a pop rock explosion in his stomach); Fake Shemp (originally used to refer to the Stooge who replaced the original Stooge on the Three Stooges, but more broadly applied to the practice of replacing one actor with another); jenkem hoax (kids were not inhaling fermented feces and urine); Huey Long (the pseudo populist governor/senator from Louisiana who was assassinated); Sophists; Trompe L'Oeil; the War of the Worlds broadcast; Yellow Journalism; and many other things. This book is recommended for the circulating collection of public libraries, though librarians will want to note the use of curse words in a few places.—**ARBA Staff Reviewer**

Digital Resources

11.   **Archives Canada http://www.archivescanada.ca/.** [Website] Free. Date reviewed: 2019.

This website reaches out to more than 800 institutions throughout Canada to gather materials related to Canadian history, culture, geography, and more. The archives access provincial and territorial resources, maps, photographs, documents, and other sources. The site additionally provides an excellent selection of cultural exhibits derived from the archives that contribute to a detailed picture of the vast and diverse nation. The Search tab or link leads to a general search field and a list of browsing options that help users find information through a variety of avenues. Archival Descriptions display information on over 61,000 items in the archive, which can be filtered by archival institution, language, creator, subject, and other selections. Authority Records lists custodial individuals and institutions with links to affiliated records. Archival Institutions alphabetically lists all museums, archives, historical societies, university collections, and more, from the 8th Hussars Museum in New Brunswick to the Musée national des beaux-arts du Québec. This area can be filtered by such things as Geographic Region or Archive Type. Subjects lists thousands of options from the general to the specific, touching on areas of both international and local concern, from Prince Edward Island Agriculture to Hockey, AIDS, and 4-H Clubs. Places helps users find materials down to the specific street. Users can alternatively browse through the archives by Digital Objects, which organizes a vast array of text, video, audio, and images from home movies to photographs. Information for each object varies, but may include title, repository, creation date, creator, related subjects, or descriptive notes. Back on the homepage, users can select either the Virtual Exhibits tab or the Browse Digital Projects link to find a long and diverse list of online exhibits produced between 2003 and 2008 that utilize materials in the archives. Organized by year, exhibits include the "Ontario Time Machine," "Persuasion: Print Advertising and Advocacy on the Prairies," "The Art of Shipbuilding, an Inherited Skill," "Democracy in Montreal from 1830 to the Present," and many others.—**ARBA Staff Reviewer**

12.   **Retraction Watch https://retractionwatch.com.** [Website] Free. Date reviewed: 2019.

Retraction Watch maintains a database of known published research retractions in an effort to hold all corners of the academic community to account. Users can discover retraction information for case reports, clinical studies, letters, dissertations, government publications, journal articles, and much more across numerous academic fields, and note details regarding the reasons for retractions, retracted author names, and other information. The site's blog, prominently featured on the homepage, adds additional context to many of the documented retractions. It is recommended that users first read through the three appendixes (Database Fields, Reasons, and Article Types) before exploring the database, which is accessible via the Retraction Watch Database User Guide link. The User Guide, in the appendixes, is quite detailed in explaining the scope and function of the Retraction Watch database, in particular the variety of fields users can fill to create their search. Users can initiate a general subject search, choosing from well over one hundred particular subjects, such as urban planning, biochemistry, international relations, pathology, climatology, alternative medicine, and history within standard academic departments such as biological sciences, humanities, business, physical sciences, and social sciences. The database will list all affiliated entries, sharing author, title, country, reasons for retraction, subject, article type, journal name, publisher, affiliation, and more. It will also convey the Retraction Watch URL if there is an accompanying blog post. The list within a chosen subject will display up to six hundred affiliated retractions at a time. Some reasons listed for retractions include plagiarism; error in analyses; forged authorship; unreliable data; duplication of image; and text or data. Other features on the homepage include The Retraction Watch Leaderboard listing thirty-two authors and the numbers of their retractions, with links to further information and the top ten most highly cited retracted papers, which includes the number of affiliated citations both before and after issued retractions.—**ARBA Staff Reviewer**

Directories

13. **The Grey House Guide to Homeland Security Resources 2018.** 14th ed. Amenia, N.Y., Grey House Publishing, 2018. 1128p. index. $225.00. ISBN 13: 978-1-68217-759-4.

  The Grey House Guide to Homeland Security Resources 2018 (14th edition) is an essential reference for anyone concerned with public safety and homeland security. Formerly known as *The Grey House Homeland Security Directory, The Grey House Guide to Homeland Security Resources* chronicles resource agencies, personalities, directories, and databases. This well-respected assemblage includes sections that document federal, state, company, and industry resources. This volume has 5,369 listings and 11,166 key executives. The volume includes federal agencies (Department of Homeland Security (DHS), Department of Health & Human Services, Department of Labor, etc); state agencies (alphabetical by state); company listings (alphabetical by company); industry resources (associations, periodical directories & databases, shows & seminars, and web sites); and Indexes (entry, key personnel, products & services). The beginning portion of the book contains a user guide, 24 pages of DHS organizational charts; an annual Flow Report from December 2017 "U.S. Lawful Permanent Residents: 2016"; a January 2018 Annual Flow Report "Refugees and Asylees: 2016"; and a December 2017 Annual Flow Report "Immigration Enforcement Actions: 2016." *The Grey House Guide to Homeland Security Resources* offers responsible inquirers a tool that satisfies their quest for updated, simplified, and straightforward information. Readers benefit from the all-encompassing scope that surpasses other publications.

  The Grey House Guide to Homeland Security Resources supports academic criminal justice and law enforcement programs, including majors in homeland security. All library acquisition decision-makers will consider this contribution an essential resource. Community college, university, and public libraries benefit. The book will also serve as a convenient desk reference that decision-makers will appreciate when performing operational duties and responsibilities.—**Thomas E. Baker**

14. **The Official Museum Directory 2018.** 48th ed. New Providence, N.J., The Official Museum Directory, 2511. 2017. index. $299.00pa. ISBN 13: 978-0-87217-065-0.

  This is the 48th edition of a directory that provides information on more than 15,300 museums, historic sites, zoos, and other institutions. The bulk of the book lists institutions by state and then by city. Information provided includes name and contact information (address, phone number, website URL, etc.); a description of collections and activities; hours; and admission prices. Longer entries for large institutions might also include key personnel, governing authority, founding dates, research fields, publications, and membership information. The directory is designed for the museum community and for the public. While professionals might use it to find contacts, travelers can use it to find out about, for example, the Pancho Villa State Park in Columbus, New Mexico, the Baton Rouge Gallery Center for Contemporary Art in Louisiana, or the Tennessee Newspaper & Printing Museum in Rogersville. There are two indexes, one an alphabetical list of institutions and one a list of institutions by category (art museums and galleries, college and university museums, history museums, archaeology museums and archaeological sites, and so forth). Those looking for an electronic version of the directory can find purchasing information at http://www.officialmuseumdirectory.com/OMD/home. This is a recommended purchase for larger public or academic libraries.—**ARBA Staff Reviewer**

Part II
SOCIAL SCIENCES

2 Social Sciences in General

General Works

Dictionaries and Encyclopedias

15. Buchanan, Ian. **A Dictionary of Critical Theory.** 2d ed. New York, Oxford University Press, 2018. 528p. $18.95pa. ISBN 13: 978-0-1987-9479-0.

The first edition of this work published in 2010. This second edition provides users with updated and revised entries along with more than 50 new entries that cover the range of subjects included under the critical theory umbrella: history, philosophy, literary theory, psychoanalysis, sociology, etc. The author is Professor of Cultural Studies at the University of Wollongong, and he strives in this dictionary to provide users (the audience here would be college and university-level students) with a straightforward resource that does not require specialist knowledge. This is accomplished through the writing and through the use of cross-references, though the task is challenging with entries on ideas such as actor-network theory, existentialism, and bare life and thinkers like Martin Heidegger and Simone de Beauvoir. The author also makes use of *see* references (e.g., BWO, *see* Body without organs). In total, there are more than 750 entries that vary in length from one to several paragraphs; a good number of these have suggestions for further reading. This is a valuable resource, especially for students unfamiliar with these concepts and thinkers. Highly recommended for academic libraries.—**ARBA Staff Reviewer**

16. **The SAGE Encyclopedia of Intellectual and Developmental Disorders.** Ellen Braaten, ed. Thousand Oaks, Calif., Sage, 2018. 4v. index. $645.00/set; $516.00 (e-book). ISBN 13: 978-1-4833-9229-5; 978-1-5063-5329-6 (e-book).

This four-volume set includes hundreds of entries on both intellectual disorders (those characterized by significantly impaired intellectual and adaptive functioning) and developmental disorders (a more broad category characterized by learning, cognitive, and physical impairments). The encyclopedia is broad in scope but coverage of individual topics is not intended to be exhaustive; rather, this should be a good place for researchers to find foundational material and sources for further research. The target audience is students in a variety of fields: psychology, psychiatry, counseling, education, social work, health sciences, and more. The book can be used for courses and research in clinical psychology, child development, health sciences, nursing, human development, and family studies. Volumes start with an alphabetic list of entries and a reader's guide, which lists topics thematically. There is also information about the editor and contributors. The signed entries vary in length, are subdivided, and include *see also* references and suggestions for further reading. If a library purchases the electronic version of the book, users will have the ability to search within entries and within the entire set. *See also* references and author names are hyperlinked as are DOIs. The subject matter included is indeed broad. Readers will discover information on syndromes like the Alice in Wonderland Syndrome or Down Syndrome; treatments like Art Therapy or Music Therapy; such disorders as Generalized Anxiety Disorder; general topics like Bullying and Homework; and much more. There is a great deal more information provided for such entries as ADHD and GAD than there is for Deafness and Hearing Loss or Peer Rejection. The book ends with lists of disorder classifications according to the *Diagnostic and Statistical Manual of Mental Disorders* (5th ed., used in the United States) and the *International Classification of Diseases* (10th ed). There is also a list of IQ classification ratings and lists of tests commonly used to evaluate developmental disorders. The book concludes with a subject index. This encyclopedia is recommended to academic libraries.—**ARBA Staff Reviewer**

Handbooks and Yearbooks

17.   **The SAGE Handbook of Consumer Culture.** Olga Kravets, Pauline Maclaran, Steven Miles, and Alladi Venkatesh, eds. Thousand Oaks, Calif., Sage, 2018. 576p. $160.00. ISBN 13: 978-1-4739-2951-7; 978-1-4739-9877-3 (e-book).

Consumption and consumer behavior have become subjects of increasing research in fields such as business, psychology and sociology, geography, and even politics. Due to the breadth and diversity of these fields, this work is arranged into 6 sections (comprising 29 chapters): the rise of consumer culture, its "geographies," marketing studies, media and cultural studies, material culture aspects, and the politics of consumer culture. The introduction provides brief summaries of the chapters, guiding readers to the portions of a large book that will most interest them. The authors come from around the world, teaching at institutions in at least 10 different countries, in a variety of disciplines. Some studies focus on individual countries, including Russia, China, and India. Two of the most important elements of this volume are a) the truly diverse approaches to the study of consumer culture at the global level, and b) the rich bibliographies provided by each of the chapters.

A note or two about the e-book: each chapter in PDF format is numbered from page 1, making citations more difficult, though one can read the HTML version, and the site will insert page numbers! If one clicks on a footnote number in either format, there is no easy way to return to the portion of the text one was reading. The reviewer found navigating the print version much easier.

This work is designed for advanced, serious scholars of the field, and is often written in dense language: "In engaging with identity projects, consumers are driven by a call to compulsory individuality and an ideology of reflexivity, self-discipline, enterprise and improvement." (p.203) "I was immersed in the world of feminist material-semiotics, actor-network theory, heterogeneous networks and agentic objects . . ." (p. 367). Academic libraries with programs in any or all of the disciplines mentioned above should consider adding this volume to their collections. Other libraries will find it outside the scope.— **Mark Schumacher**

3 Area Studies

General Works

Digital Resources

18. **Global Road Warrior https://www.globalroadwarrior.com/.** [Website] Traverse City, Mich., World Trade Press, 2019. Price negotiated by site. Date reviewed: 2019.

This database by World Trade Press provides copious information about 175 countries. Country searches can begin by clicking on the country name or by clicking on a world map. For each country, users will get information under the following sections: Overview, Business Culture, Climate, Communications, Country Facts, Culture & Society, Education, Electrical, Embassies & Consulates, Historic Famous People, Food & Recipes, Health and Medical, History, Holidays & Festivals, Human Rights, Language, Language Glossaries, Life Cycles, Maps, Money & Banking, Music, Names, National Symbols, Points of Interest, Religion, Security Briefing, Transportation, and Travel Essentials. Users will be able to click on one or several links in each of these sections. The Maps section, for instance, takes users to 9 color maps: a political map, a provinces map, a physical map, a precipitation map, an outline map, an outline map that shows provinces, a natural earth map, a temperature map, and a population map. Under Language Glossaries, users will find several different glossaries (travel, numbers, professions, etc.). The information is more broad than deep, but the database is easy to navigate and offers users a chance to download, print, and cite data.

This database is designed for use by global firms, international relocation companies, government agencies, and libraries of all sorts. It succeeds in providing something for all of those groups. Recommended.—**ARBA Staff Reviewer**

Handbooks and Yearbooks

19. Dulberger, Michael D. **America and Its Rivals: A Comparison among the Nations of China, Russia, and the United States.** Lanham, Md., Bernan Press, 2018. 394p. index. $120.00pa.; $114.00 (e-book). ISBN 13: 978-1-59888-998-7; 978-1-59888-999-4 (e-book).

This book compares and contrasts conditions in Russia, the United States, and China using several indicators, presenting its findings in easily understandable graphs in

13 chapters: "Demographics," "Immigration," "Health," "Education," "Employment," "Income and Poverty," "Crime and Incarceration," "Freedom," "Military and Defense," "Energy," "Resources and Innovations," "Economy," and "Trade." A general introduction, though short, contextualizes the data represented throughout the book, and each chapter begins with a brief overview of the chapter topic. In the demographics chapter, for example, readers will find facts on age distributions, birth and death rates, life expectances for men and women, refugee and undocumented alien numbers, suicide rates, obesity, drug usage statistics, math and science test scores, employment numbers in agriculture, services, and industry, and much more. Other graphs feature: "Pump Price for Gasoline, 2000-2014," "Private Car Theft Rate, 2003-2014," "Prison Staffing Level of Adult Correctional Institutions, 2003-2014," "Press Freedom, 2017, Freedom House Score," "Nuclear Warhead Delivery Systems Count, 2017," "Electricity Consumption, 1980-2014," "Commercial Aircraft Count, 2015," "External Debt, 2016," "United States Trade Balance with China, 2002-2016," and "Tourist Departures, 1995-2015." Each graph appears with a short textual explanation. Underneath each graph, users will see the source information. These sources include, among others, the U.S. Department of Homeland Security, the Organization for Economic Cooperation and Development (OECD), the World Bank, the CIA, the U.S. Census Bureau, the World Health Organization, the Centers for Disease Control, the U.S. Federal Reserve Bank, the United Nations, the International Monetary Fund, and the Federation of American Scientists.

This information-packed title is recommended to academic and public libraries.—**ARBA Staff Reviewer**

20.   **Whitaker's 2019.** London, Bloomsbury Yearbooks, 2019. 1184p. maps. index. $125.00. ISBN 13: 978-1-4729-4752-9.

This yearbook is well established as the authoritative work on current affairs and political issues in the United Kingdom. While it indicates that it covers the world, only one half of the content is focused on non-United Kingdom facts and statistics. This doesn't mean that it isn't useful beyond United Kingdom information; just that the focus is on the United Kingdom. As such, it contains significant statistics on all aspects of the United Kingdom political, social, and economic infrastructure, including the royal family, Parliament, peerage, local government, law and order, education, health, social welfare, utilities and transport, religion, communications, conservation and heritage, banking and finance, taxation, and the media. The second half of the yearbook focuses on the world, with a 2017-2018 year-in-review emphasis. Packed full of illustrations, charts, tables, and a number of colored plates and maps, all aspects of United Kingdom life and culture are contained in this annual update.—**Bradford Lee Eden**

United States

General Works

21.   **Grand Canyon Centennial Project https://lib.asu.edu/grand100.** [Website] Free. Date reviewed: 2019.

Gathered from three regional libraries, the material in the Grand Canyon Centennial Project documents the rich and varied history of one of the United States' most iconic natural settings. The archive holds a wide range of digital artifacts which bring together cultural, geological, administrative, and deeply personal strands of this national park's story. Users can access the materials as they scroll down through the homepage. Under Photographs, users can find a collection of over one hundred black-and-white and color prints of storms, travelers, workers, canyon panoramas, and events. Correspondence lists over two hundred items, with letters documenting purchase agreements, development deals, administration, infrastructure, politics, natural resource management, and more. Ephemera includes fifty items such as natural history notes, cultural pamphlets, tour brochures, geological surveys, personal observations, and maps. The Colorado Plateau Archives and The Grand Canyon National Park Museum Collection contain similar materials, such as grazing permits, mining claims, hotel payrolls, expedition reports, photos of Civilian Conservation Corps work on trails and bridges, and other park developments. Artifacts in all the searchable collections are displayed as thumbnail images with identifying detail—title, contributor, series, subject, date, etc. Users can click on the thumbnail or preview icon for a more detailed description and download option. The Grand Canyon Story Map (users should employ full screen mode for optimal viewing) at the bottom of the homepage allows users to explore the archive via pinned locations on a satellite map of the canyon. Clicking on a pin creates a pop-up window artifact description and image preview. The History tab links to a Grand Canyon National Park timeline (1890-1940) which provides excellent context for many of the artifacts. Resources offer links to regional historical societies, museums, research guides, and historical books organized by era. The wealth of resources makes for an excellent and informative tribute to one of America's great national parks with wide interdisciplinary appeal for students and educators.—**ARBA Staff Reviewer**

22.   Moore, Randy, and Kara Felicia Witt. **The Grand Canyon: An Encyclopedia of Geography, History, and Culture.** Santa Barbara, Calif., ABC-CLIO, 2018. 391p. illus. maps. index. $94.00. ISBN 13: 978-1-61069-839-9; 978-1-61069-840-5 (e-book).

The Grand Canyon is recognized throughout the world yet can also be considered a symbol of America. It is culturally, economically, and scientifically important to humanity. It certainly deserves to have its own encyclopedia, and this volume does it justice in the areas of the subtitle: geography, history, and culture.

The reader can open the book at any point and be intrigued. The Introduction, Chronology of Human History, and Grand Canyon at a Glance sections combine to give a good overview at the start of the book. The rest of the encyclopedia is divided into two major sections. The first is a collection of well-written thematic essays. The first three essays cover geology followed by two on first peoples and tribes. John Wesley Powell certainly deserves his own essay, which is followed by ones on water, historical sites in order (mile by mile) down the river, Christian fundamentalism, and the future of the Grand Canyon. The second section has alphabetical entries of over 160 people, places, issues, and events, including those that are notorious or bizarre. The goal of the book is to help readers appreciate the experience of the Grand Canyon. It is intended to describe what it's like to be there. Every entry has references for further reading and the selected bibliography offers more. Very clear black-and-white photos, informational boxes, and charts are scattered throughout the book. A glossary and index complete the encyclopedia.

This reviewer looks forward to a future edition that becomes a more inclusive encyclopedia with all facets of the Grand Canyon including recreation and environment. The beautiful color photo of the canyon on the cover with the rainbow makes one want more color in the text; the new edition would offer that plus more detailed maps. Every library will find this book useful.—**Georgia Briscoe**

Alaska

23. **Alaska Communities Database Online https://dcra-cdo-dcced.opendata.** [Website] Free. Date reviewed: 2019.

The Alaska Community Database Online is a state-of-the-art resource for finding and using a wide range of information on the state of Alaska. Using a base map of the large state, the site enables users to find information on municipalities, tribes, regional organizations, and more. Users can also easily find and utilize numerous individual datasets covering relevant issues, and browse a selection of innovative projects related to the story of Alaska and its diverse communities. The How To Use This Site tab offers a helpful overview of the large amount of information and the numerous ways in which to use it. From the prominent base map, users can then choose a community from the alphabetical list of Alaska locations or click a point on the map to access a pop-up outline of available information for that location. Information in the pop-up notes community type, pronunciation, incorporation date, certified population, and more, and may also offer links to community details (history, local language recordings, etc.), photos, financial documents, and other items. Users can alternatively scroll down through the homepage and select the Community Overview Storymaps tab under Interactive Applications to access an alphabetized gallery of Alaskan communities. Further down the homepage, users can find Datasets for Download covering a range of issues, including education, public safety, demographics, and climate change. For each category, datasets are listed with title, source, type, tags, a brief description, and other details. Datasets include the Alaska American Community Survey on various topics (sex, household income, etc.), Alaska Native Language Boundaries, and more. Under the Interactive Maps tab, users can find eighteen examples of data at work with a range of projects such as Alaska Transportation, showing local, regional, and federal transportation centers throughout the large state, and Traditional Livelihoods in Alaska Threatened by Climate Change, which gathers economic, sociological, and environmental data into a compelling look at the way a changing environment has affected local communities. Users can also create personalized Alaskan maps or stories incorporating selected datasets (Build your Own Maps), and find contact information for many Alaskan organizations and entities. The Alaska Community Database Online is a valuable resource for a variety of users: regional policy makers, business professionals, environmentalists, historians, and others.—**ARBA Staff Reviewer**

California

24. **Profiles of California, 2018.** 5th ed. Amenia, N.Y., Grey House Publishing, 2018. 1148p. illus. maps. index. $149.00pa. ISBN 13: 978-1-68217-752-5; 978-1-68217-753-2 (e-book).

The last edition of this reference published in 2015, so this is a welcome update. The book utilizes data from the 2012-2016 American Community Survey and the 2010 US

Census and also includes government statistics and original research. Altogether the book covers 1,709 places in California, including 212 unincorporated places. Data is presented in 7 sections: About California, Profiles, Comparative Statistics, Community Rankings, Education, Ancestry and Ethnicity, and Climate. In the About California section users will find basic state facts (state tree, state fish, state bird, highest and lowest points, name of governor, etc.) along with dozens of color maps and photographs. Here researchers will also find a brief history of California, starting with European exploration, a timeline of California history, an introduction to California government, facts about natural resources, and an energy profile. Ample information can be gleaned from the maps alone which give population statistics; black, white, Asian, and Hispanic population statistics; median ages and income by location; and much more. Starting with Alameda County and ending with Yuba County, the Profiles section is the longest section of the book. It is rounded out by a place-name index. Profiles begin with an overview of the county in general, followed by statistics on places (unincorporated postal areas, towns, cities, and census designated places) within the county. Users will find an abundance of information on population, employment, income, educational attainment, housing, health insurance, and transportation. The next section allows users to compare the one hundred largest communities in the state by dozens of such data points as population, ancestry groups, educational attainment, health insurance, and crime. Community Rankings, the next section, curates data on incorporated places and census designated places with populations over 2,500, presenting data on each topic in ascending and descending order, with a few exceptions. This section will inform users about population density, average household size, employment, and more. Those raising school-age children will be drawn to the information in the Education section which provides school district rankings. This section lets readers see things like the student/librarian ratio, expenditures per student, numbers of teachers, and much more. Useful information will also be found in the final two sections, Ancestry and Ethnicity and Climate. This is a highly recommended purchase for public libraries, especially those in California.—**ARBA Staff Reviewer**

Illinois

25. **Profiles of Illinois.** 5th ed. Amenia, N.Y., Grey House Publishing, 2017. 864p. illus. maps. index. $149.00pa. ISBN 13: 978-1-68217-375-6.

This 5th edition of *Profiles of Illinois* (one of 15 titles in Grey House's Profiles of… series) contains the type of geographical statistical data you would have paged through before the internet came around and now might write off because of that—don't be fooled. Most of the data gathered is from disparate, freely available online sources (the bulk coming from the U.S. Census, including the 2011-2015 American Community Survey Five Year Estimates); however, the volume's value lies in it being gathered and presented here in one organized volume. New for this 5th edition are statistics on children without health insurance, dentists per capita, selected monthly owner costs (dealing with housing), language spoken at home, people with disabilities, and veterans. The User Guide chapter, which should be consulted for researchers unfamiliar with the publication, explains and cites the data sources used for each chapter. The handful of color and black-and-white reproductions are of good quality. Three years of free online access is available for buyers of the print edition. Contact Grey House for link and password.—**Bruce Sarjeant**

Michigan

26.   **Profiles of Michigan.** 5th ed. Amenia, N.Y., Grey House Publishing, 2018. 1055p. illus. maps. index. $149.00pa. ISBN 13: 978-1-68217-780-8.

This reference book (one of 15 titles in the Profiles of...series) contains the sort of geographical statistical data you would have referred to in print before the internet came along (state and county statistics—population, education, employment, etc.), and now might write off because of that. From a personal viewpoint, it is so much easier to flip back and forth through a printed publication full of data such as this than to click between multiple windows on a computer. While most of this data—for all the Profiles of series—has been gathered from disparate, mostly freely available online sources (the U.S. Census for the most part, but the Department of Education and United States Geological Survey as well), the value lies in it being presented together in an organized volume. New for this 5th edition is an expanded Profiles section containing additional statistics on dentists per capita and monthly owner costs with and without a mortgage. The User Guide section explains and cites the data sources used for each chapter. The color reproductions are of good quality, but most of those in black and white are poor quality.—**Bruce Sarjeant**

New Jersey

27.   **New Jersey Digital Highway https://njdigitalhighway.org/.** [Website] Free. Date reviewed: 2018.

The New Jersey Digital Highway pulls from a variety of state institutions to offer a rich and accessible bank of information on the cultural history of the Garden State. Users can examine digital exhibits, draw from a generous selection of educational materials, explore topics, and much more. Users can access information in a variety of ways. The Electronic NJ or Electronic New Jersey tabs link to a good variety of lessons and materials covering a range of state-related subjects. Users can find lessons alphabetically or by theme, or peruse an excellent Index of Lessons for more specific lesson detail. "The American Revolution—New Jersey's Role;" "Child Labor in New Jersey;" "Jersey Homesteads;" "New Jersey: the Garden State;" "Red Scare at Rutgers;" and eighteen other topics cast a regional view on national and international issues. Each lesson may be structured differently and may incorporate materials such as maps, chronologies, journals, letters, and other primary source documents. Users can also find additional Links for Educators, including a glossary, educator resources, and the New Jersey and Core Curriculum Standards. The homepage also features two digital exhibits: "Chinese Exclusion in New Jersey" and "Invisible Restraints: Life and Labor at Seabrook Farms." Other items include a New Jersey Map Portal, leading to an excellent digital collection of geological, political, historical, and other state maps, and the New Jersey Environmental Digital Library, which gathers information on the local environment from state agencies, research institutions, and other sources. The variety and quality of the materials on the New Jersey Digital Highway makes it an excellent resource for educators, historians, and others interested in the state of New Jersey.—**ARBA Staff Reviewer**

28.   **Profiles of New Jersey.** 5th ed. Amenia, N.Y., Grey House Publishing, 2019. 654p. illus. maps. index. $149.00pa. ISBN 13: 978-1-64265-062-4; 978-1-64265-063-1 (e-book)

This is the 5th edition of *Profiles of New Jersey,* based in part on content from the 4-volume *Profiles of America* and including an updated New Jersey chapter and new information on number of dentists per capita, air quality index values, and selected monthly owner costs with and without a mortgage. The front matter includes an introduction and extensive user guide followed by section 1, About New Jersey, which includes information on such things as state flower, state bug, state governor, and state time zone. Color maps, color photographs, a brief state history, a New Jersey state timeline, basic government information, facts on the state's land and natural resources, a state energy profile, and a series of demographic maps (in color) are provided. The volume supplies profiles of 877 places based on 2010 US Census data and the most recent American Community Survey. The places are arranged alphabetically within counties. In the profiles, users will find information on the geography, population (including density, ethnicity, race, household size), employment, income, educational attainment, housing (rates of homeownership, median home value, median year structure was built, and more), health insurance, safety, transportation, and school districts (if applicable). A "Place Name Index" at the end of this section makes it easy for researchers to jump to a particular place. The Comparative Statistics section allows users to find data about the 100 largest incorporated places, townships, and CDPs (Census Designated Places) using different data points (population, commute to work, marriage status, etc.). Community Rankings provides information on 150 places with populations over 2,500, ranking them in ascending and descending order based on employment, ancestry, marital status, crime, and more. The Education section offers an overall profile of New Jersey schools, New Jersey's National Assessment of Education Progress, and school district rankings. The final sections provide profiles of ancestry, ethnicity, and climate. This curated, reliable, easy-to-use reference is recommended.— **ARBA Staff Reviewer**

Ohio

29.   **Profiles of Ohio.** 5th ed. Amenia, N.Y., Grey House Publishing, 2018. 800p. illus. maps. index. $149.00pa. ISBN 13: 978-1-68217-767-9; 978-1-68217-768-6 (e-book).

This is the fifth edition of *Profiles of Ohio;* the previous edition published in 2015. The beginning of the book provides user guides to the Profile, Education, Ancestry and Ethnicity, and Climate sections. These are followed by key facts about the state (state bird, state flower, state symbol, etc.), information about the state government structure, the state's land and natural resources, the state's energy profile, and more. A series of color demographic maps closes out the first section of the book. The demographic maps provide easy-to-read visualizations of such things as median household incomes, percentage of college graduates, and population. Profiles of counties and places (the longest section) are arranged alphabetically and are followed by a place-name index. The next section, Comparative Statistics, provides data on the largest 100 communities. The fourth section, Community Rankings, lists both the top and bottom 150 communities with a population of 2,500 or more. These rankings include such things water area, land area, marriage status, employment, education, homeownership rates, and many other indicators. Education, Ancestry and Ethnicity, and Climate sections round out the volume. In these sections, users will find answers to questions on many topics, including school district rankings, racial group rankings, and significant storm events. This is a reliable, comprehensive, one-stop resources that is recommended for public libraries, especially libraries in Ohio.—**ARBA Staff Reviewer**

Texas

30.   Haley, James L. **The Handy Texas Answer Book.** Canton, Mich., Visible Ink Press, 2019. 395p. illus. maps. index. $21.95pa. ISBN 13: 978-1-57859-634-8.

This installment in the Handy Answer series by historian James L. Haley, known for his books *The Buffalo Soldier* and *Sam Houston,* gives readers a well-written and well-informed guide to Texas history and life. The information is provided in a question-and-answer format, but the quality of the writing is such that it is easy to read from cover to cover. A timeline in the front of the book starts with c. 14,000 BCE and continues through 2017. There is also a useful section on Texas basics, such as state flower, state song, state flag, geography, population, and demographics. The chapters begin with one on Texas's native Indians, European explorers, the establishment of Spanish missions, and European immigration. The following chapters are just as interesting: "The Republic of Texas," "Texas as Antebellum State," "Reconstruction to Urbanization," "Modern Texas," "Texas Regions," "Business, Religion, and Education," "Environment and Nature," "The Big Five Cities," "Good Times, Texas Style" (sports, zoos, food, etc.), "Quirky Texas" (regional speech, legends, etc.), and "Texan Notables" (outlaws, artists, musicians, etc.). Chapters are enlivened by black-and-white photographs and maps. The back of the book contains a listing of Texas governors and presidents (1691-1846) and of Texas state governors (1846-present). A bibliography and index round out the book. Highly recommended for public and school libraries, especially those in Texas.—**ARBA Staff Reviewer**

Vermont

31.   **Vermont Life Magazine. https://archive.org/details/vermontlifemagazine?sort =titleSorter.** [Website] Free. Date reviewed: 2018.

This site accesses digital editions of 285 issues of *Vermont Life* magazine, which published quarterly for over 70 years. Starting with the first issue in 1946, the magazine emphasized bucolic landscapes, regional activities, and stories of interest pertaining to local figures. Site users have access to every page of most every issue published. Users can scroll through the list of magazine issues, sortable by publication date, views, and more. Selecting an issue allows access to its readable version. Readers simply click on a page to "turn" it, and can zoom in and out. There are a number of downloading options, including Kindle, EPub, Full Text, PDF, and others. Extended articles may highlight industry or activity unique to Vermont. "The Scatchard Pottery" in Volume 21, Issue 3, shares how clay artisans found their home in Vermont, while "Horsemen on Skis" in Volume 5, Issue 2, discusses Norwich College's Army ROTC winter training. And the more recent Volume 72, Issue 1, includes "Landmark Decision," about the role of Vermont's historic churches in a changing religious climate. Readers will note how the magazine evolved in style and content through the inclusion or exclusion of particular features, the changing emphasis on advertising, and the incorporation of new technologies. The archive would appeal to regional historians, armchair travelers, landscape photographers, and many others.—**ARBA Staff Reviewer**

Virginia

32. **Profiles of Virginia.** 4th ed. Amenia, N.Y., Grey House Publishing, 2017. 658p. illus. maps. index. $149.00pa. ISBN 13: 978-1-68217-381-7.

This fourth edition (see ARBA 2015, entry 31) provides readers with data from all populated counties and communities in Virginia, based on data included in the larger *Profiles of America.* Readers will also find data on 338 unincorporated places. A detailed user guide is followed by an About Virginia section that includes a color photo gallery, a brief history and timeline, and information on the state's government. A series of easy-to-read, color maps show congressional districts, the percent of population who voted for Donald Trump (by county), populated places, and more. These are followed by color demographic maps depicting such things as median household income, median home value, and population. The largest section of the book, Profiles, presents counties in alphabetical order, starting with Accomack County. County profiles include location within the state, statistics on population, religion, economy, employment, education, housing, and other information. County profiles are followed by profiles of cities or towns within the county. These include statistics on population, employment, income, educational attainment, housing, health insurance, and transportation. This section concludes with a place-name index for quick navigation. The Comparative Statistics section comes next and compares the 100 largest incorporated cities by several data points: marriage status, crime, population by race/Hispanic Origin, health insurance, etc. Community Rankings allows researchers to compare places based on a variety of such categories as median age, ancestry, population, elevation, rental vacancy rate, and more. There are also sections devoted to education, ancestry and ethnicity, and climate. All in all, this is a complete statistical portrait of Virginia and can serve as a resource for a variety of patrons. Recommended for public and academic libraries.—**ARBA Staff Reviewer**

Africa

General Works

33. **Africa South of the Sahara.** 47th ed. Edited by Europa Publications. New York, Routledge/Taylor & Francis Group, 2017. 1570p. index. $980.00. ISBN 13: 978-1-85743-875-8.

This detailed examination of the 53 countries south of the Sahara begins with a brief foreword, a note on sources, information about contributors, a guide to abbreviations, and a calendar of political events, 2016-2017. The remainder of the book is divided into three parts. The first, General Survey, contains a series of essays: "Economic Trends in Africa

South of the Sahara," "State Failure in Africa," "A Century of Development," "The State of Relations between France and Africa," "China Continues its Rise in Africa," and "Brazil's Engagement with Africa." The second and longest part of the book, Country Surveys, lists all 53 counties in alphabetic order starting with Angola. All entries follow the same format. A physical and social geography discussion is followed by sections on recent history and the economy. A section on statistics comes next and covers everything from area and population to industry to cost of living to tourism to trade and health. A directory of offices and officials follows the statistical data and includes information for government offices, the press, banks, political organizations, and much more. All country profiles conclude with a bibliography. The last part of the book, Regional Information, provides information on regional organizations like the UN and the Economic Community of West Africa, and on such major commodities as aluminum, cobalt, coffee, gold, iron ore, sugar, tea, and tobacco. The book concludes with a list of research institutes concerned with Africa, select bibliographies of books and periodicals, and an index of regional organizations. Those wishing for an electronic version of the content should consult www.europaworld.com. This curated collection based on reliable data is recommended for academic libraries.— **ARBA Staff Reviewer**

Angola

34. James, W. Martin. **Historical Dictionary of Angola.** 3d ed. Lanham, Md., Rowman & Littlefield, 2018. 518p. maps. (Historical Dictionaries of Africa). $125.00; $118.00 (e-book). ISBN 13: 978-1-5381-1122-2; 978-1-5381-1123-9 (e-book).

The last edition of this title published in 2011 (see ARBA 2012, entry 88). This third edition begins with an overview of Angolan history followed by a chronology, maps, and a list of acronyms. The dictionary entries include people, places, events, and social institutions covering the country's politics, economics, society, and culture. As examples of the volume's tidbits: Angola is larger than California and Texas combined—the 7th largest country in Africa. The Angolan Civil War lasted from 1975, when Portugal relinquished control over the country, to 2002. The war was an ethnic conflict as well as a battlefield of the Cold War with Cuba, the USSR, South Africa, Zaire, the US, China, Portugal, the Warsaw Pact nations, Brazil, France, Algeria, Zambia, Southwest Africa/Namibia, North Korea, Gabon, Côte d'Ivoire, and the Republic of Congo all playing a variety of roles. Peace finally came in 2002 with the MPLA, which had been backed by Cuba and the USSR, emerging as the dominant military and political force. After 26 years of civil war, the country's infrastructure is still in tatters. Angola has 2 doctors for every 10,000 people (compared to 26 per 10,000 people in the US). One in 5 children die before the age of 5. Angola is rich in diamonds and oil, yet two-thirds of the people survive on less than $2/day. Brazil has invested heavily in the Angolan economy, and Brazilian culture is influential as seen in the popularity of Brazilian soap operas and capoeira, a fusion of martial arts, music, and gymnastics that began in Africa, evolved in Brazil, and has returned to Angola. Removal of land mines is a major challenge. Because of the landmines, laid by both sides during the civil war, Angola has the highest number of amputees per capita in the world— there are more than 80,000 mine-disabled Angolans, prompting Angola to host the Miss Landmine Survivor contest in 2008. The country must import food because so much of its farmland remains mined—only 12.97% is arable. Although Angola has a long literary heritage, books are a luxury few can afford—the cost of a book varies from 750 to 1500 kwanzas (in 2017 $1 equaled 165.9 kwanzas). Appendixes include place-name changes, major government leaders since independence, provincial capitals and their populations, Angolan holidays, and an extensive bibliography (over 100 pages) with English and Portuguese titles as well as web sources.—**Adrienne Antink**

Botswana

35.   Morton, Barry, and Jeff Ramsay. **Historical Dictionary of Botswana.** Lanham, Md., Rowman & Littlefield, 2018. 460p. maps. (Historical Dictionaries of Africa). $110.00; $104.50 (e-book). ISBN 13: 978-1-5381-1132-1; 978-1-5381-1133-8 (e-book).

Part of the Historical Dictionaries of Africa series from Rowman & Littlefield, this fifth edition on the country of Botswana contains new and updated information in the dictionary section, as well as an expanded and updated bibliography. A general overview and history of the country is provided in the preface, followed by maps and an historical chronology of events. The dictionary entries provide extensive information, with *see* references bolded and *see also* references in all caps. Three appendixes present national elections, demographic trends, and indigenous languages information. Known for their bibliographies sections in this series, this book is no exception with both print and electronic resources in both general and very specialized subject areas (such as arts and crafts, literature and folklore, sciences, women and gender, and economics to name a few. An excellent resource on one of the many modern-day countries in Africa.—**Bradford Lee Eden**

Gabon

36.   Yates, Douglas A. **Historical Dictionary of Gabon.** 4th ed. Lanham, Md., Rowman & Littlefield, 2018. 606p. maps. (Historical Dictionaries of Africa). $140.00; $133.00 (e-book). ISBN 13: 978-1-5381-1011-9; 978-1-5381-1012-6 (e-book).

This fourth edition comes approximately ten years after the last one was published (see ARBA 2007, entry 86). The author, a professor of political science at the American Graduate School in Paris and a Maître de Conférences in Anglo-American Jurisprudence at the Université de Cergy-Pontoise, cowrote the third edition. The volume begins with a list of abbreviations and acronyms, three maps, a chronology from 1472 to 2017, and an introduction that includes discussion of the land and people and the country's history. There are over three hundred A-to-Z entries. Words in bold font cross-reference to other main entries within the dictionary. The dictionary also employs *see* and *see also* references. Coverage is broad, including politics, economics, health issues, culture, and important figures. The entries vary in length. Brother Dominique Fara, the first native of Gabon to be made a Catholic brother, gets a short paragraph, while the book gives President Ali Bongo and France over eleven pages each. There are several appendixes: "French Commandants, Governors, and Governors-General," "Presidents and Prime Ministers," "Roman Catholic Bishops," and "Traditional Monarchs," followed by a lengthy bibliography subdivided into General Works and Sources, Archaeology and Prehistory, Early Accounts and Exploration

Accounts, History, Government, Economy, Society, Sciences, and Arts. Recommended.—
ARBA Staff Reviewer

Asia

General Works

37.   **The Himalayas: An Encyclopedia of Geography, History, and Culture.** Andrew
J. Hund and James A. Wren, eds. Santa Barbara, Calif., ABC-CLIO, 2018. 326p. illus.
index. $94.00. ISBN 13: 978-1-4408-3938-2; 978-1-4408-3939-9 (e-book).

Say "the Himalayas" and we instantly think about the mystique surrounding Mount
Everest, but this reference reminds us that there is so much more to this region where
Hinduism, Buddhism, Islam, and animism meet and coexist. We forget that the Hindu-
Kush-Himalaya region stretches from Afghanistan and Pakistan across the continent to
Tibet, China, Sikkim, Bhutan, and Nepal. The volume begins with brief thematic essays
on a range of topics, such as Himalayan prehistoric cave people, Hindu sacred sites and
pilgrimages, climate change, NGOs, and LGBTQ communities. These essays are perhaps
too brief, tantalizing but leaving the reader wanting more. The main body of the text is
comprised of short topical entries, covering both Asian and European influences, as well
as the geography, flora and fauna, people, and events of the region. To give a taste of
what is covered, we learn that approximately one-third of the world's population gets its
water from the watersheds and rivers that originate in the Himalayas. Bhutan measures its
progress toward modernization with its Gross National Happiness index, not its GDP. The
Karakoram Range (which includes K2) is the world's most extensively glaciated landscape
outside of the polar regions. Into extreme experiences? Try one of the three marathons
held on the slopes of Mount Everest, starting at Base Camp. Board the Lhasa Express,
the high elevation railway that runs from Qinghai Province, China to Lhasa, Tibet (1,215
miles). The train offers oxygen supplies for each passenger and a doctor on each car.
Travelers must have a health registration card certifying they are healthy enough for the
trip. The book ends with excerpts from a small selection of primary documents that range
from the formation of the Himalayas as described in the ancient writing, the *Mahabharata*
to William of Rubruck's (a Flemish Franciscan missionary and explorer) *Account of the
Mongols* written from 1253 to 1255 and Nepal's 2015 constitution.—**Adrienne Antink**

Europe

Slovenia

38.   Plut-Pregelj, Leopoldina, Gregor Kranjc, Žarko Lazarević, and Carole Rogel.
Historical Dictionary of Slovenia. 3d ed. Lanham, Md., Rowman & Littlefield, 2018.
700p. maps. (Historical Dictionaries of Europe). $150.00; $142.50 (e-book). ISBN 13:
978-1-5381-1105-5; 978-1-5381-1106-2 (e-book).

This is the third edition of this volume (1996, 2007), part of the Historical Dictionaries of Europe series (see ARBA 2008, entry 130). Not only does it provide the historical information related to Slovenia covered in the first two editions, it also adds significant content and information from 2007 to 2017, especially content related to the global economic crisis of 2008, politics, migration challenges, and protest movements. With maps, a historical chronology, an extensive introduction, and three appendixes that document the rulers of Slovene lands, political parties in state assembly from 1990 to 2017, and selected macroeconomic indicators from 1995 to 2015, this extensive tome is arranged like all the dictionaries in this series. Each topic appears in bold font, as do important dates and cross-references. *See also* entries are set in all caps. A large bibliography divided into ten sections and twenty-two subsections means that this book contains everything needed to begin research on the historical and modern-day country of Slovenia.—**Bradford Lee Eden**

Turkey

39. Heper, Metin, Duygu Öztürk-Tunçel, and Nur Bilge Criss. **Historical Dictionary of Turkey.** 4th ed. Lanham, Md., Rowman & Littlefield, 2018. 796p. (Historical Dictionaries of Europe). $180.00; $171.00 (e-book). ISBN 13: 978-1-5381-0224-4; 978-1-5381-0225-1 (e-book

This is the 4th edition of the *Historical Dictionary of Turkey* (see ARBA 2010, entry 98). The Kingdom of Turkey began on the Orkhon River in Siberia in the 7th century. The Turks settled in the Anatolian area, a geographical location in Asia Minor during the Middle Ages. This Asia Minor location lies between the eastern and western cultures. The Turks were greatly influenced by the Muslims in the 10th century and became the site of the Ottoman Empire from 1299 to 1922. Today in the 21st century, Turkey has managed to bring the social periphery in the country to the center, a participant in western politics though in an eastern culture.

The dictionary covers the history of Turkey from 1261 to June 19, 2017, beginning with Kingdom of Turkey, the Ottoman Empire, and the Republic of Turkey through to the modern Turkey era. At this time President Erdogan has put tight controls in place following the July 2016 coup by members of the Turkish military. He is trying to have his Muslim country become a member of the western-influenced European Union and maintain his membership in NATO.

The dictionary has 900 A-Z entries about Turkey. There are black-and-white maps to supplement the definitions of people, places, and the history of Turkey. A chronology of the history and a timeline are provided.

The book is a good tool to aid in understanding the importance of geographic location in understanding the country of Turkey, its culture, and its political stance in today's world.—**Kay Stebbins Slattery**

Latin America and the Caribbean

Guatemala

40.   Fry, Michael F. **Historical Dictionary of Guatemala.** Lanham, Md., Rowman & Littlefield, 2018. 413p. maps. (Historical Dictionaries of the Americas). $110.00; $104.50 (e-book). ISBN 13: 978-1-5381-1130-7; 978-1-5381-1131-4 (e-book).

This entry from the Historical Dictionaries of the Americas series is an entirely new volume; a previous version by a different author appeared in 1973. The first part of the book includes a section of acronyms and abbreviations, a basic map, and a chronology running from 2000 BCE to 2017. These resources are followed by an introduction that covers the country's physical features, people, and history, including the pre-Columbian period, conquest, life as a colony, independence and the republic, the brief period under a freely elected government from 1944 to 1954, and the period of military rule and civil wars that followed the 1954 U.S.-backed coup. The more than 700 entries in the dictionary vary in length from a short sentence to a few pages and cover people, places, culture, politics, the economy, and more. The topics cover quite a bit of territory, from the kaqchikels (a large Maya ethnic and linguistic group), to Nobel Peace Prize winner Rigoberta Menchu, to Protestantism. Entries include generous cross-references. In the case of Catholicism, for instance, the list of *see also* references is longer than the entry itself. The book concludes with an extensive bibliography, divided into sections starting with an introduction and including materials on topics from the pre-Columbian period to the 21st century. A fair percentage of these materials refer to Spanish-language publications. Recommended.—**ARBA Staff Reviewer**

Trinidad and Tobago

41.   Pemberton, Rita, Debbie McCollin, Gelien Matthews, and Michael Toussaint. **Historical Dictionary of Trinidad and Tobago.** Lanham, Md., Rowman & Littlefield, 2018. 452p. (Historical Dictionaries of the Americas). $110.00; $104.50 (e-book). ISBN 13: 978-1-5381-1145-1; 978-1-5381-1146-8 (e-book).

Part of the Historical Dictionaries of the Americas series from Rowman & Littlefield, this new edition is an extensive revision of the original edition. Since the two islands of Trinidad and Tobago were separate colonies for 400 years before they were united, the editors have outlined the histories of each of these islands separately, before they present the history of their existence as a single colony from 1889/1898. As a result, the term Trinidad and Tobago as a single term or as separate terms is not cross-referenced. After the usual maps and chronology, the historical dictionary is provided. Eight appendixes are included: government officials; the reestablished Tobago House of Assembly (THA); national holidays and observances of Trinidad and Tobago; schools (secondary denominational); prominent newspapers; Panorama: Steelband Competition winners (large band category); population (2016 estimates); and population by age: 1960 and 2000. A large and comprehensive bibliography follows. Probably the most complete dictionary/history of these islands available for the academic reference shelf.—**Bradford Lee Eden**

Middle East

General Works

42.   **Digital Library of the Middle East https://dlme.clir.org.** [Website] Free. Date reviewed: 2019.

While currently under development, the Digital Library of the Middle East (DLME) is already a vital resource for students and educators and others regarding Middle Eastern history, archaeology, culture, and other topics. The site aims to digitally preserve and promote thousands of years of Middle Eastern culture by gathering information on a range of cultural materials—architecture, maps, manuscripts, sculptures, coins, weapons, and many other artifacts—which are at risk of erasure due to the ongoing conflicts in the region. Other items are dispersed throughout collections around the world. From the homepage, users can Search the Prototype to access any available materials. From here, users can choose from a list of filters including Language, Type, Creator, Source Institution, Medium, and Thumbnail, to achieve a sampling of what the full database will hopefully offer. Under the Type filter, users can currently find over six thousand artifacts with Images (and over one hundred thousand without). Information for items with Images, mostly in black and white, may include date (general), extent (dimensions), medium, provenance, spatial (general region), temporal (general era), or format (e.g., amulet, arrowhead). Clicking on the thumbnail affords a slightly larger view. Users can also access close to two hundred maps and over seven hundred examples of text (poems, letters, commentary, illuminated manuscripts, liturgical texts, and more) beneath the Type option. Outside of the database, users can select the Sample Exhibits link on the homepage to find three unique examples of ways in which artifacts from the DLME can be used in scholarship: "Qatar's Maritime History and Heritage," "Identifying Papyri with DLME," and "Piecing Together the Ritual Use of Egyptian Female Figurines." Each of these exhibits offers a scholarly essay incorporating database artifacts and other links. Although the database is still under development, there is ample material here—**ARBA Staff Reviewer**

4 Economics and Business

General Works

Dictionaries and Encyclopedias

43. **The New Palgrave Dictionary of Economics.** 3d ed. New York, Palgrave Macmillan, 2018. 20v. illus. index. $6,500/set; $6,500 (e-book). ISBN 13: 978-1-349-95188-8; 978-1-349-95190-1 (e-book).

This is the third edition of the authoritative *New Palgrave Dictionary of Economics* (the second edition published in 2008). This edition includes thousands of entries—hundreds of which are new—by approximately 1,700 authors, 36 of whom are Nobel Laureates. In print, the material comprises 20 volumes arranged in an A-to-Z format. The dictionary reflects the expansion of the field of economics and the major economic developments since 2008, including the global financial crisis. The front matter includes a publication history, a preface to this edition and prefaces to the previous two editions, the introduction to the book that started it all, the 1893 *Dictionary of Political Economy,* and editorial information. The signed entries vary in length and include reference works; many have keywords and *see also* references. Each article includes a *Journal of Economic Literature* (JEL) code. The dictionary makes extensive use of illustrations. There are 754 in total; 108 illustrations are in color. A series of appendixes includes lists of entries by author for all three editions and entries by author from the original 1893 work. The final appendix groups entries by JEL code. The electronic version has the advantage of taking up less space, and it provides search capacities not available for print. This venerable reference is highly recommended to large academic libraries looking to update their edition. The cost is $9,750 for those libraries considering the purchase of both the print and the electronic versions.—**ARBA Staff Reviewer**

44. **The SAGE Encyclopedia of Business Ethics and Society.** 2d ed. Robert W. Kolb, ed. Thousand Oaks, Calif., Sage, 2018. 7v. index. $1,295.00/set. ISBN 13: 978-1-4833-8152-7.

This 7-volume 2d edition adds more than 300 new entries to a set that contains nearly 1,200 entries overall. Entries range in length from 500 to almost 11,000 words, and all entries provide cross-references, reference lists, and suggested readings. In the front matter, users will find information about members of the editorial board and contributors along with a list of entries, a reader's guide, and an introduction. In the introduction, Editor Robert W. Kohl, finance professor at Loyola University, Chicago, discusses the interrelatedness of business ethics and business and society. Though the two disciplines use different methodologies, they are both concerned "with normative issues surrounding commerce." Kolb also explains the rationale behind the encyclopedia, which is to address "the normative dimensions of commerce." To this end, the encyclopedia embraces 24 themes and dimensions that include Accounting and Taxation; Customers and Consumers; Ethical Thought and Theory; Management; Rights and Justice; and Scandals, Failures, and Disasters, among many others. Individual entries cover concepts, legislation, judicial rulings, scandals, events, and individuals, such as the Affordable Care Act, Age Discrimination, Data Privacy, Hedge Funds, Virtual Currencies, the Madoff Scandal, the Financial Crisis, 2008-2011, the Glass Ceiling, Whistleblowing, Milton Friedman, and Employee Monitoring and Surveillance. Entries are well written and informative and coverage is wide ranging. This set is recommended for academic audiences.—**ARBA Staff Reviewer**

Digital Resources

45.   **EconBiz https://www.econbiz.de/.** [Website] Free. Date reviewed: 2019.
    EconBiz allows users to search thousands of pages of academic writing on myriad subjects within the economics and business fields. As a portal to a number of databases, users can find book chapters, journal articles, working papers, and more. For students, EconBiz additionally offers several tools to help develop research skills regarding how to search, cite, and access information in particular regard to the business and economic fields of study. Users can enter general or specific search terms in the prominent bar, conduct an advanced search, create a list of favorites, access search history, limit a search to open access materials, and perform other actions. After entering a search term(s), users can sort materials by relevance or date and can narrow their options by publication date, subject, online availability, publication type, language, institution, and more. Selected materials are listed with title, author, date, and excerpt. Materials may include a link to a full text via the original publishing source (e.g., institution, journal) with download link, abstract, and other information. There may also be a list of more access options. The Thesaurus link on the homepage is an excellent tool for use in crafting searches, with access to nearly six thousand standardized subject headings and close to twenty thousand terms concerning business and economics and any relevant concepts (law, politics, etc.). Users can peruse a long list of the most popular search terms, including economic growth, consumer behavior, China, globalization, financial crisis, portfolio management, trade liberalization, the United States, and others. Under the About EconBiz tab, users will find a list of included journals and databases which allows users to look at publications by institutions, collections, and catalog database. Users may also appreciate the beta section which highlights site features in development including scientific figure search engines and search visualizations (maps, timelines, etc.). EconBiz is available in English, French, and the original German.—**ARBA Staff Reviewer**

46.   **Hockeystick.com. https://www.hockeystick.com/.** [Website] Free. Date reviewed: 2018.

This site offers a variety of tools and resources aimed at helping Canadian companies reach "hockeystick" growth. It primarily functions as an open database of Canadian company and investor information that can be maximized in a variety of ways. From the homepage, users can search companies and investors from the central bar, or access the database straightaway via several approaches. Users can click on a map of companies and investors by province; select from a table of companies, venture capital firms, accelerators, government programs, and more; click on one of the top 5 sectors or top 10 investment verticals; or scroll through a menu of recently added companies and investors. Incorporated into appealing graphics, this gateway offers a good foundation to the greater detail of the database. The database itself lists general information for each entity: legal name, primary location, business types, operating status, year founded and website. Clicking on the company name links to a more detailed profile which may include social media, affiliated organizations, recent deals, number of employees, investors, and more. As this is an open database, users can suggest edits. Registered users gain access to a number of tools that help manage and maximize the data, such as Deal Flow, which helps users create workflow steps and gather qualitative and quantitative metrics and a Dashboard where users can build or customize data visualizations. These tools and others are described under the Features tab on the homepage. Registered users can also save searches and store information on selected entities. The Industries tab aligns these tools/features with the particular entities (e.g., accelerators, government programs) they most benefit. Hockeystick is a good way to gain an overall sense of Canadian business and investment which could appeal to entrepreneurs, investors, and educators and students of economics and affiliated disciplines.—**ARBA Staff Reviewer**

Directories

47.   **Business Information Resources 2019.** 26th ed. Amenia, N.Y., Grey House Publishing, 2019. 1978p. index. $195.00. ISBN 13: 978-1-64265-060-0.

Business Information Resources covers 102 industries and contains listings of magazines, journals, websites, associations, directories, databases, and trade shows. Since its last edition, the resource has added over 400 new records and thousands of updates; this edition contains 23,951 listings. Front matter includes "User Guide"; "User Key"; "Content Summary of Chapter Listings"; "U.S. Small Business Administration *Small Business Profile*"; "NAICS Codes: Cross-Reference Table"; and "SIC Codes: Cross-Reference Table." Entries are listed alphabetically by industry and among the industries covered are: Accounting, Aviation and Aerospace, Apparel and Accessories, Communications and Media, Engineering, Healthcare, Legal Services, Manufacturing, Marketing, Petroleum and Allied Products, and Motor Vehicles. Each industry section includes subjects; for example, the category Apparel and Accessories includes subcategories among which are Clothing Contractors, Headwear, Hosiery, Sunglasses, and Sportswear. Each industry section includes annotated lists of Associations; Newsletters, Magazines and Journals; Trade Shows; Industry Web Sites; and Directories and Databases. Each entry includes a record number, title, address, phone number, toll-free number, fax number, e-mail, web site, key executives, description , members (if association), year founded, frequency (for publications), subscription price, circulation for publications, scheduled special issues (magazines), attendees (of trade show), and month (if listing is for a trade show). Indexes are available for entries and publishers. *Business Information Resources* contains a trove of information resources for industries and should be a staple in business collections of academic, special, and public libraries. The guide should prove to be of great help to consumers searching for information about specific products and services, for researchers, faculty and students of industry information, and as a starting point to a research paper. Highly recommended to business collections.—**Lucy Heckman**

48.   **Financial Post Directory of Directors 2019.** Toronto, Grey House Publishing Canada, 2018. 1392p. $449.00. ISBN 13: 978-1-68217-838-6.

The *Financial Post Directory of Directors* is published annually each fall and "presents an up-to-date list of Canadian business people, with the directorships and offices they hold" and "also contains a list of key Canadian companies, both privately traded and publicly owned." The companies listed must meet the following criteria: incorporation in Canada; substantial revenue or assets; and Canadian residency for most of the directors for each company. Each of the entries for directors includes: name, title, degrees received, address, and previous positions. Each of the entries for companies includes name, address, telephone, website, directors, and other executive officers. Indexes include an Industrial Classification Index for Companies (e.g., banks, real estate); geographic index; and a list of abbreviations in directory listings. Additionally featured in this resource are reports: "Anatomy of a top Canadian Director"; "Canadian Board Diversity Council 2017 Annual report Card;" "The Inclusion Imperative: In 2018 building a better board means building a board that looks like Canada"; "Inbound M & A: What Directors Need to Know"; and a list of the Financial Post 500, its annual list of Canada's largest company by revenue. The *Financial Post Directory of Directors* is an excellent repository of data about directors and their companies and features results of surveys about directors in Canada. Recommended especially to larger public business libraries and academic libraries supporting advanced degrees in Business Administration.—**Lucy Heckman**

49.   **FP Survey-Industrials, 2017.** 91st ed. Toronto, Grey House Publishing Canada, 2017. 978p. index. $310.00pa. ISBN 13: 978-1-68217-536-1.

FP Survey-Industrials serves as a guide to all industrial companies publicly traded and reporting in Canada. Coverage includes companies involved in banking, manufacturing, real estate, forestry, financial management, and other areas. In each company entry, users will find a full legal name; an introductory paragraph; an address, telephone, website, and email; a profile, describing company's business and operations; recent merger and acquisition activity; directors, trustees, and other executive officers; capital stock; major shareholder information; price range for stocks; capital stock changes; dividends; long-term debt; financial statistics; and related companies (wholly owned subsidiaries, subsidiaries). Data is gathered by the Financial Post (FP) from corporate reports, news releases, company websites, filings of the Ontario Securities Commission's filings, price feeds from stock exchanges, and inquiries sent to the company. In addition to the directory information, *FP Survey-Industrials* contains: Guide to Financial Statistics Tables; Top Ten by Industry (listings of companies within various industries among which are banks, energy, utilities, and transportation); the Year in Review (including corporate name changes and dividend changes); abbreviations listing; and an index of companies. The *FP Survey-Industrials* is a comprehensive source of data for industrial companies publicly traded in Canada.

It is highly recommended to academic libraries supporting undergraduate and graduate business programs and to larger public and research libraries.—**Lucy Heckman**

50.   **FP Survey-Mines & Energy, 2017.** 91st ed. Toronto, Grey House Publishing Canada, 2017. 992p. index. $310.00pa. ISBN 13: 978-1-68217-538-5.

FP Survey-Mines & Energy is "a guide to all natural resource companies publicly traded and reporting in Canada." Included in this resource, now in its 91st edition, is a directory to companies involved in "the exploration for, development and production of base and precious metals, industrial minerals, oils and gas and electricity generation." Each entry contains: full legal name; introductory paragraph; profile of company; recent mergers and acquisitions activity; predecessor information about company; directors, trustees and other executive officers; capital stock; major shareholder; price range; dividends; long-term debt; related companies (wholly owned subsidiaries, subsidiaries); and financial statistics. Data is obtained for each company from annual reports, news releases, company websites, stock exchange bulletins, and "solicitations to the companies via data forms, telephone calls, faxes and email." In addition to the company entries, this resource contains a Guide to Financial Statements; Top Ten by Industry in each of 22 Industry Groups of the Global Industry Classification Standards; the Year in Review, a synopsis of activity from July 1, 2016, to August 8, 2017; Abbreviations; and an index of Companies. *FP Survey-Mines & Energy* provides a wealth of company information and is recommended to larger academic and research libraries.—**Lucy Heckman**

51.   **FP Survey-Predecessor & Defunct, 2017.** 33d ed. Toronto, Grey House Publishing Canada, 2017. 544p. $310.00pa. ISBN 13: 978-1-68217-540-8.

The *FP Survey-Predecessor & Defunct* is a "comprehensive collection of corporate changes which have occurred over the years since 1929 when Financial Post first began its coverage of the Canadian corporate landscape." This resource is a record of corporate changes including: amalgamations and mergers; acquisitions through purchase offers or shares exchanged; incorporation changes; many once-public companies that no longer exist; name changes; privatizations through buy-backs and redemptions; receiverships; reorganizations; and reverse takeovers. Companies are listed alphabetically and include date of establishment and date of changes made. For example, researchers can learn that the company AGIP Resources Ltd. had its name changed to Cameco Resources Ltd. on September 28, 1992, and that AISI Research Corporation was dissolved and struck off register on January 15, 1993. The records of publicly active companies are available in other FP publications in the series: *FP Survey-Industrials* and *FP Survey-Mines & Energy.* All the FP publications are recommended to larger academic and public libraries.—**Lucy Heckman**

Handbooks and Yearbooks

52.   Christensen, Mary. **Turn Your Spare Space into Serious Cash: How to Make Money on Airbnb, Homeaway, Flipkey, Booking.com, and More!.** Nashville, Tenn., AMACOM/American Management Association, 2018. 200p. index. $17.95pa. ISBN 13: 978-0-8144-3966-1.

This is an informative and easy read that is recommended for public libraries of all sizes. In it, readers will find a frank discussion of the pros and cons of renting out part or all of their home through any of the numerous hosting sites like Airbnb. The author is speaking from experience, as she and her husband rent out part of their home in Queenstown, New Zealand, to travelers from all over the world. Home sharing can be quite lucrative and is thus attractive to many looking to supplement household income, but this book paints a realistic picture of what it really means to have strangers in your family home.

The short chapters provide a roadmap for would-be hosts, discussing such essentials as setting household rules, writing honest reviews of guests, taking your neighbors into consideration, physically preparing your space, getting and increasing bookings, the importance of following local tax laws and regulations, what to do when you have unruly guests, and avoiding burning out. Stories about problematic guests will likely terrify those for whom home sharing is not the right fit. But for those would-be hosts, this is a valuable guide.—**ARBA Staff Reviewer**

53. **Handbook of Migration and Globalisation.** Anna Triandafyllidou, ed. Northampton, Mass., Edward Elgar, 2018. 487p. index. (Handbooks on Globalisation). $290.00. ISBN 13: 978-1-78536-750-2; 978-1-78536-751-9 (e-book).

This wide-ranging exploration of the interaction between the movement of people and the changing economic nature of the world draws on the knowledge and experience of forty-one academics and other researchers, from institutions such as the World Bank, and from five different continents. According to the publisher, this volume "explores the multifaceted linkages between two of the most important socioeconomic phenomena of our time."

Among the twenty-seven chapters there are both case studies and broader overviews of the political, economic, cultural, and even ecological aspects of these subjects. Several of the studies focus on situations in individual countries and regions: China, India, Russia, North Africa, South America, and Ukraine, among others. The widely diverse modes of migration governance are examined in many of the texts, as are the economic factors which affect the patterns of movement between countries. One of the underlying themes is the struggles and the challenges that migrants must face, and the efforts made to assist them. Each chapter has numerous references, sometimes close to one hundred items, and despite the highly international focus, nearly all of the cited items have been published in English.

This is a text that requires some background knowledge from its readers, as complex subjects are explored. Academic libraries with patrons involved in international studies are clearly the target of this volume. Although the price is high, they should consider it.—**Mark Schumacher**

54. **Handbook of Research on New Product Development.** Peter N. Golder and Debanjan Mitra, eds. Northampton, Mass., Edward Elgar, 2018. 447p. index. $270.00. ISBN 13: 978-1-78471-814-5; 978-1-78471-815-2 (e-book).

How are new products conceived and how do they enter the marketplace, then succeed or fail? While there are a number of books available covering new product development, the *Handbook of Research on New Product Development,* is unique in providing in one volume an overview of the existing academic research on new product development. Additionally, it identifies areas for further and future research. The handbook's editors are both professors of marketing from the Tuck School of Business at Dartmouth and the Warrington College of Business, University of Florida; the contributors hold academic positions in business, marketing, and supply chain management with expertise in aspects of new product development at prestigious business schools and colleges around the world.

Beginning with an introduction and overview of research in the field, sections cover the five common stages of new product development: idea generation (including chapters on customer-driven innovation); market analysis; product design and development (including chapters on new product demand forecasting; product enhancements, such as upgrades, add-ons, extras and accessories; sustainability, and open innovation); commercialization; and market outcomes (including chapters on word of mouth processes, crowdfunding, and best practices in new product development). The final section covers areas for new and further research such as opportunity identification, idea screening, concept and market testing, and product launch strategies among others. Each chapter includes extensive references. The handbook's primary audience is academic researchers and graduate students, although new product managers and practitioners may benefit from this thorough review of the research to date. It will be an essential addition to all large research and academic libraries that support marketing and product development programs.—**Colleen Seale**

55.   **Principles of Business: Economics.** Hackensack, N.J., Salem Press, 2017. 539p. illus. index. $165.00. ISBN 13: 978-1-68217-672-6; 978-1-68217-673-3 (e-book).

Principles of Business: Economics is part of the Principles of Business series which is "intended to introduce students and researchers to the fundamentals of important and far-reaching business topics using easy-to-understand language." Others in the series are: Finance, Marketing, Entrepreneurship, Management, and Accounting. Entries in this volume are listed in alphabetical order and among the topics presented are Special Problems in Economics, Transfer Pricing, North American Free Trade Agreement (NAFTA), Global Marketing, Microeconomics Theory, Elasticity, E-Commerce, Exchange Rate, and Labor Relations. Each entry consists of an abstract and an overview. Each entry is signed and contributors are experts in the field. Each entry covers its topic clearly and concisely; for instance, the entry for High-Frequency Trading provides an introduction to the topic, discussion of specific applications, and viewpoints regarding this topic (e.g., whether high-frequency trading will render the current stock market obsolete). In addition to the entries and an index, a glossary of terms is provided; the glossary contains definitions of terms such as antitrust law and controlled transactions as well as for specific organizations, legislation, and key individuals. *Principles of Business: Economics* is an excellent source for students taking introductory courses in business and for researchers and anyone wanting to learn more about economic concepts. Recommended to academic libraries supporting economics and social sciences curricula as well as to public libraries.—**Lucy Heckman**

56.   **Principles of Business: Entrepreneurship.** Hackensack, N.J., Salem Press, 2017. 387p. illus. index. $165.00. ISBN 13: 978-1-68217-601-6; 978-1-68217-602-3 (e-book).

In this series, Principles of Business, the publisher's intent is to provide a "comprehensive introduction" to each topic. Scholars and experts in business contribute signed articles on each topic. In this volume, sixteen contributors wrote the sixty-five articles. All contributors have master's degrees, some have doctorate degrees. Some have business experience, others have a consulting business. The articles are well written and easy to understand. Each article includes an abstract, an overview of main concepts, a discussion of the topic with issues, and a bibliography. Some of them include applications; some of them include viewpoints. Most articles run four to six pages.

Organized by title in an A-Z fashion, the table of contents and/or the index can be consulted to determine where a particular subject is addressed. For example, leadership is at the beginning under "Authentic Leadership," and is also listed under "Executive Leadership," "Inclusive Leadership," "Innovation Leadership," "Leadership" "Leadership & Motivation, "Servant Leadership," and "Transformational Leadership." That being said, this volume is appropriate for public libraries as well as academic institutions for undergraduates and could certainly be used with high school juniors and seniors.— **Ladyjane Hickey**

57. **The SAGE Handbook of Small Business and Entrepreneurship.** Robert Blackburn, Dirk De Clerq, and Jarna Heinonen, eds. Thousand Oaks, Calif., Sage, 2018. 680p. index. $175.00. ISBN 13: 978-1-4739-2523-6.

The introduction discusses the overarching goal of this handbook: to take stock of past research and to push agendas forward in the highly heterogeneous and multidisciplinary field of entrepreneurship and small business. The target audience includes postgraduates, researchers, public and private analysts, and others. Readers will find information in four parts. The first, People and Entrepreneurial Processes, offers reviews of literature on entrepreneurial leadership, the role of networks in the entrepreneurial process, the relationship between entrepreneurship and migration, social entrepreneurship, and more. The second part, Entrepreneurship and Small Business Management and Organization, includes literature reviews for such topics as the nexus between entrepreneurship and strategy, corporate entrepreneurship, and the interface between marketing and entrepreneurship. Entrepreneurial Milieu, part three, discusses several topics including the effects of government regulation on entrepreneurship and specific features of international entrepreneurship research. The last part, Researching Small Business and Entrepreneurship, has chapters that examine the possibility of a paradigm shift in entrepreneurial research, the main methodological approaches used in studies of female entrepreneurs, the challenge of assessing causality in entrepreneurship research, and other matters. Chapters are supplemented with figures and tables and include notes and references. The book provides an author index and a subject index. This well-written and authoritative handbook is recommended for academic libraries.—**ARBA Staff Reviewer**

58. Sherman, Andrew J. **Mergers and Acquisitions from A to Z.** 4th ed. New York, AMACOM/American Management Association, 2018. 364p. index. $39.95. ISBN 13: 978-0-8144-3902-9; 978-0-8144-3903-6 (e-book).

Mergers and Acquisitions from A to Z now in its 4th edition "focuses primarily on mergers and acquisitions as a means of growing," although toward the end of the book certain external means are explored as well. This resource examines the nuts and bolts of mergers and acquisitions, helping readers learn about key terms and definitions; trends; reasons why a buyer buys and a seller sells; motivations in an acquisition and a merger; and recent developments and case studies. Topics covered include: the seller's perspective; the buyer's perspective; preparing the letter of intent; due diligence; regulatory considerations (e.g., environmental laws, labor and employment law); structuring the deal (stock vs. asset purchases, method of payment); valuation and pricing of the seller's company;

financing the acquisition; the purchase agreement; avoiding the deal killers; post-closing challenges (e.g., transition, legal issues); and alternatives to mergers and acquisitions. Sherman explains clearly the processes involved and advises readers on strategies to bring a deal to fruition while avoiding pitfalls. Included are lists of resources for prospective buyers and sellers; a list of resources and guides to equity financing; sample letters; a post-Sarbanes-Oxley due diligence checklist; and figures illustrating concepts (e.g., dealing with due diligence surprises; understanding the difference between joint ventures and strategic alliances). The chapter "Alternatives to Mergers and Acquisitions" concerns strategies involving the building of external relationships and alternatives discussed are joint ventures; franchising; and technology and merchandising licensing. *Mergers and Acquisitions* is highly recommended to practitioners and faculty and students in schools of business. It is recommended to public, special, and academic libraries supporting graduate and undergraduate programs in business. It should be used as supplementary reading for students and also as a starting point for researchers.—**Lucy Heckman**

59.   **Women Entrepreneurs and Strategic Decision Making in the Global Economy.** Tomos, Florica, Naresh Kumar, Nick Clifton, and Denis Hyams-Ssekasi, eds. Hershey, Pa., IGI Global, 2019. 411p. index. $215.00. ISBN 13: 978-1-52257-479-8; 978-1-52257-480-4 (e-book).

This reference source begins with a table of contents and a detailed table of contents. Each of the 15 chapters in some way contributes to understanding not just the increase in the number of women entrepreneurs worldwide and the success of these women but also to recognizing the structural barriers (educational, political, social) that keep women from full participation in the global economy. Users of this book will also come away with an appreciation of the impact of gender on strategic management and entrepreneurship. The geographical scope of the book is broad; there are chapters on Pakistan, India, Turkey, Bosnia and Herzegovina, Malaysia, Wales, and more. While most of the chapters are more narrowly focused on single countries or regions, there are articles such as "Inequalities: A Concern for Capitalism and Global Strategy" and "Born vs. Educated Entrepreneurs: Who Are Richer and Happier?" Chapters address a vast range of issues: work-family balance, intellectual capital, financing, new emergent technologies, information communication technologies, emotional intelligence, globalization, and, of course, entrepreneurship, among many others. The book concludes with an extensive index, which makes topics easily locatable. The book can be read from cover to cover, but each chapter can stand on its own. Libraries are also able to purchase separate chapters in an electronic format. This well-curated reference source should be considered (either as a whole or in part) by academic libraries.—**ARBA Staff Reviewer**

60.   Yocum, Jeanne. **The Self-Employment Survival Guide: Proven Strategies to Succeed as Your Own Boss.** Lanham, Md., Rowman & Littlefield, 2018. 198p. index. $18.95pa.; $17.99 (e-book). ISBN 13: 978-1-5381-0871-0; 978-1-5381-0872-7 (e-book).

The Self-Employment Survival Guide offers practical step-by-step advice on how to become one's own boss and how to build a successful business. The author, Jeanne Yocum, has had nearly thirty years of experience being self-employed as a ghostwriter and a public relations consultant and draws on her own experiences and those of other businesspeople. The stated mission of the book is "to give people who are considering self-employment a full view of what being your own boss entails. By learning the ups and downs that come with being in charge of your own livelihood. I hope you are well-prepared to make the best choice for you." Yocum covers several nitty-gritty topics: adjusting to working alone; setting prices for services and products; gathering a list of clients; keeping up with new skills; time management considerations; setting timelines; dealing with clients; money management; tax issues; deadbeat clients; stress; avoiding burnout; and planning for retirement. In addition to Yocum's experiences, "other voices" who discuss their experiences at being self-employed are: Mark G. Auerbach, principal of Mark G. Auerbach Public Relations; Holly Green, independent copywriter and marketing strategist; Howie Green, illustrator and designer; Stefan Lindegaard, author speaker, strategic adviser, and entrepreneur; Pat Mullaly, who established a graphic design firm, Circle Graphics; Barbara Rodriguez, entrepreneur, educator, and businesswoman; and Carol Savage, public relations and marketing communications freelance professional. Hearing from the entrepreneurs about their experiences is especially helpful and informative. The book includes an index. Highly recommended and fills a need for students or employees considering a future of being self-employed. It is especially recommended to public library collections.—**Lucy Heckman**

Accounting

Handbooks and Yearbooks

61.   **Principles of Business: Accounting.** Hackensack, N.J., Salem Press, 2017. 506p. illus. index. $165.00. ISBN 13: 978-1-68217-670-2; 978-1-68217-671-9 (e-books).

This title is the fifth volume of the business information series Principles of Business from Salem Press. The resource is meant to be an introduction to fundamentals of accounting in an easy-to-understand format. It says the editors are from Salem Press so we're not sure on their qualifications on determining the appropriate items to include. There are several contributors from scholars and experts in and outside of the business field. For example, looking in the short biographies for each of the contributors, there are lawyers, a writer, an anthropologist, and a librarian. However, none specified having any accounting experience. The article on accounting ethics was done by a political science expert.

The book has a table of contents, introductory content, and entries for each of the topics. At the back, there is a glossary and an index. The table of contents makes it is easy to navigate the book. Since the subject area is so broad, it is difficult to know what topics are included or how they are arranged without it. However, articles are alphabetized with article titles beginning with "The" in the Ts, which is not very practical. In addition, there are articles that do not seem to have anything to do with accounting. For example, there is an article on Keynesian economics. That seems better suited for the next volume on economics.

Unfortunately, the index at the back is not very good. It does not include all the times that a topic is covered or it leaves things out entirely. For example, the article "Statistical Applications in Accounting" has a picture of the office building for the American Institute of Certified Public Accountants (AICPA) and mentions the AICPA, but that page number is not included in the index. There are multiple pictures of Federal Reserve chair Ben Bernanke, but he is not in the index. None of the contributors are in the index so users cannot see what articles they wrote unless they thumb through the entire book.

Something to note is that on the copyright or imprint page it states that no part may be reproduced or transmitted without written permission from the copyright owner. Other titles have a similar phrase but may provide an exception for fair use, which this title does not. So interlibrary loan may not be allowed without asking the copyright owner.

The articles themselves are formatted similarly with an abstract, overview, application, and conclusion with some entries varying in format. They also have sections for a bibliography and suggested readings. There are a few pictures and diagrams. It might be nice if there were more relevant pictures as it is very text heavy, but it does not take away from the content.

Overall, this title would be good for those looking for articles in the accounting, finance, and economic worlds as long as contributor qualifications are not important since it does not stick to accounting topics from experts with stated accounting experience. Undergraduate students would probably benefit the most since they would be looking for topics like this and may appreciate the additional readings part of the articles to find more resources. If the e-book version is keyword searchable, it may be a preferred format since the index omits things. However, do not expect a book on accounting principles from those in the field.—**Breezy Silver**

Business Services and Investment Guides

Handbooks and Yearbooks

62.   **FP Equities-Preferreds & Derivatives, 2018.** Toronto, Grey House Publishing Canada, 2018. 211p. $175.00pa. ISBN 13: 978-1-68217-850-8.

FP (Financial Post) Equities-Preferred & Derivatives is arranged within sections: Preferred Shares which lists outstanding publicly and privately held preferred shares "with detailed descriptions of their features"; Ratings features ratings from Dominion Bond Rating Service (dated May 8, 2018); and Derivatives which covers Preferred Securities; Structured Profits; Income Trusts; and Warrants. Each listing in the Preferred Shares section includes DBRS rating; dividend details; redemption dates; exchange; lead underwriters; transfer agent; registrar; exchange traded; symbol; and CUSIP number. Ratings section lists issuer name, rating, description, and last update. The Derivatives section listings include DBRS rating; dividend details redemption; retraction; lead underwriters; transfer agent; registrar; exchanges; symbol and CUSIP number; and tables that include warrants by issuer; trust units; and warrants by expiry date. *FP Equities-Preferred & Derivatives* also includes the articles "Evolution of the Canadian Preferred Share Market" and "Canadian Preferred Share Market." This resource should prove to be of value to investors and brokers and is recommended for larger public libraries and academic libraries supporting an advanced degree in business and finance.—**Lucy Heckman**

63.   **Weiss Ratings Investment Research Guide to Bond and Money Market Mutual Funds, Winter 2017-18.** Amenia, N.Y., Grey House Publishing, 2018. 527p. $279.00pa. (single edition); $549.00pa. (4 quarterly editions). ISBN 13: 978-1-68217-804-1.

This title is part of the Financial Ratings Series from Weiss Ratings, and it is published by Grey House Publishing. Weiss has several titles and gives ratings on different areas including insurance, mutual funds, stock, bonds, and exchange traded funds. This title gives ratings on bond and money market mutual funds. There are several companies that will provide ratings. Weiss claims to be the only "100% independent rating agency" with more accurate ratings and they are focused more on the consumer rather than companies they are rating. They promote that the U.S. Government Accountability Office (GAO) concluded they were the first to warn about future insurance company failures before any of their competitors, and the 1994 report is linked on their website. Weiss also reports on a broad number of companies both large and small in their print guide depending on the amount of research information they have. However, it does not say how many companies are specifically listed in the guide and does not give specific criteria on what companies are included except to say that it includes "nearly all" of them.

The title is well organized and easy to follow with an introduction section, the ratings organized in various ways, and an appendix. The first page after the table of contents is a terms and conditions page, which is not really expected in print material. It does have a phrase in it that makes one wonder if interlibrary loan would be allowed, but that may require more clarification with Weiss.

The introduction includes a lot of information on how to use the guide when looking at a specific bond or mutual fund. It also goes over their investment ratings A, B, C, D, and E, and how the ratings are broken down into Overall, Reward, and Risk categories. Then it goes into describing the criteria on whether users should buy, sell, or hold. It also has a warnings page that makes sure the reader understands important limitations with the guide including that the rating does not tell the whole story and ratings can change, which would be useful for newer users. Then it has a news article in it that promotes Weiss. It does seem like there is a lot of self-promotion in this piece. Something that could be added somewhere is an explanation of the different types of funds. They have different guides on stock mutual funds, bond and money market mutual funds, and exchange-traded funds. Since this is geared to consumers, it could be beneficial to explain the differences to users so they knew what guide to use.

The ratings are organized six different ways: index of all bond and money market mutual funds, detailed analysis of the 100 largest bonds and funds, best all-around bonds and funds, high performance bonds and funds, low volatility bonds and funds, and buy rated bonds and funds by category. Each section also has a contents portion that is a dictionary describing the numbers on the ratings pages. Each listing includes the fund's name, ticker symbol, stock exchange, fund type, fund category and prospectus objective, ratings, investment information, returns, performance, assets, and fees. This allows users to get a full picture of the fund. All sections include the buy-hold-sell ratings of each fund. The section that goes into details on the 100 largest bonds and funds goes into more information and financial data for the fund including information on the company and investment strategies. As for the ratings themselves, competitors will all have different opinions on a fund's performance and different ways of ranking them, so it is difficult to compare to others. However, doing a quick comparison this title seemed to have some similar results, but there are differences.

Finally, the appendix includes a glossary, a list of providers, and more information on the investment ratings series. The glossary is easy to use with words in alphabetical order. The providers list is in alphabetical order and gives company name, address, phone number, and website if available. The information on the ratings series is an advertisement of all of the titles in the different series.

Overall, this title has value in helping users navigate bond and money market mutual funds analysis all from a central location. There are competitors and additional options online including some free information, but the information may be limited or need a subscription for extended access. In this day and age, the electronic access may be a better option since information can change rapidly. Weiss may be more known for insurance ratings, but the company is not the most known provider for fund performance so it may not have the same name recognition. It also tends to be geared a bit more to consumers than researchers or other heavy users. However, this title would work if one wanted a comprehensive print directory that was easy to navigate and also could be used to build a historical collection.—**Breezy Silver**

64.   **Weiss Ratings Investment Research Guide to Exchange-Traded Funds, Winter 2017-18.** Amenia, N.Y., Grey House Publishing, 2018. 1153p. $279.00pa. (single edition); $549.00pa. (4 quarterly editions). ISBN 13: 978-1-68217-793-8.

This title is part of the Financial Ratings Series from Weiss Ratings, and it is published by Grey House Publishing. Weiss has several titles and gives ratings on different areas including insurance, mutual funds, stock, bonds, and exchange-traded funds. This title gives ratings on exchange-traded funds. There are several companies that will provide ratings. Weiss claims to be the only "100% independent rating agency" with more accurate ratings and they are focused more on the consumer rather than companies they are rating. They promote that the U.S. Government Accountability Office (GAO) concluded they were the first to warn about future insurance company failures before any of their competitors, and the 1994 report is linked on their website. Weiss also reports on a broad number of companies both large and small in their print depending on the amount of research information they have. However, it does not say how many companies are specifically listed in the guide and does not give specific criteria on what companies are included except to say that it includes "nearly all" of them.

The title is well organized and easy to follow with an introduction section, the ratings organized in various ways, and an appendix. The first page after the table of contents is a terms and conditions page, which is not really expected in print material. It does have a phrase in it that makes one wonder if interlibrary loan would be allowed, but that would require more clarification with Weiss.

The introduction includes a lot of information on how to use the guide when looking at a specific fund. It also goes over their investment ratings A, B, C, D, and E, and how the ratings are broken down into Overall, Reward, and Risk categories. Then it goes into describing the criteria on whether users should buy, sell, or hold. It also has a warnings page that makes sure the reader understands important limitations with the guide including that the rating does not tell the whole story and ratings can change, which would be useful for newer users. Finally, it has a news article in it that promotes Weiss. It does seem like there is a lot of self-promotion in this piece. Something that could be added somewhere is an explanation of the different types of funds. They have different guides on stock mutual funds, bond and money market mutual funds, and exchange-traded funds. Since this is geared to consumers, it could be beneficial to explain the differences to users so they knew what guide to use

The ratings are organized seven different ways: index of all exchange-traded funds, detailed analysis of all buy- rated funds, detailed analysis of all rated funds with assets over fifty million, one hundred largest funds, best one-year return buy-rated funds, best low-expense funds, and buy-rated funds by category. Each section also has a contents portion that is a dictionary describing the numbers on the ratings pages. Each listing includes the fund's name, ticker symbol, stock exchange, ratings, price, category and prospectus objective, returns, performance, assets, asset allocation, turnover ratio, and valuation information. This allows users to get a full picture of the fund. All sections include the buy-sell-hold ratings of each fund. The two sections that go into details on all of the buy-rated funds and those with assets over 50 million go into more information and financial data for the fund including information on the company and investment strategies. As for the ratings themselves, competitors will all have different opinions on a fund's performance and different ways of ranking them, so it is difficult to compare to others. However, doing a quick comparison this title seemed to have some similar results, but there are differences.

Finally, the appendix includes a glossary, a list of providers, and more information on the investment ratings series. The glossary is easy to use with words in alphabetical order. The providers list is in alphabetical order and gives company name, address, phone number, and website if available. The information on the ratings series is an advertisement of all of the titles in the different series.

Overall, this title has value in helping users navigate exchange-traded funds analysis all from a central location. There are competitors and additional options online including some free information, but the information may be limited or need a subscription for extended access. In this day and age, the electronic access may be a better option since information can change rapidly. Weiss may be more known for insurance ratings, but the company is not the most known provider for fund performance so it may not have the same name recognition. It also tends to be geared a bit more to consumers than researchers or other heavy users. However, this title would work if one wanted a comprehensive print directory that was easy to navigate and also could be used to build a historical collection.—**Breezy Silver**

65.   **Weiss Ratings Investment Research Guide to Stock Mutual Funds, Winter 2017-18.** Amenia, N.Y., Grey House Publishing, 2018. 1255p. $279.00pa. (single edition); $549.00a (4 quarterly editions). ISBN 13: 978-1-68217-812-6.

This title is part of the Financial Ratings Series from Weiss Ratings, and it is published by Grey House Publishing. Weiss has several titles and gives ratings on different areas including insurance, mutual funds, stock, bonds, and exchange-traded funds. This title gives ratings on stock mutual funds. There are several companies that will provide ratings. Weiss claims to be the only "100% independent rating agency" with more accurate ratings and they are focused more on the consumer rather than companies they are rating. They promote that the U.S. Government Accountability Office (GAO) concluded they were the first to warn about future insurance company failures before any of their competitors, and the 1994 report is linked on their website. Weiss also reports on a broad number of companies both large and small in their print guide depending on the amount of research information they have. However, it does not say how many companies are specifically listed in the guide and does not give specific criteria on what companies are included except to say that it includes "nearly all" of them.

The title is well organized and easy to follow with an introduction section, the ratings organized in various ways, and an appendix. The first page after the table of contents is a terms and conditions page, which is not really expected in print material. It does have a phrase in it that makes one wonder if interlibrary loan would be allowed, but that may require more clarification with Weiss.

The introduction includes a lot of information on how to use the guide when looking at a specific mutual fund. It also goes over their investment ratings A, B, C, D, and E, and how the ratings are broken down into Overall, Reward, and Risk categories. Then it goes into describing the criteria on whether users should buy, sell, or hold. It also has a warnings page that makes sure the reader understands important limitations with the guide including that the rating does not tell the whole story and ratings can change, which would be useful for newer users. Then it has a news article in it that promotes Weiss. It does seem like there is a lot of self-promotion in this piece. Something that could be added somewhere is an explanation of the different types of funds. They have different guides on stock mutual funds, bond and money market mutual funds, and exchange-traded funds. Since this is geared to consumers, it could be beneficial to explain the differences to users so they knew what guide to use.

The ratings are organized seven different ways: index of all stock mutual funds, detailed analysis of the 100 largest funds, best all-around stock mutual funds, consistent return buy funds, high performance funds, low volatility funds, and buy-rated funds by category. Each section also has a contents portion that is a dictionary describing the numbers on the ratings pages. Each listing includes the fund's name, ticker symbol, stock exchange, fund type, fund category and prospectus objective, ratings, investment information, returns, performance, assets, and fees. This allows users to get a full picture of the fund. All sections include the buy-hold-sell ratings of each fund. The section that goes into details on the one hundred largest funds goes into more information and financial data for the fund including information on the company and investment strategies. As for the ratings themselves, competitors will all have different opinions on a fund's performance and different ways of ranking them, so it is difficult to compare to others. However, doing a quick comparison this title seemed to have some similar results, but there are differences.

Finally, the appendix includes a glossary, a list of providers, and more information on the investment ratings series. The glossary is easy to use with words in alphabetical order. The providers list is in alphabetical order and gives company name, address, phone number, and website if available. The information on the ratings series is an advertisement of all of the titles in the different series.

Overall, this title has value in helping users navigate stock mutual funds analysis all from a central location. There are competitors and additional options online including some free information, but the information may be limited or need a subscription for extended access. In this day and age, the electronic access may be a better option since information can change rapidly. Weiss may be more known for insurance ratings, but the company is not the most known provider for fund performance so it may not have the same name recognition. It also tends to be geared a bit more to consumers than researchers or other heavy users. However, this title would work if one wanted a comprehensive print directory that was easy to navigate and also could be used to build a historical collection.—**Breezy Silver**

66.   **Weiss Ratings Investment Research Guide to Stocks, Winter 2017-18.** Amenia, N.Y., Grey House Publishing, 2018. 615p. $279.00 (single edition); $549.00 (4 quarterly editions). ISBN 13: 978-1-68217-789-1.

This title is part of the Financial Ratings Series from Weiss Ratings, and it is published by Grey House Publishing. Weiss has several titles and gives ratings on different areas including insurance, mutual funds, stock, bonds, and exchange traded funds. This title gives ratings on stock from publicly traded companies. There are several companies that will provide ratings. Weiss claims to be the only "100% independent rating agency" with more accurate ratings and they are focused more on the consumer rather than companies they are rating. They promote that the U.S. Government Accountability Office (GAO) concluded they were the first to warn about future insurance company failures before any of their competitors, and the 1994 report is linked on their website. Weiss also reports on a broad number of companies both large and small in their print guide depending on the amount of research information they have. However, it does not say how many companies are specifically listed in the guide and does not give specific criteria on what companies are included except to say it includes "nearly all."

The title is well organized and easy to follow with an introduction section, the ratings organized in various ways, and an appendix. The first page after the table of contents is a terms and conditions page, which is not really expected in print material. It does have a phrase in it that makes one wonder if interlibrary loan would be allowed, but that may require more clarification with Weiss.

The introduction includes a lot of information on how to use the guide when looking at a specific stock. It also goes over their investment ratings A, B, C, D, and E, and how the ratings are broken down into Overall, Reward, and Risk categories. Then it goes into whether users should buy, sell, or hold the stock. It also has a warnings page that makes sure the reader understands important limitations with the guide including that the rating does not tell the whole story and ratings can change, which would be useful for newer users. Then it has a news article in it that promotes Weiss. It does seem like there is a lot of self-promotion in this piece.

The ratings are organized seven different ways: index of all stocks, best performing stocks, high yield stocks that are rated buys, stocks with high volatility, undervalued stocks by sector, buy-rated stocks by sector, and an expanded analysis of all A-rated stock. Each section also has a contents portion that is a dictionary describing the numbers on the ratings pages. Each listing includes the companies' name, ticker symbol, stock exchange, market sector, ratings, recommendation on whether to buy, sell, or hold, and several numbers for stock and financials. This allows users to get a better view of the company. The other sections allow users to view the same companies organized in different ways as previously mentioned including listing the best performing stocks and undervalued stocks by sector. The section on the expanded analysis of companies of A-rated stocks goes into more information and financial data for the companies. As for the ratings themselves, competitors will all have different opinions on a stock's performance and different ways of ranking them, so it is difficult to compare to others. However, doing a quick comparison this title seemed to have similar results to others.

Finally, the appendix includes a glossary and more information on the investment ratings series. The glossary is easy to use with words in alphabetical order. The information on the ratings series is an advertisement of all of the titles in the different series.

Overall, this title has value in helping users navigate stock analysis all from a central location. There are competitors and additional options online including some free information, but the information may be limited or need a subscription for extended access. In this day and age, the electronic access may be a better option since information can change rapidly. Weiss may be more known for insurance ratings, but the company is not the most known provider for stock performance so it may not have the same name recognition. It also tends to be geared a bit more to consumers than researchers or other heavy users. However, this title would work if one wanted a comprehensive print directory that was easy to navigate and also could be used to build a historical collection.—**Breezy Silver**

Consumer Guides

Handbooks and Yearbooks

67.   **Weiss Ratings Consumer Box Set.** Amenia, N.Y., Grey House Publishing, 2018. 9v. $399.00pa. (single edition); $499.00pa. (2 biannual editions). ISBN 13: 978-1-68217-816-4.

Weiss Ratings' Consumer Box Set is comprised of the titles: *Consumer Guide to Automobile Insurance; Consumer Guide to Elder Care Choices; Consumer Guide to Homeowners Insurance; Consumer Guide to Long-Term Care Insurance; Consumer Guide to Medicare Prescription Drug Coverage; Consumer Guide to Medicare Supplement Insurance; Consumer Guide to Term Life Insurance; Consumer Guide to Variable Annuities;* and *Consumer Guide to Health Savings Accounts.* Weiss ratings categories are: A. Excellent; B. Good; C. Fair; D. Weak; E. Very Weak; F. Failed; and U. Unrated. Plus signs next to a rating letter indicate a company is in the upper third of a letter grade; a minus sign indicates it is in lower third of a letter grade. The *Consumer Guide to Automobile Insurance* features an overview of auto insurance options; categories of insurance coverage (e.g., bodily injury liability, property damage liability, collision, comprehensive); financial responsibility limits and enforcement by state; "no fault" insurance; how premiums are determined; and how to save money. A directory section lists recommended insurers by state. The appendix includes a quote comparison worksheet, helpful resources, state insurance commissioners' departmental contact information, and a glossary of terms. The *Consumer Guide to Elder Care Choices* teaches consumers about types of facilities available (continuing care retirement, assisted living, home health care agencies, nursing homes, etc.); payment options; finding facilities; and what questions to ask. The appendix contains a nursing home checklist. The *Consumer Guide to Homeowners Insurance* describes the types of coverage available, the basic causes of loss covered, liability coverages, dwelling coverage, personal property coverages, policy conditions, how premiums are determined, and how to shop for a policy. The directory/ratings section arranges companies by state and each entry includes contact information and safety ratings. The appendix includes a quote comparison worksheet, helpful resources, state insurance commissioners' departmental contact information, and a glossary of terms. The *Consumer Guide to Long-Term Care Insurance* covers types of long-term care needs and services (e.g. nursing homes, hospice care); what to consider when deciding on options for long-term care; Medicare coverage; alternatives to standard long-term care insurance; premium rates; and an index of long-term care insurers. Ratings listed here range from A to E. The appendix includes a long-term insurance care planner, a glossary of terms, and a list of reference organizations. The *Consumer Guide to Medicare Prescription Drug Coverage* describes the Medicare Prescription Drug Plan and how the coverage works; making a choice about prescription drug coverage; tracking drug costs throughout the year; and a directory and rating guide for drug plans approved by Medicare. Each entry includes name of organization, website, telephone, insurance company associated with the plan, states where organizations offers Medicare Advantage Prescription Plans, and states in which the organization offers a stand-alone plan. The appendix includes a list of state health insurance assistance programs and other helpful resources. The *Consumer Guide to Medicare Supplement Insurance* includes "Answers to your questions about Medigap" and what is and is not covered; selecting a Medigap policy; Medigap premium rates; and an index of Medigap insurers. The *Consumer Guide to Term Life Insurance* helps users determine if life insurance is needed, how to choose the right type of policy, and contacting an agent. The appendix includes a life insurance needs worksheets, state insurance commissioners' departmental contact information, and a glossary. The *Consumer Guide to Variable Annuities* defines annuities and discusses pros and cons. This guide rates annuities by various criteria including best low-cost variable annuities, best variable annuities with guaranteed withdrawal benefits, and worst variable annuities. The *Consumer Guide to Health Savings Accounts* covers the basics of health savings accounts (HSAs); HAS eligibility, ownership, and control; establishing a HAS; and distributions and deductibles. An index lists recommended health insurers by state and each entry includes name, address, zip code, and telephone number. The appendix includes frequently asked questions and helpful resources. This is a highly informative and practical set for consumers seeking further information on various options for insurance and healthcare needs. Recommended to public libraries and to academic libraries supporting a program in insurance.—**Lucy Heckman**

Finance and Banking

Handbooks and Yearbooks

68.   Careers in Financial Services. Hackensack, N.J., Salem Press, 2017. 359p. index. $125.00. ISBN 13: 978-1-68217-595-8; 978-1-68217-538-8 (e-book).

Careers in Financial Services supports individuals considering entering the field of finance. The related options are abundant and center on three main categories of the finance industry—public, corporate, and personal finance. Financial services is an emerging field that provides opportunities for upward mobility. The U.S. Bureau of Labor Statistics' current Occupational Outlook Handbook states that employment of financial analysts should grow by 11 percent through 2026, faster than average for all occupations.

Salem Press specifically designed this book for a high school and undergraduate audience. Its reader-friendly format encourages self-discovery and inspires interest. The book offers bold fonts, bullet formatting, short paragraphs, graphics, and highlighted boxes filled with relevant skills, duties, responsibilities, profiles, and expectations regarding work environments. Readers gain insight into earnings, career clusters, training/educational requirements, and physical requirements. A special section details associations that the reader can contact for more information. Additionally, creative presentation enhancements include fun facts, famous firsts, and numerous photos. One particular highlight included in each chapter is the "Conversation With" feature, a two-page interview with a professional who works in a related job. An extensive index system supports speedy information retrieval.

Careers in Financial Services will be a useful resource for teachers, guidance counselors, and students. Recommended.—**Thomas E. Baker**

69.   **Debt Information for Teens: Tips for a Successful Financial Life.** 3d ed. John Tilly, ed. Detroit, Omnigraphics, 2018. 346p. index. (Teen Finance Series). $69.00. ISBN 13: 978-0-7808-1569-8; 978-0-7808-1570-4 (e-book).

This 4th edition of *Debt Information for Teens* (see ARBA 2012, entry 192) addresses a growing problem among 18-24 year olds—debt. The six-part resource includes content on the economy and your wallet, personal money management, establishing and using credit, credit cards, and identifying and resolving debt-related problems. The last section, If You Need More Information, provides readers with concrete help as it includes information on where to find online calculators, interactive financial tools, and other electronic resources. The book's format works well for the targeted population—the writing is fast paced and not overwhelming, and the book makes good use of illustrations, information boxes, fonts, and bullet points. This is a recommended purchase for public, school, and academic libraries.—**Thomas E. Baker**

70.   **Financial Independence Information for Teens.** Angela L. Williams, ed. Detroit, Omnigraphics, 2019. 372p. index. (Teen Finance Series). $62.00. ISBN 13: 978-0-7808-1582-7; 978-0-7808-1581-0 (e-book).

This book is designed to give teens the information they need to achieve financial capability and literacy. Information is presented in parts and chapters. The chapters in part 1, Determining When a Teen Is Ready to Be Independent, address the meaning of financial capability and literacy, how to conduct a self-assessment, how to plan for independence (moving in costs, utility connection fees, mortgage payments, etc.), and how parents can help teens understand and handle these issues. In addition, there is information on minor emancipation, opportunities for teens with disabilities, and obstacles faced by teens in foster care. Teen Employment, part 2, discusses the legal guidelines for employing children (e.g., what hours are permissible), and includes information on such things as internships, job opportunities, networking, writing a resume, finding a career path, workplace ethics, workplace hazards, and self-employment. The third part, Creating and Living Within a Budget, gives teens tips on how and why to save money, how to make a budget, etc. Teens can also learn how to avoid such common mistakes as having too many credit cards and find advice on saving and investing, credit card rewards programs, student loans, and more. Living on Your Own, part 4, provides nuts and bolts information about leasing and subleasing an apartment or house, tenants' rights, renter's insurance, and landlord obligations, as well as advice on scholarship applications and electronic banking. The last section, Planning for the Future, expands on some of the ideas introduced earlier in the book about choosing a career and adds information about entrepreneurship, the importance of monitoring and maintaining a credit score, and the decision to take out a student loan or pursue an advanced degree. The last section supplies additional resources that include online money management tools, resources for disabled teens, and resources for financial independence. An index rounds out the work. The writing style and level is appropriate for high school students. There is some subject matter overlap with Omnigraphics' *Debt Information for Teens* (2018). Recommended.—**ARBA Staff Reviewer**

71.   **Financial Services Canada/Services Financiers au Canada, 2018-2019.** 21st ed. Toronto, Grey House Publishing Canada, 2018. 1310p. $449.00pa. ISBN 13: 978-1-68217-828-7; 978-1-68217-829-4 (e-book).

The 21st edition of *Financial Services Canada* "profiles organizations that are headquartered in Canada, and also those of significance to the Canadian financial industry that may be headquartered elsewhere, with branches or divisions in Canada." There are more than 32,000 listings arranged within eight chapters: "Banks & Depository Institutions"; "Non-Depository Institutions"; "Investment Management"; "Insurance Companies"; "Accounting & Law"; "Major Companies"; "Associations"; and "Financial Technology & Services." Each entry includes name, address, telephone, fax, e-mail address, URL, executives, profile, year founded, social media information, ownership, stock exchange membership (where applicable), and locations of branches. In addition to the directory section, this resource includes four indexes (by entry, executive name, geographic location, insurance class). Researchers will find a user's guide, list of abbreviations, information on the labor force, fast facts about the Canadian banking system, reports, the article "Recent Developments in the Canadian Economy: Fall 2017," and more in the beginning of the volume. *Financial Services Canada* is an excellent source of data in addition to its comprehensive listing of organizations. It should be considered for purchase by research libraries and academic libraries supporting an MBA program.—**Lucy Heckman**

72.   **FP Bonds-Government, 2018.** Toronto, Grey House Publishing Canada, 2018. 84p. $175.00. ISBN 13: 978-1-68217-848-5.

FP Bonds-Government "lists outstanding publicly and privately held debt securities, together with their features and provisions, issued by the Government of Canada, the provinces and selected federal and provincial agencies." Unless otherwise indicated, all issues and amounts are outstanding as of March 31, 2018. This resource is arranged into three main sections: Canada which includes details of debt issued by the Government of Canada and its federal agencies listed by maturity date plus data about Canada Savings Bonds; Provincial Debt with data on debt arranged by province; and Eurobonds, including debts offered by the European market. Also included are: a report of the Financial System Review of Canada; a report, "The Life Cycle of Government of Canada Bonds in Core Funding Markets"; a report, and "Has Liquidity in Canadian Government Bond Markets Deteriorated?" *FP Bonds-Government* provides a wealth of information and data about publicly and privately held debt securities, and it is recommended for larger public libraries, and academic libraries supporting a postgraduate program in business, and to investors and practitioners researching the bond markets.—**Lucy Heckman**

73.   **Research Handbook of Finance and Sustainability.** Sabri Boubaker, Douglas Cumming, and Duc Khuong Nguyen, eds. Northampton, Mass., Edward Elgar, 2018.

645p. index. $350.00. ISBN 13: 978-1-78643-262-9; 978-1-78643-263-6 (e-book).

The stated purpose of the *Research Handbook of Finance and Sustainability* is to explore "some of the exciting new topics in sustainable finance." The handbook is arranged within four parts: Part I, Corporate Social Responsibility, contains chapters on matters relevant to corporate social responsibility including financial and ethical effects, firm innovation, and corporate governance. Part II, Environmental and Entrepreneurial Finance, focuses on such topics as structured microfinance in China, the relationship between venture capital and growth in emerging markets, and the birth of environmental finance. Part III, Governance and Sustainable Finance, includes chapters on impact investing in social enterprises, the low-carbon transition and financial system sustainability, and climate risks and the practice of corporate valuation. The last part, Fraud, Governance, and Agency Problems, focuses on topics including corporate governance and fraud, sustainability disclosure and earnings management, and how to foster responsible corporate governance. Each chapter is a scholarly article written by expert(s) in the field and the authors/contributors represent faculty from universities worldwide which include: Victoria University of Wellington (New Zealand); University of Utah; Monash University (Australia); Villanova University; Banking Academy of Vietnam; University of Edinburgh; and Lund University (Sweden). Each chapter contains a list of references and some contain charts, tables, and figures. This resource also supplies an index and biographical information about the editors and contributors. The *Research Handbook of Finance and Sustainability* is highly recommended to faculty and students of graduate business schools and researchers. It is recommended for purchase by academic libraries supporting advanced degrees in business administration.—**Lucy Heckman**

74.   **Weiss Ratings Financial Literacy: Planning for the Future.** Amenia, N.Y., Grey House Publishing, 2018. 8v. $359.00/set. ISBN 13: 978-1-64265-020-4.

The Weiss Ratings Financial Literacy set is comprised of eight volumes, each of which "provides readers with easy-to-understand guidance on how to manage their finances." The volumes in the series are as follows: *Living Together, Getting Married, and Starting a Family*; *Buying a Home for the First Time and Mortgage Shopping*; *Insurance Strategies to Protect Your Family*; *Making the Right Healthcare Coverage Choices*; *Protect Yourself from Identity Theft*; *Steps for Career Advancement*; *Saving for Your Child's Education*; and *Retirement Planning Strategies & the Importance of Starting Early*. *Living Together, Getting Married, and Starting a Family* covers setting financial goals, setting up a long-term strategy, merging finances, splitting up expenses, financial priorities and life goals (e.g. retirement, college savings), wedding budget planner, prenuptial agreements, financial impact of parenthood, parental leave, and health insurance plus worksheets on financial planning and statistics on family expenditures. *Buying a Home for the First Time and Mortgage Shopping* covers data on the housing market today, getting mortgage preapproval, types of homes, hiring a realtor, home inspection, credit scores and loans, first-time home buyers, and homeowners insurance. This volume also features a list of helpful resources, all from Weiss Ratings, and a glossary of terms. *Insurance Strategies to Protect Your Family* discusses how life insurance works, how much life insurance one should buy, average annual life insurance rates, and disability insurance and includes a guide to helpful resources. *Making the Right Healthcare Coverage Choices* provides information on historic trends for health insurance costs, on types of plans, on Medicare, on the Affordable Care Act, and more. *Protect yourself From Identity Theft* covers securing your Social Security number, types of identity theft, securing the home computer, password security, what to do in case of identity theft, disputing fraudulent charges, and how to protect your identity by keeping personal information private. This resource also features a list of resources for further reading, a glossary of terms, and sample letters including a dispute letter to a credit bureau, a dispute Letter to a company for a new account, and an identity theft letter to a debt collector. *Steps for Career Advancement* provides advice about evaluating your career path, how to write a resume that stands out, getting ready for the interview, evaluating potential employers, how to ask for a raise, retirement plans, bonuses, and health insurance. This resource also includes a list of helpful resources and occupational statistics. *Saving for Your Child's Education* covers trusts, savings plans, savings bonds, and the 529 College Savings Plan, and includes a list of helpful resources and 529 Plans. *Retirement Savings Strategies* covers 401(k) plans, defined benefit plans, IRAs, wills, and the importance of starting planning early. The guide also features *Weiss Ratings Recommended Mutual Funds,* helpful resources, Social Security benefits estimates, a list of largest mutual fund providers, and a glossary of terms. The Weiss Ratings Financial Literacy should prove to be of great value to consumers and is recommended primarily to public library collections.—**Lucy Heckman**

75.   **Weiss Ratings Guide to Banks, Spring 2019.** Amenia, N.Y., Grey House Publishing, 2019. 300p. index. $279.00. ISBN 13: 978-1-64265-168-3.

The purpose of the *Weiss Ratings Guide to Banks* is "to provide consumers, businesses, financial institutions, and municipalities with a reliable source of banking industry ratings and analysis on a timely basis." Weiss Safety Ratings are based on five indexes: capitalization, asset quality, profitability, liquidity, and stability. Ratings use a letter-based system consisting of A. Excellent; B. Good; C. Fair; D. Weak; E. Very Weak; F. Failed; and U. Unrated. Section I, Index of Banks, is an analysis of all rated U.S. Commercial Banks and Savings Banks and each entry contains name; city; state; safety rating; prior year safety rating; safety rating two years prior; total assets, one year asset growth; commercial loans/total assets; consumer loans/total assets; home mortgage loans/total assets; securities/total assets; capitalization; leverage ratio; and risk-based capital ratio. Section II, Weiss Recommended Banks by State, is a compilation of U.S. Commercial Banks and Savings Banks receiving a Weiss Safety Ranking of A+, A, A-, or B+. Section III, Rating Upgrades and Downgrades, contains a list of all U.S. Commercial and Savings Banks receiving a rating upgrade or downgrade during the current quarter with each entry including name, new safety rating, state, and date of change. The appendix section includes a list of recent bank failures 2013-2018, a glossary, and an explanation of the differences between banks and credit unions. *Weiss ratings Guide to Banks* is recommended to special libraries, larger public libraries, and academic libraries. This contains information suitable for researchers and consumers.—**Lucy Heckman**

76.   **Weiss Ratings Guide to Credit Unions, Spring 2019.** Amenia, N.Y., Grey House Publishing, 2019. 300p. index. $279.00. ISBN 13: 978-1-64265-202-4.

The stated purpose of the *Weiss Ratings Guide to Credit Unions* is "to provide consumers, businesses, financial institutions, and municipalities with a reliable source of industry ratings and analysis on a timely basis." Evaluated in this guide are: checking, merchant banking, or other transaction accounts; an investment in a certificate of deposit or savings account; a line of credit or commercial loan; and a counterparty risk. Weiss safety ratings are based on five indexes: capitalization, asset quality, profitability, liquidity, and stability. Ratings are based on letter grades: A. Excellent; B. Good; C. Fair; D. Weak; E. Very Weak; F. Failed; and U. Unrated. Section I, Index of Credit Unions, is an analysis of all rated U.S. credit unions which are listed in alphabetical order. Entries include: institution name; city; state; safety rating; prior year safety rating; safety rating two years prior; total assets; one year asset growth; commercial loans/total assets; consumer loans/total assets; home mortgage loans/total assets; securities/total assets; capitalization index; and net worth ratio. Section II, Weiss Recommended Credit Unions by State, is a compilation of credit unions receiving a Weiss Safety Rating of A+, A, A-, or B+. Each entry includes: institution name, city, state, telephone, and safety rating. Section III, Rating Upgrades and Downgrades, is a list of all credit unions receiving an upgrade or downgrade during the current quarter. Each entry includes institution name, new safety rating, state, and date of change. The appendix includes a list of failed credit unions (2013-2018), a chart showing the differences between banks and credit unions, and a glossary. The *Weiss Ratings Guide to Credit Unions* should prove useful to researchers and consumers and is recommended especially to special libraries and larger academic and public libraries.—**Lucy Heckman**

Industry and Manufacturing

Digital Resources

77.   **Seafood Slavery Risk Tool. http://www.seafoodslaveryrisk.org/.** [Website] Free. Date reviewed: 2018.

The Seafood Slavery Risk Tool (SSRT), run jointly by the Monterey Bay Aquarium Seafood Watch program, Liberty Asia, and the Sustainable Fisheries Partnership, gathers data related to forced labor, human trafficking, and other on-the-job hazards of particular commercial fisheries around the world. The Search Database option at the bottom of the page allows users to enter a country, fishery (type of seafood), or category of risk rating to access related profiles. Alternatively, users can View All Profiles to scroll through information on thirty-five worldwide fisheries. Each profile lists species and country, notes risk level (low, high, critical), fishing method, location(s), and other information. The profile also includes a summary which relays updated data from various reports (e.g., the Trafficking in Persons—TIP—report from the U.S. Department of State) and then assesses whether the fishery meets the SSRT criteria. Users can also Download Fishery Profile for a PDF of the complete report, presenting numerous criteria, source links, and more. The tool looks at the Faroe Islands Atlantic Cod Fishery, Brazil's Lane and Yellowtail Snapper fisheries, Thailand's Cuttlefish and Bobtail Squid fisheries, Taiwan's Pacific Bluefin Tuna fisheries, and others. Under the Resources tab on the homepage, users can follow the methodology behind the SSRT (e.g., sources). They can also find good background information on seafood slavery issues (causes, modes, etc.) and a glossary.—**ARBA Staff Reviewer**

78. **The Thomas Register. https://www.thomasnet.com/.** [Website] Free. Date reviewed: 2018.

The Thomas Register is the online version of the long-established directory of manufacturing resources, product, and company information. While Thomas the company has grown substantially beyond the register into modern marketing, advertising, and data solutions, the register remains a signature achievement. The online version makes it easy for users to search and browse an expansive database of company information, product catalogs, and CAD (Computer Assisted Design) models associated with many aspects of industry. Under the Network tab or icon, users can find over five hundred thousand product and parts suppliers by selecting the Supplier Discovery link. Seventeen broad categories such as Process Equipment, Metal & Metal Products, Hardware, Adhesives & Sealants, and more help organize the extensive list of parts and services, such as Magnets, Brushes, Bolts, Extruded Plastics, Rapid Prototyping Services, Noise Control, and Calibration Services. Selecting a specific product links users with the Thomas Supplier database. Under Product Catalogs, users can browse a generous Manufacturer and Distributor Catalog Collection organized into roughly fifty categories, such as Agricultural & Farming, Chemicals & Gases, and Machinery & Machining Tools. Within each category, users will find an A-Z listing of products which they can click to present the display of associated catalogs. The CAD Models database lets users search and browse a large collection of CAD models organized into an alphabetical gallery display. Users can find models, images, schematics, and affiliated information for Automotive Parts, Bearings, Compressors, Dimmers, Filters, Hoists, Robotic Components, Valves, and much more. Within each of the three databases, users can extract supplier information such as company description, website, products/services offered, product catalog, news & press releases, and location. Additional information (key personnel, annual sales, etc.) may also be available while some detail (certifications, registrations, etc.) may be available upon registration with the Thomas website. Users can also request information, compare suppliers, create a shortlist of suppliers, contact suppliers, and perform other functions. Users will find analysis and industry news under the homepage Insights tab. Articles and White Papers (searchable by keyword) explore supply chain, engineering & design, industry trends, and other topics. Currently featured White Papers include "Glass vs. Plastic: Benefits of Using Glass Components in Biotechnology, Medical Device, Point-of-Care & Pharmaceutical Industries" and "Environmental Monitoring for Museum Curation." The website is full of information that could appeal to students, educators, and professionals within engineering, product management, industrial design, and other fields.—**ARBA Staff Reviewer**

Directories

79. **Food & Beverage Market Place, 2018.** Amenia, N.Y., Grey House Publishing, 2018. 3v. index. $695.00/set. ISBN 13: 978-1-68217-368-8.

The *Food & Beverage Market Place,* now in its 19th edition, is available online at http://gold.greyhouse.com or in 3 print volumes. The directory provides comprehensive coverage of approximately 34,000 companies related to the food and beverage industries. Included in the 34,000 listings are hundreds of new company profiles and thousands of updates. The first volume covers food and beverage manufacturers and contains 4 indexes: "Brand Name Index," "Ethnic Food Index," "Geographic Index," and "Parent Company Index." These indexes are especially helpful in a volume this size (more than 1,350 pages). Equipment, supplies, and service providers comprise volume 2, along with 2 indexes, "Brand Name Index" and "Geographic Index." In volume 3, users will find brokers, importer/exporters, transportation firms, warehouse companies, and wholesalers/distributors as well as eleven indexes, including "Import Region" and "Wholesale Product Type." The set provides users with basic contact information (address, phone number, website). Depending on the company, users may find information about type of product, the names of executives, sales numbers, number of employees, year founded, parent company, or export region. Recommended for large public or academic libraries.—**ARBA Staff Reviewer**

Handbooks and Yearbooks

80.   **The SAGE Handbook of Tourism Management.** Chris Cooper, Serena Volo, William C. Gartner, and Noel Scott, eds. Thousand Oaks, Calif., Sage, 2018. 616p. index. $185.00. ISBN 13: 978-1-5264-6113-1.

The essays in this well-crafted handbook are written by leading thinkers and international academics in the field of tourism management. The handbook succeeds in its goal of providing an accurate account of the literature in all tourism management subfields. The essays are accessible to those new to the field, though it is also quite useful for those familiar with the field. The first part, Approaching Tourism, contains opening chapters focused on the contrasting and contemporary approaches to tourism studies. These include, among many other chapters, "Critical Turns in Tourism Studies." "Tourism Gender Studies" traces this particular subfield from 1979. Destination Applications, part two, has thought-provoking chapters like "Tourism Crisis and Safety Management," which analyzes safety management from the perspective of the tourism security chain; "Tourism in Emerging Markets;" and more. The third section, Marketing Applications, is comprised of such chapters as "Destination Branding," an issue at the forefront in light of intensifying competition, and "Consumer Behaviour in Tourism." Part four, Tourism Product Markets, features essays on such topics as niche tourism and the growth of tourism centered on festivals and other leisure events. "Tourism and Social Media," "Tourism and the Internet: Marketing Perspectives," and other essays focused on technological applications make up the fifth section. For this reviewer, the sixth section, Environmental Applications, contains fascinating articles on the intersection between environmental concerns and tourism. "Tourism in a Low Carbon Energy Future," for instance, delves into a variety of topics such as the detrimental environmental impact of air travel and certain tourist activities like jet skiing and discusses possible tourism sector responses. All essays are signed by the contributors, who are listed in the front matter (names and affiliations). Tables and figures are used throughout. Lists of both can be found in the front matter. An index rounds out the work. Recommended for academic libraries.—**ARBA Staff Reviewer**

Insurance

Handbooks and Yearbooks

81.   **Weiss Ratings Guide to Health Insurers, Spring 2019.** Amenia, N.Y., Grey House Publishing, 2019. 538p. (Financial Ratings Series). $279.00. ISBN 13: 978-1-64265-180-5.

The purpose of this guide is "to provide policyholders and prospective policy purchasers with a reliable source of insurance company ratings and analyses on a timely basis." This resource evaluates and rates: medical reimbursement insurance; managed health care (PPOs and HMOs); disability income; and long-term care (nursing home) insurance and includes ratings for health insurers such as commercial not-for-profit insurers, mutual insurers, Blue Cross/Blue Shield plans, and for-profit and not-for-profit insurers. Weiss ratings are based on a series of indexes: capitalization, investment safety, reserve adequacy, profitability, liquidity, and stability. Ratings are by letter: A. Excellent; B. Good; C. Fair; D. Weak; E. Very Weak; and F. Failed with an additional U. Unrated. Section I, Index of Companies, is an analysis of over 1,466 rated and unrated U.S. Health Insurers with companies listed in alphabetical order. Each entry includes: insurance company name; domicile state; safety rating; data date (the latest quarter end that was received by the editors); total assets; total premiums; capital and surplus; risk-adjusted capital ratio #1; and risk-adjusted capital ratio #2. Section II, Analysis of Largest Companies, is a summary analysis of all rated U.S. Health Plans and Blue Cross Shield Plans plus other U.S. insurers, with companies listed in alphabetical order. Each entry includes name of company; address; telephone; domicile state; NAIC code; when commenced business; safety rating; major rating factors; principal business; member physicians; medical loss ratio; administrative expense ratio; enrollment; medical expenses per member per month; principal investments; provider compensation; total member numbers; group affiliation; and a customized graph or table depicting one of the company's major strengths or weaknesses. Section III, Weiss Recommended Companies, is a compilation of U.S. health insurers listed alphabetically receiving a Weiss Safety Rating of A+, A, A-, or B+. Each entry includes name, address, telephone number, and safety rating. Section IV, Weiss Recommended Companies by State, is a summary of those U.S. health insurers receiving a Weiss Safety Rating of A+, A, A-, or B+. Listed alphabetically by state each entry includes name, domicile state, and total assets. Section V, Long-Term Care Insurers, is a list of rated companies providing long-term care insurance with each entry including name, address, telephone number, and safety rating. Section VI, Medicare Supplement Insurance, includes parts consisting of: Answers to Your Questions about Medigap; Steps to Follow When Selecting a Medigap Policy; Medigap Premium Rates; and Medicare Supplement Insurers. Section VII, Analysis of Medicare Managed Care Complaints, is an analysis of complaints filed against U.S. Medicare managed care plans. Section VIII, Rating Upgrades and Downgrades, is a list of all U.S. health insurers receiving a rating upgrade or downgrade during the current quarter. The appendix includes a planner for long-term care, a Medicare prescription drug planner worksheet, a list of recent industry failures, and risk-adjusted capital in Weiss Ratings models. The Weis Ratings Guide contains a wealth of information about health insurers and provides ratings of various insurers. This guide belongs in all insurance special libraries and those supporting an insurance curricula. Consumers will find this of value in selection of plans, so it is also recommended to larger public libraries.—**Lucy Heckman**

Labor

Career Guides

82.   **Careers Overseas.** Hackensack, N.J., Salem Press, 2017. 506p. illus. index. $125.00. ISBN 13: 978-1-68217-597-2; 978-1-68217-598-9 (e-book).

Careers Overseas offers practical advice to those interested in working internationally in the medical field, in the Peace Corps, as English teachers, or in other occupations. Chapters include career snapshots, overviews, work environments, profiles, occupation interests, duties and responsibilities, transferable skills and abilities, education, training and advancement, earnings, employment outlooks, related occupations, photographs, and contact information. The text also explores challenges, as well as education and technical requirements for entry-level positions and career advancement. Content enhancements include fun facts, famous firsts, shadow boxes, bullet formats, and reader friendly fonts. There are also "Conversation With" features, which present interviews with professionals. Recommended.—**Thomas E. Baker**

83.   Graham, Dawn. **Switchers: How Smart Professionals Change Careers and Seize Success.** New York, AMACOM/American Management Association, 2018. 268p. index. $24.95. ISBN 13: 978-0-8144-3963-0; 978-0-8144-3965-4 (e-book).

Switchers by Dawn Graham, leading career coach and the SiriusXM's weekly show Career Talk host, is written "to specifically address the unique needs and job search challenges of career changers, who are ready to make their new career a reality but unsure of how to do it." Graham refers to the Four Rs involved in the job search: Responsibility, "taking responsibility for what happens" and oriented towards an internal locus of control; Reality, putting one's energy into dealing with reality; Risk, realizing there are no guarantees in a job switch; and Resilience in the job search process. The book is comprised of five parts: Choose Your Switch, Clarify Your Plan A, Craft Your Brand Value Proposition, Create Ambassadors, and Keep the Ball in Your Court. Chapters cover important topics like the psychology of the job search, creating a network, realizing the path to a new career may not be linear, and interview techniques. Each chapter includes a summary and "Switch Points" (main ideas and advice). The appendix is an essay "How to Choose a Career Coach." This book includes bibliographical notes and an index. *Switchers* fills a need in that it concentrates on those who wish to change careers and offers practical advice. Highly recommended to academic and public libraries and to the libraries of university career centers.—**Lucy Heckman**

Handbooks and Yearbooks

84. **Occupational Outlook Handbook, 2018-2019.** Lanham, Md., Bernan Press, 2018. 1202p. illus. index. $40.00pa.; $25.00 (e-book). ISBN 13: 978-1-59888-976-5; 978-1-59888-976-5 (e-book).

The *Occupational Outlook Handbook* is "a career resource offering information on the hundreds of occupations that provide the majority of jobs in the United States." Each occupational profile includes a summary, work environment, list of typical duties performed, pay, job outlook, state and area data, descriptions of similar occupations, and references to related associations, organizations, and other institutions. Entries are listed in alphabetical order and among the occupations covered are: Architecture and Engineering; Business and Financial; Community and Social Service; Education, Training, and Library; Healthcare; Life, Physical, and Social Science; Management; Production; Sales; and Transportation and Material Moving. Each section includes illustrations and tables. For example, the section for Healthcare covers: Athletic Trainers; Chiropractors; Dental Assistants; Dentists; EMTs and Paramedics; Home Health Care and Personal Care Aides; Optometrists; Pharmacists; and Physicians and Surgeons, among other occupations. Each occupation is described in great detail; for instance, the entry for Physicians and Surgeons includes duties, work environment, types of physicians, education needed, pay, important qualities (e.g., compassion and leadership skills), and job outlook. Also provided in the handbook are data for occupations not covered in detail (e.g., Credit Analysts, Demonstrators and Product Promoters, Farm and Home Management Advisors); an appendix, "Summary of Occupations" (a brief description of job duties, entry-level education, and median pay for occupations covered); a glossary of terms; and an index of occupations. The *Occupational Outlook Handbook* is a staple and a highly recommended source for students considering specific careers, job hunters, and those changing occupations. It is essential for university, public, and career center libraries.—**Lucy Heckman**

Management

Handbooks and Yearbooks

85.   Falcone, Paul. **96 Great Interview Questions to Ask before You Hire.** 3d ed. New York, AMACOM/American Management Association, 2018. 356p. index. $19.95pa. ISBN 13: 978-0-8144-3915-9; 978-0-8144-3916-6 (e-book).

Companies want to ensure that they hire the best candidates for their openings. The interview process, however, can pose many challenges to hiring managers—how do you ask the right questions to get the information you need to make the correct decision? In this third edition, the author explores the 96 questions advertised in the title, providing potential answers and follow up questions in-depth, with particular focus on why these questions are helpful in identifying the candidate with both the correct fit and skills for your organization and the job opening.

New to this edition are chapters on hiring middle managers, freelancers, and remote workers, as well as a chapter on effective onboarding. Approximately eight pages of new material discusses legislation affecting the hiring process at the national and state levels including fair pay laws, minimum wage considerations, and screening questions. It appears that some chapters, specifically the chapter on interviewing millennials, could have used a more substantial update in the nearly 10 years since the previous edition—aside from changing the names of some social media applications, little else changed to reflect the fact that this age group is now more experienced in the workforce. Overall, this book is geared towards those hiring in a largely traditional, corporate environment, but many of the questions make sense for a wide-range of employers. Of most value to—both interviewers and interviewees—are the strategic considerations presented for each stage of the interview process, helping to demystify the tense process of hiring, onboarding, and retaining new employees.—**Emily Lauren Mross**

86.   **Handbook of Human Resource Management in the Tourism and Hospitality Industries.** Ronald J. Burke and Julia Christensen Hughes, eds. Northampton, Mass., Edward Elgar, 2018. 429p. index. $180.00. ISBN 13: 978-1-75643-136-3; 978-1-78643-137-0 (e-book).

Tourism and hospitality are people-focused sectors—not only in focusing on those consumers they serve, but also in terms of the scores of employees who drive these service industries. Employment in the industry continues to grow, according to the Bureau of Labor Statistics. The *Handbook of Human Resource Management in the Tourism and Hospitality Industries* details traditional aspects of developing and retaining talent at hotels, resorts, and restaurants with timely focuses on gender equality and representation, diversity training, discrimination, and safety and security in light of modern threats. The seventeen chapters utilize varying methodologies to present information, including literature reviews, case studies, survey research, and meta-analyses.

The focus on diversity in the hospitality and tourism workforce is notable and novel when compared to other similar texts; however, there are some limitations across the work. Chapters do not follow one consistent format, and are not organized by nor intentionally identified by methodology. Most chapters are written by academics and provide detailed reference lists, but some vary considerably in terms of tone and content. There is no formal preface or introduction to address the audience, though the "Setting the Stage" section highlights main themes of the industry addressed in the volume. Additionally, there is no conclusion to tie the chapters together, leaving an abrupt end at the index. The *Handbook of Human Resource Management in the Tourism and Hospitality Industries* provides both traditional Human Resource Management (HRM) ideas and current trends that should be of interest to modern managers; it can supplement other works on tourism and hospitality.—**Emily Lauren Mross**

Marketing and Trade

Digital Resources

87.   **J. Walter Thompson: Advertising America. https://www.amdigital.co.uk/ themes/product/j-walter-thompson-advertising-america.** [Website] Chicago, Adam Matthew Digital, 2018. Price negotiated by site. Date reviewed: 2018.

This resource presents a wide variety of documents from the archives of an important American advertising company, material now held in the Rubenstein Rare Book & Manuscript Library at Duke University. Presenting a century of diverse items, from the 1890s to the late 1990s, the database includes complete Account Files and Corporate Vertical Files for companies such as Kodak, Kraft, Scott Paper, and the United States Marine Corps. Other items include meeting minutes, newsletters, and items from the company's research centers and its Information Center. Approximately 1,500 print advertisements are also viewable. Given the company's international presence, there are also materials from ad campaigns in Great Britain, such as for Guinness beer. Documents can provide details of meetings concerning particular ad campaigns or offer correspondence between the company and its clientele. Very useful elements of this resource are the many pages that describe the content within sections of the database, such as the wide-ranging industries for which Thompson created advertising material, including computers, electronics and telecommunications, food, automobiles, and domestic cleaning. Another page provides links to each of the 12 categories of documents, some of which are mentioned above. As with other Adam Matthew resources, this database is fairly specialized. While it is a resource most useful for researchers of American business history, others interested in graphic art in the advertising world may also find this of interest. Libraries serving these groups should investigate the cost for their institution.—**Mark Schumacher**

Handbooks and Yearbooks

88.   Bly, Robert W. **The Digital Marketing Handbook.** Irvine, Calif., Entrepreneur Press, 2018. 220p. illus. index. $21.99pa. ISBN 13: 978-1-59918-621-4; 978-1-61308-381-9 (e-book).

This concise and authoritative handbook by independent copywriter and consultant Bly, author of ninety books, provides guidance for online, brick-and-mortar, or hybrid businesses of any size. There are fifteen easy-to-follow chapters: "Choosing Your Online Business Model"; "Profits Equal Sales Minus Expenses"; three chapters on market funnels for consumer products, B2B products, and service firms; "Driving Traffic to Your Website with Online Marketing"; "Driving Traffic to Your Website with Offline Marketing"; Winning with Blogging and Social Media Marketing;" "Building Your Opt-in List"; "Hub Sites, Landing Pages, and Squeeze Pages"; "Publishing an Online Newsletter"; "Generating Leads and Sales with Email Marketing"; "Autoresponders and Upsells"; "Joint Ventures, Affiliate Marketing, and Licensing"; and "Membership Sites." Black-and-white figures throughout the book help illustrate concepts. There are a series of appendixes that provide an infographic sample, a schedule for producing a direct-mail promotion, and information about vendors and software and services. An index rounds out the book. This is a recommended purchase for public libraries, for businesses, and for individuals looking to gain more from their website.—**ARBA Staff Reviewer**

89.   Fromm, Jeff, and Angie Read. **Marketing to Gen Z: The Rules for Reaching this Vast and Very Different Generation of Influencers.** New York, AMACOM/American Management Association, 2018. 202p. index. $24.95. ISBN 13: 978-0-8144-3928-9; 978-0-8144-3927-2 (e-book).

Jeff Fromm, president of FutureCast, a division of advertising agency Barkley, and Angie Read, Vice President of Growth Insight at Barkley, have written an informative look at marketing to Gen Z, people they define as having birth years of 1996-2010. *Marketing to Gen Z* looks at the defining characteristics of a cohort that will comprise approximately 40 percent of consumers by 2020. The content for this book comes from the result of a cross-generational study conducted in September 2016 that surveyed Gen Z, Millennials, Gen X, and Boomers on their views of self, brand expectations, media habits, shopping habits, and information access. While the survey content is informative and allows the authors to create personas for members of Gen Z as well as include direct quotes from survey participants, it should be noted that the sample size of the survey was 2,039 and only 505 identified as members of Gen Z. Even given this small sample size, the authors make informative notes on how Gen Z is different from generations before it and discuss why this matters from a marketing perspective. Importantly, they discuss the strategies that will work when trying to reach Gen Z including influencers, "brand me," and other qualities that Gen Z is looking for in brands. The authors accomplish this in part by examining cultural and world shifts that have occurred and influenced Gen Z as they have grown up. Using both cultural context and survey results, the authors are able to identify and provide readers with short case studies of brands that have had success marketing to Gen Z. Each chapter concludes with a "key takeaways" section to summarize the key points. The authors also include a chapter, "What's Next?" that aims to help readers position their brand or service in the years to come. The book has a thoughtful layout with helpful graphics, larger text, and an easy-to-read and reference format and is perfect for anyone with a brand or service they want or need to market to Gen Z.—**Alexandra Hauser**

90.　　Luttrell, Regina M., and Luke W. Capizzo. **The PR Agency Handbook.** Thousand Oaks, Calif., Sage, 2018. 280p. index. $55.00pa. ISBN 13: 978-1-5063-2905-5.

According to the authors of *The PR Agency Handbook,* "the overarching goal of this book is to highlight the many different functional components found within an agency as well as reinforce the positive impact that excellent agency work can have on organizations." The book is arranged within four parts: Part I, Agency Life, covers the work environment, working with clients, and client types. The second part, Strategies & Tactics, addresses managing projects; corporate communications and agency partners; social media; marketing in a public relations agency; branding basics; designing a website; creative production; and internal communication. The Business of Agency PR, Part III, discusses client service and entrepreneurship and business development. The last part, Putting It All Together, features public relations tools and templates. Also included in handbook are a glossary, index, and bibliography. Each chapter features an interview with a practitioner; for example, the chapter "Working with Clients" features the transcript of an interview with Valerie Stachurski, founder and president of Canadian agency Charming Media. Also found in each chapter are: objectives; a list of questions for reflection and discussion; and illustrations. Chapter 14 "Public Relations Tools and Templates" includes: the PR prospective client proposal template; ROSTIR strategic planning guide; SWOT analysis; press release; and media advisory. *The PR Agency Handbook* is a practical source for students and professionals. It should prove very helpful as an assigned text for undergraduate and graduate students; this handbook is recommended primarily to academic libraries supporting a business program, especially for marketing, media, and advertising courses.—**Lucy Heckman**

91. **Principles of Business: Marketing.** Hackensack, N.J., Salem Press, 2017. 417p. index. $165.00. ISBN 13: 978-1-68217-599-6; 978-1-68217-600-9 (e-book).

In this series, Principles of Business, the publishers' intent is to provide a "comprehensive introduction" to each topic. Scholars and experts in business contribute signed articles on each topic. In this volume, sixteen contributors wrote the seventy articles. These experts are professionals in the field and hold academic degrees. Each article includes an abstract, an overview of main concepts, a discussion of the topic with issues, and a bibliography. Some of them include applications; some of them include viewpoints or issues. Most articles run four to six pages.

The glossary provides short definitions for the concepts and terms, but there are terms not included. "Product life cycle" is used as a term on page 3. It is included in the index, but it is not defined in the glossary. High school students and those with no prior information will need to supplement this work with a business dictionary to define missing terms.

Organized by title in an A-Z fashion, users can check the table of contents or index to find particular subject terms. Highly recommended for public libraries and academic libraries serving undergraduates.—**Ladyjane Hickey**

92. Westergaard, Nick. **Brand Now: How To Stand Out in a Crowded, Distracted World.** New York, AMACOM/American Management Association, 2018. 204p. illus. index. $23.00. ISBN 13: 978-0-8144-3922-7; 978-0-8144-3923-4 (e-book).

Nick Westergaard, the chief brand strategist at Brand Driven Digital, host of On Brand podcast, author of *Get Scrappy,* and teacher of branding, marketing, and communication at the University Of Iowa, has written an informative and practical guide to build a brand. *Brand Now* "uncovers the new rules of branding in our crowded, chaotic world" where it is increasingly difficult to stand out. Seven rules of branding are discussed in Part I, The Brand Now Dynamics: Meaning (grounding a brand with meaning, creating a brand that stands for something); Structure (considering "all the pieces of DNA that go into creating a brand, all the molecules or touchpoints" such as logo, slogan, and signage); Story (what is the brand's core story); Content (what makes good content in the layers of a brand's story); Community (embracing and expanding customers and "fans" of the brand); Clarity (creating a brand that is transparent and simple); and Experience (creating strong cultures which help build strong brands). Westergaard uses case studies throughout this book which illustrates what works most effectively in building a brand. Also included in addition to the chapters is the Brand Now Toolbox, designed to help readers implement "the dynamics for different types of brands or in specific situations." Covered in the Brand Now Toolbox are: Brand Now: A Summary; Humor: The BONUS Eighth Dynamic; Brand Now for B2B Brands; Brand Now for Small-Business Brands; Brand Now for Personal Brands; Brand Now for Political Brands; Brand Now Naming; Brand Now Crisis Communication; Touchpoint Checklist; and Touchpoint Map. Each section includes a nitty-gritty analysis; for instance, Brand Now Naming presents ideas for how to name the company including the features of a strong brand name (e.g., easy to pronounce and memorize). Also included are discussion group questions for a team at work or students in a classroom, bibliographical notes, and an index. *Brand Now* is highly recommended to practitioners and students and should be purchased by public libraries and by academic libraries supporting a program in business administration.—**Lucy Heckman**

Taxation

Handbooks and Yearbooks

93.   Fishman, Stephen. **Tax Guide for Short-Term Rentals: Airbnb, HomeAway, VRBO & More.** Berkeley, Calif., Nolo, 2018. 192p. index. $19.99pa. ISBN 13: 978-1-4133-2456-3; 978-1-4133-2457-0 (e-book),

The popularity of short-term rentals through online platforms like Airbnb, VRBO, and HomeAway has skyrocketed in recent years. Those who rent part or all of their homes do not necessarily have the tax knowledge necessary to maximize profits while avoiding trouble with the IRS. This book provides valuable tax advice in twelve chapters starting with an introduction and followed by: "How Short-Term Rentals Are Taxed," "Tax Free Short-Term Rentals," "Deducting Your Expenses: The Basics," "Operating Expenses," "Repairs," "Deducting Long-Term Assets," "Prorating Your Deductions," "Reporting Rental Income on Your Tax Return," "Filing IRS Form 1099 Information Returns," "Deducting Losses for Short-Term Rentals," and "Recordkeeping." Here readers will find details about what qualifies as an operating expense, how to deduct the cost of repairs, how to depreciate assets, what expenses have to be prorated, how to fill out a Schedule E, what rental loss rules apply, and so much more. An index rounds out the book. Book purchasers will find additional information about changes or updates on the nolo.com website. This timely guide, written by a lawyer, will assist the many who people who operate short-term rentals. Recommended for public libraries.—**ARBA Staff Reviewer**

5 Education

General Works

Dictionaries and Encyclopedias

94. **The SAGE Encyclopedia of Educational Research, Measurement, and Evaluation.** Bruce B. Frey, ed. Thousand Oaks, Calif., Sage, 2018. 4v. index. $645.00/set. ISBN 13: 978-1-5063-2615-3; 978-1-5063-2613-9 (e-book).

This is a multivolume reference book that covers a wide range of topics about educational research methods, statistics, assessment, and evaluation. It is important to mention that this reference book acts as a comprehensive guide that provides detailed explanations and entries. Users would otherwise have to consult several sources to find equivalent information. The following main topics are listed in the reader's guide: Assessment, Cognitive and Affective Variables, Data Visualization Methods, Disabilities and Disorders, Distributions, Educational Policies, Evaluation Concepts, Evaluation Designs, Human Development, Instrument Development, Organizations and Government Agencies, Professional Issues, Publishing, Qualitative Research, Research Concepts, Research Designs, Research Methods, Research Tools, Social and Ethical Issues, Social Network Analysis, Statistics, Teaching and Learning, Theories and Conceptual Frameworks, and Threats to Research Validity. Under each of these main topics, a reader can find related entries that describe different aspects of the main topic. The length of entries varies; some entries are compact, and some entries are long and contain several subtopics. One of the advantages is that after each entry, a reader can find resources for further reading and exploration; in the online version of the book, a reader just needs to click on the DOI link of the resource in order for it to display. Another advantage is that almost all further reading resources represent academic publications and can serve as a great theoretical foundation for people who want to broaden their knowledge about a research methodology. The total number of entries is 691. As a doctoral student, I would definitely recommend this reference book for research colleges, universities, and organizations because I believe that students, instructors, and researchers can greatly benefit from this reference guide.—**Maria Agee**

Digital Resources

95.   **Teach Online. https://teachonline.ca/home.** [Website] Free. Date reviewed: 2018.
        Teach Online acts as a hub for information on the latest in online learning technology, best practices, and other developments. It offers a number of resources and tools useful to online instruction technology integration, training, and more. Sourced out of Ontario, Canada, the information on the site could be relevant to a range of online teaching scenarios around the globe. The site is rich with ideas and best practices that users can approach either through the tabs running across the top of the homepage, or by scrolling down through the gallery. Pockets of Innovation provides users access to 185 innovative projects that connect with a variety of online teaching areas such as training, collaboration, technology, and engagement. Users can keyword search by region of origin (Ontario, Cross Canada, or International). Alternatively, users can download a 64-page PDF of all projects, some of which include "Using Blended Learning to Provide Knowledge and Skills for Caregivers of Older Adults," "Game of Genders: Using Video and Audio in an Archaeology Course," and much more. Tools and Trends offer numerous resources along thematic lines, including PDF booklets and videos on How to Use Technology Effectively, Must Read Books, and Best Practices for Design and Delivery. Users can also find links to Seven Searchable Directories for 75 EdTech Start-ups; Selected Journals in Online and Distance Learning; Vendors of Online Learning Products and Services; Online, Open and Distance Learning Associations and Consortia Throughout the World, and others. Directory information varies, but may include location, website, category, subcategory, and brief description. Webinars and Interviews offer Power Point presentations, audio recordings, and other tools covering the latest topics in online learning. The wealth of resources on this site would appeal to teachers and students interested in online education.—**ARBA Staff Reviewer**

96.   **World Inequality Database on Education https://www.education-inequalities. org/.** [Website] Free. Date reviewed: 2019.
        The UNESCO Institute for Statistics and the Global Monitoring Report jointly maintain the World Inequality Database on Education (WIDE), which is designed to monitor the UN Sustainable Development Goal (SDG) 4 to "ensure inclusive and equitable equality education and promote lifelong learning opportunities for all." The database allows researchers to track how wealth, gender, ethnicity, and location impact and shape educational opportunities. Users can compare countries and can compare groups within countries. From the homepage, users can discover the indicators used and the countries covered. The homepage also links to popular searches and examples of how to use the database. Using the indicator "Less than 4 years of schooling for age group 20-24," the database examples show how countries rank against one another. In using the same indicator to compare groups within countries, users will see that the adjacent regions of Niamey and Tillaberi in Niger, for example, are the most privileged and most deprived, respectively, in terms of the same indicator (less than 4 years of schooling). This database offers a great deal of free, customizable, and reliable information.—**ARBA Staff Reviewer**

Directories

97.   Educators Resource Guide, 2018/2019. 12th ed. Amenia, N.Y., Grey House Publishing, 2017. 793p. index. $145.00. ISBN 13: 978-1-68217-350-3.

It is truly amazing to have such a large bulk of useful information that is so neatly and thoughtfully arranged in one directory guide. The volume consists of three main sections. The first section covers different resources that are important for educators' professional development. These resources include various professional organizations, associations, conferences, teaching opportunities abroad, and information and technology resources to create positive innovative learning environments. The second section contains a vast number of tables and charts of statistics and rankings in twenty-five different educational categories, such as elementary education, secondary education, and postsecondary education; the data goes beyond the U.S. educational system and covers some aspects of the Canadian and international educational systems. The tables and charts are well-organized and formatted. The section ends with a good-sized glossary that helps identify and define important educational terms and notations. The last section offers three types of indexes: entry and publisher name index, geographic index, and subject index, which are valuable finding aids. This directory guide's visual design simplicity highly increases its practical application. The proximity between the listings is sufficient, and the titles of the listings are bolded, which facilitates navigation. This directory guide can act as a ready-reference book because everyday use can help educators discover new helpful information that can be used to improve their professional skills and increase learning motivation in their classrooms and schools. This book is suitable for anyone who is involved in education or teaching, and is highly recommended for public and academic libraries and for general or professional reading audiences.—**Maria Agee**

Handbooks and Yearbooks

98.   Chatfield, Tom. Critical Thinking: Your Guide to Effective Argument, Successful Analysis and Independent Study. Thousand Oaks, Calif., Sage, 2018. 328p. index. $27.00pa. ISBN 13: 978-1-4739-4714-6.

This primer on critical thinking expertly introduces reasoning, argumentation, rhetoric, and bias and how understanding those concepts can make us better readers, researchers, and writers. Terms are well explained, examples are plentiful, and the workbook format allows readers to respond to questions and scenarios and document their understanding. The last two chapters focus on applying what is learned when using books and online resources for research and writing for academic purposes. The layout makes information accessible and attractive, as Chatfield highlights and defines words in the margins, provides tips, uses bullet points and charts, and presents full-page illustrated quotes about critical thinking from experts and historical figures. Chatfield chooses just the right combination of formal writing and casual address, creating the feeling that readers are learning from a trusted, witty friend. Links to YouTube videos produced by Chatfield end each chapter, and he encourages social media interaction using #TalkCriticalThinking for additional discussion and questions. Librarians and teachers would benefit from self-guided study of this book, and it would make an excellent resource to explore in a PLN or to share with AP students. Back matter is extensive and includes thoughtful endnotes and a reading guide for further study. The book also includes a glossary and an index. Highly recommended.—**Michelle Glatt**

99.   Cohen, Ralph Alan. **ShakesFear and How to Cure It: The Complete Handbook for Teaching Shakespeare.** New York, Arden Shakespeare/Bloomsbury Publishing, 2018. 375p. illus. index. $29.95pa. ISBN 13: 978-1-4742-2871-8; 978-1-4742-2873-2 (e-book).

ShakesFear and How to Cure It: The Complete Handbook for Teaching Shakespeare is written from the perspective of someone who has seemingly spent his entire adult life entrenched in the world of Shakespeare. Ralph Alan Cohen's authority is undisputed, and as such, he conveys knowledge that is insightful, practical, and, above all else, immensely useful for teaching and learning.

Cohen has taken his decades of experience and created a manual of sorts to help educators learn different (perhaps better) ways to approach teaching Shakespeare in the classroom. Cohen is self-aware enough to realize others may already be great teachers of Shakespeare, but believes his ideas and words can contribute and inspire in ways foreseen and unforeseen.

ShakesFear is divided into two parts. Part 1 has 5 chapters that approach the teaching of Shakespeare on a more macro level. Cohen discusses 7 common preconceptions of teaching Shakespeare, 8 donts, 9 dos, and common student complaints regarding Shakespeare being "too hard" or boring/irrelevant. These chapters show Cohen's ability to connect and engage with the reader in a way that feels like talking with a colleague. The content is rich with practical and helpful advice, and his language is comfortable and easy to follow.

Part 2, then, explores Shakespeare's 38 plays in more detail in order to provide a reference for each specific work. Each chapter includes Cohen's personal comments, "ploys" to use when teaching, and scenes to use for alternate readings. Cohen admits his comments may say more about him than about Shakespeare, but they do provide a welcome introduction for those new to the work, or perhaps those looking for a new perspective. The "ploys" are simply exercises or techniques that Cohen has used, mostly successfully, when teaching. Finally, the alternate readings point out specific scenes that may spark discussion due to their varied interpretations.

ShakesFear may not be "complete" in the literal sense, but it is a fantastic resource for educators. Although new(er) Shakespeare teachers will probably benefit the most, I do believe the book can provide new perspectives and ideas for experienced teachers as well. Cohen has a gift for communication, allowing *ShakesFear* to be accessible and useful to a wide audience.—**Tyler Manolovitz**

100.   **Education Today: Issues, Policies & Practices.** Beryl Watnick, ed. Hackensack, N.J., Salem Press, 2018. 3v. index. $295.00/set. ISBN 13: 978-1-68217-712-9; 978-1-68217-713-6 (e-book).

This three-volume set is a gold mine of knowledge in the field of education because it introduces such a wide range of educational entries that even a very sophisticated reader will find some topics of interest. The first volume offers insights about theoretical and psychological aspects of education; the second volume uncovers the information about educational practices in educational settings, and the third volume encourages educators to think about how they can prepare students and provide the skills that are necessary for success in the 21st century. This set of volumes consists of 446 articles that are distributed among 25 sections, such as history of education, education theory, higher education, multicultural and diversity education, adult education, alternative education, ESOL, and many others. Each article in a section has a consistent structure that includes the following components: overview, applications, viewpoints, further insights, terms and concepts, bibliography, and further reading. The beauty of this set is that it provides just enough information to wake up a reader's curiosity and create hunger, so he will further explore additional resources that the volumes present as suggested readings in the end of each section. The writing style is clear and precise, and it underlines the important points of each issue without overwhelming the reader with information. However, there is one point that I found questionable. Volume 3 is the only volume that has an index, so it can be challenging to locate necessary information in volume 1 and volume 2. Despite this slightly confusing point, I think this three-volume set can serve as an excellent reference source or as a conversation or debate starter for educators, instructors, students, and educational professionals.—**Maria Agee**

101.   **U.S. National Debate Topic 2017-2018: Education Reform.** Bronx, N.Y., H. W. Wilson, 2017. 201p. illus. index. (The Reference Shelf, volume 89, number 3). $75.00pa. ISBN 13: 978-1-68217-453-1.

Like other books in the "Reference Shelf" set, this book, which is tied to the annual high school debate topic, brings together print and internet articles (30 in this case). Under the broad topic of the title, there are 5 sections: 1) The State of American Education, 2) Reform 2017, 3) In the Classroom—Skills, Knowledge, Climate, 4) Equity and the Achievement Gap, and 5) Education Technology. Interestingly, the preface points out the dangers and the threats to improved public education caused by the current political climate in the United States. As with other volumes in this series, the pieces selected offer a wide range of viewpoints: an article from *The National Review* argues that only Secretary of Education Betsy DeVos can save American schools, while another presents teachers' fears of her approach to education. Other items discuss vocational education, funding of public education, and all levels of school from kindergarten to college. Although brief, the book offers a diverse range of texts.

As with the entire "Reference Shelf" set, the "Index" only lists individuals, in this case led by DeVos (33 mentions) and Donald Trump (17). The lack of subjects, such as "charter schools," "higher education," and "vouchers," detracts somewhat from its usefulness. Also, the bibliography simply appears to bring together the references found in the 6 introductory texts (a preface and the 5 section introductions) written by Micah L. Issitt, but does not include citations from at least one of the chapters that provides some useful sources.

Institutions of all kinds should find this volume of use to their readers. Although fairly expensive for a paperback of its length, school, public and academic libraries should investigate it.—**Mark Schumacher**

Elementary and Secondary Education

Digital Resources

102.   **African Education Research Database https://essa-africa.org/AERD.** [Website] Free. Date reviewed: 2018.

This database offers a varied collection of research, including articles, chapters, PhD theses, working papers, and more, related to the topic of education in the many countries of Sub-Saharan Africa. A map of the African continent is pinned at particular locations and numbered according to amount of available research documents. Users can select a pin on the homepage map or choose by country (Nigeria, South Africa, Ghana, etc.), keyword (Arts Educations, E-learning, etc.), or method (Experimental, Quantitative, etc.). Users can also select the large green Keywords banner below the map to browse by keywords categorized by Phases & Types of Education; Students, Access & Learning; Language & Curriculum; and other categories. Search parameters yield a listing by title of the relevant research. Clicking on the title presents the abstract alongside other identifying information such as author(s), country(s), year, language, document type, research method, and full citation. There is also a link to the document in its original publishing source. Users will find a range of topics explored from such places as Somalia ("Making schools more girl-friendly: exploring the effects of 'girl friendly space' on school attendance of adolescent girls"), Malawi ("Education for democratic citizenship in Malawian secondary schools: balancing student voice and adult privilege"), Zimbabwe ("The role of politics in the migration of Zimbabwean teachers to South Africa"), and many others. The easy-to-navigate database helps focus attention on the diversity of the issues facing education in the many nations across the African continent and would be of interest to a wide audience of students, educators, and other researchers interested in the state of education in the region.—**ARBA Staff Reviewer**

Directories

103.   **The Comparative Guide to American Elementary & Secondary Schools, 2019.** Amenia, N.Y., Grey House Publishing, 2019. 1626p. index. $150.00pa. ISBN 13: 978-1-68217-776-1.

This 10th edition begins with a brief introduction and user guide before delving into state and national educational profiles. The states are arranged in alphabetic order; each profile contains four sections: a state public school educational profile; National Assessment of Educational Progress (NAEP) test scores; a school district profile; and school district rankings. Using California as an example, this means users will find ready reference facts on such things as mean ACT and SAT scores; ratios of students to teachers and to librarians; percentages of male and female students; scores on math, science, and reading for 4th and 8th grade; and average proficiencies on tests by gender and race. After these overviews, each county within California is listed in alphabetic order, subdivided by school districts within that county. In these school district profiles, users can find the number of schools and students, gender and race percentages, the percentage of English language learners, the percentage of students with individual education programs, the percentage of students eligible for the free lunch program, and more. The last section within the state profile ranks 22 pieces of data by school district (number of teachers, female and male students, Asian students Hispanic students, English language learner students, etc.). The last part of the book, National Public School Data, provides summary information about how students in public schools are faring academically in addition to national statistics based on the NAEP test scores. The end of this section ranks districts in ascending and descending order using such criteria as numbers of female and male students, student/counselor ratios, and other categories. Following the national section is a glossary, index of school districts, and a city index. This comprehensive reference is recommended to public libraries.—**ARBA Staff Reviewer**

Handbooks and Yearbooks

104.   Gyure, Dale Allen. **The Schoolroom: A Social History of Teaching and Learning.** Santa Barbara, Calif., Greenwood Press/ABC-CLIO, 2018. 218p. illus. index. (History of Human Spaces). $39.00. ISBN 13: 978-1-4408-5037-0; 978-1-4408-5038-7 (e-book).

The Schoolroom examines the history of education in America in a unique way, through the architecture of school buildings, the classroom spaces within them, and the objects within those classrooms. The first major section focuses on the history of the schoolroom from the one-room schoolroom of colonial America to the flexible, open classrooms of today. The author makes important connections between classroom spaces and curricular and pedagogical trends. In addition, the book explores how the classroom environment influences student health as well as discipline, essential components of learning. The second major section chronicles the architectural history of schoolhouses, from the Quincy Grammar schools in the mid-1800s to the first graded schools and high schools, and then the move towards standardization of school buildings. These developments are placed in historical context, such as the connection between the postwar growth of suburbs and more open, casual buildings. Gyure also describes more recent changes related to technology, disability rights, sustainability, and security. The last section of the book explores material objects within educational spaces including blackboards, desks, computers, media, and teaching projection systems. There is also a short section on ancillary spaces such as corridors and lockers. These intertwined stories of education buildings, spaces, objects, methods, and pedagogies provide a backdrop for the general history of education. The usefulness of the reference text is enhanced by the inclusion of a chronology, glossary, bibliography, and index. The book is one of five volumes in the ABC-CLIO/Greenwood Press series History of Human Spaces.—**Theresa Muraski**

105.   Zeffren, Elisheva, and Perella Perlstein. **Secrets of Great Teachers: 22 Strategies to Energize Middle and High School Classrooms.** Jefferson, N.C., McFarland, 2018. 240p. index. $35.00pa. ISBN 13: 978-1-4766-7030-0; 978-1-4766-3054-0 (e-book).

This book offers a multidimensional perspective on teaching and emphasizes a variety of strategies that can help improve overall instructional practices. The book consists of twenty-two chapters that reflect twenty-two strategies. The chapters are not arranged in any particular order and can be read independently. The writing is simple and clear; bullet points keep the reader focused on important ideas throughout. The book offers strategies that can be considered universal and can be applied to a wide range of school subjects in middle schools and high schools. The organization of each chapter is not very consistent, but the authors offer various examples, resources, and ideas that show how their suggestions and recommendations can be used in real-life instructional interventions and interactions. These strengths make this book valuable for novice teachers. However, the book title, *Secrets of Great Teachers,* is misleading because the content has been in pedagogical practice for decades and because main concepts described in the book are not secrets but well-known pedagogical concepts and methods. These include Bloom's taxonomy, using visual aids, promoting literacy, and critical and independent thinking. However, it is very useful that these twenty-two strategies are collected in one place because they serve as a convenient reference resource for teachers, especially for those in the early years of their careers. The extensive bibliography and index add value. This book is recommended for university libraries with undergraduate education students and for practicing professionals who want to improve their teaching strategies.—**Maria Agee**

Higher Education

Digital Resources

106.   **Tuition Funding Sources. Https://www.tuitionfundingsources.com/.** [Website] Free. Date reviewed: 2018.

Tuition Funding Sources is a simple and valuable resource for high school and college students with a large database of roughly seven million scholarships in addition to other college and career resources. General users can select the Careers tab found at the top or in the center of the homepage. This links to a Career Aptitude Test and an A-Z list of careers from Accountant to Zoologists and Wildlife Biologists. Users can learn general information about particular careers in such sections as Significant Points, Nature of the Work, Working Conditions, Earnings, Job Outlook, and more. General users can also examine the Scholarship of the Day on the homepage for a sample of the greater contents of the site. Users who register with the site (free) and complete a basic profile can select the Scholarship Search tab (or Get Started or Register Now) to access a list of applicable scholarships. Profile questions generally encompass interests, academic information, heritage, activities, and more. Scholarships are listed by name, and include application deadline, number, and amount of award(s). Clicking on the name links to a more detailed description of the scholarship. Users can click the star icon to the left of the scholarship name to add to their personal list. With its vast scholarship database and good foundational information on careers, Tuition Funding Sources is an excellent resource for high school and college students.—**ARBA Staff Reviewer**

Special Education

Handbooks and Yearbooks

107.   Sacks, Arlene. **Special Education: A Reference Book for Policy and Curriculum Development.** 3d ed. Amenia, N.Y., Grey House Publishing, 2018. 388p. illus. index. $165.00. ISBN 13: 978-1-68217-950-5; 978-1-68217-749-5 (e-book).

Sacks' third edition of this title has had all previous chapters reviewed and revised, has added a chapter on popular culture and advocacy and one on national statistics (some divided by state), and has divided the resources into print and nonprint. The now eleven chapters are the following: "Overview"; "Chronology"; "Special Education Curriculum"; "Special Education Programs and the Law"; "Politics and the Special Education Challenge"; "Popular Culture and Advocacy"; "Organizations, Associations, and Government Agencies"; "Selected Print Resources";" Nonprint Resources"; "Primary Documents and Quotations"; and "National Statistics." "Chronology" is especially well done with explanations of each entry. The "Primary Documents and Quotations" chapter is for the purpose of advocacy, and documents and quotations do not necessarily relate to the volume's entries. Each chapter has a list of references, but the one for "Popular Culture and Advocacy" is disappointingly short (three entries). A glossary and a general index complete the volume. Although the text is well written and approachable for majors and graduate students, the black-and-white photos and images are largely grainy, dark, and out of focus, making the interpretation of some statistical charts difficult. For libraries in which the previous editions have been well-used or that have need of such specialized reference and background sources, this is recommended.—**Rosanne M. Cordell**

6 Ethnic Studies

General Works

108. Intangible Cultural Heritage https://ich.unesco.org/en/what-is-intangible-heritage-00003. [Website] Free. Date reviewed: 2019.

This site catalogs Intangible Cultural Heritage (ICH) around the world. The project is part of the UNESCO convention for safeguarding ICH, which can include oral tradition, performing arts, social practices, rituals, festive events, knowledge and practices about nature and the universe, and knowledge and skills to produce traditional crafts. Users can find further explanation of what is meant by ICH under the Convention tab on the homepage, along with the answers to frequently asked questions and other information. There are also News and Events tabs, which are current. More details about particular projects, like one started in 2018 to compile an inventory of sacred sites and rare ritual practices in Kyrgyzstan, can be found under the Safeguarding tab. An Actors tab contains information about NGO involvement, donors, and partners. Specific country information is discoverable via the By Country tab. Using this tab, users can type in a country and the database will produce a page that provides news and events, periodic reporting requirements, the ICH inscribed elements, ongoing nominations and backlog nominations, ICH projects, and (potentially) other information like relevant legislation and NGOs active in the country. The Lists tab arranges ICH inscribed elements by date (2008-2018). In total there are 508 inscribed elements corresponding to 122 countries. Clicking on one of these, such as Shadow Play in Syria, will give users a description of the ICH, photographs, and a video of the ICH in question. There are also links to related content on the left side of the page. Lists offers another feature, Dive into Intangible Cultural Heritage, which uses web semantics and graphic visualizations to map the information in the database.—**ARBA Staff Reviewer**

109. Webb, Lois Sinaiko, Lindsay Grace Cardella, and Jeanne Jacob. International Cookbook of Life-Cycle Celebrations. Santa Barbara, Calif., Greenwood Press/ABC-CLIO, 2018. 770p. index. $105.00. ISBN 13: 978-1-61069-015-7; 978-1-61069-016-4 (e-book).

This volume updates and enlarges the 2000 edition of this text (called *Multicultural Cookbook of Life-Cycle Celebrations* and written by the late Lois Webb). There are recipes from more than 150 countries around the world, prepared for various events: births, baptisms, birthdays, weddings, and deaths. The entry for each country begins with an introductory text, including geographical, historical, and social information and comments about the place of food in its culture. The recipes themselves range from quite simple dishes to some that require exotic ingredients that might be somewhat hard to find in some places in the United States. There are recipes for breads, meat, and fish dishes, vegetable preparations, beverages and desserts, along with some more exotic dishes, such as Tunisian harissa (fiery pepper seasoning), Japanese shredded omelet, and Nepalese paneer cheena and paneer tikki (cheeses).

The opening "Getting Started" chapter is curious because it seems to indicate that this book is designed for young cooks. One part is titled "Don't Cook Alone: Have Adult Help" (p. xli). In fact, the current book evolved from a similar 1993 book written "for students." Other useful information at the outset includes a discussion of the life-cycle rituals related to all the major religions around the world and an 18-page glossary of food-related terms. Given the numerous cultural elements in this volume, it should not be considered a mere cookbook but also an interesting look at scores of countries and the events that mark the lives of their inhabitants. Readers interested in world culture, as well as delicious food, will enjoy this volume. Any library with such patrons should consider this book. And for a 770-page book it is quite reasonably priced.—**Mark Schumacher**

African Americans

110.   **Afro-Louisiana History and Genealogy. https://www.ibiblio.org/laslave/.** [Website] Free. Date reviewed: 2018.

This site gathers information from diverse archives to help shed light on 100 years of Louisiana slave history. Slave inventory documents supply names, dates, places, and other vital information. Users can easily access the information from a series of links on the homepage. Search the Database provides a series of fields to be filled with known information such as Slave Name, Master's Name, Gender, Epoch, Racial Designation, Plantation Location, and Origin. The latter two categories list generous options—34 plantation locations and over 150 places of origin to choose from, attesting to the quality and detail of the records. Data in each record may include Estate Name, Buyer's Name, Seller's Name, Document Year, Gender, Racial Designation, and Document Location in addition to details regarding family, skills and trades, emancipation status, and other details. Miscellaneous Searches provide links to three searches grouped by theme, including African Names (and explanations of them), Revolts (listing slaves known to have been involved in a conspiracy or rebellion), and Runaways. Users can click on the names in each alphabetical listing to access their records. View Original Documents offers users a look at thumbnails and brief summaries of several slave inventory sheets. Clicking on a thumbnail allows a closer examination. The Dr. Hall's Statistical Calculations link shows users how the data has been and can be used with several documents clarifying Name Frequency, Master's Name Frequency, Mother's Name Frequency, Freed Slaves, Islamic African Slave Names, and more. In addition, users can find charts depicting such things as Freed Slaves by Decade, Mean Price by Gender, Location of Africans from Various Coasts, and Percent by Origin.—**ARBA Staff Reviewer**

111.   **Black Loyalist http://www.blackloyalist.info/.** [Website] Free. Date reviewed: 2019.

During the tumultuous years of the American Revolution, blacks who hoped to escape slavery maintained loyalty to the English crown. This site shares information on roughly one thousand Black Loyalists who left New York between April and November of 1783. The site also offers a good selection of essays and other materials which help fill in the story of the Black Loyalists. Users can access the information in several ways. The Browse tab at the top of the page links to a drop down menu of options: Runaways, Owners, Events, Places, and Groups. Alternatively, users can click either the Browse the Black Loyalists tab or the Browse the Events tab on the homepage to approach the information that way. Individual names under Runaways or Owners each link to affiliated information which may include a brief descriptive paragraph, links to Related Background Information, and a Timeline of Events with more links. Users can discover fascinating detail about listed individuals, such as their name origins, their relatives, and their fates. Under Events, users can view a timeline of events bearing on or related to the story of Black Loyalists, such as the 1776 Smallpox Outbreak or the 1783 Evacuation of New York. Each event link can be followed for further detail. Groups lists nearly fifty entities/organizations involved in the story, such as Black Pioneers, Captain John Coffin's Company, Kings Americans Dragoons, and the Quakers. Users can click an entity name to access related links, dates, and more. The Places feature is not complete, but will eventually pin over eighty relevant locations (from London, England, to the Great Bridge to Ferry Point) to a Google map. In the meantime, users can select a place from the list to access links of affiliated people and events. It is important to note that the Black Loyalist website is still under development. As such, some links may not function and some information has yet to be uploaded or organized. There is, however, still a good amount of information that could shed light on the Black Loyalist refugees—an important part of the expansive postcolonial era and a crucial element of the black diaspora.—**ARBA Staff Reviewer**

112.   **Black Power Encyclopedia: From "Black Is Beautiful" to Urban Uprisings.** Umoja, Akinyele, Karin L. Stanford, and Jasmin A. Young, eds. Santa Barbara, Calif., Greenwood Press/ABC-CLIO, 2108. 2v. illus. index. (Movements of the American Mosaic). $189.00/set. ISBN 13: 978-1-4408-4006-7; 978-1-4408-4007-4 (e-book).

Although numerous monographs and encyclopedia articles have been written on the Black Power Movement (BPM), this excellent new two-volume set by editors Umoja, Stanford, and Young focuses specifically on the period between the 1950s and 1998 (the death of Stokely Carmichael) when the BPM was most active. The approximately 190 scholarly entries plus five overview essays cover a range of topics, including biographies, organizations, and general areas such as black bookstores. Each signed entry runs about three pages long, with *see also* references and secondary bibliographies (a summative bibliography would have been a good addition). Select entries also feature excerpts from or the full text of primary documents, such as Huey Newton's "In Defense of Self-Defense." Black-and-white photos are scattered throughout, and the index and movement chronology are very helpful. Entries are consistently well written, mixing factual points (names, dates) with solid critical narrative. Considering the movement's significance in addition to how these entries complement those found in more general reference works such as Carney Smith's *Complete Encyclopedia of African American History* (2015), this set is essential for U.S. cultural history collections.—**Anthony J. Adam**

113.   **Critical Insights: Martin Luther King Jr.** Robert C. Evans, ed. Hackensack, N.J., Salem Press, 2019. 272p. index. $105.00. ISBN 13: 978-1-64265-030-3; 978-1-64265-031-0 (e-book).

This book is part of the highly regarded Critical Insights series from Salem Press. This volume examines and discusses the life and work of Dr. Martin Luther King, Jr., through both the expected Critical Contexts and Critical Readings sections. After introductory remarks, an interview with Keith Miller, and a short biography of Dr. King, four chapters focus on various contexts of Dr. King's work including the use of marching, singing, and road imagery in the civil rights movement; the traits and impact of Dr. King's speeches and sermons; a pluralist analysis of Dr. King's "I Have a Dream" speech; and contraries and progression in Dr. King's writings. The Critical Readings section contains twelve chapters on Dr. King's uses of intertextuality, balanced thinking, and balanced phrasing, Dr. King's refusal to extemporize, precursors to the "I Have a Dream" speech, Dr. King's use of proverbs and "he Samaritan Way," whiteness and care for the other, poems inspired by Dr. King, critical reactions to the televised miniseries on Dr. King along with his "A Testament of Hope," and a number of interviews with people who knew him or heard him speak. An extensive bibliography along with a chronology of Dr. King's life and a list of his works makes this volume the definitive guide on the life and legacy of Dr. Martin Luther King, Jr.—**Bradford Lee Eden**

114.   Hillstrom, Laurie Collier. **Black Lives Matter: From a Moment to a Movement.** Santa Barbara, Calif., Greenwood Press/ABC-CLIO, 2018. 164p. index. $39.00. ISBN 13: 978-1-4408-6570-1; 978-1-4408-6571-8 (e-book).

This reference text on the Black Lives Matter (BLM) movement begins with an introduction and timeline which summarize the origins and major milestones of the movement. This overview is followed by seven topical chapters. First, the author provides a historical context for the movement from the civil rights movement to the fatal shooting of Trayvon Martin in 2012. Two chapters provide details about the police shooting of Michael Brown in Ferguson, Missouri, and the decentralized growth of the nationwide grassroots network, including mission, goals, and related events. The author also provides details on the tactics used to grow the movement, especially the use of social media, protest strategies, connections to political platforms, and even a police violence mapping project. The author also includes a chapter on the critical backlash towards the movement. The text concludes with short summaries on issues related to racial injustice in America and the rise of the BLM movement, including economic inequality, segregation, problems in the criminal justice system, and voter suppression. Following a conclusion, there are short biographical sketches of various figures important in the rise of the BLM movement and a few primary documents that would be useful for historical researchers. Each chapter includes notes and there is a brief, annotated bibliography as well as an index. In general, the volume supplies historical context and basic information on the origins, growth, and reactions to the BLM movement. It will be useful as a starting point for high school and lower-level undergraduate research, similar to books on the same topic in Gale's Opposing Viewpoints and Abdo's Essential Library Special Reports series.—**Theresa Muraski**

115.   **Last Seen: Finding Family after Slavery. http://www.informationwanted.org/.** [Website] Free. Date reviewed: 2019.

This project digitizes advertisements placed in African American newspapers by former slaves in search of loved ones following emancipation. The project is a joint effort by the Department of History at Villanova, the Albert LePage Center for History in the Public Interest (Villanova), and the Mother Bethel AME Church (Philadelphia). These last seen or information wanted advertisements mention family members by name, include the place the person was last seen, provide physical descriptions, and may even include the name of the former slave owner. At present, there are over 3,200 advertisements in the database. There are two ways to search the ads, either by browsing by item or browsing by collection. If browsing by item, users can choose to browse all or can use filters to conduct a narrowed search. If users choose to browse by collection, they click on the name of the newspaper in which the ad appeared. Either way, users will be taken to a clickable thumbnail of the advertisement and be provided with a description, a date, source information, tags, and a citation. Users can also click on Mapping the Ads, which shows the location of the person (indicated by a yellow dot) who placed the ad and allows users to view the distribution of the ads over time. Clicking on the dots pops up the ad placed. Valuably, there are K-12 lesson plans that align with Common Core Standards. All are downloadable and free to use. These ads are especially good for teaching students how to identify and use primary sources, how to think critically, and how to work collaboratively. The project is ongoing as a team of graduate students is painstakingly searching for more ads and digitizing them. It is possible to volunteer as a transcriber via a link on the homepage of the project. There is also a place to upload advertisements not already in the database.—**ARBA Staff Reviewer**

116.　**Milestone Documents in African American History.** 2d ed. Echol Nix, Jr. and Keturah C. Nix, eds. Hackensack, N.J., Salem Press, 2017. 4v. illus. index. $395.00/set. ISBN 13: 978-1-68217-579-8; 978-1-68217-580-4 (e-book).

The first edition of this set published in 2010 (see ARBA 2011, entry 323). This new edition includes 124 chronologically arranged full-text primary documents in African American history, ranging from John Rolfe's letter of 1619 to the 2017 Report Summary of the Ferguson Police Department Investigation. Entries include the document itself (longer documents are necessarily excerpted), critical analysis by approximately 70 field experts, brief lists of secondary print and web sources, glossaries, timelines, and "Questions for Further Study." Additional materials include a teachers' activity guide, 138 photographs and illustrations, and a list of documents by category. As the earlier edition ended with President Obama's inaugural address and only a handful of historic and recent documents have been added, libraries will discover considerable overlap. Readers also will find some significant documents missing—the Second Morrill Act, for example, or the 1836 Gag Rule which prohibited Congress from receiving antislavery petitions. However, purchase of the print edition comes with free unlimited access to the equivalent online database, which students can use at school or home. Granted that many of the documents can be found full text online (archives.gov is a highly useful entry point for full-text documents) or in-print format, the significant benefit in acquiring this four-volume set lies in the additional materials noted above, particularly the critical analyses. Compares well with White, Bay, and Martin's two-volume *Freedom on My Mind: A History of African Americans, with Documents* (2d ed., 2016).—**Anthony J. Adam**

117.　**MIT Black History. https://www.blackhistory.mit.edu/archive.** [Website] Free. Date reviewed: 2018.

This archive of over three thousand artifacts highlights the long history of black involvement at the Massachusetts Institute of Technology (MIT). Users can trace the evolution of the black experience going back nearly as far as the prestigious university's founding in the 1860s. Selecting the Archive or Explore Archive tab connects users to a search bar or a timeline display which organizes materials by decade. Users can also browse materials by MIT School, MIT Department, Life at MIT, or Career. Within the archive are photographs (including yearbook photos), videos, brochures, event programs, audio recordings, interviews, and other materials. Artifacts may be accompanied by a brief narrative description, including a biography if applicable, and other identifying information such as collection, career, and external link. Highlights include notes written by Alonzo Fields, employee under MIT President Samuel Stratton, who later served as Chief White House Butler under four U.S. Presidents; a video of President Barack Obama's 2009 visit to MIT; a 2015 photograph of the MIT Black Women's Alliance co-chairs with astronaut Yvonne Cagle; a photograph of Anselmo Krigger, class of 1917 athlete and possibly "the first black graduate of the MIT Department of Civil Engineering," and more. The Stories feature gathers artifacts into broader narratives of the black experience and legacy at MIT. NASA Figures: An MIT Constellation describes black MIT graduates and their successful affiliation with the U.S. space agency. Robert R. Taylor: First Black Student at MIT presents a biography of the first accredited African American architect. Publications present over one hundred reports, theses, articles, and books published by MIT graduates and educators related to the black experience. Larger volumes are available for purchase while some are downloadable. Here users will find the Dallas Brown 1910 thesis titled "Comparative wearing tests on different makes of globe and gate valves," a 1988 article on MIT's Minority Success Record and a children's book from 2009 titled Ron's Big Mission, recounting the story of *Challenger* astronaut Ronald McNair. Coupled together, the archive and accompanying contextual information makes the site a vital resource for students and educators of American history, Black Studies, and other disciplines.—**ARBA Staff Reviewer**

118. **New York Slavery Records Index http://nyslavery.commons.gc.cuny.edu.** [Website] Free. Date reviewed: 2018.
    The New York Slavery Records Index holds over 35,000 records regarding slavery in the state of New York. Gathering information from census records, birth certificates, ship inventories, newspapers, legal documents, and many other sources, the index offers information on enslaved individuals and the people who owned them. The index maintains records from as far back as the early 16th century. Due to the scope of the index and its sources, it is recommended that users first select the Search Instructions tab on the homepage. Users can then select SEARCH from the blue bar and contribute any known information to the corresponding field, such as Slave Last Name, Slave Birth Year, Slave Death Year, Owner Last Name, and so on. Users can narrow the search by Type of Record source: Census, Document, Enslaved Person, Ship, Site, Slave Owner, etc. The Search Tag field lists acronyms of related information, such as ABN (Slave Babies Abandoned), EMN (emancipation) and much more. Information within each record varies, but may include relevant names (slaves, owners), dates, locations, source documents, and numbers (slaves owned). Under Sources, users can find brief contextual information on Slavery Records in a listing of types of records and/or the entities which created them, such as Dutch Records of New Amsterdam, Slave Ship Records, Colonial Census Records, Runaway Slave

Advertisements and Announcements, and more. Additional resource links are available here as well. The homepage also features links to contextual essays on the "Start and End of Slavery in New York," "Sojourner Truth," and other topics. The quantity of records and additional resources make the index a good starting point for research .—**ARBA Staff Reviewer**

Arab Americans

119.   Al-Deen, Aminah. **History of Arab Americans: Exploring Diverse Roots.** Santa Barbara, Calif., Greenwood Press/ABC-CLIO, 2018. 194p. illus. index. $61.00. ISBN 13: 978-1-4408-4068-5; 978-1-4408-4069-2 (e-book).

This book explores the history of Arab Americans through a number of different lenses and approaches: the geographic, the cultural (beliefs and values), the linguistic, and the historical. After a chronology of key dates in Arab American history, 11 chapters focus on providing an unbiased discussion related to the history of this topic from 1600 to the present, with emphases on culture, faith, practices, politics, engagement, women, American media, 9/11 and post-9/11 life for Arab Americans, and challenges for the Arab American community into the future. Each chapter includes a short bibliography, along with short biographical profiles of Arab Americans who were both important and/or are well-known in American history and current life. This book would be a good introduction for any college class related to contemporary society, diversity, and culture.—**Bradford Lee Eden**

Asian Americans

120.   Lee, Jonathan H. X. **Asian American History Day by Day: A Reference Guide to Events.** Santa Barbara, Calif., Greenwood Press/ABC-CLIO, 2018. 466p. index. $94.00. ISBN 13: 978-0-313-39927-5; 978-0-313-39928-2 (e-book).

This volume presents hundreds of events, running from January 1 to December 31, involving Asian Americans, from the late 18th century to a few years ago. Each date of the year is arranged identically: a brief paragraph describing an event in a given year, one or two paragraphs of a text (from a print or online source) about the event, references to books and websites about the event, and finally an "Also Noteworthy" section, listing events on the date in other years. Occasionally, a date will present details of two events. While a few dates present famous moments, such as the attack on Pearl Harbor, December 7, 1941, most are little-known moments in American history, such as the foundation in 1919 of the Korean Liberty Congress in Philadelphia and the 1952 Supreme Court ruling in the *On Lee v. United States* case. Sikhs, Arabs, and Muslims are also included as Asian Americans, often as victims of hate crimes.

This book is best enjoyed by reading day-by-day about the events within the Asian American community throughout the country, rather than seeking related events. For example, there is not a simple way to find all the Korean or Japanese events quickly by looking through the index. (A curiosity: the cover has a large photo of Daniel Inouye, the late senator from Hawaii, but he is not mentioned in the index at all! He is mentioned briefly in a few places.) Libraries serving an Asian American population will certainly find this of interest, while other libraries should consider it as well, for its useful information on these diverse groups—**Mark Schumacher**

Indians of North America

121.   **American Indian Newspapers. https://www.amdigital.co.uk/primary-sources/ american-indian-newspapers.** [Website] Chicago, Adam Matthew Digital, 2018. Price negotiated by site. Date reviewed: 2018.

This new collection from Adam Matthew, American Indian Newspapers, provides researchers with the opportunity to explore 45 newspapers written by and for indigenous communities. The collection, comprised of 9,000 individual editions from the United States and Canada, contains national periodicals, as well as local community news and student publications. Editions include bilingual and indigenous language editions. There are opportunities to search an event over time as some titles are digitized in large runs that include more than 500 issues. Newspapers are sourced from the Newberry Library, Chicago, and the Sequoyah National Research Center at the University of Arkansas, Little Rock. Newspapers span 1828-2016, but the bulk of the newspapers in the collection cover the 1970s-2016. A series of tabs on the main page allows users to click on Introduction, Newspapers, Searching, Explore, Essays, and Help. The introduction supplies information on the selection criteria, the editorial board, the nature and scope of American Indian Newspapers, and copyright. Under the Newspapers tab, users can click on a thumbnail of each paper or search by language, publisher, publishing location, or library/archive (Newberry or Sequoyah). Searches can be conducted at the article level. An informative video provides information on how to use the collection's search features. The Explore tab connects to newspaper profiles; an additional video introduction; and photo features from the newspapers that include dates, newspaper from which it is sourced, and subject and copyright information. Here users will also find external links to publishers and news sites. The Essays tab includes seven contextualizing pieces, such as "Wounded Knee: The Spark That Ignited Tribal Publishing," by Erin Fehr, archivist at the Sequoyah National Research Center; "The Changing face of the *Indian School Journal,* 1900-1980" by K. Tsianina Lomawaima, Arizona State University; and a video essay "The History of the Cherokee Phoenix" by Executive Editor Brandon Scott and Assistant Editor Will Chavez. This will be a valuable research tool for scholars at large academic libraries. Highly recommended.—**ARBA Staff Reviewer**

122.   **Defining Documents in American History: Native Americans.** Michael Shally-Jensen, ed. Hackensack, N.J., Salem Press, 2017. 400p. illus. index. $175.00. ISBN 13: 978-1-68217-587-3; 978-1-68217-588-0 (e-book).

Editor Michael Shally-Jensen and 13 other scholars have produced this latest volume in Salem Press' Defining Documents in American History series. It contains 30 documents, many excerpted, dating from 1451 to 2017 that are organized under four categories: "Early Encounters and Conflicts"; "Western Wars and Aftermaths"; "New Lives and Circumstances"; and "Later Developments." It is important to note that the term "Native Americans" in this work apparently only includes American Indians, as one will not find a focus on other native groups, such as Hawaiians. Also noteworthy is that native peoples are the subject of some of the documents selected for inclusion, thus in those cases the perspective proffered is that of Europeans and their descendants. Examples include "Christopher Columbus: Letter to Raphael Sanxis on the Discovery of America"; "John Smith: The Generall Historie of Virginia"; and "Narrative of the Captivity and Restoration of Mrs Mary Rowlandson." Each of the documents is accompanied by analyses, biographical information about the author of the document, and bibliographical information for further research. The work concludes with a chronology that lists the documents by year of publication, a list of web resources, bibliography, and an index.

As with any reference of this type, there are quibbles about what was selected for inclusion and what was not. An explanation of the criteria utilized would have been helpful. For instance, there are three different documents included that center on the Cherokee efforts between 1829 and 1832 to stop their removal from their Southeastern homeland. Yet, the Indian Removal Act of 1830 is missing, despite it being the law used by the United States to remove not only the Cherokees west of the Mississippi River, but also other native groups including the Chickasaw, Choctaw, Creeks, Ho-Chunk, Potawatomi, and Seminole. Another curious exclusion is House Concurrent Resolution 108, which was passed in 1953 and inaugurated the federal government's Termination Policy, which did horrific damage to American Indian nations for more than 20 years and whose consequences resonate to this day. This reference will find utility in public and school libraries. Academic libraries with collections focusing on U.S. history or Native American Studies likely have many of these documents in other sources, as the majority are not very obscure.—**John R. Burch Jr.**

123. Dennis, Yvonne Wakim, and Arlene Hirschfelder. **Native American Landmarks and Festivals: A Traveler's Guide to Indigenous United States and Canada.** Canton, Mich., Visible Ink Press, 2018. 432p. illus. maps. index. $19.95pa. ISBN 13: 978-1-5785-9641-6; 978-1-5785-9694-2 (e-book).

This guidebook is a comprehensive look at the various landmarks, festivals, museums, ruins, and more that encompass Native American culture. The book is divided into chapters based on regions of the United States, such as Northeast and Southwest. While the table of contents does not say which states are under which heading, the index will help readers find information related to particular states. The text is respectful to Native Americans and acknowledges that some landmarks, such as the Penobscot Building in Detroit, incorporated Native American motifs into its art deco style but did so as more of an appropriation than a respectful tribute. The text is sprinkled with black-and-white photos and, while color photos would have been more interesting, the price tag is very reasonable for a book this comprehensive. It is not a book for the casual reader, but rather for those doing research or planning a trip. An unlikely choice for the average high school collection, but this book would work well in schools with a large Native American population or for an intensive study of Native American history and culture. Additional selection.—**Laura Younkin**

124. **Digital Paxton. https://hsp.org/history-online/digital-history-projects/digital-paxton.** [Website] Free. Date reviewed: 2018.

The Historical Society of Pennsylvania has gathered numerous colonial-era documents related to the Paxton incident, which saw European settlers stage random attacks against indigenous people as retribution for distant fort attacks. Convinced to put their concerns to paper, the settlers, their advocates, and others produced pamphlets, cartoons, broadsides, correspondence, and other artifacts which we can study today. Users can examine the digital collection of over 1,600 images, and can also engage in critical analysis of the materials in several ways. This homepage offers good foundational information on the archive, which can be accessed via several links. Once inside the archive, users can select from a list of options underneath the menu icon in the upper left corner of the page. For the Digital Collection, users can browse the collection as a whole or by media, which includes Art, Books, Broadsides, Manuscripts, Newsprint, Pamphlets, and Political Cartoons. Users can also access the Transcribed Records (88 so far) or a complete index. Under each media category, documents are listed alphabetically by titles, which users can click to view. Users can examine the digital artifact in a viewer (some with transcription) alongside available metadata which may include date of origin, description, citation, format, author/creator, and more. Users can view the "Act for Preventing Tumults and Riotous Assemblies," "A Historical Account of the Late Disturbance," a 1757 Peace Medal, and other items. The Historical Overview offers generous foundational information and analysis with five essays addressing different aspects of the Paxton incident. "Pontiac's War and the Paxton Boys," for example, goes back to set the scene as the French give up their territories to the British, opening the door to more expansion at the expense of native peoples. The Keywords section offers five essays which emphasize the interdisciplinary appeal of the artifacts in focusing on the concepts of "Material Culture," "Anonymity," "Condolence," "Elites," and "Anti-Presbyterianism." The essay on "Anonymity," for example, examines the effect of dubious or unknown pamphlet authors. Under Pedagogy, users can find lessons suitable for both high school and university settings which may incorporate discussion questions, reading suggestions, vocabulary, core concepts, multimedia, and more.—**ARBA Staff Reviewer**

125.   **Indian Treaties in the United States: An Encyclopedia and Documents Collection.** Donald L. Fixico, ed. Santa Barbara, Calif., ABC-CLIO, 2018. 422p. illus. index. $94.00. ISBN 13: 978-1-4408-6047-8; 978-1-4408-6048-5 (e-book).

Donald L. Fixico, Distinguished Foundation Professor of History, Distinguished Scholar of Sustainability in the Wrigley Global Institute of Sustainability, and Affiliate Faculty in American Indian Studies at Arizona State University, edited *Treaties with American Indians: An Encyclopedia of Rights, Conflicts, and Sovereignty.* Upon publication in 2008, it joined Vine Deloria Jr. and Raymond J. DeMallie's *Documents of American Indian Diplomacy: Treaties, Agreements and Conventions, 1775-1979* as the two core reference resources on the subject of American Indian treaties. Although comprehensive, both are multivolume resources and are priced as such. There has since been a need for a good single-volume reference on the topic that was also within the price-range of school libraries and smaller publics. Fixico has aptly and admirably filled that niche with *Indian Treaties in the United States: An Encyclopedia and Documents Collection.*

Part 1 consists of six pithy essays: "Indian Treaty Making: A Native View"; "Indian Treaties as International Agreements"; "Canadian Indian Treaties"; "Colonial and Early Treaties, 1775-1829"; "Indian Removal and Land Cessions, 1830-1849"; and "Reservations and Confederate and Unratified Treaties, 1850-1871." Interspersed within the essays are boxes containing short essays expounding on key concepts, such as one on the Reserved Rights Doctrine and another on Native American Sovereignty. At the conclusion of both the main and short essays are suggestions for further reading. Part 2 contains the text of 22 treaties, all of which are contextualized within the essays that comprised the first part of the work. While many of the treaties are well known, there are some obscure ones included, such as the 1833 Treaty of Chicago and the 1866 Reconstruction Treaties with the Cherokee, Choctaw, Chickasaw, Creeks, and Seminole. Concluding the work are two appendixes, one listing the respective treaties by tribe and another listing treaties negotiated by Canadian First Nations, and an index. This volume is an essential purchase for school, public, and academic libraries that do not already own *Treaties with American Indians: An Encyclopedia of Rights, Conflicts, and Sovereignty.* Libraries that own the previous work should strongly consider acquiring this gem for their circulating collection.—**John R. Burch Jr.**

126.   **Little Bighorn Battlefield National Monument https://npgallery.nps.gov/LIBI.** [Website] Free. Date reviewed: 2018.

The National Park Service is building this website as a digital repository for artifacts connected to the Battle of Little Bighorn. Extracted from the larger permanent collection of historical and archaeological items from the Little Bighorn Battlefield National Monument in Montana, the site currently features an interesting collection of over 1,900 photographs related to the devastating battle—a flashpoint along the long timeline of U.S.-Native American relations. The site hopes to continue to digitize items (including records, oral histories, correspondence, military artifacts, tools, and more) from the permanent collection. Users can browse All Keywords which are limited to the following terms: Richard Throssel, Crow Foot, Rain in the Face, Sitting Bull, Fort Totten, George Armstrong Custer, Curly, D.F. Barry Collection, War Bonnet, and J.A. Scholten. After selecting a term/phrase, users can select Search Archive Assets to view available materials. Items are presented in a list or a gallery view and users can click through to find accompanying metadata such as resource type, description, title, locations, creation date, and more as known. Items of note include evocative portraits of two figures central to the Little Bighorn story—the Studio Portrait of George Armstrong Custer in Fringed Buckskins and Sitting Bull (in full headdress) Standing Facing Left.—**ARBA Staff Reviewer**

127.   **The Lone Woman and Last Indians Digital Archive http://calliope.cse.sc.edu/ lonewoman/home.** [Website] Free. Date reviewed: 2018.

The Lone Woman of San Nicolas Island is a seminal tale in California history. This archive displays over 450 annotated documents—newspaper articles, magazine stories, and more—connected to her story. Users can examine a side-by-side display showing each document alongside its annotated transcription. Clicking on selected text within the transcription accesses the notes, which offer information on such topics as nearby native tribes, the California Channel Islands, the missions, and individual figures (such as George Nidever, who brought the Lone Woman to the mainland). Simply structured, the homepage displays a series of links from which to choose. Users can browse the archive by Newspaper Publication, Publishing Date, Publishing Location, Title, Literary Trope, or Document Group. Users can also conduct a basic or advanced search. Literary Tropes connects certain ideas within the accounts of the Lone Woman to the greater myth of her and other Native Americans' experience. The website identifies 14 distinct tropes that emerge throughout the documents. This link provides insight on identified tropes such as the "discovery" of the Lone Woman, the Lone Woman as a "Girl Crusoe," and others.

Users can also examine data visualizations of how tropes emerge and persist throughout time. A series of maps provide further context, and include an 1812 world map, an 1826 map of North America, an 1846 map of California and others. Maps are georeferenced for contemporary analysis. The website shows how a story can expand into legend, and offers a rich resource for students and educators of Californian and American history.—**ARBA Staff Reviewer**

128.   Martinez, Donna. **Documents of American Indian Removal.** Santa Barbara, Calif., ABC-CLIO, 2019. 268p. index. (Eyewitness to History Series). $94.00. ISBN 13: 978-1-4408-5419-4; 978-1-4408-5420-0 (e-book).

Donna Martinez, Professor of Ethnic Studies at the University of Colorado Denver and a Cherokee, frames the removal of American Indian peoples by the United States government as a form of ethnic cleansing. Recognizing that the removal processes evolved over time, she divides the 52 documents included in this work into six chapters. "Evolution of Federal Government Policies, 1778-1829" focuses on the initial development of federal Indian policy, which began with the idea of assimilating native peoples but that was soon abandoned in the early 19th century in favor of forced migrations west of the Mississippi River. "Rhetoric of Removal, 1829-1830" includes documents debating the issues that were eventually ensconced in the Indian Removal Act of 1830. Particularly notable is a circular from Catharine Beecher imploring women to oppose the legislation, as it marked an early example of women entering the nation's political sphere. "Removals, 1830-1836" and "Ethnic Cleansing, 1836-1844" focus primarily on the removal experiences of the Cherokee, Chickasaw, Choctaw, Creeks, and Seminoles. These chapters exemplify this work's major weakness, in that only two documents between the two chapters address the experiences of a native group in the nation's northern climes. "Responses to Removal, 1854-1879" turn towards the conquest of the Great Plains and beyond. The final chapter, "Who Owns the Land? 1891-1932," includes documents by both Sitting Bull and Geronimo. Within each chapter, the respective documents are contextualized by an opening essay that describes the motivations of federal authorities for whatever actions they were pursuing at the time along with explanations of how the respective American Indian groups responded to the threats to their homelands. In addition, the text of each document is preceded by a short essay describing the import and influence of that particular text and its author. Supplementary materials include a chronology and bibliography. This title is recommended for high school, public, and undergraduate libraries requiring a reasonably priced collection of primary sources on the topic. Libraries requiring a much more comprehensive work on the topic should strongly consider acquiring the *Encyclopedia of American Indian Removals,* edited by Daniel F. Littlefield Jr. and James W. Parins (see ARBA 2012, entry 405).—**John R. Burch Jr.**

129.   Watkins, Joe E. **The Story of the Choctaw Indians: From the Past to the Present.** Santa Barbara, Calif., Greenwood Press/ABC-CLIO, 2019. 120p. index. (The Story of the American Indian). $39.00. ISBN 13: 978-1-4408-6266-3; 978-1-4408-6267-0 (e-book).

ABC-CLIO/Greenwood Reference has introduced a new and unique series entitled The Story of the American Indian. Unlike most reference titles on Native Americans, this series is written from the "tribal perspective." (Series Foreword). Each author is either a member of the tribe or is a scholar who has extensive firsthand knowledge of the tribe. Each volume concentrates on a specific tribe and discusses its historical context, homelands, languages, communities, culture and traditions, contributions to American society, and current status.

To date, only two tribes have been covered: the Choctaw and the Chippewa. Since the former volume is half the length of its companion at 118 pages, the publisher seemingly has given each author the freedom to determine the amount of information to be included. The author of *The Story of the Choctaw Indians: From the Past to the Present* is Joe E. Watkins (Ph.D. Southern Methodist University); he is both a member of the Choctaw Nation of Oklahoma and a scholar. Rather than focusing on a single Choctaw group, this book tells the larger story of "the Choctaw." The tribe actually comprises three distinct groups: the Choctaw Nation of Oklahoma, the Mississippi Band of Choctaw Indians, and the Jean Band of Choctaw Indians.

The book is divided into six chapters that follow chronologically: "Deep History" (archaeology, origins), "Interactions with Europeans," "U.S. Intervention and Removal," "Post-Removal Development," "Constructing the Modern Choctaw Nation," and "Choctaw Today." Each chapter is written for a general audience. The author uses an in-text citation method with a relatively long reference list; he also includes a short bibliography of "Further Readings" and an index.

Librarians, teachers, and students of Native American history can use this book for ready reference or as a brief history, reading it cover-to-cover. As a Choctaw himself and a scholar, Dr. Watkins is a good fit for this assignment.—**John P. Stierman**

Kurds

130.   Gunter, Michael M. **Historical Dictionary of the Kurds.** 3d ed. Lanham, Md., Rowman & Littlefield, 2018. 474p. illus. maps. $110.00; $104.50 (e-book). ISBN 13: 978-1-5381-1049-2; 978-1-5381-1050-8 (e-book).

The approximately 35 million Kurds constitute the largest nation in the world without its own independent state. They are primarily dispersed in four modern nation states—Iraq, Turkey, Syria, and Iran—and their centuries-old struggle for national rights has emerged prominently in recent Middle East history. The failed states of post-Hussein Iraq and Assad Syria plus the rise and fall of ISIS have helped lead to near Kurdish statehood in Iraq (the KRG, Kurdistan Regional Government) and Kurdish autonomy in Syria (Rojava). In Turkey, temporary cease-fire with the Partiya Karkaren Kurdistan (PKK) and Haklarin Demokratik Partisi (HDP) as the first pro-Kurdish party to be elected to the Turkish parliament suggest unprecedented achievement and recognition. Gunter's (Tennessee Technological University) updated historical dictionary presents readers with a scholarly introduction on the Kurdish people and culture, and is particularly focused on contemporary trends, movers, and shakers. Intended as a reference tool for researchers, students, and interested members of the public, this volume provides approximately 700 cross-referenced entries that succinctly tell the story of present-day Kurdish national identity and destiny. Annotated entries vary in length and encapsulate parties, trends, leaders, educators, entrepreneurs, literati, politicians, revolutionaries, and religious leaders. The book concludes with an extensive 130 page topical index of articles and books on events and trends that speak about and to the persona of the text. A definitive reference work.—**Zev Garber**

131. **The Kurds: An Encyclopedia of Life, Culture, and Society.** Sebastian Maisel, ed. Santa Barbara, Calif., ABC-CLIO, 2018. 376p. illus. maps. index. $94.00. ISBN 13: 978-1-4408-4256-6; 978-1-4408-4257-3 (e-book).

Today's estimated 35 million Kurdish people are spread out among four modern nation-states—Iraq, Turkey, Syria, and Iran ("Kurdistan")—and their age-old struggle for national rights has thematically emerged as an important concern in recent Middle East history. This source work of life, culture, and society of shared history between Kurds and their surroundings is properly researched by Editor Sebastian Maisel (Grand Valley State University) and an international team of scholars who write with fortitude and fairness. Attempts at factual history, statistics, focused research, and on-site reporting permeate Parts I and II of this sparsely illustrated and reader friendly volume. Part I is parsed into chapters and covers history, geography, culture, language, literature, religion, media, food, dress, and cinema. Part II chapters profile Kurdish communities living in Middle Eastern countries, Europe, Israel (Kurdistani Jews), and the United States. Part III contains selected sections of primary documents related to culture, history, and religion which are translated and annotated. For the most part, the essays exhibit historiography, defining origins, tribal belief, and diversity before and after the emergence of Islam in Kurdistan. This book is a wellspring of facts and tidbits of a diverse people who practice different varieties of Islamic beliefs and nonbeliefs, bounded by common history, defined by land and group survival. Helpful to the nonspecialist are discussions of relevant belief claims and behavior patterns, and the effect of sacred tradition on the life of the people. Highly recommended.—**Zev Garber**

Latin Americans

132. **50 Events That Shaped Latino History.** Lilia Fernández, ed. Santa Barbara, Calif., Greenwood Press/ABC-CLIO, 2018. 2v. illus. index. $198.00/set. ISBN 13: 978-1-4408-3762-3; 978-1-4408-3763-0 (e-book).

Two handsomely produced volumes document 50 key "events" that have shaped the experience of Latinos living in the United States. "Event" must be interpreted broadly, for the broad coverage includes everything from a summary of the Spanish empire in America to the founding of Univision in 1987. Each event or capsule description includes a brief but useful chronology, sidebars highlighting special features of the discussion, a documentary excerpt, or primary source, and a brief bibliography of further readings in English. There are photos of major political and cultural figures, but there are no maps and there is no specifically statistical appendix. As one would expect in a reference work of this kind, the index is quite ample, and runs to over 80 pages.

Inevitably, the coverage of such a project must be both arbitrary and selective, so the relevance and usefulness of the volumes will depend on the needs of the user or researcher. The first volume has a distinctly more "historical" feel than the second, which is substantially, but by no means more directed at social and cultural issues, including immigration and migration, which directly or indirectly account for about a third of the volume. Again, the composition of the Latino population in the United States dictates the geographic coverage of the volumes, which is heavily (but, again, not exclusively) weighted toward Mexico, Mexicans, and Mexican Americans. About a third or more of the entries deal with Cuba, Puerto Rico, and the Caribbean, and there is a chapter exclusively devoted to "The Fall of the Trujillo Dictatorship and Dominican Migration, 1961-1990s." These weightings are all, evidently, pragmatic considerations in an attempt to appeal to the broadest audience possible, some 57 million ethnically, racially, and politically diverse people in 2015.

The quality of the scholarship varies, and while it would be unrealistic to expect refereed journal caliber work in what is essentially a popular production, even some of the more difficult, abstruse, technical, or obscure entries are generally more than worthwhile. If not all strive equally for balance or a semblance of objectivity, given the enormously controversial nature of much of the subject matter, the editor has given very little grounds for quibble or complaint. For example, the coverage of the Mexican- American War of 1847 is adequate, and indeed, gives more attention to the Southwestern United States than one normally finds. In a work dedicated to the Latino population in the United States, that only makes sense: events in California and New Mexico were more important than the usual enumeration of military campaigns in Northern and Central Mexico. Yet one does wish for a map of places, military movements, and action here. To say that one can readily be found elsewhere hardly excuses its absence. Perhaps pointing out that US military activity in the Southwest was the least of the matter where trade, diplomacy, and skullduggery counted for much more is an important point in itself.

Politics, publication lags, and genuinely new scholarly discoveries present equally thorny issues. While I do not disagree with the general description of the overall effects of the North American Free Trade Agreement (NAFTA), especially to the effect that its putative benefits were oversold in Mexico, something already evident by 1994 as the bungled devaluation and ensuing financial crisis showed. However, it is only fair to point out that the same volume that suggests that Henry B. Gonzalez was not radical enough for some Latino activists (2: 721-722) fails to mention that Gonzalez voted against HR 3450, the NAFTA Implementation Act in 1993, one of six Texas representatives to do so. For the representative from San Antonio, Texas, that took a certain amount of courage. Gonzalez understood economics well enough to understand that his constituency was not a likely beneficiary of NAFTA. As of 2016, hourly manufacturing wages are lower in Mexico than in China, and have been since 2011 (*Financial Times,* January 14, 2016). It is hard for me to believe that volumes carrying a 2018 publication date could not get this crucial fact right, whatever the long-run fate of NAFTA turns out to be. On a less critical note, Bobby Sanabria's "Birth of Latin Jazz, 1930s-1940s" is not only a pleasure to read, but remarkably informative as well. I have never before read that Mario Bauzá, who taught the inestimable Dizzy Gillespie how to blow a trumpet properly, was a clarinet player first, and only picked up trumpet as a sub. Of everything I read in both of these volumes that might be the most incredible fact of all. I assume Sanabria knows.

College and secondary school libraries will find the volumes useful for students and undergraduates. Public libraries above all would probably be interested in having the volumes available as a reference work for the nonspecialist reader curious to learn more.— **Richard Salvucci**

7   Genealogy and Heraldry

Genealogy

133.   **Anglican Record Project https://www.ireland.anglican.org/about/rcb-library/ anglican-record-project.** [Website] Free. Date reviewed: 2019.

The Anglican Record Project is the work in progress to digitize transcriptions of Anglican Church of Ireland parish records. Users can discover general information related to births, marriages, and burials throughout the counties of Ireland extending back centuries in some cases. Users can scroll through the current list of fifteen distinct Anglican parishes, presented by name and county and listed with types of available records and years covered. Users will note that the digitized records are quite random in terms of date range. The records for the Delgany parish of the Glendalough diocese (county Wicklow), for example, reach as far back as the 17th century. Selecting a parish from the list accesses a PDF of parish records, transcription notes regarding spelling variations, and other anomalies, and an index. There may also be a brief parish history, map, or a churchyard sketch. Record quality and quantity varies from parish to parish, with Dromiskin parish church holding many years of baptism, marriage, and burial information while Kiltubride offers memorial inscriptions only (quite touching when one considers the size and location of the parish). Users can generally learn names, dates, and locations, with, for example, baptism records sharing alleged date of birth, name, parents, abode, father's occupation, and minister's initials.—**ARBA Staff Reviewer**

134.   **MyHeritage.com. https://www.myheritage.com.** [Website] Free and fee. Date reviewed: 2018.

This genealogical research database launched in 2003 and has quickly grown to more than 95 million members worldwide. MyHeritage has offices in Tel Aviv, Israel, and in other countries including the United States. Though some services are free to registered users, a monthly fee is required in order to take full advantage of the services available on the site. The database quickly searches through a large array of such sources as newspapers, immigration records, church records, and government documents from the United States and other countries. Altogether, the database includes billions of documents worldwide. Most of the documents are locked unless the monthly fee is paid, but documents from the U.S. Social Security Death Index and images from BillionGraves are freely accessible. Discovered data can easily be added to a family tree. In addition, users can purchase DNA testing kits through this site to further genealogical research. The true value in this site is its ease of use in terms of both searches and construction of family trees. Even if fees are not paid, users can at least get a good idea of how often and where a potential family member appears in records. Those records that are freely available elsewhere (e.g., Chronicling America and US Census data) can then be consulted directly. MyHeritage also engages in pro bono genealogical work. The DNA Quest has reunited adopted children with their families, Tribal Quest documents family histories and cultures of remote tribes, and its restitution project attempts to restore looted World War II heirlooms to their rightful owners. This one-stop shop to researching, DNA testing, and family tree creating will most likely appeal to someone conducting intensive genealogical research.—**ARBA Staff Reviewer**

135.   **Professional Genealogy: Preparation, Practice & Standards.** Elizabeth Shown Mills, ed. Baltimore, Md., Genealogical Publishing, 2018. 678p. illus. index. $59.95. ISBN 13: 978-0-8063-2072-4.

Elizabeth Shown Mills edited and wrote five chapters in the authoritative *Professional Genealogy: A Manual for Researchers, Writers, Editors, Lecturers, and Librarians* (see ARBA 2002, entry 345), widely regarded since its publication as the standard textbook for genealogy courses and for aspiring professional genealogists and of value to individuals ranging from beginning family historians to advanced researchers, lecturers, and writers in the field. Mills' sterling qualifications alone commend this new, updated volume, designed to replace *Professional Genealogy.* Certified as a genealogist in 1976, she edited the *National Genealogical Society Quarterly* for sixteen years, is a past president of the American Society of Genealogists and of the Board for Certification of Genealogists, lectures widely, and has authored an essential manual in her field, *Evidence Explained* (see ARBA 2018, entry 545), as well as numerous other articles and books.

Professional Genealogy: Preparation, Practice & Standards, as its foreword indicates, "reexamines conventional topics through new eyes" and "addresses new areas of specialization, such as forensic and genetic genealogy" (p. 15). It is organized in six sections: Professional Preparation, Ethics & Legalities, Career Management, Professional Research Skills, Writing, Editing & Publishing, and Educational Services. Each section contains two or more individual chapters; each chapter is authored by one or two of the 23 prominent individuals in genealogy who contributed their expertise to this book and whose qualifications are supplied in brief biographical notes at the front of the volume. Extensive and complete endnotes for print and online materials appear at the end of each chapter, often along with a list of related resources for further study. Numerous attractive figures and tables dot the text. The unusually comprehensive and essential "Index to People, Places, Subjects, and Titles" occupies some 25 pages. The appendix alphabetically lists important genealogical abbreviations and acronyms. Large format pages and the typeface make the text exceptionally readable.

As Mills maintains in her preface, "a new generation of genealogical educators offers the field a new manual-new insights and new specialties, grounded in more-solid standards and wider experiences and applications" (p. 18). Some chapters are aimed squarely at professional genealogists, but others, such as the chapters on "Copyright & Fair Use," "Executing Contracts," and "Crafting Family Histories," will appeal to a much broader audience. This new handbook of genealogical work, beautifully designed, almost 700 pages in length, and priced at less than $60.00, belongs in all but the smallest libraries.—**Julienne L. Wood**

Heraldry

136.   Glossary of Terms Used in Heraldry www.heraldrynet.org/saitou/parker/. [Website] Free. Date reviewed: 2019.

This website replicates the late-19th-century volume by James Parker that offers a detailed and generously cross-referenced explanation of terms affiliated with the long-established traditions of British heraldry. Fairly straightforward in presentation, users can approach the generous material either alphabetically via the Glossary link or thematically through the Synoptical Table link. From the homepage, users can click through the list of links to navigate various website features. The Introductory link leads to the original author's introduction as well as a more contemporary preface explaining the development and structure of the online edition. Users can then proceed to A Synoptical Table which groups heraldry terms into 28 sections for a good visual understanding of the complex relationships between them. Users can scroll through the sections which organize terms by general heraldry components (e.g., Tinctures, Points of the Escutcheon), or elements within the components (e.g., Descriptive Terms Applied to Ordinaries and Charges). Users can also find information describing the most fundamental aspects of heraldry (e.g., General Heraldic Terms and Titles, Orders, Knights, Heraldic Officers, etc.) near the end of the table. The glossary itself is a straightforward alphabetical listing of terms that encompass a wide range of objects and figures such as beasts, weapons, or plants (more specifically, "unicorn," "frog," "hammer," "dagger," "thistle," etc.), in addition to basic shapes and other elements of heraldry design, such as "bend," "pale," "fess," and "ordinaries." Users can jump between letters of the alphabet for easier navigation. Information accompanying each term may include a basic description, language origins and variations, links to related terms, and a list of family name associations. Entries that describe the basic foundations of heraldry may be quite detailed, such as those for "marshalling" or "achievements." There may also be an accompanying illustration with a link to enlarge. The glossary may consider numerous versions of individual terms. For example, the term "Caps" is cross-referenced with "Chapeau," "black hat," "Lord Mayor's Cap," "Abacot," "long cap," "Morion," and more. An extensive index lists family names (original spellings) of referenced coats of arms and notes if there is an accompanying illustration. The Heraldic Gallery link accesses 20 pages of illustrations used throughout the glossary. Each thumbnail can be enlarged, although there is no cross-reference to the glossary from here. A Glossary of Terms Used in Heraldry takes great care to emphasize the authentic terminology affiliated with all components of the earliest coats of arms, crests, and more.—**ARBA Staff Reviewer**

8 Geography and Travel Guides

Geography

137. The History of Cartography Project https://geography.wisc.edu/histcart/. [Website] Free. Date reviewed: 2019.

This site is an important launching point for scholars interested in the global history of maps. It offers a number of contextual resources which serve as a good foundation for users interested in the multivolume reference *The History of Cartography,* which is available in hardcover or in an online edition accessible separately and through this site (see below). Users can find good background information via the Resources tab on the blue bar. Useful Links highlight several other cartography-related websites including the David Rumsey Historical Map Collection with over 75,000 online maps and images spanning 6 centuries and many regions across the globe. The Exploratory Essays Initiative present 10 scholarly essays such as "Allied Military Model Making During World War II," by Alastair W. Pearson and "American Promotional Road Mapping in the Twentieth Century" by James R. Akerman. There is also a generous list of Literary Selections on Cartography showcasing writers and poets views on maps, with supplemental scholarly commentary. The main draw of the site is found under the Publications tab. Here users can select a volume from *The History of Cartography* to access a summary and a link to its table of contents within the e-book website: https://www.press.uchicago.edu/books/HOC/index. Within this searchable site, users will find four volumes (some organized into "books" or "parts"), with more to come. Volumes are generally arranged by region and/or time period and cover Cartography in Prehistoric, Ancient, and Medieval Europe and the Mediterranean; Cartography in the Traditional Islamic and South Asian Societies; Cartography in the Traditional East and Southeast Asian Societies; Cartography in the Traditional African, American, Arctic, Australian and Pacific Societies; Cartography in the European Renaissance; and Cartography in the Twentieth Century. Volumes consist of essays from a range of scholars which may incorporate timelines, illustrations, photographs, and other materials. Essays include "Cartographic Content of Rock Art in Southern Africa" (Vol. 2, Book 3), "Renaissance Star Charts" (Vol. 3), "Chinese Maps in Political Culture" (Vol. 2, Book 2), and much, much more. Each volume/book opens with a Gallery of Color Illustrations (the exception to this format lies in the sixth volume, *Cartography of the Twentieth Century,* where color illustrations appear throughout alphabetical encyclopedic entries). Together, the History of Cartography site and e-book provide a comprehensive, easy-to-navigate, and reliable interdisciplinary resource.—**ARBA Staff Reviewer**

Travel Guides

138.   **Central Asia.** 7th ed. London, Lonely Planet, 2018. 512p. illus. maps. index. $34.99pa. ISBN 13: 978-4-78657-464-0.

Those travelers hoping for an adventure have found the right travel guide. This title from Lonely Planet starts with a two-page color map of Central Asia, a list of its top 15 suggested places to see, very useful general information for first-time visitors, suggested itineraries, visas and permits, and border crossings. It then provides detailed sections on each of the five countries covered: Kyrgyzstan, Tajikistan, Uzbekistan, Kazakhstan, and Turkmenistan. These country-specific chapters are divided by regions, so users can jump to the place they most want to visit, like Karakol in Kyrgyzstan, a city that serves as gateway to skiing and alpine trekking, or the Silk Road city of Samarkand in Uzbekistan. For all destinations, travelers will find data on city sights, accommodations, eating and drinking, shopping, transportation, outdoor activities, and more. The end of each country chapter details the country's history, arts, environmental concerns, social customs, environmental concerns, and current political and economic conditions. Chapters end with a country-specific A-Z survival guide that provides guidance on such things as customs regulations, etiquette, medical services, public holidays, and embassies and consulates. The guide ends with a section titled Understanding that contains a discussion of Central Asia today, which provides a more macro view than the country chapters. There is also a section on the Silk Road that traces the history of the great east-west trading route through to its current revival. Users will also find details about the people (including ethnic groups, customs, and culture), the role of Islam, the arts, architecture, and the environment. A concluding survival guide gathers information on accommodations, health, transportation, public toilets, language (including a useful dictionary), and many other topics. An index and map legend round out the work. This lightweight, portable guide is highly recommended for public libraries.—**ARBA Staff Reviewer**

139.   **China.** 6th ed. New York, DK Publishing, 2018. 660p. illus. maps. index. $30.00pa. ISBN 13: 978-1-4654-6910-6.

Following a usage guide, chapter 1, "Introducing China," provides suggested itineraries, a color country map, a portrait of the country that touches on economics, politics, family life, language, culture, and religion, and much more. The guide is divided into chapters by region: "Beijing and the North," "Central China," "The South," "The Southwest," "The Northeast," "Inner Mongolia & the Silk Road," and "Tibet." Chapters provide a great detail of information, organized around major areas. In the chapter on Beijing and the North, for example, users will find detailed information about the Beijing Opera, the Forbidden City, the Great Wall of China, shopping and entertainment, and regional food along with detailed maps of Beijing (including a street finder index) and information about temples, palaces, museums, and other tourist destinations. In this and all chapters, the included, full-color photographs are of the highest quality and do much to enhance the content. The penultimate chapter, "Travelers' Needs" has sections on where to stay, where to eat and drink, shops and markets, entertainment, and sports and special holidays. The last chapter, "Survival Guide," has practical information and travel information, with tips on when to go, visas and passports, insurance, hospitals and medical facilities, domestic air travel, traveling by bus, ferry, and train, and more. A general index and a phrase book round out the book. This travel guide to the vast and diverse country that is China is highly recommended.—**ARBA Staff Reviewer**

140.   **Essential Italy.** Brooklyn, N.Y., Fodor's Travel, 2019. 880p. illus. maps. index. $25.99pa. ISBN 13: 978-1-64097-070-0.

Following color photographs of 25 spots that showcase the beauty of Italy, the first chapter, "Experience Italy," provides sample itineraries; maps showing major regions; tips on transportation, when to go, and how to budget; and information on Italy today. Coverage is broad, with chapters on: Rome; side trips from Rome; Venice; the Veneto and Friuli-Venezia Giulia; the Dolomites; Milan, Lombardy, and the Lakes; Piedmont and Valle D'Aosta; the Italian Riviera; Emilia-Romagna; Florence; Tuscany; Umbria and the Marches; Naples and Campania; Puglia, Basilicata, and Calabria; Sicily; and Sardinia. Each chapter includes several maps and color photographs; information about eating, drinking, and shopping; where to go for entertainment; what to see; where to stay; itinerary suggestions; and more. The information is quite detailed. For example, hotels are listed along with prices, number of rooms, whether or not meals are provided, if the spot is good for families, etc. Like other Fodor travel guides, this one offers recommendations. The book ends with "Travel Smart Italy," which contains information on air, bus, car, ferry, and train travel; different types of accommodations (apartment and house rentals, convents and monasteries, farm holidays and agritourism, and home exchanges); customs and duties; eating out; emergencies; hours of operation; passports and visas; trip insurance; and other necessaries.—**ARBA Staff Reviewer**

141.   **Essential Switzerland.** Brooklyn, N.Y., Fodor's Travel, 2018. 561p. illus. maps. index. $22.99pa. ISBN 13: 978-1-64097-032-8.

This travel guide pulls readers in with its opening suggestion of 25 things to do or see in Switzerland. The main part of the book starts with "Experience Switzerland," a chapter that includes maps of the country; basic information about languages spoken; national foods; information about people, politics, the economy, sports, and gender parity; itineraries that include train trips, car trips, and hikes; and more. The rest of the book covers the following areas: Zurich, Eastern Switzerland and Liechtenstein; Graubünden; Ticino; Luzern and Central Switzerland; Basel; Fribourg and Neuchâtel; Bern; Berner Oberland; Valais; Vaud; and Geneva. All of these sections contain regionally specific details about where to stay, what and where to eat, and what to do. All of this is punctuated by color photographs and maps. There is quite a bit of information packed into this guide like the types of food and costs at restaurants, the typical clientele found at bars, the entry fees and operating hours of museums, and types of available transportation. Throughout the sections, users will see starred suggestions; these "Fodor's Choice" favorites can give travelers an added sense of confidence when booking a hotel or choosing a restaurant. "Travel Smart Switzerland" provides more details about transportation within the country, accommodations, internet availability, tipping, and other basics. The book concludes with short lists of vocabulary words in French, German, and Italian (with pronunciations) and an index. Recommended for public libraries.—**ARBA Staff Reviewer**

142.   **Fodor's Barcelona with Highlights of Catalonia.** 6th ed. Rachel Roth, ed. Brooklyn, N.Y., Fodor's Travel, 2018. 226p. illus. maps. $19.99pa. ISBN 13: 978-1-1018-7982-5; 978-1-1018-8045-6 (e-book).

This 6th edition from Fodor's is a valuable guide to one of Europe's most popular destinations. The guide covers Barcelona thoroughly and contains additional information about nearby cities and towns like Girona, Valencia, Tossa de Mar, Sitges, and Figueres. The book is broken into digestible chunks: Experience Barcelona begins with some of the many reasons to visit the city—food, architecture, climate, top attractions, and more. Exploring Barcelona focuses on sections: La Rambla, the Barri Gotic, El Ravel, the Eixample, Sant Pere and La Ribera, Gracia, Upper Barcelona, Monjüic, and La Ciutedella and Barceloneta. For each of these areas, readers find recommendations for lodging, restaurants, attraction, museums, shopping, and other activities. The book provides a detailed color map for each of these sections. Travel Smart Barcelona rounds out the book, and has details about credit cards, banks, different forms of transportation, and other essential information. The guide brings Barcelona to life with its color photographs. The book includes many color maps that travelers will find extremely useful. Highly recommended for public libraries and travelers.—**ARBA Staff Reviewer**

143.   Helmreich, William B. **The Manhattan Nobody Knows: An Urban Walking Guide.** Princeton, N.J., Princeton University Press, 2018. 354p. illus. maps. index. $24.95pa. ISBN 13: 978-0-691-16699-5.

This walking guide of Manhattan covers the thirty-one distinct neighborhoods of Manhattan, painting pictures of some of the interesting and fascinating residents and sites along the way. A map of the island, divided into the neighborhoods, is provided at the beginning of the book, and each chapter includes a map of that neighborhood with the major streets and locations where the stories provided came from. There are black-and-white pictures and photos throughout. This book is more a book of stories and people than of major sites or places to visit; while one could use this book to walk through the neighborhoods, it is more of a story book of encounters and people which the author met and recorded as he walked through each area. As such, it is more of a contemporary snapshot of the author's walks through Manhattan to be read at home, rather than a Fodor's guide to use when walking through Manhattan.—**Bradford Lee Eden**

144.   Le Nevez, Catherine, and Abigail Blasi. **Amsterdam.** 11th ed. London, Lonely Planet, 2018. 354p. illus. maps. index. $21.99pa. ISBN 13: 978-1-78701-898-3; 978-1-78657-557-9 (e-book).

This handy guide from Lonely Planet will serve travelers to Amsterdam well. Information about the city is presented in four sections: Plan Your Trip, Explore, Understand, and Survival Guide. The first part of the book lists city highlights like the Van Gogh Museum, canal trips, and the Anne Frank House. The book also includes what is new for travelers since the last edition; important tips (especially for first-time travelers) about such things as currency, language, visuals, money, mobile phones, etiquette, tipping, and what to wear; top itineraries and top events by month; drinking, eating, and shopping; and more. Detailed information for major neighborhoods includes easy-to-read maps. The Understand Amsterdam section provides information on the city today, its history, Dutch paintings, Dutch design, and Dutch architecture. There is a survival guide with information about customs, public restrooms, opening hours, money and credit, what sort of identification to carry, the type of adapter needed, and the answers to other common travel questions. There is a language section that lists the basics necessary to ask directions, to order food, to handle emergencies, etc. A series of maps and a map index rounds out the book. Recommended for public libraries.—**ARBA Staff Reviewer**

145.   **The Michelin Guide: Chicago.** Watford, England, Michelin, 2018. 232p. illus. maps. index. $18.99pa. ISBN 13: 978-2-06-723062-0.

This guide to the diverse food scene in Chicago includes approximately 190 restaurants visited anonymously by Michelin's food inspectors. The result is a curated reference to the best food for a variety of budgets. The inside front cover includes a full-color pullout map of the city. Front matter also includes information about the Michelin guides and a key to the symbols used in the guide that indicate a variety of things like wheelchair accessibility, notable cocktails/wine/beer, and valet parking. The guide is divided into neighborhood: Andersonville, Edgewater & Uptown; Bucktown & Wicker Park; Chinatown & South; Gold Coast; Humboldt Park & Logan Square; Lakeview & Wrigleyville; Lincoln Park & Old Town; Loop & Streeterville; Pilsen, University Village & Bridgeport; River North; and West Loop. Each neighborhood section provides an introduction and a full-color map that indicates the location of the restaurants included in the section. The guide lists restaurants in alphabetic order; users will find a discussion of the food and décor as well as symbols that indicate the price (from under $25 to over $75), the rating (from Bib Gourmand—inspectors' favorites for a good value—to a Michelin plate—a good meal with fresh ingredients—to three stars—exceptional cuisine worth a special journey). Descriptions also include a map coordinate for easy navigation. Color photographs of restaurant interiors, food plates, and neighborhoods enhance the content. All pages are tabbed according to neighborhood for quick navigation. A series of indexes rounds out the work: "Alphabetical List of Restaurants," "Restaurants by Cuisine," "Cuisines by Neighborhood," "Starred Restaurants," "Bib Gourmand,"and "Under $25." Recommended.—**ARBA Staff Reviewer**

146.   **The Michelin Guide: Main Cities of Europe.** Watford, England, Michelin, 2018. 936p. illus. maps. $29.99pa. ISBN 13: 978-2067223783.

The Michelin Guide to restaurants and lodging in major European cities is a useful and trustworthy reference for travelers, particularly those traveling for business or those looking for upscale restaurants and hotels. The reviews are based on anonymous inspections of hotels and restaurants, none of which is allowed to pay to be in the guide. The front matter explains the guide's inclusion criteria and the symbols used in the book; it also provides a map legend and a usage guide. The guide includes more than 2,000 hotels and 800 restaurants in the following cities and countries: Vienna and Salzburg, Austria; Brussels and Antwerp, Belgium; Prague, Czechoslovakia; Helsinki, Finland; Paris and Lyons, France; Berlin, Hamburg, and Munich, Germany; Athens, Greece; Budapest, Hungary; Dublin, Ireland; Rome and Milan, Italy; Luxembourg, Luxembourg; Amsterdam and Rotterdam, Netherlands; Oslo, Norway; Warsaw and Cracow, Poland; Lisbon, Portugal; Madrid and Barcelona, Spain; Stockholm, Gothenburg, and Malmo, Switzerland; and London, Birmingham, and Edinburgh, United Kingdom. The guide provides brief introductions to the cities and then lists ratings for restaurants and hotels. Very helpfully, the guide makes generous use of color maps. The front flap includes a European map, and the back flap provides international dialing codes. The restaurant selections are also available in an app or online at https://guide.michelin.com. Highly recommended for travelers, travel professionals, and public libraries.—**ARBA Staff Reviewer**

147.   **Russia.** London, Lonely Planet, 2018. 720p. $29.99pa. ISBN 13: 978-1-78657-362-9.

This 8th edition (light enough for travelers to carry) from Lonely Planet starts with a two-page color map; a suggested list of the top twenty sights for visitors, including The Hermitage, the Caucasus Mountains, the Black Sea, and the Trans-Siberian Railway; a "Need to Know" section, which includes information on overall trip planning (exchange rates, transportation, what you need to know about accommodations, etiquette, etc.) for those who have never been to Russia; and potential itineraries. Chapters cover cities and regions: Moscow, the Golden Ring, St. Petersburg, Western European Russia, Kaliningrad and the surrounding area, Northern European Russia, the Volga Region, the Russian Caucasus, the Urals, Western Siberia, Eastern Siberia, and the Russian Far East. Chapters include more detailed maps; color photographs; transportation maps; information about transportation, tours, cultural sights and museums, festivals, accommodations, food and drink, shopping, entertainment, safety, outdoor activities, and more. There are three concluding chapters; "Understand Russia," "Survival Guide," and "Language." "Understand Russia" starts with a current events section followed by sections on demographics, religion, performing arts and music, literature and cinema, architecture and visual arts, food and drink, and landscape and wildlife. A foldout map of Moscow and St. Petersburg is included. This guide will inspire all would-be travelers and is recommended for public libraries.—**ARBA Staff Reviewer**

148.   **USA.** 10th ed. London, Lonely Planet, 2018. 1224p. illus. maps. index. $29.99pa. ISBN 13: 978-1-78657-448-0.

This travel guide to hundreds of destinations starts with a two-page color map, a list of 25 top sights, general information (time zones, exchange rates, etc.), tips for those visiting the United States for the first time, suggested itineraries and outdoor activities, eating and drinking suggestions (including a food glossary), traveling with kids, and regional highlights. After this overview, the guide presents more in-depth information on regions in the following order: New York, New Jersey, and Pennsylvania; New England; Washington DC & the Capital Region; the South; Florida; Great Lakes; the Great Plains; Texas; Rocky Mountains; Southwest; California; Pacific Northwest; Alaska; and Hawaii. Users can skip directly to their destination of interest by using the table of contents or the index. For each region the book suggests best places to sleep and eat, times to visit, sights to see, tours, and more. Each section contains detailed maps. The last part of the book is devoted to explaining the history, culture, social customs, arts and architecture, and flora and fauna of the United States. There is a surprising amount of historical information packed into this relatively short section, certainly enough to explain the history of the country and the current social, political, and economic conditions to visitors from other countries. An index and map legend conclude the work.

This guidebook works well for both domestic and international tourists. Though it is likely too heavy to carry around in a backpack or bag, it is a great resource to keep in a car or in a hotel room. Highly recommended for public libraries.—**ARBA Staff Reviewer**

9 History

Archaeology

149. Muskett, Georgina. **Archaeology Hotspot France: Unearthing the Past for Armchair Archaeologists.** Lanham, Md., Rowman & Littlefield, 2018. 202p. illus. maps. index. (Archaeology Hotspots Series). $38.00; $36.00 (e-book). ISBN 13: 978-1-4422-6922-4; 978-1-4422-6923-1 (e-book).

This book provides an accessible review of archaeology in France for the amateur. The first chapter covers the development of archaeology in France. The next two chapters cover prehistoric France, the Iron Age, the Gallo-Roman period, and Early Medieval France. The book also includes separate chapters on French archaeology and archaeologists; debates, controversies, and scandals; and archaeological research in France in the 21st century. Black-and-white photographs illustrate each chapter. The volume contains a select bibliography, a glossary, an index, and brief biographical information about the author, an associate professor of Archaeology, Classics and Egyptology at the University of Liverpool. The author is an expert in the field, with experience in excavation, curation, research, and teaching. This work would be a useful addition to high school and undergraduate libraries.—**Joanna M. Burkhardt**

150. **Portable Antiquities Scheme. https://finds.org.uk/.** [Website] Free. Date reviewed: 2018.

This website, run by the British Museum and National Museum Wales, collects information on nearly seven hundred thousand ancient artifacts found by casual hobbyists throughout England and Wales. It offers a record of discovered coins, tools, jewelry, vessels, and more that may otherwise be undocumented, alongside a helpful set of publications, guides, and other research that help to facilitate the relationship between the amateur and the rich archaeology of the two countries. While the site requests user registration (free) for some information and capabilities (e.g., to export data), it nonetheless provides ample information on its finds for all users. Users can conduct a basic search from the bar at the center of the page, or can select the Database tab from the top of the homepage. From here, users can filter their search by All Artefacts & Coins, Hoard Search (referring to two specific finds of Iron Age and Roman coins), All Images, and more. Entering a search term or phrase displays a record listing which can be further filtered by such parameters as County of Origin, Object Type (e.g., icon, coin), Broad Period (e.g., Neolithic, Medieval), Material, and more. The display may include a thumbnail image, Record ID, list of applicable parameters, Workflow Stage (has the find been verified and published), and a summary description, among other information. Clicking on the thumbnail—of the seven hundred thousand records there are approximately three hundred thousand images—will enlarge it against a ruler for accurate size, and users can zoom in on the image and/or download it. The entry will also note if the Spatial Data has been recorded. Clicking on the Record ID provides much more detail, such as an extended description, a chronology, and dimensions & weight. There may also be a map of the find location (satellite, open street, etc.) and a timeline of associated dates. Within the database, users can also access statistics which cover finds recorded per day, per region and other information. Guides provide topical information on the identification and preservation of Byzantine Coins, Bronze Age Artefacts, and more. Treasure lays out the find reporting law (Treasure Act 1996) applicable to England, Wales, and Northern Ireland.—**ARBA Staff Reviewer**

American History

Biography

151. **American Reformers.** 2d ed. Bronx, N.Y., H. W. Wilson, 2017. 958p. index. $195.00. ISBN 13: 978-1-68217-196-7.

This volume updates the first edition, published in 1985. Nearly six hundred entries, written by eighty-six contributors, cover thirty-one areas of reform, such as abolition, education, labor unions, Native American rights, prison reform, and suffrage. The reformers presented here range from well-known individuals such as Jane Addams, John Brown, Mark Twain, Thomas Jefferson, and Martin Luther King, to little-known people who in fact changed the course of American history in their various ways. The new edition has added two categories: LGBTQ and conservative reformers. Among those additions are Harvey Milk, Patrick Buchanan, and Phyllis Schlafly. Entries run from a page to three plus pages. Given the focus on the individuals' roles as reformers, some entries leave out the details of the last years of their lives. Many entries include images (photos or paintings), mainly found in the Library of Congress.

A minor disappointment is that the references for most of the original entries in the first edition have not been updated since the first edition. Some items listed in the article bibliographies are over a century old. For example, several important studies of Jefferson, King, and Emma Goldman, published in the last decade are not mentioned. Even recent works by the authors of the articles themselves are not included. The newly added entries, of course, have many recent book, periodical, and even film references. Interestingly, the table of contents uses more complete names of many of the individuals, compared to the contents in the first edition, by adding middle and maiden names.

This volume does, however, provide excellent introductory information on hundreds of Americans who shaped numerous aspects of this country's history. Academic and public libraries seeking a wide-ranging biographical resource for this group of important Americans will be well-served. (School libraries are somewhat less likely to benefit from this book, in part because of its cost.)—**Mark Schumacher**

Dictionaries and Encyclopedias

152.   **American Revolution: The Definitive Encyclopedia and Document Collection.** Spencer C. Tucker, ed. Santa Barbara, Calif., ABC-CLIO, 2018. 5v. illus. maps. index. $546.00/set. ISBN 13: 978-1-85109-739-5; 978-1-85109-744-9 (e-book).

Spencer Tucker, Senior Fellow in Military History at ABC-CLIO, has edited an impressive series of reference titles documenting the military history of the present-day United States, beginning with *The Encyclopedia of North American Colonial Conflicts to 1775: A Political, Social, and Military History* (see ARBA 2009, entry 605) and including such notable works as *The Encyclopedia of the War of 1812* (see ARBA 2013, entry 578) and the *American Civil War: The Definitive Encyclopedia and Document Collection* (see ARBA 2014, entry 588). This five-volume set on the American Revolution is a worthy addition to the corpus.

Volumes 1-4 constitute the encyclopedic portion of the reference tool. Approximately 120 scholars wrote more than 1,300 alphabetically arranged entries. Each entry is signed and includes bibliographic citations for further research and cross-references. Although the American Revolution was fought between 1775 and 1783, coverage actually begins with the aftermath of the French and Indian War and continues with the travails of the newly founded nation through the end of the 18th century. Notable is the perspective that the American Revolution was a world war, thus numerous entries examine the European countries who joined the conflict and their motivations. Supplementing the text are numerous black-and-white maps and illustrations. The appendixes in the fourth volume include: Medals, Decorations, and Military Honors; Ranks, Military; Chronology; Glossary of Military and Naval Terms; and Bibliography. Volume 5, edited by James R. Arnold, Independent Scholar, and Roberta Wiener, managing editor of the *Journal of Military History,* contains 153 documents, some of which are excerpted. They are presented in chronological order, beginning with Cato's Letters (1721) to the Alien and Sedition Acts (1798). Following the documents is the index to all five volumes.

Although this reference set features an impressive breadth of topics produced by academics, it is written in a manner that is accessible to lay readers. High school, public, and academic libraries should strongly consider acquiring this title for their reference collection.—**John R. Burch Jr.**

153.   **Shaping North America: From Exploration to the American Revolution.** James E. Seelye and Shawn Selby, eds. Santa Barbara, Calif., ABC-CLIO, 2018. 3v. illus. index. 309.00/set. ISBN 13: 978-1-4408-3668-8; 978-1-4408-3669-5 (e-book).

Shaping North America will provide the researcher, regardless of where they come into the process, with a solid foundation to this unique period in both American and World History. This expansive multivolume set looks at both the precolonial and colonial periods of early American history, offering up players and accounts of key events that not only established a new nation in the United States of America, but set the course for its development. This work covers the pre-Colombian period through the creation of the Constitution (roughly 1400–1790), and it is written in a straightforward language with encyclopedic style entries covering thematic areas (social, political, cultural, etc.). The researcher will find information including, but not limited to, the Indian nations such as Algonquin, Aztec, Inca, and Wampanoag, North American explorers, the individuals who began settling the land, and the ideas and religions that moved the colonies closer to independence. The set provides a list of entries, a user guide to related topics, and a timeline of key events and major issues. Entries are written and signed by scholar experts. Each passage is followed by a *see also* reference and a list of further readings. It is important to note that many of the entries in this set have primary sources directly connected to the entry. The breadth of primary documents is truly amazing, including items such as personal diaries, letters, poems, images, treaties, and other legal documents. The importance of including documents written by some of the men and women who shaped American history can never be overstated as these documents allow the reader directly into the hearts and minds of the individuals who created them.

Shaping North America is truly a resource that will bring value to any libraries' collection in this area of history.—**Lawrence Joseph Mello**

154.   Snodgrass, Mary Ellen. **Frontier Women and Their Art: A Chronological Encyclopedia.** Lanham, Md., Rowman & Littlefield, 2018. 356p. illus. index. $125.00; $118.50. ISBN 13: 978-1-5381-0975-5; 978-1-5381-0976-2 (e-book).

A companion volume to the author's *American Colonial Women and Their Art* (also 2018) (see ARBA 2018, entry 519), this book covers the period from 1765 to 1899. The range of arts, presenting the "quest for self-expression" of these women, is quite wide, as there are gymnasts, gamblers, historians, prophets, and botanists included, although these women may also have engaged in other arts, such as ceramics, poetry, or other writing. The women and their backgrounds are also quite diverse: a Siberian seamstress who became a "multinational business mogul" in Alaska, the 42nd wife of Brigham Young, and Queen Liliuokalani, Hawaii's last monarch. Given its chronological organization and rather anecdotal approach, this book lends itself to simply being read as history, rather than a biographical reference book. The reader may select an era she/he is interested in and learn about the diverse activities taking place across the American frontiers.

Four appendixes cover arts, states, ethnology and present a chronology of major moments between 1610 and 1912. A glossary and an 11-page bibliography of primary and secondary resources are also included. This book should spark interest in American women whose lives are little known. Scholars and students in women's and gender studies programs, or in history departments, may well find new areas to explore after reading this volume. Academic libraries will be most interested in the content here, but other libraries might consider it.—**Mark Schumacher**

155.   **The World of Antebellum America.** Alexandra Kindell, ed. Santa Barbara, Calif., Greenwood Press/ABC-CLIO, 2018. 2v. illus. index. $198.00/set. ISBN 13: 978-1-4408-3710-4; 978-1-4408-3711-1 (e-book).

The antebellum period was an unstable and politically explosive era in which the northern and southern economies separated into diverse but polarized economies. Massive population shifts from rural plains into northern cities coincided with the rise of industrialization and manufacturing while agrarian Southern plantations focused on King Cotton, its primary crop, and the slave labor needed to harvest it. Simultaneously, westward expansion, according to the doctrine of Manifest Destiny, resulted in the acquisition of new territories and states, with the "rush" of settlers into newly acquired terrain resulting in harsh and cruel removals of Native Americans onto isolated reserves. Simultaneously, forcible tensions rose between the North and South over whether slavery should remain legal, culminating in the nation's first and only civil war to date.

This two-volume encyclopedia falls in the time period between its series partners (i.e., *The World of the American Revolution* and *The World of Civil War America*). Volume 1, *Arts to Housing and Community,* contains six of ten categories (Arts, Economies and Work, Family and Gender, Fashion and Appearance, Food and Drink, Housing and Community), and Volume 2, *Politics and Warfare to Science and Technology,* is divided into four categories, (Politics and Warfare, Recreation and Social Customs, Religion and Beliefs, Science and Technology). Categories are in alphabetical order across both volumes, with, as the author promptly notes, a particular focus on changes to American life as they occurred throughout Antebellum. Found in both volumes is the exact same table of contents listing entries by category and page number, as well as a listing of primary documents; meanwhile, Volume 1 contains a preface, formal introduction, and chronology, while Volume 2 includes a main bibliography, a listing of editors and contributors, and an index.

The size and scope of the encyclopedia seemingly reflects the myriad aspects of American society during this period. The preface in Volume 1 is usefully explanatory and carefully outlines the decisive changes the antebellum period wrought, and what those changes meant to Americans of the time. Accordingly, entries are distilled to all manner of finely tuned detail, ranging from the foreseeable ("Fatherhood, "Education - Primary and Secondary") and delightful ("Breads and Biscuits," "Bloomer Costume"), to the curious ("Sewing Societies," "John C. Calhoun") and downright foreboding ("Minstrel Shows," "Lynching"), with each complemented by relevant suggestions for further reading. Selected primary documents, forty in total, include Angelina Grimke Weld's "What Came Ye Out for to See?" and Frederic Douglass's comment on the Dred Scott decision. Making one's way through the volumes takes a close examination of how they are organized, particularly relative to one another, but the author nevertheless has written a genuinely practical and highly effective encyclopedia that well describes the antebellum period and appropriately connects the previous volumes in the series.—**Sheri Edwards**

Digital Resources

156. **American Historical Periodicals from the American Antiquarian Society, Series 6.** https://www.gale.com/primary-sources/american-historical-periodicals. [Website] Farmington Hills, Mich., Gale/Cengage Learning, 2018. Price negotiated by site. Date reviewed: 2018.

An exclusive partnership between the American Antiquarian Society and Gale, a Cengage company, digitizes and makes available the considerable Society holdings, which include journals, periodicals, and magazines. Series 6 contains almost 200 newly digitized titles, offering new content and filling gaps in coverage from Series 1-5. The collection allows researchers to discover much about American politics, society, and thought from the colonial era to the 1920s. The interface is well designed and easy to use. Researchers can select a title from a browsable list of periodical titles. Once a title is accessed, users will see links to available issues, the number of issues, the publication format and frequency of publication, the publication language, and the place of publication. If a researcher clicks on *Scientific American,* for example, and then the link for the January 13, 1900 issue (vol. 82), she can then click the links for individual articles, search within the results, or analyze the results utilizing two tools, term cluster or term frequency. Additionally, US and Canadian institutions that own a Gale Primary Source Archive will receive complimentary access to more than 6 million pages from Series 1-5. Series 1-6 is also integrated into Gale's Digital Scholar Lab, which opens new and exciting research opportunities via its textual analysis tools. Users can search within this collection or across other Gale Primary Source Collections. The American Historical Periodicals from the American Antiquarian Society, Series 6 is highly recommended for academic libraries.—**ARBA Staff Reviewer**

157. **Calisphere. https://calisphere.org/.** [Website] Free. Date reviewed: 2018.

Calisphere gathers materials from the digital collections of the ten University of California campuses as well as numerous libraries, private schools, and other institutions into one place. It is home to over a million documents, images, audio and visual recordings, and more, many reflective of the rich detail of California history. Artifacts illustrating "The Watts Rebellion," "Native Americans: Arts and Traditions in Everyday Life," "The Rise of Technology," and "Disasters in the Gold Rush Era" are just some of what is found in the broader collections on the site. Users can conduct a basic search from the bar in the center of the homepage. Alternatively, users can select from one of several tabs to help clarify their interests. Under Contributing Institutions, users will find a list of nearly fifty collections organized under the UC Partners (Berkeley, Merced, Los Angeles, Santa Barbara, Riverside, etc.) link. Selecting the Statewide Partners link displays an alphabetical directory of over one hundred fifty contributing museums, libraries, non-UC schools and other institutions representative of military, cultural, labor, Native American, scientific, ethnic and other interests. Users can click any institution to link to their collection within the Calisphere database. Alternatively, users can select the Collections tab to find materials organized contextually by subject or format. Here, users can Random Explore and scroll through a display of featured collections (the Don Pedro Project, the Chapman Family Correspondence, etc.) or select from an A-Z collection display. Exhibitions are expertly curated with items pulled from one or more Calisphere collections. Under this category, users can Random Explore from a generous gallery or Browse All through an alphabetized display which also groups exhibitions by theme: California History (California Missions, The Growth of Cities, etc.), California Cultures (African Americans, Hispanic Americans, etc.), and others. An Exhibition may include a narrative overview alongside relevant documents/artifacts from the Calisphere database. Users can closely examine digital artifacts, which include photographs from the devastating 1906 earthquake and fire in San Francisco, papers of environmental activist Kathleen Goddard Jones, the Kenneth L. Waller Bataan Prisoner of War Collection including an oral history, annotated map, photos, and much, much more. Each artifact may yield accompanying metadata such as Title, Creator, Issue Date, Contributing Institution, Collection, Description, Type, and Format. The extensive but easy to navigate Calisphere is accessible to many grade levels and would appeal to a wide range of academic interests: historical, cultural, sociological and others.—**ARBA Staff Reviewer**

158. **Civil War Washington http://civilwardc.org/.** [Website] Free. Date reviewed: 2019.

Civil War Washington hosts a generous collection of materials that look expressly at the United States Civil War and its relationship with Washington D.C. Users can easily explore maps, historical texts, and other artifacts which shine a light on scientific, political, social, and cultural issues that permeated the capital around the time of the devastating conflict. From the homepage gallery, users can find information by category. Maps allows users to examine historical Washington D.C. through the eyes of modern technology. Users can examine four base maps (three historical and one modern) with the addition of data layers that identify hospitals, forts, white churches, colored churches, railroads, streams, and more. Users can easily switch between maps, zoom, and click on icons that identify locations with further detail such as street address, data source, people, and links to further information. Users click on the Open Map Application button to access the feature. Texts offer several categories of materials to explore, including Petitions, Medical Records, Letters from Washington, and Newspapers. Users can zoom in on digital images of pages from three Civil War era hospital newspapers: *The Cripple, The Soldier's Journal,* and the *Armory Square Hospital Gazette,* but there is no transcription or keyword searching at this time. The other three categories offer digital thumbnails as well as transcriptions and other identifying information. Medical Records offer detailed and sometimes quite graphic descriptions of an individual's medical conditions and wounds, while twenty-four Letters from Washington represent Washington D.C.-based correspondence to the editors of *The Anglo-African* newspaper. Hundreds of petitions reflect the legal aspects of moving individuals from slavery to freedom. All the materials are filled with the names, places, organizations, and more which are listed in the website's Data section. Here, users can keyword search or browse over seven thousand records on People, Places, Events, Organizations, and Documents. Information in the records is generally basic, but any connections are emphasized. People lists individuals with notes, if known, on gender, race, occupation, date of birth, and date of death. Clicking on an individual's name may reveal data source and additional detail. Events list specific military engagements, large and small, while Organizations generally cover military regiments. Visual Works currently centers around a small collection of medical doctor and hospital photographs. Users can click on the thumbnail image for closer examination and to find any affiliated information such as date, creator, and source. Interpretations offer a selection of scholarly essays addressing both the union of U.S. Civil War scholarship with digital technology as well as several themes addressed across Civil War Washington. Essays include "Emancipation in the District of Columbia," "Military Hospitals in the Department of Washington," and others. Civil War Washington offers a unique approach to Civil War study in its use of various media and its focus on one city's connection to the conflict.—**ARBA Staff Reviewer**

159. **Early California Population Project https://www.huntington.org/ecpp.** [Website] Free. Date reviewed: 2019.

The Early California Population Project is an extensive database of information gathered from historic California Mission registers between the years of 1769 and 1850. Through baptism, marriage, and burial records, users can find information on the earliest European settlers in addition to native populations throughout the large state. Records from twenty-one missions in addition the Los Angeles Plaza Church and the Santa Barbara Presidio are included. Due to the size and specific nature of the records, it is recommended that users go through the Search Tips and Sample Searches, found on the left side of the launch page, before exploring the database. Mission Notes are here as well, and pertain to missing records, duplicate records, and general record organization. Basically, users select a Record Type (e.g., baptism, death) then add any known Criterion, such as Mission, Marital Status, Military Status, Officiant, Recorder, Spouse Name, and Spouse Religious

Status. The database follows a very basic structure—users must begin the search with at least some specific information in order to return records. The fact that name Criterion emphasize such a large range of options: surname, native name, or Spanish name for bride, groom, and both sets of parents speaks to the intricacies of searching old records. Available records will appear as a list and users can click to view. Records may reveal data for any number of the generous selection of Criterion options, and include a field for Notes. This site has obvious appeal to researchers and may also be a useful resource for students and educators.—**ARBA Staff Reviewer**

160. **Freedom on the Move https://freedomonthemove.org/.** [Website] Free. Date reviewed: 2019.

The Freedom on the Move project gathers information on fugitive slaves via a large and growing collection of runaway slave advertisements. Users can find names, dates, and many other details about members of a marginalized society taking desperate measures to be free. Users can edit information within the database and contribute new entries as well. All users must first create a free account with a username and password, but can then access the collection via the Crowdsource and Search Ads bar at the center of the launch page. Currently, users can search or browse over 20,000 runaway slave advertisements. The site organizes searches through four categories: Advertisement, Runaway, Enslaver, or Runaway Event, each with its own search parameters. Alternatively, users can scroll down and browse through the database which displays advertisements in a list or gallery format and includes newspaper name, newspaper location, publishing date, and a thumbnail image of advertisement if available. For each advertisement, users can examine the Original Image (if available) and the Transcribed Ad (not all advertisements are transcribed). Identifying information for the advertisements includes language, posted by, publication date, newspaper, newspaper location, and runaway event information (outside involvement, date, escapee count) if known. Users can discover fascinating detail within the advertisements, including runaway names, aliases, physical characteristics (height, weight, gender, possessions, injuries, etc.), skills (literacy, languages, etc.), and more. Other information may describe the enslaver (name, gender, location, etc.) and advertiser (*Daily Picayune, The Pennsylvania Journal,* the *Milledgeville Federal Union,* etc.). Put all together, the detail within the brief advertisements offers a clearer portrait of the many individuals desperate for freedom, such as "grille girl Madeline…creole…about five feet two inches high" or "Wilson, (of) short stature, delicate figure…seen many times near Carroliton and on board steamboats."—**ARBA Staff Reviewer**

161. **Hidden Patterns of the Civil War https://dsl.richmond.edu/civilwar.** [Website] Free. Date reviewed: 2019.

This site gathers a number of digital scholarship projects concerning the U.S. Civil War into one place. Centered mainly around Richmond, Virginia, histories, the projects within Hidden Patterns of the Civil War both work individually and collectively to expand understanding of the great conflict. Four projects emphasize text analysis while five projects use maps in an exploration of subjects such as emancipation, slavery, migration, and more. Mining the Dispatch, within the text-based projects, uses "topic modeling" to analyze frequency and changes related to the subjects covered over the course of the war in Richmond's prominent newspaper, the *Daily Dispatch.* Users can create charts and graphs that focus on coverage of key topics such as slavery, nationalism and patriotism, soldiers, and economy. Users can adjust charts to reflect number of articles with topic or topic as a percentage of print space, examine transcriptions of exemplary articles, (highest topic proportions in category), and view predictive words. A related project allows a search of the *Daily Dispatch* archive (transcribed) covering the time between November 1860 and December 1865. A good chronology with links to related news stories and a brief essay on confederate Richmond and its primary newspaper accompany the search engine. The Proceedings of the Virginia Secession Convention link lets users examine fully transcribed debates of the Virginia delegation regarding the secession question. Users can search speeches by delegate or county or conduct a basic search of all text. The project supplies contextual information through essays, timelines, and maps. The TextMapping project creates visualizations (word clouds, synchronic bar graphs, etc.) of regional archive document comparisons. The project offers a text-based analysis of Republican vs. Democrat, North vs. South, and Unionist vs. Secessionist points of view. Under the maps category, users can find five distinct projects. One of these is Visualizing Emancipation, which allows users to track or add emancipation events, Union Army locations, and the legality of slavery. This project will also offer teaching resources including a lesson plan with guiding questions and learning objectives, worksheet, and video tutorials (in development). Marriage, Migration, and Emancipation illustrates the movement of newly emancipated and married couples by Virginia county (data is currently available for 12 counties). Mapping Richmond's Slave Market, still under development, will offer a 21st-century view of 19th-century Richmond by highlighting buildings associated with the slave trade—auction houses, jails, and associated businesses—over an 1856 map. Sketches and photographs will provide additional context regarding life around the Richmond slave market. The Voting America: Civil War Elections maps depict voting patterns for the 1860 and the 1864 presidential elections. Users will find visualizations of states and counties won by party. It is important to note that the link leads to applicable pages of the Voting America site which extends its scope well beyond the Civil War years. Finally, Scale and Freedom displays six maps (black and white) emphasizing event relationships as patterns using the global cotton market, armies and escapes, migration and marriage, and more.—**ARBA Staff Reviewer**

162. **La Florida. The Interactive Digital Archive of the Americas http://laflorida. org/.** [Website] Free. Date reviewed: 2018.

La Florida is an interactive exploration of colonial Florida based upon a searchable database of information on past inhabitants of the region. Users can conduct a basic search from the blue bar in the upper right corner of the homepage or select from several links in the center of the page. Exhibits currently showcases materials from the archive of the parish of St. Augustine, the oldest city settlement in the United States. These records offer a glimpse into the lives of some of the earliest settlers of the new world; tracking marriages, births, deaths, and more. Currently, users can examine a portion of the extensive archive, which will eventually expand in content and correspond with English and Spanish transcription. People shares biographical data on close to 3,500 individuals who came ashore after 1513. Users can search from the bar or scroll down through an alphabetical list of names. Available information may include group, gender, origin, literacy, and occupation. There may also be a Google map pinned with the subject's original place of residence, a brief biographical sketch, relevant dates, and notes. The Infographics link shows a map display of known origin sites of the population database, and two other visualizations of literacy and occupation (pikeman, harquebusier, shipmaster, etc.) data. Florida Stories offers video content on select individuals within the database, offering insight into the tremendous challenges of establishing settlements in the region. Under the Mapping La Florida link, users can find an interactive map dating from 1544 that reveals names and locations of Native American settlements, and an 18th-century property map showing St. Augustine as it was just before the British took over. Users can learn names of property owners, plot sizes, types of buildings, building composition, and other information. Junior Scholars will eventually link to educational tools and activities for younger students. While La Florida is still in development, the resources it currently offers are engaging and informative. The site has broad appeal.—**ARBA Staff Reviewer**

163. **Millican Project https://millican.omeka.net/about.** [Website] Free. Date reviewed: 2019.

The Millican Project gathers materials related to a race riot occurring in Millican, Texas, in 1868, considered the largest riot of its kind in the region. Simple in structure, the site offers an important glimpse into the uneasy post-Civil War milieu, the role of journalism, and other factors. From this page, users can follow the Millican Document link to an essential essay providing background on Millican with reference to the American Civil War, voting rights, the Ku Klux Klan, railroad expansion, the Freedmen's Bureau, and the investigations, politics, and general significance of the tragic event. Users can then examine thirty-four items in two collections by selecting the Browse Items, Browse Collections, or Map tabs at the top of the page. Items mainly consist of regional newspaper accounts, editorials, and statements as well as contemporary maps of the area. Users can examine the digital artifact, and find information such as Title, Subject, Description, Creator, Publisher, Date, Type, and Tags. A text translation is generally available as well. The Map tab lets users find items by pinned location on a world map—some items originate out of state and even out of the country (there is a mention of the riots in the *Hamburger Nachrichten,* a newspaper out of the Northern German Confederation). Other standout items include a map of Brazos County from 1867 and a letter from Confederate General Henry E. McCulloch, a man determined not to allow freed blacks suffrage. Though small in scale, the archive offers compelling material about an important event along the timeline of American civil rights history. It would be of interest to historians, civil rights advocates, educators, and students.—**ARBA Staff Reviewer**

164. **Sanborn Fire Insurance Maps http://library.stanford.edu/guides/sanborn-fire-insurance-maps.** [Website] Free. Date reviewed: 2019.

Initially produced for practical reasons, the Sanborn Fire Insurance Maps are now fascinating historical artifacts. This collection from the Stanford libraries presents maps for 43 California communities (with three others out-of-state), generally dating from the first half of the 20th century. From the Sanborn Fire Insurance Maps homepage, users can conduct a general search, or browse through the gallery display of maps presented alphabetically by city/town name. Clicking on the map accesses the map page(s) in a viewer. Accompanying information includes title (generally city, county, state, and date), physical description, and place created. Users can click the More Details tab for language, issuance, type of resource, map data, and access conditions. Within the viewer, zoom and navigation capabilities are available to capture the fine detail. Users can discern street names, street numbers, lot measurements, building purposes (e.g., grocer, dance hall), and more. A key notes map markings and colorings which point out number of stories in a building, roof composition, window and door location and composition, building materials, and more. Users can also learn fire station location, relative building heights, and information on water and fire facilities. While maps for some communities may represent only a portion of their area (e.g., Carlsbad, San Marino), the maps for other communities (e.g., Compton, San Bruno) may encompasses many pages and be more reflective of the community as a whole. These larger map sets may also include an index of street names and particular buildings. An interactive index is available under the Curated Features tab on the homepage and is helpful in navigating these larger map sets. Users can also find information on the two Sanborn Atlases in the collection (for Frankfort, Kentucky and Hallowell, Maine) under Curated Features. The content in this database can be compared to ProQuest's fee-based product, Digital Sanborn Maps—**ARBA Staff Reviewer**

165. **Thomas Jefferson's Monticello https://home.monticello.org/.** [Website] Date reviewed: 2019.

Though this free-to-use site is not new, it is definitely worth a look for those who have not explored all it has to offer. The main website provides users with videos and articles regarding slavery at Monticello, a set of frequently asked questions, online exhibitions, and information for teachers via the Monticello Digital Classroom (many materials have been recently added). Drilling down from the Research Collections tab users will find a Thomas Jefferson Encyclopedia. Notably, users need to register (free) to make the most of this material. There is also a Monticello Plantation Database that uses information from Jefferson's Farm Book to provide researchers with basic information—birth dates, death dates, locations, family relationships, and occupations—for the approximately six hundred slaves owned by Jefferson.—**ARBA Staff Reviewer**

166. **Valley of the Shadow http://valley.lib.virginia.edu/.** [Website] Free. Date reviewed: 2019.

Also known as the Valley Project, this extensive digital archive gathers a range of Civil War-era materials from Augusta County, Virginia, and Franklin County, Pennsylvania. Lying at different ends of the Shenandoah Valley, the communities defended vastly different ideals throughout the war, yet dealt with many similar issues. The archive contains thousands of pages of diary entries, correspondence, speeches, church records, maps, and other materials from these two counties, expanding the view from the battlefields to the communities that supported them. Users can Enter the Valley Archive via the link on the homepage then choose a browsing option from a schematic which displays materials by category (letters & diaries, newspapers, images, etc.) and by time period: The Eve of War (1859-1861), The War Years (1861-1865), and The Aftermath (1865-1870). Users can conduct a search within a document category by keyword, author, or subject. Browsing options for each category will vary, but will be further organized by county. Users can find helpful tips on how best to navigate the materials by first clicking on the Using the Valley Project link at the bottom of the schematic page. Within each category of materials, it is always easy to return to the schematic to continue browsing. Most items within a category are listed alphabetically by family collection or author name alongside the date and a brief description. Users can jump to a particular letter in the alphabet for easy navigation. Users will also find applicable links to all related materials within other areas of the archive under any particular category. Letters and diaries are transcribed with either original or modern spelling, and some are annotated with historical, geographical, and other context. Users can find census and veterans records, soldiers records, tax records, maps and images, and other documents. Under Newspapers, users can find articles indexed by topic, such as daily life, war memories, and race relations for each time period and county. Users can also browse newspapers, like the *Republican Vindicator* from Augusta County and the *Valley Spirit* from Franklin County, by date. Users can view text transcripts for each archived paper. Maps and images add excellent context regarding geography, infrastructure, agriculture, slavery, politics, and religion to the archive. Users can find maps that illustrate the average farm value in 1860, railroads and roads in 1860, presidential voting by precinct, county comparison maps, and much more. An animated theater battle map (found under Battle Maps) follows the movement of the 5th Virginia Infantry throughout their deployment.— **ARBA Staff Reviewer**

167. **What America Ate: Preserving America's Culinary History from the Great Depression** http://whatamericaate.org/about.php. [Website] Free. Date reviewed: 2019.

One of the many government-funded projects during the Great Depression included the America Eats Project, which sent writers and photographers across the country in search of information about what Americans were eating and how these foods were prepared during a period of massive economic and social change. A planned reference book never came to fruition, and, until now, the records from the America Eats Project have been scattered across the country in various repositories. With funding from the National Endowment for the Humanities and support from the history department at Michigan State University and Matrix, The Center for Digital Humanities and Social Sciences at Michigan State, these materials are now freely available. The database offers a variety of ways to access the materials. Users can click on All Formats, America Eats, Cookbooks, and Advertising. There are a number of filters on the left side of the page. Under these different entry points, users will find a trove of material: 200 local cookbooks, thousands of advertisements, correspondence from the project, and more. Other tabs at the top of the homepage provide further information. Explore History takes users to a series of contextualizing essays, while Spotlight Sources offers guidance on how to work with primary sources, including questions that students can ask and answer. There is also a Recipes tab and a Map tab. The map is interactive and will let users click on a region to discover material. This database is easy to navigate and packed with information that can be used by educators, students, and members of the general public.—**ARBA Staff Reviewer**

168. **Woodstock Archive** https://photoarchive.museumatbethelwoods.org. [Website] Free. Date reviewed: 2019.

This archive houses user-submitted photograph and film footage collections taken during and around the Woodstock music festival. Twenty separate photo collections account for over 650 photographs (black & white and color) while 9 contributors have uploaded 18 short films (digitized from super 8). Together, the images evoke the youth-driven counterculture spirit that enveloped the normally bucolic hillsides of upstate New York over those three days in July of 1969. Users can access the materials via the Collections tab at the top of the homepage. Collection Photographs present a gallery of the individual photo collections. Users can click on a gallery image to access a specific collection and are able to view a slideshow of the entire collection or view the photograph individually.

Brief photographer, subject, and technical information introduces each collection, but other than this there is limited detail available for individual photographs. Photographs are watermarked, but can be downloaded or purchased for a price depending on resolution and/ or usage. Photos capture both intimate moments and wide-ranging landscapes that speak to the personal meaning and scope of the festival scene. The Collection Videos gallery includes similar descriptive information. Some films may contain audio. Highlights of this gallery include musical performance video, interviews with local business owners, and New York state police surveillance footage. Each collection can be keyword searched via the bar at the bottom of each gallery. The personal photographs and films are important artifacts of a changing time.—**ARBA Staff Reviewer**

Handbooks and Yearbooks

169.   **The Correspondence of Henry D. Thoreau. Volume 2: 1849-1856.** By Henry D. Thoreau. Robert N. Hudspeth, Elizabeth Hall Witherell, and Lihong Xie, eds. Princeton, N.J., Princeton University Press, 2018. 700p. index. $99.50. ISBN 13: 978-0-691-17058-9; 978-0-691-18902-4 (e-book).

Following a 2013 volume covering 1834 to 1848 and containing 163 letters, this volume presents 246 letters, half by Thoreau and half sent to him. (A third volume will complete the set.) Nearly every letter is accompanied by numerous footnotes explaining names, places, and events mentioned in the text. On many occasions the notes exceed the length of the letter. A number of the correspondents are well-known figures: Horace Greeley, Louis Agassiz, Ralph Waldo Emerson, and Charles Sumner. Understandably, family members are also frequent correspondents. The letters paint an image of the religious, literary, political, and scientific portions of the New England society that Thoreau knew during this period. Following all the letters, there are 170 pages of an "Editorial Appendix." There are three substantial introductions: General, Historical, and Textual. The first one is identical to the introduction in the first volume of the series. Other items include "Notes on the illustrations," library symbols for the various institutions housing the letters, and a bibliography.

This volume is clearly a work best suited to academic libraries; almost every library holding a print copy of the first volume is part of a college or university. Scholars in this area of 19th-century American history should find it most useful.—**Mark Schumacher**

170.   Crowder, Jack Darrell. **Women Patriots in the American Revolution: Stories of Bravery, Daring, and Compassion.** Baltimore, Md., Clearfield /Genealogical Publishing, 2018. 102p. illus. index. $24.95pa. ISBN 13: 978-0-8063-5874-1.

This book highlights the contributions of approximately ninety women to the overall success of the American Revolution. Women fulfilled various roles—washerwomen, spies, cooks, nurses, and even soldiers. After a brief introduction the book lists the women in alphabetic order. Entries vary in length, format, and content but all include sources. The shortest entry for Henrietta Maria Cole is comprised of two sentences and includes life and death dates and the fact that she carried dispatches during the war. The information is drawn from the D.A.R. Lineage Book, volume 39. One of the longest entries is for Sarah Matthews Reed Osborn Benjamin who worked as a cook, servant, and washerwoman for the troops. This entry consists largely of a deposition she gave to her grandson in 1837 as part of a pension application. The book includes fascinating narratives such as the story of Oneida Indian Polly Cooper who delivered supplies to Washington's starving troops at Valley Forge and stayed to nurse the sick and Sally St. Clair, a Creole girl who dressed as a man in order to fight alongside the one she loved. A bibliography and an index round out the work. Recommended for public libraries.—**ARBA Staff Reviewer**

171. **Defining Documents in American History: Secrets, Leaks & Scandals.** Michael Shally-Jensen, ed. Hackensack, N.J., Salem Press, 2018. 2v. illus. maps. index. $295.00/ set. ISBN 13: 978-1-68217-698-6; 978-1-68217-699-3 (e-book).

This installment in the Defining Documents in American History series contains 75 documents (speeches, memos, letters, reports, transcripts, minutes, testimony) related to secrets, leaks, and scandals throughout American history, starting with an encoded letter from American general Benedict Arnold to British major John Andre. As with the other titles in this series, the documents (presented in part or in whole) are contextualized with a summary, overview, defining moment, author biography, and analysis of document themes. Each essay has a bibliography and additional readings section. The book organizes the 75 documents into the following sections: Secrets, Conspiracies, and Scandals through the 19th Century; Controversies, Conflicts, and Communism through the mid-20th Century; Government in Hiding, from Vietnam to Watergate and After; Scandals, Scares, and Intelligence Failures in Recent Decades; Lies, Leaks, and Hacks in the Contemporary Period; and Selected Environmental Debacles. In these sections, users will find foundational information on important historical moments and topics as revealed through analysis of such documents as the Dred Scott decision, coverage of the sinking of the U.S.S. *Maine,* the articles of impeachment against President Andrew Johnson, Executive Order 9066, testimony about the My Lai Massacre, excerpts from the Clarence Thomas hearings, and the 2018 executive order separating children from families at the U.S.-Mexico border. The final section on environmental debacles contains an excerpt from Rachel Carson's *Silent Spring,* a report to the president on the *Exxon Valdez* oil spill, a record of a teleconference between President George W. Bush and others about Hurricane Katrina, and communications concerning the Flint, Michigan, water crisis. Appendixes include a chronology, a list of web resources, a general bibliography, and an index. High school and undergraduate students starting a research project or hoping to find the answers to identification questions will find this a useful set. There are also a number of black-and-white photographs, cartoons, and maps that add value to the material presented. Highly recommended.—**ARBA Staff Reviewer**

172. **Defining Documents in American History: The Legacy of 9/11.** Michael Shally-Jensen, ed. Hackensack, N.J., Salem Press, 2018. 321p. illus. maps. index. $175.00. ISBN 13: 978-1-68217-921-5; 978-1-68217-964-2 (e-book).

This title includes 44 documents (speeches, letters, government reports, treaties, correspondence, essays, minutes, sermons, and transcripts) related to 9/11 and its aftermath. The book begins with an introduction by Editor Michael Shally-Jensen, which outlines the 20th-century history of French, Russian, British, and American involvement in the Middle East, providing the book's users with scaffolding on which to hang the information provided in the documents. Shally-Jensen arranges the documents in four parts: Historic Background (13 documents); Growing Conflict and 9/11 (14 documents); War—Its

Justifications and Problems (9 documents); and The Post-9/11 World (9 documents). Each document analysis (either excerpted or printed in whole) includes a summary overview, a defining moment, a biography of the document's author or authors, document themes and analysis, and a bibliography and additional readings list. Examples of documents presented in this volume include the Balfour Declaration, a speech by Gamal Abdel Nasser on the nationalization of the Suez Canal, Colin Powell's 2003 speech to the UN on Iraqi Weapons of Mass Destruction, and a speech by an Islamic State spokesman Abu Muhammead Al-'Adnani proclaiming the creation of the caliphate. Particularly interesting are the documents relating to the 1979 Soviet invasion of Afghanistan, a topic that has recently been in the news. Each document analysis contains a glossary, and the book is enhanced overall by the use of black-and-white photographs and maps. Appendixes include a "Time Line of 9/11," which starts in 1970 and runs through 2001; a list of web resources, a bibliography, and an index. This document collection is recommended for school and public libraries. Those who own a copy of *Defining Documents in World History: The Middle East,* however, will want to look carefully at the table of contents as some of the same documents appear in both titles.—**ARBA Staff Reviewer**

173.   Derks, Scott. **Working Americans, 1880-2017. Volume VIII: Immigrants.** 2d ed. Amenia, N.Y., Grey House Publishing, 2018. 614p. illus. index. $150.00. ISBN 13: 978-1-68217-745-7; 978-1-68217-746-4 (e-book).

This volume updates the previous edition (see ARBA 2009, entry 211) with new coverage of the modern-day immigrant experience. The focus is on first-and second-generation immigrant families. Profiles are arranged chronologically, in decade chapters. Generally, each decade includes three profiles of individual immigrants. Each profile contains details about the subject's life and his or her transition to American culture and historical snapshots with information about significant events that happened during the period. Each profile contains original source documents and black-and-white photographs of the individual and other items of interest. New to this edition is a Facts & Figures section containing 24 pages of current facts and statistics from the Office of Immigration Statistics. There is a bibliography of some 50 books and articles relevant to the subject and an index to names and subjects.

The volume is a mishmash, or potpourri, of information pertaining to the immigrant experience in America from 1880 to 2017. There is a great deal of information for students motivated enough to dig it out. There is a generally positive attitude toward the individuals covered and the contributions they have made, if not towards the ordeals they have gone through, including the anti-immigrant attitude of the Trump administration. Given the price of the volume it is a luxury item for all except for large university libraries.—**Jonathan F. Husband**

174.   **Gender Roles in American Life: A Documentary History of Political, Social, and Economic Changes.** Shehan, Constance L., ed. Santa Barbara, Calif., ABC-CLIO, 2018. 2v. index. $198.00/set. ISBN 13: 978-1-4408-5958-8; 978-1-4408-5959-5 (e-book).

Students looking for an overview of the history of men and women in America and how their roles have evolved over time will find it in this comprehensive two-volume set. Each volume is divided into four chapters which cover a particular time period; for example, "1930-1955: The Great Depression, The New Deal, World War II, and Its Aftermath." Each chapter begins with an essay relating important events and how gender roles were perceived in each period, but the bulk of each chapter is a collection of primary documents which will transport the reader to that historical period as seen through the eyes of its contemporaries. The variety of documents is wide-ranging: letters, pamphlets, magazine articles, speeches, government documents, congressional hearings, and excerpts from books. Some may be familiar, such as the "Remember the Ladies" letter of Abigail Adams to her husband, but many will be new and can help round out the knowledge of young readers. The collection of documents is diverse in the gender of the author and in the opinions expressed. Each is cited at the end of the piece, so readers can see exactly where it came from. In addition, there is a list of references at the end of each chapter essay, so students can continue their learning if they choose. For high school students researching gender roles, American history, or politics, this set offers an excellent selection of primary source material. The range of documents from 1775 to 2017 will be invaluable for students investigating current attitudes and, especially, historical ones. An index rounds out the work. Highly recommended.—**Mary Northrup**

175.   Gould, Neil. **The American Revolution: Documents Decoded.** Santa Barbara, Calif., ABC-CLIO, 2018. 292p. index. $81.00. ISBN 13: 978-1-4408-3946-7; 978-1-4408-3947-4 (e-book).

Beginning with the 1765 ballad "American Taxation," this volume in ABC-Clio's Documents Decoded series broadly surveys the American Revolution through approximately 65 documents. Accompanying each are copious annotations by Neil Gould, Department of History, Government, and Economics at Duchess Community College, which fulfill such functions as defining concepts or putting events into context. The respective sources, some of which are excerpted, are organized in four sections. "The Road to Revolution" includes 20 documents, ranging from contemporary accounts of the Boston Massacre to Paul Revere reminiscing in 1783 about his famous ride. "Battles of Liberty," which provides perspectives from the battlefields, warrants 11 accounts. The third section, entitled "A Nation of Amazons," illuminates the many important roles undertaken by women during the era. The lyrics of 22 songs make up the final section, "Songs of Liberty." Supplementing the text are a chronology and suggestions for "Further Reading." It should be noted that the titles recommended for research are extremely dated, as the newest was published in 1984. Many were produced in the 19th century and would be difficult to obtain. This title is recommended for libraries serving high school and lower-level undergraduate clientele.—**John R. Burch Jr.**

176.   Hedtke, James R. **American Civil War: Facts and Fictions.** Santa Barbara, Calif., ABC-CLIO, 2018. 228p. index. (Historical Facts and Fictions series). $61.00. ISBN 13: 978-1-4408-6073-7; 978-1-4408-6074-4 (e-book).

Of all events in American history, the Civil War (1861-1865) captures the public imagination like almost no other. For over 150 years, the Civil War has been analyzed, cataloged, and debated from almost every angle—its causes, outcomes, and political, social, and technological aspects. The war remains a sensitive issue, however, with many misperceptions and fallacies still widely accepted. In *American Civil War,* author James R. Hedtke seeks to separate the facts from fictions on topics such as the Emancipation Proclamation, Civil War medicine, and the combat roles African American and women soldiers played. The book is one in a series of works highlighting historical facts and fictions (other topics include Christianity, Vikings, and the Middle Ages).

For each topic, Hedtke examines first the popular notion and then the facts, providing excerpts of relevant primary source documents and suggestions for further reading. Drawing on memoirs, newspaper articles, public documents, speeches, and the *War of the Rebellion* (a gold mine of contemporary accounts of military actions as reported by both sides), Hedtke traces the origins of historical fictions to their source. He dismantles key components of Lost Cause mythology—states' rights, not slavery, was the primary factor driving the secession movement, for example—and debunks conspiracy theories like those propagated to explain President Abraham Lincoln's assassination. Hedtke writes with scope and clarity throughout, his selection of primary sources lending his arguments an extra level of credibility, enabling him to be direct without being preachy.

Clearly written and judiciously compiled, *American Civil War* is a welcome addition to any general research collection.—**Craig Mury Keeney**

177.   Hendricks, Nancy. **Daily Life in 1950s America.** Santa Barbara, Calif., Greenwood Press/ABC-CLIO, 2019. 282p. illus. index. (The Greenwood Press Daily Life Through History Series). $61.00. ISBN 13: 978-1-4408-6441-4; 978-1-4408-6442-1 (e-book).

Part of the Greenwood Press Daily Life Through History series, this book focuses on 1950s America. It is divided into seven broad chapters, each subdivided into numerous smaller topics and one primary source document as a representation of that chapter. After a short preface, introduction, timeline, and glossary, the seven chapters are "Domestic Life," "Economic Life," "Intellectual Life," "Material Life," "Political Life," "Recreational Life," and "Religious Life." Four appendixes provide information on slang during the 1950s, various awards in sports and music, best-selling books, major Congressional legislation, and major Supreme Court decisions. As an example, the chapter on iIntellectual life discusses communication, cultural critics, education, health and health care, literature, medical advances, news media, popular culture, and science, ending with John F. Kennedy's speech at the Rockefeller Public Service Awards Luncheon in 1958. A great source book for classes on this time period in American history.—**Bradford Lee Eden**

178.   Issitt, Micah L. **Gender: Roles & Rights.** Amenia, N.Y., Grey House Publishing, 2018. 764p. illus. index. (Opinions throughout History). $195.00. ISBN 13: 978-1-68217-951-2; 978-1-68217-952-9 (e-book).

With gender identity and sexuality issues in the news, this volume in Grey House's Opinions throughout History series is a welcome reference tool. The book begins with an overview essay discussing gender concepts and a timeline from 1533 through 2018 with notable relevant events. Six major sections divided into 28 chapters follow. These sections cover major topics: citizenship & constitutional rights; sexual nonconformity & changing policy; in the workplace; LGBTQ+ rights; birth control & reproduction; and marriage & parenting. Each chapter features primary and secondary source documents such as newspaper and magazine articles, speeches, court decisions, and legislation. Commentary by scholars in the field, a conclusion, discussion questions, and a bibliography complete the chapter. A final essay on ideas about gender, notes, a complete list of sources included, a glossary, and a bibliography appear at the end of the volume. There is also a chapter of historical snapshots to situate the documents within the broader context of world events.

Since the book discusses everything from the origin of patriarchy though transgender parenting rights, it is a valuable resource for students of history, psychology, and the social sciences. It will also be very useful for debate preparation.—**Barbara M. Bibel**

179.   Issitt, Micah L. **Immigration.** Amenia, N.Y., Grey House Publishing, 2018. 814p. illus. index. (Opinions throughout History). $195.00. ISBN 13: 978-1-68217-722-8; 978-1-68217-723-5 (e-book).

Immigration is a major issue in the United States at this time. This book in Grey House's Opinions Throughout History series examines immigration through the attitudes and ideas that have shaped policy. An introductory essay presents basic concepts, and a timeline from 1492 to 2017 lists major events. The 31 chapters that follow use primary and secondary resources including magazine and newspaper articles, speeches, court decisions, and legislation to paint a picture of immigration policy and process as they evolve historically. Each chapter includes an introduction, a list of concepts covered, analysis by scholars, a conclusion, discussion questions, and a reading list. Black-and-white illustrations augment the text. Historical snapshots at the end of the book place the ideas presented within the larger context of events occurring in the country. A list of sources presented, a glossary, and a bibliography complete the work.

Since the book examines liberalism, progressivism, and conservatism in the context of immigration and looks at the idea of American identity, it is very useful and timely. By looking at everything from treaties with Native American nations to the ban on travel from Muslim-majority countries, this volume provides a comprehensive overview of major issues that American society must confront. It is a useful resource for students, debaters, and anyone who wishes to be well-informed on these issues.—**Barbara M. Bibel**

180.   Nicholson, C. Brid. **Documents of the Lewis and Clark Expedition.** Santa Barbara, Calif., ABC-CLIO, 2019. 244p. index. (Eyewitness to History Series). $94.00. ISBN 13: 978-1-4408-5455-2; 978-1-4408-5456-9 (e-book).

The ABC-CLIO Eyewitness to History series is excellent and this is another fine addition to these outstanding works. Patricia Stroud's recent book (2018) on the life of Meriwether Lewis and the Ken Burns PBS video and television series on the Lewis and Clark expedition revived interest in this remarkable journey. This collection of 114 documents and expository information allows the reader to experience the adventure of the quest to find the passage to the Pacific Ocean. Students are afforded the opportunity to see how the writing of history is based on primary sources, but the sources themselves are subject to opinions and bias about the events that they chronicle.

The volume begins with an historical introduction that explains the expedition, the purpose, the primary players, the results, the return home, accomplishments, and the aftermath. This is followed by a detailed chronology and a map of the trip. The individual chapters each begin with interesting essays that highlight the documents in that unit. Each document is followed by a citation of its source, primarily from journal excerpts and letters, and a bibliography for further reading. The appendix provides a list of all the expedition members and the Native American nations that the adventurers met along the way. A full bibliography and an index are included.

The material in this attractive volume is not readily accessible by quick online search so the book is a good addition to most libraries.—**Joe P. Dunn**

181.   Olson, James S., and Mariah Gumpert. **The 1950s: Key Themes and Documents.** Santa Barbara, Calif., ABC-CLIO, 2018. 344p. illus. index. (Unlocking American History series). $61.00. ISBN 13: 978-1-4408-6132-1; 978-1-4408-6133-8 (e-book).

In the United States (U.S.), the end of World War II ushered in an unparalleled era of vigorous expansion and growth. The Great Depression of the 1930s, along with wartime angst and uncertainty in the 1940s, gave way in the 1950s to a booming economic recovery, mass migration to suburbs, and explosive population growth. Moreover, increases in military and infrastructure spending propelled the nation to superpower status. Radio took a backseat to television as a popular form of family entertainment, and disaffected writers churned out literature and poetry that mercilessly ridiculed conformity and traditional roles between the sexes. Nevertheless, not all was well: many Americans once again found themselves fighting for the civil rights already guaranteed them by the Constitution, and tensions with the Soviet Union mounted as the two nations warily engaged in a metaphorical "cold" war, fueled largely by a struggle for economic, political, and scientific supremacy.

The bulk of the volume is comprised of alphabetized, encyclopedic entries of various aspects of U.S. history, ranging from, for example, The Abbott and Costello Show to Juvenile Delinquency, The Catcher in the Rye, and Tibet. Each entry is selected from Olson's *Historical Dictionary of the 1950s,* but modified to accommodate students in advanced placement (AP) history classes associated with the 1950s, and for those students in history classes aligned with Common Core standards. Each entry belongs to one of nine categories reflecting, as the authors note, "Key Themes" (e.g., civil rights, music). The volume also includes a section of eight primary sources derived from notable events of the time, both familiar ("Harry Truman's Declaration of National Emergency") and perhaps lesser-known ("Mrs. America in a Fallout Shelter"). The authors also provide a preface; a how-to page for interacting with the volume; an introduction interwoven with aspects of each key theme; alphabetical and topical lists of entries; a list of primary documents; sample essay questions as could be found on AP U.S. history exams; a chronology of the decade by each year within; four appendixes (e.g., "Listing of Biographical Entries"); and a bibliography and index.

The volume is comprehensive in breadth and depth of entries. The authors are explicit in outlining the volume's purpose and use, with a thoughtfully written introduction and concise but instructive directions for its application. Entries are listed alphabetically; however, each of the nine themes is categorized in the bibliography, which is helpful for pursing further research on any one topic within the volume. Moreover, the top of each page is labeled according to its corresponding entry. Students in AP history and in Common Core history classes should find the volume to be an excellent and well-organized guide to the development of the U.S. in the 1950s, and an overall rich mosaic of invaluable knowledge. A useful addition would be more photographs than are currently present.—**Sheri Edwards**

182.   Robertson, Jr., James I. **Robert E. Lee: A Reference Guide to His Life and Works.** Lanham, Md., Rowman & Littlefield, 2019. 206p. maps. index. (Significant Figures in World History). $50.00; $47.50 (e-book). ISBN 13: 978-1-5381-1348-6; 978-1-5381-1349-3 (e-book).

The front matter of this title contains a preface, two Civil War-era maps, and a chronology that starts with Lee's birth in 1807 and ends (with the exception of four dates) with his death in 1870. In the introduction, the author states that this is intended as a historical encyclopedia and not a biography. The author has made every attempt to write the entries on family and friends, military career, education, upbringing, slavery, allegiance to Virginia, religious beliefs, presidency of Washington and Lee, and postwar efforts to reconcile the country from Lee's point of view and not through a 21st-century lens. The entries are arranged in an A-to-Z format, and the author makes use of *see* references. The bibliography is extensive by design. According to Robertson, it is the most comprehensive to date on Lee and its 382 entries are divided as follows: Lee's Writings, Lee Biographies, Personal Memoirs, Lieutenants and Opponents, Family and Friends, Military Studies, Inspirational Studies, and Related Studies. Indeed there are hundreds of sources, but the bibliography does not include digital resources, which will be missed by many readers. The author holds a PhD from Emory University and has served as both executive director of the U.S. Civil War Centennial Commission and as an active member of the Virginia Civil War Sesquicentennial Commission. This reference guide/encyclopedia may be most suitable for the circulating collection at a public library in search of a new source on Lee.—**ARBA Staff Reviewer**

183.   Springer, Paul J. **Propaganda from the American Civil War.** Santa Barbara, Calif., ABC-CLIO, 2019. 316p. illus. index. $94.00. ISBN 13: 978-1-4408-6443-8; 978-1-4408-6444-5 (e-book).

Paul J. Springer, Professor of Comparative Military Studies at the Air Command and Staff College whose publications include *9/11 and the War on Terror: A Documentary and Reference Guide and Encyclopedia of Cyber Warfare,* defines propaganda as a means "to frame and shape public debate" (p. xiii). The 112 examples of propaganda selected for this work represent an eclectic mix of mediums, including books, broadsides, letters, lithographs, pamphlets, poems, songs, and speeches. All illustrations are reproduced in black and white. Notable is the decision by the editor not to include newspaper articles, which can be easily located in other sources. Introducing each document is a header that identifies the author, date of publication, where written, and the document's significance. Each entry concludes with an analysis that describes the motivations behind the document and explorations of its impacts. The respective entries are organized into six chronologically arranged chapters. The first chapter covers 1839-1860. Subsequent chapters focus on each year of the conflict, except for the last, which spans 1865-1893. Interspersed throughout are sidebars examining topics like the Nullification Crisis of 1833, Fugitive Slave Act of 1850, and Andersonville. Also included is a detailed chronology on both the history of African slavery in North America, beginning in 1619, and key events during the Civil War. Concluding the reference are a bibliography and index. Libraries serving high school students and undergraduates should strongly consider acquiring this work as it conveniently packages a wide variety of resources that will be of use in disciplines as varied as art, history, music, poetry, and political science.—**John R. Burch Jr.**

184.   **A State-by-State History of Race and Racism in the United States.** Patricia Reid-Merritt, ed. Santa Barbara, Calif., Greenwood Press/ABC-CLIO, 2019. 2v. index. $198.00/set. ISBN 13: 978-1-4408-5600-6; 978-1-4408-5601-3 (e-book).

Reid-Merritt's collection is a timely contribution to the debate on race and racism in the United States. The essay writers are a diverse lot, ranging from academic sociologists and historians to undergraduate students. Each 12-25 page essay provides a chronology of important events, an historical narrative, and a brief biographical account of at least one individual involved in the state's race question. A short secondary bibliography concludes each essay, with a more extensive general secondary bibliography in Volume 2. Coverage per state is dependent on the significance of a particular group in that state's racial diversity—South Dakota focuses on Native Americans, Michigan on African Americans, etc.—but writers also touch on other groups (Hmong and Somali in Minnesota, for example) to a lesser degree. Out of necessity, given the potential length of entries devoted to in-depth analysis and discussion of race, coverage per group cannot go into detail, and patrons with a deeper knowledge of race within each state will note significant absences (the essay on Texas, for example, makes no mention of Barbara Jordan, Julian Castro, or contemporary political leadership in Houston, Dallas, or San Antonio but does highlight President Johnson and the hate crime attack on James Byrd, Jr., in 1998). As the set is designed for high school students, undergraduates, and general readers, most academic and public libraries will find the set a useful addition in developing more comprehensive collections on race and racism.—**Anthony J. Adam**

185. **This Is Who We Were: In the 1990s.** Amenia, N.Y., Grey House Publishing, 2017. 576p. illus. maps. index. $155.00. ISBN 13: 978-1-68217-379-4; 978-1-68217-380-0 (e-book).

This is Who We Were: In the 1990s is part of Grey House Publishing's This is Who We Were series. When we look at decades as periods of uniqueness in human history, one key element often discussed is how music defined that particular decade. The decade of the seventies was known as being the decade of Disco, the eighties saw the rise of Hair Metal Rock n Roll, and the nineties witnessed the emergence of Grunge and Hip Hop music. However, while music does play a huge element in our human cultural evolution, it is not the only thing that defines or shapes any one decade. The nineties was a decade of relative peace and prosperity. The Cold War officially ended with the fall of the Soviet Union on Christmas Day 1991, and it clearly seemed a new era was born. This volume offers insight into the decade that was the 1990s by looking at America through the lens of class, occupation, or social cause for all regions of the United States. The volume provides a comprehensive look at the decade in five sections: Profiles, Historical Snapshots, Economy of the Times, All Around Us, and Census Data. The Profiles section is arranged in 3 categories: Life at Home; Life at Work; and Life in the Community. The section profiles 28 people, including a cell phone entrepreneur, an immigrant worker and striker, a high school soccer player and coach, and a hydrogen fuel cell visionary, among others. What really makes this section come alive is the original photographs and advertisements. The Historical Snapshots section is broken down into 3 areas: early 1990s, mid-1990s, and late 1990s. The section on the economy gets down to the nuts and bolts of what things cost and what people earned. The section All Around Us presents the decade through 50 primary documents. Last but surely not least in value is the section on Census Data. All data comes from the 2000 U.S. Census, broken down by state; it includes 27 census briefs and 3 special reports. While census data can be found in the official governmental record, the ability to have it in the same volume as the 28 profiles helps the researcher to delve deeper. This is a very useful way to open up the decade up to the reader regardless of their level and ability in the research process. The quality of the work is well crafted and cited. Overall this work is a very useful tool in any reference collection. It will provide more than just a gentle stroll down memory lane. Whether one is unable to remember the 1990s or was born long after the end of the Soviet Union, *This Is Who We Were: In the 1990s* is a volume you will want to add to your collection.—**Lawrence Joseph Mello**

186.   **This Is Who We Were: In the 2000s.** Amenia, N.Y., Grey House Publishing, 2018. 513p. illus. index. $160.00. ISBN 13: 978-1-68217-716-7; 978-1-68217-717-4 (e-book).

This book gives readers a look at the 2000s from several different perspectives. The book begins with a short introduction that stresses the pivotal role of the 9/11 terrorist attacks in shaping the decade. This is followed by a section that profiles 27 people, including the last known survivor from the south tower of the World Trade Center, a special forces sergeant in the war in Afghanistan, a waitress, a healer, a heavy machinery operator, a girls basketball coach, an Irish immigrant and researcher, and a surfer and surfboard manufacturer. The profiles include various tools that maintain reader interest. At the end of the story of the World Trade Center terror attack survivor, for example, there are four textboxes that contain the final words of four people who perished. Likewise, the profile of the basketball coach concludes with a timeline related to Title IX. Following this section are 11 pages of bullet point highlights from the early, mid, and late part of the 2000s. These are not contextualized but offer interesting facts. The third section, Economy of the Times, offers lots of data to those looking for things like annual income for roofers, nurses, dentists, architects, and others in 2002, 2005, and 2008, respectively. Readers can also find the prices of particular items like sleeping bags, compasses, and beach towels throughout the decade. The fourth section is comprised of 50 reprinted (original) articles—book excerpts speeches, articles, advertising copy—from *The Washington Post, Time, Wikinews,* and other sources. Articles include the date of publication. The last section reproduces statistical data from the 2010 U.S. Census and State-by-State Comparative Tables from 2000, 2010, and 2016. Here readers can find statistics on Hispanic, white, black, rural, and foreign-born residents, maps, statistics on homeownership, and profiles for every state that feature black-and-white, easy-to-read maps. A brief list of suggested further readings and a subject index conclude the book. While much of this information can be found in other places, this volume puts it together in one digestible volume. Recommended.—**ARBA Staff Reviewer**

187.   Wilson, Jamie J. **The Black Panther Party.** Santa Barbara, Calif., Greenwood Press/ABC-CLIO, 2018. 135p. illus. index. (Guides to Subcultures and Countercultures). $39.00. ISBN 13: 978-0-313-39253-5; 978-0-313-39254-2 (e-book).

Wilson, author of *The Black Panther Movement In Connecticut* (2014), here compiles a brief guide for general readers and students to the party's activities during its prominence in the mid-1960s through the 1970s. A timeline gives significant dates in the party's history, followed by five brief chapters overviewing regional and cultural differences. Biographies of Huey P. Newton, Eldridge Cleaver, and Bobby Seale are sketched, along with roughly thirty pages of primary documents (many from FBI sources) and a good secondary bibliography. Although useful as an introductory guide, this slim volume would benefit greatly from additional biographical sketches and especially more primary documents, as these are difficult to obtain for most small-to-medium sized libraries. However, the series' format apparently precludes larger numbers of documents, and Wilson has carefully chosen those he feels most important to understanding the party relevance. For additional primary documents, students should refer to Philip Foner's *The Black Panthers Speak,* 2nd ed (Da Capo, 2002), although Wilson's is the only "reference" source on the market and is thus a useful addition to all African American and cultural history collections.—**Anthony J. Adam**

African History

Rwanda

188. **Rwandan Genocide: The Essential Reference Guide.** Alexis Herr, ed. Santa Barbara, Calif., ABC-CLIO, 2018. 320p. illus. index. $94.00. ISBN 13: 978-1-4408-5560-3; 978-1-4408-5561-0 (e-book).

Rwandan Genocide: The Essential Reference Guide is both an extremely relevant and timely addition to the field of Holocaust and Genocide studies. The producer of this publication, ABC-CLIO, also has reference titles on the Bosnian and the Armenian genocides. The editor and contributors not only explore the genocide but also the events that led up to the atrocity and its aftermath. The book, edited by Holocaust scholar Alexis Herr, is a useful entry-level reference resource guide for undergraduate students. With over 100 concise entries, organized A to Z, the book's strength is found in its overall organization. The introductory essays provide a brief overview to contextualize the 1994 genocide along with essays discussing the causes, consequences, perpetrators, victims, bystanders, and international relations. The book provides an extensive index to assist in finding names or ancillary topics not provided in the list of entries at the beginning of the book. Along with the extensive indexing, researchers will find useful provision of primary documents, a thin but useful bibliography, a section dedicated to a pro-and-con debate style discussion of research topics, and a chronology. There is much to like about this volume; however, it also has its limitations. Of its 14 contributors there isn't a single Rwandan or African contributor. What also immediately stands out about the volume is the absence of maps and graphics. There are no maps of the continent, the region of East Africa, or Rwanda to visually assist in situating the Rwandan conflict. And, although the volume presents the material very well, there are some obvious omissions from the entries such as genocide memorial sites, local organizations, and an in-depth discussion of cultural production as it relates to the genocide. In all, I think entry-level undergraduate students will find the volume useful despite its limitations.—**Erik Ponder**

Ancient History

Dictionaries and Encyclopedias

189. Ermatinger, James W. **The Roman Empire: A Historical Encyclopedia.** Santa Barbara, Calif., ABC-CLIO, 2018. 2v. illus. index. (Empires of the World). $182.00/set. ISBN 13: 978-1-4408-3808-8; 978-1-4408-3809-5 (e-book).

Part of the Empires of the World series—other titles in the series are *The Ottoman Empire and The Mongol Empire*—this is a guide to various topics associated with the Roman Empire (31 BCE-476 CE), such as cities, government and politics, groups and organizations, individuals, institutions, key events, military, and objects and artifacts. Each area has an overview essay, topics ranging in length from a few paragraphs to three pages of text, arranged alphabetically, and a bibliography of two or three items. *See also* references lead to similar items. There is an introduction giving an outline of Roman imperial history, a chronology, a collection of forty-four "primary" documents, a selected bibliography of about 120 items, and a subject index. There are a few dozen black-and-white illustrations including a map. James W. Ermatinger is currently dean of the College of Liberal Arts and Sciences and professor of history at the University of Illinois-Springfield.

This set can supplement Matthew Bunsen's *Encyclopedia of Ancient Rome* (Facts on File, 2012). The text is accessible to high school students and the adult public, and it seems accurate. Browsers can pick up quite a bit of information on the Roman Empire, but the set is a luxury item for all but large public and academic libraries given that preimperial Roman history is not included.—**Jonathan F. Husband**

Digital Resources

190. **The Badian Collection. https://coins.libraries.rutgers.edu/romancoins.** [Website] Free. Date reviewed: 2018.

This site holds the digital version of the Ernst Badian Collection of Roman Republican Coins from Rutgers University. Holding over 1,200 coins, the collection traces the evolution of coinage within the republic via its display of bronze, silver, and gold pieces reflecting the influence of an array of emperors, events, and other notable figures. From the homepage, users can Search the Collection using selected fields or Browse the Collection from the bar at the top. Within the database, users can examine the entire collection by relevance or date, or group coins by name, region, denomination, and more. Users can generally examine several images of each coin, alongside such information as Moneyer, Mint Date, Denomination, Material, Authority, Weight, Method of Manufacture, and Period of Use. There will also be a description of Obverse and Reverse Type, and a series of Subject links that reference images on the coin, from gods to grains and much more. Under Resources, users will find a generous bibliography covering technical and historical subjects related to coinage. Other features are in development, including tutorials, lesson plans, a 360 degree viewing tool, and the ability to curate and annotate subcollections. The compact collection of coins provides a broad understanding of the cares and concerns of the noble classes. It is a good starting point for further research and would appeal to a range of scholars and collectors from young to old.—**ARBA Staff Reviewer**

191. **Stanford Geospatial Network Model of the Roman World http://orbis. stanford.edu/.** [Website] Free. Date reviewed: 2019.

This site offers a geospatial database that demonstrates the time and financial cost of Roman expansion throughout the ancient world. The model considers land and water routes, modes of transport, weather, terrain, and other factors as it invites users to consider discrete segments of Roman movement within their larger geographical achievements. To the left of the map, users choose parameters to employ in determining expenses between selected Roman settlements (e.g., Roma and Constantinopolis), such as departing month/ season and priority (fastest, shortest, or cheapest route). Users will also consider various Network Modes (road, river, coastal, or open sea) and transport capabilities (oxcart, foot, rapid military march, etc.). Calculate Route will determine the marked route on the map, which can be manipulated to display Terrain, settlement Sites, Paths, Regions, and more, and will provide a descriptive summary of trip length (time and distance) and cost in denarii, alongside other information. Users can also Calculate Network (via Network tab) to determine the distance/time between a user's chosen starting site and other main locations throughout the empire, or Calculate Flow (via the Flow tab) to see the most efficient segments between a user's base site and others. The generous capabilities of the model (users can employ a tutorial as they proceed throughout the database) create optimal research possibilities (the Research link under the About tab provides a few examples) that would appeal to students, educators, and anyone interested in the ancient world.—**ARBA Staff Reviewer**

Asian History

Dictionaries and Encyclopedias

192.   Buell, Paul D., and Francesca Fiaschetti. **Historical Dictionary of the Mongol World Empire.** 2d ed. Lanham, Md., Rowman & Littlefield, 2018. 388p. maps. (Historical Dictionaries of Ancient Civilizations and Historical Eras). $100.00; $95.00 (e-book). ISBN 13: 978-1-5381-1136-9; 978-1-5381-1137-6 (e-book).

Part of the Historical Dictionaries of Ancient Civilizations and Historical Eras series from Rowman & Littlefield, this second edition (see ARBA 2004, entry 462) focuses on one of the greatest empires in history, the Mongols. Besides the dictionary, which is a major accomplishment in itself, there is much here that makes it a unique reference work. Starting with the maps, dates of Chinese dynasties and states, and chronology, the introduction features seven essays on various dynasties and their accomplishments and rulers during the Mongol Empire: Mongolia before the Empire (to 1206), the Mongol Empire (1206-1260), Qanate China (1260-1368), The Golden Horde (1235-1502), Ca'adai Ulus and Qaidu (1260-1338), Ilqanate (1260-1356), and Epilogue: Mongols and the outside world. Three appendixes feature the Mongolian scripts, a glossary of Mongolian words and terms, and selected recipes from the Yinshan Zhengyao (1330). The extensive bibliography that is a feature of this series that never fails to impress. This book should be a valuable resource for any academic institution's reference shelf.—**Bradford Lee Eden**

European History

Great Britain

193.   **The British Empire: A Historical Encyclopedia.** Mark Doyle, ed. Santa Barbara, Calif., ABC-CLIO, 2018. 2v. illus. maps. index. (Empires of the World). $198.00/set. ISBN 13: 978-1-4408-4197-2; 978-1-4408-4198-9 (e-book).

At the close of the 20th century, Great Britain handed over sovereignty of Hong Kong to China, signaling the symbolic end of the British Empire that had ruled large parts of the globe in the 19th and 20th centuries. ABC-CLIO's new installment in its Empires of the World series, *The British Empire: A Historical Encyclopedia,* explores the meaning of this empire some 20 years after its final demise. The 2-volume set of over 200 articles written by 76 contributors presents the difficult history of British imperialism and colonialism, with one aim being to describe the exchange of ideas from "colonizer to colonized and back again," but no less important the aim to present the complexity of empire, imperialism, colonialism, and related events. In the preface, Editor Mark Doyle suggests a modest scope, namely to offer a representative sample of the "most interesting facets" of the British Empire. The proposed audience of high school and college students, to which I would add public library communities, will learn about the more traditional lines of inquiry, (e.g., political and military), as well as history from below, or history from marginalized people groups. The publisher's site states that the text "avoids simplistic assessments of British imperialism as merely 'good' or 'bad,' emanating an objectivity that enables readers to develop their own ideas about the nature of the empire." The introduction mirrors this objective by encouraging the reader to reject easy answers in favor of new understanding, knowledge, and scholarship.

As with any reference work, the reader will need to devote some time to the structure of this encyclopedia. Doyle aids this by outlining the book's features in the preface. For optimal use, readers should first read the short overview of British imperial history in the introduction. After glancing over the broad themes, events, people, and ideas, readers should study the table of contents for how the two-volume set is arranged and organized. Alphabetical entries have been organized into eight categories, including: Government and Politics (31 entries); Organization and Administration (27 entries); Groups and Organizations (29 entries); Individuals (30 entries) in Volume I and Key Events (30 entries); Military (30 entries); Objects and Artifacts (19 entries); and Key Places (20 entries) in Volume II. A 37-page Index printed in both volumes provides an additional layer of access by allowing the reader to look for names, places, and other key terms that could be mentioned in any of these categories as well as in the sidebars. Other helpful features include a 6-page chronology listing events from 1497 to 1997; 42 primary documents (1584-1963); a listing of British Sovereigns (1509-present) and Prime Ministers; and a 4-page select Bibliography. Typical entries are about 2-3 pages, including references and a "Further Reading" section. Entries may also have a photograph or sidebar elucidating the content.

Recommended for high school, college, and public libraries.—**Amy Koehler**

194.   Frost, Ginger S. **The Victorian World: Facts and Fictions.** Santa Barbara, Calif., ABC-CLIO, 2018. 227p. index. (Historical Facts and Fictions). $61.00. ISBN 13: 978-1-4408-5590-0; 978-1-4408-5591-7 (e-book).

The nine chapters in the latest volume in ABC-CLIO's Historical Facts and Fictions series examine topics in social history (focusing on women and families), cultural issues, and economic/political issues. The chapters are arranged identically: "What People Think Happened," "How the Story Became Popular," several primary documents, then "What Really Happened," more primary documents, and a "Further Reading" list. The chapters are clearly presented, exploring to what degree the stereotypes of Victorian England were true. Topics are diverse: sexual behavior, lack of a sense of humor, diplomatic isolation, a society riddled with crime, among others. The primary sources are quite varied as well: trial reports from *The Times* and other newspapers, texts by William Thackeray and Charles Dickens, divorce petitions, crime reports, excerpts of speeches that were later published, and numerous texts by female writers throughout the period. Each primary text is preceded by a brief introduction which situates it in its social and political context.

Any library with readers interested in the world of 19th-century Great Britain should certainly consider adding this book to their collection. Its organization and clarity will appeal to a wide range of readers.—**Mark Schumacher**

195. **Medieval Murder Map. https://www.vrc.crim.cam.ac.uk/vrcresearch/london-medieval-murder-map.** [Website] Free. Date reviewed: 2018.

Produced by Professor Manuel Eisner of the Violence Research Centre at the University of Cambridge, this interactive map of murders in medieval London pinpoints the location of 142 murders within the City of London in the first half of the 14th century. Each clickable pin opens to tell the story of the murder committed at the site based on the original records of inquests held by the coroner in front of a jury drawn from the free men of the ward in which the murder occurred or from the three neighboring wards. Researchers can use one of two maps, the Braun-Hodenberg Map of 1572 or a London map from approximately 1270. Users can also filter results by gender, location of the crime, the weapon used, and whether the crime took place in a public or private space. The site provides good contextualizing data in "The Historical Background" link, which discusses how violent medieval London was and when, where, and how murders were committed. Most murders took place in public commercial areas, most murderers were men, and the most popular weapon was a long knife. There is also information about the population of London at this time, the spatial organization of the city, markets, occupations and guilds, and the Inns of Court. The information in this database is curated, reliable, and easy to access.—**ARBA Staff Reviewer**

196. **Welsh Tithe Maps. Https://places.library.wales.** [Website] Free. Date reviewed: 2018

This site helps users find historical records related to places in Wales, the United Kingdom. The site layers data from 19th-century tithe maps (which helped administer land-use payments) over a modern geographic interface to create a more detailed representation of Wales over time. Users can fit 19th-century landowner, land occupier, parish, and land use information amidst modern expressways, golf courses, business districts, and more. Users can separately view original tithe maps and affiliated documents. From the homepage, the Search option allows users to scroll through a display of applicable records with reference to map location. The Find a Place option asks users to type in the name of a known location—village, city, town, etc.—to display a satellite, modern, or historical (1888-1913) base map pinned by apportionment information. Clicking on a pin allows users to access available documents (historical apportionment map, register) and their metadata which may include author, date, title, scale, description, or other information. Users can zoom in and out, measure distances between land apportionments, and identify land by use (arable, hay, garden, wood, bog, etc.), among other options. The documents and maps are a good historical, geographical, and genealogical reference for users interested in Wales.—**ARBA Staff Reviewer**

Ireland

197.   **Divided Society: Northern Ireland 1990-1998 https://www.dividedsociety.org/.** [Website] Price negotiated by site. Date reviewed: 2019.

This site holds the digital portion of the Northern Ireland Political Collection, which has amassed thousands of documents related to the late-20th-century conflict between Irish Nationalists and Unionists in Northern Ireland. It includes roughly 500 periodical titles, 800 political posters, and a good variety of other materials and resources. It is important to note that for users outside of the United Kingdom and Ireland, the site charges an institutional and individual subscription fee. However, while many items may not be closely examined, there are other materials general users can explore, along with previews of premium items. Scrolling through the homepage affords a good overview of site contents and structure. Users can click on a specific link: Journals, Posters, Audio, Videos, Toolkits, or Essays to access available materials (or a preview of them if one has not subscribed). Users can also access them via the Explore or Outreach tabs at the top of the homepage. Journals reflect a range of issues related to the conflict as well as a range of perspectives. General users can preview the covers of 5 of them, including *Police Beat* and *Ulster Nation.* Posters share 8 diverse examples from the handmade to the professional. General users can also listen to 25 Audio interviews capturing various personal recollections of the conflict and peace process, and view 6 Toolkits which draw from the larger archive to provide discussion questions, etc., on the 1994 Ceasefire, The Referendum, and more. Under the Explore tab, general users can also examine lists of 24 Themes, over 3,000 Topics, and nearly 2,000 People Mentioned within the greater collection. In addition to the full digital archive, subscribers can access ten scholarly essays on various subjects such as "Religion in Northern Ireland's Conflict and Peace" or "The Good Friday Agreement." While general users have only limited access to the materials, the site nonetheless offers a good sense of the quality and capabilities of the greater collection. Users can make a well-informed decision regarding subscription.—**ARBA Staff Reviewer**

198.   **Justice for Magdalenes. http://jfmresearch.com.** [Website] Free. Date reviewed: 2019.

This site works as a clearinghouse for information related to the Magdalene Laundries, the institution and rehabilitation program that housed "fallen" or otherwise destitute women and girls in Ireland for over two centuries, but has only recently been exposed as abusive and deadly. Since 2003, advocates have successfully forced an apology from the Irish government. With more work to be done in regards to compensation, this site offers valuable research data and tools that serve to educate the public about the Magdalene Laundries and their legacy. From the homepage, users can choose from a variety of tabs to access oral histories, educational materials, essays, reports, site descriptions, and more. The Preserving Magdalene History tab provides an excellent introduction to the Magdalene Laundries story, describing the people involved, the conditions within the laundries, and more. There are also brief essays on each of the Magdalene Laundry sites throughout Ireland, including Galway, Limerick, Peacock Lane, Donnybrook, and others. The Magdalene Oral History Project holds eighty-four audio files from Magdalene Laundry survivors, their relatives, members of religious orders, key informants, activists, and others. Accompanying metadata may include interview date, interviewee status, transcript link, or keyword. The Magdalene Names Project, a work in progress, gathers information about the women and girls incarcerated in the Magdalene Laundries. Within its descriptive essay, users can follow the here link to a Map of Magdalene Laundries and Graves which pins known locations across the Ireland. A table organizes available information for each of the laundries, including digitized census images and a Names Database gleaned from electoral registers. Clicking on the name of the graveyard reveals its Google map location. Under the JFMR Publications tab users will find links to documents related to the justice project including proposed legislation, briefing notes, press releases. Human Rights submissions, a report on state involvement in the Magdalene Laundries, and more. Educational Resources include a list of related links, academic and newspaper articles, videos , and other information. The site would appeal across a number of academic disciplines, including social justice, Irish history, religious studies, and more.—**ARBA Staff Reviewer**

Poland

199. Biskupski, M. B. B. **The History of Poland.** 2d ed. Santa Barbara, Calif., Greenwood Press/ABC-CLIO, 2018. 290p. illus. maps. index. (The Greenwood Histories of the Modern Nations). $63.00. ISBN 13: 978-1-4408-6225-0; 978-1-4408-6226-7 (e-book).

Published as a part of The Greenwood Histories of the Modern Nations series and written to inform Americans, interested students, laypeople, and even specialists, the second edition of *The History of Poland* tells the story of Poland through an engaging and multistranded narrative. Indeed, it wouldn't be difficult for the reader to imagine listening to the words of its author, M. B. B. Biskupski, a subject expert who aims in this volume to provide a critical interpretation of Poland's past, a task that encompasses evaluating its distinctive culture, its imagination and historical themes, and thoughts on the security of its present and future. Biskupski's prose is flowing and lucid, much like a lecture in form. He raises questions and writes provocatively on controversial subjects within the scholarship. To enter into these controversies, the reader is sometimes given an endnote but these are used sparingly. Instead, the curious should refer to the bibliographic essay for "further reading." Still, the book is not concise in every section. In this edition the author has intentionally devoted more words and pages to the 20th and 21st centuries than in earlier editions; and he has done so in the hopes that the reader will understand the issues of Poland's present and future.

All books published in this series include a bird's-eye-view introduction of the nation in question. Readers can skim these pages to learn more about Poland's geography, population, political system, economy, geopolitics, and cultural life. This volume also provides a helpful list of abbreviations, a timeline covering events from the 10th century to the present, 2 maps, a select biographical dictionary of notable people, a glossary, bibliographic essay, and index. *The History of Poland* is recommended for anyone interested in the history and future concerns of Poland.—**Amy Koehler**

Spain

200.   **Innovation and Human Rights: List of Victims of Spanish Civil War and Franco https://ihr.world/en/.** [Website] Free. Date reviewed: 2019.

The Spanish Civil War (1936-1939) often gets overlooked compared to the other devastating conflicts of the 20th century, but for many it is no less poignant. This project, translatable into English and French from the original Spanish, consolidates data on casualties, the missing, and other victims of the Spanish Civil War which, while helping clarify the historical record, may also work to offer descendants and others a greater sense of understanding. Simply structured, the site presents a list of Spanish Civil War victim names, accessible by clicking the blue Search button in the center of the homepage. Users can also type a name above the button, or scroll down the page to examine by Dataset or Author. The list is alphabetized by last name, which is presented alongside its data source. Selecting a name from the list accesses available information, which may include as much as place of death or disappearance, place of burial, and date of death or disappearance, or as little as a record number. There may also be a list of related documents (i.e., similarly named victims) and references. Clicking on the dataset underneath references links to information regarding the source and location of the data, which may illuminate more historical detail such as number of associated files, source description, etc. For example, Antoni Alcalá Reyes is a name gathered from the Register of Burials in the Cemetary of Cambrils, kept in the archive of the church of Santa Maria de Cambrils. This register recorded those who died in a field hospital nearby. The text-only website is rather bare, with no images throughout its pages. However, the effect is that of a memorial, where one can linger over the mere existence of a name.—**ARBA Staff Reviewer**

Latin America and the Caribbean

Venezuela

201.   Tarver, H. Micheal. **The History of Venezuela.** 2d ed. Santa Barbara, Calif., Greenwood Press/ABC-CLIO, 2018. 248p. index. (The Greenwood Histories of the Modern Nations). $63.00. ISBN 13: 978-1-4408-5773-7; 978-1-4408-5774-4 (e-book).

The first edition of this title focused primarily on the political and economic history of Venezuela from the arrival of the Spanish to 2005, which marked the sixth year of Hugo Chávez Frías' presidency (see ARBA 2006, entry 109). This new edition by H. Micheal Tarver, Professor of History at Arkansas Tech University, retains eleven chapters from its initial incarnation. The new content is encapsulated in three chapters: "The Age of Chavismo, 1999-2013"; "The Socialist Collapse, 2013-2018"; and "An Uncertain Future." Although coverage is extended to 2018, the narrative of Nicolás Maduro's catastrophic presidency does not adequately convey the humanitarian crisis presently unfolding in the country. Hyperinflation has resulted in poverty rates soaring, much of the populace is malnourished due to chronic food shortages, and diseases are rampant due in part to a lack of basic medicines and medical supplies. In response, hundreds of thousands of

Venezuelans have fled to neighboring countries like Brazil and Columbia. Although the rapidly expanding refugee population is a major contributor to regional instability, that issue in not addressed because it is occurring outside of Venezuela's borders. Public and school libraries should strongly consider acquiring this survey as it provides background information on an international calamity that is getting significant coverage from media outlets around the world.—**John R. Burch Jr.**

Middle Eastern History

General Works

202.   **Defining Documents in World History: The Middle East.** Michael Shally-Jensen, ed. Hackensack, N.J., Salem Press, 2018. 2v. illus. maps. index. $295.00/set. ISBN 13: 978-1-68217-702-0; 978-1-68217-703-7 (e-book).

This latest installment in the Defining Documents in World History series starts with a publisher's note, an introduction, and a list of contributors. The second volume concludes with a chronological list of entries, a list of web resources, a bibliography, and an index. The material is organized in four parts: Early, Medieval, and Early Modern History; Ottoman Endurance and Collapse; Twentieth-Century Troubles; and Recent Realities. *The Middle East* includes fifty-seven documents (either excerpts or a whole) and each is contextualized by a summary overview, defining moment, author biography, document analysis, and essential themes.

There are first-hand accounts, letters, travel accounts, imperial decrees, speeches, and treaties. Among the documents featured are: an account of the revolt of the Maccabees and Judean independence; a historical account of the capture of Jerusalem in 1099; a letter from Pliny the Younger to Emperor Trajan regarding the best way to treat Christians in Bithynia (in modern-day Turkey); the peace treaty that ended the Russo-Turkish War of 1768-74; an excerpt of Winston Churchill's book on the Battle of Omdurman in Sudan; and George W. Bush's 2003 speech to the country on military operations in Iraq. The writing is accessible to high school and college students and the entries are easy to follow. Sections are clearly labeled, documents are set in shaded text boxes, and entries include suggestions for further reading. Black-and-white illustrations are sprinkled throughout. Helpfully, documents include glossaries of terms or people that may be unfamiliar to students: kunya, zunar, antiphonal, Aquila, firman, Clauzel, etc. Recommended for public and school libraries.—**ARBA Staff Reviewer**

Syria

203.   Shoup, John A. **The History of Syria.** Santa Barbara, Calif., Greenwood Press/ABC-CLIO, 2018. 222p. illus. maps. index. (The Greenwood Histories of the Modern Nations). $63.00. ISBN 13: 978-1-4408-5834-5; 978-1-4408-5835-2 (e-book).

Most histories of Syria focus on the period after the Sykes-Picot Agreement. However, Syria has a rich history going all the way back to ancient times (before the Babylonians).

Its history can be divided into periods of ancient antiquity, Greco-Roman, Byzantium, Arab, Ottoman, World War I, World War II, and the Assad regimes. Only Paton's and Hitti's works on Syrian history (published in 1901 and 1955, respectively) substantially cover the period before World War I.

Greenwood's Histories of Modern Nations series has added *The History of Syria* to its single-volume works covering almost 50 countries. Two-thirds of the historical narrative is devoted to pre-World War I Syrian history. Like other volumes in this series, it has a timeline of events; the main portion is a succinct, well-written, and easy-to-understand chronological history from antiquity to contemporary times. This is followed by thumbnail sketches of about 50 notable Syrians. This is intended as an introductory work. Hence, it has a Bibliographic Essay section which provides an outline of references that pertain to historical periods. Most of the references are books in print, and can be easily accessed by general readers. The period covering contemporary times also includes some web resources.

For a work that covers as much breadth as this book covers, it cannot go beyond an outline of events and people. As such, it is an excellent introduction to Syrian history, and provides the tools needed for further research. Recommended as supplementary material for high school and introductory college-level courses. Also recommended for general readers wishing to get an introduction in Syrian history.—**Muhammed Hassanali**

World History

Biography

204.   **Great Lives from History: The 21st Century.** Hackensack, N.J., Salem Press, 2017. 3v. illus. index. $395.00/set. ISBN 13: 978-1-68217-589-7.

This installment in the Great Lives from History series contains biographies of 359 notable individuals, covering 2000-2017. The book includes "figures important to the historical record" of major events at the beginning of the 21st century as well as major figures from the arts and culture. Each entry is arranged within sections: Early Life; Life's Work (how the individual gained recognition); significance which "offers an overview of the importance of the individual's accomplishments and discovers the value in studying him or her"; and Further Reading, containing a brief bibliography. Some biographies include sidebars and a photograph of the individual. The entries cover 19 categories: Activism, Books and Ideas, Business, Computers and Information Technology, Diplomacy, Film and Television, International Government and Politics, U.S. Government and Politics, Journalism, Law, Literature, The Middle East, Music, Philosophy, Social Issues, Sports, Terrorism, and Visual Art. Among those profiled are: Maya Angelou, Joe Biden, Osama Bin Laden, Tony Blair, Fidel Castro, Johnny Depp, Donald Trump, Kobe Bryant, Bill Gates, Oprah Winfrey, Mark Zuckerberg, Michelle Obama, and Jane Goodall. Also included is an index of names, topics, organizations, and publications. Entries are listed alphabetically in the main section and are also grouped by the 19 categories mentioned previously; for instance, in sports among those listed are Kobe Bryant, Tom Brady, and Serena Williams. This volume is highly recommended for "quick reference" and as a starting point for a research paper on the life and accomplishments of a noted individual. It is recommended to academic and public libraries and should prove invaluable to students and faculty of universities and to anybody interested in learning more about a public figure.—**Lucy Heckman**

Chronology

205. **Timelines of History.** 2d ed. New York, DK Publishing, 2018. 512p. illus. maps. index. $27.99pa. ISBN 13: 978-1-4654-7002-7.

Following a foreword by David Parrott, University of Oxford, this 2d edition of *Timelines of History* is comprised of 7 chapters that together include timelines from 8MYA to 2017. This book is more than a series of timelines, as it provides a political, military, cultural, social, and economic narrative enlivened by hundreds of color photographs as well as color maps, graphs, and charts in addition to the timelines that run across the top and bottom of the pages. One strength of the book is that it weaves together worldwide historical strands. For the years 1721-1722, for example, readers learn that the Treaty of Nystand ended the Great Northern War between Sweden and Russia; that Dutch explorer Jacob Roggeveen stumbled on Easter Island, the Society Islands, and Samoa while searching for Terra Australis; and that the Safavid dynasty of Persia was deposed by Independent Afghans. In the years just following, 1723-1724, King Agadja in Dahomey (now Republic of Benin) conquered neighboring Allada to provide slaves for Europeans and the Indian state of Qudh achieved independence. The final portion of the book provides a chronological directory subdivided by Rulers and Leaders, History in Figures, Wars, Explorers, Inventions and Discoveries, Philosophy and Religion, Culture and Learning, Oldest Universities, Disasters, and Famines and Plagues. This is followed by a glossary and an index. This is recommended for the adult nonfiction, circulating collections of public libraries, particularly in light of the price tag.—**ARBA Staff Reviewer**

Dictionaries and Encyclopedias

206. **The United States Holocaust Memorial Museum Encyclopedia of Camps and Ghettos. Volume III: Camps and Ghettos under European Regimes Aligned with Nazi Germany.** Geoffrey P. Megargee, Joseph R. White, and Mel Hecker, eds. Bloomington, Ind., Indiana University Press, 2018. 990p. illus. maps. index. $150.00. ISBN 13: 978-0-253-02373-5; 978-0-253-02386-5 (e-book).

The third volume in this encyclopedia of camps and ghettos from the United States Holocaust Memorial Museum deals with camps run by states that were allies of and collaborators with Nazi Germany. It provides readers with information about the extent of civilian and military cooperation in carrying out Hitler's plan. A group of more than forty international contributors wrote over seven hundred articles covering sites under the control of ten countries. Black-and white illustrations and detailed maps help readers locate these sites.

The book is organized alphabetically by country. Each section begins with an introduction that provides an overview of the country's involvement with the war efforts.

Alphabetical entries for individual camps and ghettos follow. The entries discuss the history of the camp, the types of prisoners there, the type of labor performed, which military units were involved, and whether the inmates were killed. They also provide information about prisoner culture, resistance and/or escapes, when and how the site was dissolved, and whether any personnel were tried for war crimes. All entries are signed. There are notes and source lists as well. A list of abbreviations will help users locate source materials since the archives are abbreviated in the notes.

A list of approximate rank equivalents is useful for researchers who want to understand the military groups running the camps. There are separate indexes for personal names, places, and organizations and enterprises as well.

This is a very useful resource for anyone doing Holocaust research. It provides information that is difficult to find and makes it accessible. It also lays a foundation for further research.—**Barbara M. Bibel**

207. **The World's Oceans: Geography, History, and Environment.** Rainer F. Buschmann and Lance Nolde, eds. Santa Barbara, Calif., ABC-CLIO, 2018. 434p. illus. maps. index. $94.00. ISBN 13: 978-1-4408-4351-8; 978-1-4408-4352-5 (e-book).

The world's oceans cover over seventy percent of the earth's surface, but little has been written about their history in relation to the world. *The World's Oceans* seeks to change that by gathering together the disciplines of history, oceanography, anthropology, geography, transportation, linguistics, and many others. This encyclopedia fills a blank spot in bringing together information on the importance of the oceans to world history and to the development of humanity. The work is organized into two primary sections: thematic essays and topical entries. The thematic essays are longer in nature and provide a broad historical overview of the oceans and their importance to human development. The topical entries provide a more detailed look at specific topics identified in the thematic essays. The thematic essays average fifteen to twenty pages in length while most of the topical entries are three to five pages. Bibliographies for further reading appear at the end of each of the thematic essays and the topical entries; there is also a general bibliography at the end of the work. Cross-references at the end of entries are useful to readers. Black-and-white photographs and maps throughout provide a visual connection with the text and increase the appeal of the volume. An extensive index of names and subjects completes the volume.

The World's Oceans: Geography, History, and Environment will be of interest in all types of libraries—public, academic, high school—for its accessible text and its content. A sturdy hardcover binding will stand up well to repeated use by patrons. The work is probably best placed in the circulating collection, due the length of the essays and the interconnectedness of the topics explored in the two sections.—**Gregory Curtis**

Digital Resources

208. **Age of Exploration. http://www.exploration.amdigital.co.uk/.** [Website] Chicago, Adam Matthew Digital, 2018. Price negotiated by site. Date reviewed: 2018

This collection, focused broadly on exploration by sea, provides a sampling of documents over a half-millennia of discovery, collected from a dozen disparate libraries.

Given the size of the subject, one can hardly expect an exhaustive resource, but this assemblage seems remarkably scattershot: correspondence from 19th-century Arctic expeditions, ephemera related to initial circumnavigations of the globe and of Australia, early-20th-century films that describe ship life, 16th-century fragmentary documents related to English exploration, and other miscellanea. While there is little to hold these items together, the standard Adam Matthew interface does sort documents into several themes, such as "Competition," "New Territories," "Ships & Provisions," "Navigation, Scientific Observations & Instruments," and several others. The database offers a particularly effective interactive map feature, a media gallery, two video interviews with prominent maritime historians, and more. Specialized "expedition" and "ship" directories are useful, though the ship list is limited to a few resource types; it does not include images of those ships that appear elsewhere here. Unfortunately, Adam Matthew did not use their proprietary Handwritten Text Recognition technology on the included manuscripts. To be sure, any organized collection of documents related to maritime history is a useful start. While the content is interesting and might be helpful, its random nature is quite evident.—**Peter H. McCracken**

209.   **Colonial North America http://colonialnorthamerica.library.harvard.edu/ spotlight/can.** [Website] Free. Date reviewed: 2019.
     This digital collection organizes thousands of pages of materials regarding colonial North America, including maps, correspondence, diaries, financial documents, and more. From this page, users can conduct a search from the prominent bar or scroll down through the page to view featured items or curated exhibits. Users can alternatively access a menu on the side of the page from which they can Browse the entire digital collection. Materials are organized by broad category: Women, The Sea, Maps, Families, Science, and Law. Under each category, materials are displayed in a gallery of thumbnail images accompanied by title and attribution. Users can bookmark the gallery display for reference. Clicking on an item opens a viewer which users can manipulate to enlarge the item, turn pages, download, and more. Information accompanying the item may include a list of related Subjects, Content Notes, Biographical Notes, and identifying information such as Origin, Description, Type, and Date. Items in the collection are diverse, and include student notes from medical lectures, regional and local maps, astronomical tables, and papers of Samuel Ward and Julia Rush Cutler Ward, parents of Julia who grew up to pen "The Battle Hymn of the Republic." The curated exhibits, also accessible via the A Closer Look link on the menu, use items from the collection as they explore themes such as food, slavery in colonial North America, politics in the Early American Republic, and others. The exhibits incorporate scholarly essays as they highlight selected artifacts. Though all materials are related to Colonial North America, the scope of the collection includes information on other parts of North and South America, Great Britain, continental Europe, and parts of Africa. This website will continue to be updated with newly digitized items, additional information, and new features accordingly. When complete, it will contain an estimated 470,000 digitized pages.—**ARBA Staff Reviewer**

210.   **Directory of Women Historians. https://womenalsoknowhistory.com.** [Website] Free. Date reviewed: 2018.
     Encouraging and promoting women historians who work across an array of specialties, www.womenalsoknowhistory.com provides a searchable directory of individual historian

profiles. Content is supplied by women historians who have submitted a completed profile to the site's editorial board for verification and listing. The Search tab allows users to enter a name or keyword to find applicable portions of the directory (e.g., area of study, affiliated institution, etc.). Alternatively, users may choose to browse via the Expertise by Area tab at the top of the homepage. Here they can access a list organized into three categories: Geography (U.K., Spain, Middle East, Korea, etc.), Chronology (Ancient, Early Modern, 17th Century, etc.), or Topic (American Presidents, Diplomacy, Indigenous Peoples, Law, etc.). It is important to note that these categories and their contents may change with respect to current profiles in the directory. Selecting from one of the categories will display an alphabetical listing of associated women historians, with information regarding Affiliation (university, private entity, etc.), Country Focus, Keywords and Availability to media. The listing will also note if the historian has a doctorate degree. Clicking on a historian's last name links to her full profile which may include contact information, Recent Publications, Social Media, an "About Me" feature and more. Under Recent Publications users will find either a list of or link to published work. Information in the profiles will vary as they are created individually.—**ARBA Staff Reviewer**

211.   **UNESCO World Heritage Centre http://whc.unesco.org/en/list.** [Website] Free. Date reviewed: 2019.

Information via links on the homepage will take users to News & Events, About World Heritage, Activities, Publications, Partnerships, and Resources. One will find a glossary, a history of the World Heritage Sites program, answers to frequently asked questions, and more under these links, but the heart of the site's data falls under The List link. Here users will find information about all 1,092 designated World Heritage Sites. Sites are arranged alphabetically by country; a symbol that indicates status—cultural site, natural site, or mixed site. A red symbol indicates a site in danger. Clicking on the name of the site takes users to further links—description (which is available in multiple languages), maps, documents, photo gallery, a video(s) or other multimedia material about the site, and indicators. Indicators lists threats to the site by year. The description of a site includes the country in which it resides, any modifications, coordinates, the date it was designated as a World Heritage Site, links to events (if any), and links to outside resources. The number of photos varies. There are more than 70 for Palmyra, Syria, and 36 for the Old Town of Ghadamès in Libya. The World Heritage Centre and its list of World Heritage Sites are current and free to use. The database provides more information than found in book versions such as *World Heritage Sites* (Firefly, 2015).—**ARBA Staff Reviewer**

212.   **The World Remembers https://www.theworldremembers.org.** [Website] Free. Date reviewed: 2019.

The World Remembers represents an ambitious yet vital project dedicated to remembering individuals lost during World War I. On the centenary of the war, The World Remembers conceived and executed a way to honor these men and women in public displays of names within many participating countries. This website has collected those names into a searchable database which users can access via the Search the Names tab on the homepage. Users are required to enter last name, country, and date of death in the search fields, but may also include first name if known. The country field relates to the nation under which the individual served. Users may be able to discover full name, rank, date of birth, date of death, and cemetery name. It should be noted that all deceased individuals are not accounted for on the site due to a country's ability to contribute to the project, incomplete records, etc. It is worth examining each participating country's data constraints and considerations accessible under the search fields to note data sources and further database information (for example, while Germany has contributed over eight hundred thousand names to the database, it has not accounted for nearly seven hundred thousand others). Countries which have contributed to The World Remembers include Belgium, Canada, France, Germany, the United Kingdom (including the British Indian Army), the United States, Australia, Slovenia, the Czech Republic, New Zealand, China, Italy, Turkey, South Africa, and Ukraine. Other resources are also available on the site, including an extensive photograph gallery organized into the following sections: Cemeteries, Civilians, Prisoners, Refugees, Soldiers, Women, and Casualties. Users can hover over a photo (black & white) for general identification (e.g., "American Soldier," "Ukrainian Leader in Berlin," etc.) or click on it for date and source. Users can learn more about a participating country's war experience via the menu icon in the upper left corner of the homepage. Although still under development, the Countries link lets users select from a list for particular information, which may include a brief essay and educational opportunities (Canada is a good working example). The Display Locations Map will include a Google map of places that displayed the names as part of The World Remembers project.—**ARBA Staff Reviewer**

Handbooks and Yearbooks

213.   **A Cultural History of Work.** Deborah Simonton and Anne Montenach, eds. New York, Bloomsbury Academic, 2018. 6v. illus. index. $550.00/set. ISBN 13: 978-1-4742-4503-6.

This set explores the culture of work in six chronological volumes: antiquity, the "medieval age," the "early modern age," the Enlightenment, the "age of empire," and the "modern age." The focus throughout the set is on "the western world." (p. xii) In addition to the two editors listed, the six volumes have separate editors whose expertise is in the period being studied. (The volume on the Enlightenment is edited by the set's editors.) Those volume editors provide an introduction to the nine identically themed chapters that follow in the six volumes: 1) the economy of work, 2) picturing work, 3) work and workplaces, 4) workplace culture, 5) work, skill and technology, 6) work and mobility, 7) work and society, 8) the political culture of work, and 9) work and leisure. This format allows a reader to pursue a single topic within the 2,500-years of the history of work in the West, as well as probing the diverse elements of the culture of work during a particular historical period, which can run from as few as 100 years ("the modern age") to more than 1,000 years (antiquity). As an example, the chapters on workers' mobility trace a fascinating range of activity and examine the vast variety of documents and texts available to historians to analyze this topic.

Contributors come from many countries, including Canada, Italy, Belgium, Northern Ireland, Austria, and France although most are associated with universities in the United States. They work in diverse departments such as classics, art history, European history, management, and U.S. history. This set is clearly aimed at college and university libraries: programs such as economics, American and world history, women's studies, and art history will benefit from the information herein. Readers will need some prior knowledge of the eras and the topics discussed, but there are also numerous footnotes and a "Further Readings" section in each volume to guide them to other useful items. If affordable, this set will certainly enrich a library in academia.—**Mark Schumacher**

214. **Defining Documents in World History: Asia.** Michael Shally-Jensen, ed. Hackensack, N.J., Salem Press, 2018. 356p. illus. index. $175.00. ISBN 13: 978-1-68217-927-7; 978-1-68217-966-6 (e-book).

At the article level, this book has a nice structure to it. The primary document is highlighted separately from the rest of the article. The articles are standardized and consist of a brief overview, a "defining moment" detailing why the document was created, who wrote the document, and an analysis of themes. All articles are signed and helpfully provide the name of the translator. Each article has a short bibliography at the end for additional references. Articles are easy to read and would be applicable for high school through adult readers.

The overall scope of this volume is a bit problematic. Simply put, it is trying to cover too much in a slim volume. It is unclear why certain documents were selected over others. The 20th century gets the most weight in this volume; all articles related to Korea and Southeast Asia are from this period. Geographically, East Asia gets the most coverage, particularly China. The final bibliography looks to be a compilation of the bibliographies from the individual articles.

In total, this work provides a good introduction to individual documents and may be useful for a broad survey course of modern Asia. Recommended.—**Allen Reichert**

215. **Defining Documents in World History: The 18th Century.** Michael Shally-Jensen, ed. Hackensack, N.J., Salem Press, 2017. 367p. index. $175.00. ISBN 13: 978-1-68217-581-1; 978-1-68217-582-8 (e-book).

Part of the Defining Documents in World History series from Salem Press, this volume focuses on important historical documents of the 18th century, along with accompanying essays. It contains thirty-two primary source materials from this century, with each essay supported by a critical essay, summary overview, defining moment, author biography, document analysis, and essential themes. The five major sections are: The American Colonies in Resistance and Revolution; The Founding of a New Democratic Republic; Slavery and Democracy?; Rights and Revolution in France; and The British Abroad. Some of the interesting primary source manuscripts discusses include: Proclamation of 1763, Lord Dunmore's Proclamation, the Declaration of Independence, the Northwest Ordinance, George Washington's farewell address, slavery clauses in the U.S. Constitution, Declaration of the Rights of Man and of the Citizen, and the British Regulating Act, to name but a few. Appendixes include a chronology, web resources, and a bibliography. Along with the other books in this series, this is an excellent undergraduate resource for academic libraries.—**Bradford Lee Eden**

216. **Defining Documents in World History: The 19th Century.** Michael Shally-Jensen, ed. Hackensack, N.J., Salem Press, 2018. 2v. illus. index. $295.00/set. ISBN 13: 978-1-68217-696-2; 978-1-68217-697-9 (e-book).

Documents are the soil in which historians work their tiny plot in the academic garden. Without them, we have no history. While scholars go to graduate school to learn how to analyze memoirs, letters, diplomatic communications, and treaties, to name a few primary sources, students, especially at the lower levels, do not get many opportunities to do this. Salem Press has changed that with the publication of Defining Documents in World History series. A majority of the set covers modernity, devoting two volumes to every century back to and including the 17th. The volumes preceding that cover the *Renaissance and Early Era, 1308-1600*; *The Middle Ages, 476-1500*; and *The Ancient World (2700 B.C.E. - 50 C.E.)*. Three more titles are devoted to the Middle East, Asia, nationalism and populism, and women's rights.

The title under review here covers the 19th century. In two volumes there are sixty-one signed articles. All entries were prepared by a small group of yeoman scholars, about half of whom have a PhD and the rest an MA. The reader does not know in what subject area the degree was received; one assumes history. In the "Publisher's Note," the user is informed only that "The essays have been signed by scholars of history, humanities, and other disciplines related to the essays' topics."

According to Salem, the series was designed for high school and college students; the goal is to advance the study of documents as an important part of history education. The documents are divided into four regional sections: Europe, Asia, Africa, and America. Each section begins with a brief, one-page, introduction that provides the student with a thumbnail sketch of the sweep of history mostly in that region during the 19th century. There is an eclectic mix of topics, from "An Account of U.S.-China Trade Negotiation" to the "Treaty of Ghent." Treaties are the most common document, making up a quarter of the sixty-one.

Given that the century was one of colonial expansion, one is not surprised to see a majority of the documents are related to diplomacy, foreign policy, and war. Since the series is geared to an introductory level, another appendix that grouped the documents into broad categories, such as economic, legal, military, diplomatic, cultural, and political would have been helpful. Some entries could potentially wind up in more than one category, such as "Karl Marx on British Rule in India" and the "Communist Manifesto." It is refreshing to see more than "the usual suspects," such as Napoleon and the Dreyfus Affair. Young students may for the first time learn about the Taiping Rebellion and the Mexican Revolution.

Each document has a title, date, the author or authors, and genre. There are many genres including treaty, philosophical tract or manifesto, speech, report, petition, address, and memoir, to name a few. Each document entry begins with an overview, followed by its "defining moment." A short biography of the author, an excerpt of the document, a document analysis, and essential themes follow. In addition, many have interesting images and photographs. Each entry closes with a bibliography and recommendations for further reading. A chronological list of the documents, a list of web resources, bibliography, and index appear at the end of the second volume.

Defining Documents in World History: The 19th Century is recommended for high school, junior college, and undergraduate libraries. Purchase includes online access, which expands its potential audience.—**John P. Stierman**

217.   **Defining Documents in World History: The 20th Century.** Michael Shally-Jensen, ed. Hackensack, N.J., Salem Press, 2018. 2v. illus. maps. index. $295.00/set. ISBN 13: 978-1-68217-924-6; 978-1-68217-965-9 (e-book).

This set presents 72 documents important to understanding the 20th century. The scope is broad and comprehensive, and documents are arranged in the following seven sections: Africa and the African Diaspora (5 documents); Asian Affairs (11 documents); Euroamerican and World Affairs (21 documents); Latin American Affairs (13 documents); The Middle East (8 documents); Women in the World (5 documents); and Technology, Medicine, and the Environment (9 documents). Among the documents are the Boxer Protocol, a report on the Armenian Genocide, the Munich Agreement, the Zimmerman Telegram, the Balfour Declaration, an essay from Emma Goldman ("Marriage and Love"), and a letter from an army physician during the 1918 flu pandemic. Documents include letters, speeches, legislation, treaties, government documents, essays, political tracts, and even a book chapter. As with the other titles in this series, the presentation of each document makes it accessible to the reader. A summary overview, a description of the defining moment, and an author biography precede the document (which is presented in whole or excerpted). This is followed by an analysis of the document that highlights its main themes. A bibliography and suggestions for further reading wrap up each document analysis. Generous black-and-white photographs and maps enhance the material. Taken altogether the set provides a broad overview of major developments worldwide during the 20th century. This is a solid reference to consult at the beginning of a research project and would be a valuable supplement to material presented in a survey course.—**ARBA Staff Reviewer**

218.   Lederer, Laura J. **Modern Slavery: A Documentary and Reference Guide.** Santa Barbara, Calif., Greenwood Press/ABC-CLIO, 2018. 366p. index. $108.00. ISBN 13: 978-1-4408-4498-0; 978-1-4408-4499-7 (e-book).

This documentary tells the story of the antislavery movement chronologically through its documents. Terms used to describe slavery also changed over time, and these changes are noted. The book tells the history of the antislavery movement from the Germantown Petition of 1688 through the antislavery movement of the last fifty years, which is the main focus of the book. Each document or excerpts from the original document are followed by an analysis and further readings. Interesting sidebars are interspersed with stories of survivors, information about other cases, or other antislavery efforts and individuals involved.

A reader's guide groups the documents by subject matter and different perspectives so the reader can locate materials. A chronology gives additional materials not included in the book itself. A bibliography and index are included making it easy to reference particular passages or works.

This is essential to every public or academic library covering current issues, civil rights, human rights, and history.—**Ladyjane Hickey**

219.   **Modern Genocide: Analyzing the Controversies and Issues.** Paul R. Bartrop, ed. Santa Barbara, Calif., ABC-CLIO, 2018. 376p. illus. index. $94.00. ISBN 13: 978-1-4408-6467-4; 978-1-4408-6468-1 (e-book).

This encyclopedia looks at scholarly debates and academic arguments about genocide. The selected controversies—as noted, study of genocide is "fraught with debate and dissent" (p. xv)—touch on Native Americans, Australia's Aborigines, the Irish Potato Famine, southwest Africa's Hereros, Armenia, the Ukrainian famine of the 1930s, the Holocaust, and events in East Timor, Cambodia, Guatemala, Kurdistan, Bosnia, Rwanda,

Darfur, and Myanmar. A final section looks at prevention, intervention, and international law. An appendix reprints the 1948 United Nations convention on genocide. Not included are debates about Apartheid, Palestine, Tibet, or Xinjiang.

Some 100 short essays ask questions such as "Did the American Indian Wars Constitute Genocide?" and "Should the Allies Have Bombed Auschwitz?" with competing interpretations and answers. Twenty-nine chapters focus on places such as Guatemala or concepts such as intervention and are grouped in five parts that are thematic or chronological. The 57 contributors represent institutions in the United States, Australia, Canada, the United Kingdom, Germany, and Israel: a core team of 10 scholars wrote half the entries. Chapter-level bibliographies identify major works of English-language scholarship, but discussion emphasizes issues rather than review of the scholarly literature. For example, works by Daniel Goldhagen and Christopher Browning are noted but without detailed discussion of historians' debates over "ordinary Germans" as agents of the Holocaust.

Paul R. Bartrop, the lead editor, produced related works such as *Bosnian Genocide* (see ARBA 2017, entry 153) and *Encountering Genocide* (see ARBA 2015, entry 317). This single volume should not be confused with his four-volume set called *Modern Genocide: The Definitive Resource and Document Collection* (see ARBA 2016, entry 159) which combines primary sources with analysis. Comparable reference works for conceptual, theoretical, and analytical discussion include *Fifty Key Thinkers on the Holocaust and Genocide* by Bartrop and Steven L. Jacobs (Routledge, 2010) and *The Genocide Studies Reader* by Samuel Totten and Bartrop (Routledge, 2009).—**Steven W. Sowards**

220.   Taulbee, James Larry. **War Crimes and Trials: A Primary Source Guide.** Santa Barbara, Calif., ABC-CLIO, 2018. 382p. index. $94.00. ISBN 13: 978-1-4408-3800-2; 978-1-4408-3801-9 (e-book).

Beginning in the latter half of the 19th century, countries began to craft rules governing the conduct of warfare. Initially, they generally focused on the protection of the wounded and medical personnel aiding them both on the battlefield and in field hospitals. Following the horrors of World War I, much more attention was paid to the codification of rules governing how warfare was conducted. Tribunals followed to prosecute those who were deemed to be in gross violation of established international norms. James Larry Taulbee, professor emeritus of political science, Emory University, begins by exploring the evolution of the rules governing the humane conduct of war through notable documents like the 1863 Lieber Code, which concerned the conduct of Union soldiers during the American Civil War, and the Geneva Convention of 1864. Much of the book focuses on twenty-five case studies of war crime trials. Each includes detailed contextual information that describes both the atrocity and how and why the perpetrator(s) were brought to justice. Also included are excerpts or full transcripts of pertinent primary sources. A major strength of the work is the diversity of atrocities chosen for inclusion. While there are a significant number of trials emanating from World War II, one will also find chapters focusing on the My Lai Massacre during the Vietnam War, Slobodan Milošević's actions as Serbia's President from 1989 to 2000, and the prosecution of Charles Taylor, Liberia's former leader. This work is highly recommended for collections on criminal justice, military science, or world history. Libraries should also consider acquiring Taulbee's 2-volume *Genocide, Mass Atrocity, and War Crimes in Modern History: Blood and Conscience* as a complementary resource.—**John R. Burch Jr.**

221.   **U*X*L Protests, Riots, and Rebellion: Civil Unrest in the Modern World.**
Farmington Hills, Mich., Gale/Cengage Learning, 2018. 3v. illus. index. $286.00/set.
ISBN 13: 978-1-4103-3908-9.

Each volume of this series contains in-depth articles on issues in modern history
that have resulted in protests, riots, and rebellions. The broader subjects are arranged
alphabetically (animal rights, civil rights, war, etc.) and spread across all three volumes.
Some topics have more than one chapter to cover the content, though each chapter
includes excerpts and links to primary source materials, vocabulary specific to the topic,
critical thinking questions, photos, and illustrations, as well as a list of books and websites
readers can seek out for further information on that topic. The series contains research
and activity ideas, a reader's guide, chronological timeline, centralized glossary, and a
detailed, thematic table of contents that may be more useful than the general table of
contents. Most of the writing is straightforward, although in the effort not to be pedantic,
the writing occasionally sounds simplistic. The breadth of the topics presented makes this
a highly recommended resource for collections looking to strengthen their coverage of this
subject matter. Highly recommended.—**Kyla M. Johnson**

222.   **Viewpoints on Modern World History.** New York, Greenhaven Publishing, 2018.
6v. illus. index. $286.80/set. ISBN 13: 978-1-5345-0170-6.

This series covers major international events through expert analysis in six books: *AIDS
and Other Killer Viruses, The Armenian Genocide, The Arms Race and Nuclear Proliferation,
Brexit,* and *US-Iran Relations*. Each title offers an introduction to the topic before digging into
more specific discussions in chapter-length articles. The chapters are pulled from magazines,
committee hearings, interviews, and think tanks. Each chapter provides an introduction
and the source of the material. Unfortunately, only some of the articles include their own
sources. Some supply substantial footnotes while others cite statistics with no indication
of where the information originated. This series is geared towards high school and college
student researchers and therefore is very text heavy with almost no photos. The books cover
events from the 20th and 21st centuries, including President Trump's nuclear agenda, Brexit
negotiations, and the Iran deal. Though there is nothing flashy about this series, it is a simple,
informative, and effective research tool. Some topics may quickly become outdated, but much
of the information will remain useful for researchers. The book includes a bibliography and an
index. Recommended.—**Cathy DeCampli**

223.   Wolf, Kirsten, and Tristan Mueller-Vollmer. **The Vikings: Facts and Fictions.**
Santa Barbara, Calif., Greenwood Press/ABC-CLIO, 2018. 186p. index. (Historical Facts
and Fictions). $61.00. ISBN 13: 978-1-4408-6298-4; 978-1-4408-6299-1 (e-book).

This well-designed series presents contemporary fictions in a historical context to
explain both the origins of the fictions as well as the actual background stories. Eleven
beliefs about Vikings are debunked, including the idea that Vikings all shared a single
religion, that women were accorded equality in Viking society, and that Vikings drank
from skull cups. Primary source material, usually medieval poetry from Scandinavia and
western Europe, is presented in translation in order to demonstrate what Vikings considered
their own history as well as what victims of Viking raids knew and didn't know about their
attackers. Each chapter ends with a list of books and articles for further reading, and a
bibliography is included before the extensive index. Few of the resources are available
online. The volume would be an excellent research aid for advanced high school students
and undergraduates.—**Delilah R. Alexander**

10 Law

General Works

Dictionaries and Encyclopedias

224.   Law, Jonathan. **A Dictionary of Law.** 9th ed. New York, Oxford University Press, 2018. 768p. (Oxford Quick Reference). $18.95pa. ISBN 13: 978-0-19-880252-5.

The last edition of this title appeared in 2015; this new edition adds more than 100 entries, pushing the dictionary's total number of entries close to 5,000. Among the new entries are those concerned with Brexit and new case law. Articles begin with a definition of the word or words, followed by a more extensive explanation of the topic. Length varies, but all articles strive to convey information with as little jargon as possible. The dictionary is easy to navigate and utilizes *see* and *see also* references when necessary. Other noteworthy features of this edition include an appendix of internet resources and a writing and citation guide. The target audiences are legal and other professionals, students in any level law course, and laypeople who need a reliable explanation of legal concepts. The price makes this a quite reasonable purchase for libraries interested in acquiring a legal reference written for UK practitioners or for those needing to consult a UK legal reference.—**ARBA Staff Reviewer**

Digital Resources

225.   **Anglo American Legal Tradition http://aalt.law.uh.edu/.** [Website] Free. Date reviewed: 2018.

This site organizes a vast digital collection of medieval and early modern law documents from the National Archives in London. Currently, the collection spans centuries of Anglo legal thought and process regarding wills, loans, settlements, sales, disputes, leases, and much more. From the homepage, users click the Enter Site link to access an information page including an effective table of contents with links to records of roughly thirty reigns, including the Commonwealth, from Richard I in the late 12th century up through the reign of Victoria. Links are organized into Legal Systems I-IV (it appears that documents representing Legal System V and VI, covering the years after 1776 and focused on the United States, are in development). Clicking a link will generally access a table of

143

available document series which include such things as Common Pleas, Kings Bench Rolls, Exchequer of Pleas, Pipe Foreign Accounts, Chancery Order and Decrees, Duchy Decrees, Kings Bench Indictments, and Privy Council Papers. Each series may note document information such as Calendar Date, Regnal Year, Parties, Subject Matter, Roll/Case, and Number. Links within the document series may access images of the original document. Each document collection and series may vary in content and structure, and navigation may be somewhat unclear. There may be particular navigation information within each series. Users can also find generous site information and navigation help next to the table of contents, with links to tutorials, FAQs, downloading information, viewing suggestions, and excellent information on legal tradition and legal systems. Anglo American Legal Tradition would be an important resource for law and history scholars and educators.— **ARBA Staff Reviewer**

Handbooks and Yearbooks

226. **American Values and Freedoms.** Minneapolis, Minn., ABDO Publishing, 2018. 6v. index. $155.70/set.

Each title in the series addresses the historical significance of our Constitutional freedoms and the application of these freedoms since our nation's founding. Each of the books follows the same format, providing reference aids at the end that include essential facts, additional resources, and source notes. Titles include *Freedom of Religion, Freedom of the Press, Governmental Checks and Balances, Right to Bear Arms, Right to Protest,* and *Right to Vote.* In addition, each of the books includes discussion starters at the end of the chapter, captioned color and black-and-white photographs, and thought-provoking text boxes. Interspersed throughout are "perspective" pages that highlight an event through a specific lens. Aligned to Common Core standards and correlated to state standards, this series offers readers an opportunity to think critically about these freedoms as they evolved through time. The books include glossaries, indexes, and timelines. Recommended.— **Susan Yutzey**

227. **Defining Documents in American History: Supreme Court Decisions (1803-2017).** Michael Shally-Jensen, ed. Hackensack, N.J., Salem Press, 2017. 2v. index. $295.00/set. ISBN 13: 978-1-68217-585-9; 978-1-68217-586-6 (e-book).

This two-volume set will serve as a handy aid for students looking to find information on key Supreme Court decisions since the early 19th century. The book is well structured and easy to use. The front matter contains notes on contributors, an introduction, and a complete list of contents. Court cases are treated chronologically in three sections: The Founding Years to the Mid-Nineteenth Century; Maturation Pains: From Reconstruction to the Mid-Twentieth Century; and Modern Dilemmas: From the Civil Rights Era to Today. Entries range in length from approximately two pages to twenty-plus pages and each entry is comprised of a summary overview, historical context, a biography of the decision author, a historical document (in the case of this book, the documents are all or part of the decision under discussion), an analysis of the document, a discussion of essential readings, the contributor's name, and a bibliography/additional reading list. Entries include glossaries of potentially unknown words/terms, pieces of legislation, and people.

The set analyzes sixty decisions; among the decisions covered are: *Marbury v. Madison, Cherokee Nation v. Georgia, Dred Scott v. Sandford, United States v. Cruikshank, Plessy v. Ferguson, Muller v. Oregon, Korematsu v. United States, Brown v. Board of Education, Griswold v. Connecticut, Miranda v. Arizona, Loving v. Virginia, Roe V. Wade, Bush v. Gore,* and *Citizens United v. Federal Election Commission.* These decisions are highly likely to appear on standardized tests or on history exams in high school and college. The advantage of a book like this is that it uses accessible language to give students the reliable information they need to understand a decision and its importance. In fact, there is likely more information on an individual decision than students will find in a textbook (history, law, or political science). This set can also serve members of the general public interested in reading for themselves the decisions that have shaped the trajectory of the United States. Highly recommended for public, school, and academic libraries.—**ARBA Staff Reviewer**

228.   **Guns in America.** Bronx, N.Y., H. W. Wilson, 2017. 184p. illus. index. (The Reference Shelf, volume 89, number 1). $75.00pa. ISBN 13: 978-1-68217-451-7.

This slim volume reprints thirty items published between 2013 and early 2017, divided into five sections, each with an introductory text written by Micah L. Issitt (described online as "a humble, work-a-day, dollar-a-paragraph writer"). Topics include the ideology of guns, a global perspective on guns, and the future of guns in America. The original sources, both print and web-based, include *The Washington Post, The New Yorker, The New Republic, The Huffington Post,* and *The Atlantic.* The articles run from two to eight pages. The selections are well chosen and well grouped, with a wide range of points of view being provided. For example, at least one article recommends that the American public arm itself to protect itself. Another explores the disagreements and conflicts between Democrats and Republicans in Congress concerning allowing gun purchases by suspected terrorists, which apparently 91 percent of them were able to do between 2004 and 2014. Since this broad topic is among the most discussed in the United States today, all sorts of libraries (except, perhaps, special libraries in other fields) should consider adding books containing these perspectives on a subject of importance to the American people.

Curiously, the two-page "Index" has only proper names, including thirty-one references to Donald Trump, but no reference to the National Rifle Association or any other terms related to this topic, such as "background checks" or "automatic weapons," which could guide readers to texts (and points of view) that might interest them. The "Websites" section lists eleven sites, including three progun groups; among the other sites listed are the Centers for Disease Control and Snopes. (A "Betsy Maury" is mentioned as the editor of this volume, but she is never mentioned elsewhere in the volume.)—**Mark Schumacher**

229.   **Legal Issues across the Globe.** Thomas Riggs, ed. Farmington Hills, Mich., Gale/Cengage Learning, 2018. 426p. illus. maps. index. $315.00. ISBN 13: 978-1-4103-3840-2; 978-1-4103-3841-9 (e-book).

No book proves the truth of Dick the Butcher's line from Henry VI, Part 2, better than the volume under review. Dick's well-known and oft misinterpreted quip is, "The first thing we do, let's kill all the lawyers." Taken literally, the line rouses cheers from audiences because they know the trouble the lawyerly types often bring. Seen in context (the speaker is a crook), it's actually a compliment. Our modern age may well be too jaundiced to receive the latter, however.

As if ripped from the tweets of every pundit on Twitter, this volume tackles many of the vexing questions before the world today: Internet free speech, same-sex marriage, police misprisions, marijuana, women's sexual rights, and so on. Each topic is followed by twelve articles on how countries across the globe view the issue. A brief overview introduces each topic and its global venue. Internet free speech, for example, is spotlighted by China, Cuba, Fiji, Finland, France, Germany, Jordan, Russia, Sri Lanka, Uganda, the United States, and Venezuela. The issue of women's reproductive rights, in addition to the United States, is also ventilated by Brazil, Colombia, India, Iran, Ireland, Nigeria, Pakistan, Philippines, Poland, Saudi Arabia, and the Solomon Islands.

The articles provide key insights regarding the freedom, or lack thereof, each issue has in the country presented, and what the consequences may be for violations of same. To be able to compare and contrast these issues in the same volume should be enough to recommend it to any library of merit. Nevertheless, its true value may be an inadvertent one. No other volume underscores the other well-known sage advice, this one quoted by Churchill in the House of Commons in 1947, viz., that democracy is the worst form of government, except for all the rest.—**Mark Y. Herring**

230. Morton, David A., III. **Nolo's Guide to Social Security Disability: Getting & Keeping Your Benefits.** 9th ed. Berkeley, Calif., Nolo, 2018. 464p. index. $39.99pa. ISBN 13: 978-1-4133-2484-6; 978-1-4133-2485-3 (e-book).

Written by a doctor and former consultant on disability determination for the Social Security Administration (SSA), this book demystifies the complicated processes of qualifying for and maintaining disability benefits. The book is comprised of fifteen chapters, an introduction, appendixes, and an index. Book purchasers also gain free access to the Nolo website which posts updates and changes to Social Security policies as well as medical information on over two hundred conditions and disability requirements. The chapters are as follows: "What Is Social Security Disability?" "Applying for Disability Benefits," " Disability Benefits for Children," "Getting Benefits during the Application Process," "Proving Your Are Disabled," "Who Decides Your Claim," "How Claims Are Decided," "Whether You Can Do Some Work: Your RFC [Residual Functional Capacity]," "How Age, Education, and Work Experience Matter," "When Benefits Begin," "Reasons You May Be Denied Benefits," "Appealing If Your Claim Is Denied," "Once You Are Approved," "Continuing Disability Review," and "Your Right to Representation." The appendixes include a "Glossary of Bureaucratic Terms," "Medical-Vocational Rules," and "How to Use the Medical Listings on Nolo.com." The SSA forms used in this book are for illustrative purposes only. Applicants need to get forms in person from a SSA office or from the SSA website. This helpful and inexpensive guide will assist anyone who has to apply for the start or continuation of disability benefits. Recommended.—**ARBA Staff Reviewer**

231. Randolph, Mary. **The Executor's Guide: Settling a Loved One's Estate or Trust.** 8th ed. Berkeley, Calif., Nolo, 2018. 520p. index. $39.99pa. ISBN 13: 978-1-4133-2480-8; 978-1-4133-2481-5 (e-book).

This guide, written by a lawyer, is designed to assist people with no experience through the process of acting as executor of an estate. The book is divided into six sections, starting with Getting Ready, which provides readers with an overview of an executor's duties. The next part, First Steps, discusses duties that need to be fulfilled in the first week and the first month after the death of a friend or family member. Part 3, Taking Care of the Estate, focuses on basics like what to do if there is no will, how to add up debts and assets, and what to do about outstanding bills. Transferring Property, the fourth part, covers property that does not go through probate, how to transfer property, claiming money in retirement plans, and more. Part 5 focuses on trusts and the last part directs readers on where to find additional help, including government sites, legal librarians, lawyers, and other experts. The book also includes a glossary, two appendixes on state information and how to use the downloadable forms on the publisher's website, and an index. This easy-to-understand book is recommended for public libraries.—**ARBA Staff Reviewer**

Constitutional Law

Dictionaries and Encyclopedias

232.   **Bill of Rights, Second Edition.** 2d ed. Thomas Tandy Lewis, ed. Hackensack, N.J., Salem Press, 2017. 2v. $175.00/set. ISBN 13: 978-1-68217-593-4; 978-1-68217-564-4 (e-book).

This second edition "is an encyclopedic guide to the first ten amendments to the U.S. constitution—those collectively known as the U.S. Bill of Rights because of the important rights and liberties they were framed to protect." This new edition has been revised and expanded "to relate to today's current social and political climates" and is arranged in four broad sections within the two volumes: Overview of the Ten Amendments; Historical Topics and Legal Concepts; Contemporary Issues Relating to the Bill of Rights; and Court Cases. Volume 2 contains Court Cases and Appendixes (the Declaration of Independence, the Constitution of the United States, Amendments to the U.S. Constitution, Supreme Court Justices and the Bill of Rights, Time Line, Glossary, Select Bibliography, and Index). Each entry (for Overview, Historical Topics and Legal Concepts, Contemporary Issues, and Court Cases) is signed by contributors, experts in the field who represent mostly universities, including Georgetown University School of Law, Loyola University, College of New Jersey, Illinois State University, Skidmore College, and Ohio State University. Each entry for specific amendments includes: description, significance, and an entry discussing historical and legal background. For instance, the Fifth Amendment entry contains analysis of the Self-Incrimination Clause, the Due Process Clause, the Double Jeopardy Clause, the Grand Jury Clause, and the Takings Clause. The Historical Topics and Legal Concepts section contains entries for The Bill of Rights: A Brief History and Summary; Blaine Amendments; Constitutional Interpretation; Declaration of Independence; Federalism; Plea Bargaining; and War and the Bill of Rights. The Contemporary Issues section contains entries among which are Abortion Rights, Capital Punishment, Search and Seizure, Censorship, and Affirmative Action Programs. Court Cases entries include: name of case, citation, when announced, issues, relevant amendments, brief summary and history and implications of case. The *Bill of Rights* is highly recommended to public and academic libraries. It is an excellent resource for students and faculty of government and politics, social science, and law and for students studying current events. It can be used as a "quick reference" tool and as a starting point to research. Overall, this should be a key resource in reference collections.—**Lucy Heckman**

Digital Resources

233. **Mapping First Amendment Conflicts. http://firstamendmentwatchorg/ 2018/05/17/map-first-amendment-conflict/.** [Website] Free. Date reviewed: 2019.

The freedom of speech—enshrined in the U.S. Constitution's first amendment— seems to be facing more challenges than ever. This page from First Amendment Watch hosts an interactive map that pinpoints locations across the United States and Puerto Rico known to have witnessed events or incidents related to First Amendment issues. The map currently pins close to 300 First Amendment-related incidents (more are added as they are reported to the site). Users can zoom in on the national map to more clearly discern individual locations. Pins are colored to categorize the nature of the issue, which may include libel, access, censorship, assembly, prior restraint, threats, campus speech, and more. Clicking on a pin opens a profile of the First Amendment challenge, noting location, date, brief description and link to relevant news article. There may also be an update to the case. Users can click on an arrow icon to open a more detailed map. Simply structured, the page is nonetheless a good starting point for research on First Amendment issues.—**ARBA Staff Reviewer**

Handbooks and Yearbooks

234.   Hudson, Jr., David L. **Equal Protection: Documents Decoded.** Santa Barbara, Calif., ABC-CLIO, 2018. 250p. index. $81.00. ISBN 13: 978-1-4408-5804-8; 978-1-4408-5805-5 (e-book).

In this series, Documents Decoded, readers are guided through a selection of primary sources with analysis. Each document has an introduction along with an explanation of its context and significance. Interpretive comments are provided on a sidebar. The documents include significant court cases and speeches.

This volume is on the equal protection clause found in section one of the Fourteenth Amendment to the United States Constitution. "It provides that no state shall 'deny to any person within its jurisdiction the equal protection of the laws.'" (p. vii) David Hudson has done an admirable job in selecting the documents to include in this volume and in explaining each document's significance in the history of the concept of equal protection under the law.

Race, gender, sexual orientation, and affirmative action are all addressed. Libraries will appreciate the nonpartisan way the book addresses the controversy of marriage between two persons, and how the equality amendment was interpreted in *Obergefell v. Hodges* (June 26, 2015).

This volume is very well written and is easily understood at all levels, from senior high to the average person. Highly recommended to all academic and public libraries.— **Ladyjane Hickey**

235.   LeMay, Michael C. **Religious Freedom in America: A Reference Handbook.** Santa Barbara, Calif., ABC-CLIO, 2018. 350p. illus. index. (Contemporary World Issues series). $60.00. ISBN 13: 978-1-4408-5104-9; 978-1-4408-5105-6 (e-book).

Religious Freedom in America is a comprehensive book that covers the history of how freedom of religion has been treated in the United States since its enshrinement as a concept in the country's founding documents. While it is a fundamental principle, it has been difficult to deal with on an everyday basis in our country.

Religious Freedom in America tackles many issues surrounding the concept in seven chapters beginning with the "Background and History" of the issue and ending with a chapter covering the chronology of important events. The five chapters in between contain original essays from participants in the struggle to interpret the Free Exercise Clause and the Establishment Clause in the Constitution, profiles of people and organizations who are dedicated to influencing both government and society, and a wealth of other information. Illustrative tables are spread throughout the volume and a reference section is included at the end of many chapters; a detailed index rounds out the work.

Religious Freedom in America would be a valuable addition for any librarian that collects reference material on the Constitution, the law in general, or American history.—**Alicia Brillon**

Corporation Law

Handbooks and Yearbooks

236.   **Research Handbook on the History of Corporate and Company Law.** Harwell Wells, ed. Northampton, Mass., Edward Elgar, 2018. 641p. index. (Research Handbooks in Corporate Law and Governance). $290.00. ISBN 13: 978-1-78471-765-0.

According to the editor, chapters in the *Research Handbook on the History of Corporate and Company Law* "survey the growth of corporate and, more generally, business organization law from the Medieval era to the present day, addressing developments over time in jurisdictions around the globe." The volume is arranged in four parts: Part I, Taking Shape, includes chapters on Islamic law and economic development; business organizations in India prior to the British East India Company; business organization and organizational innovation in late medieval Italy; and the corporate form in the move from municipal governance to overseas trade. Part II, Modern Europe, includes chapters on the development of English company law before 1900; German corporate law in the 20th century; a history of the corporation in Spain; and classes of shares and voting rights in the history of Italian corporate law. Chapters in Part III, Asia, examine corporation law in late imperial China; the stakeholder approach to corporate law: a historical perspective from India; and Japanese corporate law and corporate governance in historical perspective. Part IV, North America, contains chapters on topics including for-profit and nonprofit special corporations in America, 1608-1860; evolutionary models of corporate law; the evolution of Mexican mercantile and corporate laws; and a brief history of modern U.S. corporate law. The contributors are experts in the field and represent universities worldwide among which are: the University of Illinois; Fordham University School of Law; University of Cambridge (UK); University of Geneva (Switzerland); Hitotsubashi University (Japan); University of Calgary (Canada); and Emory University. Each chapter contains an extensive list of bibliographical references; the book contains a list of figures and tables and an index. The *Research Handbook on the History of Corporate and Company Law* is especially recommended to faculty and students of graduate programs in business and law. Law libraries and academic libraries should consider purchasing this research handbook.—**Lucy Heckman**

237.   **Research Handbook on the Regulation of Mutual Funds.** William A. Birdthistle and John Morley, eds. Northampton, Mass., Edward Elgar, 2018. 468p. index. (Research Handbooks on Corporate Law and Governance). $270.00. ISBN 13: 978-1-78471-504-5; 978-1-78471-505-2 (e-book).

The *Research Handbook on the Regulation of Mutual Funds* "covers several topics that fall into at least four major categories central to the legal regulation of mutual funds today"; these topics are arranged within four sections: The Role and Regulation of Investment Funds; Identity and Behavior of Mutual Fund Investors; The Broader Range of Investment Funds; and International Perspective on Investment Funds. Each chapter within these sections is written by experts in the field; authors represent colleges and universities that include Duke University School of Law, Rutgers Law School, University of New South Wales Business School, Yale Law School, Melbourne Law School, and Trinity College Dublin, School of Law, Ireland. Chapters in the first section include "The Rise and Fall of the Mutual Fund Brand"; "Why Do Management Funds Have Special Securities Regulation?"; "The Fiduciary Structure of Investment Management Regulation"; and "Fiduciary Contours: Perspectives on Mutual Funds and Private Funds." In the second section, users will find such chapters as "Who are Mutual Fund Investors?"; "Protecting the Mutual Fund Investors: An Inevitable Eclecticism"; "The Past and Present of Mutual Fund Fee Litigation under Section 36 (b)"; "Toward Better Mutual Fund Governance"; and "Mutual Fund Compliance: Key Developments and Their Implications." The third section includes "Tales from the Dark Side: Money Market Funds and the Shadow Banking Debate"; "Exchange-Traded Funds: Neither Fish nor Fowl"; "Free Funds: Retirement Savings as Public Infrastructure"; and "Confluence of Mutual and Hedge Funds." "The Anatomy of European Investment Fund Law"; "Governance Aspects of Mutual Funds in Ireland"; "Regulating Collective Retail Investment Funds in the United Kingdom with the Objective of Investor Projection, and Some Implications"; and "Regulation of Mutual Funds in Australia" are among the chapters in the final section. Each chapter includes a bibliography and bibliographic notes including references to specific court cases. An index rounds out the work. The *Research Handbook of the Regulation of Mutual Funds* is a source of scholarly articles on legal aspects of mutual funds. It is recommended to law libraries and academic libraries supporting an MBA program.—**Lucy Heckman**

Criminology and Criminal Justice

Chronology

238.   Mickolus, Edward. **Terrorism Worldwide, 2016.** Jefferson, N.C., McFarland, 2018. 254p. index. $49.95pa. ISBN 13: 978-1-4766-7155-0; 978-1-4766-3026-7 (e-book).

239.   Mickolus, Edward. **Terrorism Worldwide, 2017.** Jefferson, N.C., McFarland, 2018. 212p. index. $49.95pa. ISBN 13: 978-1-4766-7562-6; 978-1-4766-3400-5 (e-book).

Taken together, these two volumes cover worldwide terrorist activities during 2016-2017. The introduction to both volumes discusses the definition of terrorism as used in this book, the book's arrangement, the activities of key terrorist groups in 2016 or 2017, innovations in terrorist methods, the fates of key terrorists, senior terrorists who were killed, captured, or surrendered in 2016 and 2017, and notes on how to use the book. Both volumes use the same format, dividing the material by region: Worldwide, Africa, Asia, Australia, Europe, Latin America and the Caribbean, Middle East, and United States and Canada. An appendix in each volume provides updates about terrorist incidents that occurred in the previous year. This information can include the outcome of trial, terrorists' fates, and information about victims. Both volumes offer bibliographies that include current works, which is quite useful for those using this volume as a place to start research on a particular topic. Both volumes of *Terrorism Worldwide,* a curated and highly reliable work, are highly recommended for public and academic libraries.—**ARBA Staff Reviewer**

Dictionaries and Encyclopedias

240.   **American Prisons and Jails: An Encyclopedia of Controversies and Trends.** Worley, Vidisha Barua and Robert M. Worley, eds. Santa Barbara, Calif., ABC-CLIO, 2019. 2v. index. $198.00/set. ISBN 13: 978-1-61069-500-8; 978-1-61069-501-5 (e-book).

There is a crisis occurring in America. Currently, the United States incarcerates more of its citizens than any other nation in the world. Not surprisingly, managing enormous jail and prison populations comes with its share of issues and challenges. *American Prisons and Jails: An Encyclopedia of Controversies and Trends* details some of these issues, while providing historical information as well as information about current developments taking place within the American correctional system.

This two-volume set covers a wide assortment of topics. These include essays referencing prison populations (e.g., inmate AIDS/HIV, conjugal visits, suicide in custody), prisons and jails (e.g., overcrowding, riots, prison industries, cost of prisons), correctional employees (e.g., misconduct by correctional employees, correctional officer subculture, sexual abuse of inmates by correctional staff), and the judicial system (e.g., federal sentencing guidelines, section 1983 lawsuits, death penalty legal issues).

The relatively short entries contributed by academics and subject specialists afford brief treatment to topics rather than exhaustive coverage and will therefore be of value to those seeking introductory material. Volumes contain a list of entries as well as a comprehensive index allowing for ease of searching. Also of value is the inclusion of *see also* subject terms and a bibliography at the conclusion of each article for further reading and research.

Given the title of this set, the presence of articles detailing the prison systems of Australia, Peru, China, England, France, Norway, and South Africa and the death penalty in the Middle East is somewhat puzzling. While serving to provide a global perspective, these contradict the implication of an exclusively American focus. This aside, the collection provides a respectable array of topics largely related American to prison and jails in one convenient set.—**Dianna L. Kim**

241.   **Encyclopedia of Rape and Sexual Violence.** Smith, Merril D., ed. Santa Barbara, Calif., ABC-CLIO, 2018. 2v. index. $182.00/set. ISBN 13: 978-1-4408-4489-8; 978-1-4408-4490-4 (e-book).

The *Encyclopedia of Rape and Sexual Violence* is a comprehensive, two-volume set that takes a multifaceted approach to a timely topic. Tackling the subject from a global perspective, this well-researched resource provides a thorough overview of rape and sexual violence. The in-depth introduction traces the historical roots of sexual violence—from the ancient tales of Greece and the Bible to the modern #MeToo movement—and offers an outline of what readers will find in the set. The twenty alphabetically arranged entries focus on a variety of issues, including acquaintance rape, campus rape, incest, marital rape, and sexual assault in the military. Each entry provides information about prevalence, obstacles to prevention, and major laws related to the issue. A list of suggested further reading at the end of each entry includes books, articles (both academic and popular), and government reports. Unique elements of this resource include a Chronology of Selected Rape and Sexual Violence Events and, in volume two, an extensive section of primary documents. These sections cover well-known incidents, federal legislation, and news stories pertaining to rape and sexual violence. The primary documents are one of this set's strongest features. This is an easily accessible resource with the table of contents, introduction, chronology, and list of primary documents repeated in each volume. Contributors include social workers, psychologists, and educators from a wide variety of disciplines and this diversity is reflected in the resource. Although it generally offers varied content, it does not address in a significant way the intertwined relationship of race and sexual violence, particularly in relation to the United States history of slavery. Supplementary materials in volume two include a list of books, films, and organizational resources for further study and a comprehensive general index with page numbers for main entries indicated by bold type. Users would be better served if the index was also included in volume one. Overall, the *Encyclopedia of Rape and Sexual Violence* is a valuable resource for students and academic researchers. This set is recommended for academic and large public libraries.—**Lisa Morgan**

242.   **Gangland: An Encyclopedia of Gang Life from Cradle to Grave.** Finley, Laura L., ed. Santa Barbara, Calif., ABC-CLIO, 2018. 2v. index. $198.00/set. ISBN 13: 978-1-4408-4473-7; 978-1-4408-4474-4 (e-book).

Gangland: An Encyclopedia of Gang Life from Cradle to Grave is a comprehensive two-volume encyclopedia on America's gangs and their fascinating histories. This ABC-CLIO encyclopedia is edited by Laura L. Finley, Associate Professor of Sociology and Criminology at Barry University. The two-volume encyclopedia is intended to provide a complete resource of the nation's most prominent gangs and an accessible guide to related topics. Entries in *Gangland* were primarily written by criminologists, students, journalists, and community experts with the majority of the writers being criminology students of Barry University. The encyclopedia accurately describes the majority of notable gangs in America and contains histories and information on the Crips, Bloods, MS-13, Latin Kings, Aryan Brotherhood, Hells Angles, and more. *Gangland* also provides detailed descriptions of the various forms of gangs like street gangs, motorcycle gangs, hate gangs, and prison gangs.

The two volumes are divided alphabetically with subjects A-M located in volume 1 and N-Z in volume 2. Volume 1 contains a brief introduction and a section on the history of gangs in the United States sections along with a chronology of significant dates in U.S. gang history. Volume 2 contains a glossary, recommended resource list, information on the editor and contributors, and an index. Along with the general descriptions, the authors have provided a list of further readings to correspond with each subject. The encyclopedia's convenient format and additional resources make this a valuable resource for anyone interested in gangs and their American heritage.—**Trent Shotwell**

243. **Mass Shootings in America: Understanding the Debates, Causes, and Responses.** Jaclyn Schildkraut, ed. Santa Barbara, Calif., ABC-CLIO, 2018. 332p. index. $94.00. ISBN 13: 978-1-4408-5624-2; 978-1-4408-5625-9 (e-book).

With the ever-increasing number of mass shootings taking place in the United States, Editor Jaclyn Schildkraut provides the reader with a one-volume reference to topics related to mass shooting. Following a foreward by the former principal of Columbine High School, the reader is taken into an excellent introduction that quickly brings the novice up to speed with this topic. The book presents topics into four major sections or blocks: Understanding Mass Shootings in America; An Encyclopedia of Mass Shooting Events 1966-2016 (subdivided by decade); A Mass Shooting Q & A, with chapters by experts that address many of the pertinent questions on this topic; and Pivotal Documents in Mass Shooting Research. A nice index and recommended readings area close out this excellent reference work.

A great example of a chapter is in the expert Q & A section: "Government Options to Stop School Shootings" by Dr. Lawrence Southwick, Jr. Eight pages cover several questions in a simple and easy-to-use format. Questions and conclusions are provided and an excellent list of references is available for those wishing to do more research.—**Scott R. DiMarco**

Digital Resources

244. **The American Prison Writing Archive. http://www.dhinitiative.org/projects/apwa.** [Website] Free. Date reviewed: 2018.

The high incarceration rate in the United States has created a distinct community made up of both prisoners and prison affiliates. Their experiences as Americans are unique and powerful. The open source American Prison Writing Archive (APWA) allows for contributions from those both currently and formerly incarcerated in addition to all varieties of prison staff and volunteers, creating a platform for voices that may otherwise go unheard. From the homepage, users can read an overview of the project begun by the Digital Humanities Initiative at Hamilton College, and then click the blue APWA button to access the archive. Once inside, users can conduct a basic search or narrow fields by essay title, author, or essay id. Users can also browse all essays within the Essays Archive box on the left side of the page, or browse via a selection of other qualifiers such as essay titles, author names, prisons, states, and author attributes (ethnicity, religions, gender identification, etc.). Essays are presented with a thumbnail image of the original submission alongside various identifying information: title, author, state, and more, in addition to a brief text excerpt. Clicking the title or thumbnail accesses the original submission that users can scroll through. Alternatively, they can select the View Transcription link to view the content in a different way. Users will find a wide range of submissions reflecting on themes like remorse, fear, corruption, anger, discrimination, and human dignity. Although some of the nearly 1,500 essays have been submitted by women, most are from men. The majority express the raw thoughts of a population with a very different perspective on life: "28 Days from Nirvana" by George Kayer is a real standout.—**ARBA Staff Reviewer**

245.   **American Violence. https://www.americanviolence.org/.** [Website] Free. Date reviewed: 2018.

American Violence is a database tracking murders across the United States. The site is simply structured, allowing users to explore a Map, Chart, or Table of trends and statistics on murders for roughly eighty of the larger U.S. cities. The homepage presents the national map with cities marked by dots sized and colored according to number of murders committed between August 2017 and July 2018. Underneath the default Map View tab in the upper left corner of the page, users can select the Chart View to track the number of murders over the same time span for ten cities with a population over one million (New York, Chicago, Phoenix, etc.). The chart can be adjusted to display cities with a population between five hundred thousand and one million (Detroit, Fresno, Memphis, etc.), cities with a population less than five hundred thousand (Baton Rouge, Kansas City, Buffalo, etc.) and all cities. The Table View lists the data shown in the other graphics using Timespan, Murders, Rate/100K, and Avg. Population as column headers. Users can find more information via the Menu icon in the upper right corner of any page. The Cities link provides general background on data collection for particular cities and states. News adds website context to several external articles and reports such as "Can Weather Help Cities Understand Violence?" from the *New York Times* and the FBI report "2017 Crime in the U.S." Still in development, American Violence hopes to incorporate violence-by-neighborhood data for some cities in the future.—**ARBA Staff Reviewer**

246.   **Behind the Badge. https://www.behindthebadgeny.org/.** [Website] Free. Date reviewed: 2018.

Behind the Badge helps educate the public about law enforcement policies across New York State (currently including information for seven cities/counties). It offers insights on how policies work within various police departments, how they originated, and how they have positively or negatively affected their communities. Users can explore the database by Police Department or Policies. The site hopes to bring policy information on sixteen other cities/counties online in the near future. To explore by Police Department, users select the By Department tab at the top of the homepage or scroll down to the New York Police Departments link. Users can continue to scroll through a list of cities/counties— Buffalo, Albany, Nassau County, Rochester, Suffolk County, Syracuse, and White Plains, or select by broader region. Users can then choose from a list of seven policy categories, including Police Misconduct; Department Diversity; Surveillance Technology; Use of Force; Stops, Field Interviews, Search & Seizure; Equitable Policing; and Enforcement of Low Level Offenses. It is interesting to note that departments do not necessarily maintain policies on every category. Supplemental information may include background on policy accessibility to the public and a "Policy Spotlight" highlighting an issue particular to each department. Clicking on a policy links to a PDF of the policy document or separate links to policy components. There may be statistical information as well. Exploring the site By Policy links to a brief and general description of the policy category, then lists the departments that maintain that policy. As it continues to develop, the site will be a good resource for researchers of criminal justice, civil liberties, law enforcement research, and more.—**ARBA Staff Reviewer**

247. **CSDE Lynching Database http://lynching.csde.washington.edu.** [Website] Free. Date reviewed: 2019.

This database, hosted by The Center for Studies in Demography and Ecology (CSDE) at the University of Washington, serves as a historical account of incidents of racial violence occurring between the years of 1877 and 1950 across the southern region of the United States. The database collects information on lynchings or attempted lynchings, generally defined by the site as illegal killings conducted by at least three people in reference to tradition, honor, or justice. The About Us tab accessed via the homepage details the people and institutions involved in gathering information and developing the database. General users can access brief descriptions of nearly four thousand (and counting) cases via the Search tab at the top of the page. Users can enter information in the corresponding fields related to subject name(s), year(s), state(s), race, and sex. Search results yield a list of subjects, locations, and dates. Alternatively, selecting the default fields (e.g., "All Years," "All States") allows users to browse the complete list of cases. Clicking a subject's name opens the record, which may include Alternate name(s), Case Status, Date, County, State, Race, Age, Mob Information, Accusation, Method of Death, Documents, and other details. Users who register with the site (free) can access quantitative data or download large groups of case files for further research capabilities. Under the Educators tab, users can find links to teaching resources such as a lesson plan, suggested readings, and more. The information on the site offers only a sketch of the events and players involved in these violent acts from the past. Nonetheless, it is an excellent, curated, and reliable springboard to further research on the subject.—**ARBA Staff Reviewer**

248. **InSight Crime. https://www.insightcrime.org/.** [Website] Free. Date reviewed: 2018.

InSight Crime gathers information on organized crime in Latin American and Caribbean countries. It offers reports, news analysis, profiles, and other information related to organized crime and its relationship to various aspects of society—the economy, politics, human rights, and more. Creatively organized, the site will appeal to researchers who study regional or national issues related to crime, law enforcement, drug policy, and much more. Users can select from a number of tabs at the top of the page to access the material. The News tab links to a chronological gallery of stories from around the region. Users can scroll through the extensive archive to find News Briefs—generally shorter pieces—and News Analysis, longer pieces including regional context and further background. All articles are tagged for reference and are accompanied by a selection of Related Articles. Recent pieces include "For Informant, a Treacherous Road to Justice in El Salvador" and "Arming Mexico Oil Company Staff is Risky Business." Investigations share thirty-five multipart reports on broader topics also accessible in a gallery display. Users can download full reports or examine reports by section. "Venezuela: A Mafia State?" is an eight-part report looking at the country's drug trafficking problem, its relationships with neighbor nations, and other issues. Other Investigations include the three-part "Illicit Campaign Financing in Guatemala" and the six-part "The MS13." InDepth repackages articles from throughout the website under six umbrella categories: Homicides; Elites and Organized

Crime; NarcoCulture; Prisons; Gangs; and Colombia, Peace, and Conflict. Users can also examine the site's articles by Countries. Clicking the name of a country or its location on the accompanying map opens a brief country profile, a gallery of related News Briefs and Analysis and an article describing the dominant crime groups in the country, their history, leadership, geography, and more. The homepage features a selection of all article categories, lists most read articles, and highlights six newsmakers (people or groups of note). The generous content on the site would be useful to anyone researching organized crime and its myriad manifestations in Latin America and the Caribbean.—**ARBA Staff Reviewer**

249. **K-12 School Shooting Database. Https://www.chds.us/ssdb/.** [Website] Free. Date reviewed: 2018.

Part of the U.S. Department of Homeland Security Digital Library, this database takes a broad look at gun violence in primary and secondary schools in the United States by tracking reported incidents of guns brandished or fired on school property. Scrolling down through the homepage accesses the national map with pinned incident locations. Bubbles are colored to reflect the nature of the gun incident (e.g., gang related, mental health, bullying), and sized to note number of incidents. Clicking on a bubble accesses incident information: date, time period, city, category, and casualty numbers. There is also a brief incident summary. Users can zoom in on the map for improved perspective, particularly helpful for locations where there are numerous incidents. The incident map is updated as incidents are reported. Selecting the yellow View the Data tab in the center of the page or the Graphs tab in the upper left corner brings users to a series of twenty-four visualizations tracking incidents by state, year, firearm type, time of day, gender of the victim, shooter's affiliation with school, and more. This website, with its sobering content, will be useful for reporters, social scientists, and student researchers, among others.— **ARBA Staff Reviewer**

250. **Lexis Nexis Community Crime Map. http://communitycrimemap.com/.** [Website] Free. Date reviewed: 2018.

The Community Crime Map offers a way for the public to monitor crime in their areas and engage with law enforcement for the purpose of increased public safety. The interactive national map displays selected cities across the country pinned with crime "events." Users manipulate the Google/satellite map with selections from the menu on the left side of the page, and can add layers of data for a fuller picture of the local crime environment. Users can input a street address or jump to a city after scrolling through a generous but noncomprehensive alphabetical-by-state list from AK-Anchorage to WY-Sheridan. The selected map will be pinned by icons indicative of particular events, including aggravated assault, homicide, fraud, theft, alcohol violation, shoplifting, and others. Clicking on the icon provides information on the crime event such as location, date, time, responding agency, and more. Users can find data according to date range, can buffer the map to track events within a certain area of the city, choose which events the map will show, and add a density layer (under analytic layers) to add population context. Agency layers will highlight such things as city limits and service areas. Above the map, users will find different views of the data. The data grid lists events and their information in a table. Analytics uses a pie and bar chart, timeline, and a heatmap to express the data. Metadata covers records and geocoding information for the reporting agency. The Community Crime Map is still developing (a city's appearance in the database does not guarantee that events will appear on the map). Nonetheless, it offers important information in an easy-to-navigate format that would appeal to a variety of researchers.—**ARBA Staff Reviewer**

Handbooks and Yearbooks

251.   Barnes-Svarney, Patricia, and Thomas E. Svarney. **The Handy Forensics Answer Book: Reading Clues at the Crime Scene, Crime Lab and in Court.** Canton, Mich., Visible Ink Press, 2019. 400p. illus. index. $21.95pa. ISBN 13: 978-1-5785-9621-8.

Thanks to shows like *CSI: Crime Scene Investigation,* the interest in forensic science has grown exponentially in recent years. Some high schools have added forensic science classes as electives, showing that science has obvious real-life applications. This book taps into that trend. Dividing most of its information into "At the Crime Scene" and "In the Crime Lab," the book contains chapters on topics such as forensic psychology, famous crimes, and forensic science in movies and on television. The information is scholarly and in-depth, yet still understandable to readers new to the subject. There are illustrations, though all are presented in black-and-white. For students doing research, the layout is a little hard to navigate for that purpose. The information is accurate and useful, especially for students studying forensic science, but the topic is pretty specific and may not be a necessary addition for schools that do not have a forensics class. Additional selection.—**Laura Younkin**

252.   O'Hear, Michael. **Prisons and Punishment in America: Examining the Facts.** Santa Barbara, Calif., ABC-CLIO, 2018. 243p. index. (Contemporary Debates). $63.00. ISBN 13: 978-1-4408-5542-9; 978-1-4408-5543-6 (e-book).

Like earlier books in this series, this volume explores its topic, prisons and punishment, by asking and answering questions about diverse aspects of that theme, including sections on alternatives to incarceration, American sentencing, and release and life after prison. The forty questions posed have two-part texts: "Answer" (a single paragraph) and "The Facts" (an elaborated discussion). Each question also has a "Further Reading" list, containing four to twenty references. The reading suggestions may be books, journal articles, or occasionally material from websites. The questions are straightforward and clear. "Is probation just a 'slap on the wrist'?" or "Does time in prison leave inmates more likely to reoffend?" or "What should be done to address racial disparities in incarceration?" are three examples of the topics explored here.

The first page of this book clearly defines its intended audience and that of the other Contemporary Debates volumes: ". . . high school and undergraduate students as well as members of the general public" (p. ix). That clearly designates the kinds of libraries that will benefit most from adding this title to their collections. This series has examined other topics of current interest: climate change, the Affordable Care Act, Muslims, marijuana, journalism and "fake news," and immigration. These other books should be of similar interest to libraries considering this one.—**Mark Schumacher**

253.   **The Palgrave Handbook of Criminal and Terrorism Financing Law.** Colin King, Clive Walker, and Jimmy Gurulé, eds. New York, Palgrave Macmillan, 2018. 1260p. index. $329.00. ISBN 13: 978-3-319-64497-4; 978-3-319-64498-1 (e-book).

This four-part book begins with an introductory section that lays out the book's purpose: to analyze more deeply the "relevant 'follow the money' policies, legislation, and institutions." The book assesses the design of institutions and the degree of accountability of these agencies, tackles issues of legitimacy, looks at the implications of crime crossing borders, and examines the adaptability of agencies in light of changes or newly introduced technologies like Bitcoin. The book's approach is comprehensive in its treatment of tainted ("dirty") assets, evaluating the interrelationships between anti-money laundering, asset recovery, and counterterrorism financing. The coverage is broad geographically; though it focuses on the United Kingdom and the United States, it also incorporates Asia and Europe. The book is multidisciplinary, including contributions from scholars in law, criminology, political science, international studies, and business. The second part evaluates anti-money laundering with specific chapters on topics like the problems of Bitcoin for the EU AML framework and money laundering in the City of London. In the third part focused on recovery, researchers will discover chapters on forfeiture law in the United States, civil recovery in England and Wales, and more. The last part on counter-terrorism financing looks at a variety of topics in such chapters as "Counter-Terrorism Financing Assemblages after 9/11," "Examining the Efficacy of Canada's Anti-Terrorist Financing Laws," "Criminal Prosecutions for Terrorism Financing in the UK," and "Kidnap and Terrorism Finances." The book includes a select bibliography and index. Chapters also have references as well as author information. Highly recommended for academic libraries.—**ARBA Staff Reviewer**

254.   **Research Handbook on Corporate Crime and Financial Misdealing.** Jennifer Arlen, ed. Northampton, Mass., Edward Elgar, 2018. 378p. index. (Research Handbooks in Corporate Law and Governance). $255.00. ISBN 13: 978-1-78347-446-2; 978-1-78347-447-9 (e-book).

Research Handbook on Corporate Crime and Financial Misdealing "brings together leading scholars from a variety of disciplines to explore mechanisms for deterring corporate crime and securities fraud through both public enforcement and private interventions." The handbook is part of the series Research Handbooks in Corporate Law and Governance. Contributors represent organizations and universities among which are New York University School of Law; George Mason University; Georgetown University Law Center; University of Michigan Law School; Yale University Harvard Law School; and the Norwegian School of Economics. The research handbook is divided into parts, Corporate and Individual Liability for Corporate Misconduct; Public Enforcement of Public Corruption and Securities Fraud; and Role of Private Actors: Compliance, Corporate Investigations, and Whistleblowing. The first part covers the "causes of corporate crime, empirical analysis of public enforcement, the liability of supervisors, and the potential cost to corporations of reputational damage from corporate criminal settlement." The second part includes chapters on topics of multijurisdictional enforcement games: the case of anti-bribery law; corruption in state administration; and securities law and its enforcers. The last part covers topics including economic analysis of effective compliance programs; behavior ethics, behavioral compliance; and when the corporation investigates itself. Chapters provide extensive bibliographical references. An index is included; some chapters have figures and charts (e.g., statistics and flow charts). The *Research Handbook on Corporate Crime and Financial Misdealing* is highly recommended to students and faculty of law and business. It contains chapters by experts in the field and contains bibliographic references for further research. Libraries supporting law schools and/or schools of business should purchase this book.—**Lucy Heckman**

255.   Steffens, Bradley. **Gun Violence and Mass Shootings.** San Diego, Calif., Reference Point Press, 2019. 80p. $29.95. ISBN 13: 978-1-6828-2515-0.

This is a needed book to address the gun problem currently roiling the United States, providing a thought-provoking look about the pros and cons of gun ownership in American society. No fancy graphics or primary colors are used to draw in the reader, and information is presented in a straightforward manner that is written for the mature reader. Numerous sidebars, illustrations, and photographs are scattered throughout to supplement and enhance the text and to explain hard-to-grasp concepts. The book begins with an introduction about the Parkland High School shooting and other mass shootings in the country, followed by four chapters: "A Uniquely American Problem," "Patchwork of Laws," "Strengthening Gun Laws," and "An Armed Citizenry." Both sides of the issue are given equal weight. The author provides numerous sobering statistics about guns in America. For example, Nicholas Kristof of the New York Times wrote in a 2015 article that from 1968 to 2015 more Americans died from guns than died in all the military conflicts in American history. At the end of the volume are sections on where to find more information on the topic. This book would be a welcome addition to any school library in need of information on this timely topic.—**Augie E. Beasley**

256.   **Terrorism: The Essential Reference Guide.** Colin P. Clarke, ed. Santa Barbara, Calif., ABC-CLIO, 2018. 348p. illus. index. $94.00. ISBN 13: 978-1-4408-5628-0; 978-1-4408-5629-7 (e-book).

Political violence is not a new phenomenon. For centuries prior to 9/11, terrorists have posed threats to nations worldwide. *Terrorism: The Essential Reference Guide,* an encyclopedia of entries edited by political scientist Colin P. Clarke, identifies individuals, organizations, and events related to terroristic activity.

In order to provide a historical context for current terrorist movements, Clarke begins this volume by providing an informative summary of the evolution of terrorism followed by a discussion of the origins and activities of the al-Qaeda terrorist network and the development and ideology of ISIS. He concludes by offering projections concerning the future of terrorism based upon current trends. Within these introductory materials, Clarke also references a number of seminal works on terrorism providing the reader with a solid base of scholarly literature upon which to rely for additional research.

Comprised of submissions from 34 scholars, this alphabetically organized encyclopedia includes 102 entries as well as 19 illustrative photographs concerning the origin, leadership, ideologies, mission, strategies, history, and evolution of domestic, European, and Middle Eastern terrorist activity. Each entry is accompanied by *see also* references and citations for further exploration. A chronology of events, 14 primary source documents, and comprehensive index add to the value of this guide.

While not revolutionary in terms of content, this volume provides a respectable overview of the progression and characteristics of terroristic activity which will be of value to undergraduates through faculty.—**Dianna L. Kim**

257.   **Transnational Crime and Global Security.** Philip Reichel and Ryan Randa, eds. Santa Barbara, Calif., Praeger/ABC-CLIO, 2018. 2v. index. $164.00/set. ISBN 13: 978-1-4408-4317-4; 978-1-4408-4318-1 (e-book).

Unquestionably, transnational crime presents a serious threat to international and national security and its worldwide ramifications for public health, safety, and economic stability have become a principal focus of criminologists. Globalization has facilitated the rapid expansion and diversification of criminal networks. Exacerbating the problem is a significant lack of effective coordinated response. In *Transnational Crime and Global Security* Editors Philip Reichel and Ryan Randa identify several types of transnational crime and the eradication initiatives nations have taken to address this global issue.

This two-volume set contains 31 submissions by 40 diverse scholars from 10 different nations. Volume one contains information concerning the dissemination of unlawful goods and services and details those crimes which jeopardize security such as transnational corruption, terrorism, and the weaponization of infectious diseases. Volume two focuses on approaches to understanding transnational crime and the consequences of and responses to this global threat.

Somewhat surprising is the absence of a chapter focusing on weapons trafficking in volume one given illicit arms' links to crime, security, and terrorism. This aside, the editors are otherwise comprehensive in their coverage of transnational crime and global security in that other relevant topics such as drug trafficking, human smuggling, intellectual property theft, and cybercrime are identified. Furthermore, the consequences of transnational crime and the manners in which nations have responded to it are also covered providing additional depth and perspective.

Of particular value is the diversity of the expert contributors which serves to appropriately afford a global perspective to the collection. This set will be of value to security students, research scholars, policy makers, and practitioners and includes editor goals, organization notes, suggestions for use, section introductions, editor/contributor information, and an index. A bibliography also accompanies each article supplying content for additional reading and research.—**Dianna L. Kim**

Human Rights

Digital Resources

258.   **American Civil Liberties Union Papers, 1912-1990, Part II: Southern Regional Office.** [Website] Farmington Hills, Mich., Gale/Cengage Learning, 2018. Price negotiated by site. Date reviewed: 2018.

This Gale database resource provides a variety of researchers, in history, women's studies, sociology, and law, with nearly 6,800 documents from the Southern Regional Office of the American Civil Liberties Union. Most of the documents date from the 1945-1990 period, and many of them contain miscellaneous documents linked to specific court cases. (The original materials in this database are now in the Mudd Manuscript Library at Princeton University, along with other ACLU files.) This archive, available online for the first time, contains diverse types of documents: memos, testimony, meeting minutes, personnel records, and several others. The subjects of these materials include school segregation, antiwar protests, sexism, and voting rights. Because the items come from individual ACLU folders, the materials can be quite varied. Fortunately, the keyword search function in the database will indicate which pages within a given folder/document contain the term that was searched.

Researchers will need some experience searching this resource, or some prior understanding of ACLU documents, before their work will move forward smoothly. One interesting feature of the database is the "Term Frequency" search, where one can enter a word or phrase, such as "Abernathy" or "Vietnam," to see how many documents contain the term, year by year. (Unfortunately, the dating of some of the folders can throw off research: the term "NAACP" is shown to be in several items which presumably predate the year of its founding. In fact, it only appears in a document decades later within the folder. Another folder lists the date range as "1795-1973" but the only 18th-century mention is a typed copy (circa 1960s?) of a Jefferson letter, connected some way to the other materials in the folder.) That being said, there is fascinating information in this resource, and libraries serving students, faculty, or researchers in this area should investigate how much it would cost for their population.—**Mark Schumacher**

259.   **Civil Rights and Restorative Justice Project https://crrj.northeastern.edu/.** [Website] Free. Date reviewed: 2019.

Northeastern School of Law's Civil Rights and Restorative Justice Project (CRRJ) is developing an archive of materials related to cases of racial violence and injustice spanning the years 1930-1970 with the goal of facilitating a community's ability to pursue restorative justice. The current digital archive uses legal documents, photographs, media accounts, and other records in support of 57 individual historical cases. The Reading Room link presents case information gathered by the CRRJ. Materials, such as photographs, death certificates, and litigation case files, vary for each case but generally include a PDF of the CRRJ case summary. There may also be a topical student essay. Accompanying metadata lists Title, Creator, Resource Type, Subjects and Keywords, and more. Some cases may display additional links to newspaper articles, related CRRJ initiatives, and other information. Clicking on the icon to the right of the case subject's name links to the Case Watch Map which provides geographical context. Users manipulate the timeline bar at the bottom of the map to enable pinned locations to appear. Clicking on the pin displays a brief description of the case as well as links to relevant materials in The Reading Room. The homepage also provides access to The Red Record, a developing podcast series devoted to the stories behind the cases. A two-part episode on Samuel Mason Bacon, a black man who was arrested and killed after refusing to give up his bus seat to a white man, is currently available. The Headlight blog shares personal reflections of victim descendants, lawyers, students, and others. Still in development, the CRRJ project will eventually allow users to register to gain access to more cases and information.—**ARBA Staff Reviewer**

260.   **Deathscapes https://www.deathscapes.org/.** [Website] Free. Date reviewed: 2019.

Deathscapes brings a modern artistic eye to a serious subject, serving as an exhibit of contemporary stories of state-sponsored custodial racial violence and injustice. It maps recorded instances of violent episodes, tracking manifestations across the landscapes of Australia, the United States, and Canada as well as the United Kingdom and European

Union. Using a variety of formats, the site tells impactful stories of racialized indigenous, migrant, and other minority populations with the goal of closer examination of reasons, methods, and implications. Case Studies are the primary feature of Deathscapes, sharing twelve global examples (some in development). Users can click on an image from the gallery or filter using a key term as defined by the project (users can first examine the terms, such as "Death by Policing," "Racial Governance," "Settler-Colonial State," etc., under the Go To Project key terms link). Case Studies may use photographs, timelines, videos, statistics, and other resources to convey incident details, victim biographies, foundational analysis, discussions of implications, and additional pieces of information. "Jimmy Mubenga and the Plane," for example, describes a event where an Angolan man, having lived and worked legally in the United Kingdom for sixteen years as a refugee, died on a commercial airliner while in custody of a private security company. The study examines the repercussions of Mubenga's death; the increased visibility of deportations, the rise of activism in opposition to the forced deportations, and more. Other studies address cases that involve targeted brutality, mental health neglect, suicides, and other issues found in such settings as immigration detention camps, prisons, and police stations. Other features on the site include Engagements, offering a selection of further reading; Galleries, organizing photographs, artworks, social media posts, and other tributes to movements and individuals; and Inspirations, sharing quotes, videos, and other reflections which honor and educate about marginalized peoples. Deathscapes challenges users with its difficult subject matter, but provides an important resource for the ongoing global civil rights movement. The site will continue to add stories.—**ARBA Staff Reviewer**

Handbooks and Yearbooks

261.   Condé, H. Victor, and Charles Gelsinger. **Human Rights and the United States.** Amenia, N.Y., Grey House Publishing, 2017. 2v. index. $250.00/set. ISBN 13: 978-1-68217-346-6.

Human Rights and the United States is a two-volume work "designed as a tool to help Americans learn about U.S. laws, policies, procedures, opinions and records within the international human rights and related law arena." The first volume contains such chapters as: "Chronology of U.S. Human Rights Moments and Events"; "U.S. State Department, Secretary of State and Human Rights"; "Organization of American States: The U.S. and the Inter-American Human Rights System"; "Equality, Non-discrimination and Racism"; and "Rights of Indigenous Peoples." There are also chapters on the rights of children, the rights of women and girls, migrant workers, refugees, and freedom of thought and belief. The second volume covers freedom of expression, the criminal justice system, climate change, health care, education, and more as these topics relate to human rights. Each chapter includes: a leader page that contains a paragraph summary of what the chapter is about and why the topic is important; Quotes and Key Text Excerpts; What You Should Know; and Primary Source Documents. There are three appendixes "U.S. Law and Legislation, Resolutions, and the Restatement of Law"; "Case Law Decisions from U.S. Courts & International Courts"; and Reports of Selected U.S. and International NGOs." Also included is a bibliography, finding guides, a primary source documents index, and a general index. *Human Rights and the United States* contains a wealth of information and access to a wide range of primary source document reprints. This invaluable work is recommended for academic and public libraries and should prove to be of great research value to students and faculty of social studies, government and politics, history, sociology, and current events. Highly recommended.—**Lucy Heckman**

262.   **Contesting Human Rights: Norms, Institutions and Practice.** Alison Brysk and Michael Stohl, eds. Northampton, Mass., Edward Elgar, 2019. 234p. index. (Elgar Studies in Human Rights). $135.00. ISBN 13: 978-1-78897-285-7; 978-1-78897-286-4 (e-book).

This scholarly volume explores numerous important aspects of human rights. The introduction by Alison Brysk spells out the studies that follow, as they connect with one another within the current status of human rights worldwide. Case studies examine the status of human rights around the world, from child marriages to LGBT rights, from human rights cities to constitutional incorporation of human rights protection. At least one essay points out the position of the current U.S. government, that wishes to "reduce America's long-standing commitment to humanitarianism, poverty reduction, democracy, women's health, and human rights" (p. 198). All of the chapters have numerous references, either as scores of footnotes or dozens of items in bibliographies, providing readers with a great deal of further information. Sources include books, scholarly articles, and in some chapters, numerous court cases.

The text throughout is quite scholarly and often quite specialized, exploring topics such as "the trans-national human rights judicial network," which requires some background knowledge of the human rights courts in Africa, Europe, and the Americas. This volume is one of three published by Elgar in 2019, and edited by these two authors, that examine aspects of human rights; the others are *Expanding Human Rights* and *Contracting Human Rights.* This will be most useful in academic libraries which support programs in gender studies, political science, history, law, and other related fields.—**Mark Schumacher**

263.   Issitt, Micah L. **National Security vs. Civil and Privacy Rights.** Amenia, N.Y., Grey House Publishing, 2017. 695p. illus. index. $195.00pa. ISBN 13: 978-1-68217-720-4; 978-1-68217-721-1 (e-book).

This is a new series from Grey House Publishing titled Opinions throughout History, and the first topic is privacy, civil rights, and national security. The book contains 29 chapters examining landmark legal cases, from the 1890 Foundations of a Constitutional Debate to the 2016-18 Section 702 Renewal. Each chapter details a specific legal debate, controversy, law enactment, or Supreme Court decision. At the bottom of each chapter, a timeline of events prior to, up to, and after the event provides a quick reference and history. There are many black-and-white pictures throughout the book, along with discussion questions for classroom and homework assignment use. Some of the events described include *Barenblatt* vs. *United States* (1959), The FISA Act of 1978, The PATRIOT Act (2001), The Snowden Leaks (2013), and the USA Freedom Act (2015), to name a few. A timely reference work with a wealth of historical information and detail on these topics.—**Bradford Lee Eden**

International Law

Dictionaries and Encyclopedias

264.   Doebbler, Curtis F. J. **Dictionary of Public International Law.** Lanham, Md., Rowman & Littlefield, 2018. 620p. $165.00; $156.50 (e-book). ISBN 13: 978-1-5381-1124-6; 978-1-5381-1125-3 (e-book).

Here readers will find more than four hundred entries on public international law. The book begins with helpful supplemental tools, such as a list of acronyms and abbreviations, a list of foreign language terms, a chronology, and a list of entries. There are entries on people, treaties, cases, international organizations, and more. Extensive cross-references enhance navigation, as does an index. Entries can range from a few paragraphs to several pages. If a term within an entry appears in boldface type, this is a cue to users that the term has its own entry. A subdivided bibliography will greatly assist researchers who want to find more information on a particular subject. This dictionary merits selection for political science and law courses. Public, high school, and university decision makers should consider including this exemplary reference.—**Thomas E. Baker**

Digital Resources

265.   **Virtual Tribunals. https://exhibits.stanford.edu/virtual-tribunals/.** [Website] Free. Date reviewed: 2018.

This site, which will eventually share a variety of document collection related to international criminal tribunals, currently allows access to the trial records from the Special Panels for Serious Crimes (SPSC) in East Timor, concerning the violence and other criminal activity borne out of the 1999 East Timorese quest for independence from Indonesia. Records are available for roughly fifty-five trials that occurred in the ensuing years. Users can learn about the SPSC and the particular crimes in East Timor via the links at the bottom of the page: Introduction to the SPSC, SPSC Cases, and SPSC Crimes. Alternatively, users can directly explore all associated documents via the Browse tab at the top of the page or via the search options on the left-hand side. Browse links to a gallery of document types: Basic Documents, Decisions and Judgments, Indictments, Judicial Orders/Notices, Motions, and Transcripts. Aside from Document Types, users can search using Crime Charged/Topic, Issuing Body, Case Title, Date Range, or Language. There may be additional subcategories to search as well. Selecting from any of these categories lists relevant documents with a thumbnail image and other identifying information such as case title, case/document number, date filed, record type, language, and extent (number of pages). Clicking on the thumbnail opens the document in a viewer, and users can zoom, download, and keyword search within it. The excellent organization of Virtual Tribunals bodes well for its future expansion. The project is currently gathering and processing records for the Extraordinary Chambers in the Courts of Cambodia, the International Criminal Tribunal for Rwanda, the International Criminal Tribunal for Yugoslavia, Post-World War II Trials (European and Pacific Theater), and the Special Court for Sierra

Leone. The site would appeal to researchers, educators, and students of international law, human rights, global studies, and more.—**ARBA Staff Reviewer**

Handbooks and Yearbooks

266.   **Protecting Migrant Children: In Search of Best Practice.** Mary Crock and Lenni B. Benson, eds. Northampton, Mass., Edward Elgar, 2018. 526p. index. $205.00. ISBN 13: 978-1-78643-025-0; 978-1-78643-026-7 (e-book).

This book offers an "interdisciplinary and multicultural" exploration of the issue of migrant children. Twenty-four chapters examine the situation in locations around the world: Australia, the United States, China, South Sudan, Central America, among others. The 33 contributors also come from around the world, many with ties to Australia. Nearly all are lawyers or have had legal experience. The introductory chapter by the editors provides an excellent overview of the studies to follow, as well as a clear statement of its focus: "The book has at its centre the millions of children who are being or have been displaced across borders by wars or other catastrophes" (p. 7). The chapters are grouped in six sections which look at displacement stories, protection frameworks (two of the sections), domestic laws, process matters, and finally challenges and solutions. Each study is highly documented with scores of footnotes citing laws, other government documents and related research.

Although this is an expensive volume, law school libraries and other higher education libraries that have students and faculty exploring these subjects should consider adding it, in print or as an e-book, to their collections. Other libraries can do without its detailed, often technical, exploration of this specialized subject.—**Mark Schumacher**

267.   **Research Handbook on International Water Law.** Stephen C. McCaffrey, Christina Leb, and Riley T. Denoon, eds. Northampton, Mass., Edward Elgar, 2019. 538p. index. (Research Handbooks in International Law). $315.00. ISBN 13: 978-1-78536-807-3; 978-1-78536-808-0 (e-book).

Editors Stephen C. McCaffrey, Distinguished Professor of Law at the University of the Pacific and recipient of the 2017 Stockholm Water Prize, Christina Leb, Senior Water Resources Specialist and Thematic Focal Point for Transboundary Waters at the World Bank, and Riley T. Denoon, a doctoral student at the University of the Pacific, are joined by 33 other contributors in producing a much needed reference on international water law. The 29 essays provide fascinating insights into international agreements forged throughout the world. Unfortunately, a thread that runs throughout the work is that the treaties are full of rhetoric but short of enforceable specifics. This is because many countries are loath to share their waters. A notable example is China, which has the headwaters of many of Southeast Asia's major rivers, such as the Mekong, within its borders. Although the respective rivers flow through many neighboring countries, China considers them to be theirs and builds huge dams on them to impound as much of the water as they desire. The Mekong River Commission, which includes representation from Cambodia, Laos, Thailand, and Vietnam, is lauded in this work as a successful example of shared governance over the Mekong River and its watershed, but its effectiveness is compromised by China's unwillingness to join or even acknowledge that they share a transnational river. Despite the obvious weaknesses of the vast majority of the agreements, the authors of the respective essays do see them as a step forward. It is hoped that as countries begin to work together, they will develop the trust necessary to forge stronger agreements. Most of the authors are specialists who have worked on transboundary water issues through international bodies so the level of expertise is impressive.

Their familiarity with the subject matter is reflected by the heavy footnoting in each essay. This work is highly recommended to academic libraries supporting graduate programs focused on the environment or the law. Undergraduate libraries should also consider acquiring this work, but be aware that most of the authors assume their readers have a basic understanding of the topic so fundamental concepts go unexplained.

[Editor's note: The e-book version is priced from £22/$31 from Google Play, ebooks.com, and other eBook vendors, while in print the book can be ordered from the Edward Elgar Publishing website.]—**John R. Burch Jr.**

11 Library and Information Science and Publishing and Bookselling

Library and Information Science

General Works

268.   Aldrich, Rebekkah Smith. **Sustainable Thinking: Ensuring Your Library's Future in an Uncertain World.** Chicago, American Library Association, 2018. 194p. index. $49.99pa.; $44.99pa. (ALA members). ISBN 13: 978-0-8989-1688-9.

Sustainable Thinking has a tougher edge than the rather innocuous title would lead the reader to believe. Yes, the book is about helping libraries understand and plan for a future with a foundation shifting underfoot. The intention and motivation behind this goal, though, are undeniably emotional and activist in nature. Far from a criticism, a book that serves as a type of call-to-arms for the entire library profession should be a welcome voice to the conversation.

Functionally, the book is divided into three main sections: a situation report, strategy, and tactics. Having worked with libraries for eighteen years in order to raise awareness and funding, Aldrich has a great perspective to share in the continuing battle of library public opinion and an increasingly unsupportive political environment. Because of its activist nature, each of the twenty-five chapters ends with a brief worksheet that encourages readers to think about the chapter content and, as a result, increase a sense of ownership in libraries, provide an understanding of their critical role in society, and stoke an activist flame for libraries to succeed. The publication ends with a section of resources that includes library resolutions, case studies, and an index.

Sustainable Thinking is a fantastic resource for many types of audiences. Library-friendly individuals will sense a renewed urgency to keep fighting for libraries in our society. Perhaps more importantly, though, would be a potential audience that could benefit from some enlightenment, knowledge, and new perspective regarding libraries.—**Tyler Manolovitz**

269.   Hirsh, Sandra. **Information Services Today: An Introduction.** Lanham, Md., Rowman & Littlefield, 2018. 574p. index. $65.00pa.; $61.50 (e-book). ISBN 13: 978-1-5381-0300-5; 978-1-5381-0301-2 (e-book).

This title first published in 2015 (see ARBA 2016, entry 185). The revised edition of Sandra Hirsh's *Information Services Today: An Introduction* is even better than the original. Information services is a broad topic that encompasses a wide variety of subjects, but the layout of the book breaks it down into manageable subtopics and includes issues particularly important today, such as diversity and social justice; ethics, licensing, copyright, privacy, and security issues; management skills; and creating and collaborating via technology. Highlights of this revised edition include new topics such as strategic planning, change management, design thinking, advocacy, and data management and analysis. This is a dense, information-heavy volume that should prove to be a valuable resource throughout the career of any information professional. Its primary audience is new students in an information school or LIS program, but this would also be useful for current information professionals who need a refresher, non-LIS professionals who want more insight into the information fields, and instructors in LIS programs. The book also includes links to an online supplement with relevant links, tools, and recommended readings, as well as a series of archived webinars that engage specifically with the content of specific chapters, often presented by the chapter authors themselves.—**Shanna Hollich**

270.   **Open Divide: Critical Studies on Open Access.** Joachim Schopfel and Ulrich Herb, eds. Sacramento, Calif., Library Juice Press, 2018. 188p. $35.00pa. ISBN 13: 978-1-63400-029-1.

Fourteen chapters by sixteen contributors around the world (although not from the United States) explore the current issues involving open access. The preface presents aspects of the current open access situation among researchers, authors, and publishers such as Elsevier whose journal prices have been prohibitive for many institutions, and the growth of options to attempt to reduce the cost of scholarly publication. Then there is an introduction (which summarizes the thirteen chapters to follow), six articles in a section labeled Global Issues, and seven articles in the North/South section which examine a variety of disparities affecting researchers and scholars in the southern hemisphere.

There are a few editing issues in the "References" lists: dates slightly off, page numbers of printed articles missing, and other minor issues. Given the important information and insights concerning the global situation of open access, these essays will nonetheless be of most interest to readers in academic libraries, where work with providing open access materials is most prevalent. The reasonable price and the breadth of the discussion make it an excellent selection.—**Mark Schumacher**

271.   **The Politics of Theory and the Practice of Critical Librarianship.** Karen P. Nicholson and Maura Seale, eds. Sacramento, Calif., Library Juice Press, 2018. 264p. index. $35.00pa. ISBN 13: 978-1-63400-030-7.

This book contains a fascinating group of essays centered on the concept of critical librarianship: a growing body of scholarship which combines both practical and theoretical knowledge to challenge the ways that libraries and the profession consciously and unconsciously support systems of oppression. The goal is to move towards a more socially just, theoretically informed praxis. Divided into four sections containing fourteen chapters, the authors explore issues related to the history of librarianship; the way the library profession classifies and categorizes print and digital objects; how disabilities are dealt with among staff and patrons in libraries; how information literacy is taught and presented to first-generation, diverse, and disadvantaged populations; and the ways that digital communities and discourse within the library profession have raised awareness and implemented change. Issues related to activism, resistance, and attitude are also explored. A great compilation of essays related to this recent and growing topic.—**Bradford Lee Eden**

Libraries

College and Research Libraries

272.   **Academic Libraries for Commuter Students: Research-Based Strategies.** Mariana Regalado and Maura A. Smale, eds. Chicago, American Library Association, 2018. 164p. index. $59.99pa.; $53.99pa. (ALA members). ISBN 13: 978-0-8389-1701-5.

This book brings together studies by librarians and researchers at community and baccalaureate colleges and universities nationwide, including schools that serve both commuter and residential students and those that serve a mostly commuter student population. The overarching goal is to help librarians design and develop services, resources, and facilities for the students they serve. There are several case studies; each case study describes the research methods used, analyzes what was learned, and discusses specific changes made as a result. Cases studies include information from Indiana University-Purdue University Indianapolis, a school that serves both commuter and residential students; the seven colleges of the City University of New York, which mainly serve commuter students; several community colleges; the University of Colorado at Boulder, which has a more traditional, noncommuter student body; and more. When one takes into account the fact that the percentage of commuter students in the college population, the need for this book becomes obvious. Recommended.—**ARBA Staff Reviewer**

273.   Budd, John M. **The Changing Academic Library: Operations, Culture, Environments.** Chicago, American Library Association, Association of College and Research Libraries, 2018. 474p. index. $88.00pa. ISBN 13: 978-0-8389-8997-5.

Part of the ACRL Publications in Librarianship series published by the Association of College and Research Libraries, this third edition of the classic volume on academic libraries, their history and operations, current challenges and opportunities, and operations and culture is a well-known and consistent reference book for academic librarians. The second edition published in 2012 (see ARBA 2012, entry 465). Divided into twelve chapters, the author has brought the previous two editions up-to-date, and has added recent information on topics of current interest. Placing academic librarianship within the broader macroenvironments of higher education, faculty governance, the history of libraries in the United States, and related communities of practice and importance, this book also touches on basic issues such as budgeting, collections, access, scholarly communication, digital information, and the role of the academic librarian in the academy. Every academic librarian needs to have access to or own a copy of this book, and it also provides provosts and presidents with an introduction to the role of libraries in higher education.—**Bradford Lee Eden**

274.   Evans, G. Edward, and Stacey Greenwell. **Academic Librarianship: Second Edition.** 2d ed. Chicago, American Library Association, 2018. 284p. index. $98.00pa.; $85.50pa. (ALA members). ISBN 13: 978-0-8389-1563-9.

This volume updates a 2010 edition, and retains the structure of that book, but with 90 fewer pages. The 14 chapters deal with faculty, students, funding, facilities, collections and service, among other topics. Each chapter also includes a "Key Points to Remember" subsection, as well as "Check This Out," "Something to Ponder," and "Keep in Mind" sidebars, as in the first edition; much of those texts remains the same, although there are also updates and refocusing of topics throughout the volume, given today's changing library world. Each chapter contains several new references from the last 2-3 years.

The stated goal of this book is to be a guide to help librarians throughout their careers "particularly in better understanding higher education institutions and how academic libraries support those institutions." (p. xiv) The book achieves that goal with its wide range of topics, a clear writing style, and numerous references to other useful readings and websites, found throughout. Students and teachers of librarianship will find this book a useful overview of the field. It is, however, disappointing that a 284-page paperback put out by the American Library Association costs $98.00; this may well reduce sales to some extent.—**Mark Schumacher**

275. **The Globalized Library: American Academic Libraries and International Students, Collections, and Practices.** Yelena Luckert and Lindsay Inge Carpenter, eds. Chicago, American Library Association, Association of College and Research Libraries, 2019. 432p. $90.00pa. ISBN 13: 978-0-8389-8951-7.

It is hard to deny that international ties are important to academic libraries, even increasingly so. The stated goals of *The Globalized Library* are to highlight current activities involving those ties, and to develop a professional vocabulary to convey their value within academic institutions. The book's chapters are divided into 5 thematic sections. Chapters in the first (on information literacy) and second sections (on outreach and inclusion) primarily describe efforts to integrate international students on US campuses, although one chapter discusses information literacy instruction for students on a satellite campus abroad. Sections 3 and 4, on collections and digital humanities and establishing libraries and services abroad, cover a range of projects including international acquisition networks, area studies collections, and libraries established abroad. Chapters in Section 5, on career and development, discuss international exchange/mentoring programs for librarians and library science students.

This book provides a good overview of international activities in North American academic libraries, which will be useful to librarians considering similar initiatives. However, the book does not provide a unified definition of what a globalized library is (is it just an academic library whose activities involve non-North Americans in some way?) or who its constituents are (refugee and immigrant students are mentioned in the introduction, but later chapters seem to focus heavily on students who come to North America specifically for educational purposes). Addressing these questions more clearly would contribute to libraries' ability to communicate the value of their international initiatives. Recommended for libraries at research institutions.—**Chana Kraus-Friedberg**

276. **Library Service and Learning: Empowering Students, Inspiring Social Responsibility, and Building Community Connections.** Theresa McDevitt and Caleb P. Finegan, eds. Chicago, American Library Association, Association of College and Research Libraries, 2018. 424p. $78.00pa. ISBN 13: 978-0-8389-4609-1.

Library Service and Learning offers readers an in-depth look at ways libraries have become actively engaged in service-learning and experiential learning. Each chapter is a detailed case study written by librarians, university faculty, and students who have developed successful service-learning experiences at their institution. The book is divided into three sections, based on whether the librarian led the learning experience, partnered with others, or the library itself served as the host. Each chapter is highly structured and includes detailed information on the activity, the people involved, and the outcomes. Appendixes include syllabi, rubrics, and other course materials that provide enough detail for readers to re-create the experience or activity described. There is a good mix of institutional type and size represented, along with subject areas and types of students, making it easy for readers to find something that will fit their own institutional need. Common among all of the case studies is the inclusion of information literacy outcomes, utilization of library resources or facilities, and service to a community partner. A discussion of the benefits to not only the instructors and students, but also the community partners and institutions, along with difficulties each faced, is especially helpful to those who may wish to develop a similar experience. A final chapter offers a review of the literature on experiential and service-learning in libraries and information literacy instruction and provides resources for further study on the benefits of these types of practices. This book is an excellent resource for those looking to partner with their library in creating service-learning experiences, as well as for librarians interested in becoming involved in the activities at their institution.— **Andrea C. Kepsel**

277.   **Motivating Students on a Time Budget: Pedagogical Frames and Lesson Plans for In-Person and Online Information Literacy Instruction.** Sarah Steiner and Miriam Rigby, eds. Chicago, American Library Association, Association of College and Research Libraries, 2019. 322p. $64.00pa. ISBN 13: 978-0-8389-8949-4.

As most instructional librarians know, it can be hard to motivate students in one-shot instruction sessions. Unlike the faculty teaching the courses, we don't always have a longer time frame in which to build relationships with the students or the power of the grading pen to frame the relevance of our subject matter. We also often teach skills that students may believe they already have, such as effective searching or source evaluation. In *Motivating Students on a Time Budget,* chapter authors aim to offer instructional librarians a set of ideas and lesson plans that will allow them to motivate students during short information literacy sessions.

The first 5 chapters of the book review current research on motivation and apply it to student learning. The authors discuss some broad principles of engagement for instructors, including the importance of understanding student perceptions of assignment relevance. The remaining 14 chapters provide examples of lessons plans for readers to use or alter in their own work. Many of the chapters in both groups refer to Keller's ARCS (Attention, Relevance, Confidence, Satisfaction) model of motivation as a framework for understanding student needs and interests. Most lesson plans are designed for in-person sessions with undergraduate students but could be altered to fit other situations as well. From creating an information literacy escape room to using list poems as starting points for research, the lesson plans in this book will offer instructional librarians some new ideas for engaging students in information literacy. Recommended for all academic libraries.— **Chana Kraus-Friedberg**

278.   Reale, Michelle. **The Indispensable Academic Librarian: Teaching and Collaborating for Change.** Chicago, American Library Association, 2018. 128p. index. $57.00pa.; $51.30pa. (ALA members). ISBN 13: 978-0-8389-1638-4.

How can subject librarians thrive on a modern college campus? Michelle Reale, the access services and outreach librarian at Arcadia University, provides a series of tested strategies in *The Indispensable Academic Librarian*. At a time when academic library services are often viewed as an afterthought, Reale illuminates a path toward heightened relevance.

To succeed, new librarians must seek out new opportunities and become "indispensable" in their work. Over the course of ten chapters Reale investigates central areas for instruction and outreach librarians: reference, teaching, fostering critical inquiry, faculty collaborations, and leadership. Reale helps contextualize how these seemingly disparate activities work together to enable professional success.

A key theme throughout the volume is taking a proactive approach to one's duties as well as having the courage to lead new library initiatives. Reale seamlessly includes practical examples learned over a successful career. "Critical Pedagogy in the Classroom" is the strongest chapter and offers a provocative examination of this topic. Each chapter concludes with several potential strategies and a short reading list.

Reale's writing is highly engaging, and passages are often sprinkled with lively anecdotes. While topics are presented with clarity and style, some sections don't go into significant depth. Regrettably, there is limited use of current research to help support Reale's recommendations.

The Indispensable Academic Librarian offers a succinct overview of the major components of successful liaison work. Despite a limited range of perspectives, this volume should provide considerable value to beginning instruction, outreach, and subject librarians. Reale's book also serves as a practical complement to the many traditional titles in this area.—**Joshua Becker**

279. **Shaping the Campus Conversation on Student Learning and Experience: Activating the Results of Assessment in Action.** Karen Brown and others. Chicago, American Library Association, Association of College and Research Libraries, 2018. 378p. $70.00. ISBN 13: 978-0-8389-8994-4.

This volume has two apparent goals. First, it provides a detailed account of the three-year "Assessment in Action" project (2013-2016) developed by the Association of College and Research Libraries (ACRL) and funded by the Institute of Museum and Library Services. (This project was a contribution to ACRL's "Value of Academic Libraries Initiative.") Three annual reports of the project are included in this first section. The 6 main chapters of this section are authored by Karen Brown and Kara Malenfant, 2 of the editors, while the last item is a June, 2016 ACRL "Value of Academic Libraries Statement."

The second section contains nine articles written by participants in the project, reporting on the activities they initiated at their institutions during this project. Studies include topics such as instruction for first-year students, working with other student support services on one's campus, assessing information literacy instruction for transfer students, and enhancing the library experience for aboriginal and international students in Alberta, Canada. The volume concludes with 11 appendixes (147 pages), which include annual reports to funding agencies, a list of participants for each of the years, and other related documents. (One minor fact to note: six items, totaling about 125 pages, only show the original page numbers of the reprinted document being presented, rather than numbers from this book itself, making referencing them somewhat tricky.)

This reasonably priced volume will be quite useful in academic libraries, particularly at institutions with graduate library/information science programs. Other types of libraries will probably not require the highly focused content found here.—**Mark Schumacher**

280.   **Transforming Libraries to Serve Graduate Students.** Crystal Renfro and Cheryl Stiles, eds. Chicago, American Library Association, Association of College and Research Libraries, 2018. 446p. $88.00pa. ISBN 13: 978-0-8389-4606-0.

The 34 chapters in this volume, written by 54 authors, present a vast range of initiatives undertaken by academic libraries to enhance the experience of graduate students in a wide range of disciplines. In recent years, many colleges and universities have developed services and study spaces for their graduate students, in part because those students often consider undergraduates "noisy and inconsiderate." (New York University students were particularly bothered by this.) Increasingly, positions such as "Graduate School Librarian" have appeared on campuses across the country, and these librarians have sought to learn what their population of grad students wishes to see done to enhance their experience. The volume is divided into four sections: the different kinds of graduate students and their needs, library functions and spaces, workshops and data services, and partnerships. Each chapter also provides a useful bibliography to lead readers to earlier studies of these issues.

The rich diversity of projects undertaken by the various institutions will provide readers with a wide range of ideas to contemplate for their own graduate student populations. All academic libraries should certainly consider this volume for their collections.—**Mark Schumacher**

Public Libraries

281.   Aldrich, Rebekkah Smith. **Resilience.** Chicago, American Library Association, 2018. 88p. (Library Future Series, Book 2). $24.99pa.; $22.49pa. (ALA members). ISBN 13: 978-0-8389-1634-6.

This slim volume explores the importance of resilience in today's society and the ways that libraries can contribute to the resilience of the people they serve. Throughout this brief text, the author paints a difficult time for the country: "our government is close to non-functioning and civic leadership is weakened by the toxicity of the political sphere" (p. 5), "given the severity of what lies ahead, particularly on the environmental front" (pp. 65-66), and the statement in the conclusion that librarians must work hard "in the face of violence, oppression, and environmental devastation" (p. 87). The book is almost completely about public libraries and the communities they serve. Instead of being gatekeepers to information, libraries need to become "catalysts and conveners" (p. 38), by leveraging their positive image in the minds of their patrons. There are at least a dozen examples of great work being done in libraries across the country to enhance the lives of the patrons they work with by building a resilient community.

In this tiny book, the 65 footnotes, which are often 100+ characters of a URL, are in a font about 1/15 of an inch and are practically unreadable. There are various bits of text in boldface: "hack the world," "social cohesion," "we need a supercharged type of collaboration," without a clear explanation of the reason for highlighting these terms rather than others. Given the book's focus, it will most useful for public libraries, but schools with library science programs could consider it as well.—**Mark Schumacher**

282.   Alessio, Amy J., Katie Lamantia, and Emily Vinci. **Pop Culture-Inspired Programs for Tweens, Teens, and Adults.** Chicago, American Library Association, 2018. 150p. $49.99pa. ISBN 13: 978-0-8389-1705-3.

This book is filled with program ideas for public libraries, although a couple might be adaptable for use in schools as well. The authors have included an introduction which explains the theme, how to understand pop culture, what still works, and how to use the book. The programs they chose cover trends mostly found in books, music, movies, fashion, games, and food. All possess very high appeal to lots of age groups. The ideas are arranged by decades from the 1950s to 2000s, with a final chapter that includes activities spanning across all of the covered eras. The same format is used for every program: each starts with a set of boxes which contain prep time, length of program, number of patrons, and suggested age range. Then comes several different sections, including supplies/shopping, activities to do, marketing, and variations by age groups. All seem straightforward and relatively easy to carry out, although several are quite time-consuming. This would make a good choice for public libraries and systems that want to work on new programming ideas, though this would probably not be a first purchase for those in a school library setting.—**Melinda W. Miller**

283.   Dowd, Ryan J. **The Librarian's Guide to Homelessness.** Chicago, American Library Association, 2018. 248p. index. $57.00pa.; $51.30pa. (ALA members). ISBN 13: 978-0-8389-1626-1.

The author, Ryan J. Dowd, is an educator and executive director of a large homeless shelter in Chicago. The subtitle of this book gives an accurate description of its contents, "An empathy-driven approach to solving problems, preventing conflict, and serving everyone." The book is divided into four parts. The first, Homelessness and Empathy, describes the causes and condition of homelessness beginning with exploding such concepts as "most homeless people are mentally ill" and "people are homeless for a long time." A later chapter in this part explores the concept of empathy ("the ability to share and understand the feelings of others") and how it applies to the treatment of the homeless. The remaining three parts deal with specific conditions and topics. Some examples: empathy vs. punishment, the many uses of body language (e.g., how to stand), verbal dos and don'ts (e.g., never say "What's the matter with you?"), and the many simple techniques available to solve difficult situations. Another part deals with specialized situations such as mental illness, substance abuse, sleeping, and personal hygiene. Part four gives advice to managers, directors, and leaders to administer the program plus a concluding summary chapter on how best to help homeless people. Each chapter ends with a brief section called, "Notes" which is a bibliography of four or five references (many are websites). The book concludes with a three-page appendix of key phases to use in difficult situations and a four-page general index. There are many factors that make this an outstanding book on the subject: the practical, everyday situations and solutions described make it extremely valuable and the presentation of this material in clear prose plus the frequent use of examples and case studies bring immediacy to the material. Most of all, the author's positive, sympathetic attitude towards his subject is contagious. Although some of the material deals with situations outside the library, most is relevant particularly in relation to medium to large public libraries. In conclusion, anyone who deals with the homeless in public libraries will benefit from a look into this valuable resource.—**John T. Gillespie**

284.   Flaherty, Mary Grace. **Promoting Individual and Community Health at the Library.** Chicago, American Library Association, 2018. 134p. index. $50.00pa.; $45.00pa. (ALA members). ISBN 13: 978-0-8389-1627-8.

According to the author, Mary Grace Flaherty, more than 90 million American adults have low health literacy. In an effort to help with this issue, many libraries are working to improve patrons' access to, and use of, health information. *Promoting Individual and Community Health at the Library* covers the strategies used by libraries in this endeavor. The author, who teaches in the graduate library program at the University of North Carolina at Chapel Hill and who has over 25 years of experience working in medical research and other libraries, argues that health reference differs from other types of questions because it involves critical information issues and needs. It is therefore crucial that libraries have the appropriate information and the means of delivering it.

The work opens with an overview of the history of public libraries and consumer health. The book then expands to discuss the provision of health information and health programming in public libraries. These topics are followed by chapters on reaching out to the community and future opportunities. The final chapter deals with staff health information training, ethics, and cultural sensitivity. The text is augmented with case studies, simple flow charts, lists of social service agencies, and websites. Each chapter concludes with a summary and a list of references. The work is indexed.

This is a well-researched and well-written book that librarians in almost all types of libraries will find very useful. Recommended.—**January Adams**

285.   Kirker, Christine. **25 Projects for Art Explorers.** Chicago, American Library Association, 2018. 49p. illus. $24.99pa. $22.49 (ALA members). ISBN 13: 978-0-8389-1739-8.

This is a good professional book for public librarians, school librarians, and art teachers interested in combining literacy and art. Each chapter focuses on a single picture book and art project. The art projects mostly involve re-creating and practicing the illustration style shown in each book with a theme that is similar to the source book's theme. This resource provides readers with a synopsis of the featured book for each art project, information about the illustrator, information about the illustration technique (often with links to watch how the illustrator does it online), programming tips, suggestions for other books to display, and listings of the materials and directions needed to complete the art project. The projects are fully explained and everything needed to take these projects from the page straight to a library program or lesson is included. While the art ideas are not particularly innovative, they are certainly fun and easily doable learning experiences for children. I would feel comfortable with doing most of these lessons, but I am not sure I would be able to demonstrate some of the techniques well enough to teach. Many different artistic styles are shown in the guide, including watercolor, gouache, cut paper, collage, ink, painted tissue paper, pulp paper-making, mixed media, and cartoons. An appendix with materials guidelines is included. Recommended.—**Michelle Bridges**

286.   Lehn, Carla Campbell. **From Library Volunteer to Library Advocate: Tapping into the Power of Community Engagement.** Santa Barbara, Calif., Libraries Unlimited/ ABC-CLIO, 2018. 188p. index. $50.00pa. ISBN 13: 978-1-4408-5670-9; 978-1-4408-5671-6 (e-book).

The author has had a distinguished career in libraries, principally in California where she became involved in a state-wide program on volunteerism that, in 2008, was unveiled in a publication, *Get Involved: Powered by Your Library.* This project and many others, both state and local, form the basis of the data and advice presented in this current, engrossing volume which, in a "how-to-do-it" fashion, reports on the purposes, design, planning, execution, and rewards involved in these new approaches to volunteerism and libraries. Although the focus of this account is on medium to large public libraries, many of these approaches and techniques could be applied in part to libraries of all types and sizes. The book is divided into eight chapters beginning with one that describes the many and varied benefits volunteers can supply (e.g., specialized skills, expanded or supplementary services, enriched community relations) and ending with a chapter that summarizes the planning and strategies necessary for creating an effective volunteer program. The middle chapters deal thoroughly with the initiating, managing, and evaluating of this new form of volunteerism with many practical, real-life examples to insure success. Topics covered include recruitment, screening applicants, orientation, staff involvement, the roles played by various elements in the library structure (e.g., the director, board members), legal issues, writing volunteer job descriptions, avoiding burnout, training tips, and methods of measuring success. Each chapter ends with a one-paragraph summary and a section called Notes that provides brief additional explanatory information. The book ends with an epilogue which supplies tips for getting started and a thirty-page appendix which is designed as a trouble-shooting guide once the program has been in place for a few months. Topics here include changing the program, solving the problem of unsuitable volunteers, recruitment issues, and replacing retiring helpers. The book ends with a four-page annotated bibliography and a brief subject index. Although the intended audience is public librarians, personnel in other types of libraries will benefit from exploring the ideas so thoroughly and convincingly presented in this book.—**John T. Gillespie**

School Libraries

287.   American Association of School Librarians. **National School Library Standards for Learners, School Librarians, and School Libraries.** Chicago, American Library Association, 2018. 320p. index. $199.00pa. ISBN 13: 978-0-8389-1579-0.

This helpful guide demonstrates how the new National School Library Standards apply to learners, school librarians, and the school library while offering examples of implementation, sample assessments, and professional learning scenarios. The new standards' integrated frameworks are based on five common components that are intended to reflect each other. They begin with six Shared Foundations: inquire, include, collaborate, curate, explore, and engage. These are each then defined by one-sentence Key Commitments and applied across four Domains. The Domains of think, create, share, and grow are then related to Competencies and Alignments, creating a progression of knowledge, skills, and dispositions that mirrors the inquiry process. For example, within the foundation of Explore, learners will progress from Think stage—in which they read, write, and reflect to satisfy personal curiosity—to the Share stage—in which they engage collaboratively with the learning community—and, finally, the Grow stage, recognizing skills that can be developed and accepting feedback for growth. Numerous charts and graphics illustrate how this alignment relates to the learner, the school librarian, and the school library. Also included are useful verbs, a list of evidence, and related professional documents. Additional resources are available through the AASL Standards website, where administrators, educators, and parents can explore from their own point of view. This hefty and essential guide will help empower school librarians and library administrators to transform their teaching and learning and continuously improve their Libraries and Library Programs. The book includes a glossary. Highly recommended.—**MaryAnn Karre**

288.   Maniotes, Leslie K. **Guided Inquiry Design in Action: Elementary School.** Santa Barbara, Calif., Libraries Unlimited/ABC-CLIO, 2018. 147p. index. $40.00pa. ISBN 13: 978-1-4408-6035-5; 978-1-4408-6036-2 (e-book).

This final book rounds out the related titles on Guided Inquiry Design (GID) and provides a cursory description of the process with emphasis on elementary school application. Instructional outline chapters preface lessons which provide basic understanding for those not familiar with GID, allowing ideas to be applied with minimal study prior to application. The lessons included walk readers through the application of inquiry-based learning while stressing collaborative, cross-disciplinary instructional practices that emphasize student driven learning. A strong correlation to makerspace ideas and learning practices in elementary school provides a strong implementation base for lessons presented in the book. Resources include suggestions for additional learning and a detailed, easy-to-read index which allows for easy referencing of ideas. Recommended.—**Peg Billing**

289.   Woolls, Blanche, and Sharon Coatney. **The School Library Manager.** 6th ed. Santa Barbara, Calif., Libraries Unlimited/ABC-CLIO, 2018. 269p. index. $60.00pa. ISBN 13: 978-1-4408-5256-5; 978-1-4408-5257-2 (e-book).

The latest edition of this title offers a comprehensive view of school librarianship today. It includes everything from how to choose a library education program to a look into what the future may hold for our profession. The book is divided into three parts: In the Beginning, Going to Work, and Keeping Up. Within these sections, readers are educated about following a budget, designing a space, and communicating with stakeholders. Every chapter concludes with relevant and useful suggested exercise to complete. For example, the chapter about professional development ends with an exercise asking readers to plan for their own professional learning network if they don't already have one. The overall theme of the book is leadership and encouraging school librarians to take on a leadership role. Recommended.—**Valerie Jankowski**

Special Libraries

290.   **Government Information Essentials.** Susanne Caro, ed. Chicago, American Library Association, 2018. 240p. illus. index. $75.00pa.; $67.50pa. (ALA Members). ISBN 13: 978-1-8389-1597-4.

Government documents, both physical and electronic, are created at the federal, sate, and local level and include such items as hearings, reports, statutes, treaties, and statistics. They are rich in historical value and provide practical statistical data. They offer valuable primary source material for everyone from the hardened researcher to the curious citizen. The Government Publishing Office (GPO), formally known as the Government Printing Office, recently changed its name to reflect the shift to the digital world. GPO's mission is to keep today's citizens informed as well as to preserve the government record for future generations. GPO is the world's largest publisher and it makes its publications available to the public through the Federal Depository Library Program (FDLP). There are approximately 1,400 depository libraries which are located in all 50 states, six territories, and the District of Columbia. The depository library system is as diverse as the libraries that make up the system, with academic libraries making up 52% of the system. With a depository system as diverse as the FDLP, it only makes sense that the people who are stewards of this information are equally diverse, and not all of them walked into such a role knowing just what it means to be a government documents librarian or professional. The author has ten years of experience working with all levels of government information and currently serves as the FDLP regional coordinator for Montana. The book is broken into five thematic parts: advice for the new document professional, collection management, working with the collections, teaching and training, and advocacy and events. Each of those five areas draws from the experiences of librarians and professionals who currently work in the field. This work contains best practices not only for managing a collection but for how to market resources to the community. Individual chapters offer endnotes and resource lists. These resource lists will give both new and/or veteran government documents professionals a place to turn to when seeking information. The book also provides more valuable information in the appendixes section.

Overall *Government Information Essentials* is a highly valuable source for all government documents librarians.—**Lawrence Joseph Mello**

291. Joseph, Claire B. **The Medical Library Association Guide to Developing Consumer Health Collections.** Lanham, Md., Rowman & Littlefield, 2018. 152p. index. (Medical Library Association Guides). $35.00pa; $33.00 (e-book). ISBN 13: 978-1-4422-8170-0; 978-1-4422-8171-4 (e-book).

The author, the director of the Medical Library at South Nassau Community Hospital and book review editor for the *Journal of Hospital Librarianship,* uses the preface to discuss the changes in the health care system, how these changes have made it necessary for patients to understand and advocate for their own care, and how librarians can provide consumers with a relevant collection of health information. The book is intended for all librarians, from students to seasoned veterans in libraries of all sorts (public, academic, medical school, law school). The book's twin aims are to connect patrons with consumer health information and to serve patrons who are underserved medically. The author intends for each chapter to stand on its own so that the book can be used for reference purposes. The book contains a wealth of information on multiple such topics as the connections between a library's physical community and health; online and print medical reference sources; writing a grant proposal; customer service; privacy and confidentiality considerations; community outreach; health literacy; how to find multicultural and inclusive consumer health information, including information in multiple languages; and how to steer patrons toward reliable sources for the best health information. Each chapter begins with a bullet-point list of main ideas covered and each chapter ends with references. There are helpful tables, figures, and sample forms throughout. Particularly helpful in chapter 3, "Building the Collection" are the recommendations for specific print and online resources. This well-supported and informative guide is highly recommended.—**ARBA Staff Reviewer**

292.   Latham, Bethany. **Finding and Using U.S. Government Information: A Practical Guide for Librarians.** Lanham, Md., Rowman & Littlefield, 2018. 233p. illus. index. (Practical Guides for Librarians, No. 41). $65.00; $61.50 (e-book). ISBN 13: 978-1-5381-0715-7; 978-1-5381-0716-4 (e-book).

The US federal government produces a massive trove of valuable information both physical and electronic. They are a valuable primary source material for either the hardened researcher or the average citizen seeking information about a certain agency. Yet due to how the information is produced and organized, government information is difficult to locate let alone effectively use. This book is a straightforward source that will provide useful information and insight to those librarians who do not work in their libraries' Government Documents Department, yet have to help patrons locate and use government information. The author sees this resource as a guidebook, one that will introduce the field of government information and provide a subject-based guide for understanding and coming to terms with the uniqueness and diversity that is the world of government documents. It is also written for a secondary audience that being of a government documents department head or depository coordinator, as it provides beneficial and useful information to be used to train staff in their department. The book is divided into three parts: Background and Context, How to find and use Government Information, and Collection Management, and Professional Development. Recommended.—**Lawrence Joseph Mello**

293.   Nappo, Christian A. **Presidential Libraries and Museums.** Lanham, Md., Rowman & Littlefield, 2018. 242p. illus. index. $75.00; $71.00 (e-book). ISBN 13: 978-1-4422-7135-7; 978-1-4422-7136-4 (e-book).

Presidents have always been an object of fascination among Americans, with many people making pilgrimages to sites related to these national leaders. The web page for presidential libraries at the U.S. National Archives (https://www.archives.gov/presidential-libraries), which one might think of to go to first, focuses only on those fourteen institutions associated with the National Archives. This sturdily bound book covers twenty-five establishments where one can either do serious research or just visit for personal enrichment. The introduction provides a brief history of these institutions, and can be supplemented by delving into academic studies such as: Benjamin Hufbauer's *Presidential Temples: How Memorials and Libraries Shape Public Memory* (University Press of Kansas, 2005), and Jodi Kanter's *Presidential Libraries as Performance: Curating American Culture from Herbert Hoover to George W. Bush* (Southern Illinois University Press, 2016). For each institution there is first directory information (address, phone number, website, and social media addresses), followed by a biography of the president, a description of how the institution was established, some highlights of the collections and exhibits, references notes, and bibliography. The contents are interesting and easy to read, providing one with enough information to start planning a visit. This volume replaces the earlier *Presidential Libraries and Museums: An Illustrated Guide* by Pat Hyland (Congressional Quarterly, 1995). Mr. Nappo teaches for the Lee County, Florida, School District, and previously published *The Librarians of Congress* (Rowman & Littlefield, 2016). This work is nicely illustrated with presidential portraits and photographs of the institution and collections. An online version is also available. While this item would certainly not look out of place on a reference shelf, it might perhaps find more use in the general circulating collection, so that patrons could take it home to read it at their leisure.—**Daniel K. Blewett**

Reference Works

Bibliography

294.   **Children's Core Collection.** 23d ed. Julie Corsaro and Kendal Spires, eds. Bronx, N.Y., H. W. Wilson, 2017. 2965p. index. (Core Collection Series). $240.00. ISBN 13: 978-1-68217-235-3.

A staple for over a hundred years, this reference resource has seen many evolutions in its name, authorship, and source lists. Since the 20th edition, *Children's Core Collection* (CCC) has carried its present-day title. Whatever its title, it remains the premier tool for maintaining and honing children's book collections. Created by librarians for librarians, its purpose is multifold. It is a device for making purchasing decisions, a curriculum support resource, a user services aid, a collection maintenance tool, and, most interestingly, a professional development tool. Numbering nearly 16,000 English-language titles, the annotated catalog entries are arranged roughly into thirds using the Dewey Classification system for nonfiction, "E" for easy books, and "Fic" for fiction works. Nonfiction comprises the bulkiest part of the catalog, while the integrated index alone takes up a third of the entire text block. Stars denote the most highly recommended titles. All entries contain at minimum a publisher's description; most also include select book review excerpts (something which rival resources may point to, but do not necessarily include).

The previous edition was necessarily split into two volumes, but thanks to an enlarged trim size and lighter-weight paper, CCC is now available once again as a single manageable volume, albeit still totaling nearly 3,000 pages. New since the 22d edition is an appendix cross-referencing the Caldecott and Newbery Award-winning authors and titles appearing inside the volume. Removed since the last edition are outdated books primarily on internet safety.

Geared toward public and school libraries, this highly usable print reference work will be essential for those libraries that do not subscribe to the simultaneously appearing EBSCOhost version of more than 49,000 titles representing "a new abundance of books on technology, social sciences and sciences." Librarians should be aware that titles online are searchable also by grade level (a feature the print edition lacks). Compare CCC not only to its digital counterpart, but also to A to Zoo (picture books only) (see ARBA 2015, entry 694) and to the "Best Books for..." print resources in the Children's and Young Adult Literature Reference series, and their supplements.

As time-consuming as collection maintenance projects can be, librarians could easily purchase this costly title every other edition and still keep their shelves fresh and relevant. And as comprehensive and authoritative as the work is, every other edition could easily serve to aid readers and educators and keep curriculum support specialists knowledgeable.—**Lucy Duhon**

295.   **Graphic Novels Core Collection, Second Edition.** Kendal Spires, ed. Bronx, N.Y., H. W. Wilson, 2018. 838p. illus. index. (Core Collection Series). $295.00. ISBN 13: 978-1-68217-662-7.

Originally only in database form, the second edition of Graphic Novels Core Collection (see ARBA 2017, entry 185) is a comprehensive resource for fiction and nonfiction comics and graphic novels for all ages. The core collection has expanded to 2,500 of the recommended levels of the Most Highly Recommended and Core Collection. Most Highly Recommended titles are referenced by a bold-faced star and are considered the best of the best. All titles in the core collection are published in the United States, Canada, or the United Kingdom, with all being available in the United States. Titles are selected by collection development librarians in academic, public, and school libraries. The multipurpose resource aids in purchasing decisions, serves as a readers' advisory, provides verification of information, provides curriculum support, aids in collection maintenance, and serves as an instructional aid. The volume is organized in two parts; part one is a list of works, while part two is an author index, title index, and subject index. Each listing includes a full biographical description. The list of works is broken down into four levels: pre-K through grade five, grades six through eight, grades nine through twelve, and adult. For ease of cataloging each entry has suggested Dewey Decimal classifications. This is an invaluable resource for anyone interested in comics and graphic novels. Highly recommended.—**Shelly Lee**

296.   **The Reference Librarian's Bible: Print and Digital Reference Resources Every Library Should Own.** Steven W. Sowards and Juneal Chenoweth, eds. Santa Barbara, Calif., Libraries Unlimited/ABC-CLIO, 2018. 456p. index. $65.00pa. ISBN 13: 978-1-4408-6061-4; 978-1-4408-6062-1 (e-book).

This volume presents five hundred reviews from past *American Reference Book Annual* volumes, nearly all from 21st-century volumes, grouped into six broad areas: General Reference Works, Social Sciences, History and Area Studies, Humanities, Sciences, and Health Sciences. The table of contents does an excellent job of directing readers to fifty subtopics within those areas, while the subject index at the end of the volume gives even more detail to the material covered, with narrower topics such as "Cats" and "Korean War, 1950-1953." The titles included are "among the most widely held titles in American libraries." (p. xi) The reviews may examine an early edition of a reference work, but useful information is provided concerning newer editions and online versions. There are scores of titles from well-known publishers of reference works: Routledge, Macmillan, Oxford University Press, and Cambridge University Press. As the title points out, there are databases and websites included; most are free sites created by government agencies and other organizations (CIA for The World Factbook, NOAA for the National Weather Service site, the International Monetary Fund for International Financial Statistics, etc.).

This will be a good checklist for many libraries, predominantly academic institutions, to use to evaluate their collections. Specialized libraries should also benefit by exploring the titles in their particular areas, such as science or the health sciences. Reasonably priced for a very useful tool, this volume should be considered by other libraries as well.—**Mark Schumacher**

297.   **Young Adult Fiction: Core Collection.** 2d ed. Kendal Spires and Julie Corsaro, eds. Bronx, N.Y., H. W. Wilson, 2018. 670p. index. (Core Collection Series). $255.00. ISBN 13: 978-1-68217-239-1.

In *Young Adult Fiction: Core Collection,* the editors, Kendal Spires and Julie Corsaro, have included over 3,000 short summaries of young adult titles gleaned from EBSCOhost databases.

In part 1 of the work, the titles are arranged alphabetically by author last name. A star icon next to the title denotes the essential titles for a YA collection. Each title includes a summary, sometimes taken from another source. Additionally, for many titles there is also an evaluation of the title from an outside source (for example, *School Library Journal*). Though the entries are organized alphabetically, finding authors is not as easy as it could be. The author's name is bolded on the page, but so are keywords, so your eye frequently rests on those rather than the author name. Entries at the top of pages denoting which letters are on the page (like in encyclopedias) would increase the user-friendliness. Part 2 is an author, subject, and title index, grouped together, alphabetically.

Also included is a list of Printz Award winners which is given annually by the Young Adult Library Services Association (YALSA), a division of the American Library Association (ALA). However, it is incomplete as it does not include nonfiction or graphic novels award winners. This is unfortunate as the 2017 winner was indeed a graphic novel (*March* by John Lewis, Andrew Aydin, and Nate Powell), as was the 2007 winner (*American Born Chinese* by Gene Luen Yang). Graphic novels are also not included in the main body of the text, which is problematic as they are not only esteemed award winners but an important component of YA literature. There is also a list of Morris Award winners. This award is given to a first-time author writing for young adults.

Though having some Printz and Morris award winners represented is beneficial, YALSA has other awards which would help a librarian build their collection, and those are not included. The Margaret Edwards award is given to an author who has contributed significantly to YA literature. Including those titles would help librarians make sure their collection has a deep scope. The Odyssey Award honors audiobooks; these audiobook awards ought to be listed separately so librarians can expand their collections beyond print. The Stonewall Awards denote worthy titles about LGBTQ youths. Also missing are some *New York Times* bestselling authors such as Kiera Cass and Rick Riordan. In a public library, in particular, these authors are important to include.

Since the titles are gleaned from databases which are updated weekly, and since it does not include graphic novels, nor many award winners or best-selling authors, this is not an essential guide for libraries.—**Elizabeth Webster**

Directories

298.   **Libraries Canada, 2017/2018.** 32d ed. Toronto, Grey House Publishing Canada, 2017. 804p. index. $369.00. ISBN 13: 978-1-68217-830-0; 978-1-68217-831-7 (e-book).

Libraries Canada (former title *Directory of Libraries in Canada*) is comprised of 6,617 entries categorized within 5 sections: Public Libraries; College and University Libraries; Special Libraries; Library Services and Resources; and Library Associations and Groups. It also contains six indexes: Entry Name Index; Archive Index; Government Libraries Index; Location Index; Personnel Index; and Subject Index. Its two appendixes consist of: a Directory of Special Collections of Research Value in Canadian Libraries and Depository Libraries of Canadian Government Information. The Introductory Material section contains a sample entry; list of abbreviations; "Library and Archives Canada 2017-2018 Departmental Plan"; "the State of Digital Publishing in Canada 2016"; "Are You Still Listening: Audio Book Use in Canada 2016"; "2015 Canadian Public Library Statistics"; and "Federal Government Library Closures and Changes." Each of the chapters representing a type of library is arranged alphabetically by provinces and regions. The chapter on library services and resources is arranged alphabetically by type of resource (e.g., periodicals) and also contains a list of e-libraries and a calendar of events. The section Library Associations, Consortia & Groups is arranged alphabetically and includes a list of regional library systems arranged by province. Each library entry contains name, address, telephone number, fax, email, URL, National Library Symbol, when founded, hours, acquisitions budget, special collections, services, subjects covered, number of personnel, and library administrators. *Libraries Canada* is an essential source for libraries of Canada and for larger research collections in the United States. It should be included in Library and Information Science collections in the United States and Canada. Highly recommended.—**Lucy Heckman**

Handbooks and Yearbooks

299.   Cassell, Kay Ann, and Uma Hiremath. **Reference and Information Services: An Introduction.** 4th ed. Chicago, American Library Association, 2018. 484p. index. $88.00pa.; $79.20pa. (ALA members). ISBN 13: 978-0-8389-1568-4.

Cassell and Hiremath's work has become a standard educational tool for LIS programs and a valued handbook for working professional librarians. It covers fundamental concepts, major reference sources, special topics, and management of reference collections and services in 23 chapters. This edition has an entirely rewritten chapter on children's and young adult reference services, an expanded chapter on ethics by a new author, and a new chapter on public programming in reference services. It retains the organization of major reference works by question topic rather than by type of resource, and includes the RUSA Outstanding Reference Sources since 2007 as an appendix. One change that is not an improvement is the streamlined table of contents; this reviewer believes readers would find the more detailed style of the TOC in the 3rd edition more useful (see ARBA 2013, entry 460). Some sections are largely unchanged, such as the one on assessment, which should be updated with the more complex views of assessment now available in the literature. Still, enough has been redone that librarians and library educators will want to update their own copies and consider assigning them as textbooks to LIS students. Essential.—**Rosanne M. Cordell**

300.   **The Portable MLIS: Insights from the Experts.** 2d ed. Ken Haycock and Mary-Jo Romaniuk, eds. Santa Barbara, Calif., Libraries Unlimited/ABC-CLIO, 2018. 378p. index. $55.00pa. ISBN 13: 978-1-4408-5203-9; 978-1-4408-5204-6 (e-book).

This is a comprehensive overview of the library profession based upon core competencies. This second edition has been updated to reflect changes in the profession as well as emerging trends and issues. The 21 chapters of the book are written by various experts in their fields. Topics start with a general introduction to the profession then move on to foundational issues, functions, and finally to globalism and the future. The appendices included are varied and range from core values to the Library Bill of Rights to sample policies and position statements. Overall, this is an excellent introduction to the profession. It is recommended for those new to the profession, considering entering the profession, and current professionals looking for a reference or refresher. Recommended.—**Darshell Silva**

301.   Tucker, Virginia M., and Marc Lampson. **Finding the Answers to Legal Questions.** 2d ed. Chicago, American Library Association, 2018. 232p. index. $75.00pa.; $67.50pa. (ALA members). ISBN 13: 978-0-8389-1569-1.

In this 2d edition, Tucker and Lampson provide an excellent resource for librarians, beginning law students, and paralegals. It is focused on small and medium sized public libraries to guide librarians in collecting and managing basic legal resources for their local community. It is designed to meet the needs of law students and paralegals learning the basics of legal research.

Legal research is complex because it is unlike any other kind of research. There are three branches of government at the federal and state level. These branches make laws, rules, and regulations. Tucker and Lampson explain the structure of the legal system in the United States, mitigating its complexities. They explain the primary sources and secondary sources at federal, state, and local levels. Overall, Tucker and Lampson address the resources needed to answer typical legal questions asked by people using their local public library.

Highly recommended for all public libraries and undergraduate academic libraries supporting prelaw curriculums or training paralegals.—**Ladyjane Hickey**

Special Topics

Archives

302.   Franks, Patricia C. **Records and Information Management.** 2d ed. Chicago, American Library Association, 2018. 498p. illus. index. $84.99pa.; $76.50pa. (ALA members). ISBN 13: 978-0-8389-1716-9.

Records and archives come in many different manifestations, and the author thoroughly covers them from ancient civilizations to present-day cloud storage and digitization. Subjects included are: records and management plans, creation, appraisal, and retrieval; electronic records and management; developing and emerging technologies; disaster preparedness and recovery; risk management; privacy and security; social media; and long -term preservation. There are many real-life examples and product comparisons. Also included are a comprehensive bibliography and a glossary.

The author discusses current archival education and training and the importance of staying up to date in records management quoting Italian educator Giovanni Vittani, who wrote, in 1913, a still highly significant message for today: "An archival school must not have the pretense of creating the complete archivist, but must make the student able to continue his education while working in any kind of archives."

Records and Information Management is not a difficult read, even for this instruction and reference librarian. This reviewer highly recommends this book for college archival and record management classes.—**Linda W. Hacker**

303.   Mooradian, Norman A. **Ethics for Records and Information Management.** Chicago, American Library Association, 2018. index. $75.00pa.; $67.50pa. (ALA members). ISBN 13: 978-1-8389-1639-1.

This book seeks to "present ethics as a systematic body of knowledge that has developed over time around the issues central to records and information management [RIM]" (p. xxv). It is a very dense text at times, dealing with concepts such as ethical reasoning, ethical judgments, professionalism, and moral obligation, first in general, then within the occupation of RIM. Various subtopics are addressed, such as whistle blowing and information leaks, information privacy, and management ethics, each in a separate chapter. (It is useful that Appendix C provides clear and brief synopses of chapters 1 through 6 in 22 pages). Throughout the volume, the author presents the ethical, moral, technological, and legal issues that come into play when dealing with records management in various settings, which the author divides into three categories: for-profit organizations (corporations), public sector organizations (governmental agencies), and not-for-profit organizations (NGOs). He also stresses the importance of ethics in the profession: "Records management has an ethical core and an ethical mandate" (p. 50).

This volume will be most useful in academic libraries, particularly those with institutional archives, and libraries in any other institutions that deal with sensitive information, such as government offices (national, statewide, or municipal) and law firms.—**Mark Schumacher**

Cataloging and Classification

304.   Brubaker, Jana. **Text, Lies and Cataloging: Ethical Treatment of Deceptive Works in the Library.** Jefferson, N.C., McFarland, 2018. 158p. index. $55.00pa. ISBN 13: 978-0-7864-9744-7; 978-1-4766-9856-8 (e-book).

Cataloging librarians invariably encounter works that are not what they appear to be on the surface: works of dubious authorship, works of satire presented as nonfiction, and the like. But how should catalogers proceed in describing materials that misrepresent their contents in an attempt to deceive audiences? In *Text, Lies and Cataloging: Ethical Treatment of Deceptive Works in the Library,* Jana Brubaker provides case studies, surveys the bibliographic records in WorldCat, and offers recommendations on how they can be edited to more accurately reflect their contents.

Having cataloged problematic works before, this reviewer admires Brubaker's knowledge on the subject, but he wishes she had expanded her scope. She focuses heavily on fictional works passed off as nonfiction but leaves works questioning well-documented historical events and commonly held scientific beliefs entirely out of the discussion. Are they not arguably also deceptive works? What about other flavors of misrepresentative works (blatantly partisan political screeds marketed under the subject heading of "political science," for example)? Where is the line for catalogers between editorializing and giving the appearance of tacit acceptance?

The reviewer likewise wishes Ms. Brubaker had adopted a broader, more philosophical, approach on the subject of editing bibliographic records. Her recommendations on adjusting fixed field codes and adding subject subdivisions and genre terms are all sensible, but they effectively underscore their limited impact (how many researchers besides librarians read text-based notes and search on subject headings?). There is also the issue of future developments. To what extent will these approaches still apply when libraries move away from the MARC format into a web-based environment?

Text, Lies and Cataloging reads more like the start of a conversation than a guide to catalogers wrestling with deceptive works.—**Craig Mury Keeney**

305.   **Coding with XML for Efficiency in Cataloging and Metadata: Practical Applications of XSD, XSLT, and Xquery.** Timothy W. Cole, Myung-Ja (MJ) Han, and

Christine Schwartz, eds. Chicago, American Library Association, 2018. 196p. index. $60.00pa; $54.00pa. (ALA members). ISBN 13: 978-0-8389-1653-7.

This volume is the direct result of an all-day preconference on the topic held at the ALA 2015 Annual Conference in San Francisco. It explores how libraries, specifically technical services and technical services librarians, can use Extensible Markup Language (XML) to make their work more efficient for themselves and their patrons. A quick review of XML basics, library metadata in XML, and XML validation using schemas moves towards an introduction to the uses of XPath and XSLT in cataloging workflows, connecting the library to the Semantic Web, using XQuery for library metadata including a number of case studies, XQuery basics and functions including regular expressions, and metadata workflow using XQuery. A number of appendixes provide numerous samples and examples of coding along with software configurations. A good book to build efficiencies using metadata in libraries.—**Bradford Lee Eden**

306.   Kelsey, Marie. **Cataloging for School Librarians.** 2d ed. Lanham, Md., Rowman & Littlefield, 2018. 396p. index. $55.00pa.; $52.50 (e-book). ISBN 13: 978-1-5381-0608-2; 978-1-5381-0609-9 (e-book).

Cataloging for School Librarians, second edition, is an invaluable addition to school librarians in training and any school librarian who needs additional information regarding RDA, which replaced AACR2. The expansive coverage of cataloging also includes information on Sears, Dewey Decimal, and FRBR. Using the MARC format, copious examples of cataloging are shown on a wide variety of materials ranging from print to nonprint items. This comprehensive edition is written in an easy to understand, conversational tone, keeping the topic interesting and the text quite readable. It is divided into four parts including Essential Information, Descriptive Cataloging, Subject Cataloging and Classification, and a Conclusion. The conclusion incorporates the correlation to the Common Core State Standards, an appendix section, glossary, bibliography, index, and a section about the author. Black boxes labeled "Special Tidbit" are dispersed throughout the book, which highlight important items to consider when cataloging. Each of the eleven chapters concludes with a summary of the chapter and a "Test Your Knowledge" quiz which helps the reader to retain the information. This is an excellent resource for any school library required to do its own cataloging.—**Shelly Lee**

307.   **Sears List of Subject Headings.** 22d ed. Barbara A. Bristow, Maria Hugger, Kendal Spires, and Claire Fielder, eds. Bronx, N.Y., H. W. Wilson, 2018. 1056p. $195.00. ISBN 13: 978-1-68217-234-6.

The last edition of this book published in 2014, so librarians will be pleased to see this update. Moreover, this is the first edition since Grey House Publishing acquired the title in 2018. Longtime users will notice welcome formatting changes; the larger book size and different typology absolutely facilitate searching.

This edition features more than 1,600 new and revised subject headings that reflect changes in materials, changes in cataloging theory and practice, changes in the demographics of library users, and changes in English language usage. This edition also incorporates the 6th edition of *The Sears List Canadian Companion.* Like the 21st edition, this new release conforms to RDA standards. New and revised subject terms include scope notes where required. Users will find a list of canceled and replaced headings in the front of the book; these include, but are not limited to: Farm Family to Farm Families, Counter Culture to

Counterculture, Transvestites to Cross-dressers, Weblogs to Blogs, and Generation Y to Millennials (Persons). Classification numbers are taken from the *Abridged WebDewey* and spellings and definitions are based on *Webster's Third New International Dictionary of the English Language, Unabridged* (1961) and the *Random House Webster's Unabridged Dictionary* (1997). In the front matter, users will also find a history of the publication, a discussion of the principles and practices of subject cataloging, a list of every subdivision used in the *Sears List,* and more. As always, librarians will appreciate the information on *see also* terms and broader and/or narrower terms as well as usage and geographical notes.

This standard and highly respected work is highly recommended for use in small and medium-size libraries.—**ARBA Staff Reviewer**

Children's and Young Adult Services

308.   Barrett, Megan E., and Rebecca J. Ranallo. **Cultivating Connected Learning: Library Programs for Youth.** Santa Barbara, Calif., Libraries Unlimited/ABC-CLIO, 2018. 135p. index. (Libraries Unlimited Professional Guides for Young Adult Librarians). $50.00pa. ISBN 13: 978-1-4408-5538-2; 978-1-4408-5539-9 (e-book).

This book is a wonderful resource for librarians who want to create library programs that help close the learning gaps in technology and digital fluency while also getting teens directly involved with the planning and implementation process. The authors describe what connected learning is; how to assess the community's or school's needs; how to create a space that encourages connected learning; developing the collection to include apps, online resources, and other equipment and technology; staffing and running the program; planning the programs that support connected learning; marketing and promotion; and assessing and evaluating connected learning at your library. Each chapter ends with a concise summary plus action steps for that particular aspect of the program, and the book concludes with a comprehensive resource section. Other features include sample surveys and forms. The book concludes with a bibliography and an index. Recommended.—**Laurie Balderson**

309.   Evans, Nancy. **Cultivating Strong Girls: Library Programming That Builds Self-Esteem and Challenges Inequality.** Santa Barbara, Calif., Libraries Unlimited/ABC-CLIO, 2018. 237p. index. (Libraries Unlimited Professional Guides for Young Adult Librarians). $45.00pa. ISBN 13: 978-1-4408-5668-6; 978-1-4408-5669-3 (e-book).

This volume provides a comprehensive look at everything that is needed to plan, promote, and run a successful program focused on many of the gender-based problems that young adult girls face today. The author begins by expanding on the many reasons why such a program is needed and why such a program belongs in a library. Evans then offers a smorgasbord of ideas, activities, and materials that address a wide variety of topics, including gender bias and inequality, body image, the media, friendships and conflict, social media, romantic relationships and violence, and more. She organizes these topics into six programs, but explains how they can be expanded or reduced to any number that fit a library's particular needs. The programs begin with ice-breakers, and include games, activities, discussion topics, videos, worksheets, suggestions for guest speakers, and ways to expand the program after it has finished. Activities and worksheets are handily repeated at the end of each chapter, and additional videos, websites, and sources are included. Since she has successfully run this program series and presented it at PLA and ALA, Evans can offer valuable suggestions for tailoring the program to a specific audience and library, deciding specifics like time and group size, and overcoming difficulties or avoiding pitfalls. From preface to index, this is a well-organized guide to creating an outstanding critical librarianship service that builds strong rapport with tween and teen girls in the library. Highly recommended.—**MaryAnn Karre**

310.   Wyckoff, Amy, and Marie Harris. **Career Programming for Today's Teens: Exploring Nontraditional and Vocational Alternatives.** Chicago, American Library Association, 2019. 200p. index. $56.99pa.; $51.29pa. (ALA members). ISBN 13: 978-0-8389-1759-6.

Written in ten chapters, *Career Programming for Today's Teens: Exploring Nontraditional and Vocational Alternatives,* is a comprehensive tool for any librarian wishing to provide alternative career programming for teens. Each chapter gives in-depth information regarding the topic at hand including, but not limited to: trade schools, career-focused programming, meeting professionals, library internships, options for partnership in the community, program assessment, and collection development. Each chapter ends with a conclusion summarizing the chapter highlights and a "Notes" section indicating sources used to obtain information within the chapter. Chapter 4, "The 'Meet a Professional' Workshop Series," is a wealth of knowledge on teen career selection. Chapter 7 provides in-depth information on how to run a successful trade school fair, including planning steps and a timeline for doing so, as well as how to market the fair. Several appendixes are provided plus evaluation tools, a sample program flier, sample e-mails, planning documents, and a list of state-based worker's resources. An alphabetical index is also provided in this easy-to-use, thorough resource. Highly recommended.—**Shelly Lee**

Collection Development

311.   Gregory, Vicki L. **Collection Development and Management for 21st Century Library Collections: An Introduction.** 2d ed. Chicago, American Library Association, 2019. 264p. index. $79.99pa.; $71.99pa. (ALA members). ISBN 13: 978-0-8389-1712-1.

The second edition (see ARBA 2012, entry 612) of this well-known volume on library collection development and management for the 21st century is packed full of useful tips, knowledge, and guidance for any librarian whose duties relate to these topics. Chapter 1 examines new elements influencing collections today such as e-books, self-publishing, and globalization. Chapter 2 assists with needs assessment and marketing plans, while chapter 3 provides the components of a good collection development policy. Chapters 4 and 5 look at the selection process, various tools, and the acquisitions process. Chapter 6 covers budgeting, fiscal accountability, and consortiums, while chapter 7 is comprised of information on weeding and deselection. Chapter 8 examines resource sharing, interlibrary loan, and cooperative collection development, while Chapter 9 discusses legal issues related to collection development. Chapter 10 discusses professional ethics and intellectual freedom, and chapter 11 examines the topic of preservation (both physical and digital). The final chapter looks at the future of collection management and development. An essential resource for any academic or public services librarian.—**Bradford Lee Eden**

312.   **Guide to Streaming Video Acquisitions.** Eric Hartnett, ed. Chicago, American Library Association, 2019. 110p. index. $59.99pa.; $53.00pa. (ALA members). ISBN 13: 978-0-8389-1766-4.

The primary purpose of the book is to address the logistics of providing streaming video for your library. The book is aimed predominantly at academic libraries, but public libraries that are interested in streaming might find parts of the book useful. Why would an academic library want to invest in streaming video? The author gives three reasons: classroom use, videos for research, and videos for entertainment. A recent survey found 68 percent of college students access and use streaming videos as part of their academic requirements and 79 percent use videos to supplement their course work, while a University of Hawaii study found 66 percent admit they have never searched for a physical video in the library catalog. So how does an academic library meet this demand without breaking the budget?

The book covers everything from the library's role in providing streaming to selection criteria, business models, workflows, licensing, classroom use, cost-assessment, accessibility for the visually or hearing impaired, and the future of streaming. Since streaming video is becoming more popular in the classroom, it's important for libraries to understand copyright, the TEACH act, and fair use. The book goes into detail on all three topics.

The book leaves the reader with perhaps more questions than answers: ownership versus access, patron driven acquisition (where you only pay for the videos that have actually been viewed), permanent streaming access (ownership for the life of the file) versus a limited term that expires with your subscription. But if your library is considering entering the world of streaming video, the book provides plenty of fodder to consider.—**Brian Clark**

313.   Johnson, Peggy. **Fundamentals of Collection Development and Management.** 4th ed. Chicago, American Library Association, 2018. 418p. index. $85.00pa.; $76.50pa. (ALA members). ISBN 13: 978-0-8389-1641-4.

Collection development is still an important aspect of librarianship, even with all the recent availability of faster, more efficient acquisitions options. Trained professionals are needed in an environment where information technology is quickly evolving. An introduction to the concept of collection development and management is followed by chapters on staff organization; planning, policies and budgets; vendor relations; managing and developing collections; marketing and outreach; accountability and valuation; and collaborative arrangements. The chapter on scholarly communication, found in previous editions, has been eliminated and incorporated into other chapters. The supplemental reading lists, glossary, and appendixes have all been updated. Helpful illustrations enhance the text and fictional case studies (a new feature) include ideas for discussion. Extensive notes sections follow each chapter and appendixes offer lists of professional resources and selection aids. The information is well researched, logically arranged, and suitable as a guide for beginners and a quick reference tool for seasoned professionals.—**Martha Lawler**

314.   **Middle & Junior High Core Collection.** 13th ed. Julie Corsaro, Kendal Spires, and Claire Fielder, eds. Bronx, N.Y., H. W. Wilson, 2018. 2120p. index. (Core Collection Series). $295.00. ISBN 13: 978-1-68217-238-4.

This significantly updated edition of a standard collection management tool has been weeded of older and less relevant titles so that it includes about 10,000 titles recommended for young people in grades 5-9 and professional aides for their librarians, as opposed to the 11,000 titles in the previous edition. The familiar organization of a Classified Collection and an Author, Title, and Subject Index remains the same. Entries include a full bibliographical description, Sears subject headings, a suggested DDC classification number, ISBN and LC numbers, a brief description of the contents, and an evaluation from a quoted source, when possible. The Core Collection Series is intended to be used as an aid in purchasing, an aid to readers' advisors, for the verification of information, in curriculum support, in collection maintenance, and as an instructional aid. "Most Highly Recommended" titles are starred. Excluded are non-English language materials except bilingual materials and dictionaries (or similar works), adult fiction, textbooks, computer program manuals, and other topics that quickly become outdated. This edition continues to include graphic novels. The entire volume is available as a regularly updated database by EBSCO. It should be noted that the print volume does not include most classics, but these may be found in EBSCOhost. This title continues to be an invaluable tool for school and public librarians and should be considered essential.—**Rosanne M. Cordell**

315.   Zellers, Jessica, Tina M. Adams, and Katherine Hill. **The ABCs of ERM: Demystifying Electronic Resource Management for Public and Academic Libraries.** Santa Barbara, Calif., Libraries Unlimited/ABC-CLIO, 2018. 244p. index. $50.00pa. ISBN 13: 978-1-4408-5580-1; 978-1-4408-5581-8 (e-book).

The ABCs of ERM attempts to tackle an immense and complex topic in a way that is accessible and instructional to public and academic librarians. Libraries continue to transition from providing access to tangible resources to providing access to intangible resources, and this book sets out to provide a concise primer on the entire concept of electronic resources.

The ABCs of ERM serves as a practical and real-life guide to the topic at hand. Chapter 1 lays the foundation for the subject (and the book) with the aptly titled "So What Are Electronic Resources Anyway?" From that point, the next 11 chapters guide the reader through as many of the ins and outs of electronic resources that one could expect in only about 250 pages. Readers will learn about electronic resource vendors, licenses, access, purchase methods, marketing, the role of the user, etc.

Each chapter is written so that all library professionals can easily comprehend the subject matter. Perhaps most important, though, is the immensely applicable and relevant way in which the information is presented. Think of this like a training guide for new librarians who will interact with electronic resources (i.e., all of them). The content is excellent, the presentation is welcoming, and the length is unintimidating. The authors have done an excellent job in creating a book that should prove invaluable to the profession, particularly in this transition period—**Tyler Manolovitz**

Copyright

316.   Harris, Leslie Ellen. **Licensing Digital Content: A Practical Guide for Librarians.** 3d ed. Chicago, American Library Association, 2018. 182p. index. $65.00pa.; $58.50pa. (ALA members). ISBN 13: 978-0-8389-1630-8; 978-0-8389-1679-7 (e-book).

This 3rd iteration of Harris' key resource on libraries' licensing electronic resources has essentially remained the same from the 1st edition. The second edition appeared in 2009 (see ARBA 2010, entry 572). Harris is enthusiastic, well-versed, and thoroughly explanatory on challenges and considerations for libraries licensing digital content. All content is written in layman's terms and is easily understandable. The eight chapters are logically organized, although it feels like Chapter 4 ("Key Licenses Clauses") and Chapter 5 ("Boilerplate Clauses") could be combined using a small visual icon to help identify which clauses are boilerplate, and therefore likely to be commonly recognized in all types of contracts, not exclusively in license agreements. As the author does workshops as well as consulting on this topic, new and updated questions and answers for Chapter 7 might be an area to expand upon in any future editions. Additionally, deliberation of how of PORTICO, CLOCKSS, or other 3rd party dark archives or preservation methods may fit into in Chapter 4's Perpetual Access/Archive clause and would be beneficial to the discussion. Furthermore information and discussion on the new updates to EU privacy laws would add valuable context in the current environment. Lastly, consideration on licensors providing usage statistics, particularly for libraries that require COUNTER compliant statistics, would also assist librarians in license negotiations. Sample wording for this unique requirement would be particularly useful.

An informative preface including a note about intended global scope is once again included in this edition as is a helpful section of free online resources for additional research on licensing electronic content. There is also an 11-page glossary in addition to the index.

Since content has not changed nor increased substantially from the first edition, this 3rd edition is not an essential resource for those that already own either of the previous editions. However, in general, this resource is invaluable for all librarians handling licenses and negotiations.—**Kat Landry Mueller**

Digitization and Digital Libraries

317.   Bannerjee, Kyle, and Terry Reese, Jr. **Building Digital Libraries: A How-To-Do-It Manual for Librarians.** 2d ed. Chicago, American Library Association, 2018. 250p. index. $85.00pa.; $76.50pa.; (ALA members). ISBN 13: 978-0-8389-1635-3.

The title *Building Digital Libraries* can be a deceiving because I do not think that the authors expect anyone to build a digital library from scratch; rather, the material in this second edition (see ARBA 2009, entry 575) is more of a guide to finding what you need from amongst various open-source and commercial resources to create your own digital library project. The introduction states that the book's goal is to familiarize the reader with a wide range of topics. *Building Digital Libraries* provides a foundation that allows you to learn enough about the various aspects of a digital library project to identify what you need to learn more about and where to look for more information.

The best feature of this book is its interactive component. It asks you questions about your digital library project, so that you can think through the many steps and decisions to be made. *Building Digital Libraries* covers topics such as metadata, discovery, sharing metadata, and access. After an introductory chapter, each chapter covers a different aspect of digital libraries, and you may be more familiar with some rather than others. This can help inform the reader about adding more people to the team who have greater understanding of those sections, and the necessity for any team thinking about creating a digital library to incorporate people of various skill sets and knowledge. *Building Digital Libraries* is recommended for a library or groups just beginning a new digital library project.—**Susan Elkins**

318.   **Digital Preservation in Libraries: Preparing for a Sustainable Future.** Jeremy Myntti and Jessalyn Zoom, eds. Chicago, American Library Association, 2019. 380p. index. $84.99pa.; $76.49pa. (ALA members). ISBN 13: 978-0-8389-1713-8.

Digital Preservation in Libraries attempts to provide a helpful compendium of research articles and case studies about one of the most important and quickly evolving aspects of libraries today: digital preservation. Libraries have only had a couple of decades to work on the task of digital preservation, as compared to the many centuries of perfecting the art of physical preservation. Compound that with the rate at which technology is advancing, and libraries have an obvious need for quality research, important lessons, and practical advice.

This volume includes 18 chapters, divided into 6 parts, exploring multiple aspects of digital preservation. Chapters include discussions about the history of digital preservation, different strategies and policies, individual library experiences, preservation of specific material types, collaboration, copyright, etc. As with most quality reference works, *Digital Preservation in Libraries* sets a foundation for the topic and explores the idea in different ways and from different perspectives.

Because of the anthology nature of this book, chapters vary in terms of voice, format, and technical jargon, but they all nibble at important aspects of the topic as a whole. Not all chapters will be useful to everyone, but everyone with interest in digital preservation should find a few relevant and worthwhile chapters, at least. As an ALA publication, the cost may be a bit on the pricey side, but quality and relevance of the content likely make it a worthwhile investment.—**Tyler Manolovitz**

319.   Kowalczyk, Stacy T. **Digital Curation for Libraries and Archives.** Santa Barbara, Calif., Libraries Unlimited/ABC-CLIO, 2018. 246p. index. $60.00pa. ISBN 13: 978-1-61069-631-9.

Digital Curation for Libraries and Archives is an introductory manual or textbook, so-to-speak, providing a foundation for understanding the varied components that go into digital curation. Even in library circles, faculty and staff often overlook and misunderstand the concept of the digital curation role. Not only can this book be used as an instructional and training guide, it can also be used as an informational lesson to help library employees understand the breadth of digital curation.

Digital Curation for Libraries and Archives is divided into four main sections that discuss an overview of preservation, preservation technology fundamentals, preservation planning, and preservation in practice. The 12 chapters share both research-based information and experiential lessons for all aspects of the preservation and curation process. Each chapter makes liberal use of figures and tables to accompany the text, as well as provides a detailed reference list and discussion questions for further exploration.

This publication is a fantastic introductory resource exploring the main components to digital curation and preservation. Because of its nature as a teaching and education tool, the language and writing can be on the technical and dry side. However, Kowalczyk has written in a way that the lessons are easy to follow and understand, which similar books should strive to achieve.—**Tyler Manolovitz**

Evaluation and Assessment

320.   **Academic Libraries and the Academy: Strategies and Approaches to Demonstate Your Value, Impact, and Return on Investment.** Marwin Britto and Kirsten Kinsley, eds. Chicago, American Library Association, Association of College and Research Libraries, 2018. 2v. index. $120.00pa/set. ISBN 13: 978-0-8389-8945-6.

In a higher education environment that increasingly asks libraries to demonstrate their value, every librarian, regardless of their institution's size and budget, needs to be thinking about assessment. This two-volume set loaded with case studies adds to the growing list of books about library assessment, but *Academic Libraries and the Academy* distinguishes itself in several ways that make it a necessary addition to the academic librarian's bookshelf.

Academic Libraries and the Academy is divided into several parts. Volume one opens with a foreword from Megan Oakleaf and an introductory chapter from Editors Marwin Britto and Kirsten Kinsley. This introduction provides an overview of the higher education landscape, along with an explanation of how the set is organized. (The foreword and introductory chapter appear again in volume 2.) The case studies are organized around the metaphor of "hanging fruit." Section 1, Seeding the Initiative, focuses on case studies of institutions beginning their assessment efforts. The "Low-Hanging Fruit" of section 2, are short, low-cost, low-stakes assessments. Volume 2 begins with "Reachable Fruit" — assessment measures that are more time—and cost-intensive. These assessments may take up to a year to conduct. The "Hard-to-Reach Fruit" in section 4 focuses on studies that will require more than a year of data collection and/or external partnerships and funding.

In Megan Oakleaf's foreword, she states that the breadth and depth of the case studies make "library assessment practice accessible to newcomers" and "provides sufficient detail to guide established practitioners" (p. xi). A summary at the beginning of each chapter makes it easy for readers to skip around to the studies that are most useful for their library. These summaries list the project focus, tools used, duration of the project, cost of the project, and size of the institution. All of the case studies have a similar structure that includes the context that led to the project and a reflection after the study was completed. In the examples where the assessment involved conducting a survey, a copy of the survey questions is included. Notes and bibliographies for each chapter provide recommendations for further reading.

Many books on assessment focus on large, public institutions, and while these types of institutions are represented in Britto and Kinsley's work, equal space is given to small private colleges, branch campuses, and community colleges. International libraries are well represented here, with case studies from Singapore Management University, Covenant University in Nigeria, and many others. Many of the projects detailed in these volumes focus on information literacy program assessment. Librarians looking for information about other assessment projects may have a more difficult time finding projects relevant to their work; however, areas such as collection assessment, accessibility, and discovery services are represented here.

This set is highly recommended for academic libraries and library science programs. The sheer variety of institutions and projects represented in these two volumes make this a must-have for academic library staff, whether or not they have "assessment" in their job title. Students in library science programs may benefit from learning about the types of assessment projects occurring in academic libraries.—**Kristin Elizabeth Cole**

321.   Matthews, Joseph R. **The Evaluation and Measurement of Library Services.** 2d ed. Santa Barbara, Calif., Libraries Unlimited/ABC-CLIO, 2017. 446p. index. $65.00pa. ISBN 13: 978-1-4408-5536-8; 978-1-4408-5537-5 (e-book).

The Evaluation and Measurement of Library Services is a second edition tome geared toward providing libraries and library employees with a foundation for understanding and implementation methods of evaluating, assessing, and measuring all aspects of library services and operations. Libraries, as in most professions, must continually provide evidence for their impact, importance, and relevance to society. As data collection becomes more advanced and complicated in a field that, not too long ago, relied on simple gate counts and check-outs, this publication provides a fantastical theoretical and practical guide to evaluating and assessing libraries.

The almost 450 pages of *The Evaluation and Measurement of Library Services* include 26 chapters throughout 5 main sections. The 5 parts explore the evaluation process and models, methodology, evaluation of library operations, evaluation of library services, and evaluation of library outcomes. Specifically, these chapters range in scope from qualitative and quantitative tools, evaluation of different library departments, information literacy, summer reading programs, social media, economic impacts, social impacts, etc.

As one would expect from a publication such as this, the text makes liberal use of evidence-based research, data and statistics, charts, graphs, etc. The book also attempts, though, to provide a foundation for those that may still not see or understand the necessity of such assessment. Both a theoretical and practical guide, *The Evaluation and Measurement of Library Services* is a great resource for all library professionals due to its impact on literally every aspect of library services and operations.—**Tyler Manolovitz**

Information Literacy

322.   Cooke, Nicole A. **Fake News and Alternative Facts: Information Literacy in a Post-Truth Era.** Chicago, American Library Association, 2018. 56p. index. $35.00pa.; $31.50pa. (ALA members). ISBN 13: 978-0-8389-1636-0.

This report on a contemporary topic is just the right length for the busy librarian or educator seeking to increase their knowledge of information literacy. It begins with a list of news headlines that the reader is asked to rate for truth and accuracy. Most readers may have trouble getting them all right, but thankfully the answers are provided in the conclusion. A nice blend of scholarly and practical information comprises the text. Sources are cited throughout, culminating in a four-page list of references at the end which includes books, articles, and websites. The concluding chapter is full of practical ideas to be used in instruction, including checklists to evaluate sources, a lesson plan, a list of sources for additional information on the issues of fake news, and multiple forms of literacy, websites for fact checking, and graphics suitable for display in a classroom or library (including one in Spanish). Librarians and teachers interested in delving into how media operates—both in its traditional and new forms—and how information is acquired will find solid information in this book. Social media and its tendency to isolate users into selective bubbles gets good treatment, as does iterative journalism, which reports on what is heard (as opposed to discovered) by reporters. Educators know that critical thinking is extremely important, especially now with the proliferation of new forms of media and increased confusion about what distinguishes truth from falsehood. This book brings it all together and provides a one-stop source for background information and practical ideas.

The book concludes with an index. Recommended.—**Mary Northrup**

323.   Dail, Jennifer S., Shelbie Witte, and Stephen T. Bickmore. **Young Adult Literature and the Digital World: Textual Engagement through Visual Literacy.** Lanham, Md., Rowman & Littlefield, 2018. 140p. index. $30.00pa.; $28.50 (e-book). ISBN 13: 978-1-4758-4083-4; 978-1-4758-4084-1 (e-book).

Today's young adult has grown up in a digital world. They have never known a world where technology and digital content was not available at their fingertips. This book demonstrates how the digital world and literacy collide. Throughout the book, there are a multitude of activities and ideas to encourage and facilitate the embracing of this collision, and to engage students in ways you may never have previously considered. Many ideas, such as Google Maps, YouTube, book trailers and graphic novels, are presented. Between this, the additional resources, and hyperlinks to online content, teachers will be able to quickly adapt their current practices to utilize some of the engaging digital formats described in the text. Recommended.—**Pamela K. Simmons**

324.   **Information Literacy and Libraries in the Age of Fake News.** Denise E. Agosto, ed. Santa Barbara, Calif., Libraries Unlimited/ABC-CLIO, 2018. 184p. $65.00pa. ISBN 13: 978-1-4408-6418-6; 978-1-4408-6419-3 (e-book).

Editor Denise Agosto asserts in chapter one that libraries have traditionally taught users to think critically and are positioned to educate users to "determine whether information they encounter online is accurate, reliable, and worthy of being shared." This reviewer heartily agrees with this assertion. This volume is short enough to be skimmed in a week but has thorough coverage of fake news as it relates to information literacy. This book starts off with introductory material including references to world events that catapulted phrases like fake news into headlines and dictionaries, definitions of key concepts, and the history of the fake news phenomenon. The primary audience for this book is librarians, and there is a heavy emphasis on content by academic library authors. However, there are also essays written by librarians in public and school libraries. As far as the authors, bios are included at the back of the book with satisfactory credentials and experience. The reader will also find information on the different kinds of literacy at play in educating consumers about evaluating and thinking critically about news. The editor also includes essays with topics that will enrich a practitioner's knowledge and give them more tools to teach and guide library users. There is additional content that addresses how the ACRL Framework concepts can be utilized in information literacy instruction, suggestions for library instruction related to fake news, and how instructors may utilize research LibGuides to teach fake news topics. This book includes good coverage on teaching and educating users on fake news as it relates to digital and media literacy. However, one suggestion might have been to include either a list of additional materials or toolkit for practitioners to use in their education efforts.—**Jessica Graves Louque**

325.   **Leveraging Wikipedia: Connecting Communities of Knowledge.** Merrilee Proffitt, ed. Chicago, American Library Association, 2018. 263p. index. $68.00pa. $61.20pa. (ALA members). ISBN 13: 978-1-8389-1632-2.

Leveraging Wikipedia is a collection of essay chapters exploring the relationship between Wikipedia and libraries. Specifically, this book surveys the premise that

Wikipedia and libraries are important to each other and exist as natural allies working toward a common goal.

The 15 chapters of *Leveraging Wikipedia* cover a wide variety of topics. Some of the more niche topics include connecting citizens with the military and bringing archival collections to Wikipedia with the Remixing Archival Metadata Project Editor. Other chapters discuss how to become a wikipedian, the librarian-supported relationship between Wikipedia and education, and edit-a-thons.

The chapters vary in terms of format and structure, simply sharing the Wikipedia theme as their connective tissue. As such, the subject matter and personal relevance can fluctuate significantly from chapter to chapter. One chapter may be a relatively short anecdotal story of a specific experience, followed by a longer prototypical research paper with dozens of references. Depending on one's outlook and expectations, this could be either a strength or a weakness. Regardless, each article is well written, understandable, and easy to follow.

Because the topic of Wikipedia and libraries is important to a certain audience, this publication will prove a useful resource to those individuals. For those interested in utilizing Wikipedia in the profession or looking toward the future of the topic, *Leveraging Wikipedia* is a very good introduction.—**Tyler Manolovitz**

326.   **Literacy Engagement through Peritextual Analysis.** Shelbie Witte, Don Latham, and Melissa Gross, eds. Chicago, American Library Association, 2019. 178p. index. $44.00pa.; $40.40pa. (ALA members). ISBN 13: 978-0-8389-1768-8.

The twelve chapters in this volume explore ways that teachers and librarians can use the Peritextual Literacy Framework (2016), developed at Florida State University, to enhance students' skills in understanding books and nonprint texts. Peritext elements include book covers, dust jackets, title pages, tables of contents, and indexes. Having students of all ages, from first grade to college, explore these features has been shown to increase their interest in reading and their ability to understand the works they read. The studies included are quite varied, from studying the covers of two graphic novels by Gene Luen Yang and exploring the role of covers in gaining an understanding of Kafka's *The Metamorphosis,* to using the framework to analyze Disney films through the study of DVD containers and exploring a film about the street artist Banksy. The collection of essays clearly demonstrates the variety of settings in which "peritextual literacy" can increase one's ability to understand and interpret texts of many kinds. Given that this is a relatively new field within both education and literary analysis, the volume will be an excellent starting point.

Teachers, future teachers, and education administrators will benefit from the studies included here. Libraries serving these populations should consider this title.—**Mark Schumacher**

327.   Mallon, Melissa N. **The Pivotal Role of Academic Librarians in Digital Learning.** Santa Barbara, Calif., Libraries Unlimited/ABC-CLIO, 2018. 152p. index. $50.00pa. ISBN 13: 978-1-4408-5217-6; 978-1-4408-5218-3 (e-book).

The Pivotal Role of Academic Librarians in Digital Learning discusses "how academic librarians, instructors, and other campus administrators can collaborate to create a learning environment that facilitates student development of the critical thinking, information, and digital literacy skills needed for engaging in the complex modern information landscape" (xiii). The book is written primarily for public services librarians, especially those in an instructional and/or distance learning capacity, or with information literacy and/or digital literacy responsibilities. The author argues that students are spending more of their time and doing more of their work in digital spaces, and academic librarians must therefore adopt new technologies, approaches, and mindsets to properly support them.

The book is divided into 8 chapters : "Communicating Academic Excellence through Librarian-Faculty Collaborations," "Outreach Strategies for Graduate and Professional Programs," "Integrating Digital Literacies in the Curriculum," "Customized Research Support for Distance Learners," "Performance-Based Assessment of Research Skills," "Promoting Transferrable Research Skills in General Education Courses," "Students as Creators: Collaboration through Connectivism," and "Tying Research Instruction to the University Strategic Plan." Certain themes are observed throughout: outreach librarians must form relationships with faculty and students (i.e., venture "outside the library"), embrace social media, provide customized content for diverse groups and individuals, be flexible, be lifelong learners, document and assess the impact of their services, align themselves with larger departmental and institutional priorities, and read and contribute to professional literature(s), etc.

The Pivotal Role of Academic Librarians in Digital Learning is a quick, informative read, with a wealth of useful references for each chapter. Librarians will find the efficient descriptions of various educational ideologies especially useful (e.g., single paragraph explanations of Constructivism, Cognitivism, and Connectivism—within the context of distance education—on pages 55-56). The author also has a significant online presence, with an active Twitter feed and a regularly updated collection of research guides, which provides additional context for the book.—**Richard Nathan Leigh**

Information Technology

328. Hennig, Nicole. **Siri, Alexa, and Other Digital Assistants: The Librarian's Quick Guide.** Santa Barbara, Calif., Libraries Unlimited/ABC-CLIO, 2018. 91p. index. $35.00pa. ISBN 13: 978-1-4408-6108-6; 978-1-4408-6726-2 (e-book).

This book examines the hot trend of voice-first computing, devices that activate systems through the use of the voice. Statistics show that 20 percent of the U.S. population have purchased and are using these devices since they appeared two years ago. An introduction to voice-first computing, devices, and advantages leads into how libraries can incorporate these devices to provide benefits for various populations such as the elderly and those who have physical challenges and concerns about privacy, ethical concerns related to their use by children, and the future of voice computing. Granted, it may be quite early in the development of this technology for its incorporation in libraries, but the author provides a good discussion of its possibilities and its challenges for those interested and willing to experiment.—**Bradford Lee Eden**

International Librarianship

329. Carlyle, Cate, and Dee Winn. **Your Passport to International Librarianship.** Chicago, American Library Association, 2018. 132p. index. $49.99pa.; $44.99 (ALA members). ISBN 13: 978-0-8389-1718-3.

Libraries have played an important part in developing and educating people in many countries for centuries but international librarianship is still a relatively new part of librarianship. It was introduced in 1927 when the International Federation of Library Association (IFLA) was founded by a few European and American librarians. It has become an important part of librarianship. The book under review is based on the practical experience of two Canadian librarians who are proponents of international librarianship and volunteering in libraries in developing countries in Africa, Asia, and Central and South America. Libraries in these countries are underdeveloped because of budget problems, lack of leadership, hunger, illiteracy, war, famines, and poverty. All chapters are well written including chapter number 7 written by an American librarian who is a very active volunteer in a library in Guatemala through the Librarians Without Boarders program. All authors are of the view that it is important to volunteer in the libraries of developing countries. It will be a good experience in spite of the fact that there will be cultural shocks, language problems, poverty, slow progress, poor living conditions, and other problems but it is worth helping libraries and librarians in these countries for the benefit of their citizens and to fulfill their information needs through technology. Chapter 8 gives a list of online sources about volunteering as an international librarian. The book also includes a bibliography and an index. It is a good addition to the library literature and is recommended for all library collections and librarians interested in contributing as volunteers to libraries and international librarianship.—**Ravindra Nath Sharma**

Library Facilities

330.   Gisolfi, Peter. **Collaborative Library Design: From Planning to Impact.** Chicago, American Library Association, 2018. 146p. illus. index. $74.99pa.; $67.50pa. (ALA members). ISBN 13: 978-0-8389-1717-6.

This is a curious book. In one way, it is an advertisement for some of the work that the author's architecture firm has done in the last twenty or so years in the northeast United States. Having said that, there is a lot of useful information here about the process of designing library facilities, whether it is a new building to replace one no longer adequate, or an addition/reconfiguration of an existing structure. The volume is divided into two equal sections: five public libraries in the first half and five academic and school libraries in the second. Each of the ten projects has three brief essays: "The Planning process," "The Design," and "The Impact." The listed author provides the design section, while members of the respective library communities furnish the other two essays. Throughout these texts the authors present the diverse ways that the library community interacts with the architects chosen for the project, from start to finish.

One of the finest elements of this volume is the collection of striking photographs showing the results of the projects, often with both before and after images so as to emphasize the enhancements that have been made. Detailed floor plans, with before and after diagrams, supplement most of the ten articles.

Librarians involved with renovation or construction planning, and those simply interested in the subject, will find useful ideas about modernizing or upgrading their facilities.—**Mark Schumacher**

Library Funding

331.   Chrastka, John, and Patrick "PC" Sweeney. **Before the Ballot: Building Political Support for Library Funding.** Chicago, American Library Association, 2019. 260p. index. $54.99pa.; $49.49pa. (ALA members). ISBN 13: 978-0-8389-1779-4.

This book is written as a companion book to *Winning Elections and Influencing Politicians for Library Funding* (2017), which was primarily written for library ballot committees and advocacy organizations. This volume specifically focuses on the work that librarians can do to influence politics in the years between elections. Divided into 2 parts and 16 chapters, it explores advocacy and influence and messaging in order to gain support for library funding and election ballots related to library fundraising. Issues such as gaining insight into voter attitudes surrounding libraries, the librarian as candidate, the library as cause, building partnerships and joining coalitions, defining audiences of potential supporters, understanding engagement with supporters and activists, why libraries lose, and the ideal 36-month campaign from "before the ballot" to election day are all covered in this book for public and private libraries whose major funding comes through election ballot initiatives.—**Bradford Lee Eden**

Library Instruction

332.   Kroski, Ellyssa. **Escape Rooms and Other Immersive Experiences in the Library.** Chicago, American Library Association, 2019. 188p. illus. index. $57.99pa.; $52.19pa. (ALA members). ISBN 13: 978-0-8389-1767-1.

This book by librarian and prolific author/editor Ellyssa Kroski provides librarians at public, school, and academic libraries with a well-written, easy-to-follow, and inspirational how-to book on creating escape rooms. As explained by the author, escape rooms promote information literacy, engage patrons, encourage critical thinking, and more. The book is divided into two main parts. Part I, Introducing Escape Rooms and Immersive Experiences, looks at how libraries are incorporating these rooms, starting with chapter 1, "Escape Rooms and Immersive Experiences Explained." This chapter has a section on escape rooms in the United States which includes descriptions and URL information. Readers will also find information on interactive museum exhibits, live action role playing games, and escape rooms in the United Kingdom and Europe. The second chapter elaborates on the opportunities provided by escape room activities (outreach, increasing information literacy and critical thinking, team building, etc.). The third chapter includes case studies of escape rooms used in school, public, and academic libraries, with patrons ranging in age from pre-tween to adult. The second part of the book, How to Create, Organize, and Run Eleven Project Types, conveys the nuts and bolts process of creating and hosting a successful escape room. Readers will learn how to host a predesigned escape room event, how to design an escape room from scratch, how to host an immersive experience, how to host a kid-friendly escape room event, how to design a digital breakout, how to host an escape room for the purposes of staff training and team building, and more. The last chapter walks readers through an escape room created by the author, *The Search for Alexander Hamilton and the Missing Librarian.* There are two appendixes, "Escape Room Set-up Document Template" and "Escape Room Puzzle Document Template." The book concludes with a list of resources and an index. Highly recommended.—**ARBA Staff Reviewer**

Library Management

333.   Henry, Jo, Joe Eshleman, and Richard Moniz. **The Dysfunctional Library: Challenges and Solutions to Workplace Relationships.** Chicago, American Library Association, 2018. 202p. index. $64.00pa.; $57.60pa. (ALA members). ISBN 13: 978-0-8389-1623-0.

This volume deals with a challenging and complex topic: dysfunction in the library, whether public, academic, or private. Libraries have always attracted both introverted and extroverted individuals, given the wide variety of tasks, services, and duties needed to keep today's libraries running. This often creates challenges due to change, innovation, teamwork, conflict, and differences of opinion, which often build and grow over time due to the long-term tenures of library staff and librarians, and the conflict avoidance tendencies of many library directors. The three authors draw on their wealth of experience to address such issues as dysfunctional organizational culture, incivility in the work environment, toxic behaviors of staff, poor communication, conflict management, ineffective collaboration, difficulties with team composition, and organizational deviance and workplace politics. A timely and much-needed book on a topic faced by many libraries.—**Bradford Lee Eden**

334.   Miller, Robin, and Kate Hinnant. **Making Surveys Work for Your Library: Guidance, Instructions, and Examples.** Santa Barbara, Calif., Libraries Unlimited/ABC-CLIO, 2019. 118p. index. $45.00pa. ISBN 13: 978-1-4408-6107-9; 978-1-4408-6108-6 (e-book).

This book provides quick guidance and tips for conducting library surveys. From initial planning to various survey methods, from writing questions to focusing on distribution and specific populations, from analyzing the results to taking action, it is written for those who are newbies to the library survey landscape. Sample questions regarding demographics, services, spaces, communication, and collections are included in appendixes. There are lots of tables, figures, examples, and illustrations throughout. A concise volume on this topic which I highly recommend.—**Bradford Lee Eden**

335.   Moran, Barbara B., and Claudia J. Morner. **Library and Information Center Management.** 9th ed. Santa Barbara, Calif., Libraries Unlimited/ABC-CLIO, 2018. 548p. index. $60.00. ISBN 13: 978-1-4408-5447-7; 978-1-4408-5448-4 (e-book).

For those teaching or learning about leading and managing libraries, this book would be a valuable resource. Written for students in library and information programs at the university level, this book offers a wealth of information about being successful in leading and managing all types of libraries. Asking learners to put what they are reading into practice is one of the best features, including a wide array of cases, quotes, and thought provoking discussion questions. These activities are sprinkled throughout the chapters, at the end of each chapter, and included in the online course companion. The online companion provides additional and expanded resources that further enrich each chapter. The online companion is good, but not always intuitive. As examined, it appears to be for instructors, not students, and I am not sure if that was the intent. Discussion questions and cases are placed in boxes of contrasting color, helping break up the volume of information encountered at one time. Likewise, each chapter includes charts, graphs, and tables to help visually reinforce content. A valuable resource for a class or as a professional reference on leading and managing libraries. Recommended.—**Michelle Hudiburg**

336.   Sannwald, William W. **Financial Management for Libraries.** Chicago, American Library Association, 2018. 200p. index. $82.00pa.; $73.80pa. (ALA members). ISBN 13: 978-0-8389-1560-8.

Librarians at any experience level benefit from financial management knowledge; however, it is a skill missing from many library educational programs. *Financial Management for Libraries* fills that gap by covering the basics of financial budgeting and strategic planning in a concise, easy-to-read format.

Three libraries are featured throughout the book demonstrating how budgets are planned, the various revenue sources, performance measures, and more. Each library serves a different sector of the population; an academic library, a public library, and a township library. Example graphs, charts, and tables are from genuine financial documents provided by the three libraries. These real-world examples offer relatable information for every reader, regardless of the type of library in which he or she works. References are located at the end of each chapter making it easy for readers to quickly find additional sources for further reading on the chapter subject.

A few issues slightly mar the readability. There is the occasional grammatical error, errant bracket, missing word, or repeated word that detailed readers will notice. Some financial documents are printed in smaller text font than the rest of the book. For readers who need the larger text font, this becomes problematic when reviewing these examples.

Recommended as an introduction to financial management for established library professionals and students. Librarians that do not directly handle budgets benefit from understanding the complexity of the process for a greater appreciation of budgetary decisions.—**Jeffrey A. Jensen**

337.   Searcy, Carly Wiggins. **Project Management in Libraries: On Time, On Budget, On Target.** Chicago, American Library Association, 2018. 124p. index. $54.99pa.; $49.49pa. (ALA members). ISBN 13: 978-0-8389-1719-0.

While day-to-day tasks of library employees are crucial to the success of the institution, one-time projects can be equally important. This book provides clear and important information on the many diverse elements of such an endeavor, such as drafting a charter, understanding stakeholders, staffing, timing, planning for funding, and facing potential risks. Although the chapters are fairly brief, readers will find useful details throughout: risks a particular project might face, diverse ways to reward stakeholders, a detailed timeline for a project, and others. Summaries and footnotes for each of the fifteen chapters and a brief bibliography at the end of the text add to the usefulness of this volume.

Any library that undertakes projects regularly should consider adding this title, despite its hefty price. Administrators and library staff will learn a great deal about the process of running smooth, fulfilling, and successful projects—**Mark Schumacher**

338.   **Short-Term Staff, Long-Term Benefits: Making the Most of Interns, Volunteers, Student Workers, and Temporary Staff in Libraries.** Nora J. Bird and Michael A. Crumpton, eds. Santa Barbara, Calif., Libraries Unlimited/ABC-CLIO, 2018. 144p. index. $65.00pa. ISBN 13: 978-1-4408-4176-7; 978-1-4408-4177-4 (e-book).

This book provides guidance and ideas for the use of short-term staff in libraries. It describes both volunteer and paid opportunities, and how to make the best use of this workforce as more libraries find themselves dealing with reduced budgets and increased workflows. After a short introduction regarding the benefits of short-term staff, eight chapters describe various types of opportunities and ideas for making the case for both volunteer and paid staff. These include working with faculty and sponsors for academic credit, working with grant funding and project-based staff, residencies, virtual internships, how to incorporate these staff opportunities in both academic and public libraries, and thinking outside the box for projects in special collections and archives. The editors describe the benefits of both volunteer and paid short-term staff for both libraries and the staff themselves. A compact book exploring new ideas for dealing with workforce issues in both public and academic libraries.—**Bradford Lee Eden**

339. Stoltz, Dorothy, Gail Griffith, Muffie Smith, and Lynn Wheeler. **Transform and Thrive: Ideas to Invigorate Your Library and Your Community.** Chicago, American Library Association, 2018. 152p. illus. index. $60.00pa.; $54.00pa. (ALA members). ISBN 13: 978-0-8389-1622-3.

This book strives to provide librarians with ideas on how to keep libraries relevant, vital, and valued parts of communities. The book is divided into four sections: Risk-Taking (3 chapters); Treasure Those You Serve…So They Will Serve You (3 chapters); Become an Outstanding Library Leader (3 chapters); and Activate Creativity (2 chapters). In these chapters, readers will find discussions on how to think laterally (an idea developed by Edward de Bono in the late 1960s), taking risks, the importance of valuing staff and customers, how to build good will among all stakeholders, how to evaluate programs, and more. The book makes generous use of black-and-white photographs and quotes from, among others, Plato, Helen Keller, Confucius, Aristotle, Shakespeare, Muhammad, Abraham Lincoln, Buddha, and Benjamin Franklin. There are nine appendixes that include a worksheet for facilitating the thinking process on intelligent risk taking, a sample checklist for events and special programs, and a guide for the first steps to interrogating a Shakespearean monologue or play scene. Appendix H, "Suggested Resources," is an unannotated list of seven organizations: the American Library Association, the Aspen Institute, the Center for the Future of Libraries, the Erikson Institute, the Global Family Research Project, the Harwood Institute of Public Innovation, and New America. "Suggested Reading," Appendix I, offers nine resources, including three works by de Bono and one each from Plato, Aristotle, Ralph Waldo Emerson, and Shakespeare. An index rounds out the work.— **ARBA Staff Reviewer**

Library Outreach

340. Berman, Erin. **Your Technology Outreach Adventure: Tools for Human-Centered Problem Solving.** Chicago, American Library Association, 2019. 188p. index. $54.99pa.; $49.49pa. (ALA members). ISBN 13: 978-0-8389-1778-7.

Librarians wanting a guide to technology outreach have come to the right place. Berman, formerly the Innovations Manager at San José Public Library and currently the Principal Librarian of the Learning Group at Alameda County Library, brings her expertise to the subject in an easy-to-follow framework that takes readers from theory and ideas through to implementation. The first chapter, "Bridging the Digital Divide," discusses some overarching issues such as technology access and the ultimate goal of technology outreach—literacy. Chapter 2, "Outreach Fundamentals," stresses the importance of gathering information about the needs and aspirations of your library community (what languages are spoken other than English, for example), what partnerships already exist, and more. "Technology-Based Outreach Planning," chapter 3, discusses things to consider in choosing an outreach project (robot building, library card sign-us, etc.), what technology to purchase, and related topics. Chapters 4-7 focus on design thinking and include the history of design thinking, best practices for design, design thinking exercises, and how to turn a prototype into a real-world outreach program. The final chapter shows technology research in practice using case studies of programs implemented at San José Public Library. These include making videos at a skate park, connecting e-books and seniors, and creating a pop-up, mobile makerspace. The book includes graphic organizers, diagrams, and other tools to support the information provided. A section of resources and an index round out the book. Highly recommended.—**ARBA Staff Reviewer**

341.   Carson, Jenn. **Get Your Community Moving: Physical Literacy Programs for All Ages.** Chicago, American Library Association, 2018. 204p. illus. index. $54.00pa.; $49.49pa. (ALA members). ISBN 13: 978-0-8389-1725-1.

Jenn Carson, yoga instructor and librarian at the L.P. Fisher Public Library in Woodstock, New Brunswick, Canada, provides librarians in public, school, and academic settings with the rationale for physical movement programs and a roadmap for how to implement physical activity programs. In the introduction, Carson relays the results of a recent survey she conducted among ALA members regarding physical activity programs in the library. Of the more than 300 who responded, 65 percent said their libraries offered physical activities. The first chapter explains what physical literacy is and why it matters. This is followed by a chapter on getting started with physical activity programs that includes funding, logistics, legal liability, and more. Chapter 3 focuses on what it calls passive play and suggests ways to introduce passive physical activities into libraries (e.g., a hopscotch mat in the children's section, alternative collections, and book displays on physical movement). Chapters 4-6 outline programs for children, teens, and adults that include everything from fun runs to Nerf battles to walking clubs to quidditch (Harry Potter) matches. These chapters discuss the activities in detail and provide information about budget, step-by-step instructions on how to start and carry out the activity, and multiple literacy tie-ins (books, films, periodicals). Chapter 7 discusses ways to involve particular communities (First Nations, seniors, low income, people with disabilities, and library staff) in physical activity programs. A concluding chapter is followed by an afterword by Dr. Denise Agosto on why it is important to expand our concept of literacy to include physical literacy. All chapters contain reference notes, and all chapters are enhanced by black-and-white photographs. Chapters also include shaded textboxes that feature "Activity All Stars" like Information Services/Health Librarian Gwen Geiger Wolfe from Lawrence (Kansas) Public Library who introduced a program that allows patrons to check out gym memberships. The book concludes with an appendix that lists movement-based holidays, a glossary of terms, a bibliography, and an index. Recommended.—**ARBA Staff Reviewer**

342.   **Genealogy and the Librarian: Perspectives on Research, Instruction, Outreach and Management.** Carol Smallwood and Vera Gubnitskaia, eds. Jefferson, N.C., McFarland, 2018. 293p. index. $55.00pa. ISBN 13: 978-1-4766-7087-4; 978-1-4766-3322-0 (e-book).

In this book more than thirty librarians offer practical suggestions on ways to expand genealogical services in public, academic, and special libraries. The first section, Overview, covers general ground, from trends in genealogy, to the usefulness of a project like Chronicling America, to how other historical sources like the Sanborn Maps and WPA records can be used to find and contextualize genealogical facts, and more. The following sections are: Collaboration, Case Studies, Research, Instruction, Family, Outreach, Management, and Finances. Within these sections, there are informative chapters on such things as strategies for finding military and court records, how to instruct patrons in using genealogical sources, how to find death records, and other tools and tips. The Outreach section contains ideas on engaging with various community members and groups using genealogical sources. The section on management focuses largely on issues surrounding digitization of records, and the last section, Finances, offers ideas about how to fund digitization projects. Most chapters include works cited. Back matter includes notes on the contributors and an index. Recommended.—**ARBA Staff Reviewer**

343.   **The Library Outreach Casebook.** Ryan L. Sittler and Terra J. Rogerson, eds. Chicago, American Library Association, Association of College and Research Libraries, 2018. 202p. illus. $56.00pa. ISBN 13: 978-0-8389-4873-6.

As academic libraries work to expand their campus presence, *The Library Outreach Casebook* provides a broad exploration into the planning and implementation of many successful events. Ryan Sittler, an original editor of the popular Library Instruction Cookbook series, has compiled this anthology with creative examples from a wide range of institutions. Time and again, this volume illustrates how imagination and persistence can lead to productive results.

The casebook is divided into three sections: starting strategies; programming and event planning; and outreach to select populations. The twenty-one readable chapters utilize a case study approach and are written by the librarians that created these events. Popular topics include: scavenger hunts, actors in the library, de-stress events, therapy dogs, game nights, and social media themed activities. Promotional materials, handouts, and photographs from these efforts are often included. Library Outreach can take many forms, and Sittler includes topics on graphic design, usability testing, and content marketing. With few exceptions these efforts were created for a broad audience and were not tied to a particular course or discipline.

Regrettably, despite a variety of interesting examples, chapters rarely provide accurate information about the time and cost associated with creating and hosting these efforts. Additionally, it's not always clear what specific factors made these events successful. Sadly, no events involved partnerships with other campus groups.

Notwithstanding these limitations, the examples in *The Library Outreach Casebook* provide a roadmap of worthwhile destinations that merit strong consideration. Events are scalable and could easily be adapted to fit different academic settings and outreach budgets. This volume is recommended for academic librarians as well as students in LIS programs.—**Joshua Becker**

344.   **The Relevant Library: Essays on Adapting to Changing Needs.** Vera Gubnitskaia and Carol Smallwood, eds. Jefferson, N.C., McFarland, 2018. 290p. illus. index. $55.00pa. ISBN 13: 978-1-4766-7029-4; 978-1-4766-3317-6 (e-book).

The thirty-four articles in this volume are grouped into nine sections such as Reevaluating Collections, Enhancing Partnerships, Transforming Programming, and Extending Accessibility. Nearly all of the articles recount efforts at libraries to accomplish change: to enhance resources and access to them, to design study spaces based on patrons' suggestions, to improve access and service for patrons, and other projects. The fifty-seven authors come from diverse library settings—colleges and universities, public libraries, school libraries and library networks—and present the projects they have undertaken. Many have served in various important roles in library organizations. This provides a very broad view of the importance of maintaining and enhancing library relevance to the user population. Many of the projects presented here could be considered outreach efforts intended to better serve the library's user population.

Librarians of all types will find ideas in this large collection of essays that they would be able to adapt to their local situation. Library science students will also get a broad look at the current approaches to enhancing library settings and programs. Any library engaging, or hoping to engage, in projects like the ones presented here should certainly get this volume.—**Mark Schumacher**

Makerspaces

345.   Cox, Marge. **The Elementary School Library Makerspace: A Start-Up Guide.** Santa Barbara, Calif., Libraries Unlimited/ABC-CLIO, 2018. 135p. index. 40.00pa. ISBN 13: 978-1-4408-5338-8; 978-1-4408-5339-5 (e-book).

This book is a well-designed, timely professional resource. It starts off with introductory material about makerspaces—a little history, what they are, and why readers might want one. Subsequent chapters feature a variety of easy-to-do activities arranged by subject. With each field, the author discusses ideas and resources in a down-to-earth manner that is easy to understand. The end of the book briefly reviews the importance of data, knowing how the space will be used, funding, PR, and getting started. After reading this, I realized it is not only a good book for getting started, but also a good book for those in search of ideas related to what is being taught in the classroom for existing library makerspaces. This is the book's strength. All activities are ready to use, simple, and follow a step-by-step design that can be copied (copyright information is included on each page). If elementary librarians are thinking of starting up a makerspace or just looking for some quick ideas for different subject areas, this is a book they will want to read. Recommended.—**Melinda W. Miller**

346.   Kroski, Ellyssa. **63 Ready-to-Use Maker Projects.** Chicago, American Library Association, 2018. 368p. index. $67.00pa.; $61.19 (ALA members). ISBN 13: 978-0-8389-1591-2.

The maker projects in this book are categorized into seven main categories: Paper, Cardboard, and Crafts; Sewing and Textiles; Circuitry, Wiring, and Wearables; Milling, Soldering, and Cutting; High-Tech Programming and Robotics; Digital Media; and 3D Printing. Over 30 librarians contributed projects to this work, which explains the variation in the amount of detail and information provided for individual projects. All entries include a project description, cost estimate, materials list, step-by-step instructions, learning outcomes, pictures of the finished project, and recommended next projects. The suggested age range, level of difficulty, and time required are notably absent in most entries, and the "step-by-step" instructions take the form of an ordered list of steps in some projects and paragraphs explaining the process in others. Projects range from the tried-and-true lava lamp, duct tape crafts, movie making, and LED projects to unique interactive displays, complex coding projects, and hacking projects that go behind the scenes of everyday items and uses. In spite of some inconsistencies, the breadth and variety of projects make this a useful source for any library or makerspace serving middle school and older students. School libraries serving advanced upper elementary students may also find some inspiration in projects that can be adapted for younger students. Recommended.—**Holly Whitt**

347.   **School Library Makerspaces in Action.** Moorefield-Lang, Heather, ed. Santa Barbara, Calif., Libraries Unlimited/ABC-CLIO, 2018. 147p. index. $45.00pa. ISBN 13: 978-1-4408-5696-9; 978-1-4408-5697-6 (e-book).

As promised by the title, this manual brings together stories of individual school librarians who are utilizing makerspaces in a variety of settings and for a variety of audiences. Going beyond computer lab coding classes or high school robotics clubs, these scenarios describe individual journeys of implementing makerspaces, often from scratch. The content represents early elementary, middle, or upper-grade experiences as well as contacts with teachers, administrators, special education students, English language learners, and public libraries—both bringing public library sources into classrooms and sharing efforts at public library sites. Part of the appeal is hearing a fresh voice in every entry, as well as enjoying the adventures as readers learn along with narrators, covering topics such as finding time, space, and materials; helpful hints such as how to woo constituents; establishing—and in some cases, abandoning—rules and regulations; results; and future plans. It's easy to find inspiration within these pages, whether reading cover to cover or dipping in for targeted articles. Rounded out with resources for further exploration—especially the blogs—this is an appealing choice for library instructors, students, and professional collections. Recommended.—**Kathleen McBroom**

348.   Seymour, Gina. **Makers with a Cause: Creative Service Projects for Library Youth.** Santa Barbara, Calif., Libraries Unlimited/ABC-CLIO, 2018. 148p. illus. index. $45.00pa. ISBN 13: 978-1-4408-5728-7; 978-1-4408-5729-4 (e-book).

Gina Seymour has done an excellent job of distilling why and how to add service learning and service projects as integral elements to your school/public library's makerspace, be it a dedicated space, mobile/cart, or pop-up event. Divided into two sections, she opens with background about makerspaces and how they help students develop entrepreneurial skills and empathy. Additionally, she addresses the importance of learning from failure. She presents strong arguments for offering these types of opportunities for disadvantaged populations, English language learners, and students with disabilities. She offers suggestions for setting up a makerspace, stresses the importance for partnering/communicating/collaborating with outside organizations, and gives guidance on how to seek outside financial support. The second section of the book offers solid programming ideas, grouped by projects for animal shelters, the homeless and hungry, health and wellness, government organizations and NGOs, and global organizations. A few of the suggested activities assume the presenter has requisite skills to teach those skills to a group (using a 3D printer, braiding, crocheting, etc.), while a couple others are vague; however, the vast majority are clear, detailed, and meaningful. For most projects, she offers relevant dates to undertake a given project, materials needed, instructions on how to implement, and cautionary considerations. Occasional black-and-white photographs illustrate some of the finished projects and help break up the text. The appendixes include templates for communicating with potential partners, a calendar of dates to help flow the year, and a list of national organizations to consider contacting. Well-conceived and executed, this tool would be helpful not only to those starting out setting up a makerspace, but also for those seeking to take theirs to the next level. A bibliography and index round out the work. Recommended.—**Stephanie Bange**

Readers' Advisory

349.   Harlan, Mary Ann. **The Girl-Positive Library: Inspiring Confidence, Creativity, and Curiosity in Young Women.** Santa Barbara, Calif., Libraries Unlimited/ABC-CLIO, 2019. 164p. index. $45.00pa. ISBN 13: 978-1-4408-6063-8; 978-1-4408-6064-5 (e-book).

Representation of diverse groups in literature is imperative for all libraries. However, the representation of girls in young adult literature has not been given the attention it deserves. Harlan focuses on the representation of girls in young adult literature and the impact it has on them. She provides information on how to look at YA books through a feminist lens to select titles that will inspire young women to develop their own confidence and creativity to have a voice in society. This resource provides some background information. However, the majority of the book provides detailed title reviews, discussion questions, and activities to encourage a healthy mindset in girls and young women. *The Girl-Positive Library* is an excellent resource for any teen services librarian wishing to encourage growth and positivity for young females. Recommended.—**Shelly Lee**

350.   Lacy, Meagan, and Pauline Dewan. **Connecting Children with Classics: A Reader-Centered Approach to Selecting and Promoting Great Literature.** Santa Barbara, Calif., Libraries Unlimited/ABC-CLIO, 2018. 482p. $60.00pa. ISBN 13: 978-1-4408-4439-3; 978-1-4408-4440-9 (e-book).

This book provides a different approach to Readers' Advisory for children by organizing children's literature titles in terms of both textual appeal and reader appeal. Research indicates that children are most inclined to read when they are allowed to choose the titles for themselves, but many need help finding books that will appeal to them. That is where this book comes in. Chapters are divided first by genre and then by Catherine Sheldrick Ross's reader-driven appeals. More than three hundred American and British titles are listed, with a summary and critical evaluation following each citation. Genres covered include adventure/survival, animal, fantasy, historical fiction, myth/legend, realism, science fiction, and toys/games. Ross's appeals include the following: Awakening, Identity, Reassurance, Connection with Others, Courage, Acceptance, and Understanding of the World. Each entry also contains themes, reading interest level, and read-alikes. The books suggested in each genre are all novels; no picture books are listed. Classic titles were chosen because they have stood the test of time and exemplify universal themes, though the authors acknowledge that one downside to focusing on classics is the lack of diversity. This is an excellent tool for any parent to give guidance to those children who have a difficult time finding a book to read or who want books similar to the one they just read. An appendix in the back lists key children's literature awards for fiction. An index rounds out the work. Recommended.—**Anne L. Hoffman**

351.   **Muslims in Story: Expanding Multicultural Understanding through Children's and Young Adult Literature.** Gauri Manglik and Sadaf Siddique, eds. Chicago, American Library Association, 2018. 248p. illus. index. $49.99pa.; $44.99pa. (ALA members). ISBN 13: 978-0-8389-1741-1.

There are plenty of books in contemporary children's and young adult literature with diverse characters. However, what is missing is a resource that brings together titles and themes for readers' advisory of Muslim Children's Literature as a subgenre. *Muslims in Story* was written to fill this gap after an increase in hate crimes against Muslims following the 2016 presidential election and the subsequent Muslim ban. This book was the result of the authors' research for their campaign named "Counter Islamophobia Through Stories." The audience for this book includes educators, school media specialists, and librarians. The book lists include an age range of preschool to young adult. The authors' purpose for the book is to provide a tool to help education and library practitioners provide programming ideas and book recommendations to help children and young adults gain cultural understanding and develop more positive views of Muslims to counter any negative views they may encounter.

Part one provides a background on the rich history of Muslims in America, Islamophobia and its impact on children, and how literature may be used to reshape the narrative about Muslims to bring about change. Part two includes book lists to aid librarians and educators in increasing reader exposure to Muslim characters, culture, and traditions through literature. Book lists are centered on themes including Muslim kids as heroes, inspiring leaders and thinkers, stories that celebrate Islam including religious practices and traditions, and Islamic folktales. Each chapter includes a theme explanation, book summary, and book awards. Many entries include ideas for further engagement, discussion starters, and book quotes, all of which would be helpful in planning book-related activities, discussions, and programs. However, the further engagement suggestions are limited and feature more suggestions for school settings. This section could have included more suggestions useful for public library programs such as activities that incorporate visual art and drama. The appendixes are thoughtfully prepared and include frequently asked questions about Islam, a timeline for Muslims in America, a glossary of unfamiliar words, and practitioner tools such as guidelines for evaluating Muslim children's literature, and suggested educational resources.—**Jessica Graves Louque**

Research

352.   Brown, Christopher C., and Suzanne S. Bell. **Librarian's Guide to Online Searching: Cultivating Database Skills for Research and Instruction.** 5th ed. Santa Barbara, Calif., Libraries Unlimited/ABC-CLIO, 2018. 376p. index. $55.00pa. ISBN 13: 978-1-4408-6156-7; 978-1-4408-6157-4 (e-book).

In the fifth edition of this venerable, graduate-level text, longstanding author Suzanne

Bell passes the mantle to Christopher Brown, a reference technology integration librarian at the University of Denver. Bell still has a role in the book, namely chapters 15 and 16 on evaluating databases and teaching other people about databases. This edition brings a number of new chapters, including ones on government information resources, controlled vocabulary, major vendors' database interfaces and common database search features, and web-scale discovery tools. As with the fourth edition, additional search tips, exercises, and tutorials are available on the publisher's website. The types of databases discussed are ones typically encountered in public or academic libraries. The first 6 chapters address the basics of databases, chapters 7 through 13 cover subject specific databases, chapter 14 addresses user needs when searching, and the last 2 chapters are those addressed by Bell and mentioned earlier. Particularly useful are the chapters on web-scale discovery tools, which discuss their virtues and shortcomings. Also useful is chapter 6 that addresses user interfaces and specific search features common to various databases. As this book often serves as a textbook, each chapter concludes with a set of exercises and references to other sources. Overall, this is an indispensable book for learning about databases. Recommended for all libraries.—**Kevin McDonough**

353.   **Research Methods for Librarians and Educators: Practical Applications in Formal and Informal Learning Environments.** Ruth V. Small and Marcia A. Mardis, eds. Santa Barbara, Calif., Libraries Unlimited/ABC-CLIO, 2018. 310p. index. $65.00pa. ISBN 13: 978-1-4408-4962-6; 978-1-4408-4962-6 (e-book).

Editors Ruth V. Small and Marcia A. Mardis have identified the "elephant in the room"—librarians are great at providing access to research but not doing research, whether in conjunction with faculty members or on our own. Unless research methods was part of their MLIS program (not mandatory in all programs) or accomplished under another discipline, many librarians have no formal methodology training.

Small and Mardis aim, in their words, to "conduct *quality* research, using *rigorous* research methods and collecting *credible* data that demonstrate *valid* and *reliable* results" (p. 4). Small and Mardis achieve their goal in this well-thought-out collection of essays from experts in the fields of social science research and, in particular, education and information science; readers will see essays from Carol Collier Kuhlthau and Megan Oakleaf, for example.

Well organized, readers can choose to use this text in a variety of ways, increasing the book's value as a go-to resource. Read straight through, Small and Mardis provide readers with a primer on research methods. Those with less time and/or a more focused goal in mind can focus on scenarios, find the one which best resembles their own research question, and then choose one from a variety of research methods. A glossary and detailed bibliography give readers additional information and avenues for further exploration.—**Rachel Meredith Minkin**

Storytelling

354.   **Storytelling Strategies for Reaching and Teaching Children with Special Needs.** Sherry Norfolk and Lyn Ford, eds. Santa Barbara, Calif., Libraries Unlimited/ABC-CLIO, 2018. 218p. index. $50.00pa. ISBN 13: 978-1-4408-5364-7; 978-1-4408-5365-4 (e-book).

Sherry Norfolk and Lyn Ford have brought together leading storytellers, teachers, and librarians who have worked with children who have special needs. Strategies and tips gained from their experiences are presented within the narratives they share. Five categories of storytelling strategies are covered based on varying types of special needs: children with emotional/behavioral disorders; children with intellectual/developmental disabilities; children with physical disabilities; children with multiple disabilities; and children with special needs who are in inclusive classrooms. Each section tells how storytellers approach a specific audience and describes what strategies worked for them with that audience. The descriptions are comprehensive. Readers will gain insights into how to tell stories and how to create stories that have multisensory props. Examples of storytelling sessions are included and provide strong foundations for the use of the strategies shared. Learning through storytelling is emphasized and covers elements of story (such as setting, characters, sequence of events, problem, and resolution), as well as encouraging children to participate in creating a new story that includes these elements. Graphic organizers, outlines for how to prepare and conduct a storytelling session, and sage advice will help guide novices and experts alike. This book is for teachers, storytellers, school and public librarians, and administrators. An index rounds out the work. Highly recommended.—**Holly Weimar**

Publishing and Bookselling

Directories

355.   **Literary Market Place 2018: The Directory of the American Book Publishing Industry with Industry Indexes.** 78th ed. Medford, N.J., Information Today, 2017. 2v. index. $429.50/set. ISBN 13: 978-1-57387-540-0.

This directory (now in its 78th edition) provides data on all aspects of publishing in two volumes. The thoroughly vetted entries incorporate information provided by the organizations included in the directory. Entries typically contain a name, address, contact information, branch offices, key personnel, and brief descriptions. The first volume (at over 1,000 pages) contains key data on publishers in the United States in 3 indexes (geographic, type of publication, subject); imprints, subsidiaries & distributors; Canadian publishers; and small presses. There are also sections devoted to Editorial Services & Agents; Associations, Events, Courses & Awards; and Books & Magazines for the Trade. Several indexes round out the work: a company index, a personnel index, a publishers toll free directory, an index to sections, and an index to advertisers (which appear at the back of the volume). Volume 2 contains directory information for the services that support the publishing industry in the following sections: Advertising, Marketing & Publicity; Book Manufacturing; Sales & Distribution; and Services & Suppliers. There are four indexes: a company index, a personnel index, an index to sections, and an index to advertisers. In total, there are more than 8,600 entries in this set. *Literary Market Place 2018* and its companion volume, *International Literary Market Place,* are available online at www. literarymarketplace.com (updated continuously). This publication is recommended to public and academic libraries.—**ARBA Staff Reviewer**

Handbooks and Yearbooks

356.   Deyrup, Marta Mestrovic. **Librarian's Guide to Writing for Professional Publication.** Santa Barbara, Calif., Libraries Unlimited/ABC-CLIO, 2019. 164p. index. $45.00pa. ISBN 13: 978-1-4408-3768-5; 978-1-4408-3769-2 (e-book).

This book is written as a discipline-specific writing and publication guide for librarians. There are nine chapters that take librarians through the basics of writing, the writing process, the template method, born digital, shorter documents, multifaceted writing projects, various types of messaging like newsletters and press releases and surveys, writing documents for obtaining jobs such as resumes and cover letters, and writing for tenure-track academic librarians. An appendix contains a workbook for each chapter with questions and specific assignments. The author has five rules for professional writing: your work only needs to be good enough, look ahead to the future, take advantage of writing conventions, repurpose your research, and work strategically. Having published professionally as a librarian for over twenty-five years, this book is great for those just beginning their career and for those whose job duties include producing documents related to outreach, communication, and marketing.—**Bradford Lee Eden**

357.   **Writers' & Artists' Yearbook 2018.** 111th ed. Alysoun Owen, ed. New York, Bloomsbury Publishing, 2017. 806p. index. $34.00pa. ISBN 13: 978-1-4729-3505-2; 978-1-4729-3504-5 (e-book).

This tried-and-true reference source is written based on information from the United Kingdom. Though directed at users in the United Kingdom, there is ample general advice that all aspiring writers and artists can use. Annual updates to listings and other material are made in consultation with the people, companies, and organizations included. The chapters are as follows: "Newspapers and Magazines," "Books," "Poetry," "Television, Film and Radio," "Theatre," "Literary Agents," "Art and Illustration," "Societies, Prizes and Festivals," "Self-Publishing," "Resources for Writers," "Copyright and Libel," and "Finance for Writers and Artists." A subject index, general index, and listings index round out the work. Chapters begin with short articles followed by listings which contain entity name, contact information, and more. The book begins with advice on knowing markets, choosing the proper publisher, the role of the editor, ISBN numbers, and other information. This is followed by listings for book publishers in the United Kingdom and Ireland, book publishers overseas (with about twenty pages of U.S. publishers), audio publishers, book packages, and book clubs. Following the listings are inspirational pieces from authors on writing short stories, romance novels, and other types of literature. There is even a one-page piece from J.K. Rowling about how the *Writers' & Artists' Yearbook* helped her as she sought a publisher for *Harry Potter and the Sorcerer's Stone*. This title is recommended for public libraries and other types of libraries in search of an inexpensive reference for aspiring writers.—**ARBA Staff Reviewer**

12 Military Studies

General Works

Dictionaries and Encyclopedias

358. Tucker, Spencer C. **The Roots and Consequences of Independence Wars: Conflicts That Changed World History.** Santa Barbara, Calif., ABC-CLIO, 2018. 422p. illus. maps. index. $105.00. ISBN 13: 978-1-4408-5598-6; 978-1-4408-5599-3 (e-book).

This volume covers twenty-six wars throughout history in which peoples have sought independence, sometimes called independence wars. The volume is not meant to include every independence war; rather, it provides a look at some well-known and representative examples. Dr. Spencer Tucker, respected encyclopedist and historian, is editor as well as contributor to this ABC-CLIO product. Each conflict is divided into: the causes, the course, and the consequences. Sections also include a timeline, further readings, occasional maps or illustrations, and tables denoting battles and various information. All of these parts, taken as a whole, provide both the novice and the expert a wonderful resource. Ranging from the Maccabean Revolt of 167-160 BC to the Tamil War of 1983 to 2009, Tucker or his contributors show both sides of the conflict and its ultimate consequences. Examples of entries include: The Jewish Revolt against Rome; The Scottish Wars of Independence; The American War of Independence; Spanish War of Independence (The Peninsular War 1808–1814); The Latin American Wars of Independence; The Greek War of Independence; The Arab Revolt; The Rif War; The Indochina War; The Algerian War of Independence; The Portuguese Colonial Wars in Africa; and the Irish War of Independence. Eight of the twenty-six struggles discussed were unsuccessful independence struggles.—**Scott R. DiMarco**

Digital Resources

359. **Service Newspapers of World War Two. http://www.servicenewspapers. amdigital.co.uk/.** [Website] Chicago, Adam Matthew Digital, 2018. Price negotiated by site. Date reviewed: 2018.

This fascinating online resource provides access to 195 newspapers published between 1936 and 1948, from 13 countries. One hundred twenty issues date from the

1930s. Newspapers from Great Britain, the United States, and New Zealand are most heavily represented. Materials are drawn from five libraries in England, Germany, New Zealand, and the United States. Items are predominantly in English, but there are materials in 9 other languages including German, French, and Russian. As the introduction to the database explains the place of these publications, "journalism played a vital role in keeping servicemen informed and connected, wherever they happened to be stationed across the world."

One useful element of this site is the detailed explanation of the process by which the database came into existence and what its content includes. Another searching functionality can be most helpful; one can limit any search by one or more of the following: date, newspaper, unit origin, unit location, service (such as Army, Auxiliaries, Pioneer Corps, POW Camp, WAAF), theatre (Asia and the Pacific, Europe, War at Sea, etc.), and by the source library. There is another useful approach to the database: three "Search Directories," for names, places, and keywords. For instance, one could select the term "Hiroshima" and limit it to the month of the atomic attack on the city. There are interesting discoveries to be made: slightly more than 70 percent of the articles containing "Pearl Harbor" in their text were published in 1944 or later, rather than soon after the 1941 attack.

This resource provides a very wide range of information about key events in a crucial moment of the 20th century. For institutions that have students and researchers interested in modern world history, this resource will certainly deserve investigation with Adam Matthew to determine the cost.—**Mark Schumacher**

Handbooks and Yearbooks

360.   **American Military Life in the 21st Century: Social, Cultural, and Economic Issues and Trends.** Eugenia L. Weiss and Carl Andrew Castro, eds. Santa Barbara, Calif., ABC-CLIO, 2019. 2v. $198.00/set. ISBN 13: 978-1-4408-5518-4; 978-1-4408-5519-1 (e-book).

Less than 10 percent of the population of the United States has served in a branch of the military, thus most are unaware of the uniqueness and stresses of life in the military for both servicepeople and their families. Eugenia L. Weiss, Clinical Associate Professor at the University of Southern California Suzanne Dworak-Peck School of Social Work and coeditor of *The Civilian Lives of U.S. Veterans: Issues and Identities,* and Carl Andrew Castro, Director of the Center for Innovation and Research on Veterans and Military Families at the University of Southern California Suzanne Dworak-Peck School of Social Work, have addressed a niche in the reference literature that has long been unfilled through the production of this valuable reference tool. Each volume is unique and can be utilized independently. Volume 1 focuses on issues related to those who are on active duty both domestically and overseas. The second volume concerns itself with topics unique to the National Guard and Reserves. In total there are 52 essays by 103 contributors on a wide range of subjects including life in the military on the home front and in combat zones, gender and ethnicity, the health and well-being of soldiers while serving and after discharge, educational and vocational opportunities, veterans organizations, and the transition to civilian life. Each signed essay includes an overview, an examination of historical trends, review of recent developments, and bibliographic citations for further research. School and public libraries should consider this title if serving military clientele or those who may be weighing joining a branch of the military. This interdisciplinary work is highly recommended for academic libraries as it has value for programs in American history, military science, political science, social work, and sociology.—**John R. Burch Jr.**

361.   **Americans at War: Eyewitness Accounts from the American Revolution to the 21st Century.** James R. Arnold, ed. Santa Barbara, Calif., ABC-CLIO, 2018. 3v. $325.00/ set. ISBN 13: 978-1-4408-4405-8; 978-1-4408-4406-5 (e-book).

For many large bound reference books that I review, I wonder why they exist because online references have supplanted them. Individuals are not likely to travel to libraries to seek out these volumes when a few computer keystrokes provide abundant, up-to-the-minute information. It is encouraging to discover a source that provides better information than the internet offers. Editor James R. Arnold, author of more than thirty military and political history books, has collected hundreds of personal eyewitness accounts of individuals at war from the American Revolution through the present day in a three-volume set. Obviously, a few pieces from the millions of individuals who were participants in all the various wars afford only a small sampling of the variety of experiences. However, on any war one selects, the reader will be absorbed in pages of captivating reminisces. The excerpts come from memoirs, from letters, and, especially in more recent times, from oral history collections. Each entry begins with a brief introduction of the individual; the end of the segment provides source information. The only complaint is that I would like to see hundreds more of these entries.

Attributes include overviews of each war, very detailed timelines of the conflicts, extensive bibliographies on each war, and a comprehensive index. The reference source is also available as an e-book.—**Joe P. Dunn**

362.   **Epidemics and War: The Impact of Disease on Major Conflicts in History.** Rebecca M. Seaman, ed. Santa Barbara, Calif., ABC-CLIO, 2018. 340p. index. $94.00. ISBN 13: 978-1-4408-5224-4; 978-1-4408-5225-1 (e-book).

This brief volume is a study on the impact of epidemics in the context of war. Editor Rebecca Seaman's goal was not to fully discuss any war, nor was it to afford the reader a thorough medical investigation of any particular disease, but rather to assess the significance of place, timing, conditions, and human-environment interaction which often leads to war and (unfortunately) epidemics.

The book is organized into four parts: contested epidemics, bacterial epidemics, viral epidemics, and epidemics of mixed origins. Part one provides three chapters (or instances) of epidemics which happened long ago and have still not been conclusively identified. Various expert opinions are weighed based upon written and translated text. Part two contains chapters discussing the outbreaks of the black death, typhus, cholera, typhoid fever, and diphtheria, while part three details viral epidemics such as smallpox, yellow, fever, measles, influenza, HIV/AIDS, and mumps. Part four tackles malaria, dysentery, and pneumonia. Within each chapter there are four common threads discussed. The first common thread is the impact of reforms and knowledge gained from previous conflicts and epidemics. The second common thread is the importance of the size of armies and their mobilization. Third is the relationship between humans and their environment, whereby despite reforms and improvements in medicine and hygiene, humans tend to get complacent and "encourage" disease. The fourth common thread amongst the chapters is the incorrect (and often irrational) human response to epidemics. While the book as a whole is not arranged chronologically, each chapter within the four parts is. An epilogue neatly sums up the four main parts of the book and ties the chapters together.

An extensive bibliography provides the reader with additional sources for further reading. Additionally, brief introductions provide the reader with worthwhile insight into the authority of the book's editor and numerous collaborators. An alphabetical index serves to quickly guide the reader to major names and subjects associated with the diffusion of epidemics and their impact on major conflicts throughout history. While not exhaustive in scope with regards to the conflicts and diseases discussed, *Epidemics and War* is a must read for those who want to understand the global effect disease can have, especially during times of war.—**Thomas O'Brien**

363.   Gibler, Douglas M. **International Conflicts, 1816-2010: Militarized Interstate Dispute Narratives.** Lanham, Md., Rowman & Littlefield, 2018. 2v. index. $275.00/set; $261.00 (e-book). ISBN 13: 978-1-4422-7558-4; 978-1-4422-7559-1 (e-book)

Military Interstate Disputes (MID) are defined as "the threat, display, or use of force by one state against another state" short of war. The Correlates of War (CoW) Project is a massive database that catalogs the myriad instances of these situations. These two volumes add a narrative to each of the coded listings of the CoW Project. Approximately 4,500 instances are covered, broken down regionally in the text. Each entry is listed by the CoW code with the date of the instance, participants, outcome and settlement (if any), fatalities, and the newly added brief paragraph explanatory narrative. Indexes provide the page numbers in the text by either code number or beginning date of the events.

To be quite blunt, I see little reason for this printed source. Yes, the brief narratives do enhance the listings in the database, but it would have been sufficient to add this information to the database. Why anyone would consult a printed or electronic volume to gain information about any of these conflicts escapes me. This is the kind of information that one should locate with a few computer keystrokes. Because the two volumes only include coverage up to 2010, it is an incomplete source upon publication, and it becomes less relevant with each passing month, let alone year.

Although the completion of these volumes entailed a tremendous amount of work done over several years, only the most highly specialized collections on security studies would have any reason to invest in this publication.—**Joe P. Dunn**

364.   **Iraq War: The Essential Reference Guide.** Brian L. Steed, ed. Santa Barbara, Calif., ABC-CLIO, 2019. 350p. illus. index. $94.00. ISBN 13: 978-1-4408-5830-7; 978-1-4408-5831-4 (e-book).

The Iraq War raged from 2003 to 2011. Among those engaged in the theater was Editor Brian L. Steed, a retired U.S. Army Lieutenant Colonel who served in Iraq in 2005, 2010-2011, and December 2014-February 2015. He is a Middle East specialist whose final military posting was as assistant professor of military history at the U.S. Army Command and General Staff College. Among his notable publications are *ISIS: An Introduction and Guide to the Islamic State* and *Voices of the Iraq War: Contemporary Accounts of Daily Life.* His latest work includes approximately 100 alphabetically arranged articles authored by 54 contributors. Each signed article includes citations for further research and cross-references. Thirteen primary documents are also included, three of which are included in their entirety. Context is provided by three essays: "Overview of the Iraq War (2003-2011)"; "Causes of the Iraq War"; and "Consequences of the Iraq War." Also included are a detailed chronology that begins in 1990 with Iraq's invasion of Kuwait and concludes with ISIS's defeat at the Battle of Mosul in 2017 and a bibliography including books, films, and television shows. This excellent single-volume reference on the conflict is recommended for school, public, and undergraduate libraries.—**John R. Burch Jr.**

365.   Wadle, Ryan. **Afghanistan War: A Documentary and Reference Guide.** Santa Barbara, Calif., Greenwood Press/ABC-CLIO, 2018. 361p. index. $108.00. ISBN 13: 978-1-4408-5746-1; 978-1-4408-5747-8 (e-book).

The nation of Afghanistan has been at war many times in its long history. One recent war began in December 1979 when the Soviet Union invaded to place a Communist, Babrak Kamal, as their selected head of government. In 1989, the Soviets withdrew in a defeat that many consider a cause of the collapse of the Soviet Union. By 2001, the religiously conservative Taliban emerged as the power in that country and violence reigned. Following the September 11, 2001, attacks in the United States, Afghanistan was again dragged into a war that has been going on for 17 years.

This work is all it claims to be—a documentary and reference guide. Dr. Wadle provides the reader with more than 86 clearly written and organized documents that range from the Soviet Invasion through the early days of the Operation Enduring Freedom to the Return of the Taliban and the Insurgency, to the Surge and Present Day. Documents range from U.S. Congressional Testimony to Afghan Government Documents, to International Agreements, to NATO Statements, to Press Conferences and Statements, to Speeches, Resolutions, Intelligence Reports, and Investigations. While this sounds very dense, Dr. Wadle makes it clear and easy to understand with every document being given a noted sources and analysis, including dates and significance. Recommended.—**Scott R. DiMarco**

Army

366.   Collins, Darrell L. **The Army of the Cumberland: Organization, Strength, Casualties, 1862-1865.** Jefferson, N.C., McFarland, 2019. 194p. index. $49.95pa. ISBN 13: 978-1-4766-7507-7; 978-1-4766-3405-0 (e-book).

Darrell Collins, the author of several other Civil War books, including *The Army of Tennessee* and *The Army of Northern Virginia,* here presents the organization, strength, and casualties of the Army of the Cumberland from 1862 to 1865. The material is drawn from the 128-volume *The War of the Rebellion: A Compilation of the Official Records of the Union and Confederate Armies.* The first section, Organization, lists army/department, corps, division, brigade, regiment, battalion, and battery levels in chronological order. Section 2, Strength, provides chronological reports by unit; reports include numbers of officers and enlisted men present, as well as artillery numbers. The third section, Casualties, reports by unit (and in chronological order) the numbers of those killed, wounded, or missing in action. The Army of the Cumberland served mainly in Tennessee, Georgia, and the Carolinas during the war and participated in such battles and campaigns as the Siege of Corinth, Mississippi; Shiloh, Tennessee; the 1864 Atlanta Campaign; the 1864 March to the Sea; and the 1865 Carolinas Campaign. The book concludes with references, a commander index, and a unit index.—**ARBA Staff Reviewer**

Navy

367.   Smith, Jr., Myron J. **Ironclad Captains of the Civil War.** Jefferson, N.C., McFarland, 2018. 254p. illus. index. $75.00pa. ISBN 13: 978-1-4766-6636-5; 978-1-4766-3129-5 (e-book).

On March 9, 1862, the ironclad warships USS *Monitor* and CSS *Virginia* faced off, the first ships of their kind used in modern warfare. Ironclads signaled a new era in naval technology, challenging their crews to quickly improvise and adapt. As inherently interesting as the ships may be, however, historian Myron J. Smith, Jr., contends that their captains are equally deserving of attention. In *Ironclad Captains of the Civil War,* Smith profiles 158 captains who served in the Union and Confederate Navies, building on his previous works *Civil War Biographies from the Western Waters* (see ARBA 2015, entry 258) and *Joseph Brown and His Civil War Ironclads* (2017). In compiling information, he draws on primary and secondary sources including archival collections, city and county histories, genealogical resources, and newspapers. The profiles vary somewhat in their level of detail (depending on the availability of information) but generally include birth and death dates, names of ships commanded, and individual accomplishments before, during, and after the Civil War.

Its title aside, *Ironclad Captains of the Civil War* reads as much like a miniature history of the US Navy in the 19th century as it does a history of the Civil War. Navy captains, Smith demonstrates, were highly educated, civic-minded, and often engaged in noteworthy endeavors. Before the Civil War, for example, Thomas Jefferson Page (Confederate States Navy) explored coasts and rivers in Bolivia, Brazil, and Paraguay. After the war, George Eugene Belknap (United States Navy) went on to become an inventor and hydrographic researcher. These officers knew each other as comrades and family members as well as adversaries.

Naval historians owe Myron Smith a debt of gratitude for compiling such a wealth of information from so many disparate sources and distilling it in a highly readable manner.—**Craig Mury Keeney**

Weapons and Warfare

368.   Bond, Henry. **Flight Accidents in the 21st Century U.S. Air Force: The Facts of 40 Non-Combat Events.** Jefferson, N.C., McFarland, 2016. 194p. illus. index. $39.95pa. ISBN 13: 978-1-4766-7402-5; 978-1-4766-3350-3 (e-book).

Pulling together data from forty U.S. Air Force (USAF) noncombat air accidents, Bond (Kingston University) provides an in-depth snapshot of costly loss of life and aircraft between 2003 and 2016, the majority after 2010. In forty separate accounts, Bond provides the where and when of each accident, the cost in dollars and lives, and a brief account of what led to each incident—there is no mention of the aftermath of investigation. He details what led to the incident from official USAF accident reports and secondary sources. All but one of these accidents cost over one million dollars; one cost as much as $317 million. Locales are global, ranging from Italy, South Korea, and Iraq, to the United States—over half were in the United States. Lives lost total forty. Though Bond points out that the

USAF reports are not written in user-friendly language, he at times he falls into the same trap of being too technical. Nevertheless, he manages to convey what happened and why. The small volume is quite a contribution to the "Virilian Museum of the Accident," a body of literature attributed to French cultural theorist Paul Virilio who analyzed the impact of technology on social disasters and accidents. The book includes a preface, cursory list of sources, and a brief index.—**Boyd Childress**

369.   Brafill-Cook, Roger. **River Gunboats: An Illustrated History.** Annapolis, Md., Naval Institute Press, 2018. 320p. illus. $54.95. ISBN 13: 978-1-5911-4614-8.

This encyclopedia covers the more than 150-year history of river gunboats. Entries are arranged primarily by country and coverage is international—Asia, Africa, North America, South America, and Europe. The introduction relays the history of river gunboats, the goals of this book, and notes on sources, plans, and specifications. Under a particular country, users will find something about the history of gunboats in that nation and information about particular gunboats, including where it was built, when it launched, dimensions, crew numbers, power and speed, guns and armor, and the fate of the boat. The author includes a photograph or drawing of the boat, which enhances the content. The author explains his decision to not include the originally planned color maps, though this reviewer wishes they were part of the encyclopedia. A concluding bibliography is a treasure trove for those who want to pursue further research. The encyclopedia also has two appendixes: "River and Lake Gunboats in Popular Culture" and "River Gunboats Camouflage Schemes." Recommended.—**ARBA Staff Reviewer**

370.   Dean, William Patrick. **Ultra-Large Aircraft, 1940-1970: The Development of Guppy and Expanded Fuselage Transports.** Jefferson, N.C., McFarland, 2018. 304p. illus. index. $49.95pa. ISBN 13: 978-1-4766-6503-0; 978-1-4766-3015-1 (e-book).

Aviation history consists of a tremendous variety of aircraft from today's emphasis on unpiloted aircraft to a variety of civil and military aircraft with various sizes and purposes. Documenting the history of these aircraft requires deep investigation into their historic successes and failures using a variety of information resources. This work focuses on ultra-large aircraft originating from the logistical needs of World War II and its aftermath.

Contents provide detailed technical and operational information on these aircraft including the Consolidated Vultee; the Douglas Globemaster Series; Douglas Aircraft and Aviation Traders Ltd.; and the Boeing Strate Series and Aero Spacelines. Examples of specific aircraft documented and analyzed within these categories include the Convair B-36 Peacemaker, C-124 Globemaster II, DC-4 (C-54)/ATL-98 Corvair, and B-29 and B-50 Superfortress.

Entries for individual aircraft describe the factors responsible for their creation, information about the number built, armament and other technical features, supply problems, photographs, flight testing and military evaluation, interactions with foreign customers, and the types of civilian and military missions they performed. Topics addressed in the multiple appendixes include aircraft size comparisons, aircraft volume, and payload comparisons, production schedules, partial listings of scheduled flights, and a glossary of terms such as TACAN Tactical Air Navigation System.

This high quality work is further buttressed by an extensive bibliography of books, popular press magazine and newspaper articles, government reports, technical rnanuals, interviews, listings of websites, and letters and emails. Entries include documentation of problems with these programs resulting in accident investigations, legal proceedings, congressional hearings, and audits by government agencies such as the General Accounting Office and NASA.

This work is recommended for anyone interested in aviation history and the complex relationships between aviation companies, the military, and various government agencies including Congress and other federal agencies with civilian aviation policymaking responsibilities.—**Bert Chapman**

371.　Johnson, E. R. Illustrated by Thomas S. Doll. **United States Marine Corps Aircraft since 1913.** Jefferson, N.C., McFarland, 2018. 580p. illus. index. $49.95pa. ISBN 13: 978-1-4766-6347-0; 978-1-4766-3065-6 (e-book).

All U.S. armed service branches have aviation divisions. Most people will instinctively associate U.S. military aviation with the Air Force and then the Navy. However, the Army and Marine Corps also include aviation components and this work provides a detailed historical overview of Marine Corps aircraft over the past century.

This effort begins with a historical synopsis of Marine Corps aviation starting prior to World War I, through 1920s operations in the Caribbean and Central America, World War II, Korea, Vietnam, and post-1975 developments emphasizing the Marine Air Ground Task Force (MAGTF). The heart of this volume is broken up into sections covering Fixed-Wing Tactical Aircraft, Fixed-Wing Transport, Trainer, and Utility Aircraft, and Rotary-Wing Aircraft. Entries in these sections describe specific aircraft including the Vought VE 7 and 9 (1920); the Douglass C-118 (R6D) Liftmaster 1960; and the Lockheed Martin F-35 Lightning II. Characteristics of these entries include technical specifications including weapons, physical dimensions, speed, cost, manufacturer, power plant (engines), drawings and photographs, and some programmatic history. Appendixes include unmanned air systems, aviation-related ships and installations, aircraft squadrons and aircraft assignments, aviation unit organization, organization of expeditionary and amphibious operations, aircraft weapons and tactics, aviation designations, terms, and abbreviations, glossary, and bibliography.

This is a very helpful introduction to the critical role played by Marine Corps aircraft in historical and contemporary operations. It is exhaustively researched and detailed and will benefit anyone interested in military aviation. Ways it could be strengthened further are examining procurement, purchasing, and development problems which have occurred in planes like the F-35 Lightning, the role played by DOD organizations such as the Office of Test and Evaluation in assessing weapon system performance, the role of congressional oversight in the development and funding of these programs, and the geographic dispersion of the manufacturers and contractors involved in building and maintaining these aircraft.—**Bert Chapman**

372.　**Weapons of Mass Destruction: The Essential Reference Guide.** Eric A. Croddy, Jeffrey A. Larsen, and James J. Wirtz, eds. Santa Barbara, Calif., ABC-CLIO, 2018. 360p. index. $94.00. ISBN 13: 978-1-4408-5574-0; 978-1-4408-5575-7 (e-book).

Eric A. Croddy, Jeffrey A. Larsen, and James J. Wirtz coedited *Weapons of Mass Destruction: An Encyclopedia of Worldwide Policy, Technology, and History.* It was divided into two volumes, one that focused on biological and chemical weapons and the other on nuclear weapons. Although their latest collaboration is a one-volume work, it maintains the same divide. There are two introductory essays: "Chemical and Biological

Warfare as Weapons of Mass Destruction: A U.S. Perspective," and "Nuclear Weapons." There are also two chronologies. While there is one bibliography, it is divided into two sections.

Included are 124 signed encyclopedia entries on such varied topics as Aum Shinrikyo, Deterrence and Defense Posture Review, Fissile Material Cutoff Treaty, Hemorrhagic Fever Viruses, and North Korea. The primary documents section includes the text or excerpts of 33 documents, such as the Biological and Toxin Weapons Convention (1972) and the Peaceful Nuclear Explosions Treaty (1976). A major weakness of this work is that it is heavily slanted towards the nuclear threat, as evidenced by the inclusion of only three primary sources concerning biological or chemical weapons. Although its coverage of the topic is unbalanced, this reference tool would still be useful in libraries serving high school or undergraduate clientele.—**John R. Burch Jr.**

13 Political Science

General Works

Dictionaries and Encyclopedias

373. **The Concise Oxford Dictionary of Politics and International Relations.** 4th ed. Garrett Brown, Iain McLean, and Alistair McMillan, eds. New York, Oxford University Press, 2018. 640p. $18.95pa. ISBN 13: 978-0-19-967084-0; 978-0-19-254584-8 (e-book).

The last edition of this dictionary appeared in 2009 (see ARBA 2010, entry 651). The biggest change from that edition to this one is the inclusion of international relations. The editors and authors have made many changes to already-existing entries and added new ones. To make room for the material on international relations, the editors decided to eliminate from print the list of primary office holders by country.

In the front matter, users will find the prefaces to all four editions, information about editors and contributors, and an alphabetical list of entries. The more than 1,700 entries are signed and include *see* and *see also* references when necessary. Entries vary in length from a single paragraph to several paragraphs. Users will find easy-to-understand entries for Mussolini, Franco, Stalinism, Hitler, Social Darwinism, historicism, Marxism, Mao Zedong, the World Bank, zero-sum game, September 11, 2001, the Afghanistan War (1979-1989 and 2001), Shining Path, Castroism, the 1917 Russian Revolution, and many other politicians, theories, political thinkers, and important events.

The dictionary, though not exhaustive, provides accurate and reliable data. Highly recommended for public and academic libraries.—**ARBA Staff Reviewer**

Digital Resources

374. **Freedom House https://freedomhouse.org.** [Website] Free. Date reviewed: 2019.

Freedom House, an independent watchdog association, was established in New York City in 1941 and in 1997 merged with the National Forum Foundation. Its mission is to advance and support democracies across the globe. Freedom House offers generous information and analysis related to the preservation and promotion of freedom and democratic ideals throughout the world. It focuses on contemporary issues affecting these ideals—press freedom, the internet, gender inequality, and more, and highlights regions where democracy has eroded. Freedom House has studied the state of freedom across six global regions and offers a series of Signature Reports and Special Reports alongside global news capsules shared via blog posts, press releases, initiatives, and other means. Users can scroll down through the homepage gallery of featured Reports, News and Analysis, Blog Posts, and Press Releases on topical stories (e.g. "Russia: Interpol Should Not Elect Russian Official as President") to get a good idea of site content. From the Reports tab at the top of the homepage, users can access links to Signature Reports covering Freedom in the World ("a comparative assessment of global political rights and civil liberties"), Freedom of the Press regarding media independence, Nations in Transit regarding countries emerging out of repressive regimes, and more. There are also a good number of Special Reports covering regional issues, such as "Far Right Extremism as a Threat to Ukrainian Democracy." Each report is structured differently, but all offer generous, easy-to-navigate information which may include interactive maps colored to convey the Freedom House rating applicable to the topic (e.g., regarding Freedom of the Press, a country is rated between 1-100 in regards to being free, partly free, or not free). The Freedom on the Net report is particularly compelling, as it looks at the role of the internet in allowing the free flow of information and points to regions that are tightening restrictions and engaging in misinformation ("fake news") campaigns that have called trust in the media into question. This report allows users to view Major Developments regarding internet freedom around the world and to Explore the Map to find a country profile. Each profile includes a Freedom House internet freedom score, which considers basic characteristics such as content limits, obstacles to access, and more. Users can also Explore Countries which lists relevant nations and their scores at a glance. Clicking on a country accesses a full profile with Quick Facts, Key Developments, and an extensive, well-researched essay.—**ARBA Staff Reviewer**

375.   **Political Extremism & Radicalism in the Twentieth Century. https://www. gale.com/c/political-extremism-and-radicalism-in-the-twentieth-century.** [Website] Farmington Hills, Mich., Gale/Cengage Learning, 2018. Price negotiated by site. Date reviewed: 2018.

Researchers will find information on both the far left and the far right in this new standalone database from Gale. The collection offers more than 600,000 pages of content and over 40 oral histories drawn from several collections: The American Radicalism Collection at Michigan State University, the Hall-Hoag Collection of Dissenting and Extremist Propaganda at Brown University, the Searchlight Archives, housed at the University of Northampton (UK), and the National Archives at Kew (UK). While the database focuses largely on the radical and extreme movements in the United Kingdom (UK) and the United States, there are materials that cover other European and Australian movements. The collection spans an approximately 100-year period from the 1900s to the 2010s and includes materials that are typically hard to find as they were created for a small, select audience. On the whole, users will find information on such topics as the formation of women's rights and other movements and a slew of groups (anti-Catholic, communist, Socialist, environmentalist, hate, new left, etc.). What sets this database apart are the extra features that facilitate comprehension and searching. There are a series of contextual essays accessible via the Essays and Resources tab from the homepage. Here users will find, among other topics, scholarly articles about the radical right in Britain and about John Sinclair and the White Panther Party in the United States. There are both basic and advanced searches, which can be filtered, or users can choose to search the subcollections comprising the database. Users can also search term frequency by year. The database creates a graph with clickables that reveal the associated documents. Users can also utilize subject indexing; the downloadable optical character recognition (OCR); the image viewer, which allows searchers to zoom, adjust contrast and brightness, and the creation of custom views; and cross-searching across other primary source products. Purchasers can also opt to include Gale's Digital Humanities Support feature, which provides data and metadata associated with Gale Primary Source collections. Highly recommended for academic libraries.—**ARBA Staff Reviewer**

376.   **Transparency International https://www.transparency.org/.** [Website] Free. Date reviewed: 2019.

Transparency International (TI) aims to educate a global audience on corruption, showing how it permeates the many layers of even civilized societies. TI, founded in 1993 by Peter Eigen (formerly of the World Bank), is a non-profit, non-governmental agency that receives its funding from individuals, foundations, government agencies, and multilateral bodies. More about TI, its funding, and its mission can be found under the About tab on the homepage. Its website offers copious materials and tools for identifying, understanding, and combating corruption in its various manifestations, and inspires a range of users to hold the corrupt accountable through public engagement, education, networking, and more. Researchers can find a trove of materials underneath the What We Do tab, beginning with the excellent foundational information within the What is Corruption link, such as its general overview on how corruption is defined and how it affects society. An Anti-Corruption Glossary is an A-Z display of terms and phrases key to understanding different types of corruption. It includes sixty entries for terms such as bribery, collusion, ethics, whistleblower, and tax haven. Each entry includes a brief, cross-referenced definition, a short animation, and links to related materials on the website. Users can also choose to examine Corruption by Topic or Corruption by Country, the former offering a gallery of eighteen umbrella topics which include Climate Change, Judiciary, Private Sector, Politics & Government, Sport, Health, and more. For each topic, the site identifies the key problem and potential solution, and gathers projects and activities, related blog posts, related news, related publications, and key publications. Under Corruption by Country users will find another A-Z listing of countries and territories with links to a snapshot of relevant articles and more. The Our Research tab offers materials mentioned above in addition to other proprietary tools, such as the Corruption Perception Index (CPI) 2018. The index ranks 180 countries and territories with mind to public sector corruption. Users can examine the global map shaded to reflect CPI score; click on a country to access its score, rank, and CP direction; and note improvers, decliners, and countries to watch. Users can also examine Transparency International's Global Analysis and Regional Analysis, find the index report for each year going back to 1995, download the full dataset, and more. The index makes excellent use of infographics, charts, and other media. The Anti-Corruption Knowledge Hub, also found under Our Research, gathers different research products such as topic guides, queries from the Anti-Corruption Helpdesk, and other materials into one area. Users can filter a search by topic, country, or document type. The Global Corruption Barometer is a survey regarding personal experience with corruption, again using bright infographics and other interactive media. Other materials found under Our

Research include the Global Corruption Report, covering 10 topics (Health, Education, Sport, Climate Change, and others), and national assessments, examining the structure and practice of elements (media, political parties, business, etc.) within a nation's governance system. Users can also access these reports, in addition to working papers and more, via the Our Publications tab. This area is searchable by document type or topic. Under News, users can find blog posts ("This week in corruption"), features ("The Alarming Message of Egypt's Constitutional Amendments"), press releases, and a good number of true stories that offer specific examples of regional corruption ("The Plight of Migrant Workers in the Maldives").—**ARBA Staff Reviewer**

Handbooks and Yearbooks

377. **Princeton Readings in Political Thought.** 2d ed. Mitchell Cohen, ed. Princeton, N.J., Princeton University Press, 2018. 762p. index. $39.95pa. ISBN 13: 978-0-691-15997-3.

The 700+ page tome before us reads more like a textbook than a reference book but its value should not be limited to a textbook alone. The sheer convenience of having so many crucial and critical texts in one place is too valuable to dismiss it to the dustbin of textbook reading, a current oxymoron if even there as one given today's aversion to textbooks by university students.

The volume is divided in to five eras of political thought: the classical, the Middle Ages, the modern, the century of turmoil, and changing horizons. Although the volume leans decidedly toward left-of-center thinkers, there is a smattering of thinkers on the right. The classical age offers up the usual suspects Aristotle and Plato among them. The very thin Middle Ages gives us Augustine, Aquinas, and Pizan, only. The very large modern part offers two dozen thinkers, among them unsurprisingly Calvin, Hobbes, Machiavelli, Locke, Rousseau, Burke, Kant, Smith, Hegel, Mill, de Tocqueville, Marx, and Nietzsche, but also, somewhat oddly, Wollstonecraft, de Gouges, and Douglas. The century of turmoil is a hodgepodge of Lenin, Mosca, Mussolini, Dewey, Orwell, Strauss, de Beauvoir, Malcom X, and the volume's editor, Cohen, to name a few. The last section, Horizons, serves up Habermas, Singer, and Foucault but also Young, Sen, and Müller.

Brief introductions commence each political thinker's selection but the absence of a topical or subject index detracts from the volume's utility.—**Mark Y. Herring**

Ideologies

378. **The Oxford Handbook on the Radical Right.** Jens Rydgren, ed. New York, Oxford University Press, 2018. 760p. illus. index. $150.00. ISBN 13: 978-0-19027-455-9.

This extremely timely handbook (available as part Oxford Handbooks Online), edited by Chaired Professor of Sociology at Stockholm University, Jens Rydgren, includes information on all the major theoretical and methodological strands on the radical right but focuses as well on topics that to this point have been written about less frequently: the right as it manifests as a social rather than a political movement and the interaction between the party sector and the nonparty sector. The book also analyzes the role think tanks, informal circles of intellectuals, the party press, the internet, and radio stations play in the radical right's ability to mobilize an electorate.

The introduction discusses a number of important topics in a well-written and easy-to-understand manner, explaining the differences and overlaps between the extreme right and the radical right; nationalism and ethnic exclusion; populism; the claim by some that the radical right is a modern manifestation of fascism; and why people support radical right-wing movements. Three parts comprise the bulk of the book. In the first part, Ideology and Discourse, readers will find such chapters as "The Radical Right and Nationalism," "The Radical Right and Populism," and "The Radical Right and Islamophobia." Issues, Part II, has chapters on "Globalization, Cleavages, and the Radical Right," "Media and the Radical Right," "Youth and the Radical Right," and "Political Violence and the Radical Right." The last part provides fascinating case studies on France, Germany, Austria, Switzerland, Belgium, the Netherlands, Southern Europe, the United Kingdom, the Nordic Countries, post-Soviet Russia, post-Soviet Ukraine, the United States, Australia, Israel, and Japan.

Recommended for academic libraries.—**ARBA Staff Reviewer**

379. **The SAGE Handbook of Neoliberalism.** Damien Cahill, Melinda Cooper, Martijn Konings, and David Primrose, eds. Thousand Oaks, Calif., Sage, 2018. 720p. index. $175.00. ISBN 13: 978-1-4729-6172-1; 978-1-5264-1600-1 (e-book).

A preface and introduction discuss the complexities of neoliberalism and the goals of the editors, all of whom hail from the University of Sydney. The book is divided into seven parts: Perspectives, Sources, Variations and Diffusions, The State, Social and Economic Restructuring, Cultural Dimensions, and Neoliberalism and Beyond. The geographic scope is broad—Latin America, Eastern and Western Europe, the former Soviet Union, China, and North America. The content casts an equally wide net, with such articles as "Foucault, Neoliberalism and Europe," "Neoliberalism: Rise, Decline and Future Prospects," "The Neoliberal Remaking of the Middle Class," and "Neoliberalism and Media." The 48 essays include references and most range in length from 10 to 15 pages. Figures and tables enhance the work. The content is most suitable for an academic library. This well-researched, academically rigorous work is recommended.—**ARBA Staff Reviewer**

International Organizations

380.   **United Nations Digital Library. https://digitallibrary.un.org/.** [Website] Free. Date reviewed: 2018.

This site serves as a portal to the vast material holdings of the United Nations. The page allows a general search from the prominent bar or a search filtered by Resource Type (documents and publications, maps, images and sounds, voting data, or speeches) or UN Bodies, which include UN Security Council, Secretariat, General Assembly, Human Rights Bodies International Court of Justice, and many others. Materials may be sorted into additional categories within the two general collections. Users can conduct a simple, advanced, or expert search. Items in a selected collection are presented as a sortable listing by title. To the right of the title, an icon will denote whether material is available for viewing/downloading (many items are not yet available). A thumbnail photograph of an item may accompany the title, but at this time many are marked only by placeholders. Information listed for selected items may include resource type, title, call number, author(s), subject(s), description, or notes. Through the portal, users can find a wide range of such materials as legal opinions, correspondence, meeting records, agendas, reports, lists, draft resolutions, speeches, and interviews. Specific topics may include border security, use of torture, sustainable development, humanitarian aid, population issues, and world food program. Users who create an account can save searches, create alerts, and perform other functions under the Personalize tab. It appears likely that more digital materials will be accessible in the near future.—**ARBA Staff Reviewer**

381. **Washington D.C. Embassies http://www.embassy.org/embassies.** [Website] Free. Date reviewed: 2018.

This site offers general information about foreign embassies in Washington D.C. in addition to basic information about the area which may be useful to foreign embassy missions. The main feature is an A-Z listing of nearly two hundred countries and other independent entities such as the Holy See. Selecting a nation from the list accesses available embassy contact information (address, phone number, email address, website, etc.), Personnel (e.g., Chief of Mission), links to Consular and Other Offices, and social media information. Anecdotal quotes from Plato, Mark Twain, Thomas Jefferson, and others are incorporated into the directory listing for a historical flourish. Other links located on the menu bar may also be of interest to users. Under the Embassies tab, users may take an Embassy Row Tour which provides brief foundational material on the foreign diplomatic mission and the embassy's role within it. The tour includes thumbnail photographs. Business Directories target particular users such as Diplomats, Americans Traveling Abroad, Educators & Students, and others who may be seeking information. This area also groups listings by services (D.C. Area Hotels, Restaurants, Visa & Passport Services, etc.). As these are paid listings, it is important to note that this is not a comprehensive directory. Resources host Travel Tips, FAQs, a Virtual Library with recommended readings on diplomacy, espionage, foreign affairs, and more, and a Virtual Gallery highlighting art, architecture, and monuments within the embassy community. While the site does not offer much depth in terms of the individual international missions, it would nonetheless appeal to those who wish to familiarize themselves with basic information about foreign embassies and their locations in Washington D.C.—**ARBA Staff Reviewer**

International Relations

382. **Carnegie Endowment for International Peace. https://carnegieendowment. org/.** [Website] Free. Date reviewed: 2018.

Long established as a top resource for international affairs research, the Carnegie Endowment for International Peace (CEIP) administers a website offering up-to-the-minute information on topics affecting all corners of the globe. Users can access this information in a variety of ways. The Topics tab on the right side of the menu bar would be an excellent starting point for general research. Users can search by Regions (Middle East, Americas, etc.) and Countries or alternatively by Issues both general (e.g., Society & Culture) and specific (e.g., Religion, Civil Society). Within these categories, information gathered from a variety of global sources is organized into Opinion, Research, Media, and Events. Links to related topics, blog posts, and work from CEIP experts are included as well. Under the category of Climate Change, for example, users can read the Strategic Europe blog post "Working Around Trump on Climate," read highlights from the Carnegie moderated discussion "Managing Business and Environmental Sustainability," watch a video interview with former Secretary of State John Kerry noting "The Absurdity of Leaving the Paris Agreement," and much more. Other tabs on the homepage access both similar and supplemental information. Research allows access to topical Papers and Blogs (China Financial Markets, Strategic Europe). Projects presents a listing of broader CEIP pursuits such as Reforming Ukraine, Security in Europe, and Rising Democracies Network. Programs include much of the same materials found within Topics, but incorporate CEIP tools such as indexes, bibliographies, and networks. Aside from the great variety of materials, the immediate response to current world issues makes this site a valuable resource for students and educators across many disciplines.—**ARBA Staff Reviewer**

383.   **Handbook on the United States in Asia: Managing Hegemonic Decline, Retaining Influence in the Trump Era.** Andrew T.H. Tan, ed. Northampton, Mass., Edward Elgar, 2018. 514p. index. $240.00. ISBN 13: 978-1-78811-065-5; 978-1-78811-066-2 (e-book).

The geopolitical changes in the Asia/Pacific region have taken on a new speed and urgency these past few years, with the decline in American power relative to other countries in the region. There have been a multitude of books and articles addressing the various diplomatic, economic, and military conundrums facing the United States today. This is not a quick answer reference book, but rather one that analyzes various issues. The 22 academic experts are mostly drawn from the Pacific region, and so provide a different outlook than that found in many American-authored publications. The 23 essays cover topics such as Trump's diplomatic and military strategies, relations with both rivals and supposed allies, and perceptions of the United States by worried governments. Unfortunately, the many problems affecting the Philippines do not get a separate chapter examination. Chapter reference notes are good. This item is for university and research collections, as some of the arguments and writing are aimed at a high level of knowledge of this important subject. The high price–another limiter to its wider availability—may mean that it is kept in restricted or reserve collections, someplace with more security controls, so that it does not get stolen. Otherwise it should be in the circulating collection, for interested patrons to take home and ponder at their leisure.—**Daniel K. Blewett**

384.   Rubenzer, Trevor. **Today's Foreign Policy Issues: Democrats and Republicans.** Santa Barbara, Calif., ABC-CLIO, 2018. 402p. index. (Across the Aisle Series). $97.00. ISBN 13: 978-1-4408-4366-2; 978-1-4408-4367-9 (e-book).

Occasionally, individuals examining contemporary U.S. political debate may ask where the two major U.S. political parties stand on various public policy issues. This can be a difficult question to answer depending on the nature of the issues being discussed, but this compendium from ABC-CLIO's Across the Aisle Series gives the dedicated user a reasonably comprehensive answer to where Democrats and Republicans stand on contemporary U.S. foreign policy issues.

Following an introduction discussing broad outlines in U.S. foreign policy since World War II, this work takes a list of alphabetically arranged subjects ranging from Afghanistan to the United Nations and discusses how Democrats and Republicans, in general, view foreign policy issues confronting the United States during the 115th Congress in 2017-2018. Individual entries begin with an At a Glance section that provides an overview. Each entry then lists perceived Democratic and Republican policy objectives, which can include similarities along with differences. Entries include longitudinal overviews of U.S. policy developments represented by speeches or policy documents prepared by presidents or other policy makers of both parties. Entries conclude with bibliographies featuring newspaper, scholarly journal, and magazine articles on these topics.

Subjects addressed in this compendium include Ballistic Missile Defense, Brexit and the European Union, climate change, cyber terrorism and security, defense spending, foreign aid, human rights, ISIS/ISIL, Latin America, military intervention, narcotics and drug policy, North Korea, refugees, Syria, and Ukraine. Entries are succinctly written and the work concludes with a glossary defining foreign policy terms such as the American Israel Public Affairs Committee (AIPAC), Arab Spring, Clean Power Plan, Crimea, Foreign Direct Investment, grand strategy, International Monetary Fund (IMF), power of the purse, and Trans-Pacific Partnership.

Today's Foreign Policy Issues generally does a good job describing Republican and Democratic political stances on a multifaceted array of foreign policy issues confronting the United States during the Trump Administration. Readers should understand that individual Republicans and Democrats may disagree with their parties usual foreign policy stances for reasons of personal conviction or political expediency. Shortcomings include failing to list religious freedom as an important Republican foreign policy concern in the human rights section on p. 131; incorrectly listing 1874 instead of 1884 as the year the U.S. Supreme Court determined federal government immigration policy supremacy in the Head Money Cases (p. 142); and failing to list the fixation of many Democrats that Russian conspiracies produced the 2016 election of Donald Trump as U.S. President (p.291).

Recommended for undergraduate students.—**Bert Chapman**

385.   **U.S. Department of State. https://www.state.gov.** [Website] Free. Date reviewed: 2019.

The Department of State provides users with a valuable array of freely accessible data about the department itself, but also contains useful reference information. From the homepage, users can find travel advisories for countries worldwide (either from a list of countries or via a clickable map). Researchers can also access the latest (March 2019) human rights report, with information on countries for 2018. The A-Z List of Country and Other Area Pages offers a variety of information about nations worldwide. For those interested in Afghanistan, for example, there is information about US-Afghan relations, US security support for Afghanistan, US assistance for Afghanistan, bilateral economic relations, political relations, Afghan membership in international organizations, and more, along with links to the CIA Factbook, a report on the history of US-Afghan relations, and other materials. The information on the site is easy to navigate and can provide information for general users (travelers, businesspeople), but can also serve as a good start for student research.—**ARBA Staff Reviewer**

Politics and Government

Canada

Digital Resources

386. **Syrian Refugee Settlement in Canada https://scalar.library.yorku.ca/syrian-refugee-resettlement-in-canada/index.** [Website] Free. Date reviewed: 2019.

This website offers a scholarly examination of the history and development of Canada's Refugee Resettlement Program in particular regard to the arrival of close to forty thousand Syrian refugees in recent years. The project analyzes positive and negative impacts and attitudes of the program. Users simply scroll down to access the entire report. Alternatively, users can jump to a particular chapter via the menu in the upper left corner of the page. Chapters include "The Syrian Refugee Crisis in Global Context," "Political Debates in Canada," "The History of Private Sponsorship and Private-Public Partnership Programs for Resettlement," "Drawbacks of Hybrid/Blended Refugee Resettlement Schemes" and "Back to the Future." Within each chapter, users can find a generous amount of embedded links and hyperlinks that access government policy pages, advocacy documents, news releases, and articles from the *Globe & Mail,* Canadian Broadcasting Corporation, the *Calgary Herald,* and other news outlets. (Many of the articles are accessed via the Internet Archive). Some link content is difficult to discern, which may be a result of the archived (no further updates) report. However, determined researchers can find infographics detailing the "Summary of Commitments For Syrian and Iraqi Refugees," more government policy statements, and additional news articles. The report explores particular topics such as political party response, Islamophobia in Canada, and administrative and regulatory challenges to private refugee sponsorship. Aside from its linking issues, the report is a succinct but informative examination of Canada's response to the recent refugee crisis and will send users in the direction of further resources.—**ARBA Staff Reviewer**

United States

Atlases

387. **Atlas of the 2016 Elections.** Robert H. Watrel and others. Lanham, Md., Rowman & Littlefield, 2018. 270p. maps. index. $95.00; $90.00 (e-book). ISBN 13: 978-1-5381-0422-4; 978-1-5381-0423-1 (e-book).

Hyperbole often flows when pundits characterize a particular presidential election: it is the most "rancorous" and/or "significant" election in modern American history. Some might claim that is an accurate description of the 2016 election. Divided into nine chapters, this atlas analyzes more than 150 maps of voting patterns at the local, county, state, and national level. The contributors are political scientists, geographers, and historians who have written lucid and informative text to accompany the large number of maps.

Although it makes no claim to be comprehensive, the work provides an eclectic range of material: "flipped counties"; Asian American vote; marijuana legalization referenda; Obamacare and the election, etc. Bibliographic web and print references at the end of the sections inform the reader of sources that might not easily be found in an Internet search. Illustrated in multiple colors with easy-to-read type and printed on durable coated paper, this beautifully designed unique work should become an important reference work on this election.—**Donald Altschiller**

Dictionaries and Encyclopedias

388.   Balleck, Barry J. **Modern American Extremism and Domestic Terrorism: An Encyclopedia of Extremists and Extremist Groups.** Santa Barbara, Calif., ABC-CLIO, 2018. 435p. index. $95.00. ISBN 13: 978-1-4408-5274-9; 978-1-4408-5275-6 (e-book).

In the introduction, the author (Professor, Georgia State University) discusses the difficulty in precisely defining extremists and extremist groups. So he relies on the research and long-standing work and reputation of two major monitoring organizations (The Anti-Defamation League and the Southern Poverty Law Center) along with the Federal Bureau of Investigation, to identify and describe the views and activities of extremist individuals and groups. Although there is a large literature on extremists in American history dating to at least the early 19th century (anti-Catholic, anti-Jewish, anti-Black), this work concentrates on the post-World War II era, although the KKK, which sadly still exists, originated after the Civil War. The entries are arranged alphabetically and range in length from a few paragraphs to several pages. The text is enhanced with black-and-white illustrations and photographs. Since no contributors are mentioned, the author is to be commended for researching and writing the entire work. Nevertheless, a volume including so much information will inevitably suffer some deficiencies. The most serious: the bibliography almost entirely lists electronic resources, even though book-length sources provide much more historical and background information than many websites, which frequently feature only recent easily accessible material that is of limited use to serious researchers.—**Donald Altschiller**

389.   **Famous First Facts about American Politics.** 2d ed. Bronx, N.Y., H. W. Wilson, 2017. 780p. index. $195.00. ISBN 13: 978-1-68217-466-1.

The present volume falls within the long-standing tradition of H. W. Wilson's Famous First Facts series. *Famous First Facts* was itself a volume first published in 1933 and quickly became the librarian's salvation for those niggling, intractable questions that, before the internet, consumed most of every librarian's day. With the advent of the internet, first facts are somewhat easier to get a grip on, and volumes such as these are not immediately the staple they once were.

Famous First Facts about American Politics zeroes in on more than four thousand "firsts" in U.S. political history. Categories are arranged alphabetically, and all entries included therein are listed chronologically. Subject, year, personal name, and geographic location indexes make finding the material easier still, though likely not as easily located as searching electronically. Users can search the indexes or go to one of the forty-two categories. Thus, if a fact about presidential elections is sought, that category might be consulted first. Categories range from, for example, the American Revolution, to cities and counties, Congress, monuments, political movements, advocacy groups, public welfare (subdivided prolifically), women, and many more. Broad categories are subdivided yet again.

Even print volumes like this have a place in our digital age, and leafing through this volume reminds one just how delightful serendipity can be when held in the palm of your hand.—**Mark Y. Herring**

390.   **Money in American Politics: An Encyclopedia.** David Schultz, ed. Santa Barbara, Calif., ABC-CLIO, 2018. 368p. index. $94.00. ISBN 13: 978-1-4408-5176-6; 978-1-4408-5177-3 (e-book).

The relationship between money and politics in America is complex and multilayered and an issue of ongoing significance to any person interested in processes of trust, accountability, and jurisprudence throughout society. This encyclopedia defines the landscape of money and politics in America and how money impacts campaigns, elections, special interest agenda setting, and public policy making. The strength of this work is the variety of subjects defined and explained. There are descriptions given for the key body of laws and court cases that outline the legal parameters of the relationship between donors and politicians; key pieces of legislation that have been passed that attempt, in many cases, to control the influence of money; and, profiles of the people who have most influenced policy. In addition, the work provides descriptions of key concepts, such as hard money, and issues, such as campaign finance reform, that are useful in understanding the historical and the contemporary relationships between money and American politics. Arranged alphabetically, the entries offer a basic introduction to the topic, followed by a list of further readings that facilitate deeper analysis for the reader. The essays vary in length but cover the essential historical, social, economic, and financial aspects of the issues related to money in politics. Particularly useful are the descriptions of legal cases because they are written in easily accessible language to accommodate introductory research reading levels. Front matter includes a complete list of entries and a chronology of events. Back matter includes names and affiliations of editors and contributors and a detailed index. Compiled from an impressive variety of scholars and researchers, this work is recommended for any researcher seeking essential information about money in American politics.—**Robert V. Labaree**

391.   **Political Corruption in America: An Encyclopedia of Scandals, Power, and Greed.** 3d ed. Mark Grossman, ed. Amenia, N.Y., Grey House Publishing, 2017. 2v. illus. index. $255.00/set. ISBN 13: 978-1-68217-548-4.

Corruption is like death and taxes: inevitable and never ending. Three hundred thirty eight alphabetically arranged entries cover people, important legal issues, and court cases, relevant concepts (e.g., obstruction of justice), scandals and events, public laws, and government committees and agencies. Sex scandals (like that of John Edwards) are not really mentioned, even if they are exploited by one's political rivals. New entries cover things like the Russian hacking during the 2016 presidential election and false election signatures. The writing is aimed at a general public or undergraduate audience, not at graduate students or faculty. The prefaces for each edition are found in the first volume, and contain some interesting observations and quotations about greed and politics. This set is useful for gaining good background information for before proceeding on to more specialized resources. At the end of the entries one finds *see also* notes and a short list of references. Appendixes include lists of governors and mayors involved with corruption, special and independent counsel investigations, and cases of expulsion and censure from Congress. The set concludes with a chronology (1635-2017), a 43-page bibliography, and an index. Access to the online version on the Salem Press platform is included with the purchase of the print volumes, which is a nice bonus. The first edition was published by ABC-CLIO (see ARBA 2005, entry 699), with the second edition coming out from Grey House in 2008 (see ARBA 2009, entry 644). This product can be supplemented by the more focused *Dirty Deals? An Encyclopedia of Lobbying, Political Influence, and Corruption* (see ARBA 2015, entry 503). It is suitable for all reference collections, especially if one does not have the earlier editions.—**Daniel K. Blewett**

392.   Pomante, Michael J., II, and Scot Schraufnagel. **Historical Dictionary of the Barack Obama Administration.** 2d ed. Lanham, Md., Rowman & Littlefield, 2018. 450p. illus. $105.00; $99.50 (e-book). ISBN 13: 978-1-5381-1151-2; 978-1-5381-1152-9 9 (e-book).

This enlarged edition of the 2014 version examines the Obama presidency now that it is over. Following a twelve-page chronology, the introduction provides a clear and concise biography of Obama: his family members, his education in Hawaii and later in college, his law school years, and his work in Chicago leading up to his political career culminating with the presidency. Six appendixes provide information on Obama's cabinet choices across the eight years, his election victories, midterm results, executive orders, and vetoes and public approval ratings, compared with other presidents. A twenty-page bibliography, divided into several sections, provides references to books and periodical texts, from 1988 (an early essay by Obama on community organizing) to 2016.

The diverse entries in the central portion of the volume range from the personnel connected to Obama (as members of the government or personal colleagues during Obama's pre-presidential years) to agencies, laws enacted during his administration, and other key events, such as pipeline controversies, the death of Osama Bin Laden, and the growing opioid epidemic. Other entries discuss such topics as foreign policy in various regions of the worlds, women and their roles, and midterm elections. Political figures also appear throughout the volume: Donald Trump, Hillary and Bill Clinton, Vladimir Putin, and George W. Bush.

Concise and clearly written, the information provided here will be very useful to all those interested in this landmark time in American political history. Academic, school, and public libraries should certainly consider adding this work, either in paper or as an e-book.—**Mark Schumacher**

393.   Vile, John R. **The American Flag: An Encyclopedia of the Stars and Stripes in U.S. History, Culture, and Law.** Santa Barbara, Calif., ABC-CLIO, 2018. 440p. illus. index. $94.00. ISBN 13: 978-1-4408-5788-1; 978-1-4408-5789-8 (e-book).

This volume includes just about everything that anyone would want to know about American flags, and more. The author, a professor of political science, suggests that America's enthusiasm for flags is fairly unique among nations, and he offers the abiding truth that individuals and community interpret symbols and ceremonies differently, which is basis for the huge amount of controversy and emotion about flags.

After a very fine introduction, the volume includes several excellent lengthy essays on subjects such as the creation and symbolism of the Stars and Stripes, flag etiquette, historic flag museums, Confederate flags, and the U.S. flag in American art, music, journalism, and politics. These are followed by over 200 individual entries on subjects that I could not even have imagined. Some of the most valuable are on Constitutional questions and cases involving the flag. A chronological timeline, glossary, contents listed both alphabetically and topically, and an index are extremely useful. The bibliographies at the end of each entry and the collective bibliography at the end of the volume are invaluable. The volume was compiled by a limited number of contributors—only nine including the editor and almost half of whom are at the editor's home institution. Others might have connections to the school although it is not mentioned in their biographical sketches.

In many of my reviews of encyclopedias, I note that prospective patrons would be as well served by consulting free online sources, so libraries might use limited resources in other ways. However, this volume is different. It is inexpensive and it should be in schools and public libraries across the nation. More importantly, American citizens should actually read this volume for a better understanding of the issues and a wider appreciation of how the adoration of the U.S. flag and other flags can be employed for both good and less savory purposes.—**Joe P. Dunn**

Digital Resources

394.   **Black Women in Politics https://blackwomeninpolitics.com.** [Website] Free. Date reviewed: 2019.

The 2018 elections in the United States saw sweeping changes throughout the candidate pool, with record numbers of women of color making their claim for a seat. This database centralizes information on over 450 black women who ran for office in 2018. Users can click on a selection of tabs at the top of the homepage or as they scroll down through the page that link to particular information. Tabs link to the same display of states and a searchable list of candidate categories—federal seats, state seats, local seats, red state candidates, blue state candidates, incumbents, and challengers. This list includes numbers of known candidates within each category. The A-Z link accesses an alphabetical directory of candidates. Selecting a state lists candidates alphabetically for that state. Clicking under type of seat lists candidates who ran for that particular office. Information for each candidate generally includes office sought, challenger/incumbent status, political party affiliation, election status (primary etc.), and links to website and social media. There are also links to update campaign status or candidate information, and information will vary depending on what is submitted. While the information is limited to a basic candidate profile, and is not comprehensive, the site is nevertheless an important tally of 2018 black women candidates.—**ARBA Staff Reviewer**

395.   **Google Transparency Report https://transparencyreport.google.com/political-ads-library.** [Website] Free. Date reviewed: 2019.

This database contains information on political advertisements concerning elections, federal candidates, or officeholders that have appeared on the Google platform or its affiliates. From this page, users can scroll through the Overview to find data in several ways. Under the By Location tab users will find the national map with states colored in regards to amounts spent in their congressional races. An accompanying table alphabetically lists the states with their total race expenditures. Clicking on a state shows its congressional district breakdown. Users can insert a name in the search bar under the By Top Advertiser Nationwide option to find information for those who have spent more than five hundred dollars on Google ads during the recent U.S. election cycle (forward from May, 2018). Alternatively they can examine the list, which places largest spending entities at the top. Users can also note spending By Top Keywords affiliated with the current U.S. election cycle, currently referencing Beto O'Rourke, Rick Scott, Ted Cruz, Bill Nelson, and Josh Hawley, certainly speaking to the popularity of the Texas and Florida races. Next to the Overview tab, users can select the Explore Political Ads option to view a gallery of political ads which can be arranged by launch date (default), money spent, or number of impressions. The ad gallery can also be filtered by ad type: video, image, or text, in addition to money spent, impressions, and date range. Each ad image in the gallery notes funding source, running dates, number of impressions, and amount spent. The What are Political Ads link offers helpful information in regards to Google's definitions and methodologies.—**ARBA Staff Reviewer**

396.   **Kentucky State Digital Archives https://kdla.access.preservica.com.** [Website] Free. Date reviewed: 2018.

This site allows access to documents related to a large number of Kentucky state government and administration offices. Users can conduct a basic or filtered search from the bar at the top of the page. To browse, users can simply scroll down through the gallery of government entities, presented alphabetically by name and with an accompanying logo or other image. The gallery can also be viewed as a list or table. Users can access documents related to The Boiler Board, Board of Veterinary Examiners, Bar Association, Board of Dentistry, Coal Council, Department of Education, Division of Historic Properties, Parole Board, Office of Financial Management, State Board of Elections, Supreme Court of Kentucky, and many other Kentucky government entities. Materials within the archive may include such items as photographs, meeting minutes, annual reports, fact sheets, policy statements, directories, and marketing materials. Information available for each entity varies, but will generally include identifying metadata alongside a series of links to PDF versions of related materials. Users can examine several years' worth of coal industry pocket guides, annual reports from the Crime Victim's Compensation Board, and a series of Executive Journals going back to the 18th century within which are Executive Orders carried out during a particular governor's term. The trove of materials will have broad appeal.—**ARBA Staff Reviewer**

397.   **Project Stand http://standarchives.com.** [Website] Free. Date reviewed: 2018.

Started by Lae'l Hughes-Watkins, University Archivist at Kent State University, Project Stand is gathering materials from academic institutions across the United States that document student activism related to underrepresented groups such as ethnic minorities and LGBTQs. While the website still appears to be in development, there are a few resources here which can serve as a good launching point for research. Under the Collections tab, users can select Collections by Theme to find data visualizations related to African American and LGBTQ categories. Users will note archive collections within the national map and can scroll through a table listing all relevant institutions. The table includes general descriptive information such as Size of Collection, Dates of Collection, Activism Topics, Format (manuscripts, photographs, etc.) of Collection, and more. Users can also hover over a pinned location on the map for a brief institution archive summary. Within the LGBTQ collection there is also an alphabetized list of collections (by name) and their affiliated institution. The options to examine Collections by Institution and Collections by Chronology are still under development. The Data link measures the popularity of topics within the student activism umbrella theme, from African American at the top of the scale to the "Other" category referencing topics such as freedom of expressions, tenure, arms control, ROTC, and animal research. Two additional graphs mark top collection Formats and Collections by Decade. Back on the homepage, the Institutions tab lists the twenty-four contributing institutions with links to a brief description of their student activism-related materials. Among these schools are Stanford University, University of Michigan, and University of North Carolina. The description may include an example from a featured collection and a link to the institution's online archive. While Project Stand is still under development, it offers a unique approach to understanding public discourse and civic engagement at the student level.—**ARBA Staff Reviewer**

Handbooks and Yearbooks

398.   **Defining Documents in American History: Political Campaigns, Candidates, and Debates (1787-2017).** Hackensack, N.J., Salem Press, 2018. 2v. illus. index. $295.00/set. ISBN 13: 978-1-68217-700-6.

This 2-volume set on political campaigns, candidates, and debates from 1787 to 2017 follows the same format as other titles in the Defining Documents in American History series. Each of the 64 documents (speeches, letters, inaugural addresses, pamphlets, debates, Supreme Court decisions) is analyzed in a discussion that includes a summary, an overview, a defining moment, an author bibliography, a document analysis, and a discussion of essential themes. Each analysis is followed by suggestions for further reading. The first volume contains a publisher's note, an introduction, and information about contributors; the second volume has four appendixes: a chronology, a list of web resources, a bibliography, and an index.

The 2 volumes are divided into 7 sections: The First and Second Party Systems, 1787-1854; The Third Party System, 1854-96; The Fourth Party System, 1896-1932; Fifth Party System, 1932-60; The Sixth Party System, Part I, 1960-74 and Part II, 1974-2016; and The Seventh Party System?, 2016-.Helpfully, each section begins with an introduction. Among many other documents, users will find James Madison's *Federalist No. 10*; the 1854 Kansas-Nebraska Act, authored by Stephen Douglas; the text of the Lincoln-Douglas Debates; William Jennings Bryan's 1896 Cross of Gold speech; the platform of the Progressive Party, attributed to Theodore Roosevelt; a Fireside Chat from Franklin Roosevelt, entitled "The Forgotten Man"; Herbert Hoover's speech against the New Deal; Richard Nixon's second inaugural address; the text of the 2010 Supreme Court decision in *Citizens United v. Federal Election Commission*; and Donald J. Trump's 2016 inaugural address. Scattered throughout are black-and-white illustrations and glossaries which help hold reader interest and increase comprehension.

The concluding bibliography contains up-to-date sources, and the web resources are useful. This book is highly recommended to its intended audience of high school and college students.—**ARBA Staff Reviewer**

399.   Derks, Scott. **Working Americans, 1880-2018. Vol. XV: Politics & Politicians.** Amenia, N.Y., Grey House Publishing, 2018. 400p. illus. index. $150.00. ISBN 13: 978-1-68217-715-0.

This volume in the Working Americans series focuses on 29 individuals involved in the political sphere. Politics here is defined broadly as an appointed or elected official, someone who works for a politician, or someone engaged in political activity. The profiles are preceded by an introduction and two reports: "The Public, the Political System & American democracy" and "Congressional Apportionment." The profiles are arranged chronologically. Each profile has a caption-length introduction and runs approximately 12-15 pages in length. Profiles include black-and-white photographs of the person profiled and three main sections: Life at Home, Life at Work, and Life in the Community. In these sections, information (date and place of birth, employment, personality, and much more) is presented using bullet point formatting. After these sections, users will find a Historical Snapshot of happenings contemporaneous to the person profiled. For Maria Kupka, whose grant writing in the 1980s provided ten million dollars to the New York police department to fight the crack epidemic, the Historical Snapshot includes such highlights as Pete Rose breaking Ty Cobb's record with his 4,192nd hit, the introduction of New Coke, and the television premiers of *The Golden Girls, Spencer for Hire,* and *The Oprah Winfrey Show.* The 29 profiles include a diverse array from Thomas Yup, who organized opposition in Los Angeles to the 1882 Chinese Exclusion Act, to Margaret Haley, who organized and advocated for Chicago's teachers in the first decade of the 20th century, to Martin Shortsburg, Senator from California in the 1920s, to Elliot Warner, Secretary of Defense under Eisenhower, to 1980s anti-nuclear weapons protestor Anna Delgado, to political cartoonist Bill Dithers who was fired from the *Pittsburgh Times Union* for his pieces critical of President Donald Trump. A Presidential Timeline starting with George Washington is followed by a glossary of political terms, suggestions for further reading, and an index.—**ARBA Staff Reviewer**

400.   **Government Support Index Handbook 2019.** Connie Harrison, ed. Detroit, Omnigraphics, 2019. 1074p. index. $275.00pa. ISBN 13: 978-0-7808-1674-9.

The "*Government Support Index Handbook* provides encyclopedic entries of all domestic programs that offer financial and non-financial assistance from federal agencies, and helps readers distinguish which programs are administered to the public via local offices, from those administered from the federal agency headquarters." This handbook provides information for 1,892 federal programs summarized from data included in the Catalog of Federal Domestic Assistance (CFDA) maintained by the General Services Administration. The section Programs Administered by Federal Headquarters provides directory information in alphabetical order; among the programs covered are Emergency Management Performance Grants; Rail and Transit Security Grant Program "TSGP/IPR (AMTRAK)"; Shelter Plus Care; The Health Insurance Enforcement & Consumer Protections Grant Program; Youth Gang Prevention; Native American Outreach; Hurricane Sandy Disaster Relief—Coastal Resiliency Grants; Healthy Start Initiative; and Career & Technical Education—National Programs. Each entry provides: agency abbreviation and program number; program name and popular name, when applicable; award type(s); purpose and objectives; applicant and beneficiary eligibility rules; award range and average values awarded applicable to financial awards; funding values of recent awards by fiscal year; and headquarters office address and contact. Each program entry features an identifying graphic block which contains the agency abbreviation and program number of five digits (e.g., DOJ 16.583 is listed for the Department of Justice's program number regarding Children's Justice Act Partnerships for Indian Communities). The section Programs Administered by Regional, State, Local Offices "contains programs administered by regional, state and local agencies which are the first point of contact when both headquarters and regional offices are applicable." These agencies are listed numerically by agency and number. For example, the Environmental Protection Agency section lists research headquarters by region and entries for programs are listed by EPA plus number assigned (e.g., the Climate Showcase Communities Grant Program is assigned the number: EPA 66.041). Indexes include the "Agency Index," which lists agencies and their divisions (e.g., the Department of State lists its divisions among which are the Federal Aviation Administration, Federal Railroad Administration; and Federal Highway Administration) and the "Federal Headquarters Index." The *Government Support Index Handbook"* should prove useful for those seeking grant awards from government agencies. It is especially recommended to larger public and academic libraries.—**Lucy Heckman**

401.   Haerens, Margaret. **The NFL National Anthem Protests.** Santa Barbara, Calif., ABC-CLIO, 2019. 142p. (21st-Century Turning Points). $39.00. ISBN 13: 978-1-4408-6903-7; 978-1-4408-6904-4 (e-book).

ABC-CLIO's new 21st-Century Turning Points series is aimed at providing high school, undergraduate, and general readers with "a clear, authoritative, and unbiased understanding of major fast-breaking events….that are transforming American life, culture, and politics…." This recent volume focusing on the NFL National Anthem protests follows a format standardized for the series. After a brief introduction, author Haerens, who has written a number of books for Cengage Gale's "Opposing Viewpoints" series, devotes roughly a third of her text to "Landmark Events" from the origins of the "Star-Spangled Banner" in sporting events to the present day. Another third considers the "Impacts" of the protests, followed by a final third consisting of biographical "Profiles" that summarize the lives and beliefs of the key players in the event. A short list of further resources and an index conclude the volume. Although well-presented and even-handed as this volume and indeed the entire series purports to be, libraries with limited budgets must consider how ephemeral such topics are and whether local need justifies the expense of the relatively short volumes. In comparison on this topic, libraries might consider Eric Burin, ed., *Protesting on Bended Knee: Race, Dissent, and Patriotism in 21st Century America* (The Digital Press at The University of North Dakota, 2018), a collection of essays by thirty-one authors ranging from attorneys to athletic directors. Recommended for comprehensive undergraduate collections on social issues.—**Anthony J. Adam**

402.   **Handbook of Political Party Funding.** Jonathan Mendilow and Eric Phélippeau, eds. Northampton, Mass., Edward Elgar, 2018. 541p. index. $290.00. ISBN 13: 978-1-78536-796-0; 978-1-78536-797-7 (e-book).

One would think a volume covering political party funding would be at least a large as Gibbon's *The Decline and Fall of the Roman Empire*! Certainly during election season—assuming that it actually ends—it would appear that only a handful of us are not trying to collect funds.

On closer inspection, however, this handbook attempts to explain the conundrum surrounding political funding, not the many places from whence it may come. The handbook is in three parts. Part one covers contentious issues surrounding political funding by eight experts covering topics like funding and propaganda, corporate funding, political funding and trust, and so on. Part two covers party finance and various eminentoes weigh in on its diverse facets: from New Jersey, the European Union, state funding and party primaries, and so on. The last section focuses on various case studies: funding in the United States, Germany, France, South Korea, India, Russia, and more.

National and international experts included in the volume are all identified and each entry is signed. Affiliations and associations are given in the contributors section. Entries are rarely shorter than ten pages and often much longer, making a detailed index a necessary first step unless one is familiar with the topic investigated. In this sense, the volume may better serve those in political science courses than the beleaguered reference librarian.—**Mark Y. Herring**

403.   **Hatred of America's Presidents: Personal Attacks on the White House from Washington to Trump.** Han, Lori Cox, ed. Santa Barbara, Calif., ABC-CLIO, 2018. 396p. index. $94.00. ISBN 13: 978-1-4408-5436-1; 978-1-4408-5437-8 (e-book).

The current criticisms of the 45th president often inspire hyperbole—he is the worst person to ever hold that office in American history. While history might later confirm this assessment, it is important to remember that many American presidents have been subjected to merciless attacks and extremely harsh judgments. Written by political scientists and historians, this work contains 44 individual essays focusing on the "most prevalent personal and political lines of attack and each president's most prominent enemies and scandals or controversies that generated significant volumes of vitriol toward the president in question." Each essay contains a narrative of about 4-6 pages (unsurprisingly, Nixon and Clinton garnered many more pages); a useful bibliography and short facts about their time in office; election statistics; and family information. Illustrations would have visually enhanced the text. Of particular note: the introduction offers a useful overview and nuanced definition of "hatred" of the presidents. The literature on the American presidency is enormous so a volume solely devoted to this narrow historical aspect should benefit students, researchers, and general readers.—**Donald Altschiller**

404.   LeMay, Michael C. **Homeland Security: A Reference Handbook.** Santa Barbara, Calif., ABC-CLIO, 2018. 376p. illus. index. (Contemporary World Issues series). $60.00. ISBN 13: 978-1-4408-5409-5; 978-1-4408-5410-1 (e-book).

This book delivers information on activities related to preparedness, response, and recovery, focusing on the years since the 9/11 terrorist attack. Passages are comprehensive and concise; information is divided into seven sections as is typical of books in the Contemporary World Issues series. The first section, Background and History, includes examinations of such key legislation as the 1965 Immigration and Naturalization Act and the 2001 Patriot Act along with discussions of Homeland Security actions during the Obama and Trump administrations and other topics. Problems, Controversies, and Solutions, section 2, casts a broad net with examinations of issues like immigration reform, the impact of federalism, climate change and natural disasters, and more. Section 3, Perspectives, provides further coverage of a wide range of topics from the evolution of emergency management in the United States, to the legacy of nuclear and chemical waste, to congressional oversight of the Department of Homeland Security. The Profiles section showcases approximately 45 individuals and organizations including the American Civil

Liberties Union, the American Library Association, The CATO Institute, the Heritage Foundation, and the RAND Corporation, and about the same number of people, starting with John Ashcroft, and including Osama bin Laden, Bill Clinton, Orrin Hatch, John McCain, Jeff Sessions, and Donald Trump. Profiles are typically a page in length. Data and Documents, section 6, gives readers selected information related to the Department of Homeland Security, FEMA, hate crimes, terrorism, immigration, and border control. The book concludes with a resources section, a chronology, a glossary, an index, and information about the authors.

This easy-to-read book provides researchers with a wealth of valuable information. Recommend for public, school, and academic libraries.—**Thomas E. Baker**

405.   Mulroy, Steven. **Rethinking US Election Law: Unskewing the System.** Northampton, Mass., Edward Elgar, 2018. 188p. maps. index. (Rethinking Law). $115.00. ISBN 13: 978-1-78811-750-0; 978-1-78811-751-7 (e-book).

If we heard it once, we heard it a dozens of times: Hillary Clinton won the popular vote by about 3 million votes. What we don't hear is that the popular vote is not how presidents are elected in this country, and it's not how they have been elected since 1787. What we also hear little about is how Hillary Clinton won only 500 counties to President Trump's 2600. Of those 500, 100 counties were the most populated. Without all 100 of those, she would have lost the popular vote by almost 11 million votes.

Make no mistake about it. All the brouhaha about the Electoral College (EC) today are from those who lost the last election. Democrats are most vocal about it now, still smarting over an election they thought they locked up six months before it was over. But Republicans also cry over the EC when they lose elections.

Mulroy takes readers on this academic exercise, hoping to lure those in who have not much thought about the EC process. It's a fascinating book with an interesting blueprint but one that would skew elections to a popular vote alone and using the "exotic" (the author's own word), for moving elections to Ranked Choice Voting and Single Transferable Vote.

That this is a partisan book is unfortunate with almost all the examples clearly titling in favor of the Democratic Party. But I suspect a book by a partisan Republican might well lean toward a new strategy that would favor the GOP.

For now, we can rest assured the Electoral College is here for the time being, and its benefit is clearly slanted in favor of balancing heavily populated areas with smaller rural ones. We may not like who ends up in the White House, and that's understandable. But abolishing the EC means that all future presidential elections would be determined by fewer than a dozen very large cities, clearly what the Founding Fathers wished to protect against.—**Mark Y. Herring**

406.   **Speeches of the American Presidents.** 3d ed. Bronx, N.Y., H. W. Wilson, 2018. 1094p. illus. index. $196.00. ISBN 13: 978-1-68217-882-9.

This new edition of presidential speeches is the first since 2001. Most of the speeches are published in full. The publisher also notes that speeches were chosen to reflect the character of the president, and to reflect contemporary concerns. As would be expected, the most significant change to this edition is the inclusion of speeches from Barak Obama and Donald Trump, along with substantially expanding the section on George Walker Bush. Another five speeches have been added for some of the earlier presidents. However, American presidents and their speeches are well represented online. Given this availability, a new edition doesn't seem altogether necessary. The entries on the presidents, which stress their oratory skills, could differentiate this collection. Unfortunately, these entries are too brief and only give a cursory overview of any particular president's skills at speaking. This is a useful volume only if a ready collection of speeches is needed at hand.—**Allen Reichert**

407.   **The United States Government Manual 2017.** Lanham, Md., Bernan Press, 2018. 568p. $35.00pa. ISBN 13: 978-1-59888-977-2.

Originally published yearly by the Government Publishing Office since 1935, *The United States Government Manual* ceased as a print edition in 2013. Since 2016, Bernan Press has taken up the reigns and produced the print version, so those users who are familiar with the printed edition can rejoice in its revival. As "the official handbook of the Federal Government," it is a handy resource, listing the numerous offices and departments that fall under the responsibility of the Legislative, Judicial, and Executive branches. Each office/department entry contains citations to the enacting laws, its brief history, what activities they are responsible for, sources of information (web addresses and publications), and who their key personnel are at time of publication. Of note: there are two different, freely available current versions online from the Government Publishing Office—one is a regularly updated database and the other a captured version of the database. Neither is comparable to the ease at which the print version can easily show, via the table of contents, what offices and departments are under each branch of the government.—**Bruce Sarjeant**

408.   **An Unprecedented Election: Media, Communication, and the Electorate in the 2016 Campaign.** Benjamin Warner, Dianne G. Bystrom, Mitchell S. McKinney, and Mary C. Banwart, eds. Santa Barbara, Calif., Praeger/ABC-CLIO, 2018. 450p. index. $73.00. ISBN 13: 978-1-4408-6065-2; 978-1-4408-6066-9 (e-book).

This reference studies the unexpected outcome of the 2016 presidential election. The volume opens with an overview that reminds the reader why the election was unprecedented—a political outsider with no elected experience won the presidency, the race featured the first woman presidential candidate from a major political party, the election was targeted by Russia, the campaign was uncivil, and scandals and gaffes plagued both candidates. The twenty-three articles that follow focus on how traditional and social media were used; Clinton's and Trump's campaigns and communication strategies; how electorate attitudes towards the candidates were shaped; and the resulting impact of electorate attitudes on voter behavior. The research topics range from the effect of political satire and comedic impersonations, to mobilization of partisan media, use of religious rhetoric, gender issues, effectiveness of endorsements, how well the media "fact-checked" the candidates, Trump's rejection of longstanding political norms, the rise of political cynicism, and more. These academic studies are built around carefully defined hypotheses with narrowly drawn results and therefore do not provide a blueprint for future candidates to follow. Their value is to portray how the 2016 election broke all the rules. Because this research was conducted soon after the election, the dynamics of the campaign and the perceptions and opinions of the American electorate were captured while the campaign cycle was still fresh in the public mind, providing a rich resource for scholars as we get further removed from this tumultuous election.—**Adrienne Antink**

Public Policy and Administration

Handbooks and Yearbooks

409. Mast, Jerald C. **Climate Change Politics and Policies in America: Historical and Modern Documents in Context.** Santa Barbara, Calif., ABC-CLIO, 2019. 2v. index. $182.00/set. ISBN 13: 978-1-4408-5970-0; 978-1-4408-5971-7 (e-book).

Climate change is a politically charged subject at this point in time, but, as *Climate Change Politics and Policies in America* makes clear, climate change has been a politically charge subject since the mid-20th century. This multivolume set provides more than one hundred primary documents (scientific papers, political speeches, government reports, etc.) on thoughts and writings about climate change over the past half century. The set's initial chapter includes documents from the first part of the 20th century. The rest of the chapters are arranged by presidential term: the Reagan and Bush I years, the Clinton years, the Bush II years, Obama's first and second terms, and the first two years of the Trump presidency. Each historical period presented begins with an overview of the politics and policy discussions that drove the thinking during that era. This introductory material runs to approximately ten pages for each time period. Each entry begins with a brief introduction and summary of the entry, typically a paragraph or two. This is followed by the remarks or the executive summary of the legislative bill or policy brief as presented at that point in the president's term of office. Source citation information completes the entry. A subject and name index completes the two-volume set.

The work will be useful in many library settings: academic, public, special with emphasis on the environment, climate change dynamics and public policy, and politics. Considering the nature of the subject matter and the length of each included entry, this set should be placed in the general circulating collection.—**Gregory Curtis**

Indexes

410. **Global Think Tank Index. https://www.gotothinktank.com/glabal-goto-think-tank-index.** [Website] Free. Date reviewed: 2018.

The Think Tank and Civil Societies Program (TTCSP) produces the Global Think Tank Index, an annual report which ranks public policy research organizations from around the world across a variety of categories. This page offers access to ten years of PDF reports. Users can select from a list of reports by year, with the most recent covering 2017. The 2017 report organizes index information into clearly defined sections, including Think Tank Statistics; Ranking Categories; and Ranking Results by Region, Areas of Research, and Special Achievement. Think Tank Statistics offer several visualizations including the Global Distribution of Think Tanks by Region map and Distribution by Country charts. The Ranking Categories section presents a list of close to fifty categories (followed by individual category descriptions) for which think tanks are considered, including Region (Sub-Saharan Africa, United States, Southeast Asia and the Pacific, and seven others) and Research Area (Global and Domestic Health Policy; Environment; Defense and National

Security; International Economic Policy; Social Policy, and more). Ranking Categories also considers a variety of Special Achievements, such as Best Government-Affiliated, Best Managed, Best Think Tank Network, Best Policy Study/Report Produced by a Think Tank, Best University-Affiliated Think Tank, and others. The Global Go To Ranking Results for all categories follow this section, providing the name and the country of the ranked think tank. Other information in the 2017 report covers Methodology and Timeline, Trends and Transitions in Think Tanks and Policy Advice, Modifications and Enhancements to 2017 Global Go To Think Tank Index, and more. It is important to note that reports from prior years may be structured differently. The TTCSP is currently developing a Think Tank Directory which may provide a more complete look at the featured think tanks, as there is currently no profile or description of the listed think tanks. The site is nonetheless a good research starting point for users across a number of academic and professional disciplines.—**ARBA Staff Reviewer**

14 Psychology, Parapsychology, and Occultism

Psychology

Bibliography

411.   Dolan, Deborah. **A Research Guide to Psychology: Print and Electronic Sources.** Lanham, Md., Rowman & Littlefield, 2018. 184p. index. $100.00; $95.00 (e-book). ISBN 13: 978-1-4422-7601-7; 978-1-4422-7602-4 (e-book).

Written by an academic librarian who serves as subject specialist for psychology, this is a thorough guide to finding information in psychology, suitable for upper-level undergraduates, grad students, and researchers. The format of the book's chapters varies based on content and intended use. The first chapter provides a brief narrative introduction to types of resources. The second chapter provides an annotated bibliography of reference sources. These would be an excellent source of information for a library looking to update its collection as well as for a researcher who might want to flesh out a personal collection. Chapter 3 provides an orientation to finding articles in psychology, and highlights the importance of considering other databases in adjacent disciplines such as business, education, medicine, and sociology. An annotated bibliography of relevant databases in these areas follows, along with an in-depth explanation of developing search strategies and other tips for searching. Numerous screenshots supplement the text to clarify what might be confusing on its own. This chapter includes approximately thirty pages that cover Tests and Measures. It's not clear why this was not its own chapter—tests and measures are significant tools in psychology research—but the materials included are highly relevant. Importantly, the author also includes a section on resources containing the full texts of tests and measures, which will benefit researchers and institutions without the ability to collect their own libraries of diagnostic tools. A short chapter on theses and dissertations (and how to find them), a list of relevant bibliographies, and recommended style and writing guides completes the expected collection of research tools. Dolan also includes lists of core US government agencies and biographical resources, and those looking at the discipline as a career will benefit from the chapter covering career resources. She closes with a list of museums and archives housing materials related to psychology. Overall, highly recommended for libraries supporting researchers in psychology and mental health fields.—**Amanda Izenstark**

Dictionaries and Encyclopedias

412. **Encyclopedia of Clinical Neuropsychology.** 2d ed. Jeffrey S. Kreutzer, John DeLuca, and Bruce Caplan, eds. New York, Springer Publishing, 2018. 5v. illus. $899.99/ set. ISBN 13: 978-3-319-57110-2; 978-3-319-57111-9 (e-book).

This 2d edition contains nearly 2,200 entries. This total includes 230 completely new entries and 1,600 updated entries from the first edition. The goal is to provide users with a comprehensive reference that provides information on evaluation, diagnosis, and rehabilitation. The set is designed for professionals working with adults and children and for students and researchers. The front matter supplies a preface and a list of the academic editors and contributors along with their affiliations. The front matter also groups the entries by topic (Pediatrics, Brain Injury, Dementia, etc). This edition incorporates 3 new topical sections— neuroimaging, military neuropsychology, and DSM-5. It is worth noting that each of the sections has its own topical editor. The articles are arranged in alphabetical order and vary in length depending on topic. All articles are signed and contain some or all of the following: cross-references, synonyms, and references and reading. The entry for Abasia, for example, is two sentences and includes author information along with cross-references. Obsessive-Compulsive Disorder takes up almost 1.5 pages and includes author information, a definition, categorization, current knowledge, neurobiology and associated conditions, assessment and treatment, *see also* references, and references and reading. The entry for Unexplained Illness is more than twice as long, at just over 3 pages. Here users will find author information, synonyms, definition, categorization, epidemiology, natural history, prognostic factors and outcomes, psychology and neuropsychology of Unexplained Illness, evaluation, treatment, cross-references, and references and reading. This reliable and comprehensive reference is highly recommended for academic libraries.—**ARBA Staff Reviewer**

Directories

413. **The Complete Mental Health Resource Guide, 2018/2019.** 11th ed. Amenia, N.Y., Grey House Publishing, 2018. 566p. illus. maps. index. $165.00pa. ISBN 13: 978-1-68217-733-4.

This 11th edition begins with an introduction that explains the format of the book. This is followed by a report, "The State of Mental Health in America 2018," which provides rankings by state. At over twenty pages, the information included is extensive. The beginning of the volume contains another report, "The Doctor Is Out: Continuing Disparities in Access to Mental and Physical Health Care," which conveys the results of a 2016 survey by the National Alliance on Mental Health, a six-page analysis. The opening portion of the book closes with a list of disorders by diagnostic category, a user's guide, and a user's key. The bulk of the book is comprised of eight sections: Disorders, Associations & Organizations; Government Agencies; Professional & Support Services; Publishers; Facilities; Clinical Management; and Pharmaceutical Companies. There are four indexes. Among the disorders covered are autism spectrum disorders, feeding and eating disorders, obsessive compulsive disorder, and tic disorder. Disorders contain introductions that discuss symptoms and associated features, prevalence, and treatment options. Following introductions are lists of associations and agencies, books, audio and video resources, support groups, and web resources all related to the disorder. Each is described in a short paragraph and contact and/or publisher information is provided where appropriate. The second section on associations and organizations first includes national groups and then lists associations and organizations by state. The section on government agencies lists federal agencies followed by state agencies. Section four, Professional & Support Services, includes a variety of resources, such as books, periodicals and pamphlets, and databases and directories. This comprehensive resource is recommended to public libraries.—**ARBA Staff Reviewer**

Handbooks and Yearbooks

414.   Aguirre, Balise. **Mindfulness and Meditation: Your Questions Answered.** Santa Barbara, Calif., Greenwood Press/ABC-CLIO, 2018. 128p. index. (Q&A Health Guides). $39.00. ISBN 13: 978-1-4408-5296-1; 978-1-4408-5297-8 (e-book).

This is part of the Q&A Health Guides series. All the volumes in this series follow the same general outline, including an opening eight-page essay on health literacy. Each also contains a brief sketch of five common myths related to the subject, case studies, a glossary, and an index. The bulk of this volume is a set of questions and answers arranged by topic so that readers can quickly find information related to their own interests. Topics covered include the history of mindfulness, and individual questions relate to contemporary issues of interest to high school and college students such as how apps can be used in mindfulness practice and how social media impacts mindfulness. Case studies include subjects from age 18 to age 61; case studies feature students (high school, college, graduate school). This book will be most useful for high school and college students seeking specific information about mindfulness, and would serve as a good reference guide for guidance counselors.—**Delilah R. Alexander**

415.   Demos, John N. **Getting Started with EEG Neurofeedback.** 2d ed. New York, W. W. Norton, 2019. 346p. illus. index. $35.99. ISBN 13: 978-0-393-71253-7.

This second edition (the first published in 2005) provides users with a major update necessitated by growth in the field. The front matter includes a list of figures and a list of abbreviations prior to the introduction, which discusses targeted users (either those licensed professionals new to EEG Neurofeedback or experienced licensed professionals looking to learn more); common questions about EEG Neurofeedback; advances in assessment and training; and more. The book is comprised of six parts: Getting Started with the Basics; Amplifying and Filtering to Match EEG Signatures to Common Symptoms; Editing the Raw EEG; the Dynamic Brain: Regions of Interest; Advanced Training and Protocol Generation; and EEG Neurofeedback in Clinical Practice. Not only will readers find easy-to-understand basic information about where to place electrodes, editing examples and EEG signatures, and the functions of different parts of the brain, they will also find case studies of people suffering from ADHD, PTSD, and other conditions as well as suggested treatment plans and much more. Valuably, the illustrations are in color. This book is recommended for individual practitioners and is highly recommended for public and academic libraries, especially considering the modest price.—**ARBA Staff Reviewer**

416.   **Mental Health Disorders Sourcebook.** 7th ed. Angela L. Williams, ed. Detroit, Omnigraphics, 2019. 634p. illus. index. $85.00. ISBN 13: 978-0-7808-1679-4; 978-0-7808-1680-0 (e-book).

This 7th edition of the *Mental Health Disorders Sourcebook* (see ARBA 2017, entry 502) provides straightforward and reliable information on conditions that affect millions of Americans. The preface discusses the content, how to use the book, the bibliography, spelling and style, the advisory board, and the medical review team. This is followed by an easy-to-use book that is divided into parts, chapters, and sections: The Brain and Mental Health (7 chapters); Mental Illnesses (13 chapters); Mental-Health Treatments (8 chapters); Pediatric Mental-Health Concerns (13 chapters); Other Populations with Distinctive Mental-Health Concerns (6 chapters); Mental Illness Co-Occurring with Other Disorders (8 chapters); Living with a Mental-Health Condition (4 chapters); and Additional Help and Information (3 chapters). Within these chapters, readers can find answers to questions about brain structure, eating well and mental health, the different types of mental illness, depressive disorders, anxiety disorders, phobias, personality disorders, eating and body image disorders, addictions, medications, the potential impact of technology on mental health treatment, obsessive-compulsive behavior and children, mental health among minority populations, how different health conditions (cancer, stroke, diabetes, etc.) affect mental health, the hope provided by research into mental health conditions, a glossary of mental health terms, contact information for crisis helplines and hotlines, and information about mental health organization. Black-and-white tables and figures supplement the material. This book provides readers with a reliable source for finding basic information. The organization of the book makes it possible for users to jump to an area of interest. Those looking for in-depth discussions can use this book to point them in the right direction. Recommended.—**ARBA Staff Reviewer**

417.   Morris, Marcia. **The Campus Cure: A Parent's Guide to Mental Health and Wellness for College Students.** Lanham, Md., Rowman & Littlefield, 2018. 236p. index. $34.00; $32.00 (e-book). ISBN 13: 978-1-5381-0452-1; 978-1-5381-0453-8 (e-book).

The author, with 20-plus years of experience working with college/university students, presents straightforward advice for parents. She examines issues such as anxiety, depression, substance abuse, loneliness, suicidal behaviors, and eating disorders. One key element of her advice, throughout, is that working with professionals, whether counselors, psychologists, or psychiatrists, at the institution their child attends is important for parents who want to help their children have a successful college experience. This book is very clearly written and understandable. Parents of college students should find it useful in dealing with a variety of possible issues, such as failing grades or antisocial behavior that their children might face. The author uses numerous events from her experience to provide readers with real-life examples of situations that might arise with their children and how these problems might be lessened and remedied.—**Mark Schumacher**

418.   Nydegger, Rudy. **Clocking In: The Psychology of Work.** Santa Barbara, Calif., Greenwood Press/ABC-CLIO, 2018. 200p. index. (The Psychology of Everyday Life). $38.00. ISBN 13: 978-1-4408-5003-5; 978-1-4408-5003-5 (e-book).

This volume is the sixth title in the Psychology of Everyday Life series published by Greenwood. Other topics include sex and dating, conflict, and eating. The format here repeats that of earlier volumes: the main section has six chapters, labeled What, Why,

How, Who, When and Where, that examine various dimensions of the subject. In this case, the forms of work, the importance of work, psychologists' theories about work (discussing people from Sigmund Freud and Alfred Adler to Albert Bandura), and the positive and negative effects of work are among the topics explored. Next there is a series of five "Scenarios" which examine options for individuals in diverse situations concerning their work status. The final section of the book, "Controversies and Debates," presents two points of view concerning three topics, such as "Does setting goals help or harm workers' performance?" As with the earlier volumes, a single author is listed on the title page, but other "contributors" are listed, with brief biographies, at the end of the volume, having provided brief texts in this final portion of the book. Somewhat curiously, the author makes numerous pessimistic comments about the current and future worlds of work: " . . . This does not bode well for the future of the work environment for most employees or potential employees." (p. 18)

As occurs too frequently, the copy editing needs more attention: words are misspelled, verb tenses are incorrect, and punctuation occasionally needs correction. As many as three mistakes occur on a single page. Nonetheless, the information is clearly presented throughout the book, quite readable for all sorts of readers. It will be useful for those seeking an introduction to the elements that create the work experience and how that experience can be enhanced by actions of both workers and supervisors. Any library with patrons interested in this topic should consider adding it to its collection.—**Mark Schumacher**

419.   **Quickies: The Handbook of Brief Sex Therapy.** 3d ed. Shelley Green and Douglas Flemons, eds. New York, W. W. Norton, 2018. 405p. index. $28.95pa. ISBN 13: 978-0-393-71156-1.

The third edition of this book has eight new chapters along with significant updating of those chapters from the previous two editions. Divided into five sections and fifteen chapters, models of brief sex therapy and cultural/sexual minorities are discussed along with monogamy, sexual violence, and the roots of brief therapy. Chapter topics include therapeutic quickies in brief relational therapy, the bad orgasm, healing the relational wounds from infidelity, challenging the status quo with consensually nonmonogamous couples, the internet as "other" in personal relationships, multicultural considerations in brief sex therapy with same-sex couples, trans-affirming sex therapy, crossing borders in brief sex therapy, addressing intimate partner violence in sex therapy, transforming stories when treating sexual offenders, an Ericksonian hypnosis approach to sex therapy, and John Weakland at work at the Brief Therapy Center at the Mental Research Institute. Geared towards students and practitioners in brief sex therapy, the third edition of this book is an essential tool and reference work.—**Bradford Lee Eden**

420.   **Take Control of Your Depression: Strategies to Help You Feel Better Now.** Noonan, Susan J. Baltimore, Md., Johns Hopkins University Press, 2018. 196p. index. $19.95pa. ISBN 13: 978-1-4214-2629-7; 978-1-4214-2630-3 (e-book).

This is an updated edition of Noonan's 2013 book, *Managing Your Depression.* The book is intended to provide members of the general public with comprehensive information and a how-to guide for understanding and managing depression. In light of the fact that depression can affect one's ability to concentrate, the book is written in digestible parts and includes checklists and worksheets. According to Noonan, approximately 15 percent of the American population will suffer from depression at some point in their lives, and not everyone will have the ability to receive expensive and sometimes scarce medical care. Twelve chapters comprise the book: "Mental Health Basics," "Mood Disorders," "Common Obstacles in Depression," "Defining Your Baseline," "Managing Your Mood Disorder," "What Is the Goal?" "Relapse Prevention," "Cognitive Behavioral Therapy," "Strategies to Get You through the Tough Times," "Dealing with Family and Friends," "Pulling It All Together," and "Collective Wisdom." The book is both informative and easy to read. The inclusion of textboxes, like Box 1.2 on sleep hygiene and Box 8.1 on distorted thinking are valuable additions. The final chapter evaluates nutrition, exercise, sleep, and support group websites; provides guidance on how to evaluate health information on the internet; and makes suggestions for further reading. There is an appendix on medications, a glossary, and an index. Highly recommended for public libraries.—**ARBA Staff Reviewer**

421.   Zwillenberg, Daniel. **Anxiety and Panic Attacks: Your Questions Answered.** Santa Barbara, Calif., Greenwood Press/ABC-CLIO, 2018. 161p. index. (Q&A Health Guides). $39.00. ISBN 13: 978-1-4408-5298-5; 978-1-4408-5299-2 (e-book).

Anxious teens are vulnerable to panic attacks, which could eventually lead to panic disorder. This book provides young readers with accurate information about the causes and symptoms of anxiety and panic attacks and with valuable information about coping mechanisms. The book uses bold fonts, an age-appropriate writing style, graphics, and bullet formatting. Readers will also find a glossary, directory of resources, and impressive index. The chapters present solid answers to pertinent questions; case studies encourage understanding and continued reading. The book also provides information about where readers can find professional help. *Anxiety and Panic Attacks* explores its subject matter with compassion, dignity, and sensitivity. Recommended.—**Thomas E. Baker**

Parapsychology

422.   Clark, Jerome. **The UFO Encyclopedia: The Phenomenon from the Beginning.** 3d ed. Detroit, Omnigraphics, 2018. 2v. index. $139.00/set. ISBN 13: 978-0-7808-1659-6; 978-0-7808-1660-2 (e-book).

This two-volume omnibus tome was originally published in three books, *UFOs in the 1980s* (1990), *The Emergence of a Phenomenon: UFOs from the Beginning through 1959* (1992), and *High Strangeness: UFOs from 1960 through 1979* (1996) and as a two-volume set in 1998 (see ARBA 2000, entry 697). This new edition includes more than sixty new entries, many declassified UFO-related documents from the United States and Brazil, in particular, and UFO-related phenomenon in all of its aspects. Each entry is highly detailed, including eyewitness accounts and the contents of many investigations and symposia, along with extensive bibliographies. Some of the more interesting entries include NASA and UFOs, International Flying Saucer Bureau, the Varginha Contact Incident, the Ummo Hoax, Ancient Astronauts in the UFO Literature, the Flatwoods Monster, and Great Taboo, to mention but a few. Probably the most comprehensive and up-to-date reference work on UFOs available at this time. Recommended for libraries in search of a title on this subject.—**Bradford Lee Eden**

15 Recreation and Sports

General Works

423. Gitlin, Martin. **100 Greatest American Athletes.** Lanham, Md., Rowman & Littlefield, 2018. 398p. illus. index. $38.00. ISBN 13: 978-1-5381-1027-0; 978-1-5381-1026-3 (e-book).

This interesting book ranks American athletes in terms of greatness from 1 to 100 using a point-based system: 35 points for achievements, 25 points for athleticism, 20 points for athletic requirements of the sport and position/event/division, 15 points for clutch factor/ mental and emotional toughness/intangibles, and 5 points for versatility. Using this point system, Gitlin's top five athletes in order are Jim Thorp, Michael Jordan, Bob Mathias, Jim Brown, and Michael Phelps. Tiger Woods rounds out the list of 100. Readers are provided with a biography for each athlete that focuses on their athletic achievements and an explanation of why they received a certain amount of points for each of the categories listed above. Athletes are included from such sports as football, baseball, basketball, track and field, golf, swimming, boxing, surfing, tennis, soccer, snow boarding, speed skating, skateboarding, and ice skating. There are more men than women included; the list also includes one horse, Secretariat. Recommended for school and public libraries.—**ARBA Staff Reviewer**

Biography

424. **Great Athletes of the Twenty-First Century.** Hackensack, N.J., Salem Press, 2018. 3v. illus. index. $395.00/set. ISBN 13: 978-1-68217-674-0; 978-1-68217-675-7 (e-book).

These three volumes update and supplement the thirteen-volume 2009 set *Great Athletes.* There are athletes from football, baseball, Olympic sports, basketball, golf, tennis, boxing, soccer, reading, racing, and individual sports. The set focuses on sports popular in North America but coverage is worldwide. The approximately four hundred biographies range in length from two to five pages and are divided into sections: Early Life, Road to Excellence, Emerging Champion, Continuing Story, and Summary. Biographies also include suggestions for further reading. The front matter includes a publisher's note, introduction, and contributor information. Volume 3 includes a glossary, extensive bibliography, and several other appendixes. The entries are easy to read and well organized. This is a good resource for those wanting basic information or for those who want to find further avenues for research. This set is recommended for public and school libraries.—**Thomas E. Baker**

Directories

425.   **Sports Market Place 2018.** Amenia, N.Y., Grey House Publishing, 2018. 1802p. index. $295.00pa. ISBN 13: 978-1-68217-766-2.

This annual from Grey House Publishing provides users with a one-stop shop for sports information for the United States and Canada in the following sections: Single Sports, Multiple Sports, College Sports, Media, Sports Sponsors, Professional Services, Facilities, Manufacturers & Retailers, Events, and Meetings & Trade Shows. Each of these sections begins with an alphabetical index. This year's edition includes approximately 14,000 listings. At the beginning of the book, users will find "Deloitte's Sports Industry Starting Lineup," "ESP Properties Top Sponsors Report," and the "11th Annual Canadian Sponsorship Landscape Study." Information varies from section to section and from entry to entry. For example, in the Single Sports section entries all contain contact information and may contain the names of key manager or executives, the nature of the service, member services, the number of members, the year founded, a description of the organization, and more. The listings in the College Sports section have contact information and may include such things as school mascot, school enrollment, and year founded for an individual institution and a description of member services and the names of member schools for an association like the New England Intercollegiate Amateur Athletic Association. The Media section gives contact information and frequency data for different outlets. Users will discover contact information, the names of executives, the names of teams sponsored, and the sponsorship budget of many organizations in the Sports Sponsors section and the capacity of certain venues in the Facilities section. The volume concludes with an entry index, an executive index, and a geographic index. Recommended.—**ARBA Staff Reviewer**

Handbooks and Yearbooks

426.   Newton, David E. **Steroids and Doping in Sports.** 2d ed. Santa Barbara, Calif., ABC-CLIO, 2018. 354p. illus. index. (Contemporary World Issues series). $60.00. ISBN 13: 978-1-4408-5481-1; 978-1-4408-5482-8 (e-book).

Steroids and Doping in Sports provides readers with an advanced understanding of steroid use in a reader friendly format. Cheating in sport is nothing new, and there is a long history of athletes using performance-enhancing drugs to run faster, jump higher, etc. This book discusses the current state of steroid and doping use among athletes and others. Moreover, the author addresses the dangers of misuse and overdose, as well as legal and governmental regulations. The book examines the challenge of detecting drug use, as new designer drugs constantly emerge and allow users to evade detection. The first section, Background and History, includes such things as the risk and therapeutic uses of anabolic steroids and a discussion of doping in the modern era. Section 2, Problems, Issues, and

Solutions, covers doping in the 1870s, the scandal involving the Bay Area Laboratory Cooperative (BALCO), which involved famous such athletes as Barry Bonds and Marion Jones, and doping in horse racing. Next comes a Perspectives section with essays like "The Politicization of Doping in Sports." A Profiles section features more than twenty individuals and organizations. The book also includes data and documents, resources, a glossary, and an index. Recommended.—**Thomas E. Baker**

427.   **Youth Sports in America: The Most Important Issues in Youth Sports Today.** Skye G. Arthur-Banning, ed. Santa Barbara, Calif., ABC-CLIO, 2018. 412p. index. $94.00. ISBN 13: 978-1-4408-4301-3; 978-1-4408-4302-0 (e-book).

Youth Sports in America is a series of essays examining the multiple issues, constituents, and components that surround the topic of young athletes in America. The essays include perspectives from coaches, parents, officials, trainers, and others in American society who shape, support, manage, and direct youth sports. The essays are written with a sociological context, connecting the many relationships of all types of groups that support and work with young athletes. There are 37 entries that cover issues such as goal setting and character development as well as economic impacts, LGBT athletes, media coverage, and sports for people with disabilities. There is an entry entitled "Parent Education" that discusses the issue of unruly parents, a topic that has been in the news recently. Corresponding timely topics include bullying, burnout, failure, concussions, body image, and eating disorders. Each entry is loaded with citations for further explorations into these topics. Included at the end is a bibliography of sources, an appendix, and an index. The appendix includes historical information describing where and when specific sports originated and also includes some notable statistical information. The sports in the appendix include baseball, football, hockey, golf, cheerleading, ultimate Frisbee, and a number of others. This collection of essays would benefit a researcher, both in undergraduate and public libraries, in search of a more "social-science-flavored" analysis of topics surrounding youth sports in America.—**Amy B. Parsons**

Backpacking

428.   Horjus, Maren. **Backpacker Hidden Gems: 100 Greatest Undiscovered Hikes across America.** Guilford, Conn., Falcon Guides, 2018. 336p. illus. maps. index. $28.00pa. ISBN 13: 978-1-4930-3386-7; 978-1-4930-3387-4 (e-book).

Author and *Backpacker* magazine Destinations Editor Maren Horjus provides readers with descriptions of one hundred lesser-known trips from across the country, arranged regionally: the West, the Pacific Northwest, the Southwest, the Mountain West, the Midwest, the Mid-Atlantic, the Southeast, and the Northeast. The introductions for each hike make it clear why the author chose them for inclusion. Excursions include such magnificent places as Central California's Channel Islands; the Yapashi Pueblo, Bandelier National Monument, New Mexico; the San Juan Mountains, Colorado; Little Missouri River, Theodore Roosevelt National Park, North Dakota; the Daniel Boone National Forest in Kentucky; and the Green Mountains in Vermont. Users will also find easy-to-follow trail maps, directions and distances, and a trip planner textbox that will provide contact, permit, and transportation information along with a suggestion on which season is best for backpacking. Extra information on flora and fauna, gear, and more is provided throughout the book. The color photographs showcase the wonder and beauty of these outdoor spaces. This is a fine place to discover a vast number of backpacking trails, which can all be modified for trail runners or day hikers. Highly recommended for public libraries.—**ARBA Staff Reviewer**

Baseball

429.   Baker, Dirk. **Baseball and Softball Drills: More Than 200 Games and Activities for Preschool to College Players.** 3d ed. Jefferson, N.C., McFarland, 2019. 2129. illus. index. $25.00pa. ISBN 13: 978-1-4766-7214-4; 978-1-4766-3315-2 (e-book).

This third edition by the head baseball coach at Worcester State University is written for coaches. The more than two hundred drills explained in the book can be adapted for use with players of any age. The book is well written and engagingly illustrated. A short foreword and preface are followed by eight chapters: "Running a Baseball Camp, Clinic, Class or Practice: Tips from A to Z"; "Baserunning"; "Bunting"; "Catching"; "Fielding"; "Hitting"; "Throwing and Pitching"; and "Closing Words." The chapters on baserunning, bunting, catching, fielding, hitting, and throwing and pitching begin with a short section on the basics of that skill. Within these chapters, the author uses the same layout for each drill—the name of the drill is followed by age range, object, equipment, and rules. This clearly and engagingly written book is recommended for public libraries or for any coach of a baseball or softball team in search of ideas.—**ARBA Staff Reviewer**

430.   Kaiser, David. **Baseball Greatness: Top Players and Teams According to Wins Above Average, 1901-2017.** Jefferson, N.C., McFarland, 2018. 240p. index. $35.00pa. ISBN 13: 978-1-4766-6383-8; 978-1-4766-2862-2 (e-book).

Baseball Greatness is a unique historical contribution for baseball enthusiasts, written by David Kaiser, who taught history at Harvard, Carnegie Mellon, Williams College, and the Naval War College. The information is contemporary in scope and acknowledges fresh breakthroughs in computer-based analysis. The content serves as a bridge for fans who may feel overwhelmed by new statistical approaches. Chapters provide well-ordered statistical facts concerning individual player contributions, and the author fills the void by compiling an abundance of facts, human comparisons, and team performance information.

Six scholarly chronological chapters, starting with "The Missionary and Lost Generation Era, 1901-1924" and finishing with "The Gen X and Millennial Era, 2005-2017," suggest opportunities for advanced insight and learning. The appendix briefly explores difficult issues that the author faced while writing the book.

Baseball Greatness represents an outstanding achievement. The author describes the logic underlying improved Major League Baseball calculations. Fans benefit in their search for objective information regarding baseball performance. Highly recommended for public, school, and academic libraries.—**Thomas E. Baker**

431.   Mitchell, Eddie. **Baseball Rowdies of the 19th Century: Brawlers, Drinkers, Pranksters and Cheats in the Early Days of the Major Leagues.** Jefferson, N.C., McFarland, 2018. 226p. illus. index. $29.95pa. ISBN 13: 978-1-4766-6487-3; 978-1-4766-2962-9. (e-book).

This book focuses on misbehavior on the part of professional baseball players in the late 19th century. The book is organized into four categories: managers, owners, players, and umpires. The largest group, players, is further subdivided into pitchers, infielders, and outfielders. Sections present individuals alphabetically. The type and extent of information included varies, but focuses mostly on the person's connection to the game. There are typically no biographic details. Entries vary in length from a few sentences to many pages. Black-and-white photographs appear throughout the work. The longer entries, such as those on Adrien "Cap" Ansen and John "Mugsy" McGraw, are the most interesting. One learns, for example, that Cap Ansen was largely responsible for keeping black players out of organized baseball and also reviled Irish Americans. Mugsy McGraw earned renown for his physical violence, among other things. The shorter entries do not provide as much detail, leaving readers wanting to know more about people like pitcher Tony Suck who changed his name from Zuck and was not a good hitter. Much of the rowdiness described by the author concerns the misuse/overuse of alcohol. A few rowdies come across as purely tragic, as in the case of infielder Marty Bergen whose undiagnosed mental illness led him to kill his family before committing suicide. The last chapter contains a few pages on "other rowdies," including the groundskeepers for the Baltimore Orioles, who mixed soap flakes into the mound dirt to make the ball slippery for the visiting team's pitchers. There is a short appendix of awards given by the author for the smartest, best looking, toughest, worst family man, and foulest mouth. A bibliography and an index round out the work.—**ARBA Staff Reviewer**

432.   **Ron Shandler's 2019 Baseball Forecaster.** 33rd ed. Brent Hershey, Brandon Kruse, Ray Murphy, and Ron Shandler, eds. Chicago, Triumph Books, 2018. 272p. $26.95pa. ISBN 13: 978-162937-613-4.

Ron Shandler's *Baseball Forecaster* is designed for participants in fantasy baseball. Shandler devised the unique system used for forecasting which players to pick. This year, the 33rd edition begins with an essay by Shandler on his losing 2018 fantasy season and the lessons learned from this experience. This is followed by the *Encyclopedia of Fanalytics,* Research Abstracts, the Major Leagues (Batters, Pitchers, Injuries), Prospects, Leaderboards, and Draft Guides. Regular updates are available at Baseball HQ (https://www.baseballhq.com/), and are complimentary for those who purchase the book. The *Baseball Forecaster* is recommended for public libraries and for individuals who play fantasy baseball.—**ARBA Staff Reviewer**

433.   **Seamheads http://seamheads.com/blog.** [Website] Free. Date reviewed: 2019.

Seamheads is home to reminisces, analyses, anecdotes, and plenty of statistics connected with the truly American sport of baseball. With contributions from a long list of baseball writers, the site offers something for everyone whether interested in AAA ball or the big leagues. Much of the content consists of topical essays, rich with statistics, which pay detailed attention to magic moments in the outfield, on the mound, and at the plate. Amidst this content, two databases stand out as particularly useful resources for the researcher. The Ball Parks Database offers information on every known ball park past to present, from Washington D.C.'s Swampdoodle Grounds and Richmond, Virginia's Allen's Pasture, to Los Angeles' legendary Dodger Stadium or Chicago's historic Wrigley Field. Users can manipulate a Google map with pinned ballpark locations to find a generous amount of data on over two hundred parks which saw play sometime between the years of 1871 and 2017. The map can be filtered to display ballparks within a span of time, active or inactive parks, or by state/region. Beneath the map, a table lists ballparks by name and includes location, first game, last game, seasons (number of), games (number of), and geographical data in addition to links to current and historical maps. Clicking on the ballpark name links to information on years of operation, affiliated teams, maps and capacity, outfield dimensions at several points, wall heights, and more for each year. But that's not all! Users can also examine data on Park Factors (homeruns, hits, singles, etc.), Park Events, and No Hitters, including all game statistics plus information on such things as opposing starter, plate umpire, and attendance numbers. Users can also access information in the Ballparks Database by Years (numbers of parks by year with details such as average capacity), Teams (listing teams alphabetically from the Altoona Pride to the Worcester Ruby Legs and providing relevant dates and affiliated statistics), and Cities (featuring a link to a historic aerial view map and allowing users to see where a ball park of old would sit in a city of today). Seamheads has also compiled a Negro Leagues Database, similarly packed with information about the segregated leagues and teams playing before Jackie Robinson's groundbreaking appearance with the Brooklyn Dodgers. Users can find copious detail regarding managers, Hall of Famers, game statistics, and much more, for teams such as the Kansas City Monarchs, The Memphis Red Sox, and The Philadelphia Stars as well as a number of Cuban and International league teams. Data can be examined by Teams or Seasons, and may include categories such as Top Position Player, Top Pitcher, batting, and fielding numbers. The Negro Leagues Database also includes generous historical and biographical material, player photographs, information on league leaders, and other material. Although each database is clearly delineated, the abundance of data can make navigation a bit tricky. Nonetheless, the rich and meticulous detail shows a genuine respect for the game of baseball that makes Seamheads a vital resource for cultural historians, statisticians, educators, students, and fans of America's pastime.—**ARBA Staff Reviewer**

434.   Spatz, Lyle. **New York Yankees Openers: An Opening Day History of Baseball's Most Famous Team, 1903-2017.** 2d ed. Jefferson, N.C., McFarland, 2018. 472p. index. $39.95pa. ISBN 13: 978-1-4766-6765-2; 978-1-4766-3247-6 (e-book).

The beloved American sport of baseball is filled with stories, and this hearty (and full of heart) book tells an engaging one: how have the inimitable New York Yankees fared over 114 years of opening days?

The author, Lyle Spatz, meticulously takes readers year by year through every first day of Yankee baseball, from 1903 through 2017 (with a brief glance at 2018's victory versus the Toronto Blue Jays). Twelve chapters separate decades of Yankee action and follow them from American League Park in Washington D.C., where they lost 3-1, to Tropicana Field in Florida and a 7-3 loss to Tampa Bay (diehard Yankee fans should not worry: there are plenty of victories in between).

Each opening day is described with deep knowledge and affection, and chapters are filled with colorful details (What was the weather like? Who sang the national anthem?) alongside an effective game summary. Adding to the richness of the recaps is excellent historical attention to individual players, the state of the baseball, and the state of the nation and the world.

Opening day 1981, for example, found 34-year-old pinch hitter Bobby Murcer, on the backside of his career, hitting a grand slam after being inspired by a raucous home crowd reception. We also learn that the attendance that day at 55,123 was the largest at the new stadium up to that point, and while the crowd got to witness stars Tommy John and Dave Winfield show their stuff in what was ultimately a 10-3 Yankee victory, a looming strike would cut the season short and inflict lasting damage on America's game.

Year to year, the book is jam packed with illuminating detail. In 1983 the Yankees faced Gaylord Perry of Seattle, at 44 the oldest player in the Major Leagues. In 1966 the crowd booed Roger Maris whose prior year had been marred by injuries. Opening day in 1936 saw both the Vice President and the President of the United States in attendance, while in 1925, Babe Ruth was a no-show due to an intestinal abscess (or was it too many hot dogs?). Along the way, readers meet all the Yankee legends: Lou Gehrig, Joe DiMaggio, Mickey Mantle, Babe Ruth, Reggie Jackson, Derek Jeter, Alex Rodriguez, and many others.

Spatz makes good use of both player and manager quotes, and lists both team line-ups with stats and additional game miscellany, followed by a brief paragraph recapping the season for each opening day essay. Baseball fans, cultural historians, and others will enjoy learning from this rich reminiscence of an iconic team's opening days. Recommended.— **ARBA Staff Reviewer**

Football

435.   Benkin, Ed. **The First 50 Super Bowls: How Football's Championships Were Won.** Jefferson, N.C., McFarland, 2018. 288p. index. $35.00pa. ISBN 13: 978-1-4766-7057-7; 978-1-4766-3072-4 (e-book).

Simply stated the Super Bowl is the most popular sporting event in the world—more popular than the World Series, the NCAA Final Four, or the World Cup. Broadcast in over 180 countries in twenty-five languages, the Super Bowl is the ultimate in sports. These fifty vignettes average five to seven pages per game, the author providing unique insight into key players and plays, unburdened by numbers and facts. Instead Benkin utilizes interviews with players and coaches to profile what influenced the outcome. A perfect example is Super Bowl III (1969), Joe Namath's guaranteed win for the New York Jets, with interviews with key players from both sides. Another is Super Bowl XXII (1988) where the Washington Redskins led by Doug Williams dominated Denver—Williams was the first African American to quarterback a Super Bowl winner. These types of vignettes make this an excellent guide to THE game. A brief list of sources and a ten-page index close the volume.—**Boyd Childress**

436.   Pollak, Mark. **The Playing Grounds of College Football: A Comprehensive Directory, 1869 to Today.** Jefferson, N.C., McFarland, 2019. 464p. $95.00pa. ISBN 13: 978-1-4766-7362-2; 978-1-4766-3260-5 (e-book).

A football field—120 yards long and 53 1/3 yards wide. For fans of college football across the nation, these simple dimensions do not do justice to the stadiums they populate every Saturday in the fall. This massive compilation of over 1,000 football playing institutions is quite an achievement listing schools alphabetically, including the years they played football, conference affiliations, and where they play and played games. A brief preface, introduction, and abbreviations offer the volume's game plan. What follows is nearly 450 pages of schools and their stadiums, some spanning the years before 1900.

From the sacred to the iconic, the book includes stadiums from Notre Dame Stadium (81,000 seats) to Ohio State's "the Big House" Stadium (104,000) to Alabama's Bryant Denny Stadium (102,000) all the way to Morehouse's Harvey Stadium (9,000) and Adams Stadium at Ferrum College (5,500). The volume also lists where schools have played charity and bowl games, who they played, and when they played. Stadiums and fields no longer in existence are included. Although the print is small and the text is jammed together, this is such a unique reference users can overlook these minor flaws with such extensive information.—**Boyd Childress**

Hiking

437.   Davis, Ren, and Helen Davis. **Best Hikes Atlanta: The Greatest Views, Wildlife, and Historic Sites.** Guilford, Conn., Falcon Guides, 2018. 204p. illus. maps. index. $24.95pa. ISBN 13: 978-1-4930-3493-2.

This book provides users with a guide to 37 hikes near the growing metropolitan area of Atlanta, an increasingly popular tourist destination. None of the hikes starts more than an hour from the city, and hikers can easily access all of the trails from one of the three interstate highways that intersect downtown Atlanta. The introduction discusses the area's geology, the amount of open space in Atlanta, the natural and human history, and the weather. Front matter includes a two-page, color map that shows the location of each hike, a map legend, and a trail finder that indicates the best hikes for particular purposes (hiking with children and/or dogs, finding mountain views or waterfalls, looking at nature, etc.) Readers will also find trail rules and tips on planning the hike, bringing adequate provisions, and more. The authors present the hikes in four sections: National Park Service Units, US Army Corps of Engineers, Georgia Department of Natural Resources, and Local Parks and Gardens. In addition to the main hikes in these sections, the authors also have several honorable mention hikes. The authors rank each hike from easy to strenuous. Hike descriptions include color photographs and a color trail map that is easy to follow. Hikers will also see directions for finding the trailhead, distances and the time it takes to hike, whether or not dogs are allowed, step-by-step directions for completing the hike, hours of operation, trail contact information, and a generous prose description of the hike and what it has to offer. The book concludes with Appendix A, "Land Use Management Agencies and Organization," Appendix B, "Outdoor Recreation and Environmental Protection," and Appendix C, "Additional Resources," a hike index, and information about the authors. Recommended for individual purchase and for public libraries, particularly those in the Atlanta area.—**ARBA Staff Reviewer**

438.   Hamilton, Linda. **Hiking the San Francisco Bay Area: A Guide to the Bay Area's Greatest Hiking Adventures.** 2d ed. Guilford, Conn., Falcon Guides, 2018. 304p. illus. maps. index. $24.95pa. ISBN 13: 978-1-4930-2983-9; 978-1-4930-2984-6 (e-book).

This is the second edition (the first published in 2003) of a hiking guide to the wonder and beauty of the San Francisco Bay Area, an amazingly diverse region with a significant amount of open space. The author, a Bay Area native, begins the book with tips for hiking in the Bay Area, map and icon legends, her top five hikes, and advice to heed before hitting the trail. Advice includes, among other tips, a reminder to get an early start if you want to avoid crowds and to keep hikes fun and short if children are in the group. A chart lists the names of the 40 trails covered in the book and indicates if they are good for photos, families, water features, dogs, or solitude. The guide provides an informative explanation of the flora and fauna, climate, efforts that resulted in the creation of more than a million acres of open space, and wilderness restrictions and regulations. The hikes are arranged by area: Point Reyes; Mount Tamalpais and Its Foothills; San Francisco and the Bay; San Mateo County Coastline; The Northern Santa Cruz Mountains; and Mount Diablo and Las Trampas Foothills. Hikes include those along the National Seashore and Tomales Bay, Angel Island, the Presidio, Ano Nuevo (and its sea lions), Big Basin Redwoods State Park, Joaquin Miller Park, and the John Muir National Historic Site. A separate chart lists hikes by those best for beachgoers, redwood lovers, animal and bird watchers, history lovers, and those who want a hike that burns the calves. An index rounds out the work. Hike maps are easy to read and follow, and the high-quality, color photographs are an enormous bonus. This is highly recommended for public libraries.—**ARBA Staff Reviewer**

439.   Massong, Tamara. **60 Short Hikes in the Sandias.** Albuquerque, N.Mex., University of New Mexico Press, 2018. 254p. illus. maps. index. $19.95pa. ISBN 13: 978-0-8263-5885-1.

Residents and visitors to Albuquerque now have an excellent new guide to hiking the nearby trails. To be in Albuquerque is to be surrounded by foothills, rivers, national monuments, volcanoes, deserts, and mountains. This book offers 60 opportunities to find a nearby hike that will be roughly 2-4 miles in length and take less than 2 hours.

The book has a thorough 25-page introduction that covers natural history, geology, Native Americans, landownership, safety, gear, trail etiquette, websites, contact information for the US Forest Service and the City of Albuquerque, and even the ten essentials. The last page of the introduction lists hikes according to special characteristics such as: most challenging, most likely to see large wildlife, hikes with water falls, ruins, etc.

The guide is divided into three sections by geographic area. Northern Trails are north of the Sandia Peak Tram; Central Trails are between the Tram and the Embudito trailhead; and South Central Trails are south of the Embudito Trailhead to I-40.

Each hike is numbered and named. The 3-4 pages on each hike starts with a table of pertinent data concerning difficulty, distance, time, elevation gain, conditions, best time, fees, and parking lot. A general summary of the hike with a color picture and a color map as well as detailed hiking instructions leaves nothing uncovered. GPS data points and yellow boxes with special interesting info to know about the area are included. There is also an "If you like this hike, try this hike" section.

Valuable appendixes include directions to parking areas, a timeline of post-Pueblo revolt land ownership, and how to use digital data with your smart phone.

Any library with patrons who would visit Albuquerque should buy this superb guidebook.—**Georgia Briscoe**

Hobbies

440.   Frost, Jeff. **The Backyard Railroader: Building and Operating a Miniature Steam Locomotive.** Jefferson, N.C., McFarland, 2019. 298p. illus. index. $49.95pa. ISBN 13: 978-1-4766-7281-6; 978-1-4766-3164-6 (e-book).

This book provides guidance for anyone who wants to get jump into a very exciting hobby—building and operating a miniature steam railroad. The author is well positioned to write this book. He learned the craft from his father, he runs his own backyard railroad, and he works at the Strasburg Rail Road in Strasburg, Pennsylvania, as machinist, mechanic, engineer, fireman, and conductor. The book's chapters cover safety; how to get started and how to operate a steam engine; valve gears; boilers; and systems, improvements, and why things are done in a certain way. This informative book is thorough and very detailed, especially for those new to backyard railroading. For instance, in the second chapter, "Getting Started," the author lists the 24 things he looks for when buying a steam engine. This chapter also has information on suppliers of steam locomotives, diesel locomotives, cars, other parts, machinery, tooling, metal, and nuts and bolts. The last chapter, "My Experiences in the Hobby" conveys the author's enthusiasm. The book includes a generous number of black-and-white photographs and diagrams. There are several appendixes: "Major Parts of a Steam Locomotive," "Common Questions" (how does a steam locomotive work?, how are the wheels held in place?), "Common Myths," "Inspections," and "Tracktive Effort and What an Engine Can Pull." An index rounds out the work. Recommended for individuals and for public libraries.—**ARBA Staff Reviewer**

Outdoor Life

441.   Romaine, Garret. **Gold Panning Colorado: A Guide to the State's Best Sites for Gold.** Guilford, Conn., Falcon Guides, 2018. 276p. illus. maps. $25.95pa. ISBN 13: 978-1-4930-2856-6.

Families or individuals looking to try their hand at mining for gold in Colorado will find this a valuable guide to the necessary tools and best sites. The book begins with a map indicating the sites discussed, an introduction, tips for getting started and for how to pan for gold, and a map legend. The guide includes information about 75 sites, which are arranged geographically into three sections: Southwest Colorado, Central Colorado, and Northeast Colorado. For each place, the guide provides information about land type (park, riverbank, seasonal creek, dry gulches, river canyon, mountain pass, tailings, lode mine, etc.), county in which it is located, elevation, GPS coordinates, best season to visit, land manager, material, tools, type of vehicle required, special attractions, accommodations (if available), how to find the site, and prospecting details. Color photographs and maps are included. More than a dozen of the sites are mine tours. For example, number 17, the Old Hundred Gold Mine Tour, in San Juan County takes visitors via electric train into the mine where they learn more about the former mining operation and have an opportunity to pan for gold. There are also four museums included, the National Mining Hall of Fame and Musuem, the Creede Underground Mining Museum, the Colorado School of Mines Geology Museum, and the Denver Museum of Nature & Science. A series of appendixes offer information about modern mining tools, websites, clubs and organizations, and further references and suggested readings. Recommended for individuals and public libraries.—**ARBA Staff Reviewer**

Tennis

442.   **The Wimbledon Archive. https://www.imgreplay.com/client/Wimbledon.** [Website] Free and fee. Date reviewed: 2018.

The Wimbledon Archive from IMG Replay has collected years of video content related to England's famous tennis tournament. Accessible to registered users, the content includes match footage, interviews, special features, and more that cover over a century of tournament play and captures moments that brought fame to the likes of Chris Evert, Bjorn Borg, Arthur Ashe, Roger Federer, Serena Williams, and others. While more recent content is freely available upon site registration, content originating before 2007 is subject to IMG's licensing agreement. The Licensing tab on the homepage offers information about this arrangement—users can Download PDF Resources or scroll to the bottom of the homepage and click on the Rights & Clearances link. Under the Content tab, users can choose from the five Wimbledon draws—Gentlemen's Singles, Ladies' Singles, Gentlemen's Doubles, Ladies' Doubles or Mixed Doubles—to access affiliated material which is then arranged by Footage or Programming. Under Footage, users can toggle a timeline reaching back to 1900 to pinpoint the year of interest. For each year, users can select an icon denoting the round of play (fourth round, final, etc.) they would like to view. Users can also view the match scores for the selected round. The page will then display a gallery of affiliated content, or a message noting footage availability through licensing agreement. Programming offers a more varied selection of content, including Official Films, Individual Round Footage, a "Golden Moment" highlight clip, Classic Matches and Documentaries. Selections within each category are presented in a gallery format and can be filtered by year or video quality.—**ARBA Staff Reviewer**

Wrestling

443.   Freedman, Lew. **Pro Wrestling: A Comprehensive Reference Guide.** Santa Barbara, Calif., Greenwood Press/ABC-CLIO, 2018. 308p. illus. index. $94.00. ISBN 13: 978-1-4408-5350-0; 978-1-4408-5351-7 (e-book).

The preface, introduction, and chronology seek to tie contemporary professional wrestling to athletic events depicted in prehistoric art, but also explain that the entertainment aspect of wrestling began in both Europe and America in the 1800s with traveling shows and carnivals. The bulk of the text includes alphabetically arranged entries; most of the entries focus on professional wrestlers, but films about wrestling, famous arenas, and organizations are included. Some entries provide photographs, and each supplies lists of books and articles for further reference. The book would be of interest to middle school and high school students, especially those already interested in professional wrestling. Commendably, the volume includes many entries about female wrestlers. Despite the focus on contemporary American entertainment, the book also covers events in Asia and Europe. Another fine feature is found in the index, where bold print distinguishes the main entry under a heading from other pages where the entry is discussed.—**Delilah R. Alexander**

16 Sociology

General Works

Dictionaries & Encyclopedias

444.   **The SAGE Encyclopedia of Lifespan Human Development.** Marc H. Bornstein, ed. Thousand Oaks, Calif., Sage, 2018. 5v. index. $945.00/set; $756.00 (e-book). ISBN 13: 978-1-5063-0765-7; 978-1-5063-5331-9 (e-book).

This encyclopedia (5 volumes) takes on an immensely broad subject in just over eight hundred signed entries by more than six hundred scholarly contributors. The task the editor and editorial board set was to create an overview of all areas of human life from before birth to death. Well-written entries range in length from 1,000 to 5,000 words. The entries include *see also* references and suggestions for further reading. The set also utilizes *see* references. Topics are easily locatable, thanks to a list of entries and a readers' guide that appear in each volume. The list is alphabetic, but the readers' guide groups entries into fourteen topics: aging, behavior, cognitive development, community and culture, developmental issues, genetics and biology, health and illness, methods, personal characteristics, relationships and the social world, services, sociocultural constructs, socioemotional development, and theory. Entries can and do appear in multiple categories in the readers' guide. Such entries as food insecurity, late versus early parenthood, nursing homes, physical activity, retirement, sexuality, toys and games, heredity, and central nervous system are both interesting and accessible. An extensive index, which appears in volume 5 of the print set, will also facilitate navigation through this work. Altogether, this encyclopedia should give users not only an overview of lifespan development but also a firm grounding in the theory and research underpinning the ideas. The editorial board selected the entries and crafted the book for use by community college, undergraduate and graduate students as well as scholars and researchers in the social sciences, humanities, life sciences, and natural sciences worldwide. Highly recommended for academic libraries.— **ARBA Staff Reviewer**

Handbooks and Yearbooks

445. **Principles of Sociology: Group Relations & Behavior.** Kimberly Ortiz-Hartman, ed. Hackensack, N.J., Salem Press, 2018. 562p. illus. index. (Principles of Sociology). $165.00. ISBN 13: 978-1-64265-111-9; 978-1-64265-112-6 (e-book).

This volume is the second in the series. While the first series volume focuses on personal relationships and behavior, this installment examines group relationships and behavior. The volume begins with a short introduction, publisher's note, table of contents, and list of contributors, and the bulk of the book is organized into four sections: Social Movements & Collective Behavior (16 entries); Stratification & Class in the U.S. (21 entries); Social Interaction in Groups & Organizations (35 entries); and Sociology of Religion (17 entries). Each section starts with a general introduction. Most entries run 5-7 pages and all include an abstract, overview, a presentation of the topic, a definition of key terms and concepts, a bibliography, and suggestions for further reading. Each is signed by one of the contributors listed in the front matter. The topic coverage is broad. Users will find entries on Contagion Theory, Emergent-Norm Theory, Mass Hysteria, the Sociology of the Internet, the Middle Class in America, Bureaucratic Inertia, Groupthink, Social Media as Social Interaction, Civil Religion, and Religious Nationalism, just to name a few. A thorough index rounds out the work. The writing style is accessible to both upper-level high school students and undergraduates. The key terms and concepts enhance understanding and the bibliographies and suggested readings offer directions for further research. This would be a useful resource for someone taking a sociology course for the first time or for someone who needs a refresher on key concepts. Recommended for school and academic libraries.—**ARBA Staff Reviewer**

446. **Principles of Sociology: Personal Relationships & Behavior.** Kimberly Ortiz-Hartman, ed. Hackensack, N.J., Salem Press, 2018. 574p. index. $165.00. ISBN 13: 978-1-64265-109-6; 978-1-64265-110-2 (e-book).

Principles of Sociology: Personal Relationships & Behavior, edited by Kimberly Ortiz-Hartman, is a wide-ranging reference work about human behavior surrounding personal interactions and relationships with a sociological lens. The book is part of a series published by Salem Press, with the two other titles covering *Group Relationships & Behavior* and *Societal Issues & Behavior.* The book is broken up into five sections by topic: Day-to-Day Interaction, Family & Relationships, Socialization, Social Change, and Aging & Elderly Issues. Prefaced with an introduction by the editor, each section includes several encyclopedia-style entries pertinent to their category. The entries themselves also contain an abstract, an overview, terms and concepts, a bibliography, and further readings. Many entries also have sections called Viewpoints and Further Insights, although this is inconsistent.

Although far reaching and accessible, there are some issues with this text. As mentioned above, the large number of contributing authors—27 not including the editor—have inconsistent style and approach, although those on theory seem most well written. Additionally, there are major problems regarding two categories: issues with citations and insufficient proofreading.

First, some of the authors in this book chose to write in the style common to many reference books where in-text citations are only given for direct quotes. I find this to be troubling in many ways, primarily how it leads to some fairly astounding statements about human behavior and opinion without a direct link to the article or book from which the author was drawing. For example, it is stated in one article that before it was socially acceptable for women to join the workforce, women "quite happily raised families and supported their husbands" (p. 180). No in-text citation is given. In another example, an author states that "Hispanics often express emotion through tears" (p.529), Again, no in-text citation is given.

Another troubling issue regarding citations is that some cited materials are inappropriate given the context. Citations are consistently out-of-date when dealing with topics and technologies that are continuously evolving. In the article on "Internet Dating," less than 20 percent of the bibliography was published after 2010 and the majority of in-text citations range from 1995 to 2005. Another article cited an example from another introductory sociology textbook instead of the original researcher, Margaret Mead, a seminal figure in her field (p. 183). In yet another article, the author cited a quote attributed to William Thomson Kelvin from the website anecdotage.com (p. 413). According to the Web Archive, this website has not been accessible since around April 2014. Additionally, one of the quotes the authors cited is generally considered to be misattributed. Another data point in a different article is credited to a study at the University of Northwestern, but the authors chose to instead reference the website Statistic Brain, which is behind a paywall (p. 4).

Second, this book is troubled by an insufficient level of proofreading. Some issues are simple typos, like missing words in a sentence ("individuals who had come to terms with the impending death of a loved before the fact" p. 530), wrong word forms ("enable the patient to life" p. 517), the wrong plural ("these phemonenon seem" p. 201), and two citations merged into one with incorrect volume information (p. 6). More substantial are the nonsequiturs (p. 5), conclusions that introduce new information not tied to the conclusion of the article (p. 202), quotes with no in-text citation (p. 259), references to the incorrect government agency (p. 258), and consistently referring to the article as a "paper" as if the initial proposal was copy/pasted into the abstract and conclusion (p. 413 & 417).

Regrettably, all of these factors lead me to not recommend this book for purchase by other libraries, although I reserve judgment on the other two books in the series. The authors of this text would have been better served by more investment and input from the publisher and/or editor.—**Carin Graves**

Abortion

447.   McBride, Dorothy E., and Jennifer L. Keys. **Abortion in the United States.** 2d ed. Santa Barbara, Calif., ABC-CLIO, 2018. 390p. illus. index. (Contemporary World Issues). $60.00. ISBN 13: 978-1-4408-5336-4; 978-1-4408-5337-1 (e-book).

This volume updates the first edition published in 2008 (see ARBA 2008, entry 716), with almost 90 more pages of information. There are diverse sections; among them are Problems, Controversies, and Solutions, the largest section of the volume; Perspectives, written by seven authors; Profiles, 99 entries of individuals and organizations from both the prolife and prochoice sides of the debate; and Resources, providing an annotated list of books, films, and Internet resources on the subject. This subject is of course one with strong opinions on both sides of the issue; this book provides viewpoints and resources for the reader to explore the various positions. A 24-page chronology, running from 1821 to 2017, provides one way to follow this subject's evolution in the United States. The index (40+ pages) can then take the reader to additional information about items/people mentioned there. Reference lists at the end of most sections provide additional readings from a variety of sources.

Over 800 public and academic libraries own the previous edition of this work. This updated and expanded version should be considered by any institution having that book in their collection, as well as by other libraries with readers interested in the topic.—**Mark Schumacher**

Aging

448.   **Older Americans Information Resource.** 12th ed. Amenia, N.Y., Grey House Publishing, 2018. 1126p. index. $165.00pa. ISBN 13: 978-1-68217-734-1.

Older Americans Information Resource "is designed for one of America's largest growing populations, with resources to help aging Americans lead happy and productive lives." This guide contains 10,000 listings and is organized within chapters: National Organizations & Federal Agencies; State Organizations & Government Agencies; Awards, Honors & Prizes; Continuing Education; Disability Aids & Assistive Devices; Health Conditions; Assisted Living Facilities; Independent Living Centers; Legal Aid Resources; Libraries & Information Centers; Print Resources for Older Americans; and Travel & Recreation. In addition to the directory entries, this resource features an introduction; a "Profile of Older Americans: 2016" from the U.S. Department of Health and Human Services. There are two appendixes, one a glossary of health and medical terms and one a glossary of legal terms. There is also an entry name index, a geographic index, and a subject index. Each organization's entry includes name, address, telephone, website, directors/president; description; and year founded. Each print material's entry includes: title, publisher, address, telephone, fax, website, number of pages, and brief description. This title provides information on a wide variety of topics among which are: locating newsletters and pamphlets on various healthcare issues; researching assisted living facilities; locating information about tours and travel services; and deciding on a continuing education course. The *Older Americans Information Resource* is a treasure trove of resources for senior citizens. Highly recommended for public library collections.—**Lucy Heckman**

Death

449.   Shreeve, Michelle. **Parental Death: The Ultimate Teen Guide.** Lanham, Md., Rowman & Littlefield, 2018. 222p. illus. index. (It Happened To Me series). $45.00; $42.50 (e-book). ISBN 13: 978-1-4422-7087-9; 978-1-4422-7088-6 (e-book).

Parental Death is a compassionate resource that addresses topics often ignored in the midst of chaos, grief, and uncertainty. Teens struggling with the death of a parent will find the reading sensitive to their needs. This book offers insightful case studies that provide support to teen readers whose coping skills may be underdeveloped and who feel overwhelmed by new and raw emotions. The author, Michelle Shreeve, offers thoughtful and authentic advice, having lost her own parent while still a young child.

This contribution provides navigational pathways to adjustment, support systems, and frank discussions regarding changes that affect family dynamics. The book's transition points and organization are flawless. The author begins by placing an emphasis on the first year after a parent's death. Discussion includes holidays, birthdays, and numerous other trigger points. Final chapters address transitioning through high school and beyond. Highlighted learning boxes frame personal experiences. A glossary and a resource section further benefit readers. Overall, the writing is clear, concise, and age appropriate.

Parental Death: The Ultimate Teen Guide is an essential bookstore offering for self-help shelves. Public, high school, middle school, and college libraries will benefit by including this book in their collection.—**Thomas E. Baker**

Disabled

450. **The Complete Resource Guide for People with Disabilities, 2019.** 27th ed. Amenia, N.Y., Grey House Publishing, 2018. 1042p. illus. maps. index. $165.00. ISBN 13: 978-1-68217-777-8.

This is the 27th edition of this guide (formerly published as *The Complete Directory for People with Disabilities*). This comprehensive reference tool starts with a brief introduction, glossary of disability-related terms, user guide, and user key. Following are two reports "National Disability Policy: A Progress Report" and "2017 Disability Statistics Annual Report." These reports include color maps, tables, and charts along with quick facts. Further ready reference information is included in the appendix (new to this edition) "2017 Annual Disability Statistics Compendium," which provides state-by-state statistics. Inside the heart of the volume users will find more than 9,000 descriptive listings, over 24,000 key contacts, and thousands of websites, fax numbers, and email addresses. There are 21 subject-specific sections, starting with Arts & Entertainment and including such other sections as Camps (arranged by state), Clothing, Education, Foundations & Funding Resources (arranged by state), Government Agencies (arranged by state), Travel & Transportation, Aging, Blind & Deaf, and Visual. There are three indexes: subject, geographic, and publisher. Libraries will receive a free year of online access along with the purchase of the print volume. Recommended for public libraries.—**ARBA Staff Reviewer**

451. **The Oxford Handbook of Disability History.** Michael Rembis, Catherine Kudlick, and Kim E. Nielsen, eds. New York, Oxford University Press, 2018. 552p. illus. index. $150.00. ISBN 13: 978-0-19023-495-9; 978-0-19023-497-3 (e-book).

This title includes 27 articles by 30 experts (mostly historians) on the global history of disability. The introduction discusses the development of the field in the 1980s and its evolution since then. The text is separated into five parts: Concepts and Questions, Work, Institutions, Representations, and Movements and Identities. The first part includes chapters on disability biography; the ethical questions with which disability historians must grapple; disability and the history of eugenics; disability in the European Middle Ages, in Greco-Roman history, and in the premodern Arab world; and more. The second section looks at disability and work in several times and places: during the Industrial Revolution in Britain; in South Asia and the United Kingdom; in British West Africa;

and in Progressive Era and post-World War II America. Section 3, Institutions, offers four articles: "Deaf-Blindness and the Institutionalization of Special Education in Nineteenth-Century Europe," "Disability and Madness in Colonial Asylum Records in Australia and New Zealand," "Madness, Transnationalism, and Emotions in Nineteenth-and Early Twentieth-Century New Zealand," and "Institutions for People with Disability in North America." The fourth section, Representation, includes information on the ways disability was pictured in 18th-century England, on the antebellum American stage, in Cold War Hungary, in modern Chinese cinema, and more. The last section, Movements, includes four articles: "Transnational Interconnections in Nineteenth-Century Western Deaf Communities," "The Disability Rights Movement in the United States," "The Rise of Gay Rights and the Disavowal of Disability in the United States," and "Disabled Veterans and the Wounds of War." Articles include notes and bibliographies, and an index rounds out the work. The introduction to the title points out that most disability history has focused on and come from North America, the United Kingdom, Australia, and New Zealand, but this title demonstrates the expansion and importance of the field. Recommended.—**ARBA Staff Reviewer**

Family, Marriage, and Divorce

452.   **Domestic Violence Sourcebook.** 6th ed. Detroit, Omnigraphics, 2019. 476p. index. $85.00. ISBN 13: 978-0-7808-1654-1; 978-0-7808-1655-8 (e-book).

This volume, the third edition in the past five years, resembles the fifth edition (2016), but with 145 fewer pages. The format remains similar: sections include Facts About Domestic Violence, Intimate Partner Abuse, Abuse in Specific Populations, Preventing and Intervening in Domestic Violence, and finally, Emergency Management, Moving Out, and Moving On. A final chapter provides "Additional Help and Information." For some reason, some of the chapters have evolved substantially since the last edition: the "Intervention by Faith Communities" text went from eight to two pages, while other sections went from 36 to 12 and 28 to 6 pages in the current edition. The reason for this change is not explained. Nearly all the 107 sections begin with this statement: "This section includes text excerpted from . . .". For instance, Section13.1, "Types of Child Abuse" comes practically verbatim from a 10-page document from the Department of Health and Human Services. Much of the information comes from resources created by the federal government, and it would be useful to include the web addresses of the documents mentioned, as many are available. That being said, this information will be quite useful to anyone dealing with, or aware of others wrestling with, domestic violence, particularly because the frequency of domestic violence in the United States is 10 million attacks per year, and 1 in 3 women and 1 in 4 men will be a victim during their lifetime. It is presented very well, in manageable sections of a few pages, with clear headings and bullet points. If a public or academic library does not own the 4th or 5th edition, it should certainly consider adding this volume to its collection.—**Mark Schumacher**

Gay and Lesbian Studies

453.   **Defining Documents in American History: LGBTQ+ (1923-2017).** Michael Shally-Jensen, ed. Hackensack, N.J., Salem Press, 2018. 2v. illus. index. $295.00/set. ISBN 13: 978-1-68217-894-2.

The Defining Documents in American History series aligns primary source documents with current contextual analysis to help foster a fundamental understanding of events and issues. Materials are selected to neither promote nor dissuade readers, but rather to well represent the trajectory of the general subject. This two-volume collection highlights a good variety of historical materials, including complete or excerpted speeches, letters, reports, mission statements, court opinions, and laws related to LGTBQ+ rights.

The editor's introduction provides a good overview of the volume's chronological structure as it presents the more notable moments in the American LGTBQ+ story through today. Documents include an excerpt from Hollywood icon Mae West's play titled *The Drag,* the first issue of *The Los Angeles Advocate* newspaper, the Don't Ask, Don't Tell law from 1993 regarding homosexuals in the military, excerpts from the opinion and dissents in 2015's *Obergefell* v. *Hodges,* and much more. Volume I's documents help expose the first tentative moments in the long fight toward equal treatment and culminate with the call to arms so to speak of the Stonewall Inn episode and the first national march for lesbian and gay rights (drawing close to 100,000 people). Volume II brings readers up to the present, pointing to pivotal court rulings and other impactful moments, such as Ellen DeGeneres coming out to a prime time television audience. The second volume is capped with documents related to the election of the first openly transgender state government official.

A concise, multifaceted essay accompanies each document and organizes information by subheading: Summary Overview, Defining Moment, Author Biography, Document Analysis, and Essential Themes. Chapters may also include photographs or illustrations, a glossary, a bibliography, and supplemental historical documents.

Appendixes at the end of the second volume include a more extensive glossary, a chronology reaching back to the mid-19th century, topical ideas for further reading, web resources, and a subject index. The volumes are also available online. Though many of the documents in this title are available online, this is recommended for those school libraries in search of a curated collection on this subject.—**ARBA Staff Reviewer**

454.   Devor, Aaron, and Ardel Haefele-Thomas. **Transgender: A Reference Handbook.** Santa Barbara, Calif., ABC-CLIO, 2019. 364p. illus. index. (Contemporary World Issues). $60.00. ISBN 13: 978-1-4408-5690-7; 978-1-4408-5691- (e-book).

This volume is organized like many of the other books in the Contemporary World Issues series, which dates back to the late 1980s. The first section is Background and History, followed by Problems, Controversies, and Solutions. The section on Perspectives presents 12 texts by as many authors, some looking at personal experiences of the transgender population in several countries and cultures. The essays in this section are quite moving, as they often explore quite closely the challenges and struggles facing transgender individuals and their families. There follow 90 pages of "Profiles," of both individuals, from Joan of Arc to Chaz Bono, and organizations, in the United States as well as in Europe and Africa. The volume ends with a Data and Documents section, a list of diverse resources (with annotations of the entries there), a chronology, glossary, and index. The text does an excellent job explaining the difference between sex and gender (or gender identity and sexual orientation) in this community, and the numerous terms that describe the diversity of people that make up this group. The Data and Documents section presents discouraging statistics about the treatment of the transgender population in the United States and around the world, along with supporting statements from the World Professional Association for Transgender Health.

Many of the earlier volumes in the "Contemporary World Issues" series are owned by a wide range of public, community college, and university libraries. Given the importance of this subject, this book will be useful in all those types of libraries.—**Mark Schumacher**

455. **Global Encyclopedia of Lesbian, Gay, Bisexual, Transgender, and Queer (LGBTQ) History.** Howard Chiang, ed. New York, Charles Scribner's Sons/Gale Group, 2019. 3v. illus. index. $692.00/set. ISBN 13: 978-0-6843-2553-8; 978-0-6843-2554-5 (e-book).

When it was first published in 2004, the *Encyclopedia of Lesbian, Gay, Bisexual, and Transgender History in America* provided coverage of one country (see ARBA 2005, entry 804). This companion title looks at the world. The three volumes contain more than 380 signed entries by an international group of over 360 contributors. They examine the LGBTQ communities in 70 countries, including places in Africa, which have less-developed historical documentation.

The alphabetical entries are several pages long with bibliographies. They cover a wide range of topics and are often divided into sections devoted to specific countries or regions. The arts (cinema, theatre, literature, music, and popular culture), biography (Khookha McQueer, Chevalier d'Eon or Mademoiselle Beaumont), events, demonstrations, and memorials (AIDS Memorial Quilt-The NAMES project, Pride Parades and Marches), geographical profiles (Australia and New Zealand, Uganda), and organizations (ACT UP, Transgender Organizations in Mainland China, Hong Kong, and Taiwan) are among the subjects included. Illustrations and sidebars offer further insights. The vast amount of information available here is interdisciplinary, examining everything from transgender athletes to the relationships between Anti-Semitism and anti-LGBTQ discrimination to queer diasporas. The approach is academic, so the reading level is vey high. This is a valuable addition to all academic libraries.—**Barbara M. Bibel**

456. **Great Events from History: LGBTQ Events.** 2d ed. Robert C. Evans, ed. Hackensack, N.J., Salem Press, 2017. 2v. illus. index. $175.00/set. ISBN 13: 978-1-68217-591-0.

This handsome, oversized, two-volume set, part of the publishers extensive series Great Events from History, is an updated revision of the title *Great Events from History: Gay Lesbian, Bisexual and Transgender Events* (Salem, 2006) which began coverage with the year 1848 (roughly when the term homosexual came into being) with a report on the Seneca Falls Convention on Women's Rights of that year and continued in 280 chronologically arranged entries that end in March, 2006, with coverage on the release of the film *Brokeback Mountain.* All of this material is included (with only slight revisions) in this second edition that includes 13 new entries ending with three covering events that occurred in 2015 (Caitlyn Jenner's transgender, the legalization of gay marriages by the Supreme Court, and China's crackdown on depiction of gays on television). Many of the topics covered involve legal or governmental actions but, as the examples show, others deal with social or cultural events. Each entry is signed and is two or three double-columned pages in length. Most of the more than 100 contributors have academic affiliations. Some entries have accompanying blackand-white photographs and over half also have sidebars that usually contain valuable excerpts from background primary sources. Articles are divided into three parts. The first gives a brief summary of the event (three or four lines), its date, locale, categories covered (e.g., civil rights, economics), and key figures. Part two, the longest, gives a factual summary of the event, while part three describes its significance. The choice of subjects covered is, in general, judicious and well rounded. Although the coverage is international in scope, the emphasis is on American-related topics. Each article concludes with an extensive bibliography (average about a dozen items) called "For Further Reading" that includes books, articles, and a few websites. Next comes a lengthy list of *see also* related articles, titles, and dates. Volume two ends with valuable additional material. First, an extensive 10-page annotated general bibliography arranged under such subjects as sports and religion that is reprinted from the first edition, with an additional, listing of books (not annotated) published from 2006 to 2017. This is followed by a chronological listing of events covered in the set, and a "Category Index" that lists the entries under 23 main subjects such as "civil rights," "crime," and "television." The set ends with a thorough 25-page general index. This is a user friendly, highly readable reference work that is recommended for public and academic libraries and, where needed, some high school libraries. However, if the library already owns the original 2006 edition, the limited changes in coverage offered in the new edition might not warrant this additional purchase.—**John T. Gillespie**

457.   **LGBTQ in the 21st Century.** Bronx, N.Y., H. W. Wilson, 2017. 184p. illus. index. (The Reference Shelf, volume 89, number 4). $75.00pa. ISBN 13: 978-1-68217-455-5.

This volume brings together thirty-four texts drawn from print publications, media sources (NPR, PBS, etc.) and several websites. The items are grouped into five key sections: LGBTQ and the Law, LGBTQ and the World, LGBTQ Culture, LBGTQ in the Schools, and LGBTQ and the Family. The sources range from the conservative "Daily Signal" to more liberal publications and media. The topics are very wide-ranging, from a debate in Minnesota as to whether kindergarten children should be taught about gender identity, to an examination of the current status of the LGBTQ community in the Middle East and to the torture of gays in Chechnya. Texts also explore the history the LGBTQ world, from ancient Greece to the present.

A list of nine websites includes both pro- and antigay groups, while the bibliography brings together often useful references found in the six introductory texts (a preface and five section introductions) written by Micah L. Issitt. Curiously, the volume provides citation format information (Chicago, MLA, APA) for the reprints, but not for Issitt's texts. And as in other "Reference Shelf" volumes, the "Index" only lists personal names, including twenty references to President Trump. Most of the other names will be unfamiliar to readers. Given that this topic is one of frequent discussion in many venues, from national publications and news outlets to schools and colleges, libraries of all kinds should consider adding it to their collections.—**Mark Schumacher**

458.   Stewart, Chuck. **Documents of the LGBT Movement.** Santa Barbara, Calif., ABC-CLIO, 2018. 250p. index. (Eyewitness to History Series). $94.00. ISBN 13: 978-1-4408-5501-6; 978-1-4408-5502-3 (e-book).

Chuck Stewart, the author-editor of this anthology of 149 documents related to the history of the LGBT (Lesbian, Gay, Bisexual, Transsexual) movement in the United States, has written extensively on this subject in a number of books like *Gay and Lesbian Issues: A Reference Handbook* (see ARBA 2005, entry 806). The documents in this anthology are arranged chronologically into 11 chapters ("Early America" to "2010s") and consist of such sources as texts of legislative and court documents from federal to state and local levels, archival material from organizations and agencies, newspaper and periodical articles, and various speeches and websites. Some examples: "New Haven Law Prohibits Lesbianism (1655)," "Supreme Court Excludes Homosexual Immigrants (1967)," "The Stonewall Inn Riots (1969)," and "Westboro Baptist Church and its God Hates Fags Message (2000)." The last document in this volume is from 2017 and deals with court ordered anti-workplace discrimination. Most documents are about one page in length and are preceded by an introductory paragraph giving background information and an indication of the document's significance. The book provides the source for each document. Each chapter begins with a brief historical overview and ends with a bibliography of eight to ten books or articles for further reading. Of particular interest is the introductory material which includes a 40-page history of LGBT rights and issues in the United States, a 2-page general bibliography, and a chronology of important events. The book ends with an extensive 20-page index. There is some duplication of material with this book with that in *Gay and Lesbian Rights in the United States: A Documentary History* (Greenwood, 2003) by Walter Williams and Yolanda Retter but coverage in the Williams and Retter book ends with 2000, while the Stewart volume contains 30 documents from the 21st century. Both volumes, however, will be of continued use. *Documents of the LGBT Movement* is a valuable supplement to histories on this topic and is recommended for all libraries where there is a demand for material on this timely subject.—**John T. Gillespie**

Philanthropy

459.   **Foundation   Maps   https://maps.foundationcenter.org/home.php.**   [Website] Free. Date reviewed: 2019.

Foundation Maps offers a state-of-the-art tool for understanding and facilitating global funding relationships. It gathers and updates data on millions of grants, thousands of grant recipients, and the charitable foundations that support them. The site requires a paid Professional or Custom subscription for access; however, general users can gain essential information about site capabilities via the Features or Tour tabs and preview the site via Free Trial with professional registration. The site uses a global map with generous and easy-to-navigate interactive features to help users find desired information about who is giving dollars and who is receiving them. Users can search numerous grant recipients, foundations, and the locations around the world served by this philanthropy. Users can further narrow their search by subject areas (e.g., arts and culture, humanities, media and communications), dollar value of grants, grant years, population group, keywords, and more. Users can also view aggregate figures regarding foundation funding, such as total number of grants, total dollar value of grants, number of funders, and number of recipients. General descriptive information can also be found regarding foundations (e.g., Bill and

Melinda Gates Foundation, Ford Foundation) and grant recipients (e.g., Global Fund to Fight Aids, Tuberculosis, and Malaria), including mission, country, financial data (assets, expenditures, etc.), contact information, and other information. All users can select the Tour tab at the top of the page which offers an excellent Foundation Maps primer, and users can explore by section such as Navigating the Map, Charts, and Funding Pathways. The Features tab provides additional detail regarding website components, including its Map, List, Charts, Demographic Overlay, and other site features.—**ARBA Staff Reviewer**

Poverty

460.   Burch, John R., Jr. **Poverty in the United States: A Documentary and Reference Guide.** Santa Barbara, Calif., Greenwood Press/ABC-CLIO, 2018. 408p. index. (Documentary and Reference Guides series). $108.00. ISBN 13: 978-1-4408-5849-9; 978-1-4408-5850-5 (e-book).

In *Poverty in the United States: A Documentary and Reference Guide,* John R. Burch Jr. presents a far-ranging analysis of how poverty has been addressed by government. The main text of this book is broken up into seven chapters preceded by an introduction. The introduction is very helpful in providing more narrative to the documents included and analyzed. The first chapter addresses policies concerning Native American poverty throughout United States history while the remaining six chapters are roughly broken up into chronological periods and associated presidential administrations. As such, the book covers a large swath of American history. The oldest document discussed is the Quincy Report of 1821, and the newest document discussed is an Executive Order from the Trump Administration in 2017. The chapters include sections on different policies or documents. Each section has an excerpt of the document, analysis of the document, and further reading. There is also the occasional "Did You Know?" sidebar included.

Besides the table of contents and the index, there are two additional tools for discovering issues within the text. The first is the "Reader's Guide to Related Documents and Sidebars" (p. ix). As an alternative to grouping the documents by their chronological chapters, the guide groups documents by topics like "Children and Juveniles" (p. ix) and "Medical Care" (p. x). The second tool for discovery is a chronology listed at the back of the book before the index. Both of these tools not only enhance discoverability of documents within the text, but also provide a more contextual understanding of the documents beyond their chaptered chronology.

In the preface, the author highlights the recent efforts to repeal the Patient Protection and Affordable Care Act (PPACA) as a guiding principle for including documents. The author believes that the failure to repeal the PPACA represents the commitment in the United States to providing for the vulnerable throughout history. The author's inclusion of historical alongside more current documents is part of what makes this text such an interesting read. The more recent documents and trends would be particularly helpful to those interested in current policy and social issues. I would recommend this book for its usefulness in uniting these documents into a historical and topical narrative.—**Carin Graves**

Sex Studies

461. **Gale Archives of Sexuality and Gender https://www.gale.com/c/archives-of-sexuality-and-gender-lgbtq-part-iii.** [Website] Farmington Hills, Mich., Gale/Cengage Learning, 2019. Price negotiated by site. Date reviewed: 2019.

This database, available to registered users, organizes three renowned and diverse collections of materials on sex and sexuality during the 16th-20th centuries. Authoritative and fictional texts, photographs, essays, letters, and other materials, originating from many countries around the world, relate the development of sexual ideals, mores, and general knowledge about numerous sex-related topics, including adultery, sexual physiology, and homosexuality. From the homepage, users can choose to search primary sources or conduct an advanced search from the central bar. From the Explore the Collections link in the top left corner of the page, users can choose from one of the three collections sourced from the British Library, the Kinsey Institute, or the New York Academy of Medicine. Within each collection, users will find an overview with select item examples. Users can additionally scroll through a display of featured collection items and access the full collection via the View All... link at the bottom of the page. Each collection lists its contents (sortable by relevance, date, author, etc.), including information such as title, author, publication date, publication location, and number of pages. The list display can be filtered by language, document types, publication year, and a generous list of subjects. Some translation is available. Clicking on a title displays the item in a viewer alongside full and source citation information and a list of related subjects and notes (if available). Within the viewer users can jump to a specific page, use arrows to navigate, zoom in and out, and otherwise adjust the image. A general table of contents, list of illustrations, and search within option are available to the right of the viewer. Users can create public and private tags for reference within an item, save search history, bookmark, download, print, use citation tools, and employ the term frequency tool which graphs usage of terms within the archive and its collections. With this tool, users can chart the number of documents by year that include the selected terms and more. Within the New York Academy of Medicine collection, users can find over 1,500 items covering the subjects of marriage, prostitution, sexual hygiene, psychology, erotic literature, sexual disorders, and more. Items include "The Physiology of Marriage" by Honoré de Balzac and "The Four Epochs of Woman's Life: A Study in Hygiene" by Anna M. Galbraith. The Kinsey Collection contains over 1,400 items exploring sexual attitudes, behaviors, and mores against the broader topics of law, medicine, and the humanities. Users will encounter information on such topics as homosexuality, adultery, celibacy, and rape within classic literature, 18th-century trial accounts, essays, and more. The Kinsey Collection features such titles as "An Essay towards a General History of Whoring" from 1697, and "The Dictionary of Love" from 1753 which defines terms such as "matrimony," "declaration," "amorous," and "lease of love." Within the Private Case of the British Library, once highly restricted, users can explore over 2,500 items with an emphasis on erotic print books. The collection opens with an extensive overview, explaining the acquisition of many rare examples of early erotica, early homosexual erotica, and more. Select titles include "Julie, ou J'ai sauvé ma rose" from 1807, "Memoirs of Madame Madeleine, etc." from 1968 and works by the Marquis de Sade, Lord Byron, and other notables.

Together, the collections comprise an essential resource to the study of human sexuality, erotic literature, sociology, and a range of other academic fields. Highly recommended for academic libraries.—**ARBA Staff Reviewer**

Substance Abuse

462.   Issitt, Micah L. **Drug Use & Abuse.** Amenia, N.Y., Grey House Publishing, 2018. 720p. illus. index. (Opinions throughout History). $195.00. ISBN 13: 978-1-68217-724-2.

Part of the Opinions throughout History series, this title by independent scholar, historian, journalist, editor, and author Micah Issitt, provides a historical treatment of drug use and abuse, starting in the late 18th century and continuing to the present. The introduction is followed by a historical timeline that starts in antiquity and runs to 2018. The book is comprised of 28 chapters that start with "The Opium Odyssey." Like all the chapters, this one contains an introduction and list of topics covered, followed by a historical discussion, a reprinted document (in this case an 1860 letter to the editor from the *New York Times,* a conclusion, a set of discussion questions (e.g., Is opioid addiction the most important drug issue in the United States? Explain your answer), and works cited in the chapter. Other chapters cover such topics as alcohol, cannabis, the beginnings of drug rehabilitation, cocaine, Prohibition, mandatory minimum sentences for drug crimes, the impact of the rise of the Colombian drug cartels in the late 20th century, medical marijuana and the legalization of marijuana, and the new (resurgent) opioid problem. There is an overall conclusion, a section of notes, a glossary, a bibliography, and an index. The end of the book also provides a long section (nearly 75 pages) called Historical Snapshots. These start with the year 1858 and run through 2018. These history highlights are not necessarily tied to drug use and abuse. For example, one 1858 snapshot lets readers know that Minnesota became the 32d state in that year. The large font, wide margins, and generous use of black-and-white images will appeal to many readers turned off by walls of text. Recommended for school libraries.—**ARBA Staff Reviewer**

463.   Newton, David E. **The Opioid Crisis: A Reference Handbook.** Santa Barbara, Calif., ABC-CLIO, 2018. 358p. illus. index. (Contemporary World Issues). $60.00. ISBN 13: 978-1-4408-6435-3; 978-1-4408-6436-0 (e-book).

This thorough volume provides an outline of topics related to the ongoing opioid crisis. Even the first section on the history of opium, with references to ancient and medieval texts, consistently relates the information to the current situation. The first half of the book consists of three sections: a history, a discussion of potential solutions, and a set of first-person essays from individuals touched by the crisis. Each of these sections contains ample in-text citations and lengthy reference lists. The second half of the book contains four reference sections. The most notable is the Profiles section, which consists of short entries on institutions and individuals related to the opioid crisis, such as Advocates for Opioid Recovery and Hamilton Wright, who helped shape American drug laws. High school and college students would benefit from this volume, and the detailed information in the Profiles section would be useful to graduate students.—**Delilah R. Alexander**

464.   **Prescription Drug Abuse.** Bronx, N.Y., H. W. Wilson, 2017. 215p. illus. index. (The Reference Shelf, volume 89, number 5). $75.00pa. ISBN 13: 978-1-68217-454-8.

Thirty-two items—print articles and broadcast and website texts—explore aspects of the current sad situation in the United States surrounding the abuse of prescription drugs. The sections are entitled 1) Pain and Anxiety in America, 2) Drugs for Young and Old, 3) Doctors, Big Pharma and the Gateway to Abuse, 4) A Search for Solutions—Treatment, and 5) A Search for Solutions—Policy. The items range from 2 to 15 pages, and date from December 2013 to September 2017. Some of the items recount tragic individual stories of drug abuse, while others explore possible ways to conquer, or at least battle, the growing epidemic of opioid use which is killing tens of thousands of Americans each year. Articles present examples from teenage users to the elderly population.

The "Bibliography" simply relists the items cited in the introductory texts by Micah Issitt, but they could be useful references for readers exploring this topic. The "Index" only lists personal names; subject terms like ADHD, recovery, or Oxycontin/oxycodone and Percocet are not included. A minor shortcoming of volumes in the "Reference Shelf" set is that no information is provided about the authors of the pieces included. In fact, one of the items in this volume indicates nothing about its origin. All in all, however, this book brings together useful information on important aspects of this epidemic in the United States that students and interested adults (certainly parents and teachers) would benefit from reading. All sorts of libraries should consider adding this volume to their collections.—**Mark Schumacher**

17 Statistics, Demography, and Urban Studies

Demography

465. International Diaspora Engagement Alliance. http://www.diasporaalliance. org/. [Website] Free. Date reviewed: 2018.

The International Diaspora Engagement Alliance (IdEA) has brought together myriad public and private entities to collaborate on mutually beneficial social and economic relationships between emigrant communities (the diaspora) and their home regions. The website offers blog posts, several initiatives, and a large number of other resources which have helped to lay the groundwork for solidifying opportunities around the globe. A key feature of the website is the Diaspora Map which illustrates the locations of diaspora organizations around the world. Clicking on a pinned location accesses information such as contact, organization type, general description, activities, and industries. The website notes that in the future, the map will also pinpoint engagement opportunities, enhancing the value of this educational and networking tool. The Blogs tab presents a generous selection of topical posts that shine a light on IdEA concerns, such as "Women in Technology: Focus on Africa" or "Five Keys to Engaging Diaspora Millennials," in addition to reports on diaspora economic forums, workshops, investment opportunities, summits, and multiple IdEA projects such as "Migrant Stories" and "Mapping Kenyan Communities in the Diaspora." Resources are generous, and encompass various links and materials regarding Diaspora Business & Investment (e.g., "Silicon Valley's New Immigrant Entrepreneurs"), Diaspora Philanthropy and Volunteering ("Diaspora Philanthropy: The Colombia Experience"), Diaspora Diplomacy (e.g., "Engaging Diaspora Communities in the Peace Process"), and Regional & Country Studies examining numerous locations (e.g., "The Cuban Diaspora in the 21st Century"). Resources also include Research & Tools such as links to the Global Diaspora Strategies Toolkit, Migration Data Hub, and the World Bank's Migration and Remittances Factbook 2016, as well as materials (slide decks, webinars, video, etc.) related to one of IdEA's signature initiatives—Capacity Building—that works to empower diaspora organizations to their utmost potential. As of late 2016, IdEA has been incorporated into the U.S. Department of State mission and it is unclear if content on the site is maintained (the most recent blog entry is September of 2016). Nonetheless, the wealth of quality information on the site would certainly appeal to international business leaders, scholars, entrepreneurs, activists, and others.—**ARBA Staff Reviewer**

Urban Studies

466.   **America's Top-Rated Cities, 2018.** 25th ed. Amenia, N.Y., Grey House Publishing, 2018. 4v. illus. maps. index. $295.00/set. ISBN 13: 978-1-68217-760-0.

America's Top Rated Cities is "a concise, statistical, 4-volume work identifying America's top-rated cities with estimated populations of approximately 100,000 or more." It presents profiles of 100 cities that "have received high marks for business and living from prominent sources such as *Forbes, Fortune, U.S. News & World Report,* The Brookings Institution, U.S. Conference of Mayors, *The Wall Street Journal,* and CNN Money." The four volumes represent different regions of the country: Southern, Western, Central, and Eastern. Among major cities covered are Athens, Georgia; New Orleans, Louisiana; New York, New York; Charleston, South Carolina; San Antonio, Texas; Richmond, Virginia; Tulsa, Oklahoma; San Francisco, California; and Los Angeles, California. Each entry for a top-rated city includes: background, which includes history, business and economic conditions, population, climate, and neighborhoods; rankings, meaning how the city ranks in various sources (e.g., *Forbes,* Milken Institute) by business/finance, education, environmental, health/fitness, real estate, and seniors/retirement; and statistical tables representing the city's business and living environments. Maps are included of the country and regions. Appendixes are available for each regional volume and include: Comparative Statistics; Metropolitan Area Definitions; Government Type and County; Chambers of Commerce and Economic Development Organizations; and State Departments of Labor and Employment. Each city entry contains a wealth of information. Researchers learn, for example, that Orlando, Florida, was selected as one of America's best cities for food truck cuisine. Information is also included on population growth, ancestry, income, employment by industry, cost of living, health risk factors, crime rate, and air and water quality. *America's Top-Rated Cities* is an excellent source for those wanting to relocate, seek employment in another part of the country, or find a place to retire. It is also a good resource for those who just want to research a city for a possible visit or vacation. It is recommended highly to larger public and academic libraries.—**Lucy Heckman**

467.   **America's Top-Rated Smaller Cities, 2018/19: A Statistical Handbook.** 12th ed. Amenia, N.Y., Grey House Publishing, 2018. 2v. maps. $225.00/set. ISBN 13: 978-1-68217-773-0; 978-1-68217-774-7 (e-book).

The fact that this massive reference tool is now in its twelfth edition suggests its continuing value and importance despite the rise of various Internet sites and print publications attempting similar but less detailed rankings of various cities, states, and other geographical areas. Volume 1 covers Alabama to Nebraska while Volume 2 runs from Nevada through Wyoming. A total of 130 cities are included, 65 in each volume. Some 55 cities are new to this 2018-2019 edition. Background summaries introduce each city. The large format pages, packed with numbers, tables, and charts, permit the inclusion of dozens of variables for each of the cities examined. For example, Business Environment variables appear in 39 tables and 42 tables present Living Environment statistics. The cities included appear alphabetically by state and also alphabetically within states. Small cities, towns, or townships are included provided their population ranges from 25,000 to 100,000 residents.

Grey House employs a "unique rating system" (p. xxv) to rank the cities with 17 categories based primarily on population growth, income, housing affordability, crime rate, educational attainment, and unemployment. Statistics have been culled from 257 books, articles, and research reports and range from the Cleanest Metro Areas to the Recreational Marijuana Tax to the Fittest Cities. Also included in these volumes are a list of 100 "Honorable Mention Cities," five color maps showing city locations, and five appendixes with 77 tables comparing cities plus definitions of metropolitan areas and contact information for State Departments of Labor and the relevant Chambers of Commerce.

Some users will need a magnifying glass to view all of the dense statistical data, but careful readers ranging from business executives and real estate developers to retirees seeking new homes and job seekers of all ages will find the search rewarding. This set is an essential purchase for all but the smallest public and academic libraries as well as business collections in special libraries.—**Julienne L. Wood**

468.   **The Comparative Guide to American Suburbs, 2017-2018.** 9th ed. Amenia, N.Y., Grey House Publishing, 2017. 2283p. index. $210.00/set. ISBN 13: 978-1-61925-372-5; 978-1-61925-373-2 (e-book).

The 9th edition of *The Comparative Guide to American Suburbs* covers 3,131 suburban communities in the 80 largest metro areas with populations of 10,000 or more. This reference source is arranged alphabetically by metro area and "pulls together the most current statistics and demographic information available to create consolidated, comprehensive profiles of suburban communities, plus Comparative Statistics and Rankings that are not available elsewhere." Each metro area section contains maps of Core Based Statistical Areas (CBSAs) and Counties and a map of the metro area. Each metro area contains a list of divisions and counties included in the CBSA, weather statistics (high and low temperatures, precipitation data for each month), demographics, income, educational attainment, housing, religion, health insurance, and Air Quality Index (AQI). Each metro area suburb contains information on land area, demographics, history, economic indicators, employment by occupation, educational attainment, housing (e.g., average mortgage cost, rental costs), health insurance, and transportation. For instance, the entry for Cortlandt, New York, provides facts and figures including that it is the site of the Bear Mountain Bridge Road and Toll House and of the Old Croton Dam, both of which are listed on the National Register of Historic places. The entry also lists city property taxes per capita, home ownership rate, and how many residents have private health insurance. Each metro area section also includes rankings lists by land area, water area, elevation, population growth 2000-2015, population density, population by race and ethnic group, median age, ancestry, marital status, veterans, individuals with disabilities, unemployment rate, homeowner vacancy rate, occupation, household income, home value, and means of transportation to work. Additionally national rankings, which rank all 3,131 suburbs, are included for population, marital status, ethnic background, average household size, ancestry, city property taxes, education, and other variables. For instance, in the national rankings it can be determined that Hillsborough, California, has the largest median home value. The Metropolitan Area rankings section ranks all 80 metro areas by topics including race and ethnicity, median age, income, air quality, and health insurance coverage. Two indexes are provided: "Metropolitan Area Index" and "Suburb Index." Sources of the data include the American Community Survey; the U.S Census 2010; and the U.S. Census

Bureau: State and Local Government Finances. *The Comparative Guide to American Suburbs* provides a wealth of data on United States metro areas and suburbs. It provides quick reference material and is a starting point to further research. Highly recommended to larger public, research, and academic libraries.—**Lucy Heckman**

469.   **World Cities Culture Report http://www.worldcitiescultureforum.com/assets/ others/181108_SCRR_2018_low_res.pdf.** [Website] Free. Date reviewed: 2019.

The World Cities Culture Report is the result of collaboration between 35 cities around the world working to promote a discussion of culture as a key force in successful urban policy. The report details the importance of culture to a city's ability to thrive and considers positive and negative aspects of a city's cultural profile. Brightly colored pages with an abundance of appealing photographs guide readers through the roughly 150-page report, which profiles both long established and rapidly advancing cultural centers around the globe: Austin, Sydney, Cape Town, Buenos Aires, Los Angeles, Amsterdam, Vienna, Lagos, Singapore, and others. Introductory pages offer Report Headlines with a bullet point summation of cultural policy and where it fits in contemporary society. A list of Featured Innovative Programmes draws highlights from various countries working within a variety of cultural missions such as cultural access and inclusion, cultural diversity and representation, and culture and climate change. The bulk of the report presents 35 City Profiles, each opening with an essay that briefly describes a city's cultural history and innovations alongside its own unique challenges. Following the essay, users can find information on each city's innovative programmes, cultural infrastructure, and trends. Live and open source data rounds out the profile. The profile on the city of Amsterdam, for example, examines the need for cultural expansion beyond its crowded city center, as well as enhanced cultural options that appeal to an aging population. Information on several programs set to address these and other issues follows. Trends for Amsterdam, for example, show the city adding more artist work and display space; renovating and adding museums, libraries and other cultural centers; and other actions. Cultural Infrastructure lists a city's highlights relating to its improved spaces open to culture such as parks, theatres, and museums. Data covers 5 categories: people & talent, cultural and natural heritage, performing arts, film & games, and vitality. Icons and numbers provide an easy reference for such points as the percentage of green space and the quantities of international tourists per year, museums, bars, and festivals/celebrations. Categories may vary depending on each city.—**ARBA Staff Reviewer**

18 Women's Studies

Biography

470. **The New Biographical Dictionary of Scottish Women.** Elizabeth Ewan, Rose Pipes, Jane Rendall, and Siân Reynolds, eds. Edinburgh, Edinburgh University Press, 2018. 448p. index. $54.95. ISBN 13: 978-1-4744-3628-1; 978-1-4744-3630-4 (e-book).

This edition adds 181 entries to the original 825 entries in the 2006 1st edition (see ARBA 2007, entry 388). In the front matter, users will find a preface to the current edition, a readers' guide, and the original introduction. Read together, they provide notes on nomenclature, the system of alphabetization, the use of bold type within entries to indicate co-subjects (sisters, colleagues, partners, etc.), the use of an asterisk before a person's name to indicate a cross-reference, the rationale for inclusion (no living women are featured), the length of entries, and the reason for the book. The front matter also contains a list of advisers and contributors and their affiliations, a list of new entries, and a list of abbreviations used. There are also 60 black-and-white plates featuring some of the women in the dictionary. These are presented alphabetically. Entries are signed with the author's initials (provided in the list of contributors) and include a source note. They vary in length from one to several paragraphs. The entry for someone as important as Mary, Queen of Scots, comprises approximately 2 pages. The system of co-subjects and cross-references allows users to trace connections between women in the dictionary. There are also *see* references (e.g., Lady Macbeth, *see* Gruoch, Queen of Scotland). A thematic index rounds out the work and provides another avenue for navigation. Highly recommended to academic libraries.—**ARBA Staff Reviewer**

Dictionaries and Encyclopedias

471. Sankey, Margaret D. **Women and War in the 21st Century: A Country-by-Country Guide.** Santa Barbara, Calif., ABC-CLIO, 2018. 322p. index. $61.00. ISBN 13: 978-1-4408-5765-2; 978-1-4408-5766-9 (e-book).

Though it does not bill itself so, *Woman and War in the 21st Century: A Country-by-Country Guide* reads like an encyclopedia that is simply arranged geographically. The title focuses on the 21st century, but the included chronology begins with 1791—the date of Olympe de Gouges' "Declaration of the Rights of Women and the Female Citizen" (written in response to the French Revolutionary publication "Declaration of the Rights of Man and Citizen"). This starting point appears intended to demonstrate the history of women in the military and war prior to the start of the 21st century. It highlights significant incidents like the discovery of Nadezhda Durova serving in the Russian Army in the guise of male clothing; Durova was subsequently rewarded by Czar Alexander I and was allowed to continue to serve. The title also provides a regional guide to the entries. The entries themselves follow a similar pattern: background; specific wars; and the integration of women into war in the 21st century. Some entries contain inserts which contain information such as war memorials, events (like protests), or other special topics (like contractors). The length of the entries varies from two pages to five or more. Every entry contains a list of "further reading" resources. The entries are well written and well organized. They provide historical contexts for women in war in the 21st century and offer adequate overviews of pertinent topics. There is a smattering of pictures throughout; the title would have been served by the inclusion of more images. A more consistent application of the sections would have been appreciated as well—some entries only contain background and the integration of women into war in the 21st century without really commenting on specific wars or events. Some entries are particularly robust while others are almost skeletal (the entry on Great Britain is nine pages long; the entry on Egypt is just a little over two pages long). One wonders if the author could not have provided more sociocultural context for the lack of participation during specific wars or events in the histories of the countries that have such short entries. Other than this concern regarding the imbalance between content for the entries, the title is otherwise a good resource. It provides a good overview of the topic of women in war and the military. While not necessarily ideal for the in-depth researcher, the title provides a good introduction to the topic and is recommended for public, school, and academic libraries.—**Megan W. Lowe**

Digital Resources

472.　**Bibliographies in Gender and Women's Studies https://www.library.wisc.edu/ gwslibrarian/bibliographies.** [Website] Free. Date reviewed: 2019.

This site hosts a curated collection of 80 bibliographies covering a range of subjects under the Gender and Women's Studies umbrella. The collection spans 23 years from 1977 through 2000, with several new bibliographies dealing with current topics in progress. Users can scroll down through a list of the bibliographies with those in progress listed first. The list includes name/subject of the bibliographies, creator of the bibliography, and the year created. Some bibliographies will link to the full digital version. Bibliographies with links include "Management, Gender, Race"; "Gender and Creative Writing: A Bibliography"; "Sterilization of Puerto Rican Women: A Selected, Partially Annotated Bibliography"; "Brave, Active, Resourceful Females in Picture Books"; and many others. Those that do not link include several from the 1980s: "Racism and Homophobia: Readings to Raise Awareness"; "Asian Women in America: A Bibliography"; "Goddesses and Goddess Worship: A Selected Reading List"; and others. Many of the unlinked bibliographies may be requested from the University of Wisconsin, Madison, Gender and Women's Studies librarian. Some of the online bibliographies offer good background information in addition to their suggested readings. With its wide selection of topics, this website would be an excellent starting point for a range of women's studies and gender research.—**ARBA Staff Reviewer**

473.   **Gender: Identity and Social Change.** https://www.amdigital.co.uk/primary-sources/gender-identity-and-social-change. [Website] Chicago, Adam Matthew Digital, 2018. Price negotiated by site. Date reviewed: 2018.

Gender: Identity and Social Change provides researchers with a curated collection of primary documents (19th century-present) from participating libraries and archives in the United States, Canada, the United Kingdom, and Australia. The database is searchable from the homepage via a series of tabs (Introduction, Documents, Explore, Image Gallery, and Help). The database organizes documents into 13 thematic areas: Women's Suffrage, Feminism, The Men's Movement, Education and Training, Employment and Labour, The Body, Conduct and Politeness, Domesticity and the Family, Government and Politics, Legislation and Legal Cases, Leisure and Entertainment, Organisations, Associations, and Societies, and Sex and Sexuality. Documents can be accessed by library or by type. Users can also click on a thumbnail image associated with each thematic area or click on the "List View" tab. Information associated with documents includes, among other things, the name of the library/archive, collection name, and collection overview, date of creation, document type, and a description. Users can print, download, or "add [article] to my archive." Documents are searchable; the database utilizes Handwritten Text Recognition, which makes it possible and quite easy to search handwritten materials. Documents also feature citation/export tools. Other features of the database include an Image Gallery that allows searches of all images or images by theme and a chronology (1803-2016) that cross-references to documents. Under the Explore tab users will find a variety of materials, such as video interviews with three of the scholars behind the selection of the documents, highlighted biographies, featured organizations, and a series of essays highlighting the document collections (e.g., "Sex, class and gender in Victorian Society: the Case of Arthur Munby" and "Late Twentieth Century Feminist Movements in the United States: Women's Bodies in Contention."). Highly recommended for academic libraries.—**ARBA Staff Reviewer**

Handbooks and Yearbooks

474.   **Defining Documents in World History: Women's Rights.** Michael Shally-Jensen, ed. Hackensack, N.J., Salem Press, 2017. 2v. index. $295.00/set. ISBN 13: 978-1-68217-583-5.

This two-volume set contains 63 articles focused on particular primary sources related to women's history, particularly women's struggles for suffrage and equality. There are four sections in the two volumes. Precursors, section 1, starts with a 15th-century letter from Joan of Arc to the King of England. Among the remaining 6 articles in this section, are Abigail Adams's famous "Remember the Ladies" letter to her husband. There are 24 articles in Suffrage and Sensibility, part 2. Here users will find documents from Elizabeth Cady Stanton, Victoria Woodhull, Sojourner Truth, Eleanor Roosevelt, Margaret Sanger, and Emma Goldman. Part 3, Equality Now!, offers documents by Betty Friedan, Simone de Beauvoir, and Gloria Steinem, the founding statement of the National Organization of Women, and the text of Title IX and *Roe v. Wade*. The 12 articles in the last part, The Personal Is Political, include Anita Hill's opening statement at the Senate confirmation hearing of Clarence Thomas and Ruth Bader Ginsburg's concurrence in *Stenberg, Attorney General of Nebraska, v. Carhart*. As with all the other titles in the Defining Documents series, the articles in this title include a summary overview, an explanation of the defining moment, an author biography, document analysis, and essential themes. A variety of documents are analyzed—pamphlets, essays, a constitutional amendment, letters, speeches, court decisions, court decisions, and book excerpts. Well-placed illustrations supplement the material, and each article includes a bibliography and suggestions for further reading. Appendixes include a document timeline, web resources, a bibliography, and an index. These volumes will help students learn how to closely read primary sources. It is important to note that, despite the title, this set is largely focused on American women's history.—**ARBA Staff Reviewer**

475. Hanold, Maylon. **Women in Sports: A Reference Handbook.** Santa Barbara, Calif., ABC-CLIO, 2018. 324p. illus. index. (Contemporary World Issues series). $60.00. ISBN 13: 978-1-4408-5369-2; 978-1-4408-5370-8 (e-book).

Women in Sports discusses the issues and history of the female athlete. There are 7 chapters, and each one highlights different aspects of this topic. The first chapter presents a brief overview and history of women in sports. There are 12 subtopics within chapter 1 that include: women's bodies, early history of clothing/sportswear for women, Title IX and collegiate sport leadership, extreme sports, and symbolic moments. The second chapter includes issues and controversies readers may have heard about in the media. Eleven subtopics examine gender equality, sex-segregated sports, the experiences of black female athletes, and women in sports media. Chapter 3 includes essays discussing various viewpoints surrounding collegiate athletics, the complex relationship female athletes have had with their bodies, and transgender athletes. A collection of brief biographies of women athletes is included in chapter 4. Chapter 5 is a collection of statistical data. There are 12 tables/figures which provide participation numbers of high school athletes by gender, methods of compensation in women's sports, and mainstream media coverage in women's sports. Reference lists of sources are included at the end of most entries. Chapter 6 provides resources (books, articles, reports, web resources) on such topics as eating disorders, LGBT advocacy, and Title IX. A timeline/chronology (1866-2017) of various significant events/controversies pertaining to women in sports rounds out chapter 7. The book includes a specialized, gender-based glossary.

Women in Sports is relevant for middle school and high school researchers who are writing an argumentative or critical analysis type of paper on any of these issues within the broader context of women in sports.—**Amy B. Parsons**

476. **Misogyny in American Culture: Causes, Trends, and Solutions.** Guglielmo, Letiza, ed. Santa Barbara, Calif., ABC-CLIO, 2018. 2v. illus. index. $198.00/set. ISBN 13: 978-1-4408-5381-4; 978-1-4408-5382-1 (e-book).

The recent increase in the occurrence of misogynistic words and actions, across all aspects of society, is the inspiration for this collection of 23 essays by various authors. Each essay examines a particular area or aspect of the widespread and prolific incidents, including such topics as the arts, advertising, education, employment and workplace, health and medicine, the justice system, the military, politics and public policy, and the media. An introduction gives an overview of the history of misogynistic attitudes and explains how the current political environment has caused an increase in incidents. Each essay offers a history of a topic as it relates to the treatment of women, the current societal and political trends, the responses to the situations, the lasting impacts that result, and a conclusion.

Brief, but thorough, bibliographies complete each essay. A chronology of significant events (ranging from 1607 to 2017), a list of organizations with contact information, a general bibliography, information about the editor and contributors, and an index complete the second volume. The extensive information contained in the essays is thorough and logical. Some black-and-white illustrations and sidebars enhance the presentation. This collection would be an excellent start for further research or as a quick overview.—**Martha Lawler**

Part III
HUMANITIES

19 Humanities in General

General Works

Digital Resources

477. Carolina Digital Humanities: Digital Innovation Lab https://cdh.unc.edu/. [Website] Free. Date reviewed: 2019.

Carolina Digital Humanities demonstrates how digital technologies help expand educational potential beyond traditional classroom learning by showcasing a number of digital research projects alongside a suite of tools and resources with which to facilitate and enhance digital scholarship. Under the Resources tab users can select the Tools link and scroll through a list of products that include Multi-use Toolkits, Collaboration Tools, Web Publishing, Data Visualization Tools, Timeline and Mapping Tools, and more. Users can read through descriptions to find the right resources for navigating, managing, and showcasing information through maps, manuscripts, visualizations, and other multimedia platforms. Users can find information on the Omeka web publishing platform, the Word Press blogging platform, Tableau Public for data visualization, Chronos Timeline, and the foremost UNC data visualization toolkit, Prospect. A gallery of thirty-three diverse examples of these tools at work can be found under the Projects tab. Several projects highlight regional studies (e.g., "Digital Feminists of Carolina," "Documenting the American South," "Main Street Carolina"), while others expand scholarship into broader topics ("Exploring Celtic Civilization," "Living with Oil in Ecuador," "Nancy Drew Digital Project," and others). Further information may be found for some, but not all projects, by clicking on its title. There may also be links to a project's webpage, although it is not clear if all projects have launched or continue to operate. While offering a helpful description of the various digital resources available today, the addition of more active project examples could inspire scholars from the range of humanities disciplines.—**ARBA Staff Reviewer**

478. Dictionary of Digital Humanities http://medium.com/dictionary-of-digital-humanities. [Website] Free. Date reviewed: 2019.

The Dictionary of Digital Humanities is a collection of vocabulary borne out of and affiliated with digital culture. Users can scroll through the simple and straightforward page for entry samples or choose from an alphabet grouping to find entries or posts in a particular range. These entries—currently numbered at 183—display the term or phrase in bold lettering with a brief definition following. The name and avatar of the entry contributor also appears, alongside the posting date. Users can bookmark the entry and "like" it. Some of the terms may be recognizable across nondigital disciplines (Mass Communication, McGuffin, Nerd, Cyborg, etc.), while others seem to strictly relate to contemporary digital culture (Meme, Wandalism, Doxing, etc.). Entries may be cross-referenced (*see* Android, Droid, Automaton for Robot) and may include links to sources or to further information. While information is basic, the dictionary can be a useful tool for educators and students.—**ARBA Staff Reviewer**

479. **Digital Scholar Lab. https://www.gale.com/primary-sources/digital-scholar-lab.** Farmington Hills, Mich., Gale/Cengage Learning, 2018. Price negotiated by site. Date reviewed: 2018.

The new Digital Scholar Lab from Gale/Cengage provides students and researchers with a powerful toolkit for conducting digital humanities scholarship. The Digital Scholar Lab utilizes a few of the most popular digital humanities tools to allow analysis of the raw data in Gale's primary source collections (e.g., Archives of Sexuality & Gender, Associated Press Collections, Nineteenth Century Collections, The Telegraph Historical Archive, and many more). Using the Digital Scholar Lab, students and researchers first create a corpus of documents. Gale's Optical Character Recognition feature allows users to quickly preview the documents as they consider which ones to include. The next step is to analyze content sets using textual analysis tools to create graphs, charts, and other visualizations. The Digital Scholar Lab also offers creators ways to manage and share their outputs while retaining all intellectual property rights. The Digital Scholar Lab operates in a Cloud-based research environment, which provides libraries with valuable savings, but, maybe more importantly, the Digital Scholar Lab will encourage students and scholars to use library resources to complete projects. It is hard not to be excited about the possibilities opened up by digital humanities generally and by the Digital Scholar Lab in particular. The appeal to graduate students and scholars is obvious, but the Digital Scholar Lab also has the potential to make in-depth research accessible to undergraduates. Highly recommended for academic libraries.—**ARBA Staff Reviewer**

480. **Saturday Evening Post https://www.saturdayeveningpost.com/.** [Website] $15.00 (annual subscription). Date reviewed: 2019.

The venerable *Saturday Evening Post* began publishing over two hundred years ago, bringing a distinctively American eye to issues and events of the day. Famous for its cover illustrations, the magazine continues to weigh in on a diverse selection of newsworthy stories and to entertain readers via literary and humor features. Visitors to the website can get an introductory look at both current and archived issues, but those who pay a $15.00/year subscription fee will have full access to decades of distinct content. Materials are well organized and accessible via the tabs at the top of the homepage. Articles, Fiction, Humor, and Art each contain numerous essays, articles, and galleries, each tagged topically—history, music, culture, food, cartoon collections, economy, American life, and more—for easy reference. The real gem of the site is, of course, its extensive archive of full issues and cover art. Under the Archive tab, users can find thumbnail images of dated issues, with full access granted to paid subscribers. The online archive goes back to 1821. Users can Browse by Year via the bar. Underneath the Art tab, users can find a number of resources, including bright replications of the *Saturday Evening Post's* renowned cover art. Users can scroll through Cover Collections, curated by themes such as "Back to School," "Bad Neighbors," "Happy New Year," and others. Some collections are available to all users, while some require subscription. Cover images are full-color, sized to page, and accompanied by publishing date, title, and name of artist. Users can additionally Browse Cover Art by artist, year, or theme, with access to thumbnail images, date, and artist. Again, full issue access is available to subscribers. Scrolling further through the Art category, users can find brief biographical essays on cover artists including J.C. Leyendecker, Stevan Dohanos, and the inimitable Norman Rockwell. Art Articles are found at the bottom of this section as well. While the website certainly offers a good browsing experience to casual users, it may be worth the small subscription fee to access the entire archive as it is steeped in the evolving narrative of the American experience. Librarians should inquire about institutional subscription pricing.—**ARBA Staff Reviewer**

481.   **Story Maps and the Digital Humanities https://www.esri.com/arcgis-blog/ products/story-maps/sharing-collaboration/story-maps-and-the-digital-humanities/.** [Website] Free. Date reviewed: 2019.

This site offers a showcase of digital storytelling projects—Story Maps—covering a range of styles and topics that blend innovative digital resources with compelling research in the humanities. Visitors to the Story Maps site can scroll through a gallery of eighty diverse projects that feature creative use of digital artifacts, text, photographs, mapping, and more. Together, the projects emphasize the boundless possibilities of digital research and presentation, spanning place and time to explore topics such as the Battle of Agincourt, the Slave Trade, Ernest Hemingway, Texas Cattle Trails, Punk Rock, Copernicus, and other subjects. Projects in the gallery are identified by title, creator, and related image. Users click the title for access. Projects can expand one's view of a familiar topic, such as "The Life and Words of Dr. Martin Luther King, Jr." or "Presidential Birthplaces," which adds geographic context to an American president's story. Projects can also open eyes to lesser-known figures and events in history, such as "Keeng Kumu: Indigenous Cartographer" or "Mary Edwards Walker," who battled convention in the U.S. Civil War as the first female field surgeon and Medal of Honor recipient. Through text, photographs, and mapping imagery, users can trace Walker's journey from an upstate New York medical school to the gruesome battlefields and prisons behind the front lines. Projects also capture the efficiency and style of digital research and presentation. "The American Experience in 737 Novels" pins examples of classic American literature to their distinct American setting. Users can select a location on the national map to display a gallery of related novels. Clicking on the novel enlarges the book cover and presents author, publishing date, story setting, and a brief descriptive paragraph. "Very Large Art" finds art in unusual and far-flung places: central Turkey, the Nevada desert, the Andean foothills, and more, bringing large scale and difficult to access art across miles and centuries to reach an online audience. Users can explore Ancient, Land, Low, Garden, Airport, and Farm Art by selecting the related tab, or scroll through the entire exhibit. Users can alternatively scroll through the entire gallery to access a global map pinned at locations featured in the Story Maps projects. Story Maps is enjoyable to explore as it educates within an expansive humanities domain and demonstrates the many new ways in which knowledge can be expressed and shared.—**ARBA Staff Reviewer**

Handbooks and Yearbooks

482.   **The Bloomsbury Handbook of Literary and Cultural Theory.** Jeffrey R. Di Leo, ed. New York, Bloomsbury Academic, 2019. 784p. index. (Bloomsbury Handbooks in Literary Studies). $176.00. ISBN 13: 978-1-3500-1280-6; 978-1-3500-1281-3 (e-book).

This volume contains 27 extensive and scholarly chapters on various topics and aspects of literary and cultural theory. Essays are on topics such as early theory, narrative and narratology, historicisms, rhetoric, feminism, postmodernism, ecocriticism, biopower and biopolitics, translation, digital humanities, identity studies, university studies, and antitheory, to name but a few. In addition, over 300 terms and figures are provided to complement the essays which are much more subjective in their construction and openly reveal the opinions and concerns of their authors. A name and subject index provide comprehensive cross-listing and referencing. This book is an essential reference work on current thought and opinion on this topic, and both faculty and students of cultural and literary theory will enjoy perusal and deep exploration of its contents.—**Bradford Lee Eden**

20 Communication and Mass Media

General Works

Dictionaries and Encyclopedias

483. Caradec, François (translated by Chris Clarke). Illustrated by Philippe Cousin. **Dictionary of Gestures: Expressive Comportments and Movements in Use around the World.** Cambridge, Mass., MIT Press, 2018. 324p. illus. index. $24.95. ISBN 13: 978-0-262-03849-2.

This delightful dictionary of international gestures is a translation from the original, published in French as *Dictionnaire des gestes* (Librarie Artheme Fayard, 2005). Inside, users will find approximately 850 gestures divided into 37 sections grouped by head, hand, feet, lips, and other body parts; gestures are accompanied by descriptive sketches and meanings. Though the dictionary includes gestures used in the Western, Eastern, and Mediterranean world, it is not intended to be comprehensive. The information provided varies from entry to entry, but none are more than a few lines. In "The Head" users will learn that if a woman in Spain pulls a strand of her hair between thumb and index finger, it can signify deception or frustration. In Turkey, tapping one's ear with a finger means something similar to "knock on wood" in the United States. Rubbing the forehead with a closed fist can mean "he's crazy" to a Native American, and in North Africa placing an index finger below a lower eyelid and pulling down can mean "watch it." Not surprisingly the largest number of gestures corresponds to the hands. Recommended for public libraries.—**ARBA Staff Reviewer**

484. **Emoji Dictionary. https://emojidictionary.emojifoundation.com/.** [Website] Free. Date reviewed: 2018.

This site gathers information from users to help define and contextualize the growing language of emojis, or pictorial symbols of objects, people, and more. As it is crowdsourced, however, it is important to note that some information may not be totally reliable. Users can search the Emoji Dictionary via the bar at the top of the homepage, or select from a display of Top Emoji (e.g., Love Letter, Smiling Face with Heart Eyes, etc.) or a display of seven general categories: People & Smileys, Animals & Nature, Objects, Food, Places & Travel, and Flags and Symbols. Selecting an emoji provides its associated parts of speech, definition, and example of usage. While these categories may result in generous contextual information for each emoji, it is important to note that the information may not be complete or properly vetted. For example, the U.S. flag emoji, while tagged with terms like "American Flag," "red, white, and blue," "freedom," and "America," is also tagged with phrases such as "fluffy," "it is cool," "fun," and others of questionable intent. It is also important to note that information may not be complete, as users have not contributed entries under definitions or parts of speech for all emojis. While the Emoji Dictionary would not be the definitive source for information on emojis, it could nevertheless offer perspective on the cultural phenomenon that is changing the way people communicate.—**ARBA Staff Reviewer**

485.   **Emojipedia. www.emojipedia.org.** [Website] Free. Date reviewed: 2018.

Emojis—a pictorial symbol of objects, feelings, and more—are fast becoming the new global language of electronic communication. This website defines each symbol and provides further contextual information. Users can conduct a search from the central bar or select from one of the eight general emoji categories located on the left side of the homepage. Categories include Smileys & People, Animals & Nature, Food & Drink, Activity, Travel & Places, and Objects, Symbols, and Flags. Smileys, by the way, capture a wide range of human emotions, including star struck, confused, fearful, sleepy, angry, and expressionless, among others. Users can then select from a listing which matches the emoji symbol with its name and serves as a link to the emoji's more complete definition. This page is particularly helpful as emojis—in common use since around 2010—may not represent traditional meanings (although many do). For example, an emoji defined as "sweat droplets" may also be used to represent splashing water, etc. Definitions are also helpful due to the many graphic similarities between the typically tiny images. For each emoji, users can scroll through a display of its appearance in different operating systems (Microsoft, Google, Apple, etc.). There may also be source information for each emoji, along with other contextual information. Other features on the homepage include a listing of the Most Popular emojis and links to the Latest News in the world of emojis. While certainly whimsical, emojis are an undeniably popular mode of communication. This website is simple to use and valuable resource in understanding the development and use of the emoji.—**ARBA Staff Reviewer**

486.   **The Oxford Encyclopedia of Intergroup Communication.** Howard Giles and Jake Harwood, eds. New York, Oxford University Press, 2018. 2v. index. $295.00/set. ISBN 13: 978-0-1904-5452-4.

This two-volume set is designed for academic use (undergrads, graduate students, and researchers). Though available as a print title, the book is part of the larger *Oxford Research Encyclopedia of Communication,* a digital resource. The print edition of this work focuses on how communication processes are influenced by groups and how human communication processes influence groups. It starts with a list of articles and a topical outline of articles. The dozens of entries vary in length, but all are substantial and at least ten pages; all include suggestions for further reading and references. The entries are international in scope and cover a wide range of topics, such as Apprehension and Anxiety in Crisis Communication, Dress Style Code and Fashion, Identity and Online Groups, Jokes and Humor in Intergroup Relations, Music and Intergroup Communication, Migrants and Migrant Workers, Political Correctness, and so much more. The book's editors are both communication professors at the University of California, Santa Barbara, and all (signed) entries are authored by academic contributors. There is sparing use of tables and figures. An extensive index (nearly sixty pages) concludes the work. The page numbers of major entries appear in bold type and "f" and "t" indicate if a term refers to a table or figure. This is a recommended purchase for academic libraries in print or as part of the larger Oxford Research Encyclopedias collection.—**ARBA Staff Reviewer**

Digital Resources

487. **Alt-Press Watch https://www.proquest.com/products-services/alt_presswatch. html.** [Website] New York, Proquest, Price negotiated by site. Date reviewed: 2019.

Alt-Press Watch gives researchers access to views from more than 230 independent newspapers, magazines, and journals from *The Advocate* in Los Angeles to the *Memphis Flyer* to the *Texas Journal on Civil Liberties & Civil Rights* in Austin. The database of more than 670,000 articles is easy to navigate by using the basic search, advanced search, or search by publication features. Users can filter results by language, date of publication, source type, document type, and whether the database includes the full text of the article. There are options to cite (according to many different style guidelines), email, save, or print once an article is selected. Content is current. A basic search for "border wall funding," for example, produced results from early 2019 as did an advanced search for family separation at the border. Recommended.—**ARBA Staff Reviewer**

488. **Facebook/Instagram Ad Archive https://www.facebook.com/ads/archive/? active_status=all&ad_type=political_and_issue_ads&country=US.** [Website] Free. Date reviewed: 2018.

This page allows users to track information related to political and national issues advertisements that have appeared on social media sites Facebook and Instagram. Users can find weekly summary reports with information on advertisers and the people and issues driving the ads. Users can view archives extending back to May of 2018 for the United States, United Kingdom, or Brazil. Users can conduct a general search from the bar at the center of the homepage or go to the Ad Archive Report link. On this page users can select a week (e.g., December 2 through December 8) from the upper right corner. Alternatively, users can scroll through the page to view the well-organized data results. The Overview summarizes the Number of Ads placed and the Amount Spent on both platforms since May 2018. Spending by Advertisers shows page name, disclaimer (advertiser and other information), amount spent and number of ads in archive. The table reflects the largest spenders of the selected time period, but users can download a PDF report of the full six and half months of the archive if desired. Weekly Spending shows most current results with the same table by advertiser listed from highest spender to lowest. Search Terms display the five most popular terms of the selected week (for the week of December 2 through December 8—they were Trump, Elizabeth Warren, Kamala Harris, Beto O' Rourke, and Cory Booker). Users can click on a term to find the related ad gallery, which can be filtered by country, type of ad, or ad status (whether it is still active). Users can click on the particular Page Name to display a gallery of its launched ads. For each ad, users can learn its status, advertiser, running date, and Ad Performance, which tracks number of impressions, money spent, and estimated audience by gender, age, and location. The site is a good way to gauge the interest in national issues, view sources of advertising, and more.—**ARBA Staff Reviewer**

489.   **Is This True? A Fake News Database https://www.politico.com/interactives/ 2018/is-this-true/.** [Website] Free. Date reviewed: 2019.

This relatively new web page from Politico examines disinformation in media; it gathers news reports, social media posts, websites, and other sources related to the "fake news" phenomenon. The site is still under development, and users are invited to submit instances of "fake news" to be included in the growing database (alongside Politico staff-vetted examples). These "fake news" incidents are classified into three categories. A Hoax is an entirely false report or claim, while an Impostor relates to a website or social media user that takes on a false identity or pretends to be a reliable source of information. The Doctored category encompasses images that have been intentionally manipulated. Users can Search from the bar or Quick Search using a selection of terms familiar from the news, including (as of this review) "Donald Trump," "White House," "Congress" and each classification mentioned above. Users can then scroll down through the affiliated examples. Under the Hoax category, for example, users see the disseminated image alongside its primary source (e.g. Facebook, Twitter) and a link to a brief descriptive paragraph. Descriptions may note number of times the false image has been shared (although it is not clear if the shares are limited to one platform). As it develops, this site will likely become a valuable reference for teachers and students.—**ARBA Staff Reviewer**

Directories

490.   **Hudson's Washington News Media Contacts Guide.** 51st ed. Amenia, N.Y., Grey House Publishing, 2018. 250p. index. $289.00pa. ISBN 13: 978-1-68217-754-9.

Despite the vast amount of information online, direct contact to media outlets can still be difficult to discover. *Hudson's Washington News Media Contacts Guide* provides this information in a compact guidebook that lets journalists and researchers know points of contact in the greatest concentration of media professionals in the world. This guide provides information for a variety of media outlets including major news services, newspapers, magazines, syndicates, TV, radio stations, and periodicals. This 51st edition is easy to navigate and has over 4,000 key media contacts. The table of contents and media guide help steer users through 6 categories and 20 subcategories. The sections range from contacts in photo services and columnists to city wires and foreign news. There are a variety of detailed indexes based on name, geography, personnel, and subject. Key telephone numbers are included for governmental contacts, as well as for important contacts at the National Press Club. Entries include information like emails, addresses, and telephone numbers. Depending on the outlet, the guide lists various staff by department so users can pinpoint the contact they need immediately. *Hudson's Washington News Media Contacts Guide* continues to be a valuable resource and is recommended as a reference guide for press offices, media professionals, government officials, and academic libraries in and around the metro D.C. area.—**Jessica Crossfield McIntosh**

Handbooks and Yearbooks

491.   **Careers in Social Media.** Hackensack, N.J., Salem Press, 2017. 324p. illus. index. $125.00. ISBN 13: 978-1-68217-666-5.

Careers in Social Media provides timely information that assists career decision making in an easy-to-read format that serves novice as well as experienced learners. Chapters include information on journalists, advertisers, marketing managers, software developers, copyrighters, writers, photographers, and more. Social media career pathways are fluid, continue to transition, and integrate into other field destinations. Chapters identify skills that have application across occupations. Brief descriptions transcend the factual into vivid explorations that include: sphere of work, work environment, daily responsibilities, education, training, advancement, and employment outlook, etc. Within chapters, "Conversations With" and "Conversations About" highlight professionals who communicate insight regarding their work experiences. Black-and-white photographs, creative design layouts, easy-to-read fonts, charts, tables, and bullet formatting peak interest and hook readers. The Guide to Holland Code (at the back of the book) helps readers discover if a particular career path is a match for their personality. The book includes a collection of suggested readings and lists transferable skills and abilities. Additionally, the subject Index assists readers in their examination of concepts, technologies, terms, and specific occupations.—**Thomas E. Baker**

492.　**Representative American Speeches 2016-2017.** Bronx, N.Y., H. W. Wilson, 2017. 197p. illus. index. (The Reference Shelf, volume 89, number 6). $75.00pa. ISBN 13: 978-1-68217-456-2.

As with other volumes in this set, these thirty-two speeches have been topically grouped into six categories: "To the Graduating Class," "Making America Great Again," "The Year in Review," "Resistance and Persistence 2017," "Free Speech on Campus," and "DREAMers and DACA." Among the speakers are Donald Trump (three speeches), Barack Obama (two speeches), several senators in a variety of settings, and figures such as Angela Davis, Mark Zuckerberg, and conservative commentator Ben Shapiro. There is a presidential inauguration speech, a farewell speech, a commencement speech, and many others on diverse political, economic, and sociolegal subjects. The selection of speeches offers a wide range of perspectives on issues important to American readers, such as immigration, health care, and climate change.

As in other titles in this series, the "Index" is curiously only proper names, featuring Donald Trump thirty-four times and thirteen names of comedians mentioned in a single paragraph of Will Ferrell's address. Phil Hartman is included but the Syrian president is not listed. There are no subject terms, such as immigration, health care, women's rights, and so on, which would certainly benefit readers as they read this book. That said, this remains a useful group of speeches which paints a picture of the events and issues in the United States in 2017. Public, academic, and probably school libraries should consider it for their collections.—**Mark Schumacher**

493.　Smith, Stephanie A. **Careers in Media & Communication.** Thousand Oaks, Calif., Sage, 2018. 167p. index. $28.00pa. ISBN 13: 978-1-5063-6092-8; 978-1-5443-2078-6 (e-book).

A must-read for anyone considering a career in media or the communications industry. The book provides a straightforward, no-nonsense approach to the various avenues available for anyone considering entering this profession. The book begins with a somewhat academic overview of mass communication, its theories and methods, and trends. The book then leaves the academe and speaks realistically about various careers including: advertising and marketing, public relations, journalism, mass communication, telecommunications and visual communications, public administration, and nonprofits.

Each chapter begins with a short but insightful history of that particular profession. That profession is then broken down into different career paths. For example, under publishing there are sections on editorial work, production, marketing, promotion, and sales. A highlight of the book is that it contains information from current professionals describing their work experience, what to expect from an entry-level job, and advice for anyone seeking a career in that industry. These sections are highlighted by shading, making it easy to peruse a particular chapter and read the professionals' point of view. Each chapter includes a section called "By the Numbers" which contains basic salary information, what, if any, degree is required or preferred, skills needed, job search terms, and the predicted growth or decline of that field.

The book concludes with chapters on skills, preparation, and tips on searching for jobs and interviewing techniques, including what aptitude those who do the hiring are seeking. The book includes eight pages of references for anyone wishing to delve deeper and a seven-page index.—**Brian Clark**

Authorship

Style Manuals

494.   Long, Priscilla. **The Writer's Portable Mentor: A Guide to Art, Craft, and the Writing Life.** 2d ed. Albuquerque, N.Mex., University of New Mexico Press, 2018. 340p. index. $24.95pa. ISBN 13: 978-0-8263-6005-2; 978-0-8263-6006-9 (e-book).

The second edition of this popular and successful book updates many of the examples, along with incorporating many of the new changes and requirements in the marketplace. The book is divided into five major sections: Your Move; Finding a Structure; The Art of the Sentence and the Art of the Paragraph; Honing, Deepening, Stretching; and Getting the Work into the World. The content is geared towards assisting a writer with grammar, plot development, syntax, speaking voice, punctuation, metaphor, simile, and various other devices and procedures which are the basics of writing. The last section discusses literary vs. commercial writing, writing buddies and critique groups, and aspects of self-publishing. There are many examples illustrating what the author is trying to get across. This book is great for aspiring writers, and a good introduction to developing style and content which grabs and captures attention from a reading audience.—**Bradford Lee Eden**

495.   Saleh, Naveed. **The Writer's Guide to Self-Editing: Essential Tips for Online and Print Publication.** Jefferson, N.C., McFarland, 2019. 270p. index. $29.95pa. ISBN 13: 978-1-4766-7159-8; 978-1-4766-3404-3 (e-book).

This book presents 75 short chapters, divided into 7 "Parts," discussing diverse topics involved in editing written documents, whether for publication in print or in various online settings. Chapter subjects include tenses, plurals, jargon, wordiness, italics, commas, sentence length, photos, and paraphrasing. Most of the topics present numerous, useful examples, sometimes showing an incorrect sentence construction, then presenting the correct one. Occasionally, however, the subjects are quite specialized: core modals, left-branching sentences, and discussing "the mandative subjunctive" in the chapter dealing with the subjunctive mood. Language is at times obscure: "Headings . . . Divide the text of an article . . .into moieties . . ." (p. 163). The last two sections, Parts 6 and 7 look at "Online Publication" and "Global Considerations," rather than the earlier, more specific areas such as "Diction" and "Punctuation."

Ironically, this book itself needs some editing. On page 2, the author speaks of "the advent of the Google." A few pages later, he states that there is "only one type of definite article: the," when in fact "the" is the only definite article. Many direct quotations lack page references, and some of the books mentioned are absent from the bibliography at the end of the volume. Still, authors/readers can find useful information in this reasonably priced book. Public libraries and possibly school libraries should consider it.—**Mark Schumacher**

496.   Sides, Charles H. **How to Write and Present Technical Information.** 4th ed. Santa Barbara, Calif., Greenwood Press/ABC-CLIO, 2017. 244p. index. $61.00. ISBN 13: 978-1-4408-5505-4; 978-1-4408-5507-8 (e-book).

How to Write and Present Technical Information, 4th edition, has been written for the professional employee whose job requires writing technical communications. It is divided into nine parts, each subdivided into chapters, with an index at the end of the book. Part I briefly identifies different personality types and how each type affects work style. This is followed by a definition of high-quality documentation and a chapter focused on defining an audience. Part II provides general writing advice, such as the steps to organizing and starting a project, conducting informational interviews, explaining a chosen subject, graphics usage in reports and papers, and electronic authoring tools. Part III focuses on paper and report writing with chapters on organizing a paper and writing the body of an article, the conclusion, and the introduction. Each chapter in Part IV discusses a specific type of document including specifications, procedures, proposals, analysis reports, and product descriptions. Part V tackles writing and designing for digital media, and Part VI is divided into chapters about public relations documents, marketing and advertising documents, and designing training programs. Part VII talks about common writing problems and editing, while Part VIII takes on presentations and meetings. Finally, Part IX sums the book up with an ethical overview.

This relatively short book is a useful resource for someone who needs a brief overview of writing different kinds of documents in a technology-driven workplace. Each topic is discussed just enough to promote understanding, but anyone wanting more in-depth coverage on a specific area may need to look elsewhere.—**Cynthia Goode**

497.   Turabian, Kate L. **A Manual for Writers of Research Papers, Theses, and Dissertations.** 9th ed. Chicago, University of Chicago Press, 2018. 462p. index. $18.00pa. ISBN 13: 978-0-226-43057-7.

Turabian's *A Manual for Writers of Research Papers, Theses, and Dissertations* continues a tradition of providing one of the best interpretations of *The Chicago Manual of Style* for higher education students and researchers in this ninth edition. The writing style is clear and easy to read, with examples illustrating proper formatting of items. The manual is divided into three parts: "Research and Writing," "Source Citation," and "Style."

"Part I: Research and Writing" discusses how to find a research topic, define it, find informational sources, drafting, and presenting the research in various formats including orally, in poster presentations, and at conferences. "Part II: Source Citations" describes the notes-bibliography and the author-date styles of citations, providing instructions for specific types of sources not just for traditional print media, but for their digital counterparts as well, including websites, blogs, and social media. "Part III: Style" hones in on the finer details of writing concerning spelling, punctuation, numbers, abbreviations, quotations, and table and figure creation. At the back of the book is the "Appendix," "Bibliography," "Authors," and "Index." The "Appendix" reviews common submission format instructions with examples, while the "Bibliography" lists subject area resources to aid research and style issues specific for various disciplines. Finally, the "Authors" page lists brief biographies of each of Turabian's authors, while the "Index" contains an alphabetized listing of subject terms with page numbers.

Changes to this text from previous editions include a concluding subsection in Chapter 5 that ties together an argument structure. Also, Chapters 17 and 19 have been reorganized, dividing the notes-bibliography and the author-date styles of citation subsections differently to reflect current electronic sources. As expected, *A Manual for Writers of Research Papers, Theses, and Dissertations* has been updated to reflect current research practices and it continues to be an excellent go-to resource for students and researchers who need guidance on following *The Chicago Manual of Style* rules of formatting.—**Cynthia Goode**

Journalism

Digital Resources

498. **UNESCO Observatory of Killed Journalists https://en.unesco.org/themes/ safety-journalists/observatory.** [Website] Free. Date reviewed: 2019.

The UNESCO Observatory of Killed Journalists presents its sobering facts via a no-frills interface that allows users to search by year, gender, type of media, and judicial status (new request, no information received so far, ongoing/unresolved, etc.). The site reports that (as of March 2019) 1,319 journalists have been killed since 1993. The main page also has a map with clickable links for those who prefer this search method. Selecting a search by year (e.g., 2018-2019) will produce a list of all those killed in that time frame (109 to this point). Clicking on the name produces the following information: date killed, gender, nationality, country in which killed, status (local or foreign), staff or freelance, type of media, and link to the DG (UN Directory-General) Condemnation. The sad statistics reveal high numbers of journalists killed in Mexico (103), Syria (103), Iraq (196), Afghanistan (66), Pakistan (71), Somalia (68), Brazil (46), and the Philippines (100).—**ARBA Staff Reviewer**

Handbooks and Yearbooks

499.   Kanigel, Rachele. **The Diversity Style Guide.** Hoboken, N.J., John Wiley & Sons, Inc., 2019. 424p. index. $94.95; $39.99 (e-book). ISBN 13: 978-1-119-05524-2; 978-1-119-05515-0 (e-book).

Rachele Kanigel, professor of journalism at San Francisco State, has created a diversity style guide for journalists, journalism students, and media writers in order to help them recognize bias and understand what words mean and why they matter. The information is presented in two parts, Covering a Diverse Society and The Journalist's Diversity Toolbox. The first chapter "Why is Diversity so Important," and the second chapter, "Implicit Bias—Addressing the Bias within Us," are followed by chapters on specific groups and issues: "Black Americans," "Native People," "Hispanics and Latinos," "Asian Americans and Pacific Islanders," "Arab Americans and Muslim Americans," "Covering Immigrants and Immigration," "Gender Identity and Sexual Orientation," "People with Disabilities," "Gender Equality in the News Media," " Mental Illness, Substance Abuse and Suicide," and "Diversity and Inclusion in a Changing Industry." Within these chapters, users will find discussions of pertinent issues, timelines of news coverage, references to further sources, discussion questions, and more. For instance, the chapter on Black Americans discusses such subjects as whether or not to hyphenate African Americans, how African Americans are portrayed in the media today, and the history of terminology from Colored to Negro to Black to African American. The second part of the book contains suggestions for diversity and inclusion activities, a cultural competence test, and a diversity calendar, but an A-Z Diversity Style Guide comprises most of this section. The guide includes more than five hundred items; some concern usage ("Black or African American," "American Indian, Native American, Native," "Third World") while some are straight definitions ("Burqa," "Kwanzaa," "Executive Order 9066," "Halal," "The Middle Passage"). The subject matter is timely and delivered in a style that is not heavy handed. Though designed for journalists, this guide would appeal to students and scholars in other disciplines. It is highly recommended for academic libraries (especially those supporting schools of journalism), for public libraries, for newsrooms, and for individuals.—**ARBA Staff Reviewer**

500.   Paron, Katrina, and Javier Güelfi. **A Newshound's Guide to Student Journalism.** Jefferson, N.C., McFarland, 2018. 194p. illus. index. $19.99pa. ISBN 13: 978-1-4766-7591-6; 978-1-4766-3440-1 (e-book).

This handy guide from journalism instructor Katrina Paron and cartoonist, illustrator, and graphic designer Javier Güelfi presents journalism students and teachers with a valuable guide to the craft divided into ten chapters: "Verification," "Understanding Conflicts of Interest," "New Rules for a New Journalism: Journalism in the 21st Century," "The Power of Journalism Making a Difference and Making a Change," "Follow the Shuttlecock: The Nature of Independent Sources," "The Folly of Blair Jayson: Resisting the Pull of Plagiarism," "It Can't All Be Broccoli: Enterprise and Feature Reporting," "All Together Now: Group Reporting," "The First Amendment and You," and "But Wait! There's More." These chapters provide valuable guidance on tips for interviews, notetaking, and sources; the anatomy of a story; examples of how to edit a first draft; maintaining neutrality; how to avoid copyright infringement; how to avoid libel; what constitutes plagiarism; how to write a review; how to use the active voice in writing; and where to find public domain resources. Each chapter includes a classroom activity that focuses on the chapter's major points. The delivery of this material will make the book appealing to students as it conveys and/or reinforces information in a variety of ways—comic strips, graphic organizers, etc. The book concludes with internet resources by chapter, a bibliography, and an index. Recommended for public libraries, school libraries, and academic libraries, particularly those that support schools of journalism.—**ARBA Staff Reviewer**

Newspapers and Magazines

Digital Resources

501.   **Bay Area Reporter https://www.glbthistory.org/online-collections.** [Website] Free. Date reviewed: 2019.

The archive of the venerable *Bay Area Reporter,* a weekly newspaper serving the LGTBQ community of the San Francisco Bay Area, is easily accessible online through the GLBT Historical Society and its links to both the California Digital Newspaper Collection (CDNC) and the Internet Archive. First published in 1971, the paper's content encompasses politics, sports, entertainment, local news, and more attuned with the LGBTQ perspective, with years of coverage focused on such topics as AIDS, gays in the military, hate crimes, and the struggle for basic rights. Users can find information on notable figures in the community such as San Francisco board of supervisors member Harvey Milk alongside stories of everyday members of the greater community. Under the Archives tab on the GLBT Historical Society homepage, users can select the Online Collections link to access the *Bay Area Reporter* Archive through either the CDNC or the Internet Archive. Users can find issues published after August 2005 at www.ebar.com/archives. Within the CDNC (https://cdnc.ucr/edu), users can find issues published between 1973 and 2005. From the link above, users can Browse by Title and select *Bay Area Reporter* (San Francisco) from the list. Users can browse editions by month and year, or keyword search within the newspaper which will create a listing of affiliated pages. The pages can be sorted in a variety of ways, and can be filtered by word count and decade. Pages are accompanied by computer-generated transcriptions, although the accuracy of the transcriptions cannot be ensured. Users can examine whole issues—side scrolling through the pages—or individual pages within a viewer. Users who register with the CDNC (free) may download the issue PDF. The Internet Archive (https://archive.org/details/bayareareporter&tab=collection) contains issues from 1971-2005 in a straightforward gallery display that can be sorted by number of views, publishing date, and more. The gallery presents colored thumbnails identified by edition volume and number. The display can be filtered by year or collection. The Internet Archive reader provides several viewing options including a one-page view, a two-page view, a thumbnail view, or an audio playback. Pages can by "turned" using an arrow key. *Bay Area Reporter* issues on the Internet Archive can be downloaded in a number of ways: PDF, kindle, full text, and more. An Online Searchable Obituary Database may also interest users, and is also available on the GLBT Historical Society Online Collections page. Users can search by name or date or visit a random obituary.

Users will find the obituary image in addition to guestbook access, where they can add their own remembrance or examine others. The *Bay Area Reporter* is an important artifact of identity, emanating from a city at the heart of the LGBTQ story. Its easily accessible archive would appeal to journalists, historians, civil rights advocates, LGBTQ advocates, educators, and students.—**ARBA Staff Reviewer**

502.   **The British Colonist http://britishcolonist.ca/index.html.** [Website] Free. Date reviewed: 2019.

This website holds over 100 years of the *British Colonist*—the major chronicle of life in British Colombia from the mid-19th century to the mid-20th century. The paper captures the early frontier days of the Northern Pacific trapping, trading, and mining outpost through the region's development as an independent province of a new nation. Users can conduct a basic or advanced search from the bar at the top of the homepage. Context links to a brief foundational essay which tracks the development of the *British Colonist* (for a time, the "only publication that receives telegraphic dispatches") alongside that of its governing nation. Links include related resources such as the Index of Historical Victorian Newspapers 1858-1922 (see review), British Colombia Historical Newspapers, and more. The Browse by Date option lets users select from a calendar display to find editions of interest. Selecting a calendar day and year displays the newspaper in a viewer. Within the viewer, users can zoom in and out, download, alter page views, scroll through pages, and perform other operations. Users can also use the audio function to hear the newspaper read aloud. It is important to consider, however, that as the application is computer generated it may be unreliable. The newspaper is rich in period advertisements (North Western Smelting and Refining Company, Searby & Moore Dispensing Chemists) and local, domestic, and international stories. Users can also find headlines such as "Canadians in Action on the Beaches of Normandy," "Local Ships Crash in Haze of San Juan Island," "Victoria Marksman Shoots Brilliantly to Win Competition" and coverage of the world wars, the stock market crash, John F. Kennedy's assassination, and more. This would be a good place to find primary material for a digital humanities project.—**ARBA Staff Reviewer**

503.   **Chattanooga Newspapers http://chattanooga.advantage-preservation.com.** [Website] Free. Date reviewed: 2019.

This site hosts thousands of digitized pages from 37 historic Chattanooga, Tennessee, newspapers. The archive holds pages published between 1838 and 1912 with the bulk of the pages collected after 1860, from a lone page of the *Chattanooga Times* to nearly 9,000 pages of the *Chattanooga News*. Users can find news, editorials, social notes, advertisements, and more. Users can search people, places, and events (filtered by dates) or can Browse by Title or Browse by Year, grouping pages by decade. The Browse by Title option allows users to select a paper to access its particular archive (in general order by publishing date). Pages within each archive are generally displayed in order of publication date and further identified by a page excerpt transcription (although, at the time of this review, it appears that all excerpts may not be accurately transcribed). Clicking on the newspaper name will access the page in the viewer, and users can download, crop, search page content, and zoom in to enlarge the very small print of the historic publications. Users can additionally keyword search within each newspaper's archive and filter display by date or decade—very useful considering the large number of pages available for some newspapers.—**ARBA Staff Reviewer**

504. **Georgia Historic Newspapers https://gahistoricnewspapers.galileo.usg.edu/.** [Website] Free. Date reviewed: 2019.

Georgia Historic Newspapers represents a significant digitization project of Georgia newspaper pages published between the years of 1786 and 1986. The project has digitized titles from each of the state's counties, and continues to add pages frequently. The database is sophisticated and easy to use. Users can Search Newspaper Contents via the bar at the top of the homepage, or conduct an advanced search from the tab. An interactive map of the state allows users to search or browse by region (South Georgia, Metro Atlanta, etc.). Additionally, users can browse newspapers by title, date, city, county, or type (school, community, African American, religious, Native American, and paper of record). Selecting a region on the map links to excellent contextual information including a brief descriptive essay on the area that touches on historical and contemporary features, lists of counties included and cities included, and lists (with links) of titles by county. Each newspaper title links to an introductory page in the database displaying a front page image, a brief paragraph about the paper, and general identifying information such as place of publication, geographic coverage, dates of publication, language(s), subject(s), and more. There are various ways in which to view the pages—All Issues Front Pages, First Issue, or Last Issue. Users can also access a calendar view of available pages. Clicking on the newspaper image accesses an enlarged page in a viewer. Users can easily navigate to the previous page, next page, or next issue from here, and can also view page text and view PDF. The project has digitized pages of *The Wolverine Observer, The Atlanta Daily Herald, The Athens Daily Banner, The Georgia Pioneer, The Southern Baptist Messenger, The Savannah Morning News,* and many, many more.—**ARBA Staff Reviewer**

505. **Index of Historical Victoria Newspapers http://webuvic.ca/vv/newspaper/ index.php.** [Website] Free. Date reviewed: 2019.

The Index of Historical Victoria Newspapers presents four unique indexes which organize summarized article transcripts from the *British Colonist,* as well as several other newspapers from the Vancouver Island, Canada, area. Users can find several specialized indexes focused regionally, locally, and topically in addition to a broad index to roughly eighty years of the *British Colonist,* also known as the *Daily Colonist,* the region's oldest daily newspaper. Users can find a brief description of each index's contents under the About tab. The General Index emphasizes the social history of Victoria and neighboring areas. The West Coast Vancouver Island Index aims to create a more definitive picture of west coast residents. A Boer War Index contains articles that reference Victoria Island residents involved in the Boer War (1899-1902). Finally, a Built Environment Index contains articles which reference buildings, architects, building material suppliers, and basically anything related to the building trade and building landscape in Victoria. This index draws from other newspapers in addition to the *British Colonist,* including the *Victoria Gazette, The Victoria Daily Chronicle,* and the *Evening Express.* There is no browse option through the site. Users must employ one of several search functions via the tab at the top of the page. It is recommended that users first read through the link explaining how the website works before they begin their basic or advanced search. Searches yield tabular data listing transcribed newspaper excerpts which can be sorted by publication date, newspaper, event date, collection, and more. Users can examine available transcripts, with search term/ phrase highlighted within the text, and click on the adjacent symbol to access the page's metadata. Clicking on the date link will access a digital image of the newspaper page if available. In conjunction with the website for the *British Colonist* (see review in ARBA 2019), the Index of Historical Victoria Newspapers is an immensely helpful tool.—**ARBA Staff Reviewer**

506.   **Queer Zine Archive Project http://archive.qzap.org/.** [Website] Free. Date reviewed: 2019.

This archive houses a diverse collection of over six hundred self-published journals or "zines"—generated by and for the queer community around the world. Epitomizing the unique and underground voice of a marginalized population, the zine incorporates homemade drawings, poetry, comics, photography, and more in a raw jumble of book reviews, articles, announcements, essays, and whatever else is on the mind of the publisher. Users can scroll down to examine the Random Object, the Recently Viewed zine, or the Recently Added zine, or can conduct a basic or advanced search. Users can browse the archive by selecting from a list of categories: Object Types (zines, flyers, audio zines, and ephemera), People, Places, Centuries, Decades, Years, and Collections. The People category provides an A-Z directory of individuals and groups (e.g., the Student Women's Action Coalition) who have published zines. Places lets users choose from a long list of cities home to zine publishing: Tel Aviv, Dublin, Buenos Aires, and many cities across the United States. Collections help group zines alphabetically or numerically in addition to listing individual donor collections. For each zine, users can scroll through and zoom on each page, presented alongside identifying information such as number of pages, languages, creator, place created, related collections, keywords (with links), format (digest, mini-zine, standard, etc.), and more. It is important to note that some of the zines are sexually explicit, with graphic language and images.—**ARBA Staff Reviewer**

21 Decorative Arts

Collecting

507. Keurajian, Ron. **Baseball Hall of Fame Autographs: A Reference Guide.** 2d ed. Jefferson, N.C., McFarland, 2018. 304p. illus. index. $49.95pa. ISBN 13: 978-1-4766-7140-6; 978-1-4766-3418-0 (e-book).

The first edition of this guide to collecting baseball Hall of Fame autographs appeared in 2012 (see ARBA 2013, entry 676). In this new and expanded edition, the author, a commercial banker, attorney, and author of many articles on baseball and vintage golf autographs, updates existing signature studies with the latest information, a price guide and selected prices realized at auction, and a new chapter about the 50 most-desired, non-Hall of Famers autographs. He also expands the chapters on building a collection and forgeries. The guide is designed for anyone involved in autograph collecting from novices to advanced collectors. The first part of the book, Building a Collection, has chapters on what to collect, forgeries and authentication, obtaining signatures and the auction process, and provenance and the black market. In these chapters, users will get detailed advice about what autographs to get, how to determine if a signature is forged, and if an item is authentic. The third chapter contains very good advice on navigating eBay. Chapter 5, "Signature Studies," is the longest in the book (approximately 200 pages) and is arranged by player name. For each player, there is a signature study, a signature population (how many are available), known forgeries, and a pricing guide. All of these have black-and-white examples of the player's signature. This is followed by a chapter on the top 50 non-Hall of Famers that follows the same format. The last chapter focuses on the 1919 White Sox scandal and the signatures of those involved. There is a short appendix of rare to ultra-rare Hall of Fame signatures followed by a list of recommended readings and an index. Highly recommended for public libraries and for anyone who collects baseball autographs.—**ARBA Staff Reviewer**

508. Kovel, Terry, and Kim Kovel. **Kovel's Antiques & Collectibles Price Guide 2018.** New York, Black Dog & Leventhal Publishers, 2017. 546p. illus. index. $29.99pa. ISBN 13: 978-0-316-47194-7.

This 50th anniversary edition contains the prices for 20,000 collectible items based on actual 2016-2017 sales figures. The majority of the items listed sold for under $10,000. An introduction discusses general trends, commenting on what is hot and what is not. It also has a section of record prices for 2016-2017 for such items as clocks, watches, glass, and silver. A section on how to use the book is important to read as it lays out policies such as leaving off dollar amounts and the fact that the book does not include fine art paintings, antiques, stamps, coins, or most types of books. There are numerous cross-references (e.g., Sterling Silver *see* Silver Sterling or American dinnerware *see* Dinnerware), an index, guide words, and page tabs, which help users navigate through the large amount of data in this book. Items are listed by category and contain a description. If one of the 2,500 color photographs corresponds to the listed item, this is indicated by *illus.* This anniversary edition contains a special section in which the authors reflect on their 50-year collection career. There are also hot tips throughout the book on numerous such things as how to remove masking tape from an item, how to wash and store dishes, and how to frame a poster. There are also many reproduced maker's marks and/or signatures. This is a must have book for anyone who pursues collecting as a hobby or business. Highly recommended for public libraries.—**ARBA Staff Reviewer**

509.   Pollio, T.N. **Ancient Rings: An Illustrated Collector's Guide.** Jefferson, N.C., McFarland, 2018. 172p. illus. index. $55.00pa. ISBN 13: 978-1-4766-7385-1; 978-1-4766-3268-1 (e-book).

The author has compiled information from his own research as a collector. Items made of expensive materials, such as gold and precious jewels, usually get the most attention, but there has been an increased interest among collectors for items made of lesser materials, such as iron and bronze. Since most people owned fewer and less-expensive rings, these pieces offer a more accurate picture of everyday life and the people who owned them. The main text begins with discussion of certain aspects, such as terminology, materials used, decorative details, considerations of identifying and dating pieces, and ethical issues. Historical periods and styles, starting with the Neolithic Period to the Modern/Industrial Age, reflect variations in styles and types of rings from different periods and places. The general information includes discussions of the meaning behind the symbols used in designs and the cleaning and conservation of the rings. A useful glossary, notes, bibliography, and index complete the text and a large number of intricate, detailed black-and-white illustrations greatly enhance the text. The writing is concise, knowledgeable, and very informative.—**Martha Lawler**

510.   Wade, John. **Retro Cameras: The Collector's Guide to Vintage Film Photography.** New York, Thames and Hudson, 2018. 288p. illus. index. $27.95. ISBN 13: 978-0-5005-4490-7.

This volume is a camera buff's version of book heaven. Chock full of both color and black-and-white pictures, it is a comprehensive guide to retro cameras and vintage film photography. After brief introductory chapters on value and rarity, basics, and formats and focal lengths, the bulk of the book is devoted to descriptions and detailed backgrounds on over one hundred cameras and all their usable film formats divided into eleven sections: 35mm single-lens reflexes, 35mm Rangefinder cameras, 35mm Viewfinder cameras, roll-film single-lens reflexes, sheet and roll-film folding cameras, twin-lens reflexes, Instamatic cartridge cameras, stereo cameras, panoramic and wide-angle cameras, miniature cameras, and instant-picture cameras. Each section contains a shooting guide which provides basic instructions and techniques for the use of cameras in that section. A final chapter discusses retro accessories such as rangefinders, flashguns, tripods, and focal-length adapters, to name but a few. This book is for collectors, owners, and aficionados of cameras.—**Bradford Lee Eden**

511. Yeoman, R.S. Garrett, Jeff, ed. **A Guide Book of United States Coins.** Pelham, Ala., Whitman Publishing, LLC, 2018. 463p. illus. index. $17.95pa. ISBN 13: 978-0-7948-4567-4.

This guidebook ("the official Red Book"), now in its 72d edition, is a treasure trove of reliable information for coin collectors and/or those interested in U.S. numismatic history. The introduction relays a good deal of information about many such topics as the evolution of coin collection, the history of this book (first published in 1946), the terms used to describe the conditions of coins (Mint State, Choice Very Fine, etc.), and the history of U.S. coinage since the colonial period. The book is organized into the following sections: Pre-Federal Issues; Federal Issues (1793-present); Bullion; United States Pattern Pieces (5 pages of significant U.S. patterns like the 1907 Indian head double eagle (J-1905, gold); and Other Issues, which has information on such things as Confederate Issues, Hawaiian and Pueblo Rican Issues, and Private Tokens. Hundreds of high-quality photographs add considerable value to this title. Five appendixes follow: "Mistakes and Errors," "Collectible Red and Blue Books," "Bullion Values," "Top 250 Coin Prices Realized at Auction," and "Modern U.S. Mint Medals." The book's table of contents, guide words, and index make it easy to jump to a particular topic. The book also provides a glossary and bibliography. This standard and reliable reference is highly recommended for individual collectors and for public libraries.—**ARBA Staff Reviewer**

Crafts

512. **Quilt Index http://quiltindex.org/2018/welcome.php.** [Website] Free. Date reviewed: 2019.

This open access database offers an updated version of the original Quilt Index (launched in 2003). Users can continue to access the old version of the Quilt Index, but all new material will appear only on the new site. The Quilt Index is a digital humanities and education project of the Michigan State University Museum and Matrix, The Center for Digital Humanities and Social Sciences at Michigan State. This straightforward database is easy to navigate from tabs at the top of the homepage: Quilts, Stories, Artists, Collections, Resources, Ephemera, About, and Search (basic or advanced). Altogether, researchers will discover thousands of images and information about quilts and their makers from hundreds of public and private collections around the world. This is also a great resource for educators as there are lesson plans accessible via the Resources tab along with contextualizing essays.—**ARBA Staff Reviewer**

513. Stanfield, Lesley, and Melody Griffiths. **The Encyclopedia of Knitting Techniques: A Unique Visual Directory of Knitting Techniques, with Guidance on How to Use Them.** Tunbridge Wells, Kent,, UK, Search Books, 2018. 160p. illus. index. $19.95. ISBN 13: 978-1-78221-644-5.

After a short introduction, this encyclopedia presents information for novices and experienced knitters in three parts: Knitting Skills; Stitch Collection; and Design and Inspiration. Within the first section users will find information on such topics as equipment and yarn, casting on and casting off, how to read knitting charts, turning rows, fastening, and embroidery. Under Knitting Skills, information is provided on cables, twists, and more. The last section discusses designs for sweaters and jackets, texture and pattern, how to calculate stitches and rows, and other knitting-relating issues. There are many supporting visuals throughout the encyclopedia. These include color photographs and color diagrams of such things as knitting charts, finished products, and diagrams of stitches. Knitting methods are explained in written step-by-step instructions, which are fully explained and supported by visual instructions. There are textboxes with tips throughout the main part of the book on topics like knitting with ribbon trim. Usability is also enhanced by the inclusion of *see also* references. The book concludes with a glossary and an index. Recommended to public libraries.—**ARBA Staff Reviewer**

Fashion and Costume

514.   Ellison, Jo. **Vogue: the Gown.** New York, Firefly Books, 2017. 304p. illus. index. $49.95. ISBN 13: 978-0-2281-0008-9.

Gowns are possibly the most dramatic of garments and serve as the inspiration and reflection of the most intense moments in life. The significance of designs—as they change, fade away, and reemerge—as well as the people who create them and those who wear them—form the focus of this collection of images, mostly in color and with informative captions. The presentation is arranged in five basic categories: classical, fantasy, drama, decorative, and modern. Each section begins with a brief overview of the category, including historical development and key figures (designers, models, etc.) and the captions offer further information. There is no definite arrangement to the presentation, which is a bit jarring. The often-iconic images are lovely, impressive, and inspiring, but the overall feeling is more of a beautiful picture book than an actual reference. An index and list of picture credits follow at the end.—**Martha Lawler**

515.   **The Handbook of Textile Culture.** Janis Jeffries, Diana Wood Conroy, and Hazel Clark, eds. New York, Bloomsbury Academic, 2018. 478p. illus. index. $49.95pa. ISBN 13: 978-1-3500-7489-7; 978-1-4742-7579-8 (e-book).

This state-of-the-art handbook on the field of textile studies is an excellent reference work for any higher education arts program. Divided into six major sections and twenty-eight separate essays ranging from the history, ethnicities, countries, materials, curation, collection, and individual artistic styles and personages of textiles, it is also accompanied by a number of color plates along with a transcription of a roundtable discussion held in Chicago in February 2014. It is a fascinating group of scholarly and practical essays on textiles and related topics such as dress, feminism and gender, cultural history, costume, fashion, and art and design. Interviews with major figures in the field such as Kay Lawrence, Joan Livingstone, and Lisa Vinebaum, to name but a few are also included.—**Bradford Lee Eden**

516.   North, Susan. **18th-Century Fashion in Detail.** New York, Thames and Hudson, 2018. 224p. illus. index. $40.00pa. ISBN 13: 978-0-500-29263-1.

This update to the 1998 volume *Historical Fashion in Detail* finally gives 18th-century fashion its own volume. Susan North, Curator of Fashion, 1550-1800, for the Victoria and Albert Museum, includes 137 items from the museum's collection, many of which are new to this work. North's brief introduction begins with an overview of the importance of dressing well in 18th-century society and the effect that one's dress could have on the wearer's social standing. From there, North takes the reader through the garment creation process, from the drapers that furnished the textiles to the embroiderers who created some of the fine details featured in this volume. North also highlights the importance of Britain's trade with China and India to the development of European fashion and art in the 18th century. Each chapter of the volume focuses on the decorations and adornments of 18th-century fashion, such as collars, lacework, pleats, and buttons. Each entry is labeled clearly with the type of garment, sex of wearer, country of origin, and time period. North gives equal attention to men's and women's fashion and includes accessories, such as caps and aprons, where necessary. All entries include beautiful full-color photographs by Henrietta Clare and Richard Davis that zoom in on the fine details of the garment. The pictures are so crisp and clear that the reader may feel as if they could touch the individual stitches. Leonie Davis and Deborah Mallinson's line drawings supplement the photographs and provide a look at the garment as a whole. For some entries, drawings are used to show how details such as buttons functioned on the garment. The text that accompanies each entry includes definitions of unfamiliar terms, a description of the garment's essential features, and some details about how the garment was constructed. North's captions go beyond just a physical description of each garment. The author provides historical context and quotations to add to the reader's understanding of this garment's place in European life. For example, an entry about a man's silk coat (p. 18) includes information about the Lyons silk industry. An additional touch is the inclusion of information about the item's provenance. These notes are fascinating and occasionally humorous. The volume concludes with a list of references for each chapter, recommendations for further reading, and a glossary. This volume is an excellent introduction to 18th-century fashion history. The brief entries and full color photographs make this a book a highly recommended addition to academic libraries, particularly libraries that support undergraduate programs in fashion, theatre, and museum studies. Large public libraries also may find this volume to be a worthwhile addition to their collection.—**Kristin Elizabeth Cole**

Interior Design

517.   Langan, Alana, and Jacqui Vidal. **Plant Style: How to Greenify Your Space.** New York, Thames and Hudson, 2018. 160p. illus. index. $25.00. ISBN 13: 978-0-500-50103-0.

Plant Style: How to Greenify Your Space seeks to guide its readers in the selection and arrangement of houseplants to help "greenify" their homes. Authors Alana Langan and Jacqui Vidal are the proprietors of the Australian firm Ivy Muse Botanical Boutique and are very familiar with creatively working with plants and accessories. Citing the trend towards minimalism in contemporary homes, they believe that greenery is needed to soften these spaces and connect with nature. Langan and Vidal note that all of the plants featured in *Plant Style* were chosen for their ease of care and hardy temperaments.

The work is divided into chapters on defining plant styling, choosing plant gangs, plant accessories, plant styling principles, styling solutions for every room, and caring for plants. The book concludes with a plant index of the authors' seventy-three favorite plants. Information in this section includes each plant's common and Latin name, and its watering, lighting, and humidity requirements.

The focus of this attractive book is on the striking photographs that illustrate the concepts the authors are describing. Hence, the text is limited.

Plant Style is a wonderful source of creative decorating ideas with plants. As such, it would serve libraries best by being located in the circulating collection rather than in the reference area.—**January Adams**

22 Fine Arts

General Works

Biography

518.   Morris, Desmond. **The Lives of the Surrealists.** New York, Thames and Hudson, 2018. 272p. illus. index. $39.95. ISBN 13: 978-0-500-02136-0.

This volume draws on the author's personal knowledge of the individuals who became known as the Surrealists, rebels against the world after the atrocities of World War I, mainly Europeans who used art and philosophy to construct and deconstruct their lives and their world visions. Short biographies and often witty comments comprise the thirty-two Surrealist artists who are highlighted in the book. Interspersed with both color and black-and-white photographs of the artists and their works, it is very entertaining reading. Some of the Surrealists discussed include Francis Bacon, Alexander Calder, Salvador Dali, Marcel Duchamp, Max Ernst, Conroy Maddox, Joan Miro, Pablo Picasso, and Dorothea Tanning, to name a few. The author himself has been called the last surviving Surrealist, and his interactions and adventures with this group of 20th-century artists are more of a Broadway play than a book.—**Bradford Lee Eden**

Dictionaries and Encyclopedias

519.   Zirpolo, Lilian H. **Historical Dictionary of Baroque Art and Architecture.** 2d ed. Lanham, Md., Rowman & Littlefield, 2018. 654p. illus. (Historical Dictionaries of Literature and the Arts). $145.00; $137.50 (e-book). ISBN 13: 978-1-5381-1128-4; 978-1-5381-1129-1 (e-book).

Part of the Historical Dictionaries of Literature and the Arts series from Rowman & Littlefield, this second edition (see ARBA 2011, entry 862) on baroque art and architecture includes eighty-five new entries. It is intended as a reference tool for college professors, art history students, and those interested in baroque art. Each entry focuses on a topic, place, work, or artist, and provides a succinct description which includes bolded cross-references to other entries. The chronology of this period, provided at the front of the volume, goes from 1580 to 1718. The impressive bibliography is divided into twelve sections, providing resources by country (Italy, France, Flanders, Holland, Spain and Portugal, England,

Germany, and other countries) as well as topic (treatises, artist biographies, emblem books, academies, art training, artistic identity, and art patronage and collecting). This book would be an excellent addition to any college and university reference shelf.—**Bradford Lee Eden**

Digital Resources

520.   **The Art Institute of Chicago https://www.artic.edu/collection.** [Website] Free. Date reviewed: 2019.

The Art Institute of Chicago (AIC) has digitized numerous pieces from its world-renowned collection, with paintings by Picasso, O'Keefe, Pollack, Monet, Chagall, and many others alongside fine examples of sculpture, decorative arts, and more. The AIC additionally offers writings and resources in this well-organized database within the museum's website. From the homepage, users can select The Collection link to access all digital materials. Users can Keyword, Artist, or Reference search from the bar, or scroll through the gallery which can be customized by theme: Cityscapes, Impressionism, Animals, Essentials, African Diaspora, Fashion, Chicago, Pop Art, and Mythology—a generous array of categories that attests to the range and quality of the AIC's holdings. Users can additionally incorporate a number of filters into their search, including date, places, medium, artists, subjects, and styles. Users may recognize a good number of artworks that exemplify a wide range of styles: Grant Wood's *American Gothic,* Pierre-August Renoir's *Two Sisters,* Andy Warhol's *Mao,* El Greco's *The Assumption of the Virgin,* and Van Gogh's *The Bedroom.* Clicking on an artwork title accesses related information as well as a viewer for up-close examination. A brief descriptive essay may accompany each artwork, in addition to information about the artwork origin, medium, inscriptions, and dimensions. Users can also find affiliated publication history, exhibition history, provenance, multimedia, and educational resources. Educational resources offer a diverse selection of materials that vary from artwork to artwork, but can include links to essays, topical teacher manuals, activities, and full resource packets (see below). Teachers can incorporate the educational resources filter option into their initial search to expedite those artists/artworks with affiliated materials. A diverse selection of blog posts can be found under the Writings tab on The Collection homepage. Posts will generally be categorized by museum history, collection spotlight (e.g., "One of Sargent's Good Things," "Portraits of Folk"), From the Archives, Inside an Exhibition, and much more. Resources for the researcher and educator are abundant. Many materials in the institute's archival collections have been digitized, with more to come. Users can select the Explore the Collection tab, which includes a good selection of fully digitized materials such as the Chicago Architects Oral History Project, the New York World's Fair Collection 1937-1940, and the Tribune Tower Collection. Users can also examine lists of materials that are partially digitized or not digitized. The Tools for My Classroom link offers nearly thirty downloadable resource packets on particular artworks or artists, which may include tools like essays, discussion questions, activities, and glossaries. The AIC offers a rich digital viewing experience of some of the most studied art in the world alongside valuable educational resources.—**ARBA Staff Reviewer**

521.   **Artsy https://www.artsy.net/.** [Website] Date reviewed: 2019.

Artsy seeks to bring the art market to more people by offering virtual galleries of painting, architecture, design, and more. Artsy's vast database contains information and digital images on roughly one million works from some one hundred thousand artists with some of the best examples of medieval, modern, and contemporary works from all corners of the globe. Within its digital galleries, users can discover basic information about the art and the artist, in addition to collection, sale, and auction information if applicable. Users can search artists, titles of artwork, gallery, or more from the top left corner of the page, or can explore the immense range of content in several ways. Scrolling down through the homepage discovers a selection of categories such as Works by Popular Artists, Emerging Photography, Pop Prints and Multiples, Artists to Follow, Abstract Painting, Figurative Painting, Geometric, Street Art, and Landscapes. Choosing the Explore Now link from the homepage slideshow allows users to Browse by Collection, which expands on many of the categories listed above. Collections is a good place to explore a wide variety of curated art available to purchase. The Artworks tab at the top of the page presents an extensive virtual gallery of individual art for sale, which users can filter by price, medium, or time period. Images are accompanied by artist name, title, date, and gallery name. Artwork price may also be included. Clicking on the image links to further information regarding the artist, other work from the artists, other works from the show, and more. Users can use the search bar to find particular artists, art styles (e.g., German Expressionism), and galleries, along with other data. Users can "follow" an artist, a gallery, or an art style which can be a helpful tool when conducting research. Information for renowned artists, whose works may be off the market (e.g., Munch, Renoir, Picasso, Giotto, etc.) may include a brief biography with mentions of the more famous works, a digital gallery, a list of selected exhibitions, high auction record, and major museum collections. There may also be a gallery of Related Works and Related Artists. The Articles link accesses artist-affiliated writings from the Artsy blog. Under the More tab at the top of the page, users can browse Galleries, Artists, or Museums. The inclusion of auction and general sale information enhances the descriptive material and sets Artsy apart from other art databases.—**ARBA Staff Reviewer**

522.   **Canadian Women Artists History Initiative https://cwahi.concordia.ca/.** [Website] Free. Date reviewed: 2019.

The Canadian Women Artists History Initiative helps promote and preserve the work of Canadian women artists in a variety of ways, ensuring their place within a rich and diverse Canadian culture. This website, available in French and English, provides information about Canadian women artists born before 1925, hosting a database of 260 (and counting) artists. From the Artist Database tab on the homepage, users can Search by Artist, search Biographical Information (e.g., place of birth or death), or search by a generous list of Media options, including photography, pottery, textiles, wood carving, painting, moosehair, and more. Users may also choose to search by Educational Background, selecting from a long list of Canadian and international institutions, association memberships (Alberta Society of Artists, The Canadian Crafts Council, and others), or bibliographies. Users can alternatively click Browse to search a list of artists from painter Phyllis Campbell Abbott to illustrator and watercolorist Mary Marguerite Porter Zwicker. Artist entries generally consist of a Biography Synopsis, with information about their art, awards, affiliated galleries, and more. Entries may also include information about an artist's education, memberships, preferred media, and file & archive locations. A bibliography of writings about and by the artist, as well as links to any associated Exhibition Review PDFs, are also included. Further information is available through the Reviews Database link, which has amassed roughly 1,000 reviews of database artists' work from close to 30 publications (*Globe and Mail, Canadian Spectator, Toronto Star,* etc.). The reviews encompass three major art exhibitions: the Art Association of Montreal Spring Exhibition, the Ontario Society of Artists Art Exhibition, and the Royal Canadian Academy of Arts. Users can fill in relevant fields, including artist, exhibition location, newspaper title, and more to explore the reviews. While information on some artists may be sparse, the website provides a vital record of women who capture the breadth of the Canadian experience through art and is a good place to find initial information.—**ARBA Staff Reviewer**

523.   **Delaware Art Museum. https://www.delart.org/.** [Website] Free. Date reviewed: 2018.

The Delaware Art Museum has created a generous digital gallery with which to showcase a significant collection of 19th- and 20th-century American art in addition to a fine collection of British Pre-Raphaelite painting. Users will find a wide range of paintings, sculpture, mixed media, illustration, photography, and more. The Collections tab on the menu bar at the top of the homepage lists a number of museum collections. Alternatively, users can simply select the Search the Collection tab near the bottom of the homepage to access a gallery of six collections: "American Art to 1945," "American Illustration," "Contemporary Art Collection," the "Copeland Sculpture Garden," "Highlights of the Eight," and the "Pre-Raphaelite Brotherhood." From here, users can conduct a basic or advanced search from the bar, or browse through an A-Z list of artists. Each collection shows a list or grid display of its artworks, with thumbnail image, title, date, artists, and object number. Selecting an artwork by clicking on its thumbnail or title slightly enlarges the image and provides expanded information such as medium, dimensions, and permalink. Browsing by artist will sometimes access brief biographical information as well. Users will find works by Robert Motherwell, Louise Nevelson, Ansel Adams, George Inness, Dante Gabriel Rossetti, Andrew Wyeth, and many others. The variety of the online collections— from portraiture to lush landscapes or a modern sculpture garden—helps users appreciate the scope of the museum's holdings and gives them a good sense of American art in particular.—**ARBA Staff Reviewer**

524.   **Google Arts & Culture https://artsandculture.google.com/.** [Website] Free. Date reviewed: 2019.

Students are able to experience natural history, arts, and culture in ways they never could before using the free resource Google Arts and Culture. This resource contains over 32,000 works with 31 mediums and materials from over 151 museums and art organizations located all over the globe. A small team of employees created the concept following a discussion on how to adapt Google technology to make museums' artwork more easily available to the public. In early 2018, the resulting product went viral after releasing its "art selfie" platform. The concept of the "art selfie" allowed users to find their art likeness by matching user faces to art museum portraits compiled within its vast database. Google Arts and Culture can be used in a plethora of ways within an educational setting and can be readily used across all content areas. Two of its best features include the sheer volume of work available through simple searching as well as the interactive features that allow users to experience artwork and history first-hand without ever having to leave the classroom.

On the main page users are directed in a simple visual display to their various and robust activity options. Included in the platform are virtual reality experiences of a variety of art galleries and of cultural locations from around the world. One noteworthy experience involves a VR Story in 3D video from the Museum für Naturkunde Berlin. It is narrated in English and features the original bones of a Brachiosaurus, the highest mounted dinosaur in the world. In the video the dinosaur walks off the platform and comes to life. This experience is truly something to be seen with or without virtual reality headsets. Another unique experience for users is the ability to zoom in on some of the greatest works of art of all time. Users can magnify a variety of selected art works for a high-definition visual experience, and see high-quality personal details up-close from artists like Monet and Van Gogh. The "Street View" feature also takes users on virtual field trips to some of the world's most iconic locations such as The Taj Mahal and St. Paul's Cathedral.

Educators and school library media specialists will find a variety of educational videos through the resource's built-in YouTube channel as well as a "DIY" section which allows students to experience a routine day in the life of a museum curator. Also included in this section are interactive activities for students which are similar to those available if touring a museum in person. The "What's Next" page lists resources and links to history timelines, art toolkits, and lesson plan ideas. When users are logged into their Google accounts they can also "favorite" items within the platform and add works of art to their own galleries, which would make a great foundation for long-term projects and art lessons involving research. The possibilities for cross-curricular digital integration as well as the expansive collection of resources and information make this a resource to be shared often and utilized in a variety of content areas throughout the school year.

Highly recommended.—**Angela Wojtecki**

525. **Guggenheim Collection Online.** https://www.guggenheim.org/collection-online. [Website] Free. Date reviewed: 2018.

This website features over 1,700 artworks from the formidable Guggenheim Museum and collections in New York City, Venice, and Bilbao. Representing over 600 artists, the works selected for the online collection offer a broad view of the groundbreaking style that defines the Guggenheim. Users will appreciate the array of browsing options, as artworks are organized by Artists, Dates, Mediums, Movements, Venues, or by Special Collections. Selecting the Artists gallery presents an alphabetical listing of such individuals as Ai Weiwei, Georges Braque, Christo, Salvador Dali, Sharon Hayes, Paul Klee, Loretta Lux, Rene Magritte, Pablo Picasso, and Sam Taylor-Wood. Mediums lets users choose to view art within Film/Video, Photography, Sculpture, Painting, and other categories. Movements offers a generous listing of viewing categories, reflecting the wide span of the Guggenheim focus and including the more familiar styles of Expressionism, Dada, or Cubism alongside the perhaps less understood Suprematism, Process Art, or Hard-Edge Painting. A brief introductory essay describes the movement and its prime cultivators. Within all these categories, users can examine an enlarged image of a selected artwork, which comes with identifying information such as Artist, Title, Date, Medium, and Dimensions. There may also be a link to the artist biography.—**ARBA Staff Reviewer**

526.   **International Dada Archive https://www.lib.uiowa.edu/dada/.** [Website] Free. Date reviewed 2019.

Born out of a rejection of the early-20th-century cultural and political establishment, Dadaism—the art of the absurd—permeated painting, film, music, literature, sculpture, and more. The International Dada Archive at the University of Iowa Libraries provides access to materials from an array of sources prominent in the world of Dada.

Users can select the Digital Dada Library tab to access digital versions of periodicals and books published in both European and North American centers of the movement. Each periodical title—*Aventure, Z,* the well-known *Cabaret Voltaire,* and others, links to a page display of all available issues, each one opened via the View tab. Users can examine individual pages or select the Full Issue tab to see each page displayed together. Many images showcase the striking graphic design emblematic of the Dada style; however, aside from the general date and publishing location, there is little contextual information.

Users can also find a selection of books and ephemera which can be viewed page by page, organized by author. Titles include *Dada Wins, The Technique of Luck, The Dadaistic Corruption,* and more. Users may recognize artists such as Max Ernst, Man Ray, George Grosz, and others as notable within Dada and other art movements of the time. For all materials, there is limited translation available from the original German or French.

The Bibliography/Catalog tab links to the Online Bibliography page where users can find basic bibliographical information for many Dada-affiliated materials. Users can search or browse by title, author, subject, and more, and can find information for essays, sound recordings, books, articles, and many other materials. The Dadaists tab leads to a generous list of individuals in the Dada movement. Users can find brief biographical information, a list of related works in the Digital Dada Library, and a list of other internet resources for artists like Alfred Stieglitz, Beatrice Wood, Otto Dix, and others.

The Dada/Surrealism Journal hosts essays, reviews, and other interdisciplinary Dada scholarship that connects the movement with history, literature, film and more. Several contributions to the most recent edition, "Dada, War and Peace" (Issue #22, 2018), address the impact of World War I on art and the artist. Users can download PDF versions of each essay, browse Most Popular Papers, and perform other functions.

Although primary materials are limited to the pages in the Digital Dada Library, the greater International Dada Archive is a good starting point for research into the movement, with the journal in particular providing diverse examples of Dada study.—**ARBA Staff Reviewer**

527.   **National Portrait Gallery https://npg.si.edu/portraits.** [Website] Free. Date reviewed: 2019.

This website offers a digital gallery of selected portraits from the Smithsonian's National Portrait Gallery. Housing portraits of a wide array of distinguished Americans, the National Portrait Gallery is a treasured institution, and this website helps bring its collection to virtual tourists, historians, and scholars across many disciplines. The site currently showcases over 15,000 works of various media, from traditional oil painting to modern digital portraiture. Users can scroll through the homepage to examine National Portrait Gallery Highlights, including Presidential Portraits in View, and selections From Our Blog, which may provide helpful context. Under the Portraits tab, users can Search the Collection via the prominent field or scroll through the page of collection samples (singer Lena Horne, abolitionist John Brown, innovator Steve Jobs, etc.). Searches can be filtered by Portraits with Images or Portraits on View at the Museum, or refined further by Theme/ Topic, Cultural Affiliation, Date, and filters. Information for each portrait may include artist name, subject, date, type/medium, dimensions, and provenance. There may be additional information conveyed through the Exhibition label. Users can examine a thumbnail of the portrait or click the link to View in Browser. For some subjects, such as President John F. Kennedy, there may be several portraits to examine. For educators, the site provides ample resources like "U.S. History–1600 to Gilded Age High School Self-Guide" and "The First Reading of the Emancipation Proclamation."—**ARBA Staff Reviewer**

528.   **Victoria and Albert Museum https://www.vam.ac.uk/.** [Website] Free. Date reviewed: 2018.

The Victoria and Albert Museum is home to some of the finest examples of art and design amassed through roughly five thousand years of creation. This website allows users to examine some of the London museum's diverse collections encompassing architecture, fashion, photography, glasswork, theatre, and jewelry. The Collections tab on the menu bar lets users examine an array of examples from the interchanging worlds of art and design, presenting a number of categories. Users can explore by various mediums as described above or from other categories. Periods and Styles features Medieval, Modernism, Art Nouveau, Renaissance, and 1960s Fashion, among others. People displays collections from iconic leaders of art and style, such as David Bowie, Vivienne Westwood, and Auguste Rodin. Under Materials & Techniques users can find Textiles, Ceramics, Quilting & Patchwork, Glass, Painting, and more. Places presents a choice of Japan, China, Islamic Middle East, South Asia, Korea, and Europe 1600-1815. Users can read a general description of each specific category (e.g., "About Textiles," etc.) before examining the digital collection. For each available item in the collection, users can download an image and discover information such as Place of Origin, Date, Artist, Materials & Techniques, and Event. There may also be a summary description to provide good contextual information. Alternatively, users can select a featured collection category from the gallery (e.g., Frames, Architecture, Fashion in Motion, etc.) or scroll to the bottom of the page and select the yellow Search the Collections tab, allowing access to the general online holdings. Notable items in the online collection include items like "The Great Wave" woodblock print from the Japan collection, David Bowie's "Aladdin Sane" album cover, a pair of white leather ankle boots from 1965, and Queen Victoria funeral ephemera. Users may also be interested in several links at the far bottom of the homepage. The Research link outlines online research guidelines and resources, projects, and more, while the International Work link explains ReACH (Reproduction of Art and Cultural Heritage), the program fostering global dialogue on digital reproduction and sharing of art and design artifacts. These resources, alongside the quality and diversity of the Victoria and Albert Museum digital collections, would assure the site's appeal to historians, educators, students, and others in the art and design world.—**ARBA Staff Reviewer**

529.   **Web Gallery of Art. https://www.wga.hu/.** [Website] Free. Date reviewed: 2017.

Recently updated, the Web Gallery of Art presents digital reproductions of over 44,000 works of art and architecture spanning the 8th-19th centuries. The site offers generous supplementary information and organizes the large collections well, making the art extremely approachable. Basic in structure, the site is easy to navigate. Users can select from a variety of tabs or links once they access the site from the Enter Here button on the homepage. An A-Z Artist Index at the bottom of the page lets users find art by artists or three style categories (Medieval, Decorative, Architecture). Selecting a letter presents an alphabetical (last name) table of artists with birthdate, death, period, and school (if applicable). Selecting the Artists tab at the top of the page lets users create lists of artists by chosen search parameters. Users can conduct a more focused search directly from the Search tab. The Web Gallery of Art also offers 16 guided tours through notable places in the art world (e.g., Sistine Chapel, Low Countries) or genres such as international gothic or women artists. Each tour may be structured differently depending on subject but will generally include good historical and artistic context with links to associated artists and their work. Users are encouraged to listen to curated music selections matched to the appropriate era as they embark on their tours or browse the art on their own. Dual Mode displays two different web pages at the same time, allowing users to compare images representative of different eras, styles, artists, subjects, and more. An extensive glossary defines artistic and historical terms from "abacus" and "acanthus" to "woodcut" and "zoomorphic ornament." Users can access additional glossaries, with information on popes, families of the Italian Renaissance, and other subjects under the Database tab. Here, users can also find lists of Museums and Churches, statistical data on the art, and other details. Limiting the content to art created between the 8th and 19th centuries helps focus the browsing experience. The site is an excellent resource for humanities educators and students whether they are just beginning to explore art or wish to expand a foundational knowledge.—**ARBA Staff Reviewer**

Handbooks and Yearbooks

530.   Dempsey, Amy. **Modern Art.** New York, Thames and Hudson, 2018. 176p. illus. index. (Art Essentials series). $16.95pa. ISBN 13: 978-0-500-29322-5.

Billing itself as "smart, beautiful…essential," Dempsey's *Modern Art* provides a brief and chronological overview of the modern art period. Dempsey begins with the rise of the avant-gardes movement in 1860 and ends with what the author characterizes as "beyond the avant-gardes," which includes 1965 through the present. The book is arranged in large chronological blocks which include the avant-gardes (1860-1900); modernisms (1900-1918); new order movements (1918-1945); what Dempsey refers to as "a new disorder" (1945-1965); and the "beyond the avant-gardes" (1965 – present). Within each of these blocks of time, the author has listed the major movements that characterize the time period. For example, modernisms includes Cubism, Futurism, and Dadaism. "A new disorder" includes Beat Art, Neo-Dadism, and Nouveau Réalisme. The content of the sections themselves may be characterized as encyclopedic: each movement include contains a brief description of the defining characteristics; a list of key artists; key features of works from that movement; the primary media or formats used; and key collections containing such works. Each entry contains one representative work from the period. Entries are typically two pages long: one page for the representative work, one page for the content. As a brief resource for the casual art viewer or enthusiast, Dempsey's title is perfect. It provides a brief explanation of the movement and provides a general overview of the kinds of works encompassed by the movement. This is not a title for serious researchers, art students, art historians, or other individuals looking for in-depth analysis. This title is recommended for public and school libraries.—**Megan W. Lowe**

531.   **The Handbook to the Bloomsbury Group.** Derek Ryan and Stephen Ross, eds. New York, Bloomsbury Academic, 2018. 316p. illus. index. $176.00. ISBN 13: 978-1-3500-1491-6; 978-1-3500-1492-3 (e-book).

This book explores the Bloomsbury Group, comprised of a number of writers, intellectuals, philosophers, and artists who lived and worked together near Bloomsbury, London, in the early 20th century. It included Virginia Woolf, E.M. Forster, John Maynard Keynes, and Lytton Strachey, to name but a few. They shared a deep interest in the importance of the arts, and each member brought a unique and faceted approach to the dynamics of the group. This volume contains ten essays, each accompanied by a case study to support the essay. The topics of the essays, in relation to the Bloomsbury Group, are: sexuality, the arts, empire, feminism, philosophy, class, Jewishness, nature, politics, and war. It is a dense and detailed examination of the interactions, writings, behaviors, and influences of this diverse and eclectic group of individuals on both their own time period and succeeding generations.—**Bradford Lee Eden**

Architecture

532.   **Archipedia Classic Buildings https://sah-archipedia.org.** [Website] Free. Date reviewed: 2019.

Archipedia is an online encyclopedia of classic American architecture, with information on architects, design styles, materials, and buildings from each of the 50 states. While noncomprehensive, the site contains information on well over 4,000 buildings, offering a representative look at the best examples of building design across a range of categories. Users can choose a state from the national map to access its individual gallery or examine site contents by Material, Style, Century, Architect, or Type. Browsing within any of these categories (except Century) allows users to choose from a generous A-Z list of tag options. For example, under the Type category, users can select from abbey churches, factories, tract houses, ice cream parlors, saloons, and other categories. A Material may include adobe brick, redwood, steel, glass, limestone, or paneling, while Style incorporates Arts & Crafts, Desert Tradition, German Renaissance Revival, Native American, and Regency among many others. Within the Architect category, users will find information on Joseph L. Eichler, Julia Morgan, Frank Lloyd Wright, and many other individuals and firms. Exploring by State displays a Google map with pinned locations above a gallery of specific building examples (most with photos). Alongside the gallery is a generous list of tags within the following general categories: Top 10 Cities, Top Ten Styles & Periods, Decades, Top 10 Building Types, Top 10 Materials, and Top 10 People and Firms. Users can hover over many of the specific tags for definitions and other detail. Available information for each building varies but may include a substantial essay on the building, architect or style, a thumbnail gallery, or a satellite map of building location.—**ARBA Staff Reviewer**

533.   Greene, Elizabeth B., and Edward Salo. **Buildings and Landmarks of 20th- and 21st-Century America: American Society Revealed.** Santa Barbara, Calif., Greenwood Press/ABC-CLIO, 2018. 324p. illus. index. $105.00. ISBN 13: 978-1-4408-3992-4; 978-1-4408-3993-1 (e-book).

This volume looks at 37 buildings and landmarks in the United States that typify aspects of the time period during which they were built. The building/landmark types are broken up into five categories: Civic, Commercial, Domestic, Military, and Memorial. Within those categories, buildings are presented chronologically from 1901 to 2014. The commercial category covers the largest number of examples (20), followed by the civic category (8). There are 5 examples for the domestic category, and 2 for both military and memorial categories.

The preface to the volume sets the stage by giving a brief overview of the big issues of the century, and how those issues are reflected in our built environment. The introduction goes on to discuss the "Advent of the Consumer Economy," "Expansion of Government Power Domestically and Internationally," "Social Issues, Suburbanization, and Civil Rights," and "Technology and Modernist Designs." The next introductory section explains how a lay person can evaluate buildings and structures by looking at the size, shape, materials used, and decorative elements to place a building or structure in an architectural framework. A chronological list of events of the century completes the introductory material. This section offers dates for significant events in the history of the United States and for the construction of buildings and monuments.

A black-and-white photo of each site begins each entry. The text gives the background for the building/landmark, including the social setting, the political situation, and the means by which the building/landmark came into being. This is followed by a description of the characteristics and functionality, key statistics, cultural significance, and sources for further reading. The final section includes information about how each site has been maintained and/or upgraded or presents a story about the unique use of the building. (For example, the section about the Empire State Building includes a description of the "Run-up event" that has occurred annually since 1978, where runners climb the 1,576 stairs in the building.) The site descriptions are followed by a biographical appendix that offers a very short entry on every person named. A glossary of mostly architectural terms, a comprehensive bibliography, and an index complete the volume.

Using a small and selective group of examples, the author captures changes in the architectural landscape that reflect some of the significant changes in life in the United States during the 20th century and the early years of the 21st century. This work is recommended for general reference collections of all kinds.—**Joanna M. Burkhardt**

534.   Hill, John. **How to Build a Skyscraper.** New York, Firefly Books, 2017. 192p. illus. maps. index. $24.95. ISBN 13: 978-1-77085-960-9.

The design and construction of forty-six buildings from five continents reflect consideration of economics, natural phenomena, functionality, and aesthetic preferences. The choice of buildings includes those with particularly ambitious design and awe-inspiring architectural detailing, ranging from older buildings, such as the Chrysler and Empire State buildings, to newer buildings, such as One World Trade Center and the Shanghai Tower. The two-four page entries for each building include such information as historical background, information about the people involved (the architects and the owners), basic and detailed design information, comparison to similar buildings, materials used, site location, etc. Color illustrations, some with cut-away views of certain cross-sections, provide interesting details. A glossary at the end helps with some of the architectural terminology that may be unfamiliar to most readers and is followed by an index. This resource would serve as a very informative beginning to further research.—**Martha Lawler**

535.   Kimball, Hoke P., and Bruce Henson. **Governor's Houses and State Houses of British Colonial America, 1607-1783.** Jefferson, N.C., McFarland, 2017. 480p. illus. maps. index. $49.95pa. ISBN 13: 978-0-7864-7051-8; 978-1-4766-2593-5 (e-book).

This volume provides a comprehensive reference guide to the houses lived in by British colonial governors and the buildings used as state house or capitols in the North American colonies from 1607 to 1783. In addition to the 13 original colonies, the volume includes East and West Florida and the Province of Quebec (ceded to the British after the French and Indian War). The scope is intentionally broad, and the book includes houses lived in by governors during their tenure and buildings used to fulfill some of the functions of a state house in addition to official, government-funded buildings. Descriptions include the following information if available: location of the building; name of the builder and architect or designer; construction dates; date a building was destroyed, rebuilt, or restored; building materials; floor plan descriptions; exterior and any architectural/historical highlight;, whether a building was used as a governor's residence or state house; other building owners or other building uses; what other information is available about the building; and whether buildings are open to the public or are in private hands.

The beginning of the book contains a brief introduction on colonial government and the different sorts of governor's houses and state houses and how they were funded and built. This is followed by two chapters that provide valuable information to the novice on historic preservation and architecture in the American colonies. Each colony receives its own chapter, which begins with a contextualizing essay on the colony's history. East and West Florida and the Province of Quebec are treated in one chapter. Within chapters, the book provides ample black-and-white illustrations or photographs of structures and floor plans. There are also a number of black-and-white maps that enhance the content. The book concludes with a glossary of architectural terms, an appendix of terms of British governors, 1607-1783, arranged chronologically and by chapter, more than 40 pages of notes, a bibliography, and an index. Highly recommended for public and academic libraries.—**ARBA Staff Reviewer**

536.   **A Spotter's Guide to Amazing Architecture.** London, Lonely Planet, 2018. 128p. illus. maps. $11.99pa. ISBN 13: 978-1-78701-342-1.

This book includes 120 amazing examples of architecture. The coverage is worldwide and equally vast in terms of time period covered and type of building. Each entry has a color picture of the structure in question along with a brief description, a location map, architect (if available), date(s) built, and physical location. Readers will find the Chrysler Building in New York, Frank Lloyd Wright's Fallingwater in Pennsylvania, the Parkroyal on Pickering in Singapore, the Sydney Opera House, Angkor Wat in Cambodia, The Burj luxury hotel in Dubai, La Sagrada Familia in Barcelona, the Chapel of the Rosary in Vence, France, Petra in Jordan, the Yinchuan Museum of Contemporary Art in Yinchuan, China, and many other marvels of human invention. This is probably as much a coffee table book and place to find ideas for where to travel as it is a guide to architecture. Recommended for public libraries.—**ARBA Staff Reviewer**

Graphic Arts

537.   Fonts in Use. https://fontsinuse.com/. [Website] Free. Date reviewed: 2018.

This site offers a vast, searchable collection of typography and the designs it helps define. Users can search the large database of over 11,000 examples of unique typefaces/ fonts and the greater design projects within which they work. A Blog offers unique perspectives on the myriad design pieces and their particular typography. Users can conduct a basic or advanced search from the bar at the top right corner of the homepage, or browse through a gallery of images representing a range of design formats (book covers, album covers, posters, marketing materials, signs, and much more) with identified fonts listed underneath. Users can search and browse through the entire collection, or narrow it to over 2,000 staff picks, representing a subjective selection of the best examples of particular typeface and design. Users can also browse by Topics, Formats, or Typefaces. Topics group the fonts according to design projects associated with Kids, Architecture, Literature, Food/Beverage, Travel, Politics, and other topics. Under Formats, users can select from a list of various media such as Newspapers, Packaging, Album Art, Magazines, and Posters/Flyers. A list of approximately 120 typefaces includes the common Times New Roman, Arial, or Helvetica alongside the more obscure Maax or Motter Ombra. The list reflects the most popular fonts—users may access additional fonts with a matching search term. Users can examine fonts within the individual design image or separately listed next to it. Accompanying information may include contributor, contribution date, publishing date, formats, topics, designers/agencies, artwork location, and tags. Additional images, as well as a narrative description, may also accompany the selection. It is important to note that as many of the images are user-submitted, accompanying information may vary. Registering with the site allows users to contribute their own examples of fonts in design, "like" an image/font, post a comment, and create a personal set (collection).—**ARBA Staff Reviewer**

Photography

538.   Photographer's Market 2018: How and Where to Sell Your Photography. Noel Rivera, ed. Cincinnati, Ohio, North Light Books, 2017. 608p. illus. index. $34.99pa. ISBN 13: 978-1-4403-5253-9.

This is the 41st edition of a reference designed specifically for photographers who want to develop a business. The book begins with a usage guide, advice on how to start selling work, and information for running a photography business, which includes how much to charge, how to self-promote, how to protect copyright, and more. This initial information is followed by 13 articles and interviews, such as "Juggling Life as a Freelancer" and "DIY Marketing," that cover many aspects of the business. The heart of the book provides information on publications and businesses that serve as markets: consumer publications, newspapers, trade publications, stock photo agencies, advertising, design, and related markets, galleries, and art fairs. Some of the information for the markets is conveyed through the system of symbols explained in the book's usage guide. The symbols indicate location, what they buy, how much they pay, etc. Entries for each market contain some or all of the following: information and location, information about the product (newspaper, magazine etc.), needs and specs, and tips on submitting. Those who want a representative to act as agent will find approximately two dozen agencies. Photographers who want to hone their skills will find a section on workshops and photo tours. The Resources portion of the book includes information about stock photography portals, available grants, professional organizations, websites, and a glossary. The book concludes with a geographic index, subject index, and general index. This specialized resource is highly recommended for individuals embarking on photography careers, for schools of photography, and for public libraries.—**ARBA Staff Reviewer**

23 Language and Linguistics

General Works

Digital Resources

539. **Austlang: Australian Indigenous Languages Database http://cdhr.cass.anu. edu.au/research/projects/austlang-australian-indigenous-languages-database.** [Website] Free. Date reviewed: 2019.

The homepage of this freely available database of Aboriginal and Torres Strait Island languages provides readers with a history of the development of the database, abbreviations used, data source, information on how to understand the information discoverable on the database, and directions regarding basic search functions (keyword, proximity, location, or language status). A search takes users to a map with clickables that lead to information on individual languages and dialects (the database does not always distinguish between a language and a dialect). Once a researcher clicks on a particular language, the database provides comments about the language, references, the location(s) where a language is spoken, estimated numbers of people who speak the language, language classification, and links to MURA, the Library and Audio-Visual Archive Catalogue of the Australian Institute of Aboriginal and Torres Strait Islander Studies, and OZBIB, a linguistic bibliography of published works on Australian Institute of Aboriginal and Torres Strait Islander languages.—**ARBA Staff Reviewer**

540. **Corpus of Contemporary American English https://corpus.byu.edu/coca/.** [Website] Free. Date reviewed: 2019.

This extensive database contains information on words and word form usage for American English. It contains over 560,000,000 words from a wide array of texts of spoken word, magazines, academic works, fiction, and newspapers. The corpus (COCA), last updated in 2017, can be used to compare words, find new usage, find subtle differences in meanings, and much more. The database can be accessed in several ways, but may be tricky to navigate. It is recommended that first-time users take advantage of the various help options available throughout the database. General users can certainly find a generous amount of information, but users who create free accounts can create their own personalized virtual corpus, save searches, and perform other functions. Through the basic interface, users can insert a word(s) in the field to explore the search options. Information on singular word frequency, word forms, matching patterns within words, and more can be displayed as a list. A Chart display sectionalizes word frequency information, tracking it across years and sources. The Collocates display shows words that appear either before or after a base word, while the Compare link examines collocates of two words, an excellent tool for gleaning subtle differences between words. There is also a Keyword in Context (KWIC) display which sorts surrounding words to find patterns in word occurrence. As some of these searches and displays can be quite technical, the help option on the right of the page becomes quite essential. The most basic operation of entering a word in the field (for example, "water"), allows users to view the word in context ("…spill into a nearby river that she violates with criminal prohibition against contaminating a municipal water supply…") with source information (*Vanderbilt Law Review*), year of addition to the corpus (2017), and more. Numbered entries can be clicked for further context and information. There are quite a few other data analysis options available via link throughout the database, such as customized word lists, part of speech, and combining words. Of note is a link to the iWeb corpus, which offers word synonyms, definitions, sounds, collocates, topics, clusters, websites, and much more. It is recommended that users first examine the PDF overview or five-minute tour before using the iWeb. COCA and its affiliated iWeb corpus would be a vital resource to educators, linguists, lexicographers, writers, language historians, and others interested in American English.—**ARBA Staff Reviewer**

541.   **Endangered Languages Project. www.endangered languages.com.** [Website] Free. Date reviewed: 2019.

The Endangered Languages Project (ELP) devotes itself to preventing the extinction of the world's endangered languages; an estimated 40 percent of the world's 7,000 languages are considered at risk. Google oversaw the development and launch of the ELP, but site information is curated by the First People's Cultural Council, the Institute for Language Information and Technology at Eastern Michigan University, the Endangered Languages Catalogue/Endangered Languages Project at the University of Hawaii at Manoa, and the Alliance for Linguistic Diversity. The vast amount of information on this site is discoverable in various ways. Users can click on an interactive world map or select a language from a dropdown menu under the Languages link on the homepage. As users drill down, they will find metadata, resources (videos, for example), bibliographic information, and more. To directly jump to things like dictionaries and videos, users can click on the Resources tab on the homepage. Those users who create free accounts have the ability to contribute information. Languages (and thus cultural heritage) are quickly disappearing. ELP gives individuals and organizations the tools to confront language extinction and to revitalize at-risk languages. It is also a reliable place to begin research about world languages.—**ARBA Staff Reviewer**

Handbooks and Yearbooks

542.   **The Oxford Handbook of Endangered Languages.** Kenneth L. Rehg and Lyle Campbell, eds. New York, Oxford University Press, 2018. 976p. index. $175.00. ISBN 13: 978-0-19-061002-9.

Under the editorship of Rehg, Associate Professor of Linguistics at the University of Hawaii at Manoa and Campbell, professor emeritus at the University of Hawaii at Manoa, the overarching goals of this handbook are threefold: to create a reasonably comprehensive reference for endangered languages that conveys the broad scope of the field; to highlight the range of thinking about endangered languages and the responses to it; and to increase understanding of language endangerment, language documentation, and language revitalization, encouraging fresh thinking and new findings. The thorough introduction provides readers with a solid understanding of the issues associated with endangered languages and is quite accessible (even for readers new to the subject). The problems of endangered languages have long been acknowledged by some linguists but more attention was paid to the problem in the wake of Michael Krauss's 1992 paper "The world's languages in crisis" in which he effectively argued that barring intervention 90% of the world's languages would disappear in the coming century. The introduction is subdivided into parts: How Many Languages Are Endangered?; Causes of Language Endangerment; Why Should We Care?; Responses to Language Endangerment; and The Structure of This Handbook. The book's 39 chapters are arranged in five parts: Endangered Languages; Language Documentation; Language Revitalization; Endangered Language and Biocultural Diversity; and Looking to the Future. In the first section (four chapters), readers will find information about such issues as determining the number of the world's endangered languages and indigenous language rights. The second section (14 chapters) conveys a wealth of information on the nuts and bolts of recording and documenting languages. Language Revitalization (10 chapters) includes discussion of new media and endangered languages, different language revitalization practices, stages of language recovery, and much more. The fourth section a variety of topics, including chapters on "Congruence between species and language diversity," "Sustaining biocultural diversity," "Traditional and local knowledge systems as language legacies critical for conservation," and "Interdisciplinary language documentation." The final section looks at such things as teaching linguists to document endangered languages and developing mobile applications for endangered languages. Chapters are fully referenced, and the book concludes with an extensive index. Coverage of this important topic is worldwide, and this book is comprehensive, forward-thinking, and well curated. Highly recommended to academic libraries.—**ARBA Staff Reviewer**

Non-English-Language Dictionaries

Chinese

543.   Cheng, Ma. **15-Minute Mandarin Chinese: Learn in Just 12 Weeks.** Rev ed. New York, DK Publishing, 2018. 160p. illus. $12.95pa. ISBN 13: 978-1-4654-6297-8.

This book, dedicated to helping people learn Mandarin Chinese, begins with a usage guide and a guide on how to use the downloadable audio app. Part of the app download requires users to scan the QR cover on the back of the book. The book is arranged into 12 weeks (chapters) and each week contains (lessons) designed to take 15 minutes each. A lesson from week 5 serves as a good example of how the book works. In this lesson, users will find these sections: Warm up (1 minute); Useful phrases (4 minutes); In conversation

(4 minutes); Words to Remember (4 minutes) and Say it (2 minutes). There is some variation in these sections day to day and week to week. The audio app allows users to hear the words and phrases as spoken by a native speaker and the opportunity to record themselves speaking. There are also pronunciation guides below words and phrases in all the chapters. There are ample color photographs throughout; some depict words and phrases in visual dictionary style and some pair the phrases in the lesson within real-life conversational settings. Chapters also provide conversational and cultural tips. Chapters cover most situations that could be faced by an exchange student, businessperson, or traveler, including introductions, eating and drinking, making arrangements, travel, getting around, accommodation, shopping, work and study, health, at home, services, and leisure and socializing. There is a menu guide at the end of the book, followed by an English to Chinese dictionary and a section on the Chinese writing system. Recommended to public libraries.—**ARBA Staff Reviewer**

French

544.   Lemoine, Caroline. **15-Minute French: Learn in Just 12 Weeks.** Rev ed. New York, DK Publishing, 2018. 160p. illus. $12.95pa. ISBN 13: 978-1-4654-6294-7.

This easy-to-use guide is designed to help students, travelers, and businesspeople learn to speak French in 15 minutes per day over the course of 12 weeks. The first few pages present a usage guide and information on how to use the free audio app that is downloadable at the App Store. Users only need to scan the QR code on the back of the book once the app is downloaded. The 12 weeks cover introductions, eating and drinking, making arrangements, travel, getting around, accommodation, shopping, work and study, health, at home, services, and leisure and socializing. Each week has lessons broken into parts designed to take a set number of minutes. A typical day will have the following sections: Warm up (1 minute); Useful phrases (4 minutes); In conversation (4 minutes); Words to Remember (4 minutes) and Say it (2 minutes). Color photographs enhance comprehension. For instance, the In conversation section will have photographs of people having the conversation in a real-life setting. Each lesson also includes pronunciation guides. The free audio app allows users to hear words and phrases as pronounced by native speakers and the ability to record themselves saying the words and phrases. Throughout users will find cultural and conversational tips. A menu guide and English to French and French to English dictionaries round out the book. Recommended to public libraries.— **ARBA Staff Reviewer**

German

545.   Goulding, Sylvia. **15-Minute German: Learn in Just 12 Weeks.** Rev ed. New York, DK Publishing, 2018. 160p. illus. $12.95pa. ISBN 13: 978-1-4654-6295-4.

This book provides users with the necessary information to learn enough German to function in many situations. Chapters are arranged in twelve weeks that cover introductions, eating and drinking, making arrangements, travel, getting around, accommodation, shopping, work and study, health, the home, services, and leisure and socializing. A user guide includes a section on using the free audio app that is easily downloaded from the App Store. The QR code on the back of the book needs to be scanned in order for the app to work. Each week has timed lessons that include various exercises. A typical week could have the following sections: Warm up (1 minute); Useful phrases (4 minutes); In conversation (4 minutes); Words to Remember (4 minutes) and Say it (2 minutes). Each exercise is supported by color photographs using the words and phrases contained in the lesson. Comprehension is also supported by the audio app which allows users to hear how native speakers pronounce words and phrases. The app also allows users record themselves saying words and phrases. The conversational and cultural tips in textboxes throughout the book enhance the usefulness of the book. One such cultural tip is that many German dogs are working dogs that are often not leashed. Thus, it is always best to approach a rural house with caution, looking out for a sign that says Warnung vor dem Hunde (Beware of the Dog). English to German and German to English dictionaries follow a menu guide and round out the work. Recommended for public libraries.—**ARBA Staff Reviewer**

Japanese

546.   **Japanese English Visual Bilingual Dictionary.** 3d ed. New York, DK Publishing, 2018. 360p. illus. index. $14.95pa. ISBN 13: 978-1-4654-6918-2.

This third edition of the *Japanese English Visual Bilingual Dictionary* uses hundreds of color photographs to help users learn words and phrases necessary to communicate about a variety of things and activities encountered in everyday life. The book is designed with ease of use in mind. In addition to two indexes, one in English and one in Japanese, the chapters are organized thematically in the following order: People, Appearance, Health, Home, Services, Shopping, Food, Eating Out, Study, Work, Transportation, Sports, Leisure, Environment, and Reference. The last section includes time, calendar, numbers, weights and measures, maps, particles and antonyms, and useful phrases. Under each of the hundreds of high-quality, photographs, users will find the word in Japanese, Romaji (the Romanization system familiar to most learners of Japanese), and English. There are textboxes throughout that contain vocabulary and/or phrases that are also ordered with Japanese first followed by Romaji and then English. Pronunciations are not printed in the book but are available via a free app that employs native speakers. This user friendly guide is recommended to public libraries.—**ARBA Staff Reviewer**

Polish

547.   **Polish English Visual Bilingual Dictionary.** Rev ed. New York, DK Publishing, 2018. 360p. illus. index. $14.95pa. ISBN 13: 978-1-4654-6916-8.

This revised and updated edition from DK publishing provides users with a well-written and easy-to-understand visual dictionary of more than six thousand words and phrases. A free accompanying audio app provides correct pronunciation by native speakers. A table of contents is followed by information about the dictionary and how to use it as well as the audio app. The app is easy to download by finding Bilingual Visual Dictionary in the app store and then scanning the book's barcode. Once downloaded, users can search for a page number, open a list of words from that page, and tap on any word to hear the pronunciation. Users can download all the English words, all the Polish words, or both. There are chapters that cover almost any conceivable situation: people, appearance, health, home, services, shipping, study, transportation, environment, food, eating out, leisure, sports, and references. The references chapter includes such things as a world map, numbers, and a calendar, and this is also where users will find useful phrases and particles and antonyms. There are extra textboxes throughout that include additional vocabulary. For example, the page on media has a textbox with words for channel, news, press, soap opera, cartoon, and more. The visuals are all in color and are clear and easy to read. The layouts of the pages make it clear which pictures or parts of pictures go with which words. A Polish word index and an English word index round out the book. Recommended.— **ARBA Staff Reviewer**

Portuguese

548. **Portuguese English Visual Bilingual Dictionary.** 3d ed. New York, DK Publishing, 2018. 360p. illus. maps. index. $14.95pa. ISBN 13: 978-1-4654-6920-5.

This compact Portuguese-English visual bilingual dictionary contains approximately 6,000 Portuguese words and phrases. The material is presented in Portuguese first and English second. Pronunciation is not provided in the text, but an accompanying audio app allows users to hear the words and phrases as pronounced by native English and Portuguese speakers. The sections are as follows: Health, Home, Services (e.g., banking and emergency services), Shopping, Food, Eating Out, Study (e.g., school supplies, math terms), Work, Transportation, Sports, Leisure, Environment (e.g., landscape, weather, architecture, animals), and a reference section that includes basic words and phrases, maps (both world and continental), and more. A short section on adjectives and antonyms and useful phrases precedes a Portuguese index and an English index. The book's layout and high-quality color photographs and illustrations facilitate use. Recommended.—**ARBA Staff Reviewer**

Spanish

549. Brémon, Ana. **15-Minute Spanish: Learn in Just 12 Weeks.** Rev ed. New York, DK Publishing, 2018. 160p. illus. index. $12.95pa. ISBN 13: 978-1-4654-6298-5.

This small book packs a lot into its 160 pages, divided into 12 weeks (chapters) starting with "Introductions" and moving through every subject from eating and drinking to travel to accommodations to leisure and socializing. At the end of the book are a menu and two dictionaries, Spanish to English and English to Spanish. The front matter includes a 3-page guide on how to best use the book. Each chapter includes a series of numbered exercises. Week 3, for example, begins by teaching users about the days and months. It begins with a warm-up exercise designed to take 1 minute, followed by 4 minutes practicing times of the day, 2 minutes practicing useful phrases, 2 minutes on saying certain phrases, and 6 minutes working on higher numbers. Pronunciation is provided on the page along with color photographs and black-and-white clock illustrations. Users can also get practice listening to native speakers pronounce words by downloading the free app (the QR code on the back of the book needs to be scanned). Users can record themselves pronouncing words and phrases as well. The front matter includes a page on using the app features. It is important to note that this book's references are to Spanish as spoken in Spain. An as added bonus, the book includes cultural tips, such as how to greet people, and other advice on things like grocery shopping and camping. Recommended for public libraries.—**ARBA Staff Reviewer**

550. **Fast Talk Latin American Spanish: Guaranteed to Get You Talking.** 2d ed. London, Lonely Planet, 2018. 96p. index. $5.99pa. ISBN 13: 978-1-78657-385-8.

551. **Fast Talk Spanish: Guaranteed to Get You Talking.** 4th ed. London, Lonely Planet, 2018. 96p. index. $5.99pa. ISBN 13: 978-1-78657-385-8.

These two handy phrase books are tailored for travelers to Spanish-speaking countries. Both books are arranged into the following sections: Chatting & Basics, Airport & Transport, Accommodation, Eating & Drinking, Sightseeing, Shopping, Entertainment, Practicalities, and Dictionary. The pages are tabbed with the appropriate chapter heading, so users can quickly find necessary phrases. Fortunately, the phrases are accompanied by pronunciation guides. Most travel-related situations are covered, including introductions, directions, buses and trains, checking in and checking out, ordering food and drinks (and conveying special diet requests and allergies), galleries and museums, bargaining, emergencies, and more. Examples of phrases include: "Does anyone speak English?" "What's the direction?" "What time is checkout?" "How much is this" and "Please bring the bill." There is also a menu decoder at the end of the chapter on eating and drinking. Sections provide easy-to-find fast phrase and phrase builder sections. For instance, the phrase builder in the Practicalities section instructs users in how to say "I have (a/an) cold, cough, fever, etc. The two titles contain much of the same information; the biggest difference between the two books concerns pronunciations. Both phrase books conclude with short English to Spanish and Spanish to English dictionaries and indexes. These small books (approximately five inches by three inches) are ideal travel companions and are highly recommended for public libraries.—**ARBA Staff Reviewer**

552. **Spanish Phrase Book & Dictionary.** Spring House, Pa., Berlitz Publishing Co., 2018. 224p. illus. $9.99pa. ISBN 13: 978-178-004-488-0.

The phrase book and dictionary, written for travelers to Spain, begins with a pronunciation guide and a usage guide before delving into the main sections: Survival, People, Leisure Time, Special Requirements, and In an Emergency. In these sections, users will find information about money, conversation, shopping, going out on the town, business travel, disabled travelers, basic information (conversion tables, grammar, numbers, etc.), and much more. Textboxes throughout the book highlight essential phrases and key words that travelers will likely see and hear. Other textboxes contain information on a variety of topics (the popularity of fútbol, skiing, how to identify a pharmacy, etc.). Pronunciation guides accompany all words and phrases. An English to Spanish dictionary and a Spanish to English dictionary round out the work. In total, this small, easy-to-carry book contains

8,000 words and phrases. Additionally, buyers can access a free app that provides essential words and phrases. This is a recommended purchase for travelers to Spain and for public libraries, especially considering the low cost.—**ARBA Staff Reviewer**

24 Literature

General Works

Bibliography

553. Brown, Sherri L., Carol Senf, and Ellen J. Stockstill. **A Research Guide to Gothic Literature in English: Print and Electronic Sources.** Lanham, Md., Rowman & Littlefield, 2018. 236p. illus. index. 90.00; $85.50 (e-book). ISBN 13: 978-1-4422-7747-2; 978-1-4422-7748-9 (e-book).

This book is a reference guide for librarians tasked with building a collection of print and electronic resources on Gothic literature. Divided into fourteen chapters providing in-depth information and insights on the topic, along with an introduction and timeline of the genre from 1764 to the present, this is probably the most detailed and comprehensive volume on this topic. A chapter on defining the genre itself leads into various collection areas such as handbooks and dictionaries, encyclopedias, biographies and biographical information, literary societies and organizations, various general and specific anthologies and critical editions, periodicals, monographs on various subaspects, edited collections, theses and dissertations, special collections, digital archives, films and television series, comics and graphic novels, and video games. An excellent collection guide for public and academic librarians and libraries on this genre.—**Bradford Lee Eden**

Digital Resources

554. **Bibliomania. http://www.bibliomania.com/bibliomania-static/index.html.** [Website] Free. Date reviewed: 2018.

Bibliomania is a free online source of information on general literature and authors, reference books, and more. Users select from the basic menu on the left column of the homepage or a specific link within the introductory paragraph on the homepage to access digital versions of classic fiction, poems, articles, plays, short stories, etc., in addition to information about them. The site is simply structured: users click through a series of links to discover relevant information. Clicking the Read link displays two fields from which users can search through six genres or individual topics. Selecting a genre (fiction, poetry, short stories, etc.) displays a brief description followed by a listing of links to available titles and related authors. It is important to note that while the available titles are generous they are by no means comprehensive. Short Stories, for example, are gathered from a limited number of writers such as O. Henry, Mark Twain, Ambrose Bierce, Anton Chekhov, and others of their time. Information under the Author link includes a brief biography, links to supplementary information, and a list of their titles available on the site. The Study link on the homepage allows users to search through a listing of topics (Linguistics, Islam, Gothic Authors, etc.) or particular authors (D.H. Lawrence, Jane Austen, Charles Dickens, etc.) sorted into Study Guides or Teacher Resources. Study Guides may include Character Lists, Themes, Further Reading, or other aids. The Research link is where users can find nonfiction classics such as Machiavelli's *The Prince,* Freud's *The Interpretation of Dreams,* Paine's *Rights of Man,* and twenty-one others. The site plans to expand its limited Biography section, which currently includes books on Ben Franklin, Abraham Lincoln, engineer Sir Henry Bessemer, and a few others. Reference materials are also available under the Research link, including Webster's dictionary, Soule's *Book of Synonyms, Roget's Thesaurus,* and more. Although the current inventory is not comprehensive, Bibliomania plans to add new titles and resources in the future. As much of the available literature is considered classic, the site would appeal to educators and students at many levels.—**ARBA Staff Reviewer**

555.   **Bloom's Literature. https://www.infobase.com/wp-content/uploads/2018/02/ FS_Blooms_S.pdf.** [Website] New York, Infobase Publishing, 2018. Price negotiated by site. Date reviewed: 2018.

This high-level database of literary resources explores the most significant classic and contemporary Western novels and plays. Entries include mostly text-based resources with discussion questions, critical articles from Harold Bloom himself, and full-text versions of works, but also use related images, video snippets of reproductions, or the entire work in full feature versions. The site is easy to navigate, enabling users to search and browse broadly by genre or time period and more specifically by author, character, or the work itself. Information from historical timelines and literary themes and movements gives readers an added layer of browsing and connecting works and related concepts in literature. Tools for students address important issues within this subject—such as plagiarism, making citations, evaluating resources, and writing papers—but the text-heavy format will be challenging for more developing writers and readers. Tools for educators are also directed at helping students avoid plagiarism and offer aid in teaching about literature using films. A special resource is the Shakespeare Center, which is a well-organized database tailored to help students understand and write about The Bard and his works. While the database describes itself as focusing on the niche of the classical Western canon, a search of various author nationalities reveals a breadth of global perspectives represented by writers' backgrounds. Librarians and educators working in depth with classic Western literature should take time to review this comprehensive literary resource. Recommended.—**Kasey Garrison**

556.   **PEN America Digital Archive. https://archive.pen.org/.** [Website] Free. Date reviewed: 2018.

PEN America has long been a rich source of literary discussion and analysis. This archive brings to light over fifty years of PEN work through readings, lectures, interviews, performances, conferences, and more, touching on the style, business, and politics of literature. Users can examine the featured collection—"Thirty Years of Toni Morrison"—on the homepage, or they can access further content by conducting a keyword or advanced search from the bar. Alternatively, users can browse the Archive Index by Subject Headings (e.g., Asian American Literature, Editors, Realism, etc.) or Author/Participant. Users can also browse the Entire Archive where they will find signature PEN programming (e.g., PEN International Congress, New Writers Evening, Conversations With..., etc.) alongside individual features such as "Green Thoughts: Writers on the Environment," "The Future of Journalism," and "The Art of the Memoir." Content features writers such as Zadie Smith, Neil Gaiman, Marilynne Robinson, Salman Rushdie, Dave Eggers, Chimamanda Ngoozi Adichie, and many others. Much of the content is available as audio or video files which include information such as participant/author, subject(s), date, genre(s), and media type in addition to a display of related content. Beyond its literary implications, the PEN America Archive broaches subjects of social reform, science, economics, civil rights and, above, all, freedom of expression.—**ARBA Staff Reviewer**

Handbooks and Yearbooks

557.   **Bloomsbury Companion to Modernist Literature.** Ulrika Maude and Mark Nixon, eds. New York, Bloomsbury Academic, 2018. 546p. index. $176.00. ISBN 13: 978-1-7809-3641-3; 978-1-7809-3655-0 (e-book).

The *Bloomsbury Companion to Modernist Literature,* edited by Ulrika Maude and Mark Nixon, provides fresh insights. By viewing Modernist Literature through the prism of seemingly unrelated disciplines, such as economics, the Theory of Relativity, and neurology, the *Bloomsbury Companion,* published by Bloomsbury Academic in 2018, reveals research synergies and provides opportunities for discovery. The editors, Maude (who wrote both the introduction and a chapter), Reader in Modernism and Twentieth Century Literature at the University of Exeter, and Nixon, Associate Professor in Modern Literature at the University of Reading, divide the main body of the *Bloomsbury Companion* into four thematic sections: The Modernist Everyday; The Arts and Cultures of Modernism; The Sciences and Technologies of Modernism; and The Geopolitics and Economics of Modernism. Excluding Maude's thorough introduction from the count, the volume contains twenty-one well-researched chapters, divided into, with one exception, groups of five that support each thematic section into which the chapters are gathered. At the conclusion of each chapter, a bibliography is provided and, in some cases, the author also provides the reader with both notes and a bibliography. The second section includes an annotated bibliography of selected criticism and an A-Z of key terms—substantial definitions accompanied by bibliographies. A timeline placing Modernism within the context of historical events is also provided as is an index. While geared towards the more advanced researcher, this book would certainly assist those less familiar with Modernist Literature when taking those first steps from casual readership into research. The *Bloomsbury Companion to Modernist Literature* makes it new and keeps it real.—**Brian T. Gallagher**

558.   **Critical Approaches to Literature: Feminist.** Robert C. Evans, ed. Hackensack, N.J., Salem Press, 2017. 330p. index. $125.00. ISBN 13: 978-1-68217-557-4; 978-1-68217-578-1 (e-book).

This is the fourth volume in the Salem Press series Critical Approaches to Literature, all edited by Robert C. Evans, a professor of literature at Auburn University and prolific author and editor of works on world literature. Like the other titles in this series (these deal respectively with moral, multicultural, and psychological issues), the body of the work is divided into two parts. The first and shorter part, entitled Critical Contexts, contains four general essays on the subject of about fifteen pages each. The second part, Critical Readings, consists of twelve essays that analyze individual works on specific topics. These essays average twenty pages in length. Each essay is by a different contributor whose credentials are given in separate appendix (most are academics). In this volume, coverage begins with an introductory essay on feminism in Renaissance love poems written by the editor. This is followed by the four Critical Contexts chapters which do not deliver the general overview as intended but instead deal with specific works and authors related to feminism including Margaret Fuller, contemporary poets Margaret Walker and Muriel Rukeyser, and Arthur Miller (one essay deals with the importance of Willy Loman's wife in *Death of a Salesman*). The 12 essays in the Critical Readings section also cover a wide range: Jane Austen's *Emma* and *Mansfield Park,* and separate essays on feminism as exhibited in such works as Kate Chopin's fiction, Zora Neale Hurston's *The Gilded Six-Bits,* Christina Rossetti's poems, Katherine Anne Porter's *Pale Horse, Pale Rider,* Doris Lessing's *The Golden Notebook,* and Zadie Smith's *NW.* The editor has contributed a completely unnecessary chapter on how Desdemona was smothered in six different films of Shakespeare's *Othello.* The gaps in coverage are unfortunate. For example, there is no mention of such important female characters in literature as Medea, Andromache, Becky Sharpe, Scarlett O'Hara, or even Lolita! There is also no mention of Virginia Wolff's ground-breaking book on the subject, *A Room of One's Own.* Each of the essays in this volume concludes with a section on footnotes and a bibliography of works cited. The latter consists chiefly of books and periodical articles and vary in length from six or seven entries to two pages. The book concludes with several appendixes. The first is a four-page chronology of important works and events in the history of feminism, followed by a glossary of terms, and two bibliographies (one called "General" and the other "Additional Works"—these should have been combined). Coverage in these sections ends roughly in the mid 1990s. Due to its erratic coverage and slipshod editing, this book can be recommended only for large collections where material on feminism is in demand.—**John T. Gillespie**

559.   **Critical Approaches to Literature: Multicultural.** Robert C. Evans, ed. Hackensack, N.J., Salem Press, 2017. 301p. index. $125.00. ISBN 13: 978-198217-575-0; 978-1-68217-576-7 (e-book),

The 18 chapters in this book offer an eclectic presentation of the possible modes of multicultural study of literature. From drinking in texts of the Elizabethan era, to Jewish elements in recent Latino literature, connections between Langston Hughes and Tyler Perry, and analyses of works by Wilfred Owen, Zora Neale Hurston, and Sherman Alexie, these authors explore numerous dimensions of literary research. In a number of chapters, the broader sociocultural setting of the text or of the performance plays a key role, analyzing the role of literary texts within diverse communities. The chapter by Melissa D. Carden ("Introduction to Multicultural Criticism: An Overview") offers a useful framework for the book, drawing on five recent books on approaches to literary analysis.

The copyediting, alas, has been poor in places: incomplete entries in a reference list, a repeatedly misspelled author's name, a missing biography in the "Contributors" section, and so on. Although an occasional distraction, this does not lessen the value of this volume, and libraries with patrons studying literature should consider adding it to their collections, if it fits within their budget.—**Mark Schumacher**

560.   **Critical Insights: Inequality.** Kimberly Drake, ed. Hackensack, N.J., Salem Press, 2018. 238p. index. $105.00. ISBN 13: 978-1-68217-690-0; 978-1-68217-691-7 (e-book).

The fourteen essays in this volume explore diverse elements of inequality presented in literature, film, and art. The authors discussed range from the well-known, such as George Orwell, Toni Morrison, James Baldwin, and Frederick Douglass, to somewhat less-well-known figures such as Anders Lustgarten and Nora Okja Keller. The way that inequality is presented in these works varies greatly from one work to the next. For example, Orwell's science fiction is quite different from Morrison's poignant depiction of a collective condition facing African American women. The role and power of inequality resonate through these essays.

The introductory texts by the editor set the stage well for the studies that follow. She explains that the works being analyzed "focus primarily on the effects of or the resistance to inequality and to the violence that often accompanies it (page vii)." Brief summaries of the following chapters are also quite useful, allowing readers to focus on the elements of this broad topic that interest them most.

As sometimes the case with this series, copy editing needs improvement. A few words are misspelled, a few references out of order, etc. Otherwise there is much useful information about the subject of inequality as it treated in literature and art. This text will be most useful to academic libraries; unfortunately, its cost may challenge some libraries.—**Mark Schumacher**

561.   **Critical Insights: Post-Colonial Literature.** Jeremiah J. Garsha, ed. Hackensack, N.J., Salem Press, 2017. 269p. index. $105.00. ISBN 13: 978-1-68217-559-0; 978-1-68217-560-6 (e-book).

The field of postcolonial literature is so vast and encompassing that it can sometimes be difficult to make decisions when choosing course texts. For those of us who do not necessarily specialize in the field, choosing an appropriate survey text can be daunting. It is nearly impossible to cover every aspect of the field with any one volume used in an introductory course.

Critical Insights: Post-Colonial Literature is a rare text. It has managed to introduce core philosophies of the field in such a way that neophyte students will be engaged. The rich bibliography section(s) will allow students to continue their research into more advanced topics. Edited by Jeremiah Garsha, a postdoctorate researcher at the University of Cambridge, this is an essential text for anyone teaching undergraduate postcolonial literature.

Garsha has set out to develop a text that will "explore postcolonial literature in its most broad sense" (vii). For those of you "entirely unfamiliar with postcolonial literary tradition" (vii), this book is for you. That is a crucial pedagogical theme that needs to be more prevalent in literature studies. At a time that students are becoming more aware of the world around them and are attempting to engage with subject matter that is by and large unfamiliar to them, *Post-Colonial Literature* would be a suitable candidate to capture the intellectual attention of curious students.

Divided into four main sections, Garsha has enlisted specialists from across the field. In the preface to this volume, Garsha writes that each contributor has been shaped by postcolonialism. It is refreshing to see so many varied voices brought together in one volume. This speaks to the editor's wish to educate and engage with students. In this respect, he has done a masterful job. Students will not only gain insight into a variety of texts and authors that quite possibly would have been unknown to them before reading this volume, but will also have a better understanding of the three general eras of postcolonialism. Speaking to these eras in the preface, Garsha's intent was to give as many themes and authors equal time as possible (xviii). Covering as much ground as this volume does is to be commended. What is also to be commended here is the notion that graduate students and postdocs can add to the conversation about postcolonialism. Garsha, himself a postdoc researcher, made the right decision to include a fair amount of graduate students' contributions. That is something that would be worth mentioning to students if using this book.

The first section of the text outside of the powerful preface by Garsha and introduction by Egodi Uchendu and Chinonye Ekwueme-Ugwu is a broad overview of the field with several essays on issues ranging from the use of graphic novels to represent the subaltern to an excellent take on the postcolonial reception of *The Tempest* by Dhrubajyoti Sarkar.

The second main section of the text covers critical readings. Starting off with an excellent argument on how to view *Sir Gawain and the Green Knight* from a postcolonial lens, the following essays delve into the heavyweights of postcolonial theory and touch on some of the essential texts of the field. What makes this section so engaging, from a pedagogy standpoint, is that it challenges students to view postcolonial literature on a global scale. By including texts from not only Africa and India, but the United Kingdom and Hawaii, we are shown that the field of postcolonial literature is immense and that there truly is something out there for those students hungry to engage with these texts.—**Lucas P. Berrini**

562.   **Critical Insights: Rebellion.** Robert C. Evans, ed. Hackensack, N.J., Salem Press, 2017. 278p. index. $105.00. ISBN 13: 978-1-68217-557-6; 978-1-68217-558-3 (e-book).

Part of the Critical Insights series from Salem Press, this book focuses on the topic of rebels and rebellion in literature. After an introductory essay, the volume is divided into two major sections, Critical Contexts and Critical Readings. Besides examining stalkers in Renaissance love poetry, the figure of Falstaff, John Donne's *The Perfume,* and Herman Melville's *Billy Budd,* there are a plethora of books discussed along with their rebels: Robin Hood, John Donne's "Holy Sonnet XIV," the short fiction of Mary Wilkins Freeman, Ibsen's *An Enemy of the People,* Camus's *The Plague,* Nella Larsen's *Quicksand,* the fiction of Robert A. Heinlein, Jack Kerouac's *On the Road,* Kurt Vonnegut's "Harrison Bergeron," Harlan Ellison's "Repent, Harlequin!" *Star Wars and the Rebel Alliance,* and *The Hunger Games.* This is an excellent resource for any undergraduate class examining politics, rebellion, and rebellious characters in literature.—**Bradford Lee Eden**

563.   **Critical Insights: Survival.** Robert C. Evans, ed. Hackensack, N.J., Salem Press, 2018. 250p. index. $105.00. ISBN 13: 978-1-68217-920-8; 978-1-68217-963-5 (e-book).

Part of the Critical Insights series from Salem Press, this book focuses on the topic of survival in the literature and science fiction genre. As with all books in this series, chapters are divided into two primary sections: Critical Contexts and Critical Readings.

Four chapters comprise the Critical Contexts section, dealing with survival psychology in Zora Neale Hurston's *Barracoon,* an overview of the survival theme in literature, survival in American short fiction, and survival in two works by Rudyard Kipling and Robert Louis Stevenson. Ten chapters are contained in the Critical Readings section, examining the works of Shakespeare, Mark Twain, Bram Stoker, Jack London, John Steinbeck, Philip Larkin, Octavia Butler, Margaret Atwood, and the true story of Christopher McCandless. This volume provides an extensive exploration of the topic of survival in literature, and would assist as an excellent textbook or reference for an undergraduate class on this topic.—**Bradford Lee Eden**

564.   **Critical Insights: The Immigrant Experience.** Maryse Jayasuriya, ed. Hackensack, N.J., Salem Press, 2018. 268p. illus. index. $105.00. ISBN 13: 978-1-68217-692-4; 978-1-68217-693-1 (e-book).

This work is one of dozens of volumes in the Themes group of the Critical Insights series (other titles include *Modern Japanese Literature, Contemporary Immigrant Short Fiction,* and *Violence in Literature.*) Thirteen contributors, including the editor, offer analyses of individual works by immigrant authors, or discussions of broader topics, such as contemporary Arab American literature, narratives of undocumented young people in the DACA era, Latina or Latino young adult literature, or immigrants in Jewish American literature." A major contribution of this book is the introduction to the reader of many less-known authors from a wide range of immigrant backgrounds, including India, Pakistan, and Lebanon, among others. In more focused studies, Junot Diaz's *The Brief Wondrous Life of Oscar Wao* and Ha Jin's *A Free Life* are examined closely within the framework of immigration events and themes. Following the articles, two lists provide titles of books by immigrant authors and secondary research on the themes explored here.

As with other volumes in this and similar series from this publisher, copyediting needs some improvement. In one chapter, a sentence misnames the author of a text being analyzed and the word "position" is misspelled. In another article, one sentence has nine words run together without a single space. That being said, there is much useful information about a kind of writing with which that many Americans are not familiar. This book will certainly broaden the reader's view of "the richness of the literature of the immigrant experience in the United States" (p. xi). Most academic and many public libraries should consider adding the book if it falls within their budget.—**Mark Schumacher**

565.   **Critical Survey of World Literature.** 3d ed. Robert C. Evans, ed. Hackensack, N.J., Salem Press, 2017. 6v. illus. index. $499.00/set. ISBN 13: 978-1-68217-615-3; 978-1-68217-638-2 (e-book).

This six-volume set is the third revised edition of the work previously published in 1993 and 2009 as *Magill's Choice of World Literature.* The new edition has been expanded to include more women writers and young adult authors; this edition also updates biographical and bibliographical information.

The work is organized alphabetically by authors, featuring around four hundred writers of fiction, nonfiction, poetry, and drama, spanning almost fifty different countries and all time periods, back to the 6th century BCE.

Each profile includes a brief block of quick facts including the author's nationality, birth and death dates, and a one-sentence summary of their place on the literary landscape. This is followed by a biography section, an analysis of the author's work as a whole, a detailed outline of two or three selected works, a final summary, a list of suggested discussion topics, and a bibliography of works by and about the author. The final volume offers some robust reference features, including an extensive glossary, author and work title indexes, and lists of profiled authors grouped by geographical location and by various categories ("Jewish writers," "Women," etc.).

In all, this work is an excellent comprehensive source for concise, authoritative information about authors of world literature, but of course only offers basic starting points for those pursuing serious research on particular writers.—**Autumn Faulkner**

566.   DeLong, Anne. **The Victorian World: A Historical Exploration of Literature.** Santa Barbara, Calif., Greenwood Press/ABC-CLIO, 2019. 238p. index. (Historical Explorations of Literature). $63.00. ISBN 13: 978-1-4408-6043-0; 978-1-4408-6044-7 (e-book).

Like the ten other titles in this series, which examine topics such as the Jazz Age, the Civil War era, Shakespeare, and the Harlem Renaissance, this book focuses on a small group of works. In this case, they are *Jane Eyre (1847), Wuthering Heights (1847), A Tale of Two Cities (1859),* and Victorian poetry and social justice, focusing on Elizabeth Barrett Browning's work. A brief introduction and a chronology begin the text, providing a context for the information to follow. The four chapters each have a biographical section, a synopsis of the work, a "historical background" of three or four pages, and a "Why We Read This Work" essay. The bulk of each chapter is comprised of a group of historical documents which address the themes of the work being presented. The topics presented in these texts include women's work (Charlotte Brontë), marriage, property, and inheritance laws (Emily Brontë), the French Revolution and social class, and urban poverty (Dickens), and child labor and workers' rights (Browning).

Academic and high school libraries will find this text quite useful for English literature classes studying the 19th century. Public libraries should also consider it for their patrons.—**Mark Schumacher**

567.   **Magill's Literary Annual 2018.** Jennifer Sawtelle, ed. Hackensack, N.J., Salem Press, 2018. 2v. illus. index. $210.00/set. ISBN 13: 978-1-68217-680-1; 978-1-68217-681-8 (e-book).

This latest edition provides readers with in-depth reviews of 150 works of literature published in 2017. Entries appear in alphabetical order and include title information, author name and birth year (death year if necessary), publisher name, type of work, and period and location depicted. For each book, readers will find a summary in italics. This is followed by a list of primary characters for novels and short fiction. The front matter of both volumes contains a "Complete Annotated List of Contents" in alphabetic order. The second volume concludes with three indexes, "Category Index," which groups books according to type—biography, current affairs, memoir, novel, short fiction, true crime, etc.; a title index; and an author index. Entries range from four to five pages; all are signed by the contributors listed in the front matter of volume one (though it should be noted that contributor names appear without affiliations). On the whole entries are informative, providing readers with an understanding of the book's contents as well as a sense of where it fits in the larger literary scene. Purchasers of the print receive access to a complimentary archive comprised of the last forty years of literary annuals. It appears that ongoing access depends on an annual purchase of the print version. This set is recommended for academic and public libraries.—**ARBA Staff Reviewer**

568.   **Masterplots, 2010-2018: Supplement.** Hackensack, N.J., Salem Press, 2018. 2v. illus. index. $225.00/set. ISBN 13: 978-1-64265-032-7; 978-1-64265-033-4 (e-book).

The newest two-volume supplement to this important and extremely popular title documents and critically evaluates 187 examples of serious fiction published in English between 2010 and 2018 worldwide. They are arranged alphabetically by title, and each review is approximately 4 pages in length and begins with a block of reference material in the following order: full book title, author(s), birth and death dates (as appropriate), first published, first performed, type of work, type of plot, time of plot, locale(s), and list of principal characters with brief descriptions. The summary of each essay-review examines the author(s) plot, intent, and focus along with a critical evaluation. A number of appendixes are provided at the end of volume 2 which includes a title index, author index, chronological index, type of plots, and cumulative title and author indexes for the 12-volume series. An updated supplement to this wonderful reference work.—**Bradford Lee Eden**

Children's and Young Adult Literature

General Works

Handbooks and Yearbooks

569.   Cave, Roderick, and Sara Ayad. **A History of Children's Books in 100 Books.** New York, Firefly Books, 2017. 272p. illus. index. $29.95. ISBN 13: 978-1-77085-957-9.

Cave (*Impressions of Nature: A History of Nature Printing*), a print historian, and Ayad, an art historian, have produced a significant history of children's books with a focus on the former British Empire, the United States, and Europe. The 100 books chosen for discussion are interesting for a variety of reasons and are not necessarily examples of the best children's literature. The authors' approach is thematic rather than chronological, with 11 eleven chapters covering "First Steps: Oral Traditions and Pre-Literacy"; "Once Upon a Time, in a Land Far Away"; "Abecedarias and Battledores"; "The 'Childe's First Tutor': The Education of the Young"; "Small Books for Small People: The Growth of Publishing for the Young"; "Tales of Tails: Animal Stories for Children"; "Innocence, Experience and Old-Fashioned Nonsense"; "Fairies and Frighteners: Tempters, Tearaways and Cautionary Tales"; "Heroes in Action: Time Travel, Detections and Derring-Do"; "The War Years and Beyond"; and "Growing Up Fast: Comics, TV and New Media." Each chapter is divided into clearly labeled major sections that delve into various aspects of the topics, demonstrating the authors' considerable expertise. A 2-page supplement on children's books as historical artifacts is followed by a lengthy bibliography, a glossary, and the general index. The entire volume is richly illustrated in high quality photos from children's books and artifacts on thick, glossy paper with an eye-pleasing layout. The writing is scholarly but easily followed by a general adult audience. This reviewer wonders why other publishers' less-impressive productions are so much more expensive. At this price, every library with a children's collection or readers interested in children's literature, and every librarian with this interest should consider this an essential purchase. LIS faculty might consider it as a textbook.—**Rosanne M. Cordell**

Bibliography

570. **Children's Picture Book Database at Miami University https://dlp.lib. miamioh.edu/picturebook/.** [Website] Free. Date reviewed: 2018.

This database organizes information on over 5,800 children's picture books that would appeal to students between preschool and third grade. Simply structured, users can search topics, concepts, or skill-levels via over 1,000 keywords or browse in several ways. Browse A-Z List offers an extensive alphabetized list of subject terms covering issues or concepts (self-esteem, friendship, monsters, etc.), places (Antarctica, Egypt, etc.), emotions (envy, homesickness, etc.), animals (blue jay, starfish, etc.), activities (karate, Cinco de Mayo, etc.), and other simple or complex ideas conveyed throughout picture books. Browse Categories enables users to find keywords within 6 broad umbrella categories: Health & Medicine; Literature, Language & Communication; Mathematics; Natural History and Natural Science; Social Studies; and Visual & Performing Arts. Browse Abstracts organizes nearly 6,000 brief picture book profiles alphabetically. Information generally includes title, author, brief synopsis of the story, and list of applicable keywords. Clicking on the picture book title links to a book cover thumbnail and expanded publishing and citation information. The search bar would be helpful to those who would like information by author. Users will find many recognizable titles and familiar authors such as Eric Carle, Eve Bunting, Dr. Seuss, Leo Leonni, Cynthia Rylant, and others. The site's simple structure helps users find relevant information quickly.—**ARBA Staff Reviewer**

571. Dorr, Christina, and Liz Deskins. **LGBTQAI+ Books for Children and Teens.** Chicago, American Library Association, 2018. 132p. illus. index. $45.00pa.; $40.50pa. (ALA members). ISBN 13: 978-0-8389-1649-0.

This slim, informative volume will be helpful to new and more experienced librarians alike. It is particularly helpful, and necessary, to those for whom dealing with LGBTQAI+ literature and/or issues poses a challenge. The foreword, introduction, and "Final Thoughts" sections are must-reads, as they provide support for librarians concerned with any aspects of LGBTQAI+ and make many salient points that practitioners can take to heart as they serve these demographics in their library communities. Annotated book lists for three categories—Young, Middle Grade, and Teen Readers—provide plot summaries, comments on illustrations, evaluation of content and back matter, awards and honors (if applicable), discussion questions, related resources, and bibliographic information for each title, along with insight and rationale regarding selection for each age group. The history of LGBTQIA+ literature for children and teens is discussed. The authors acknowledge that society as a whole has "turned a corner" regarding acceptance, but still has work to do. Readers need to see themselves reflected in the literature they read as well as be able to engage with characters that are different than they are in order to develop empathy and fully experience the diversity of the real world. The books included in this volume, along with others, will provide mirrors, windows, and doors for readers into an important and vital subject. There is a wealth of professional support and collection development assistance here. Recommended.—**Cynthia Ortiz**

572.   Thomas, Rebecca L. **A to Zoo: Subject Access to Children's Picture Books.** 10th ed. Santa Barbara, Calif., Libraries Unlimited/ABC-CLIO, 2018. 1638p. index. (Children's and Young Adult Literature Reference Series). $95.00. ISBN 13: 978-1-4408-3434-9; 978-1-4408-3435-6 (e-book).

This guide to picture books for preschool children to second graders remains the most comprehensive and versatile such information tool for librarians, teachers, and parents. Children's literature scholar and retired elementary school librarian Rebecca L. Thomas continues her solo effort keeping this long-standing resource up-to-date and relevant. Following nearly the same growth rate as the previous edition (see ARBA 2015, entry 694), this new volume has increased yet again by over 15 percent—both in the number of entries (19,716) and by page count. Yet it is still a manageable volume. This resource makes it easy to build lists of books on defined topics as well as locate specific books by subject—even by title, illustrator, or author name alone (the main "bibliographic guide" doubles as the author listing).

Most listings continue to be imprints from the 2000s, with 2016 and 2017 titles newly added, as well as incorporations from the last supplement (see ARBA 2015, entry 694). Interestingly, despite the significant increase in content, the entries are cataloged under nearly the same number of subjects. In fact, at 1,223 subjects, this volume contains two fewer than the last edition. This suggests an updated and more streamlined arrangement, although in some ways the subject guide has become more focused. For example, with 55 total "Birds" headings and subheadings (versus 54, last edition) the term "roosters" now falls under the "Birds—chickens, roosters" subheading rather than as a standalone term. The heading "Homosexuality" has been replaced by "LGBTQ" (with a *see also* to the new term, "Gender identity"). For so many new books to file into the existing subject arrangement with little need for update or expansion also suggests it was well designed in the first place.

Compared to *Children's Core Collection* (23rd ed.) (see ARBA 2019, entry 83), which excels at providing annotations and reviews, *A to Zoo* gives users a more expedient look-up of picture book titles by subject heading and more concise entries. That *A to Zoo* lacks reviews is of little consequence because the building of its catalog necessarily included the vetting of children's literature review sources. *A to Zoo* remains the single best reference resource for quick and comprehensive access to children's picture books by subject. It continues to support the varied programming, curricular, and entertainment needs of librarians, teachers, homeschoolers, and parents and should have a place in every public library.—**Lucy Duhon**

Drama

Handbooks and Yearbooks

573.   **Critical Survey of Drama.** 3d ed. Carl Rollyson, ed. Hackensack, N.J., Salem Press, 2017. 8v. index. $599.00/set. ISBN 13: 978-1-68217-622-1; 978-1-68217-639-9 (e-book).

The *Critical Survey of Drama,* third edition, has been revised and updated to include significant playwrights who have emerged since the 2003 second edition (see ARBA 2004, entry 1015) and reorganized so that it now begins with a series of overview essays followed by dramatist profiles before ending in appendixes. The appendixes include a listing by year of major awards in drama, a geographical index of dramatists, dramatic terms and movements, a timeline, a bibliography, and a subject index. The eight-volume set now provides 638 essays, 64 covering broad themes leaving the remaining 574 essays to individual dramatists in alphabetical order. Forty-five of these are new to this edition and cover dramatists such as Annie Baker, Lin-Manuel Miranda, and Lynn Nottage who have "recently come to be regarded as established figures in the theater." It would be helpful to have a clearer understanding of the criteria for these additions so that any omissions would be better understood. Seventy-two profiles that appeared in the previous edition have been updated to include new works or current research and the bibliographies in all of the entries have been revised and annotated. Essays on dramatists are standardized into seven distinct sections "to allow predictable and easy access to the types of information of interest to a variety of users" and this format proves very successful. The 7 sections include Principal Drama, Other Literary Forms, Achievements, Biography, Analysis, Bibliography, and Contributor Byline. It is a valuable feature that the first production date and the publication date of every play are provided, and the analysis section of the entries are particularly helpful as they are carefully considered and often articulate the nuances and focus of a given dramatist while placing them within critical context. The bibliography in the appendix focuses on 4 broader dramatic themes; criticism, historical, world regions, and technique. Again, how these themes were settled on and defined could be better explained. Also, it must be noted that this bibliography contains few contemporary titles. The sole editor on this edition, Rollyson has accomplished an admirable feat as the essays are accessible yet astute and cover an exhaustive, if conventional, array of subjects throughout the 8 volumes. This set is a solid cornerstone to any reference collection which seeks to include drama as a subject area and would be appropriate to both larger public and academic libraries, especially those in support of theater arts programs.—**Todd Simpson**

Fiction

General Works

574.   **Companion to Victorian Popular Fiction.** Kevin A. Morrison, ed. Jefferson, N.C., McFarland, 2018. 312p. index. $45.00pa. ISBN 13: 978-1-4766-6903-8; 978-1-4766-3359-6 (e-book).

The *Companion to Victorian Popular Fiction,* published by McFarland in 2018, offers an appreciative and well-cited assessment of the Victorian literary landscape, a landscape that might surprise novice researchers for whom this very competent and informative companion is suitably geared with its unexpected twists and dark passages and grudging empathy. Under the editorial guidance of Kevin Morrison, a distinguished professor in the School of Foreign Languages at Henan University in Kaifeng, China, and author of two other books on Victorian literature, the 156 contributing authors create a cohesive narrative structure by focusing on these stable basics: authors; select titles; and subjects such as publishers, libraries, social issues, and genres. Featured authors are used to explore a genre or the cultural aspects of the time period through an examination of either their work or their lives or both the author's professional and personal persona. Many of these featured writers will be unknown to the reader, and that is one of the many pleasures proffered by the companion: the opportunity for new readers to discover forgotten writers and find that the issues and themes they wrote about are still relevant today, issues such as gender issues, women's rights, mental illness, poverty, and addiction. Morrison's brief preface provides the reader with a succinct guide to arrangement and topic coverage. Morrison also includes a "Works Cited" for those readers who want to explore further. An index of the authors, titles, and subjects featured in the companion concludes the book. To sum up: the *Companion to Victorian Popular Fiction* weaves together an alphabetical listing of entries to create a literary and social narrative that bridges the gap between the Victorian Era and the students' present, making this guide a welcome addition to any library's shelves.—**Brian T. Gallagher**

575.   **The 1950s: A Decade of Modern British Fiction.** Nick Bentley, Alice Ferrebe, and Nick Hubble, eds. New York, Bloomsbury Academic, 2019. 302p. index. (The Decades Series). $136.00. ISBN 13: 978-1-3500-1151-9; 978-1-3500-1152-6 (e-book).

Part of The Decades Series from Bloomsbury Academic, this volume focuses on British fiction published in the 1950s. The series attempts to provide a contextual framework for the study of British fiction from the 1950s to the present. The introduction discusses how the 1950s were a decade of change in British society, and how the fiction writing was both affected by and influenced these changes. Eight essays explore the many authors and books of this decade, from the works of C.S. Lewis and J.R.R. Tolkien, to topics such as angry young men and female fiction, homosexual novels and race/anti-racism, the politics of youth and detective fiction, and the uncertainty of the literary canon and literary establishment during this decade. Appendixes include a timeline of works, a timeline of national events, a timeline of international events, and biographies of all the authors discussed in the essays. A timely and nicely framed collection of essays on British fiction written in the 1950s.—**Bradford Lee Eden**

576.   **The 1960s: A Decade of Modern British Fiction.** Philip Tew, James Riley, and Melanie Seddon, eds. New York, Bloomsbury Academic, 2018. 332p. illus. index. (The Decades Series). $136.00. ISBN 13: 978-1-350-01168-7; 978-1-350-01169-4 (e-book).

These essays explore 1960s British fiction within the historical and cultural context of the decade to convey why the selected works were influential at the time and why they continue to give insight into postwar and postcolonial Britain. The volume's introductory essay portrays a vibrant Britain, emerging from the ruins of war and shaking up the old order—from the end of rationing, to new educational opportunities, the breaking down of class lines, and the start of relative affluence—a time of youthful rebellion, open sexuality, and changing women's roles—all of which shows up in the fiction of the decade. Subsequent essays focus on specific topics with an overview of key writers and themes. As just a few examples: the "youthquake" that hit London, the genre of National Service (conscription) novels, female novelists that became popular because of their "talent, good looks, and racy writing," the archetype of the "swinging single girl," gay fiction, novels about the changing education system like *To Sir with Love,* the New Wave of British Science Fiction, and more. The essay on black writers explains how the 1948 Nationality Act gave former colonials the right to live and work in Britain as full citizens, setting off a wave of Caribbean, African, and South Asian migration and, with it, novels about adjusting to life in the new multicultural Britain. Existential and experimental novelists, like John Fowles (*The French Lieutenant's Woman* 1969) and Muriel Sparks (*The Prime of Miss Jean Brodie* 1961), are considered in detail, showing how these writers reinvigorated the British novel, after the genre had abdicated the role of storyteller to the movies. The 1960 obscenity trial resulting from Penguin's decision to publish D. H. Lawrence's *Lady Chatterley's Lover* in an unexpurgated paperback edition is discussed by several of the contributors. Penguin's legal victory is considered a watershed moment in the start of the 60's sexual revolution. Not only was this titillating book available in its full version for the first time, but even more importantly, because it was in paperback, it was affordable to all. Features include three helpful timelines: major works of the 1960s, key national events, and significant international events. Revisiting the richness of 1960s British fiction gives new insights into the life and changing culture of the time, particularly for those who did not experience this exuberant decade first-hand.—**Adrienne Antink**

577.   Wyatt, Neal, and Joyce G. Saricks. **The Readers' Advisory Guide to Genre Fiction.** 3d ed. Chicago, American Library Association, 2019. 312p. index. $64.99pa.; $58.49pa. (ALA members). ISBN 13: 978-0-8389-1781-7.

This third edition, part of the Reader's Advisory Guide series from ALA Editions, provides both depth and breadth to librarians on the topic of genre fiction. Issues examined include the relationship of genre fiction on subgenres and other literature genres and subjects; a brief history of the topic; descriptions of key authors and titles with explanations; how to conduct a conversation with readers, listeners, and viewers in order to learn the tools and skills between a genre fiction collection and your patrons; a crash course on genre fiction as well as a quick overview and key authors; resources and techniques for keeping up-to-date on new developments in genre fiction; and tips for marketing a genre fiction collection. The various genre fictions covered in this book include adrenaline, psychological suspense, mystery, literary fiction, science fiction, fantasy, westerns, historical fiction, relationship fiction, romance, and horror. A great guide for librarians building collections in these areas.—**Bradford Lee Eden**

Crime and Mystery

578.   **100 Greatest Literary Detectives.** Eric Sandberg, ed. Lanham, Md., Rowman & Littlefield, 2018. 232p. index. $45.00; $42.50 (e-book). ISBN 13: 978-1-4422-7822-6; 978-1-4422-7823-3 (e-book).

This enormously important gift to scholars, edited by Eric Sandberg, sets a benchmark for scholars and scholarship in detective literary fiction. The excellent 7-page introduction focuses much needed attention on, and gives poignant recognition to, this literary stepchild. This reference volume may in fact be a catalyst that moves detective literature from literary stepchild status to provide it a genuine and legitimate place in literary scholarship. This is decidedly not an all-inclusive list; however, the mere presence of these 100 builds a credible core for the genre. Content intentionally spans the globe, accurately drawing from this detective genre that is found in most cultures. The contributors are scholars, authors, and professors who provide a plethora of varied geographical resonance in their entries. Each entry is clearly focused, whether on the detective as authorial character, problem-solver, or as a reflection of others—such as Shanghai detective Huo Sang who is assisted by Bao Lang (p. 94-96) and closely parallels the more widely known Holmes and Watson. The unique perspective and instilled vision of each contributor to their detective makes this a rich and valuable literary resource. The uniformly brief entries are arranged alphabetically by detective and consist of about two pages each. Each entry finishes with a brief "Selected Bibliography." These are enriched with 12 pages of "Notes." Then a thorough Index of about 6 pages gives quick guidance to the reader's further search. A final 6 pages provide brief information about the editor and 66 contributors. This excellent monograph should be added to academic library collections from high school through community college and university. Large public libraries and special libraries that serve fiction readers should also acquire this resource.—**James W. Agee**

Historical Fiction

579.   **Critical Insights: Historical Fiction.** Virginia Brackett, ed. Hackensack, N.J., Salem Press, 2018. 258p. index. $105.00. ISBN 13: 978-1-68217-710-5; 978-1-68217-711-2 (e-book).

This book, part of the Critical Insights series by Salem Press, focuses on historical fiction. While many books in this series are geared towards college students, the majority of essays in this volume are written for the teaching and reading programs of students in middle and senior high schools. A short introduction detailing the parameters of the book is followed by the Critical Contexts section comprised of four essays, which discuss the historicization of the historical novel, criticism, female protagonists of young adult historical fiction, and identity formation in young adult historical fiction. The Critical Readings section is comprised of eleven essays ranging from a comparative analysis of medieval romance, the Gothic novel, legend and history, translating history for young readers, crossover in Chinese and Chinese American fiction, the American Civil War in historical fiction for young readers, the African American historical novel, Depression Era historical fiction, and real figures in historical biographical fiction. This book helps to explain the differences between real history and historical fiction for young readers, and thus is an essential book for teachers in middle to high school education.—**Bradford Lee Eden**

Romance Fiction

580.   **Encyclopedia of Romance Fiction.** Kristin Ramsdell, ed. Santa Barbara, Calif., Greenwood Press/ABC-CLIO, 2018. 496p. index. $94.00. ISBN 13: 978-0-313-33572-3; 978-0-313-05405-1 (e-book).

This monograph bridges two worlds. Edited by a librarian the book is a boon to reference and readers' advisory librarians not familiar with the genre but wanting to gain familiarity quickly and succinctly. The text is also extremely helpful to fans and aspiring writers of romance because it provides a straightforward wide angle view of the genre. As an encyclopedia the entries are in alphabetical order with entries ranging from half a page to multiple pages. Each entry includes a further reading section and may include *see also* suggested entries. Entries are signed and topics range from typical plot patterns, the evolution of the genre, biographical sketches of prominent authors, and industry jargon. One of the most refreshing things about the monograph is its professional approach to the genre. Appendix 1 contains a list of Rita award winners that introduces readers to the recognized best of the genre for different years. Appendix 2 titled "Testing the Waters" is a short core list of well-known romances from subgenres that can help readers gain familiarity with these subgenres. Lastly, there is a brief bibliography for further research and a list of contributors. Most contributors are affiliated with universities. The volume concludes with a thorough index. The physical volume is hardback with thick pages and good size typeface. This is a must have for public libraries and colleges and universities with creative writing programs.—**Melissa M. Johnson**

Science Fiction, Fantasy, and Horror

581.   **Critical Insights: Ray Bradbury.** Rafeeq O. McGiveron, ed. Hackensack, N.J., Salem Press, 2017. 300p. index. $105.00. ISBN 13: 978-1-68217-571-2; 978-1-68217-572-9 (e-book).

Critical Insights: Ray Bradbury examines the work of a writer who famously helped define literary science fiction, but also helped shaped fantasy, horror, and other strange narratives throughout novels, short stories, plays, and more. The volume offers general background information on the writer and his work, contextual information on relevant cultural, historical, and critical issues, and diverse analysis of both themes and techniques of the multidimensional author. Essays discuss many of Bradbury's most notable works, including *Fahrenheit 451, Something Wicked This Way Comes,* and *The Martian Chronicles.*

Two opening chapters offer a basic sketch of Bradbury's life alongside a general overview of his work and themes. The four essays within the Critical Contexts section offer a survey of Bradbury criticism ("From Dark Carnival to 'Carnivalization': The Critical Reception of Ray Bradbury's Works"), set the scene of his writing environment within the fear and suspicion of the nuclear age ("Big Brother, Little Sister: Ray Bradbury, Social Pressure and the Challenges to Free Speech").

Critical Readings presents ten essays covering recurring elements (nuclear devastation, robots, books, etc.) and how they relate to broader themes throughout Bradbury's fiction, teleplays, and more. A chapter by Guido Laino—"A Golem in the Family: Robotic Technologies and Artificial Intelligence in Ray Bradbury's Short Stories"—looks at the role of technology in several stories and questions Bradbury's position on it. "Faith and Religion in the Novels of Ray Bradbury" by Timothy E. Kelley notes how faith lurks underneath the surface of seemingly faithless societies. Among other things, chapters explore Bradbury's interpretation of other worlds (in particular Mars), compare original short stories to their television adaptations, and describe Bradbury's use of the unconventional hero.

A closing Resources section includes a chronology of Bradbury's life; a list of major works; a bibliography; and an index.—**ARBA Staff Reviewer**

582.   **Critical Survey of Science Fiction and Fantasy Literature.** 3d ed. Paul Di Filippo, ed. Hackensack, N.J., Salem Press, 2017. 3v. index. $295.00/set. ISBN 13: 978-1-68217-278-0; 978-1-68217-279-7 (e-book).

Alphabetically arranged by book or series title, the third edition of the *Critical Survey of Science Fiction and Fantasy Literature* includes the plot summaries and analyses of 842 prevalent and widely taught science fiction and fantasy books and series. This three-volume set contains 50 currently published works along with updated material from *Magill's Guide to Science Fiction and Fantasy Literature* (1996). Each title begins with a one-sentence summary and reference information that includes the author, genre, subgenre, first published information, type of work, time of work, and the locale of the work. Each title includes an article comprised of "The Story" and the "Analyses." "The Story" contains a summary of the title's or series' plot and characters while the "Analyses" includes literary devices and themes that are incorporated into the work. Each volume comes equipped with a contents section for the given volume as well as a complete list of contents for all three volumes. There is also a title index, a genre index, and an author index. The third volume also incorporates a section for selected science fiction and fantasy awards, a bibliography, and a section for science fiction and fantasy websites. Highly recommended.—**Shelly Lee**

583.   DeLong, Anne. **Classic Horror: A Historical Exploration of Literature.** Santa Barbara, Calif., Greenwood Press/ABC-CLIO, 2018. 238p. index. (Historical Explorations of Literature). $63.00. ISBN 13: 978-1-4408-5842-0; 978-1-4408-5843-7 (e-book).

Gothic Horror as a genre has captured the imagination of readers and moviegoers alike for close to three hundred years. Its ability to speak to both ancient primal fears as well as to provide a terrifying examination of the changing of civilization through time has allowed its popularity to persist with different generations of readers. In *Classic Horror: A Historical Exploration of Literature* by Anne DeLong we focus on four prototypical works of literature that formed the bedrock of the gothic storytelling we love today. This work allows the student to gain a new appreciation and understanding for the themes that still drive this beloved segment of fiction.

The book begins with a detailed table of contents that lists chapter sections and individual documents along with authors and year of publication. In addition the reader will find a brief introduction to the work and a chronology beginning in 1719 and detailing from there the publication of important works as well as other events that had an effect on gothic horror. The bulk of the text is divided into four chapters each discussing one work that contributed to the genre. These include *The Rime of the Ancient Mariner, Frankenstein, The Strange Case of Dr. Jekyll and Mr. Hyde,* and, finally, *Dracula.* Each chapter is separated into identical sections beginning with a synopsis of the story, followed by a historical background for the time period in which the novel was written. This then continues with a discussion of the author, a section on why this work is still read and studied today, and a description of historical themes associated with it. The final sections of each chapter provide an impressive list of primary resources with such documents as official laws, scientific theories, engineering descriptions, and philosophy and a list of suggested reading finishing the chapter. The book comes equipped with a comprehensive index but not a concluding bibliography.

This work would make an excellent addition to either a public, academic, or school library. The text is written to appeal to a wide range of readers, understandable to younger students or those with a general interest in the subject while also providing primary source material and discussion of themes that would appeal to students of higher education and academics. While the lack of a comprehensive bibliography might be seen as a detractor it is well mitigated by the detailed nature of the beginning contents and thus a returning reader will quite easily find a previously discovered document or section.—**W. Cole Williamson**

584.   **Encyclopedia of Science Fiction http://www.sf-encyclopedia.com/.** [Website] Free. Date reviewed: 2019.

This site presents over 17,000 entries on topics within the expansive world (or worlds) of science fiction. Users can find information on thousands of writers (Ray Bradbury, Neil Gaiman, Ursula K. Le Guin, etc.), concepts (androids, little green men, inner space, etc.), formats (comics, films, games), and much more. This is the third edition of the website, which continues to add new entries and expand on current content. Users can conduct a general search or narrow their options within several umbrella categories: Authors, Media, Themes, and Culture. Selecting a category links to a page listing subcategories, if any. For example, the Authors category further sorts entries by Art, Author, Critic, Editor, House Name (pseudonyms), and People (notable in science fiction media). Users can learn how many entries fall under each subcategory (there are over 11,000 Authors, over 300 Critics, etc.), find links to sample entries, and access an A-Z directory of specific entry subjects within each subcategory. Entries generally consist of a descriptive essay—some quite lengthy—focused on the subject's relationship to science fiction, with extensive cross-references to related topics and subject areas and a list of links to previous entry versions. There may also be a list of affiliated topics and, for creators, basic biographical information (birthdate, birthplace, etc.), a list of works (either alphabetical or chronological), and related links to photo galleries and further resources. Other site features include On This Day, which records important dates in science fiction and includes a searchable Timeline of science fiction creators' birth or death dates; a searchable Gallery of over 23,000 images (mostly book covers); and access to a random entry, a random new entry, and the latest entries via the What's New link. Jam packed with information from a wide range of contributors, the Encyclopedia of Science Fiction is nonetheless easy to navigate and enjoyable to explore as a repository of fantastic cultural history.—**ARBA Staff Reviewer**

585.   Gunn, James. **Alternate Worlds: The Illustrated History of Science Fiction.** 3d ed. Jefferson, N.C., McFarland, 2018. 304p. illus. index. $49.95pa. ISBN 13: 978-1-4766-7353-0; 978-1-4766-3332-9 (e-book).

First published in 1975, James Gunn's *Alternate Worlds: The Illustrated History of*

Science Fiction is considered a classic by those who study science fiction. This edition, published some 40 years after the last, has been updated with the latest iterations of an ever-changing genre, including a new chapter on how the world has shaped—or been shaped by—science fiction.

Gunn, in his preface, admits that while this is meant to be an illustrated history book, it is more than that, containing a method to examine the history and "describe what science fiction is and how it differs from other kinds of fiction...how it got to be what it is, and how it achieves its effects" (Gunn 1). He explains why he focused on science fiction as a genre, and how he decided on which authors and books to include. After the preface comes the introduction, penned by Isaac Asimov. Originally written for the first edition of the book in 1975, Asimov's introduction is a love letter to science fiction in all its forms, and well worth the read.

Containing 14 chapters, 3 appendixes, an index, and 62 color photographs (as well as many black-and-white photos), this book is well organized and thoughtfully arranged. The first chapter, which seems to be new to this edition, discusses the way science fiction is now an everyday occurrence. However, starting with chapter 2, each chapter focuses on a different historical era, as defined by science fiction literature. Each chapter is accompanied by years, in order to give the reader a better sense of time (for example, "The Rise of the Pulps: 1911-1926"). Each color photograph in the color plates set between chapters is dated, and the scattered black-and-white photos are titled to explain their relevance. The first appendix is "Science Fiction Themes" and contains a list of the main themes found in science fiction, complete with examples of books from various eras. The second appendix is called "A Basic Science Fiction Library." Here the reader will find an alphabetized list of prominent science fiction authors, each with a small blurb on their achievements and examples of their books. The third appendix is "A Short History of Western Civilization, Science, Technology, and Science Fiction" and is a multipage graph that tracks and compares various elements of history—such as major events, scientific achievements, and important historical figures—alongside literary works and authors, starting in prehistory and ending in 2017.

Gunn examines not only what modern scholars would consider science fiction literature, but also traces the genre's historical origins and discusses its effect on the world as "the literature of change" (Gunn, 249). While this text does not, and truly cannot, contain information on every piece of science fiction written, it is an excellent resource for those studying both literature in general, and science fiction in particular.—**Mary Rebecca Yantis**

586.   Palumbo, Donald E. **A Dune Companion: Characters, Places and Terms in Frank Herbert's Original Six Novels.** Jefferson, N.C., McFarland, 2018. 190p. index. (Critical Explorations in Science Fiction and Fantasy, 62). $35.00pa. ISBN 13: 978-1-4766-6960-1; 978-1-4766-3329-9 (e-book).

In his book, *A Dune Companion: Characters, Places and Terms in Frank Herbert's Original Six Novels,* Donald E. Palumbo mines those six novels, exposing a rich vein of thematic mélange that will transport the *Dune* fan—seasoned or novice—through the landscape of Herbert's imagination, without entanglements in the dense plotlines, to themes that were not mapped when Herbert created his world. Palumbo explores this landscape in his extensive introduction to *The Dune Companion,* first guiding the reader through the known region of Herbert's ecological theme, and then going beyond, revealing the existence of chaos theory, pointing out monomythic structures in the novels' narrative, structures fortified with fractal plotting elements. While Palumbo does marvel at Herbert's artistic precognition of the existence of the scientific concept of chaos theory, he does not neglect the main purpose of this book, the 62d book in the series, Critical Explorations in Science Fiction and Fantasy,: presenting characters, places, and terms in those six novel in a light that both clearly shows how they all fit together within those six novels and in a light that illuminates them in shades of new themes. And, like any good editor (Palumbo, a professor of English at East Carolina University, edits the Critical Exploration series with C.W. Sullivan, III), Palumbo shines that light on possible fault lines within Herbert's narrative structure and explains how, despite those few faults, the novels retain their integrity. The next section, "The Companion," is an alphabetical glossary of the characters, places, and terms in the six novels. At the end of every entry, the novel in which this character or place or term appeared or was used, is provided. For example, mélange appears in *Dune, Children of Dune, God Emperor of Dune, Heretics of Dune,* and *Chapterhouse: Dune.* Life dates precede all character entries. This applies to both significant and minor characters, both brief and detailed entries. For example, Shakkad the Wise lived from 9006 to 9118. His brief entry informs the reader that "the geriatric properties of mélange were discovered" during his reign. The combination of the author's introduction, with its careful mapping of the novels' landscape, and the glossary, with its people and places and customs to pay attention to, make this book an essential travel guide either for a reader's first exploration of *Dune* or umpteenth trek across that world. Finally, Palumbo includes both a bibliography of sources cited for his introduction and a one-page index at the end.—**Brian T. Gallagher**

National Literature

American Literature

Dictionaries and Encyclopedias

587.   **Encyclopedia of African-American Writing: Five Centuries of Contribution: Trials & Triumphs of Writers, Poets, Publications and Organizations.** 3d ed. Bryan Conn and Tara Bynum, eds. Amenia, N.Y., Grey House Publishing, 2018. 1112p. illus. index. $165.00. ISBN 13: 978-1-68217-718-1.

Editors Conn and Bynum update Shari Dorantes Hatch's 2009 second edition (see ARBA 2010, entry 978) by featuring 800 detailed profiles of writers, newspapers, journals, movements, publishers, awards, and other areas related to the history of African American writing from 1635 to the present. Hundreds of entries are updated, and 30 brand-new entries are included. Entries vary in length from a brief paragraph for minor or lesser-known writers to 6 or more pages for more significant writers and topics. Each biographical entry features birth/death dates and an assessment of the writer's contributions along with a brief secondary bibliography or web citation. However, no comprehensive primary bibliographies are presented. The quality of the unsigned entries varies, although overall the writing is fairly objective. The greatest benefit of this work is the inclusion of nonliterary writers and many lesser-known figures. The volume concludes with a collection of primary documents from 42 writers, a chronology of writers listed by birth date, a chronology of "firsts," lists of writers by genre or occupation (for example, talk show host), and a timeline. Black-and-white photos are included for some entries. A useful companion to the five-volume *Greenwood Encyclopedia of African American Literature* (see ARBA 2007, entry 941) and Samuels' one-volume *Encyclopedia of African-American Literature* (see ARBA 2009, entry 956). Recommended for all academic and public library collections.—**Anthony J. Adam**

Handbooks and Yearbooks

588.   **Critical Insights: Social Justice and American Literature.** Robert C. Hauhart and Jeff Birkenstein, eds. Hackensack, N.J., Salem Press, 2017. 280p. index. $105.00. ISBN 13: 978-1-68217-565-1; 978-1-68217-566-8 (e-book).

This volume, part of the Critical Insights series from Salem Press, explores the topic of social justice in American literature. Divided into two major sections, there are fifteen essays which discuss and dissect social justice as a topic within specific genres and books. These essays cover a wide range: post-Civil War rights black feminism in the works of June Jordan, Audre Lorde, and Alice Walker; Appalachian literature; the body as an embattled terrain in American literature; early indigenous American women's literature; hidden correspondence by Frederick Douglass to Anna Murray; William Dean Howells's *A Hazard of New Fortunes*; the "tragic mulatto" theme; western expansion in the writings of Laura Ingalls Wilder and Louise Erdrich; feminism, body policing, and women's suicide; early Philip Roth writings; social justice and legal cleavage in modern American literature; morality in the works of Walter Dean Myers; narrative in Chang-Rae Lee's *Native Speaker;* Colson Whitehead's *The Intuitionist;* and women's dystopic fiction and Margaret Atwood. This eclectic group of essays truly provides an in-depth exploration of social justice in American literature.—**Bradford Lee Eden**

Individual Authors

589.   **Critical Insights: Edith Wharton.** Myrto Drizou, ed. Hackensack, N.J., Salem Press, 2017. 254p. index. $105.00. ISBN 13: 978-1-68217-573-6; 978-1-68217-574-3 (e-book).

Wharton is one of the most prolific and acclaimed writers of 20th-century American fiction. Her works have inspired thousands of articles and books of literary criticism and been seen through many lenses, including modernism, cosmopolitanism, realism, naturalism, and feminism. This volume takes the view of contemporary scholars who emphasize the vast range of Wharton's canon. It focuses on her less frequently taught or discussed works, like *The Fruit of the Tree* (1907) and *The Children* (1928) as well as her signature works, like *The House of Mirth* (1905) and *The Age of Innocence* (1920). Several essays cover interesting new ground, such as Wharton's views on the law, especially concerning marriage, divorce, incest, and birth control; classical Greco-Roman themes in *The House of Mirth,* and victimhood in works by Wharton and Edith Summers Kelley.

The editor is associate professor of English at Valdosta State University and on the executive board of the Edith Wharton Society. The contributors are scholars, mostly of English but also law, classics, and African American studies.

Part of the Salem Press Critical Insights series, the volume follows its in-depth, analytical style of coverage and is aimed at college and high school readers. The student-friendly structure includes the editor's introduction to Wharton studies, a biography, and sections on critical contexts, critical readings, and resources. The latter include a chronology of Wharton's life, major works, general bibliography, editor and contributor information, and an index. Essays are 2,500-5,000 words and include a list of works cited. Purchasers of the print edition receive free online access which is helpful for classroom use. Recommended for college and high school libraries.—**Madeleine Nash**

590. **Critical Insights: James McBride.** Mildred R. Mickle, ed. Hackensack, N.J., Salem Press, 2018. 292p. index. $105.00. ISBN 13: 978-1-68217-694-8; 978-1-68217-695-5 (e-book).

Raised fatherless by his Polish-Jewish mother, James McBride adds a unique and important voice to contemporary African American Literature. This volume in the Critical Insights series examines selections from McBride's diverse repertoire of short stories, music, screenplays, articles, and more, alongside 1996's resonant *The Color of Water: A Black Man's Tribute to His White Mother.*

The volume organizes chapters into three sections and opens with a biographical sketch of the writer which connects his impoverished childhood as one of twelve children to his prolific and diversely creative adulthood as a writer and composer. The following piece discusses McBride more exclusively in the context of his memoir *The Color of Water.*

The following Critical Contexts section offers four essays which examine McBride's work against a broader contextual background. The opening essay by Robert C. Evans shows how McBride's writing expands within a pluralistic critique invoking structuralism, feminism, postmodernism, and other critical theories. Martin Kich then gathers an array of reviewer's thoughts on McBride to give a good sense of his national and international impact.

The largest section—Critical Readings—offers ten essays. While opening pieces by Robert C. Evans and Tahirah Duncan Walker continue the discussion on *The Color of Water,* other contributors look at pieces in McBride's larger body of work. Briana Toth explores the theme of superstition within the movie *Miracle at St. Anna* (2008) which tells the story of a 92nd Infantry (Buffalo Soldiers) unit trapped in German-controlled Italy during World War II. The essay "James McBride and James Brown: The Varied Appeal of Kill 'Em and Leave," by Johnathon T. Lawrence examines creative devices at work in McBride's book on soul singer Brown. And several essays look at McBride's National Book Award winning *The Good Lord Bird* (on the last days of abolitionist John Brown), comparing it to both William Styron's *The Confessions of Nat Turner* and Thomas Berger's *Little Big Man* and offering author interview excerpts and more. Other works discussed in this section include *Song Yet Sung* and "Father Abe."

The closing resources section offers a select chronology of McBride's life, a list of his works, a bibliography, and more. Recommended.—**ARBA Staff Reviewer**

591. **Critical Insights: Richard Wright.** Kimberly Drake, ed. Hackensack, N.J., Salem Press, 2019. 232p. index. $105.00. ISBN 13: 978-1-68217-917-8; 978-1-68217-960-4 (e-book).

Under the editorship of Kimberly Drake, Associate Professor and Chair of the Writing and Rhetoric Major at Scripps College, this volume in the Critical Insights series provides users with an understanding of important American author Richard Wright. The volume starts with two chapters by Drake that discuss critical views of Wright's work and his early life and work. The next section, Critical Contexts, contains four essays and is arranged chronologically. One essay by Robert C. Evans examines a 1944 piece that explains Wright's connection with the Communist Party starting in 1933 and how his opinion of the party and communism changed over time. Other chapters in this section are: "The Meaning of Rape in Richard Wright's *Native Son*"; "Richard Wright's Readers"; and "Heidegger and *The Outsider, Savage Holiday,* and *The Long Dream."* This last chapter deals with Wright's efforts to translate Sartre's French existentialism into his understanding of black existentialism. The Critical Readings section, also arranged chronologically, begins with an analysis of Wright's 1938 *Uncle Tom's Children* in light of literary naturalism, followed by chapters that examine *Native Son* as a protest novel and *Black Boy* in terms of black consciousness, artistic expression, and social justice. The last three chapters in this section examine Wright's career after his move to Paris, a point at which many critics consider his career to have been in decline. All chapters include a works cited section. The remainder of the book is divided into a Resources section that includes a chronology of Wright's life, a list of his works, a bibliography, further reading suggestions, information about the editor and contributors, and an index. Recommended for academic libraries.—**ARBA Staff Reviewer**

592.   **Critical Insights: The Crucible.** Robert C. Evans, ed. Hackensack, N.J., Salem Press, 2018. 308p. index. (Critical Insights series). $105.00. ISBN 13: 978-1-68217-684-9; 978-1-68217-685-6 (e-book).

This volume is part of the Critical Insights series from Salem Press which focuses on important texts and issues in literature. There are two introductory essays: one discusses the influence of *The Crucible* in the last six decades and one provides a short biography of the author Arthur Miller. The next section, Critical Contexts, contains four essays that explore various topics related to the content of the text: primogeniture, skepticism and tragedy, the 1996 film version, and recent scholarship. The Critical Readings section has twelve essays on issues such as scapegoats, satanism, communism, Marxism, postwar aesthetics, post World-War II dystopian writings, anti-Communist criticism, reviews of the 1996 film, the 2016 Broadway production, non-Broadway stagings, and audio readings of the book. Resources included at the back of the book include a chronology of the author's life, other works by the author, and an extensive bibliography. A concise presentation of opinion and scholarship on this important text.—**Bradford Lee Eden**

593.   **Critical Insights: The Outsiders.** M. Katherine Grimes, ed. Hackensack, N.J., Salem Press, 2018. 288p. index. $105.00. ISBN 13: 978-1-68217-686-3; 978-1-68217-687-0 (e-book).

This installment in the Critical Insights series from Salem Press examines *The Outsiders,* the 1967 novel by S. E. (Susan Eloise) Hinton. The book begins with three essays that contextualize the novel. These are followed by a Critical Contexts section that contains four essays: "Lawyer Up, Ponyboy: Reconciling Delinquency Outcomes in S. E. Hinton's *The Outsiders* with Trends in Modern Juvenile Justice"; "Critical Reception: *The Outsiders*"; "'You greasers have a different set of values': Othering, Violence, and the Promise of Reconciliation in S. E. Hinton's *The Outsiders*"; and "'Things Are Rough All Over' Indeed: Suffering and Salvation in James Baldwin's "Sonny's Blues" and S. E. Hinton's *The Outsiders*." As can be gleaned from the essay titles, the material is appropriate for a college-level course. The essay on othering, for example, utilizes the theories of Jacques Derrida as analytical tools. The next section, Critical Readings, examines the novel in ten essays. One is a compendium of Hinton's interview answers on a variety of topics, such as her childhood and parents, her character creation and focus on male characters, and her high school experiences. Readers will find discussions of identity and authenticity, YA novels and the fraternal lens, binaries, hierarchy, and privilege, and *The Outsiders* as Kunstlerroman, among other things. The kunstlerroman essay draws comparisons between Hinton's character Ponyboy Curtis and Stephen Dedalus in James Joyce's *A Portrait of the Artist as a Young Man.* All essays conclude with works cited. The book closes with a Resources section that has a chronology, a list of Hinton's works, a bibliography, and an index. The wealth of material in this volume of Critical Insights will give readers not only an increased appreciation for *The Outsiders* but also several ideas on how to further research and analyze the material in what is considered by many as the first YA novel. Recommended for academic libraries.—**ARBA Staff Reviewer**

594.   **The Historian's Awakening: Reading Kate Chopin's Classic Novel as Social and Cultural History.** Bernard Koloski, ed. Santa Barbara, Calif., Praeger/ABC-CLIO, 2019. 178p. index. (The Historian's Annotated Classics). $37.00. ISBN 13: 978-1-4408-5716-4; 978-1-4408-5717-1 (e-book).

Although *The Awakening* may be described as a story of one woman's lonely psychological journey, there is much to be analyzed in the novel's rich historical backdrop. And indeed, as this work's apt framing explores in insightful detail, the social and cultural realities of Edna Pontellier's life form the architecture of her individual struggle.

The Historian's Awakening is going to be most useful for instructors teaching this text with an eye to historical, sociological, and/or cultural analysis. The preface offers section-by-section guides to the novel's chapters with suggested topics for discussion, while the included chronology details both major historical events and events in Chopin's personal life that are relevant to novel's historical landscape. Two critical essays precede the text—one on Chopin's life and works, and one on *The Awakening's* social and cultural settings. Both offer multiple angles for analysis; for instance, in terms of Chopin as a feminist writer, or in terms of the social class structures in place at the time of her writing, and so forth.

Finally, an annotated text features extensive footnotes providing detailed historical context for various aspects of the story, as well as some exploration of the text's literary characteristics. This is a tightly constructed critical edition—concise but robust in its offerings.—**Autumn Faulkner**

595.   **The Historian's Passing: Reading Nella Larsen's Classic Novel as Social and Cultural History.** Lynn Domina, ed. Santa Barbara, Calif., Praeger/ABC-CLIO, 2018. 140p. index. $37.00. ISBN 13: 978-1-4408-5710-2; 978-1-4408-5711-9 (e-book).

This slim volume, the fifth in the publisher's series, following books on works by Mark Twain, Frederick Douglass, Joseph Conrad, and Nathaniel Hawthorne, begins by offering two useful essays that situate the work that is being presented, one concerning the life of Nella Larsen and the other exploring the 1920s in Harlem. These essays provide a clear image of both the events in the life of the author and the life in New York City for many of the African Americans living there. The rest of the book is a highly annotated text of Larsen's *Passing*. Over 130 footnotes explain and analyze this important work, which was first published in 1929. From briefly explaining terms that are seldom used today to a detailed discussion of the legal setting of race in both the 19th and early 20th centuries, this way to examine texts provides readers with an excellent context within which to fully appreciate the novel as they read it.

Any library with patrons interested in African American history or American literature should certainly consider adding this book to its collection. The approach to literary analysis presented in The Historian's Annotated Classics series offers perspectives not always seen in other analyses. Focusing on the social and historical aspects of the text, rather than literary themes and techniques, this series should broaden the reader's understanding of the text.—**Mark Schumacher**

596.   **The Historian's Scarlet Letter: Reading Nathaniel Hawthorne's Masterpiece as Social and Cultural History.** Melissa McFarland Pennell, ed. Santa Barbara, Calif., Praeger/ABC-CLIO, 2018. 263p. illus. index. (The Historian's Annotated Classics). $35.00pa. ISBN 13: 978-1-4408-4700-4; 978-1-4408-4699-1 (e-book).

This scholarly edition of an American classic contains extensive information contextualizing Hester Prynne's fictional experiences in Puritan New England. Two introductory essays describe Hawthorne's biography and the legal and religious practices in the 1600s in the American colonies. Copious footnotes accompanying the text of the novel provide additional information about historical connections to details included by Hawthorne, and a table within the preface links specific chapters with topics in American history. In addition to text, several visual aids in the novel provide photographs of buildings described in the book and pieces of art from the time period. The volume includes a chronology of key events in American history and the life of Nathaniel Hawthorne. The detailed index and lengthy bibliography make the text valuable for graduate students and scholars, while the essays and footnotes are accessible to high school and university students.—**Delilah R. Alexander**

597.   Johnson, Claudia Durst. **Reading Harper Lee: Understanding *To Kill a Mockingbird* and *Go Set a Watchman*.** Santa Barbara, Calif., Greenwood Press/ABC-CLIO, 2018. 184p. index. $39.00. ISBN 13: 978-1-4408-6127-7; 978-1-4408-6128-4 (e-book).

Many periodicals carried stories about the decision to publish the manuscript on which Harper Lee based *To Kill a Mockingbird*. In this volume, the context of that decision is meticulously examined, and historical context is provided for both novels. The ten chapters include discussion of censorship of the classic novel, and the self-imposed censorship of many readers who refuse to read *Go Set a Watchman*. The volume also provides a close analysis of literary structure, as well as sections on gender and social class. The final chapter addressing the relevance of Lee's work to contemporary racial injustice and police brutality is perhaps the finest and most compelling. The book includes a detailed chronology. The Notes on Sources section amounts to an excellent annotated bibliography and the index is very detailed. This work should be available for high school and college students working on either or both of Harper Lee's books.—**Delilah R. Alexander**

598. Snodgrass, Mary Ellen. **Gary Paulsen: A Companion to the Young Adult Literature.** Jefferson, N.C., McFarland, 2018. 199p. index. (McFarland Companions to Young Adult Literature). $39.95pa. ISBN 13: 978-1-4766-7331-8.

This volume in the McFarland Companions to Young Adult Literature series focuses on author Gary Paulsen, writer of best-selling titles that broach a range of topics from war to coming-of-age. The volume offers general analysis and insight into both the author's works and his life within a highly approachable format.

The book opens with an excellent chronology of Paulsen's extraordinary and rather insatiable life, and pairs his extensive writing achievements with personal detail. The bulk of the book's content is found in sixty-four A-Z entries on Paulsen's individual works, themes, and other topics concerning the literature.

Entries are concise but provide good information on thematic subjects like integrity and survival as well as more particular points such as Paulsen's choice of character names, showing how they can evoke heritage or a "masculine energy" among other personality traits. Other entries offer brief analysis and plot synopsis for works such as *Call Me Francis Tucket, Nightjohn, Hatchet, Harris and Me,* and many others.

The companion also includes a brief genealogy, a glossary of over two hundred terms cross-referenced to the works in which they appear, a timeline of historical references, a generous selection of writing, art and research topics, and an extensive bibliography. The volume is ideal for high school educators and librarians, students, and others interested in the literature of Gary Paulsen and the genres he explores—YA fiction, adventure stories, or even American fiction in general.—**ARBA Staff Reviewer**

599. Snodgrass, Mary Ellen. **A Literary Lee Smith Companion.** Jefferson, N.C., McFarland, 2019. 194p. index. (McFarland Literary Companions). $39.95pa. ISBN 13: 978-1-4766-7330-1; 978-1-4766-3666-5 (e-book).

This companion is designed for readers, teachers, researchers, and reviewers of author Lee Smith. The Companion section comprises the majority of the book following a short introduction. Entries in this section are about Lee's works (*Cakewalk, Family Linen, The Last Girls, Black Mountain Breakdown, On Agate Hill,* etc.); major themes in Lee's works—belonging, coming of age, Gothicism, healing and death, mental incurables, and more; and the genealogies of the families in her works. A chronology, a glossary, two appendixes, a bibliography, and an index follow. The chronology of Lee's life and works (nearly 20 pages long) gives users insight into the major events in Lee's life and how they shaped her work. The glossary (312 terms) includes foreign words and phrases, idioms, and more that are found in Lee's writings. Helpfully, each term or phrase in the glossary refers to the work in which it appears. There are also two appendixes: "Historical Events" and "Writing, Art and Research Topics." The first appendix includes the major events referenced by Lee in her works, and the second has 39 suggestions for how to analyze Lee's oeuvre. Overall, this book provides its target audience with the tools necessary for approaching and understanding this important American author. Recommended.—**ARBA Staff Reviewer**

British Literature

Handbooks and Yearbooks

600.   **Critical Insights: Lord of the Flies.** Sarah Fredericks, ed. Hackensack, N.J., Salem Press, 2017. 300p. index. $105.00. ISBN 13: 978-1-68217-567-5; 978-1-68217-568-2 (e-book).

The *Lord of the Flies* takes a compelling look at a number of unsettling ideas, including the human capacity for evil and the shocking disruption of innocence, among others. This volume in the Critical Insights series offers a survey of past popular criticism of the novel while introducing new and innovative explorations. In addition, the volume connects the experiences within *Lord of the Flies* to those of its author, William Golding, and provides other contextual material which helps explain the novel's tremendous literary impact.

Opening chapters offer a brief biography of Golding alongside the establishment of the novel's most apparent element of violence as it moves between fantasy and hard reality. The volume then moves into the Critical Contexts section, with essays discussing foundational concepts around the novel, primarily the effects of World War II and character maturity, and also establishing the need for multiple points-of-view ("The Conclusion of *Lord of the Flies:* Multiple Critical Perspectives" by Robert C. Evans).

The larger section of the book—Critical Readings—includes three chapters devoted to surveying the range of *Lord of the Flies* criticism, encompassing the years 1954 to 2010. Other essays here draw connections between the novel and Tolkien's *Lord of the Rings* (also published in 1954), look at the novel's treatment of obesity, discuss film adaptations, and more. One essay, Joan-Mari Barendse's "William Golding's *Lord of the Flies:* A Glimmer of Hope in this Dystopia?" examines the novel's few suggestions of salvation as epitomized by a pair of glasses and a conch shell.

Resources include a chronology of William Golding's life and works, a list of the author's complete works, which include poetry, drama, nonfiction, and more, and a bibliography.—**ARBA Staff Reviewer**

601.   Harding, Tim. **British Chess Literature to 1914: A Handbook for Historians.** Jefferson, N.C., McFarland, 2018. 394p. illus. index. $49.95pa. ISBN 13: 978-1-4766-6839-0; 978-1-4766-3169-1 (e-book).

Who would have known that the history of British chess could be so rich and diverse? This book certainly provides a wealth of information related to this topic prior to 1914. Eight chapters discuss the development of British chess in the late 19th and early 20th centuries, exploring important people related to the game either through writing or through playing: George Walker, Howard Staunton, Robert Wormald, Thomas Rowland, and Charles Stanley, to name but a few. The author walks the reader through the history of British chess and the importance of chess columns and writers in newspapers and magazines. He also provides a listing of historical chess books as well as resources for more information both online and in print. Six appendixes provide a number of annotated lists and contents of various chess columns and magazines. There are also lots of black-and-white illustrations, portraits, and reproductions from chess columns. Definitely a book for chess enthusiasts, especially those interested in the history of British chess.—**Bradford Lee Eden**

Individual Authors

602. Clark, Sandra. **Shakespeare and Domestic Life: A Dictionary.** New York, Arden Shakespeare/Bloomsbury Publishing, 2018. 440p. index. (Arden Shakespeare Dictionaries). $176.00. ISBN 13: 978-1-4725-8180-8; 978-1-4725-8181-5 (e-book).

This volume, the 16th in the Arden (formerly Continuum) Shakespeare Dictionary Series dating back to 2001, is written by the series editor. Other volumes have addressed topics such as military language, legal language, demonology, and class and society. Entries in this volume, over 300 terms, run from a few lines to more than 10 pages. All entries, "except for the most straightforward" (p. 3), are divided into 3 sections. The first defines the term as used in early modern England, the second presents Shakespeare's usage of the term, and the third provides selective further reading suggestions, referring to the 20-page bibliography at the end of the book. While most entries are fairly easily recognized and understood, a number of words are rarely heard today: sarcenet, posset, pantler, and kersey among others.

The concept of domestic life was becoming a topic of reflection and discussion during Shakespeare's era. Conduct books and household manuals appeared to guide and teach the English population in various ways: William Gouge's *Of Domesticall Duties* (1622) is such a text. The author of this volume explains that within that setting, she has selected "terms relating to the material processes of household life, domestic activities and implements as well as those of roles and relationships" (p. 3). Words that happen to appear in an entry, and that have an entry of their own, are highlighted once in the text of the first entry. The author selects examples of these numerous terms from not only the plays, but the sonnets and other less-known texts, such as the brief text "The Phoenix and the Turtle." The 14-page index that concludes the volume provides, among other information, the pages in the book where each work by Shakespeare is mentioned, should a reader wish to explore an individual play.

Designed for literary scholars, this book will clearly be most useful in academic libraries. Some other libraries may wish to consider it, but professors and college students seem to be those who will most benefit from this information.—**Mark Schumacher**

603. Connelly, Mark. **George Orwell: A Literary Companion.** Jefferson, N.C., McFarland, 2018. 202p. index. $39.95pa. ISBN 13: 978-1-4766-6677-8; 978-1-4766-3454-8 (e-book).

This clearly written and well-organized volume provides a great deal of useful information about the life and the writings of the important 20th-century English author, George Orwell. A 22-page chronology of the author's life and work provides excellent information that sets the context for the works discussed in the following pages. The entries range from 5- to 7-page discussions of major works, such as *Animal Farm, 1984,* and *The Road to Wigan Pier,* to much briefer texts on individual Orwell essays, characters, and sites in his writing. The longer pieces, including the opening chronology, often have a "Further Reading" list, whose items are compiled into a 278-item bibliography at the end of the volume. The bibliography that ends the volume is very complete, indicating for instance the 20 references to Adolf Hitler to be found in the text, and the 20 mentions of propaganda.

This book will enhance the collections of academic and high school libraries, in part because a list of 43 "Writing and Research Topics" will provide their patrons with diverse

approaches to Orwell's texts. Public libraries will also find this a valuable acquisition.—
Mark Schumacher

604.   **Critical Insights: Animal Farm.** Thomas Horan, ed. Hackensack, N.J., Salem Press, 2018. 222p. index. $105.00. ISBN 13: 978-1-68217-918-5; 978-1-68217-961-1 (e-book).

Like other books in the Critical Insights series devoted to a single literary work, this volume begins with brief essays by the editor, on George Orwell's life and on *Animal Farm,* and his summary of the 14 chapters that follow. The first 4 texts "cover *Animal Farm's* literary, historical, and political importance as well as its ongoing relevance to contemporary readers" (p. vii). The following 10 essays explore a diverse range of topics, such as humor, biopolitics of totalitarianism, religious text and subtext, and metaphor and allegory. All 14 chapters provide rich "Works cited" lists, leading readers to other useful texts. There are a few editorial issues that need attention. A quotation said to be on "page 5-6" of the cited source is actually on page 144. Several quotes said to be in chapter 1 of a source are in chapter 2; the author's last name is also incorrect. Another quote dropped words from the original text, without indicating that. Despite these matters, the text remains fascinating on the broad range of topics explored here.

Most academic and many public libraries should consider adding this book, as well as the other titles in this series, which now has 66 to choose from, if it falls within their budget.—**Mark Schumacher**

605.   **Critical Insights: Hamlet.** Robert C. Evans, ed. Hackensack, N.J., Salem Press, 2019. 298p. index. $105.00. ISBN 13: 978-1-64265-026-6; 978-1-64265-027-3 (e-book).

This volume, devoted to one of Shakespeare's most-read and most-performed plays begins with a question-and-answer essay with Maurice Hunt (Baylor University) in which he discusses several topics including what aspects of the play he finds most compelling. A biography of William Shakespeare by the volume's editor comes next. This is followed by the Critical Contexts section, which features four essays: the first discusses which traces of the Protestant Reformation can be found in the play; the second examines editors' introductions to the play starting in the 1970s; the third analyzes Ophelia in terms of trauma theory; and the last surveys notable film depictions (1948-2017) of Ophelia's first mad scene. Ten essays comprise the next section, Critical Readings. Among these are "Birth, Death, Rebirth: Fathers and Mothers in *Hamlet,*" "A Healthy Hamlet: A Jungian Defense of the Introverted Hero," and "Hamlet in Helmand: Wild Justice" (which concerns the story of a British Royal Marine who quoted Hamlet while killing his Afghan prisoner), "Critics' Reactions to the Filmed Version of the Doran/Tennant" (staged in 2008), and "A *Hamlet* Self-Interview" by Kent Cartwright, professor of English at the University of Maryland. A Resources section provides a chronology of Shakespeare's life and a chronology of Shakespeare's work, a selective survey of recent editions of *Hamlet,* a bibliography, information about the editor and contributors, and an index. Recommended to academic libraries.—**ARBA Staff Reviewer**

606.   **Critical Insights: Macbeth.** William W. Weber, ed. Hackensack, N.J., Salem Press, 2017. 226p. illus. index. $105.00. ISBN 13: 978-1-68217-563-7; 978-1-68217-564-4 (e-book).

This installment in the Critical Insights series examines Shakespeare's *Macbeth*. The book begins with an explanation of the volume's organization followed by a general essay on the play and a biography of Shakespeare. This is followed by a section of four critical essays that analyze the play's reception as it has evolved over time; the play's historical context; the play as seen through the lens of Alfred Mele's psychological theory of self-deception; and the play as contrasted and compared to *Hamlet*. The second section, Critical Readings, includes nine essays "on a wide range of subjects touching on *Macbeth* and its broader cultural significance." (p. ix) Among the nine essays are "Interpreting the Weird Sisters: Page, Stage, and Screen" and "Blood and Milk: The Masculinity of Motherhood in Shakespeare's *Macbeth.*" The last section of the book includes an annotated chronology of Shakespeare's life, a list of his works, a bibliography, information about the editor and authors, and an index. Like the other volumes in this series, this one provides the necessary context to make an enduring classic accessible to students entirely unfamiliar with the text while offering interesting insights to those much more familiar with the work. Recommended.—**ARBA Staff Reviewer**

607. **Critical Insights: Paradise Lost.** Robert C. Evans, ed. Hackensack, N.J., Salem Press, 2019. 308p. index. $105.00. ISBN 13: 978-1-64265-024-2.

This volume examines the circumstances, history, context, and importance of John Milton's (1608-75) *Paradise Lost,* written/dictated when the author was completely blind and at the end of two very bloody civil wars in England's history. As with all of the books in the Critical Insight series by Salem Press, two major sections (Critical Contexts and Critical Readings) provide a number of insightful essays and discussions on various aspects of the author, this piece of literature, and its influence on subsequent society and culture. Four essays in the Critical Contexts section focus on various editions, the narrative of trauma, and postlapsarian landscapes. The Critical Readings section has eleven essays on topics such as new Milton criticism, the poem as a dictated text, theology, angelic intelligence and human culpability, a play based on the poem by Erin Shield, and recent art and adaptation related to the poem. An excellent volume of insight and research on this epic and important piece of literature.—**Bradford Lee Eden**

608. **Frankenbook https://www.frankenbook.org/.** [Website] Free. Date reviewed: 2019.

Frankenbook presents an online annotated version of Mary Shelley's classic novel *Frankenstein* which incorporates contributions from experts across a range of disciplines that focus on the scientific, technological, political, and ethical themes appearing throughout the groundbreaking work. While general users have access to the full annotated text, users who create a free account have greater text interaction capabilities as they are able to contribute their own annotations and replies to thematic discussion. Users can scroll down through the homepage to access the text, and then scroll down through the text with expert annotations and/or user replies descending down the right side of the page. Clicking on an annotation highlights the applicable text, and presents the annotation (or reply) in full along with its thematic tag. Annotations generally fall into eight thematic categories: Equity & Inclusion, Health & Medicine, Influences & Adaptations, Mary Shelley, Motivations & Sentiments, Philosophy & Politics, and Science and Technology. Throughout the text, users can filter themes to focus on personal areas of interest. At the beginning of the text, users can click on the Volume 1/Preface button to navigate to another chapter or a good list of discussion questions that touch on the general thematic ideas mentioned above (e.g., "Why does Victor choose not to reveal his discovery to anyone or to consult with anyone about his determination to animate a creature based on his discovery?" or "Does Victor use both human and animal material in making his creature? What is the textual evidence, one way or the other? Does it matter to your understanding of the creature's status if it has animal as well as human parts?"). The website also includes seven scholarly essays including "I've Created a Monster! (And So Can You)" by Cory Doctorow—a humorous yet important piece on our relationship with technology. The Media tab links to a generous selection of games, videos, podcasts, and more which further explore the ideas in *Frankenstein*. Frankenbook is a valuable resource that helps show how literature can bridge the humanities with the sciences.—**ARBA Staff Reviewer**

609.   King, Douglas J. **Shakespeare's World: The Tragedies.** Santa Barbara, Calif., Greenwood Press/ABC-CLIO, 2018. 225p. index. (Historical Explorations of Literature). $63.00. ISBN 13: 978-1-4408-5794-2; 978-1-4408-5795-9 (e-book).

One of the latest volumes in a series that began in 2015, this book explores four of Shakespeare's tragedies: *Romeo and Juliet, Julius Caesar, Hamlet,* and *Macbeth*. These plays are placed "in the context of history, society, and culture through historical essays, literary analysis, chronologies, primary source documents . . ." (p. xiii) A brief introductory chronology of the English Renaissance, and synopses and "Suggested Readings" (from 17 to 26 items, largely books) for each play help to guide the reader throughout the volume. The book, as its series title indicates, also provides a rich literary and historical setting for the plays, from the development of the revenge tragedy by Seneca in the 1st century and the work of English Renaissance authors before Shakespeare to medicine in the Elizabethan era and warfare, focused on the battles with the Spanish Armada in the 1580s.

The primary sources, in fact, make up almost 50 percent of the text and are quite diverse. They include a speech by Elizabeth I, two texts on melancholy, Thomas Heywood's *An Apology for Actors* (1614), Reginald Scot's *The Discovery of Witchcraft* (1584), and texts by Martin Luther and Erasmus from the early 16th century. [A minor note: the language of some of the texts may be challenging to 21st-century readers. "Neither doth faith only bind us to this sincerity, but oftentimes also charity, as we touched before." (p. 199)]

Academic libraries will certainly find this useful for numerous literature classes, whether focused on Shakespeare or broader courses on English literature. High schools and public libraries should consider it as well.—**Mark Schumacher**

610.   **Open Source Shakespeare http://www.opensourceshakespeare.org/.** [Website] Free. Date reviewed: 2019.

Open Source Shakespeare (OSS) originated as a master's thesis at George Mason University. The site allows free access to the complete works of English playwright and poet William Shakespeare in addition to several tools for use in text analysis. Users can access the works and special features via specific links throughout the homepage. A list of thirty-seven plays, five poems, and three groups of sonnets runs down the left side of the homepage, each title a link to the work. At the top of the page, users can access plays by genre, by number of words, and by number of speeches. Clicking on the play title links to an introductory page listing acts and scenes alongside a complete list of characters. Users can navigate the play by clicking on a scene, while clicking on a character name links to all of their speeches in the play. Sonnets are selected by number or users can scroll down through all sonnet transcriptions in numerical order. Additionally, users can opt to compare two sonnets side-by-side. Users can conduct a Keyword Search or Advanced Search from the top of the page, but a good variety of specialized searches exist as well. Users can conduct a Text Search within specific works or all works. For the Character Search, users enter a name or a part of a name to find where a particular character appears as well as the number of affiliated speeches. Clicking on the play link here lists the relevant speeches, noting act, scene, and line. Character speeches can be filtered to show cue speeches or full speeches. A Concordance Search allows users to search by word form, that is, any version or part of a word. This option lets users trace word usage through all works. From the link at the top of the page, users can choose a letter to see how many word forms exist for it (e.g., over 1,000 word forms exist for the letter "E"), find a list of word forms beginning with that letter, and see how many times the word form appears. Selecting a word form from the list leads to more data, such as the number of occurrences, number of speeches, possibly related words, number of searches, and more.—**ARBA Staff Reviewer**

611.   Ponzio, Peter J. **Themes in Dickens: Seven Recurring Concerns in the Writings.** Jefferson, N.C., McFarland, 2018. 188p. illus. index. $39.95pa. ISBN 13: 978-1-4766-7257-1; 978-1-4766-3135-6 (e-book).

This volume offers different looks at subjects of importance to Charles Dickens by examining not only his novels but other texts of his as well. The themes examined include class, prison, dreams and dreaming, and ineffectual institutions. In his introduction, an excellent presentation of the settings in which Dickens grew up, lived, and wrote, the author describes the best audience for this work: "readers who have a working knowledge of Dickens's writing as well as a familiarity with his life and times." (p. 6) This book does a fine job of examining the literary elements of Dickens's work while interweaving the socioeconomic situation of his time. The chapter on prisons demonstrates the interplay of Dickens's own life, his nonfiction writings, and his novels. Having seen his family in Marshalsea Debtor's Prison in London, when he was a child, Dickens later wrote in *Sketches by Boz* about the nature of imprisonment. Later, his depiction of prisons appears in *Pickwick Papers, Little Dorrit,* and *A Tale of Two Cities,* much of which is based both on his childhood experiences and the prisons he saw during his travels in the United States, written about in *American Notes.* The other topics discussed in this book have the same intermingling of life experiences and literary skill.

A brief note about the subtitle, "Seven Recurring Themes" in a straightforward six-chapter book: the publisher created the title and thought that "society" and "social pretension" were two separate themes, hence the confusion. (This comes from the author.) Any library which serves students of English literature will find this book useful. In fact, this book should be considered by all libraries whose patrons enjoy literature.—**Mark Schumacher**

Irish Literature

Individual Authors

612. Broderick, James F. **James Joyce: A Literary Companion.** Jefferson, N.C., McFarland, 2018. 175p. index. (McFarland Literary Companions). $39.95pa. ISBN 13: 978-1-4766-6693-8; 978-1-4766-3166-0 (e-book).

Joyce's complex style and delivery have been somewhat clarified by ongoing examinations of his work, such as this overview of his life and writings. An introduction provides a basic analysis of what motivated and inspired Joyce. A biographical timeline continues these ideas with a brief discussion and a listing of quick, informative entries. The main body of the text examines, individually, each of Joyce's four main novels, starting with some background information and then discussing each chapter, focusing on character and textual progression. The presentation style is reminiscent of Joyce's own free-flowing, sometimes whimsical wording. Following the main text is an A-Z Literary Companion, an alphabetical listing including people, places, literary works, etc. that influenced Joyce and his writing. Most of these entries include suggestions for further reading. Two appendixes include annotated lists of sources considered most helpful for deciphering Joyce and his work and film adaptations of his works. An extensive bibliography and an index complete the work. This collection of material should serve as a quick reference or as a starting point to further research.—**Martha Lawler**

Latin American Literature

Handbooks and Yearbooks

613. **Critical Insights: Contemporary Latin American Fiction.** Ignacio López-Calvo, ed. Hackensack, N.J., Salem Press, 2017. 279p. index. $105.00. ISBN 13: 978-1-68217-561-3; 978-1-68217-562-0 (e-book).

This volume in the Critical Insights series presents essays which examine the works of twelve contemporary Latin American authors. Divided into Critical Contexts and Critical Readings sections, the volume encapsulates a range of scholarship on the themes, techniques, and other attributes featuring in select literature from Costa Rica, Colombia, Brazil, Cuba, Argentina, Peru, Chile, and Mexico.

Four essays in the Critical Contexts section establish an analytical foundation which can be considered alongside many of the later pieces. Essays from Melissa Fitch ("Latin American Literature and New Technology") and Ignacio López-Calvo ("World Literature and the Marketing of Roberto Bolaño's Posthumous Works"), for example, look at the influence of digital literature, social media, global marketing demands and more on Latin American literature.

The larger Critical Readings section houses nine essays. Some take an in-depth look at individual authors ("Daniel Sada and the Everyday Baroque") while others examine unique themes and innovative techniques found within the genre. In her contribution, Traci Roberts-Camps discusses novelist Barbará Jacobs' emphasis on language and writing mechanics. Paula C. Park looks at the writings of science fiction writer Daína Chaviano, who explores the need to preserve history even as one blends it into the modern multicultural society. Many of the essays touch on recurring themes in the literature, from violence and feminism to migration and urbanization, and show how modern Latin American writers react against magical realism and other frequently discussed styles of the past.

The volume has limited space with which to cover the breadth of contemporary Latin American fiction, but readers will appreciate the suggestions for further reading that follow the essays. Recommended.—**ARBA Staff Reviewer**

Russian Literature

Individual Authors

614.   **Critical Insights: Leo Tolstoy.** Rachel Stauffer, ed. Hackensack, N.J., Salem Press, 2017. 300p. Index. $105.00. ISBN 13: 978-1-68217-611-5; 78-1-68217-612-2 (e-book).

This volume in the Critical Insights series gathers essays from a range of scholars on Russian novelist Leo Tolstoy and his seminal works. The volume offers contextual foundations for understanding the 19th-century writer's novels and stories alongside modern perspectives on themes, technique, and other elements of Tolstoy's writing.

Two opening chapters offer a brief biography of the writer and a general discussion of his place in literature (in particular, Russian literature). The four essays in the following Critical Contexts section expand on this background in both providing historical context and surveying common scholarship. "Topics and Trends in Tolstoy Studies" by Joseph Schlegel admirably performs the latter, while The J. Alexander Ogden piece "The Great Brain's Brawn: Tolstoy at the Gym" focuses on a particular detail of the writer's life—his enjoyment of physical activity—and attaches it to Tolstoy's broader artistic outlook.

The ten chapters that follow within the Critical Readings section bring much of Tolstoy's major works, including *War and Peace* and *Anna Karenina,* to light in strikingly different ways. "'Similar to a Feverish Delirium:'" The Fantastic Worlds of Battle as Tolstoy's Criticism of War in *War and Peace*" by Natalya Sukhonos examines the battlefield as one of the writer's most vivid settings. Others ("From Christ to Krishna: Tolstoy and Eastern Philosophies" and "The Path of Life: A Guidebook to Tolstoy's Philosophical Source Material and the Mysticism of His Latter Years") explore the influence of eastern philosophies on Tolstoy's work. The section culminates with a more technical analysis of Tolstoy's writing—"Tolstoy's Narrative Technique: Listing People, Objects and Events"—noting the connection of list making with Tolstoy's views on contemporary society.

Supplemental material within the Resources portion of this Critical Insights volume includes a list of Tolstoy's major works, a bibliography, information about the contributors, and an index. The volume, which can also be viewed online, works as both a good introduction to contemporary Tolstoy criticism and a modern supplement to long existing analyses.—**ARBA Staff Reviewer**

Poetry

Digital Resources

615. **Emily Dickinson Lexicon http://edl.byu.edu/index.php.** [Website] Free. Date reviewed: 2019.

This website explores the language within Emily Dickinson's 1,700 plus poems with its dictionary of over 9,000 words and word forms found throughout them. The dictionary is a novel if not necessary approach to the prolific writer, whose short works encompass an abundant and diverse display of literary craft. The lexicon (EDL) was created from a variety of sources including the concurrent Webster 1844 Dictionary and the Oxford English Dictionary, in addition to Dickinson's works. Users can select the EDLexicon tab at the top of the page to access the alphabetical dictionary, which uniquely includes proper nouns, person names, and place-names. Alternatively, users can enter a term in the search field in the upper-right corner of the page. Users can navigate by selecting a letter of the alphabet to jump to that section and/or a number that jumps to the page within a letter's section. Each entry conveys a word's inflected forms, part of speech, basic etymology, word collocations (from Webster), definition(s), citation examples from poems, and further reference. For detailed description of each of these particular categories, users can select the Introduction tab from the homepage. The Webster tab leads to the eponymous dictionary of 1844—with over 82,000 thousand entries, the dictionary is an important resource for Dickinson study as it is believed to have been a resource for the poet. Under additional Resources, users will find a spreadsheet listing person names within Emily Dickinson's letters; information on Dutch, Italian, Chinese and other translations; and more.—**ARBA Staff Reviewer**

Handbooks and Yearbooks

616. Mattingly, Greg. **Emily Dickinson as a Second Language: Demystifying the Poetry.** Jefferson, N.C., McFarland, 2018. 250p. illus. index. $39.95pa. ISBN 13: 978-1-4766-6655-6; 978-1-4766-3195-0 (e-book).

This slim volume is an admirable companion to the elusive but groundbreaking work of 19th-century American poet Emily Dickinson. The book takes several approaches towards bridging the world of Dickinson's unconventional sense of poetry with the modern 21st-century reader.

Nine well-organized chapters focus on both distinct components of the poetry; word usage, symbols, allusion, punctuation, and more, and the broader environment within which Dickinson lived and wrote. Early chapters explore Dickinson's use of language and vocabulary in respect to the meanings of her era and personal domain. Later, the book explores issues of context and influence, such as the poet's education, religion, and family of lawyers and politicians. Chapters also mesh her work with the historical context of the Second Great Awakening and the American Civil War.

Closing chapters draw connections throughout all her writing, including her many letters. Here the author examines Dickinson's repetition of certain words and points to differences between various published editions of her poetry. Throughout the book, the author employs ample poem excerpts in addition to fragments from personal letters and diaries, specialized Emily Dickinson Lexicon dictionary entries, and black-and-white illustrations and photographs.

The author's preface provides essential background to understanding the organization of Dickinson's work and this volume's treatment of it. Supplemental material at the back of the book is also enlightening, and includes an appendix of whole pieces and excerpts from Dickinson's contemporaries such as Elizabeth Barrett Browning, a tutorial to the online Emily Dickinson Lexicon, chapter notes, a bibliography, and an index of first lines.

Recommended to academic libraries.—**ARBA Staff Reviewer**

617.   **The Variorum Edition of the Poetry of John Donne: Volume 4.1. The Songs and Sonnets: General and Topical Commentary.** Gary A. Stringer, ed. Bloomington, Ind., Indiana University Press, 2017. 416p. index. $80.00. ISBN 13: 978-0-253-03417-5.

Not a reference work per se, this book is part of a broad series first started over 25 years ago to bring out critical editions of the poetry of John Donne (1572-1631), considered the preeminent representative of the metaphysical poets of the English Renaissance period. This particular volume (4.1) is devoted to critical scholarship of Donne's Songs and Sonnets (some 2,224 whole or partial transcriptions of poems in 209 17th-century manuscripts and printed editions). Besides providing general commentary on the poems, Donne's autobiography and persona, the critical reception of his poems, and aspects related to dating and publication history, the book provides numerous essays on a number of subject areas and influences: these include dramatic elements, imagery, language and rhetoric, love and sexual imagery, mannerism and the Baroque, medievalism, paradox, Petrarchism, Platonism, psychological analysis, realism, science and the new learning, versification, wit and metaphysical conceit, and women. For scholars interested in this particular author, the English Renaissance, and 16th- and 17th-century English writing and poetry, this book is a wealth of information.—**Bradford Lee Eden**

618.   **W.B. Yeats's Robartes-Aherne Writings: Featuring the Making of His "Stories of Michael Robartes and His Friends".** Wayne K. Chapman, ed. New York, Bloomsbury Publishing, 2018. 373p. index. (Modernist Archives Series). $176.00. ISBN 13: 978-1-4725-9513-3; 978-1-4725-9514-0 (e-book).

Part of the Modernist Archives series from Bloomsbury Academic, this book explores a subsection of the writings of W.B. Yeats (1865-1939), an Irish poet and one of the foremost writers of 20th-century literature. In particular, two literary characters of Yeats's creation are focused upon and their subsequent development throughout Yeats's literary oeuvre are documented and studied. These two characters are Michael Robartes and Owen Aherne. After an extensive introduction which provides information on editorial principles, abbreviations, and background, the book is divided into five sections: 1896-1897, 1917-1920, 1919-1925, 1929-1931, and 1932-1937. During each of these time periods, Yeats weaves these two characters, either separately or together, into various writings and stories. The editor does a fantastic job of documenting, detailing, and describing the uses, interactions, and character development of these two literary creations throughout Yeats's published and unpublished output, providing the reader with a unique glimpse into the intricate mind of one of the greatest writers in recent history.—**Bradford Lee Eden**

25 Music

General Works

Digital Resources

619. **International Music Score Library Project https://imslp.org/.** [Website] Free. Date reviewed: 2019.

Since its creation in 2006, the International Music Score Library Project, or IMSLP, has allowed users free access to hundreds of thousands of music scores, from the well-known to the obscure, in the public domain. Its database contains millions of pages of music by nearly 17,000 composers, facilitates discussion on music through its forums, and offers copious information on associated people, styles, performances, and more. The homepage offers numerous search options including a general search from the central bar. Underneath the bar, users can narrow their search by category and subcategory (Composer Name, Genre, Composer Nationality, Time Period, and Melody) by clicking on the "book" icon. Each of these categories is structured differently. Searching by Composer Name presents a lengthy yet easily navigated alphabetical listing which can be limited to editors, arrangers, librettists, and translators. Genres are divided by Work Types (e.g., polkas, sacred hymns, anthems, jazz), Instrumentation (e.g., orchestral, vocal), Featured Instruments (e.g., mandolin, oboe, banjo), Languages and Period/Style (e.g., Baroque, Medieval). Under Composer Nationality, users have 89 choices between Albanian and Welsh; and for Time Period, users can choose along a timeline from the ancient to the present era. Users can alternatively focus on scores with recordings by selecting the "headphone" icon then searching between scores by composer or performer. Selecting an item from any of these lists accesses a general profile page which consolidates information on all relevant scores, listing them in addition to a selection of external links (biographies, discographies, websites, etc.). For each composition title, users can find lists of Performances, Sheet Music, and General Information (opus/catalog number, movement/section, date of composition, first performance). For performances, users can play or download MP3 audio files, and for sheet music users can view or download PDFs. Each title version is accompanied by generous reference information regarding publishing, purchasing, copyright, and more. There is also a list of all relevant category tags. First-time users can browse Featured scores, New Scores, or New Recordings on the homepage for a good overall sampling of what the IMSLP offers. While the site is not comprehensive—it continues to seek submissions—it is nonetheless rich in quantity and quality.—**ARBA Staff Reviewer**

620.   **ReSounding the Archives https://resoundingthearchives.org/.** [Website] Free. Date reviewed: 2019.

ReSounding the Archives, a joint project of George Mason University, University of Virginia, and Virginia Tech, produces contemporary performance recordings and other materials based upon World War I era sheet music. Songs such as "Good Morning Mr. Zip-Zip-Zip!", "K-K-K-Katy", and the famous "Over There" were heard frequently as troops shipped overseas and Americans on the home front rallied around the cause. The website information is based upon these songs and fourteen others. From the homepage, users can watch a brief introductory video or select a featured sheet music cover image— showcasing iconic turn-of-the-century art—to access materials. Users can alternatively select the Browse tab from the top of the page to access the whole collection. Within the archive, users can conduct a keyword search or click on any sheet music image in the gallery. For each song, users can sample a modern recording or view all available materials. Users can listen to or download audio for studio or live performances of the song. They can additionally view or download sheet music and find the following sections: Student Essay, Song Information, Recording Information, and Song Transcription. Song Information may include publishing date, publisher, publishing location, composer(s,) and a link to the archival record. The Recording Information tab includes brief performer and producer biographies, recording date, and location. Generally brief, Student Essays offer insightful context connecting the song to the American World War I effort, both musically and lyrically. Each essay also includes a list of related resources.—**ARBA Staff Reviewer**

Discography

621.   **Field Recordings of Black Singers and Musicians: An Annotated Discography of Artists from West Africa, the Caribbean and the Eastern and Southern United States, 1901-1943.** Craig Martin Gibbs, comp. Jefferson, N.C., McFarland, 2018. 460p. index. $95.00pa. ISBN 13: 978-1-4766-7338-7; 978-1-4766-3187-5 (e-book).

This unique and highly specialized volume is focused on providing an annotated discography of black singers and musicians recorded in West Africa, the Caribbean, and the eastern and southern United States from 1901 to 1943. As an ethnomusicological reference work, it would be highly sought after in most higher education research universities and music conservatories that have classes and degrees in ethnomusicology and the history of recorded sound. The organization of the discography is highly detailed, and is fundamental to understanding and interpreting the information contained within the book. Entries are organized chronologically, with an appendix documenting the audio sources, and three indexes which provide access to the information via artists and group names; recording titles; and labels, archives, collectors, university collections, major institutions, and websites. For those doing research and scholarship in this specific topic area, this is an essential resource.—**Bradford Lee Eden**

Instruments

General Works

Digital Resources

622.   **MINIM UK: Historic Musical Instruments http://minim.ac.uk.** [Website] Free. Date reviewed: 2019.

MINIM is the Musical Instruments Interface for Museums and Collections containing information on close to twenty thousand unique instruments held around one hundred locations in the United Kingdom. Users can find instrument images, select recordings, descriptive information, and more on historic instruments such as bagpipes, bugles, organs, castanets, gongs, flutes, lyres, and clavichords from countries all over the world. Users can search collections by scrolling down to the United Kingdom map and zooming in on pinned locations or Search for Instruments from the bar at the top of the page. Alternatively, users can Browse by Collection and select from a list of institutions such as the Ashmolean Museum, The College of Piping, and many National Trust locations. Users can also click the Browse by Instrument Family link to display a list of nine categories of instrument, including Stringed, Percussion, Wind, Keyboard, Mechanical, and others. Within the database, Facets (search filters) include Locality, Country (of instrument origin), Dynamic Resources (audio/video), Type, Instrument Maker, Date, and other categories. Information for selected instrument varies but may include an image/photograph, inventory number, brief description, collection, maker, measurements, acoustic measure, and materials. Aside from the instrument archive, users can peruse the Stories link for excellent contextual materials including essays and video. The three-part chronological series "Our Musical Heritage: 3,000 years of British music through musical instruments" is particularly compelling in its description of objects ranging from the Celtic Warhorn to the Bond Electraglide Guitar. Users can also Explore All Audio and Video, to see and hear those instruments in the database with Dynamic Resources (see above). Considering the nature of the database, it would be helpful for more audio materials to be added. .—**ARBA Staff Reviewer**

Guitar

623.   **Electric Guitars: The Illustrated Encyclopedia.** New York, Chartwell Books, 2018. 320p. illus. index. $24.99. ISBN 13: 978-0-7858-3572-1; 978-0-76036-360-7 (e-book).

A history of the guitar precedes this directory of electric guitars and electric guitar makers. The alphabetically arranged entries vary in length from a short paragraph (like the one on guitar maker Brian Moore) to a substantial entry for Fender (nearly 40 pages). Over one thousand color and black-and-white photographs enhance the work; many photographs capture key players of the guitar under discussion. An index rounds out the work. There is something in this book for everyone from the novice to the more serious researcher. There is no chronology, but coverage extends back to the early part of the 20th century. Recommended for public libraries.—**ARBA Staff Reviewer**

Piano

624.   Phemister, William. **The American Piano Concerto Compendium.** 2d ed. Lanham, Md., Rowman & Littlefield, 2018. 304p. index. $95.00; $90.00 (e-book). ISBN 13: 978-1-5381-1233-5; 978-1-5381-1234-2 (e-book).

This second edition of the 1985 classic work has expanded from 1,123 concertos written by 801 composers to 1,634 concertos written by 1,056 composers. The detailed alphabetical list by composer provides extensive information related to timing, instrumentation, reviews, date, and place of composition, information related to its first performance, and short quotes from performance reviews. Fourteen appendixes take this information and present it in various formats, from first performance or recording timelines, to various concertos and their instrumentation, to concertos for student pianists or by immigrant Americans, and withdrawn concertos or concertos by Works Progress Administration (WPA) composers. This book might be more usable as an online database, but even as a fixed entity in time it will be an invaluable resource for musicians, composers, conductors, music historians, teachers, and orchestras.—**Bradford Lee Eden**

625.   Shockley, Alan. **The Contemporary Piano: A Performer and Composer's Guide to Techniques and Resources.** Lanham, Md., Rowman & Littlefield, 2018. 250p. illus. index. $60.00pa; $57.00 (e-book). ISBN 13: 978-1-4422-8189-9; 978-1-4422-8188-2 (e-book).

This book is a welcome comprehensive guide to nontraditional techniques for the piano, and for pianists who are interested in playing repertoire which requires techniques and/or implements unfamiliar to both the instrument and to the performer. The first fifty pages provide a history of the piano and its mechanisms, how it operates, and various techniques. The remainder of the book details various ways to perform contemporary repertoire in which all of the mechanisms of the piano are used in unusual and unique ways. From a chapter on plucking, strumming, scraping, and rubbing the strings on the inside of the piano; to muting the sound of the piano through various implements; to harmonics and partials; to the piano as a percussion instrument; to various bowing techniques and implements; to preparing the piano due to compositional requirements; all of these intricate notational and compositional rules for performance are provided. There is even a chapter on the toy piano, its uses and techniques in contemporary composition. This book is a must-have resource for any performance pianist or orchestra playing contemporary music for the piano.—**Bradford Lee Eden**

Musical Forms

Blues

626.   Perone, James E. **Listen to the Blues: Exploring a Musical Genre.** Santa Barbara, Calif., Greenwood Press/ABC-CLIO, 2019. 240p. illus. index. (Exploring Musical Genres). $61.00. ISBN 13: 978-1-4408-6614-2; 978-1-4408-6615-9 (e-book).

The third installment of Exploring Musical Genres is authored by the series editor, James E. Perone, a performer and professor of music at University of Mount Union. *Listen to the Blues!* is intended as a general overview of the blues, with description and assessment of dozens of examples of performers, songs, and subgenres. It also incorporates historical and cultural context, accounting for the blues' complex interplay with other genres like rock, gospel, and country. Perone is focused primarily on the recorded era of blues: the 20th and 21st centuries. Geographically, his focus is on the United States, with some attention to the influence of the blues on British rock bands of the early 1960s.

The book's first chapter deals with the historical background of the blues, discussing some of the diverging theories on its origins in African and/or Native American music. Characteristics of blues structure and themes are introduced here as are some key figures. The core of the book follows, in the "Must Hear Music" chapter, which includes 50 encyclopedic entries primarily covering individual performers, but also three individual songs and a handful of subgenres or focused assessments of blues' connection to other genres. Perone allows himself some flexibility in these latter entries to mention performers who are not given fuller treatment elsewhere in the volume. He admits at the outset that the series' limitation of 50 entries is a challenge in covering the breadth of available blues information—nearly a century of steady recorded work. The final chapters discuss the cultural impact and the legacy of the blues.

Perone cites primary and secondary sources throughout, includes some images of performers discussed, and links to YouTube videos of performances and recordings. The index includes *see* and *see also* references.

As with earlier volumes in the series, *Listen to the Blues!* is both authoritative and accessible. It will be a useful addition to public and school libraries, or in other settings where such a general introduction is desired.—**Joshua Barton**

Classical

627.   **The Classical Music Book: Big Ideas Simply Explained.** New York, DK Publishing, 2018. 352p. illus. index. $25.00. ISBN 13: 978-1-4654-7342-4.

This 19th volume in DK's Big Ideas series looks at more than 90 key pieces of music. The book begins with a foreword by Katie Derham, classical music coordinator, who suggests that this examination of more than 1,000 years of music and the social, political, and economic context in which this music was written may bring a new level of appreciation to the music a listener already loves. The following introduction discusses the development of classical music, the role of the Church, elements of music, musical forms, and the various periods covered in the book. The book is divided into sections: Early Music (1000-1400); Renaissance (1400-1600); Baroque (1600-1750); Classical (1750-1820); Romantic (1810-1920); Nationalism (1830-1920); Modern (1900-1950); and Contemporary. Each section includes its own introduction and a timeline. Each article within the various sections features a piece of music by well-known or lesser-known composers that illustrates a particular development. Articles include "In Context" sidebars and *see also* references to other relevant pieces of music. Users will find a directory of significant composers and their work at the end of the book along with a glossary, quote attributions, and an index. The graphics and other illustrations used throughout the book enhance comprehension and keep reader attention focused. Highly recommended.—**ARBA Staff Reviewer**

Folk

628. **James Madison Carpenter Collection** **https://www.vwml.org/archives-catalogue/JMC.** [Website] Free. Date reviewed: 2019.

The James Madison Carpenter Collection has recently been added to the Vaughan Williams Memorial Library (VWML)—a renowned folk music resource. The collection is the result of many miles of travel through the far reaches of Great Britain, where between 1928 and 1935 Carpenter gathered information and recordings of traditional folk music in a variety of forms, such as fiddle tunes, shanties, ballads, and more along with children's games, folk customs, Mummers' Plays, and more. Carpenter was one of the first collectors to obtain sound recordings, many of which users can access alongside printed materials like manuscripts, lectures, and music notations. This webpage from the greater library website presents a list of eleven James Madison Carpenter Collection components, which users can access by clicking the arrow corresponding to their interest. Components include Songs, Ballads, Mummers Plays and Shanties; Cylinder Recordings; Scottish National Dictionary, Notes and Papers, Games and Music; Two volumes of Ballads—Index and Text; and six others. As collection components are rather generically labeled, it may require some digging around to find particular items. Users can conduct a basic or advanced search, but it would appear to include the entire VWML archive. Components are catalogued with extent, date created, notes, and more. Each specific item within the collection components is also catalogued and described. Under the Games category of the Scottish National Dictionary, Notes and Papers, Games and Music component, for example, users can find images of handwritten notecards with text of children's games such as "King William" or "Ole Dan Tucker." Under English Melodies (within the Music Notations, Songs and Notes component), users can find sheet music for tunes such as "Blow the Man Down," "Haul for the Grog," "Shamrock Shores," and many others. Clicking on an image enlarges it, and users can easily navigate to the next similar item from here. Recordings can be easily found on the original component list and generally selected by type and/or area (e.g., Galway, Newcastle). Users can listen to and download the recording within the player.—**ARBA Staff Reviewer**

Hip-Hop and Rap

629. **Hip Hop around the World: An Encyclopedia.** Melissa Ursula Dawn Goldsmith and Anthony J. Fonseca, eds. Santa Barbara, Calif., Greenwood Press/ABC-CLIO, 2019. 2v. illus. index. $198.00/set. ISBN 13: 978-0-313-35758-9; 978-0-313-35759-6 (e-book).

This 2-volume reference set is a comprehensive collection of essays on the global hip hop culture and its artists. Its main audience is high school and college/university students, but educators and teachers at all levels will find these volumes helpful. Over 450 entries under topics such as artists, countries, concepts, and styles are provided in alphabetical order, with a listing of entries, grouping of entries under related topics, and a historical chronology prefacing the encyclopedia proper. Each entry includes *see also* references and a short Further Reading/Further Listening section. Numerous black-and-white photographs of artists and bands are interspersed throughout the two volumes. At the end of volume 2 a number of appendixes are included: frequently mentioned hip hop artists, the 100 most influential global hip hop record labels, editor-recommended top hip hop videos worldwide, hip hop films and documentaries, and countries with severely restricted underground activity. A welcome reference source for both high school and college/university libraries.—**Bradford Lee Eden**

630. **St. James Encyclopedia of Hip Hop Culture.** Thomas Riggs, ed. Farmington Hills, Mich., St. James Press and Gale/Cengage, 2018. 579p. illus. index. $285.00. ISBN 13: 978-1-41-038081-4.

This book explores the subject of hip hop culture from its roots on the streets of New York City in the 1970s up to the present. There are 210 entries on a variety of topics such as visual arts, history, business, music, fashion, language, and dance. Entries are arranged alphabetically, and cross-references are provided. Each entry starts with an introductory paragraph that flows into an explanation of the topic's importance to hip hop culture. A bibliography is provided after each entry. Offensive language has been edited throughout with asterisks, not as a critique of the language but out of sensitivity to the users. In the "Nine Elements of Hip Hop" essay, the most important components of hip hop are discussed: hip hop dance (breakdancing), MCing (rapping), graffiti art, DJing, beatboxing, street fashion, street language, street knowledge, and street entrepreneurialism. Various cultural expressions of hip hop are also explored. What is nice about this volume is the rich number of color photographs. I highly recommend this book for the reference collections of high schools and universities.—**Bradford Lee Eden**

Opera

631. Griffel, Margaret Ross. **Operas in German: A Dictionary.** Rev ed. Lanham, Md., Rowman & Littlefield, 2018. 2v. $180.00/set. ISBN 13: 978-1-4422-4796-3; 978-1-4422-4797-0 (e-book).

This 2-volume revised version of the 1989 book contains over 4,000 detailed essays on operas written in the German language. Volume 1 contains an alphabetical dictionary of all the operas, starting with the title, description, composition dates, important performance dates, important singers and performers, and conductors. Depending on the opera, a short or extensive description of the plot follows, ending with published score information, bibliography, and discography if available. Volume 2, just as large as volume 1, contains 4 appendixes listing composers, librettists, authors and sources, and chronology. A selective bibliography, index of characters, and index of names is included. The level of detail and specificity contained in the various appendixes and indexes of volume 2 are very important for any researcher of German opera; both volumes together make this an important reference work for any college, university, or music school.—**Bradford Lee Eden**

Popular Music

632.   **Colección Gladys Palmera http://gladyspalmera.com/coleccion/.** [Website] Free. Date reviewed: 2019.

This website hosts a unique and varied collection of Latin American music recordings assembled by a Spanish super fan and radio host Alejandra Fierro Eleta (using the pseudonym of Gladys Palmera). The collection of over 50,000 hard-to-find titles spans close to a century of passionate rhythms, dynamic beats, and soulful stories in Mexican, Afro-Cuban, and other Latin American styles. The Gladys Palmera Colección has digitized roughly 5,000 titles from the larger collection, offering information, commentary, and musical excerpts. The website, which can be translated to English from the original Spanish, is still being developed. Users can select the menu icon from the upper right corner of the homepage to access several useful links. From the Catalogue tab, users will find a gallery display of full color album covers or disc images, along with song/album title, artist, and record label. Users can click the image for more information, which may include format, seal, country of edition and date, recording, style, and genres. Users can examine multiple images of the album in addition to its Tracklist, including song title, author, and featured voice. There is also a list of musicians featured on the album/track, related tags, and a gallery of related discs. Featured discs are also displayed as a gallery and include basic identifying information as above in addition to a brief descriptive essay. While there does not appear to be a direct way to hear selected music at this time, users can listen to a good variety of Latin styles via the Collection Playlist tab. Twenty-five playlists feature titles such as "Gems of Vinyl—Panama," "Women of Cinema—Movie Divas and Cha Cha Cha," "Afro-Cuban Fairy Tales—Arabian Nights with Rhythm," and more. Playlists may be accompanied by a brief introduction (in Spanish), Tracklist, Tags, Related Podcasts, and a play button. The Gems of Gladys presents a gallery of 24 personally curated selections, with brief commentary (in Spanish) and musical excerpt. It is hoped that future development of the site will enhance navigation, provide more information, and offer more listening opportunities. Nonetheless, the unique collection is a vital record of musical history and the wide range of Latin American culture.—**ARBA Staff Reviewer**

633.   Perone, James E. **Listen to Pop! Exploring a Musical Genre.** Santa Barbara, Calif., Greenwood Press/ABC-CLIO, 2018. 250p. illus. index. (Exploring Musical Genres). $61.00; $. ISBN 13: 978-1-4408-6376-9; 978-1-4408-6377-6 (e-book).

Part of the Exploring Musical Genres series, this book is a succinct yet in-depth examination of pop music from the 1950s to the present. After the series foreword and the preface, the author provides encyclopedic entries for fifty performers, songs, bands, stand-out hits, and various pop trends. These include ABBA, Beyonce, Mariah Carey, "Gangnam Style," "Like a Virgin," Barry Manilow, Motown, Saturday Night Fever, British invasion ballads, and Stevie Wonder, to name but a few. The last two chapters examine pop music's influence on popular culture, along with its legacy. This last chapter explores various interactions of pop music with American culture and society, including new versions of old hits, jukebox musicals, persistent music, Hollywood and its use of pop songs, and celebrity status. Overall, this book provides basic information on the pop genre and its background, and would be welcome in any high school or undergraduate library for introductory research.—**Bradford Lee Eden**

634.   Simmons, Rick. **Carolina Beach Music Encyclopedia.** Jefferson, N.C., McFarland, 2018. 322p. illus. index. $49.95pa. ISBN 13: 978-1-4766-6767-6; 978-1-4766-3153-0 (e-book).

This biographical encyclopedia of 220 musical groups and artists is edited by scholar and beach music enthusiast Rick Simmons. It includes artists who issued singles between 1940 and 1980 where those singles are judged by Simmons to be part of the Carolina Beach Music canon. Artists profiled therefore include groups known primarily as beach music performers, but also others, such as Marvin Gaye, for example, who are known more widely in pop and R&B, but who issued singles that can properly be understood as beach music.

Each entry ranges from 1-2 pages and includes biographical information and a relevant singles discography. The biographical coverage includes information on recordings with a focus on beach music, but may also make mention of other, more general career information. The discographies include song title, catalog number, year of release, and a Billboard Pop or R&B chart number, if the song charted. The entries are arranged alphabetically by artist, with individual artists arranged by surname. Selected artists and records are accompanied by black-and-white illustrations: either portraits of the artist or images of 45 labels. A selective index is included, covering many named individuals, cities, labels, and records.

Simmons's brief preface and introduction to the encyclopedia give some background on the history and evolution of beach music and some context as to his own personal involvement and authority with it. Apart from his work as a professor of English, Simmons has authored two books on South Carolinian history, as well as two books on the history of Carolina beach music. The introduction also elucidates an apparently contentious dichotomy between beach music and shag music. Simmons frames the latter as extra-regional music with rhythms conducive to shag dancing (the dance inextricably linked with Carolina beach music), but as generally an unwelcome, dilutive addition to beach music repertoire. Such songs are omitted from this work.

The encyclopedia endeavors to be a scholarly reference source for the beach music genre where none had previously existed. One can expect that some may quibble at the inclusion or exclusion of certain songs in Simmons's assembled canon, but the work unquestionably fulfills its purpose as a scholarly, well-formed source. It will most likely be of interest to scholars of popular music and libraries who support them, as well as to beach music enthusiasts.—**Joshua Barton**

Rock

635.   Burns, Robert G. H. **Experiencing Progressive Rock: A Listener's Companion.** Lanham, Md., Rowman & Littlefield, 2018. 182p. index. (The Listener's Companion series). $40.00; $38.00 (e-book). ISBN 13: 978-1-4422-6602-5; 978-1-4422-6603-2 (e-book).

Progressive, or prog, rock was an industry label applied to bands that were more likely to draw inspiration from Beethoven than Chuck Berry. Eschewing blues-based rock rhythms for symphonic instrumentation and virtuosic guitar solos, bands such as Electric Light Orchestra and Procol Harum often fell outside of the mainstream rock genre. Here, Burns provides a journey through the complicated history of progressive rock, both in definition and sound. As both a scholar and bassist, Burns melds a professional musician's ear with a musicologist's analytical pen to produce a tribute and history of the genre. In a lengthy introduction, Burns situates himself within the narrative, as many of the interviewees were professional colleagues and friends. Though numerous bands are profiled or discussed in the book, from Porcupine Tree to Rammstein, this is by no means an exhaustive history of the genre. Rather, the book provides a sampling of bands from the 1970s to the 2000s within the genre's wave and crash in popularity over a thirty-year period. Throughout the nine chapters that constitute the companion, Burns muses on the validity and necessity of "progressive" rock as a label, underscoring many musicians' frustration with the classification. Whereas Will Romano's *Mountains Come Out of the Sky: The Illustrated History of Prog Rock* touched upon the difficulty of defining prog in a single chapter, Burns forces the reader to grapple with defining the genre through its disparate instruments, musicians, and recordings. The inclusion of both an extensive reading and listening lists invites the reader to indulge in complex instrumentals and reverberating Mellotrons to truly understand the meaning of progressive rock.—**Josh Eugene Finnell**

636.   Perone, James E. **Listen to New Wave Rock! Exploring a Musical Genre.** Santa Barbara, Calif., Greenwood Press/ABC-CLIO, 2018. 220p. illus. index. (Exploring Musical Genres). $61.00. ISBN 13: 978-1-4408-5968-7; 978-1-4408-5968-7 (e-book).

James E. Perone, performer and professor of music at University of Mount Union, is both series editor of the Exploring a Musical Genre series and the author of its first installment, *Listen to New Wave Rock!* The volume provides a general overview of the genre via historical background, explanations of its complex boundaries, and the description and assessment of dozens of key examples of performers and individual songs. Perone's focus is on new wave rock from the late 1970s through the 1980s in the United States and United Kingdom, with some examples also from Australia and New Zealand. Though executed with scholarly knowledge, the text is intended for the general reader, with the series forward declaring that this will be the goal of the larger series.

The book's first chapter provides historical background, discussing new wave's roots in punk, its development, and its complex status as a genre of varying sounds and styles. Fifty individual entries follow, ranging from 2 to 4 pages. Each is intended as a standalone encyclopedic description and analysis of an individual song from the era. There are a few exceptions: two entries discuss entire albums (The Go-Go's *The Beauty and the Beat* and Cindi Lauper's *She's So Unusual*) and one discusses a group in general (Ramones). In total, 41 performers or groups are covered with some content repeated if groups have multiple individual songs described (such as the Talking Heads and Men at Work). Perone analyzes the songs lyrically and musically and provides an assessment of the value and impact of each within new wave broadly. The final chapters describe the cultural impact and legacy of new wave.

Perone provides citations to primary and secondary sources throughout. The book includes images of nearly all of the performers discussed. It also includes an index.

Listen to New Wave Rock! is written with authority, but succeeds at its goal of being accessible. It will be a useful addition to public and school library collections or other settings where a general introduction to new wave is desired.—**Joshua Barton**

637. Rusten, Ian M. **The Rolling Stones in Concert, 1962-1982.** Jefferson, N.C., McFarland, 2018. 332p. illus. index. $49.95pa. ISBN 13: 978-1-4766-7392-9; 978-1-4766-3443-2 (e-book).

Biographical information and tour coverage of The Rolling Stones is not in short supply. However, while Ian M. Rusten's work is not a first of its kind in concept, it is certainly original in its depth of coverage. Rusten chronicles in entirety 20 years of public performances by The Rolling Stones, beginning with the band's first gigs in 1962.

Each chapter covers a single year, beginning with an introduction that highlights other relevant, concurrent events, such as personal information of the band's members or if any records were released by the band that year. Individual concert entries form the majority of each chapter, consisting of around 200 words apiece. Entry data consists of the concert date, venue, city, and, if there were multiple shows for a given engagement, the hour is provided as well. Some description then follows, which can vary in content, either relating details of the performance or paraphrasing the Stones' interactions with journalists on the date. The sources of the descriptions are not explicitly cited. Rusten's bibliography does include selected primary and secondary sources, and he lists many serial publications consulted as primary sources for concert data and for their reportage. However, he does not list all articles or columns used in this way.

The book is enhanced by a rich selection of illustrations: photographs, concert posters, and ticket stubs. Two appendixes describe radio and television appearances respectively. It also includes an index.

Rusten names Rolling Stones fans as the primary audience for the work, but scholars and historians of the band will find it useful as well. For the latter, there may be hesitation about the work's authoritativeness given the inability to trace its content to specific sources. Nevertheless, it will be a valuable addition to any popular music collection.—**Joshua Barton**

638. **Shake It Up: Great American Writing on Rock and Pop from Elvis to Jay Z.** Jonathan Lethem and Kevin Dettmar, eds. New York, Library Classics, 2017. 603p. index. $40.00. ISBN 13: 978-1-59853-531-0.

This book provides readers with fifty iconic pieces of American writing on rock and pop from 1963 to 2014. The writings are not intended as either a complete picture of writing on rock and pop or as a complete history of rock and pop during the fifty years covered. Rather, the writings represent the diversity of voices that made up the rock and pop scene. The first piece is from Nat Henthoff's 1963 liner notes for *The Freewheelin' Bob Dylan*; the last piece is "Guitar Drag" from Greil Marcus's 2014 *The History of Rock 'n' Roll in Ten Songs.* In a field dominated by white men, this collection includes the voices of women and African American writers. Each piece begins with a brief introduction of the author and his or her career. Entries vary in length from approximately two-and-a-half pages to more than twenty-five pages. Each of the pieces is reprinted as it originally appeared. Full bibliographic citations are provided at the end of the book, as is a generous index. This curated collection of writings on rock and pop is recommended for public libraries.—**ARBA Staff Reviewer**

26 Mythology, Folklore, and Popular Culture

Mythology

Dictionaries and Encyclopedias

639.   **Critical Survey of Mythology and Folklore: Gods & Goddesses.** Michael Shally-Jensen, ed. Hackensack, N.J., Salem Press, 2019. 2v. illus. index. $295.00/set. ISBN 13: 978-1-64265-115-7; 978-1-64265-116-4 (e-book).

This guide is the fourth in the Salem Press series Critical Surveys of Mythology and Folklore, and while the others are dedicated to heroes, mythology, and sexuality, the present one deals with the gods and goddesses of the world. Aimed primarily at a high school and undergraduate student readership, this survey offers a broad review of the most important religious traditions, from China to the Americas and from Africa to Scandinavia. The guide does a great job at placing the discussion about gods and goddesses in broader contexts that include geography (with maps attached), cultural history, mythology, folklore, and literature. Interesting facts and unanswered questions are integrated alongside the interpretative segments, tale synopses, and the bibliography, making it easier to navigate both for the students, who might find entertaining reading material, and for the teachers, who can more easily plan their teaching around specific material. Compared to other similar reference sources recently published in English, such as Coulter and Turner's *Encyclopedia of Ancient Deities* (see ARBA 2001, entry 1269), Jordan's *Dictionary of Gods and Goddesses* (see ARBA 2005, entry 1160), and Lurker's *Dictionary of Gods and Goddesses, Devils and Demons* (originally in German), the present survey is less comprehensive, containing fewer entries, but better suited for educational purposes due to its emphasis on contextual interpretations and to its topic organization.—**Rares G. Piloiu**

Handbooks and Yearbooks

640.   **The Mythology Book: Big Ideas Simply Explained.** New York, DK Publishing, 2018. 352p. illus. index. $25.00. ISBN 13: 978-1-4654-7337-0.

This installment of the Big Ideas series from DK Publishing focuses on myths in the ancient world. The book begins with an introduction that examines the nature and purpose of myths in concise and easy-to-understand language. The book is then divided into sections: Ancient Greece, Ancient Rome, Northern Europe, Asia, The Americas,

Ancient Egypt and Africa, and Oceania. Sections have timelines and introductions that contextualize the myths that follow. Each myth is introduced with a textbox that conveys the theme, sources, settings, and key figures involved. The myths themselves employ a variety of textual and visual additions, like a graphic organizer describing the 12 Olympians and their symbols. Entries conclude with *see also* references. Like all books in this series, the graphics, photographs, font, and layout enhance the information and retain reader attention. The book ends with a directory, index, and information on quote attribution. Though the book is accessible for a wide range of readers, the vocabulary can be advanced (e.g., one textbox focuses on the meaning and definition of syncretism). This title is highly recommended.—**ARBA Staff Reviewer**

Popular Culture

Dictionaries and Encyclopedias

641.   **Critical Survey of Graphic Novels: Heroes & Superheroes.** 2d ed. Beaty, Bart H. and Stephen Weiner, eds. Hackensack, N.J., Salem Press, 2018. 2v. illus. index. $295.00/ set. ISBN 13: 978-1-68217-908-6; 978-1-68217-956-7 (e-book).

Although the literary art form recognized today has been around since the 1930s, graphic novels are receiving renewed interest in the library world, perhaps as a natural need to compete with patrons' engagement in digital media. The study of graphic novels has simultaneously gained a new level of respect in the academic world. In accordance, the past decade seems to have produced a spate of new reference books on comics and graphic novels. This new 2-volume encyclopedic set is one such critical work that continues to take the subject seriously. Updated and expanded from the first edition (see ARBA 2013, entry 1019) but employing the same number of contributors, it contains "20 brand new essays," totaling nearly 160 listings showcasing the hero or superhero genre. As the editors remind us, the graphic novel is a medium, not a genre. This distinction allows them to dive deep into their subject.

Each title's entry summarizes its bibliographic information—publication history (including distinct volumes), plot, characters, theme, and artistic style—as well as the impact the title has made on the landscape of graphic novels. Entries average 4-5 pages and include black-and-white photographs of the creators. Notable artists and writers receive additional sidebar treatment. Each essay closes with a list of secondary resources for further study. The wide variety of titles presented include those from major publishing houses (Earth X, Marvel Comics) as well as those from alternative and independent presses, such as The Goon by Avatar Press.

Many existing reference works covering graphic novels include hero comics, but generally only as one of many genres critiqued. Beaty and Weiner's work fills a gap, not only by its depth of coverage, but also by its narrow scope and the breadth of titles covered, thus providing a deep history and linkage across the genre and beyond. It deserves a place in public libraries collecting the genre as well as in academic libraries with curricular interest in the study of the overall literary art form. The set also contains an extensive bibliography, a guide to online resources, major award listings back to the late 1980s, a timeline, separate indexes for works by artist and author, and an integrated index. Compare to the less selective *Graphic Novels: A Guide to Comic Books, Manga, and More* (see ARBA 2018, entry 590) which offers a substantial but concise chapter on the genre, with approximately 500 listings.—**Lucy Duhon**

642. **Critical Survey of Graphic Novels: Manga.** 2d ed. Bart H. Beaty and Stephen Weiner, eds. Hackensack, N.J., Salem Press, 2018. 398p. illus. index. $195.00. ISBN 13: 978-1-68217-912-3; 978-1-68217-957-4 (e-book).

The second edition of this popular reference work discusses sixty-five highly regarded works in the manga medium. Each essay is between three and four pages in length, with bibliographic information leading into a structured text divided into the following sections: publication history, plot, volumes, characters, style, themes, and impact. Adaptations into various mediums and a bibliography are included, along with cross-references. Black-and-white photos and pictures are interspersed throughout the volume. Appendixes include an overall bibliography, timeline, works by artist, works by author, and works by publisher. Some of the novels described include *Astro Boy, Death Note, Dragon Ball, Naruto, Phoenix, Sailor Moon,* and *Tsubasa: Reservoir Chronicle,* to name but a few. For those interested in manga, this book provides comprehensive information on the most popular and influential manga novels of recent years.—**Bradford Lee Eden**

643. Hall, Richard A. **The American Superhero: Encyclopedia of Caped Crusaders in History.** Santa Barbara, Calif., Greenwood Press/ABC-CLIO, 2019. 370p. illus. index. $94.00. ISBN 13: 978-1-4408-6123-9; 978-1-4408-6124-6 (e-book).

The American Superhero: Encyclopedia of Caped Crusaders in History is a clear passion project for Richard A. Hall, who has been researching and writing about superheroes since 2007. Not only does Hall have a passion for this topic, but the knowledge and expertise necessary to harness that passion and turn it into this insightful, informative academic primer on American superheroes.

The bulk of the book is devoted to 100 alphabetical entries about superheroes or superhero groups. From Ant-Man and the Avengers to Wonder Woman and X-Men, including everything in between that doesn't have a major motion picture (Sub-Mariner, Blue Beetle, The Question, etc.), Hall explores a list both broad enough to cover a lot of ground, and concise enough to squeeze into a single volume. Each entry begins with basic detail covering such information as first appearance, publishers, key allies/enemies, secret identities, etc., followed by a concise encyclopedic overview ranging from a couple paragraphs to a couple pages. Particularly helpful, though, are the sections for further reading and cross-reference, which help readers connect the dots.

In addition, *The American Superhero* pleasantly includes five thematic essays covering the history and evolution of comics and superheroes from 1938 to the post 9/11 world. Because Hall writes all five essays, they fit together and flow both stylistically and thematically in order to establish the foundation and background for all of the entries to come. A chronology of important events, glossary, bibliography, and index round out the helpful research tools.

The information is well written, easy to understand, and organized as well as one could expect. Although the volume includes a reasonable smattering of illustrations, the black-and-white printing does not do much to highlight the creativity, artistic ability, or beauty of these creations. With that said, considering the enormous popularity of everything superhero, this volume would be a welcome addition to almost any collection.—**Tyler Manolovitz**

644. Hendricks, Nancy. **Popular Fads and Crazes through American History.** Santa Barbara, Calif., Greenwood Press/ABC-CLIO, 2018. 2v. illus. index. $198.00/set. ISBN 13: 978-1-4408-5182-7; 978-1-4408-5183-4 (e-book).

This two-volume set outlines major trends that attracted public attention and time throughout American history. The first volume starts before and includes the first half of the 20th century; the second volume covers the second half and extends into the 2010s. Each volume begins with a list of topics covered in both volumes, and includes a thematic list of related topics that would aid the researcher curious about trends related to fashion, food, music, transportation, and more.

The trends are organized in sections by decade. Each section begins with an introductory essay that provides a condensed history of the time period along with cultural context worth considering alongside the featured crazes and fads. For example, the essay introducing the first section of the first volume discusses the reality that daily survival was perhaps the most important priority for most Americans early in the country's history. Therefore, the trends outlined start later in the period, once a certain level of material comfort was attained by many.

Articles include overviews of the fad or craze, and are accompanied by brief suggestions for further reading. These are mostly popular monographs, but some include links to YouTube videos or websites. Occasional black-and-white photographs and sidebars with related information appear in the text to supplement the articles.

Not all of the fads or crazes are about products. For example, an entry titled "Little Gloria" describes the sensational 1930s custody battle over Gloria Vanderbilt, and, much later, another entry covers the Ice Bucket Challenge.

The set concludes with definitions of popular slang terms over the decades, a bibliography, and a substantial index to persons, places, and things described in the text. With its clear and concise writing style, this is an excellent addition to high school and academic libraries serving beginning students in American Studies and 20th-century American history.—**Amanda Izenstark**

645. **Holidays around the World: Detailing More Than 3,400 Observances from All 50 States and More Than 100 Nations.** 6th ed. Detroit, Omnigraphics, 2018. 1514p. index. $159.00. ISBN 13: 978-0-7808-1619-0; 978-0-7808-1658-9 (e-book).

A self-described "comprehensive reference guide" that details "more than 3,400 observances" from the United States and more than 100 nations, *Holidays Around the World* does not exaggerate when it uses the word comprehensive. This weighty singular tome hearkens back to the days of traditional reference resources of thick volumes and dense content (though there is an e-book version). The title is arranged in an alphabetic fashion and is part dictionary, part encyclopedia, and part directory, as the guide includes contact information and social media details pertaining to the holidays/observances in question, in addition to the expected material of dates, history, culture, and other such details. For example, the entry for the Angkor Wat Photography Festival contains the typical date of occurrence (late November), its significance, the history of the festival, contact information for the organization responsible for the festival, and social media details related to Facebook and Twitter. The inclusion of the Angkor Wat Photography

Festival reveals the broad interpretation of the notion of holiday employed by the editors. Whereas one might expect the inclusion of social, cultural, and/or religious celebrations like Mardi Gras, Oman National Day, and Omizutori Matsuri (the Water-Drawing Festival), the guide also includes less-historically-based traditions like the photography festival. Such inclusions are interesting and point to the elastic concept of holiday. Nevertheless, given the brevity of most of the entries, the comprehensive aspect of the title clearly relates more to the sheer number of events included rather than the title's coverage of the events themselves. Nevertheless, this resource is excellent for appreciating the sheer number of anniversaries, festivals, feasts, and carnivals that human societies celebrate and for gaining an introductory understanding of those celebrations. This title is highly recommended for public, school, and community college libraries.—**Megan W. Lowe**

Handbooks and Yearbooks

646.   **100 Greatest Video Game Characters.** Jaime Banks, Robert Mejia, and Aubrie Adams, eds. Lanham, Md., Rowman & Littlefield, 2017. 266p. Index. $45.00; $42.50 (e-book). ISBN 13: 978-1-4422-7812-; 978-1-4422-7813-4 (e-book).

Whether a hero, a villain, an alien creature, or a sidekick, a good character can help drive a story and connect players with the virtual world of a video game. *100 Greatest Video Game Characters* is an informative and engaging volume that examines characters from a wide variety of video games played over numerous platforms and spanning years of video game production.

Alphabetized entries (there is no actual ranking of the video game characters), written by a diverse group of contributors, discuss the importance of the characters in the context of the game in which they exist, exploring issues of aesthetics, personality, roles, and more.

Entries may further address broader issues of cultural impact, such as the hypersexualization and gender stereotyping of female characters, censorship, mental illness, cultural identification, social status, and violence. Each entry also lists the franchise publishing date, game developer, and related characters. There are no photographs or illustrations in the book, but a visual of the character would be a good accompaniment to the essay and offer more accessibility to general readers.

Supplemental material includes an appendix sorting video games characters by category (developer, genre, gender, species, etc.), extensive notes, a bibliography, and an index. The book would certainly appeal to gamers, but also to students and educators in media studies, computer science, and the visual or narrative arts. Readers may also be interested in the companion book *100 Greatest Video Game Franchises.*—**ARBA Staff Reviewer**

647.   **100 Greatest Video Game Franchises.** Robert Mejia, Jaime Banks, and Aubrie Adams, eds. Lanham, Md., Rowman & Littlefield, 2017. 266p. index. $45.00; $42.50 (e-book). ISBN 13: 978-1-4422-7814-1; 978-1-4422-7815-8 (e-book).

This book offers a collection of contributor essays on 100 video game franchises that have best defined and shaped the booming industry and the culture around it. Essays alphabetically chronicle games from Ace Attorney to Zork (there is no actual ranking of the game franchises) and offer general discussion of game play, narrative, aesthetics, and mechanics.

Essays additionally draw connections with a wide range of other media, such as anime, literature, and film and touch on broader issues that might merit further research, such as multimedia education, industry regulation, and feminism. Essays discuss games played across a range of platforms like Game Boy, Windows, Playstation, and Xbox. Each essay lists game publishing date, platform, developer, and similar franchises.

As there is a fair amount of specialized language relating to game worlds and technology within each essay (e.g., eSports, interface, text-adventure, cRPGs, MMO, etc.), the volume might benefit from the addition of a glossary. An accompanying screen shot of the game (there are no photographs or illustrations in the book) may also lend more accessibility to general readers.

Supplemental material includes extensive notes, a bibliography, and an index. An appendix also organizes the included franchises by category (Developer, Publishers, Genre, etc.). The book would certainly appeal to gamers, but also to students and educators in media studies, computer science, and the visual or narrative arts. Readers may also be interested in the companion book *100 Greatest Video Game Characters.*—**ARBA Staff Reviewer**

648.   **Violence in Popular Culture: American and Global Perspectives.** Finley, Laura L., ed. Santa Barbara, Calif., Greenwood Press/ABC-CLIO, 2019. 308p. index. $94.00. ISBN 13: 978-1-4408-5432-3.; 978-1-4408-5433-0 (e-book).

This book explores the topic of violence in contemporary society and media. After an extensive introduction to the topic and a chronology of violence in American popular culture, over 110 entries are detailed on violence in radio, film, television, music, literature, and video games. Each entry provides a brief discussion of the topic along with a "Further Reading" bibliography. There are no pictures or illustrations included. Some of the interesting entries include Limbaugh, Rush; Blaxploitation Films; Dystopian Young Adult Literature and Film; Superhero Films; British Television; Mexican Wrestling; Soccer/Football Hooligans; Goth and Industrial Music; Jamaican Reggae Music; Narcocorridos; King, Stephen; Scandinavian Crime Novels; Walker, Alice; *Final Fantasy*; *World of Warcraft*; and *Diablo*, to name but a few. An excellent compilation of essays and scholarship on violence in current American and global society.—**Bradford Lee Eden**

27 Performing Arts

General Works

Directories

649. **The Grey House Performing Arts Industry Guide 2019/2020.** Amenia, N.Y., Grey House Publishing, 2019. 1192p. index. $195.00pa. ISBN 13: 978-1-64265-061-7.

Now in its 11th edition, this guide (formerly known as *The Grey House Performing Arts Directory*) includes entries for 9,412 performing arts organizations and resources and the names of 36,643 key contacts. The information is presented in several sections: Dance (702 entries), Instrumental Music (1,124 entries), Vocal Music (553 entries), Theatre (1,718 entries), and Series & Festivals (1,714 entries). These are followed by listings for Performance Facilities (2,823 entries) and Information Resources (778 entries). The entries in the first five sections provide contact information (email, address, phone, fax, etc.), and much more (founding dates, organizational mission, income sources, nonprofit status, number of paid and unpaid staff, names of management and other officials, and more). The information regarding performance facilities will include contact information and other data (type of stage and stage dimensions, rental contact, staff numbers and budget, seating capacity, etc.). The entries in these first six parts are arranged by state and then by city. Part 7, Information Resources, arranges information alphabetically under 6 subheadings: Associations, Newsletters, Magazines & Journals, Trade Shows, Directories & Databases, and Industry Websites. The book concludes with six indexes: entry name, executive name, facilities, specialized field, geographic, and information resources. Recommended.— **ARBA Staff Reviewer**

Handbooks and Yearbooks

650. **Careers in the Arts: Fine, Performing & Visual.** Michael Shally-Jensen, ed. Hackensack, N.J., Salem Press, 2017. 300p. index. $125.00. ISBN 13: 978-1-68217-320-6; 978-1-68217-321-3 (e-book).

This series offers a well-organized, easy-to-use reference with general information on a variety of careers. This volume focuses on a range of jobs within the varied arts sector, encompassing specialties from acting to writing and more.

Opening pages lay a good foundation regarding the current state of the arts sector, discussing its adaptation to advancing technologies, growth potential, and other topics. The alphabetically arranged chapters that follow guide readers through twenty-seven individual occupations. Within each chapter, readers will find ample information compartmentalized into topical sections. An Overview provides an occupation's general work description with brief coverage of duties and responsibilities. Occupation Specialties lists specializations within the broader job definition. Work Environment looks at physical, interpersonal, and technical expectations of the occupation. The Education, Training, and Advancement section discusses such things as academic programs and professional requirements. Earnings and Advancement offers general assessment of salaries and benefits and the Employment and Outlook section describes current professional trends.

Chapters are succinct, and employ a generous use of bullet points, headers, tables, shaded text boxes, and other tools for ease of navigation. Additional features may include historical information, fun facts, interviews with professionals, a description of an average day on the job, a snapshot, and affiliated educational and professional resources.

The volume also includes a subject index and two appendixes providing the Holland Code career matching tool and a general bibliography. The straightforward, positive approach to the material will engage high school students, university students, and other readers considering entry into the arts field.—**ARBA Staff Reviewer**

Film, Television, and Video

Biography

651.   Lisanti, Tom. **Glamour Girls of Sixties Hollywood: Seventy-Five Profiles.** Jefferson, N.C., McFarland, 2018. 242p. illus. index. $29.95pa. ISBN 13: 978-1-4766-7233-5; 978-1-4766-1241-6 (e-book).

This book pays tribute to 75 actresses who during the 1960s were popular pinups that played minor acting roles in film and television. Labeled "glamour girls" by the media, they were known for their sexy outfits featuring plenty of curves and cleavage. Listed and featured in alphabetical order by last name, each woman is provided an extensive profile along with at least one black-and-white glamour picture. Those women who provided extensive interviews for this book are bolded in the table of contents and given a longer entry in the book. Many of these women were or became *Playboy* centerfolds and models, beauty queens, and Las Vegas showgirls before and after their various acting careers. It may be hard to keep this book on the shelves or from being stolen, given the numerous revealing photographs contained within it.—**Bradford Lee Eden**

Dictionaries and Encyclopedias

652.   **The Encyclopedia of Contemporary Spanish Films.** Salvador Jimenez Murguía, ed. Lanham, Md., Rowman & Littlefield, 2018. 558p. illus. index. $125.00; $188.50. ISBN 13: 978-1-4422-7132-6; 978-1-4422-7133-3 (e-book).

Part of the National Cinema Series from Rowman & Littlefield, this encyclopedia focuses on Spanish films produced from 1976 to 2016. The encyclopedia's more than 300 entries cover the post-Franco period. It is unique in that it is geared towards the English-speaking market and in the fact that it is international in the scope of its authorship. Each entry provides the name of the film in both Spanish and English, the date, the director, the screenplay authors, and the specs. A plot synopsis is provided, along with a black-and-white photo from the film and a short bibliography. If the film won any major awards, this information is included. Two appendixes provide select biographical profiles of outstanding Spanish actors and directors and Goya Award winners from 1987 to 2017. This reference work will enhance the diversity and comprehensiveness of any college and university film studies collection.—**Bradford Lee Eden**

653.   **The Encyclopedia of Racism in American Films.** Salvador Jimenez Murguía, ed. Lanham, Md., Rowman & Littlefield, 2018. 806p. illus. index. (National Cinemas series). $125.00; $118.50 (e-book). ISBN 13: 978-1-4422-6905-7; 978-1-4422-6906-4 (e-book).

This new collection of essays by Akita International University sociologist Jimenez Murguía explores the racism in film through contributions on specific films by over 100 scholars and critics. Exploring 3 general categories—explicit and implicit racism and critical productions that delineate how racism operates in society—the authors cover approximately 120 US feature films ranging from *Birth of a Nation* to *Get Out,* and most of the alphabetically arranged films will be familiar to anyone with an interest in race and film. Each article is roughly 2 pages in length, with varying balance in each between criticism and plot retelling. Little technical information is provided, beyond release year, director, writer(s), and length. Although occasionally lesser-known films such as *Red Tails* are covered, there are no entries for *Putney Swope, Shock Corridor,* or the Mr. Wong or Charlie Chan features. Good appendixes with articles on themes and biographical profiles conclude the volume, along with an index. A chronological listing of films would enhance future editions. A quick scan comparing this volume with Bernardi and Green's 240 film, 3-volume *Race In American Film* from Greenwood (see ARBA 2018, entry 127) shows that about one-third of the entries in the two books overlap. With those caveats acknowledged, however, libraries would do well to include both titles in their ethnic studies and film collections.—**Anthony J. Adam**

654.   **Novels into Film: Adaptations & Interpretations.** D. Alan Dean, ed. Hackensack, N.J., Salem Press, 2018. 405p. illus. index. $185.00. ISBN 13: 978-1-68217-907-9; 978-1-68217-955-0 (e-book).

The adaptation of literature into film reflects a profound and continuous, yet sometimes contentious, partnership of storytelling and narrative. As novels have become more contemporary and modern so, too, has cinematic technology, although literature and film remain forever entwined in a push-pull of often-uncompromising differences that can both transform and limit the adaptation process. Reading is typically solitary; watching films is an inherently collective experience. Reading requires us to decode words and phrases for meaning; films allow us to listen to and observe dialog to discover definition and context. The structure of a literary work can contradict that of its corresponding film; for example, characters in novels often develop over time and share their internal thoughts, while characters in adapted films often come and go as the writers see fit, with little insight into those characters' essences. Nevertheless, as the film industry continues to advance technologically, it still looks to literature, classic and contemporary alike, for both vision and content.

This book is a first edition, modeled after previous works about adaptations of literary works into film. The edition covers 100 novels, arranged alphabetically into individual entries by their corresponding film titles. Each "essay," as the entries are described, details how an adaptation came to be ("Context"); provides an in-depth analysis of a film ("Film Analysis"); and briefly notes a film's importance ("Significance"). Also included with each essay are suggestions for additional reading and short bibliographies. Meanwhile, front matter consists of a "Publisher's Note," which outlines the book content and organization, and an introduction, which describes general principles for adapting novels into film against a backdrop of an historical analysis of the process of adaptation. Finally, back matter contains six indexes, three of which provide listings of literary works by title, author, and date of publication, with the remaining three indexes similarly listing films by screenwriter, director, and release date.

Undoubtedly, the book is unique in its subject matter, and thus it likely fills a distinct gap for those who study novel-to-film adaptation. Perhaps the most notable feature of the edition are the in-depth analyses enclosed with each of the essays, which provide the context of a literary work, and describe the extent to which a film adaptation holds true to that work. As such, the analyses provide an insightful historical context to film adaptation, adding depth to the topic and thus moving beyond mere categorization. Lending credibility to the analyses are the aforementioned sections of suggested further reading and bibliographies, largely consisting of books, book chapters, and popular articles. In sum, readers can expect a diverse collection of titles ranging from the 8th century to 2016, with well-researched histories and analyses and a user-friendly arrangement.—**Sheri Edwards**

655.   Perlmutter, David. **The Encyclopedia of American Animated Television Shows.** Lanham, Md., Rowman & Littlefield, 2018. 774p. illus. index. $125.00; $118.50 (e-book). ISBN 13: 978-1-5381-0373-9; 978-1-5381-0374-6 (e-book).

Animation and animated television shows are so ingrained in modern life that we rarely consider just how new animation is as an art form, nor how prevalent these shows are on television. There is a plethora of animated shows, from cartoons aimed at young children to those created specifically for adults, and to create a reference work on them is an overwhelming endeavor. However, in *The Encyclopedia of American Animated Television Shows,* David Perlmutter has set boundaries for himself, and thus produced an excellent reference work.

In his preface, Perlmutter is quick to define exactly what the book contains and does not contain. The information contained in the book spans from 1948 to 2016, centering on animated shows that aired on television networks and cable channels in both the United States and Canada. He continues to explain how he determined which shows to include and what terms he used when creating the encyclopedia entries. Separate from the preface, the introduction is an overview of the history of animation and the rise of animated shows on television. Many of the names and terms used in the entries are present and explained within the introduction; however, while the information contained in the preface and introduction is useful in explaining Perlmutter's organizational style and the book's content, the entries themselves are straightforward and easy to follow, even without the preface.

Each entry is arranged alphabetically (ignoring definite articles such as "the" or "a") and, when such information is available, contains up to eight different pieces of information outside the title and years: the studio; distributors; producers; directors; writers; voice actors; synopsis; and commentary by the author. Some entries are shorter than others, depending on the available information as well as the length of the show's run. "Dragon Tales," for instance, takes up only half a page, whereas "Spongebob Squarepants" takes the equivalent of three full pages. There are also black-and-white images scattered throughout the book, showcasing the animation styles of different shows.

This encyclopedia is easy to read and understand and contains quite a variety of animated television shows. While more images, or perhaps colored images, would have been appreciated, the lack is understandable due to the already large size of the book. It is an excellent resource for those studying animation, television, or perhaps even the rise of the media influence on modern society.—**Mary Rebecca Yantis**

656.   Rubin, Steven Jay. **The Twilight Zone Encyclopedia.** Chicago, Chicago Review Press, 2018. 432p. illus. $29.99pa. ISBN 13: 978-1-61373-888-7.

This encyclopedia provides biographies of principal actors and behind-the-scenes personnel, information about individual episodes, and other facts about *The Twilight Zone,* the ground-breaking Rod Serling series that debuted in 1959. The entries vary in length depending on type. Those that describe the episodes are approximately one to two pages and include the air date, the opening narration, an episode description, and lists of cast and crew. The biographical entries can be anywhere from one to several paragraphs and include life and death dates, episode appearances, pay received, and career information. There are entries for objects used in the series, like a World War II B-25 medium bomber, and there are entries for ideas and things like the hour-long format, a less-than-successful idea tried for one season. The longest entry is for Serling himself; this entry includes his last interview from March 1975. A bibliography that includes books, interviews, and magazine and newspaper articles rounds out the work. Fans of the series would appreciate this treasure trove of information. Highly recommended for public libraries.—**ARBA Staff Reviewer**

657.   Terrace, Vincent. **Encyclopedia of Unaired Television Pilots, 1945-2018.** Jefferson, N.C., McFarland, 2018. 352p. index. $95.00pa. ISBN 13: 978-1-4766-7206-9; 978-1-4766-3349-7 (e-book).

This book is clearly aimed at very serious television fans or media scholars focused on television. The main text lists over 1,900 television pilots that were never produced or whose shows never aired as a series. Each entry indicates the network involved, the year the pilot was created, the cast and the director and/or producer of the program, as well as the concept behind the show. The latter can be as short as a sentence, or as long as a substantial paragraph. There are also appendixes which list over 1,000 pilots that a) differed from the final version of the show, b) were "projected television series" from 1950 to 1970 about which few details are available, or c) pilots created for produced but never-aired television shows.

The index lists well over 8,000 names, including famous figures such as Fred Astaire, Mae West, Jamie Lee Curtis, Jeff Goldblum, and Norman Lear. The vast majority, however, were unknown to this reviewer. This is a highly specialized volume, designed for those readers seriously interested in the pilot creation aspect of the television production process. Libraries of any kind will need to determine whether enough of their patrons will want to explore this topic to warrant its purchase.—**Mark Schumacher**

Digital Resources

658. **Archive of American Television. http://emmytvlegends.org.** [Website] Free. Date reviewed: 2018.

The Archive of American Television is home to over eight hundred oral history interviews with television actors, writers, directors, and others. From the homepage, users can view the slide show of new oral histories, search from the bar at the top right corner, or select the About the Interviews or How to Browse the Collection tabs for helpful background. Beneath these links, users can scroll through select interviews or click the Go to all Interviews tab to access an A-Z list of figures involved in the industry, either behind the scenes or in front of the camera. Interviews are accompanied by an About This Interview paragraph, marked by an excerpted quote by the subject. Interviews can be broken down into smaller segments or viewed as a whole, and each interview is cross-referenced to Shows, Topics, Professions, and Genres for ease of navigation. Interviews run the gamut of television genres, including drama, journalism, comedy, public television, soap operas, and game shows. The archive includes interviews with such television legends as Alan Alda, Steve Allen, Joseph Barbera, Mary Tyler Moore, and Carol Burnett alongside more contemporary figures like Anthony Bourdain, Ken Burns, or Julia Louis-Dreyfus.—**ARBA Staff Reviewer**

659. **Sponsored Films. Https://www.filmpreservation.org/sponsored-films.** [Website] Free. Date reviewed: 2018.

While sponsored films, or "message driven motion pictures" may represent a less-glamorous genre in American filmmaking, they are nonetheless a significant historical resource. This website allows users to view 135 sponsored films from public service agencies, manufacturers, religious groups, schools, and other organizations. Users can scroll through a gallery of films which are sortable by title, production date, and sponsoring entity. Selecting a film presents a film description which generally includes sponsor identification, production company, director, writer, transfer note, content description/storyline, and additional resources. Users can view, download, or share these obscure films. Sponsored by such entities as The American Social Hygiene Association, the Mental Health Film Board, the National Child Labor Committee, the City of St. Louis, Bristol-Meyers, and others, the films take a wide variety of approaches when conveying messages designed to educate and persuade audiences. For example, "Admiral Cigarette" (1897) uses rudimentary special effects and sex appeal to inform viewers that cigarette smoking is the American way (a smoking woman magically bursts from a large cigarette pack to rain cigarettes down upon Uncle Sam and other American symbols), while the 1966 feature length "Anarchy, U.S.A.," produced by the John Birch Society, uses newsreel footage and somewhat incendiary narration to try to connect the civil rights movement with communism. Users can also view or download a PDF edition of *The Field Guide to Sponsored Films* which provides further context and production information on a total of 452 sponsored films.—**ARBA Staff Reviewer**

Filmography

660.   **BFI Filmography. https://filmography.bfi.org.uk.** [Website] Free. Date reviewed: 2018.

The British Film Industry (BFI) Filmography is a database of information on over 10,000 British feature films across many genres and the people who made them. Employing a good mix of maps, tables, graphs, and other visualizations, the site helps users answer myriad questions about British films. The simply structured site allows easy access to a good range of data. From the homepage, users select from the brightly colored buttons marked Films, Roles, or People. Within the Films category, users can scroll through such data as "number of films by genre" and "box office takings over time." Visualizations may then allow users to click on particular points to retrieve lists of affiliated films. For example, clicking on a country in the map exploring foreign coproductions accesses a listing of those coproduced films. Clicking on a film provides general production information (e.g., date, genres, synopsis), main cast and crew, and additional data charts. The Roles and People buttons emphasize data around gender balance, with visualizations addressing questions such as "how many credited roles have there been, and what is the gender balance?" There is also a chart titled "Gender balance within film departments and role" which examines male and female representation across close to forty film jobs (animation, design, editing, etc.). Data here also captures "most prolific people in cast and crew (top 20)" among five job categories: cast, directors, producers, screenwriters, and editors. Users can discover information on individuals such as birth date, death date, time span of film activity, and films. It is important to note, however, that this data only refers to British productions and is not a comprehensive look at an individual's career. The gallery of questions on the homepage offers instructive examples of database range, and includes questions such as "which subjects feature in the horror genre?", "what are the highest grossing British films of the 21st century?", and "who is the most prolific female director?"—**ARBA Staff Reviewer**

661.   Craig, Rob. **American International Pictures: A Comprehensive Filmography.** Jefferson, N.C., McFarland, 2019. 444p. illus. index. $75.00pa. ISBN 13: 978-1-4766-6631-0; 978-1-4766-3522-4 (e-book).

This book catalogs over 800 films, produced or distributed by American International Pictures (AIP), from 1954 to 1979, including products created directly for television. Two introductory essays discuss 1) the AIP film enterprise, both making films in the US and acquiring foreign films, and 2) their television production and TV film syndication projects. Each of the entries includes the date, length, director, producer, and major cast members of the film. A brief synopsis is provided, either by the press at the time or by the author. The rest of the entry discusses elements of the production and the impact of the film, if any, and relates the film to others being made at the same time. There are numerous photos, either stills from the films or advertising items: newspaper ads, flyers, and posters. Comparing this volume with Robert Ottoson's 1985 AIP filmography, this book contains much more text, includes more films, but offers fewer details about the casts of the films. Together they provide a world of information. Editing could be more careful: "principle" for "principal" on page 5, three different ways of writing the company's name within three or four pages, famous French singer/actor Charles Aznavour's name misspelled in the text and in the index, and many names from the text absent from the index. That being said, students of the American film industry will find useful information about the operation of this company in the decades after World War II. Libraries that serve them should consider purchasing it.—**Mark Schumacher**

662.   Holston, Kim R., and Tom Winchester. **Science Fiction, Fantasy and Horror Film Sequels, Series and Remakes. An Illustrated Filmography, Volume II (1996-2016).** Jefferson, N.C., McFarland, 2018. 366p. illus. index. $150.00. ISBN 13: 978-0-7864-9685-3; 978-1-4766-2985-8 (e-book).

This volume continues to provide the information found in its 1997 predecessor, which had the same title, was by the same authors and publisher, and which presented 400 films produced between 1931 and 1995. This volume presents 334 films. Occasionally a pre-1996 movie appears if it was not listed in the first volume and a sequel appeared between 1996 and 2016. Each entry begins with the film's credits (including as many as 61 actors in a single production!), followed by a synopsis, reviews, and a paragraph of analysis.

All the "expected" film series, both those with older origins and the newer ones, are included: Batman, Star Wars, Harry Potter, and Planet of the Apes, among others. Even two recent versions of the Frankenstein tale are here, after 29 such films were included in the earlier volume. There are also numerous photographs throughout, mostly stills from the movie, but occasionally poster art. The index includes movie titles and actors' and directors' names, although not necessarily the names of every actor listed in the casts of the movies.

Libraries with patrons interested in film, whether a school, public, or academic library, and certainly libraries with the 1997 volume, should consider adding this title, if it is within their budget. The popularity of many of the movies included here should generate patron interest.—**Mark Schumacher**

663.   Pitts, Michael R. **Thrills Untapped: Neglected Horror, Science Fiction and Fantasy Films, 1928-1936.** Jefferson, N.C., McFarland, 2019. 340p. illus. index. $49.95pa. ISBN 13: 978-1-4766-7351-6; 978-1-4766-3289-6 (e-book).

This book chronicles nearly 150 horror, science fiction, and fantasy films which have been ignored or forgotten from the dawn of the sound era (1928) to the British film ban on cinematic horror movies (1936). These eclectic films and movies are here described in bibliographic and content detail, many for the first time ever. Title, film studio, date, length, credits, cast, and extensive descriptions along with black-and-white photographs of scenes and cinematic marketing billboards will delight film aficionados and history buffs. A helpful appendix of all the movies discussed by month and year release date is included, along with a bibliography and index. Recommended.—**Bradford Lee Eden**

Handbooks and Yearbooks

664.   Barrett, Michael S. **Foreign Language Films and the Oscar: The Nominees and Winners, 1948-2017.** Jefferson, N.C., McFarland, 2018. 216p. illus. index. $45.00pa. ISBN 13: 978-1-4766-7420-9; 978-1-4766-3275-9 (e-book).

This book presents information on 312 foreign language films. Nine were recognized between 1948 and 1956 by an "Honorary Award" selection made by the Board of Governors of the Academy of Motion Picture Arts and Sciences (AMPAS). Beginning in 1957, five films were nominated each year in the Best Foreign Language Film category and then voted on by AMPAS members. The volume is arranged chronologically. A synopsis of each film is given, along with information about the director (his or her other works, for example), the actors (their other roles and awards), and occasionally the cost of making the film and some box office figures for the film in the United States. Eighty black-and-white photos from the films are also included. Each film has been given a grade, from a single A+ (for *Mon Oncle* in 1959) to nine Ds. Interestingly, for 18 of the years, the Oscar-winning film did not receive the best grade for that year.

The author clearly was deeply committed to this project. He had to hunt down, or research, a number of films that were extremely difficult to find in order to complete his text. The Argentinean film *Course Completed* (1987) is one of the difficult ones, where he had to use the Spanish Google site to locate some of his information!

This volume will be both useful and enjoyable for patrons at many kinds of libraries, except lower-level school libraries. It serves as a wonderful introduction to a fascinating cinematic world and will introduce readers to scores of important movies.—**Mark Schumacher**

665.   Duvall, John A. **The Environmental Documentary: Cinema Activism in the 21st Century.** New York, Bloomsbury Academic, 2018. 358p. illus. index. $143.00. ISBN 13: 978-1-4411-7611-0.

The opening chapters of this book provide useful general information on 1) the elements of a documentary film, 2) "ecocritical perspectives" in the analysis of environmental documentaries, and 3) the history of such films, from *Nanook of the North* (1922) to the end of the 20th century. In seven chapters, the rest of the book analyzes 44 films, grouped by themes such as climate change, pollution and waste, food and water, and animals and extinction. Following a paragraph of introduction to the theme of the chapter, the entries vary from 3 pages for several films to 16 pages for the well-known *An Inconvenient Truth* (2006) narrated by Al Gore. Each entry begins with a set of data including the date it was released, film length, directors, producers, and narrators. There follows an analysis of the film's content, critical response to the film, and information about the production, including the challenges in the creation of the film, particularly in foreign countries: political unrest, violence, etc. For most of the films, there is a still photo included in the entry. Most of the films are made by companies from the United States. Other countries of origin include the United Kingdom, Canada, France, and China, with a few films made by international partnerships. A 22-page reference list at the end of the book details all the print and online items cited throughout the text.

This volume will be useful both for readers interested in documentary filmmaking and those interested in the health of the planet and the environmental movement trying to preserve it. Any library that can afford this book should certainly consider adding it.—**Mark Schumacher**

666.   Hischak, Thomas S. **100 Greatest American and British Animated Films.** Lanham, Md., Rowman & Littlefield, 2018. 380p. illus. index. $45.00; $42.50 (e-book). ISBN 13: 978-1-5381-0568-9; 978-1-5381-0569-6 (e-book).

Presenting information on films from 1937 (*Snow White and the Seven Dwarfs*) to 2016 (*Moana, Zootopia,* and *Kubo and the Two Strings*), each entry in this volume provides, along with a substantial text, the credits for the film, the actors who voiced the characters, songs when applicable, a brief piece of dialogue, awards or nominations the film received, and a "Did You Know . . .?" bit at the end, providing a curious fact or two about the production. The entries run from three to four pages; there is also one black-and-white image from each of the films. One interesting part of some of the entries is that there was at times the need to replace the director, also occasionally having to change actors, and thus having to re-record large portions of the sound track. It is also fascinating to see the names of the actors doing some of the voices: Mel Gibson, Eva Gabor, Bob Newhart, Kenneth Branagh, Johnny Depp, and even Walt Disney himself. The wide variety of films included over eight decades paints a rich canvas of the medium of animated films. It should be noted, however, that only seven of the one hundred films are "British" and that three of those also had US companies involved in the production.

A four-page bibliography of over one hundred books offers a wide range of useful information sources, ranging from works on the Walt Disney Studio's early animation work to recent Pixar and DreamWorks creations. The scope of these works goes from the analysis of a single film to broad histories of the animated film, giving readers many other resources to explore. Quite reasonably priced, this book should be considered by all sorts of libraries, particularly those in institutions (colleges or high schools) offering courses in media/cinema studies.—**Mark Schumacher**

667.   **Hollywood Heroines: The Most Influential Women in Film History.** Laura L. S. Bauer, ed. Santa Barbara, Calif., Greenwood Press/ABC-CLIO, 2019. 408p. illus. index. $94.00. ISBN 13: 978-1-4408-3648-0; 978-1-4408-3649-7 (e-book).

In its preface, *Hollywood Heroines* notes that several of the women and the categories listed in the title have been sufficiently appreciated or recognized in prior works on women in Hollywood and purports to be an introduction into the concept of women in Hollywood cinema, which it characterizes as "broad yet complex." The introduction emphasizes the importance of feminism and the contributions that the women included in the title have made. Additionally, it acknowledges that while the title seems to presuppose two genders only (i.e., male and female), that "gender and identity exist on a continuum." Nevertheless, the emphasis on women in the title is intended to promote the discussion of women in film. These qualifications and acknowledgements are important (and appreciated), especially given the nature of the title. The title is arranged into broad categories reflecting different aspects of the film industry and film history. These categories include obvious categories like actresses, directors, and producers. They also include categories that the editor and authors suggest do not receive sufficient attention, such as stuntwomen and makeup and hairstyling artists. These categories are arranged alphabetically in the book. Within the categories key women are highlighted; these individuals are also arranged alphabetically. Each category section begins with a brief introduction that explains the significance of the category and its historical development. Some introductions provide overviews of key time periods in film history. The entries on the individuals themselves run from a single page to several pages. There is some cross-referencing in entries. Entries also contain further reading. The entries are well written. However, each section contains an interview with one individual from that section. These interviews are placed at the ends of the sections rather than with the individual being interviewed, so if one does not read the title's introduction, it may seem like the interview belongs with the last entry and is being conducted by the person whose name is included. For example, the section on casting directors ends with Juliet Taylor. However, the interview from that section is with Avy Kaufman. At first glance, it may appear that the interview is between Ms. Taylor and Ms. Kaufman. Furthermore, little context is provided for these interviews. This seems disorganized and represents this critic's main complaint of the title. In addition to the organization issue, the title is a little pricey—$94.00—in comparison to its length and content. While this critic appreciates the analyses included in the entries and that the title purports to include individuals who are underrepresented, the price tag still seems rather steep. Other than these two concerns, the title is recommended for public libraries and academic libraries, particularly at institutions with film and gender studies programs.—**Megan W. Lowe**

668.   Lawson, Matt, and Laurence Macdonald. **100 Greatest Film Scores.** Lanham, Md., Rowman & Littlefield, 2018. 336p. illus. index. $50.00; $48.00 (e-book). ISBN 13: 978-1-5381-0367-8; 978-1-5381-0368-5 (e-book).

The authors undertook the arduous task of selecting the top 100 original film scores from 1931 to 2014. The authors selected from narrative films, leaving out documentaries and musical films. The selection process was a collaborative effort between the authors and the editorial team and came down to choosing scores that the authors refer to as "especially significant." Lawson or MacDonald's initials appear at the end of the entries they wrote (50 each). As a testament to the difficulty of selecting the top 100 film scores, an appendix presents 100 films that have great scores but did not make the authors' top 100 list.

In each entry, users will find a brief synopsis of the film followed by a detailed article on the music, and analysis "of the thematic materials and how they are used." Entries also include the release date, a black-and-white photograph, public recognition and any awards, and recommendations for recordings in the CD format. Select entries include bibliographic information. Entries vary in length from 2 to 4 pages and include a range of film scores from *Star Wars* to *The Mission, Casablanca, The Bride of Frankenstein, Chariots of Fire,* and *Titanic.* In addition to the appendix of 100 other film scores, the book contains composer biographies, a glossary of film and music terms, a select bibliography, and an index. Recommended.—**ARBA Staff Reviewer**

669.   Leszczak, Bob. **Single Season Sitcoms of the 1990s: A Complete Guide.** Jefferson, N.C., McFarland, 2018. 284p. illus. index. $49.95pa. ISBN 13: 978-1-4766-7077-5; 978-1-4766-3198-1 (e-book).

This title focuses on sitcoms (situation comedies) that ran for a single TV season or less during the 1990s. The entries are listed alphabetically by show titles, and the information includes: production company; network; weekday and time aired (including month, day and year of debut and last episode); total number of episodes; whether or not the show was filmed in front of an audience; synopsis of the storyline (sometimes using 1990s semantics); details on the filming; guest stars; an analysis of the show; and insight into the title by actors and/or others involved with the show. Occasionally a black-and-white photo accompanies some entries. Two appendixes are included, a rather large one listing shows with a short and/or vastly different second season, and one listing such facts as actors in the most single-season sitcoms, animated sitcoms, movie-based sitcoms, school-based sitcoms, etc. An index of actors and show titles finishes up the work. Fans of sitcoms and scholars of television will find this title of interest.—**Denise A. Garofalo**

670.   Macnaughtan, Don. **The Whedonverse Catalog: A Complete Guide to Works in All Media.** Jefferson, N.C., McFarland, 2018. 270p. index. $45.00pa. ISBN 13: 978-1-4766-7059-1; 978-1-4766-3160-8 (e-book).

Joseph Hill "Joss" Whedon is a television and movie screenwriter and director as well as comic book writer, producer, business executive, composer, occasional performer, Hollywood celebrity, and political activist. He is best known as the creator of the Buffy the Vampire television series and is credited with scripts for *Buffy the Vampire Slayer* movie; *Roseanne, Toy Story, The Cabin in the Woods,* and *Dr. Horrible.* Additionally, he has written comics in the Marvel and Buffyverse canons and received an Oscar nomination for cowriting *Toy Story.* The Whedonverse refers to the works of Joss Whedon. This reference book provides a complete inventory of all his work from 1989 to December 2017 as well as a bibliography of books, articles, essays, and chapters about Whedon. *The Whedonverse Catalog* is arranged within eighteen sections, the first containing bibliographic citations for the works of Joss Whedon. The remaining sections include lists of scripts and writings he did in the early years, including for the television series Roseanne and Parenthood; among the other sections are those concerning specific projects among which are *Buffy the Vampire Slayer* (movie); *Buffy the Vampire Slayer* (television); *Angel; Agents of S.H.I.E.L.D; Justice League* (movie); and miscellaneous projects including acting appearances and articles by Whedon. Each section includes an introduction to the project; episodes (including title and air date); DVD release information; tie-in books; TV or movie reviews; books and book reviews; theses and dissertations; and reliable web resources. An index is included for this resource. This is an essential book for those interested in the works of Joss Whedon. It is especially recommended for public library collections and to academic library collections supporting programs in media and film studies.—**Lucy Heckman**

671.   Maxford, Howard. **Hammer Complete: The Films, the Personnel, the Company.** Jefferson, N.C., McFarland, 2019. 984p. illus. index. $95.00. ISBN 13: 978-1-4766-7007-2; 978-1-4766-2914-8 (e-book).

An undeniably weighty tome, Howard Maxford's *Hammer Complete: The Films, the Personnel, the Company* attempts to provide a comprehensive overview of one of the industry's most significant and unique studios. Though best known for its classic horror films, Hammer Films also produced many films in other genres, far from horror. However, one cannot ignore the tremendous contribution that Hammer Films made to the horror genre and the film industry. To that end, Maxford attempts to provide an in-depth look at the studio, covering a breadth and depth of topics, individuals, and films unprecedented in previous publications about the studio. Johnson and Del Vecchio's *Hammer Films: An Exhaustive Filmography* only covers the filmography, while Maxford attempts to delve deep into the company's profile, personnel, and films, pursuing all with careful, detailed precision. Entries for actors highlight the films and characters they played, identifying their Hammer credits. Most are rather brief, though Hammer Films staple Christopher Lee has a lengthy and substantive entry (as one might expect). Entries for films include basic plot summary, cast, production details, and often images such as still shots or movie posters. Entries on collaborators like Pathé, the film processing and equipment company, indicate their relationship with the studio and film credits. The main complaint this reviewer has about this title is that the illustrations are black and white. Some color photos and reproductions of movie posters would have been greatly appreciated. Otherwise, this title is highly recommended, particularly for academic libraries with mass communication/ media communication programs and public libraries.—**Megan W. Lowe**

672.   Niemi, Robert. **100 Great War Movies: The Real History behind the Films.** Santa Barbara, Calif., ABC-CLIO, 2018. 375p. illus. index. $94.00. ISBN 13: 978-1-4408-3385-4; 978-1-4408-3386-1 (e-book).

The 100 movies selected for inclusion in this reference range from the 1930 version of *All Quiet on the Western Front* to 2017's *Dunkirk.* Most were produced in the United States, although there are selections from such countries as England, Finland, France, Germany, Japan, Italy, Russia, and Spain. Robert Niemi, Professor of English and American Studies at St. Michael's College and author of *Inspired by True Events: An Illustrated Guide to More Than 500 History-Based Films,* organizes the film entries in alphabetical order. Each contains six components: "Synopsis"; "Background"; "Production"; "Plot Summary"; "Reception"; and "Reel History Versus Real History." It is the final element that focuses specifically on historical accuracy. Some films, such as *The Battle of Algiers* are lauded for hewing closely to the historical record. Others, most notably *Braveheart,* are eviscerated for basically using historical names but presenting fiction. This work should be considered by public libraries that serve cinephiles, as this book not only serves as reference but also provides much fodder for spirited discussion as to the merits of the respective films. Academic libraries supporting film media or history programs would also benefit from acquiring this work.—**John R. Burch Jr.**

673.   Nott, Robert. **The Films of Bud Boetticher.** Jefferson, N.C., McFarland, 2018. 192p. illus. index. $39.95pa. ISBN 13: 978-1-4766-6707-2; 978-1-4766-3521-7 (e-book).

This book is a labor of love by someone whose life was strongly influenced by the acting and directing career of Bud Boetticher (1916-2001). The introduction and biography describes this influence on the author, along with nostalgic writing on various interviews and meetings with the actor/director before his death. All 33 films in which Boetticher participated in, from bit parts to major roles, from gopher to director, are detailed along with various comments, quotes, production challenges, interviews, and costar interactions both on and off screen. From the 1950s to the 1960s, Boetticher westerns were a staple of American film culture, with both heroes and bad guys who weren't afraid to kill and go against the so-called "Code of the West." Boetticher's partnership with Randolph Scott was similar to Jimmy Stewart's partnership with Anthony Mann in the early 1950s. This volume would be of interest to anyone who loves spaghetti Westerns made during the early years of modern television.—**Bradford Lee Eden**

674.   Olson, Christopher J. **100 Greatest Cult Films.** Lanham, Md., Rowman & Littlefield, 2018. 330p. illus. index. $45.00; $42.50 (e-book). ISBN 13: 978-1-4422-0822-3; 978-1-4422-1104-9 (e-book).

This volume provides basic reference material and plots for one hundred cult films, determined by the author to be the greatest. After a short introduction which defines the term and outlines the contents and organization of the book, along with a chronological list of the featured films, each entry begins with basic information such as title, date, director, screenplay, cast, specs, genre, and availability. A short plot description, background, and commentary follow, along with a black-and-white photo from the film and a number of *see also* references. Five appendixes provide brief information on ten great international cult films, ten great exploitation films, ten great midnight films, ten great camp classics, and the ten worst cult films. The index is interestingly arranged by the letters of the alphabet based on the titles of the films. A nice volume for ready access to undergraduates and aficionados of popular movies and films.—**Bradford Lee Eden**

675.   Quart, Leonard, and Albert Auster. **American Film and Society since 1945.** 5th ed. Santa Barbara, Calif., Praeger/ABC-CLIO, 2018. 364p. illus. index. $73.00. ISBN 13: 978-1-4408-3321-2; 978-1-4408-3322-9 (e-book).

The fifth edition of this popular and scholarly examination of the intersections between movies and society since 1945 has been expanded to include a significant chapter on film in the second decade of the 21st century. This chapter discusses the politics of the 2016 presidential election, the state of the economy since the 2008 recession, and the growth of Islamist terrorism. In addition, the rise of streaming services like Netflix and Hulu are described in relation to film attendance and audiences, along with diversity in Hollywood. The aim of this book is to provide both public and academic constituencies with an understandable, critically incisive, and accessible approach to American film. With an introduction and eight chapters dealing with American film and society by decade (1940s to 2010s), this book provides not only a history of American film and American society and how each affects the other, but also offers cogent essays on the growth of the American film industry as well as significant individual films and their impacts. Film studies programs will find this to be an indispensable tome, and public libraries will value the book's significant analyses and perceptions about both American society and its film industry.—**Bradford Lee Eden**

676.   Shelley, Peter. **Gene Hackman: The Life and Work.** Jefferson, N.C., McFarland, 2018. 194p. illus. index. $39.95pa. ISBN 13: 978-1-4766-7047-8; 978-1-4766-3369-5 (e-book).

This book is a comprehensive biography of the life and work of actor Gene Hackman (1930-present). It is presented chronologically, with chapters framed around his major films and other important events. Hackman's early family life and career are presented before discussions of the films *Bonnie and Clyde, The Poseidon Adventure,* and *The French Connection II.* After a chapter on semiretirement, chapters on *Twice in a Lifetime, Superman IV,* and *Narrow Margin* precede a chapter on Hackman's second Academy Award. *Extreme Measures* and *Heist* follow, with a final chapter on Hackman's supposed retirement. Chapters also include many of the other films within Hackman's extensive movie career. This book will be prized by all Gene Hackman fans as well as aficionados of Hollywood film history—**Bradford Lee Eden**

677.   Terrace, Vincent. **Television Series of the 1990s: Essential Facts and Quirky Details.** Lanham, Md., Rowman & Littlefield, 2018. 252p. illus. index. $40.00; $38.00 (e-book). ISBN 13: 978-1-5381-0377-7.; 978-1-5381-0378-4 (e-book).

A must-have book for any television addict who grew up watching TV in the 90s. The book highlights some 60 shows that premiered between January 1, 1990, and December 31, 1999. The manuscript is put together like an encyclopedia, in alphabetical order, making it easy to look for a particular favorite show. In the introduction the author states that this is not a book of essays or opinions, but strictly facts for the assorted TV series.

Each section begins with the name of the program, network or networks on which it was broadcasted, years the show aired, followed by a cast list, and a brief description of the program. Then there is a breakdown of each major character including such items as that character's place and year of birth, measurements, height, address, family members, education, occupation, phone number, car and/or vehicle license plate number, catch phrases, favorite food, talents, and pets.

The book is a stroll down memory lane; however, like an encyclopedia, you probably won't want to read this book cover to cover. The minutia on a show you've never heard of, or did not watch, will probably hold little interest for the reader.

This is the fifth edition of a series that includes television series of the 50s, 60s, 70s, and 80s. Shows that premiered in the 1980s but continued their run into the 90s can be found in the earlier edition, *Television Series of the 1980s.*—**Brian Clark**

678.   Terrace, Vincent. **Television Series of the 2000s: Essential Facts and Quirky Details.** Lanham, Md., Rowman & Littlefield, 2018. 246p. illus. index. $40.00; $38.00 (e-book). ISBN 13: 978-1-5381-0379-1; 978-1-5381-0380-7 (e-book).

This is the sixth in a series of books by Terrace. This installment features programs that aired from January 2000 to December 2009. Terrace includes shows that started their runs in the 1990s and continued into the 2000s in the earlier volume devoted to shows of the 1990s. Here readers will find a treasure trove of details about such 2000s shows as *Dexter, Gilmore Girls, The Closer, The Mentalist, The Office, Parks & Recreation,* and *Burn Notice.* Entries include the network (15 are represented), the years the show aired, a summary of the show, and biographical information on main characters that can include family, habits, place of birth, education, favorite items, hobbies, and much more. Entries vary in length from 2 pages to approximately 10 pages. An index and information about the author round out the work. This book is recommended for public and academic libraries.—**ARBA Staff Reviewer**

679.   West, Alexandra. **The 1990s Teen Horror Cycle.** Jefferson, N.C., McFarland, 2018. 195p. illus. index. $29.95pa. ISBN 13: 978-1-4766-7064-5; 978-1-4766-3128-8 (e-book).

This slim volume examines 1990s Hollywood teen horror films as a way to explain the youthful sensibilities of the culminating decade of the 20th century, and to show how the teen angst of the time fed a modern and mass-market take on evil and dread. Thirteen chapters discuss a range of high-style commercial studio releases, including such touchstones as *Buffy the Vampire Slayer, I Know What You Did Last Summer, Scream,* and others. The chapters delve into production details (casting, writing, themes, etc.), summarize plots, and place films square in the center of 1990s politics, culture, and social issues. Chapter 5 ("Generation Hex"), for example, analyzes the 1996 film *The Craft* against the backdrop of female empowerment, social ostracism, and religious morality, while Chapter 11 ("Lust for Life") discusses two films (*Wicked* and *Idle Hands*) with the Bill Clinton-Monica Lewinsky scandal and an obsessive media in mind. Interspersed with author analysis are excerpts from scripts, critic's reviews, production interviews, and more. The book is certain to interest film buffs and historians; however, students and educators of other disciplines (sociology, politics, psychology, etc.) may also find the book appealing.—**ARBA Staff Reviewer**

680.   Wiggins, Steve A. **Holy Horror: The Bible and Fear in Movies.** Jefferson, N.C., McFarland, 2018. 206p. index. $45.00pa. ISBN 13: 978-1-4766-7466-7; 978-1-4766-9971-8 (e-book).

This book provides an overview of horror in films, particularly related to those movies which have religion, the Bible, and other religious themes as their plot lines. The author incorporates a friendly narrator approach throughout, guiding the reader through a variety of chapters which narrow down movie topics, allowing for more detailed plot and character analyses of various religious horror movies. From *Alien* to *Lovely Molly,* from *The Fog* to *The Lazarus Effect*, from *Pet Sematary* to *White Zombie*, to name but a few, the author takes the reader through his personal catalog of horror movies related to religion and the Bible. Approximately 100 movies are described, and while one cannot characterize this book as scholarly, it is a delightful tome which encapsulates one author's passion and interests.—**Bradford Lee Eden**

Theater

Dictionaries and Encyclopedias

681.   Dietz, Dan. **The Complete Book of 1930s Broadway Musicals.** Lanham, Md., Rowman & Littlefield, 2018. 695p. index. $135.00; $128.00 (e-book). ISBN 13: 978-1-5381-0276-3; 978-1-5381-0277-0 (e-book).

The 1930s marked unprecedented changes in the Western world. While anti-Semitic forces and the rise of fascism raged in Europe uncontrollably, the Great Depression ushered in an economic downturn so severe it ravaged economic output, employment, and consumer demand across the globe. Unsurprisingly, theater in the United States suffered huge losses in the form of shrinking audiences, as well as starving artists who migrated to Hollywood looking for work in the film industry. Despite such dire hardships, ensuing federal responses to the economic crisis in the United States resulted in a series of large-scale initiatives. Known collectively as the New Deal, these initiatives included programs that funded theatrical performances and helped artists find work, heralding a new crop of receptive audiences looking for distractions from their economic plight, and theatrical artists eager to lend their voices to this profound transformation in U.S. theater.

The book contains 314 entries profiling musicals, revues, operas, ballets and dances, and other types of productions, staged during Broadway theater seasons 1930-1939. Entries vary in length and scope, and contain information ranging from the standard (e.g., production title, cast, and director) to the contingent (e.g., sketches, musical numbers, and number of performances). The book is organized first by an introduction and an alphabetized list of shows, followed by production entries, chronological listings of productions by season ("1930-31") and classification ("Book Musicals with New Music," "Imports," "Return Engagements"), and nine appendixes covering various angles ("Black-Themed Shows," "Gilbert and Sullivan Operettas"). Rounding out the book are a bibliography, an index, and background information on the author.

The book is well-researched, to the extent that its coverage and extent of supportive details likely is unrivaled within similar books on this topic; the book's breadth and depth is particularly notable given that Broadway theater in the 1930s lost massive numbers of audiences and performance venues. On that note, perhaps most striking are the descriptive narratives included in many of the entries. The details within the narratives are painstaking and include historical backgrounds and first-person quotations from the performances' original critics and reviewers. Meanwhile, entries are not individually numbered, making the "Alphabetical List of Shows" with page numbers necessary for finding particular entries. Moreover, as with other of the author's decade-specific monographs of Broadway musicals, the book does not contain accompanying photographs, although the lack of such visual accessories in this particular book likely has no effect on its utility, given that 1930s Broadway was not particularly well-known for its optics. Nonetheless, the book is entirely comprehensive, and anyone with even a modicum of interest on the topic should find the book both interesting and useful.—**Sheri Edwards**

682.   Hill, Anthony D. **Historical Dictionary of African American Theater.** 2d ed. Lanham, Md., Rowman & Littlefield, 2018. 754p. (Historical Dictionaries of Literature and the Arts). $165.00; $156.50 (e-book). ISBN 13: 978-1-5381-1729-3; 978-1-5381-1728-6 (e-book).

In this second edition (see ARBA 2009, entry 1075), author Hill provides nearly 1,000 entries on playwrights, actors, theater-producing organizations, directors, and design technicians, nearly doubling the total of entries in the first edition. The entries, arranged alphabetically, cover the 200-year history of African American theater. The book begins with a preface, chronology, list of abbreviations and acronyms, and introduction on the history of African American theater. The entries vary in length and are extensively cross-referenced. The information provided depends on the subject. An entry on a particular theater, for example, may contain the date of establishment, location, and name(s) of artistic director(s) while biographical entries will contain life and death dates, information on family and relationships, career highlights, theatrical education and training, and more. The book has 8 appendixes that comprise nearly 100 pages: African American Theaters (2006-2016); Audience Development Committee (Audelco) Award Winners (1974-2017); Broadway: the Black Presence (1889-2018); Black Theater Alliance Award (BTAA) Recipients (1995-2015); Design Tech: Costumes, Lighting, and Scenic Design (A Select Listing); Drama Desk Award Winners (1960-2017); Tony Award Winners (1970-2016); and Winona Lee Fletcher Awards (1998-2012). The book concludes with an extensive and useful bibliography. Highly recommended for public and academic libraries. Those that already own the first edition will still want to consider this update.—**ARBA Staff Reviewer**

Digital Resources

683.   **Shakespeare's Globe Archive: Theatres, Players & Performance https://www. amdigital.co.uk/primary-sources/shakespeares-globe-archive.** [Website] Chicago, Adam Matthew Digital, 2019. Price negotiated by site. Date reviewed: 2019.

Shakespeare's Globe Theatre in London, alongside its neighbor, the Sam Wanamaker Playhouse, have certainly told many unique stories, but their own are equally compelling. Through a vast archive of play programs, photographs, prompt books, costume notes, architectural renderings, and more, this database illuminates the many facets of a thriving and essential theatre, from its architectural design, marketing, and press to its actors, props, and technicians. Users can find materials that provide information about these two wholly unique and historically vital theatres, both designed to create the foremost theatrical experience during productions of the scope of Shakespeare's work (*Othello,*

Coriolanus, The Merry Wives of Windsor, and so on) and other non-Shakespeare works (e.g., *A Chaste Maid in Cheapside, Bedlam*). In addition to the special archive, the site provides a variety of fine scholarly resources and tools that could facilitate a wide range of research into theatrical history, architecture, entertainment marketing, costume design, acting, and much, much more.

The site allows a basic search from the central bar or an advanced search from the upper-right-hand corner link. Users can also Search Directories to find a particular category of information. Browsing options are numerous, with the archive grouping materials in several ways. An introduction offers essential foundational information about the two theatres and site contents. Under the Documents tab, users can find information in several ways. Choosing View All the Documents will reveal a full list of all materials which can be accessed alphabetically or filtered by date, document type, season, theatre, play, author, director, and other qualifiers. Documents are presented with a thumbnail image, title, date, and reference number. Clicking on an item displays a thumbnail gallery of all item pages, which can be enlarged within a viewer. Users can zoom, rotate, download as a PDF, or add to My Archive. Information accompanying the item may include related cast and production lists, links to related materials, and other information. Users can also Search Directories, focusing on documents by Production, Play, Playwright, Cast, Director, Creatives, Season, or Subject. Each directory will alphabetize its materials. From the Browse by Collection link, users can simply select the type of materials they wish to examine: Posters, Programmes, Music, Prompt Books, Show Reports, Wardrobe Notes & Jottings, Performance Photographs, Props, Around the Globe, Architectural Material, Globe Research, Oral Histories, Annual Reports, 360 Object, and June Everett Artwork. Finally, users can Browse the History of Shakespeare's Globe, focusing on materials such as oral histories, interviews, architectural plans, and correspondence specifically related to the origins and development of Shakespeare's Globe. Under the Explore tab, users can find excellent contextual information for collection materials. Collection Guides are brief essays that define and describe each archive category (Programmes, Music, Prompt Books, etc.). Information here shows how materials relate to each other and the theatre as a whole, providing essential understanding for even the novice researcher. For example, the Prompt Book, an essential archive resource, is described as containing copious detail on script, cues, timing, character, props, and more. The guides may also include links to particular items in the collection. The well-rendered Interactive Chronology from 1564 offers additional context as it notes events related to births, marriages and deaths, writing and poetry, theatres and performances, and publications. Users can examine all events together or focus on only one area, with easy navigation through time. Users can also create personalized timelines via the Add to List View button. Lastly, Essays & Video Interviews touch on the history of the new Globe Theatre, the various ways to study the archive items, and other topics. The essay "Original Practices at Shakespeare's Globe" by Dr. Farah Karim-Cooper, in particular, discusses such things as the creative philosophy of the theatre and the connection between the performance and the performance space. An Image Gallery offers easy access to a trove of thumbnail photographs which can also be sorted by play, season, etc., as well as by particular image category (Performance Photographs, Architecture, Props, Posters, etc.). 360 Objects provides a state-of-the art look at select models and props, such as a small crown from the 1997 production of *Henry V.*

Recommended for academic libraries.—**ARBA Staff Reviewer**

Handbooks and Yearbooks

684. Decades of Modern American Drama: Playwriting from the 1930s to 2009. Brenda Murphy and Julia Listengarten, eds. New York, Bloomsbury Academic, 2018. 8v. index. $628.00/set. ISBN 13: 978-1-4725-7264-6.

Each of the books in this eight-volume series on American theater and drama focuses on a particular decade during the period between 1930 and 2010. Each book follows the same structure: an overview of life and culture during the decade, an overview of the decade's theater and drama, four essays on the playwrights chosen for examination along with their works, a section of documents, an afterword bringing the playwrights' careers up to date, and a bibliography of works both on the individual playwrights and on the decade in general. The principles used in selecting the playwrights for representation were guided as follows: highlighting the most significant playwrights of that decade in both aesthetic and historical terms, who contributed at least two interesting and important plays during the decade; an inclusion of both alternative venues and Broadway productions; a reflection of diversity in gender and ethnicity; and an examination of historical trends in theatrical production and playwriting during the decade. Some examples of playwrights and their works included in this series: from the 1930s, Gertrude Stein with *Four Saints in Three Acts, Doctor Faustus Lights the Lights,* and *Listen to Me*; from the 1950s, Stephen Sondheim with *West Side Story* and *Gypsy*; from the 1970s, Ntozake Shange with *For colored girls who have considered suicide/when the rainbow is enuf, Spell #7,* and *boogie woogie landscapes*; and from the 1990s, Paula Vogel with *The Baltimore Waltz, Hot 'n' Throbbing, The Mineola Twins,* and *How I Learned to Drive.* This series is essential for any college or university library collection; it can be used in any fine arts, theater, and cultural history class as an introductory text as well as for individual examination and research on major American playwrights and their works.—**Bradford Lee Eden**

28 Philosophy and Religion

Philosophy

Dictionaries and Encyclopedias

685.   Brown, Stephen F., and Juan Carlos Flores. **Historical Dictionary of Medieval Philosophy and Theology.** 2d ed. Lanham, Md., Rowman & Littlefield, 2018. 452p. (Historical Dictionaries of Religions, Philosophies, and Movements Series). $110.00; $104.50 (e-book). ISBN 13: 978-1-5381-1430-8; 978-1-5381-1431-5 (e-book).

This second edition (see ARBA 2008, entry 1044) begins with a foreword, preface, chronology (500-1617), list of acronyms and abbreviations, notes on name usage within entries, and a lengthy introduction that covers many topics, such as the influence of Plato and Aristotle on medieval thought, the defining feature of medieval philosophy, an overview of the world of medieval theology and philosophy, parallels between Judaism and Islam, the birth of medieval Christian theology, declarative and reductive theology, and modern criticisms of medieval philosophy and theology. In the main part of the dictionary, users will find more than 300 entries on people, ideas, and terms that vary in length. As the usage note at the beginning explains, the dictionary lists authors under their first name unless they are commonly known by their second name. Entries provide *see also* and *see* references. A bolded term within an entry has its own entry so users can see connections as they move back and forth between the entries. There are two appendixes "Honorific Titles of Philosophers and Theologians in the University Tradition" and "Condemnations of 1277." The nearly 100-page bibliography is updated and subdivided. Recommended for libraries that do not already own a copy of the first edition.—**ARBA Staff Reviewer**

Handbooks and Yearbooks

686.   **The Oxford Handbook of Spinoza.** Michael Della Rocca, ed. New York, Oxford University Press, 2018. 688p. index. $150.00. ISBN 13: 978-0-19-533582-8; 978-0-19-998473-2 (e-book).

This handbook is dedicated to examining the work, influences on, and impact of philosopher Baruch Spinoza (1632-1677). As the introduction says, Spinoza is enjoying a renewed interest in Anglo-American circles, so a text devoted to decoding his thinking and impact is quite timely. The well-written introduction suggests the reasons behind the increased interest in Spinoza and lays out the goals of the book, "to present Spinoza's systematic thinking"; to demonstrate the influences of previous philosophy, particularly Descartes and Jewish philosophy prior to the 17th century, on Spinoza; and to examine Spinoza's impact on subsequent philosophers. The 27 chapters by scholarly contributors (including the editor) include those that focus on Spinoza's thinking (e.g., "The Principle of Sufficient Reason in Spinoza," "Spinoza on Skepticism," and "Spinoza's Political Philosophy"); those that focus on influences (e.g., "Descartes and Spinoza"): and those that focus on Spinoza's ongoing influence (e.g., "Spinoza's Relevance to Contemporary Metaphysics"). The handbook concludes with an index. Recommended to academic libraries.—**ARBA Staff Reviewer**

687.   **Theism and Atheism: Opposing Arguments and Philosophy.** Joseph W. Koterski and Graham Oppy, eds. Farmington Hills, Mich., Gale/Cengage Learning, 2019. 718p. index. $295.00. ISBN 13: 978-0-02-866445-3; 978-0-02-866446-0 (e-book).

This large one-volume reference work provides opposing arguments on specific questions and topics within theism and atheism, and is meant to illustrate the broad range of opinions, thought, and arguments for and against these concepts and constructs. Each of the twenty topics includes two essays, one regarding theism and one regarding atheism. The major topics are: Definition, Method, Logic, Doxastic Foundations, Religious Experience, Faith and Revelation, Miracles, Religious Diversity, Causation and Sufficient Reason, A Priori, Our Universe, Human History, Human Beings, Ethics, Meaning, Suffering, Science, Theories of Religion, Prudential/Pragmatic Arguments, and Final Reckonings. Each essay includes an extensive bibliography, and there are a number of grey boxes throughout listing key concepts for exploration in each of the topic areas. While the arguments and opinions can seem quite dense at times, one must remember that these topics are being addressed from a philosophical perspective, not theological. A nice reference work for any academic library and for inquiring minds wishing opinions related to arguments for and against theism and atheism. Recommended.—**Bradford Lee Eden**

Religion

General Works

Dictionaries and Encyclopedias

688.   **Encyclopedia of Women in World Religions: Faith and Culture across History.** Susan de-Gaia, ed. Santa Barbara, Calif., ABC-CLIO, 2019. 2v. $198.00/set. ISBN 13: 978-1-4408-4849-0; 978-1-4408-4850-6 (e-book).

As the editor's introduction notes, the *Encyclopedia of Women in World Religions* fills a major gap in the reference literature of religion by focusing on the contributions of women in world religions from ancient times to the present. Until recently, very little of the scholarship has integrated the contributions of women into the record in a comprehensive way. By concentrating on women, this reference work aims to provide a fuller understanding of religion and, by extension, humanity.

To meet this objective, editor Susan de-Gaia employs a three-form structure developed by scholar of religions Joachim Wach. Entries illustrate what the religion says about itself (theoretical), what believers of it do (practical), and how it is organized internally as well as in society and culture (sociological). Within this larger framework, the contributors explicitly bracket their own beliefs and assumptions in order to achieve critical distance in their exposition, even as they strive, de-Gaia explains, to promote the voices of women who need to be heard and in some cases vindicated. One additional goal is to foster greater tolerance by increasing knowledge and understanding. To that end, contributors critically analyze sources and avoid language that reifies old prejudices, e.g. pagan vs. Pagan. Included are many issues of special relevance to the study of women in religion, such as ordination, gendered language, and the relinquishing of tradition to form new religious institutions and practices favorable to women.

Seventeen topical sections give structure to 300 alphabetically arranged reference entries in this 2-volume set, which was produced by 125 contributors from academia and experts outside of higher education. The reader benefits from an alphabetical list of entries and a comprehensive index. Bibliographies after each entry and at the end of each volume provide further direction where one's curiosity is opened by the entries. The timeline is less helpful given the density of text. Overall, the work should be commended as a worthy addition to religious studies reference material at the college level, with the caveat that many of the definitions emphasize boldness over nuance, and any research project should utilize additional scholarly articles and monographs for more a richer perspective.—**Amy Koehler**

689.   **The World's Greatest Religious Leaders: How Religious Figures Helped Shape World History.** Scott E. Hendrix and Uchenna Okeja, eds. Santa Barbara, Calif., ABC-CLIO, 2018. 2v. index. $198.00/set. ISBN 13: 978-1-4408-4137-8; 978-1-4408-4138-5 (e-book).

Religion is rooted in faith, yet manifested in society by influential leaders. This set investigates such leaders in their religious and societal contexts. Having this focus allows for exploring individuals whose impact has stood the test of time (some have been more temporary), as well as how they have created positive change in their community: Marcus Garvey is an example of this. Although this has naturally led to a more historical focus, there are some important nods to the present, such as Munira al-Qubasyi's promotion of religious education for women in Syria today. Christianity has a dominant presence (along with Catholicism and Protestantism), but there is more diversity (Native American independent faiths, Thelema) than expected. Both volumes are arranged similarly: a full list of entries arranged alphabetically (then again by religion) and timeline precede the entries. Most entries are readable and short (three to four pages), providing analysis and historical context along with related entries, bibliography, and a sidebar for more specific information (occasionally an excerpt from a major work). This fresh look at the intersection of religion and society from the view of the personality frames the discussion in a way that will be most useful for introductory students interested in the topic.—**Stephen J. Shaw**

Bible Studies

Dictionaries and Encyclopedias

690. **Theological Dictionary of the Old Testament. Volume XVI: Aramaic Dictionary.** Holger Gzella, ed. Grand Rapids, Mich., William B. Eerdmans, 2018. 884p. (Theological Dictionary of the Old Testament). $75.00. ISBN 13: 978-0-8028-7281-4.

This volume is number sixteen and the final volume in the acclaimed scholarly series on the languages and words of the books of the Old Testament. It is a companion of the recent Kittel-Friedrich *Theological Dictionary of the New Testament* multivolume series. This final volume is a comprehensive lexicon of Biblical Aramaic accompanied by other cultural, theological, and historical terms contained in various ancient Aramaic writings. Each entry is a detailed discussion of the term's usage and meaning with full annotations and a bibliography with cross-references to all previous fifteen volumes in the series. Words are considered both semantically and linguistically in various Aramaic dialects such as Old, Imperial, and Targumic. Other sources in other traditions such as Akkadian, Ethiopic, Ugaritic, and especially Hebrew are included. This edition is geared towards Old Testament students without the linguistic background of more advanced scholars, without sacrificing the needs of the latter group.—**Bradford Lee Eden**

Handbooks and Yearbooks

691. Alexander, T. Desmond. **Exodus.** Downers Grove, Ill., InterVarsity Press, 2018. 764p. index. (Apollos Old Testament Commentary, 2). $45.00. ISBN 13: 978-0-8308-2502-8; 978-0-8308-9191-7 (e-book).

The targeted audience of the Apollos Old Testament Commentary Series is Christian, particularly preachers, teachers, and students. T. Desmond Alexander's (Union Theological College, Belfast, Northern Ireland, UK) introduction to Exodus explicates a three-fold paradigmatic agenda stitched by salvation theology. Exegetically, recounting the slavery and freedom theme of the biblical Exodus story which instructs that divine intervention rescued an enslaved, weakened, and downtrodden people; instructively, showing how the encounter of a just and compassionate God transformed the fate, faith, and destiny of a victimized people (Israel); and, theologically, the themes of historical freedom (Egypt narrative) and divine revelation (Sinai, Decalogue) are Torah/Commandments/Law anticipating an even greater freedom (flesh and spirit) that will come through God's grace rewarding identity and belief in the life, death, and resurrection of all in and through Jesus Christ. The layout of this voluptuous commentary is neither the standard lengthy commentary nor the verse by verse variety. Rather it is parsed into four sections: text translation (author's); selected notes on text, form, and structure; comment; and explanation. Alexander's translation, meaning, structure, and syntax of the text are extensively examined in and of themselves and by referring to their relationships within the Pentateuch and with other biblical books. His textual study scrutinizes vocabulary and phrases, time sequences, communication pattern, and movements within the text and complement his impressive knowledge and cross citing of texts. Likewise impressive is his detailed grammatical, syntactic, and semantic analysis of key words, phrases, and clauses.

Exegetical and theological comments are very impressive; overabundant Protestant/New Testament layers withstanding in secular academia.—**Zev Garber**

692.   **Jeremiah, Lamentations.** Tyler, J. Jeffery, ed. Downers Grove, Ill., InterVarsity Press, 2018. 610p. index. (Reformation Commentary on Scripture: Old Testament, XI). $60.00. ISBN 13: 978-0-8308-2961-3; 978-0-8308-8730-9 (e-book).

The Prophet Jeremiah's ministry extended from the thirteenth year of King Josiah's reign (640-609/8 BCE) until after the destruction of the First Temple and the overthrow of the Judean state in 586 BCE. Three sections (chapters 1-45, 46-51, 52) comprise the synopsis of Jeremiah's prophecies. Prophecies relate to Jeremiah's calling, the kings of Judah and the false prophets, foreign nations, the fall of Jerusalem, messages of comfort, and an added appendix ending with a message of destruction and redemption. Lamenting the destruction of Judea and Jerusalem, and the suffering of inhabitants during and after the siege caused by the sins of the people and their leaders, Jeremiah resigns himself to divine history and appeals to prayer that God might again look with favor on Israel and restore its people to grace (Echah, Lamentation). Protestant reformers envisioned the turbulent realities of their own 16th century in the Jeremiads of woe and calamity and reflected in Christological terms on the renewal of Spiritual Israel (Protestant Reformation) restored in prophetic promise for the coming of the Messiah. The voluptuous commentary by J. Jeffery Tyler (Hope College) features titled sections of Scripture (ESV) in an overview of the Reformation sources which are drawn, commented, and footnoted from commentaries, sermons, treatises, and confessions of known and less known reformers mirroring Lutheran, Reformed, Radical, Anglican, and Roman Catholic perspectives. In sum, a source-laden Reformation commentary on God's intervention and mercies to catastrophic events in 6th century Judah as inspired and interpreted by the turbulence of the Protestant century.—**Zev Garber**

693.   **Psalms, 73-150.** Herman J. Selderhuis, ed. Downers Grove, Ill., InterVarsity Press, 2018. 488p. index. (Reformation Commentary on Scripture: Old Testament, VIII). $60.00. ISBN 13: 978-0-8308-2958-3.

This book is volume 8 in a 28-volume series of Biblical commentaries titled *Reformation Commentary on Scripture.* About half of this series has been published thus far, and while this review will only comment on this particular volume, it is apparent that the entire series would be highly prized and of interest for any religiously affiliated educational environment as well as for individual pastors and religious leaders who regularly write sermons and Biblical-related content. Beginning with a guide to the series and a general introduction on the organization and content of the volume, each Psalm is then given and provided with an interpretation by 3 to 4 well-known Reformation figures. The goals of the series are to renew contemporary Biblical interpretation, strengthen contemporary preaching, deepen understanding of the Reformation, and advance Christian scholarship. A gem for any religious or theological program and for any Protestant religious leader.— **Bradford Lee Eden**

694.   Shuchat, Wilfred. **Abraham and the Challenge of Faith According to the Midrash Rabbah.** Jerusalem, Urim Publications/Independent Publishers Group, 2017. 567p. $34.95. ISBN 13: 978-965-524-273-7.

This volume represents a committed pastoral effort by Rabbi Emeritus Wilfred Shuchat (Congregation Shaar Hashomayim, Montreal, Canada) to disseminate the rabbinic wisdom of Genesis Rabba related to the patriarch Abraham to today's clergy and learned laity. In Abraham, the author focuses on the two following weekly synagogue biblical parashiyyot (scriptural readings): Lekh Lekha, which narrates the call and covenant of Abram/Abraham by settlement, family, progeny, and historical destiny (Gen 12-17), and Vayeira, which begins with the destruction of Sodom and Gomorrah (Gen 18-19) and ends with the Binding of Isaac (Gen 22). Genesis Rabba (redacted ca. 350-400 C.E.) represents aggadic midrash, that is, nonlegal ethical and hermeneutical pronouncements peppered with philosophical wisdom and a vast amount of folk tradition tied to a historical context (Second Temple period) though aspects of it are legal and very close to the halakhic strands of the Talmud. Rabbi Shuchat's psychological and philosophical interpretation and application of the narrative to contemporary times accompanied by selected rabbinical interpretation are the format of the volume. His inductive midrashic approach reflects primarily on what the text contains and less on why the text is what it is. However, the objective to apply the midrashic Abraham idea to the dignity and continuity of Israel (Abrahamic Covenant) lacks discussion on the contemporary Roman catastrophe and the triumph of Gentile Christianity indispensable for interpreting Sodom and Gomorrah (divine justice), priest-king Melchizedek (Jerusalem), Isaac-Ishmael (sibling rivalry), and Binding of Isaac (burnt offering, holocaust). Nonetheless an erstwhile read in classical rabbinical hermeneutics.—**Zev Garber**

695.   Wilson, Lindsay. **Proverbs: An Introduction and Commentary.** Downers Grove, Ill., InterVarsity Press, 2018. 324p. index. (Tyndale Old Testament Commentaries, Volume 17). $22.00pa. ISBN 13: 978-0-8308-4267-4; 978-0-8308-8755-2 (e-book).

Jewish tradition references Sefer Mishlei (the Book of Proverbs), Job, and Ecclesiastes as "The Wisdom Literature" of the Hebrew Bible. Ezekiel 7:26 speaks of three sources of spiritual guidance: the word/vision of the prophet; the torah (instruction) of the priest in the function of religious practice; and advice/council from the zekeinim (elders). Proverbs is a compilation of documents extended-written-edited from Solomon (Prov 1:1; see 1Kgs 5:12) to Hezekiah (Prov 25), and additional sources (Prov 30-31). Rules of practical ethics, discourses of wisdom, and original aphorisms expressed in poetic synonymous-antithetic-synthetic parallelisms characterize the mishlei of Proverbs. Textual content, compilation of a number of documents, and the absence of "Thus speak the Lord," suggest wisdom-writing of sages/zekeinim who exchange not lofty ideals nor abstractions but practical advice tested in common sense and rewarding life experience. In this new Tyndale Commentary, Lindsay Wilson tackles issues of composition, interpretation, and message for Christian guidance in secular contemporary times. From marked divisions of Proverbs (Introduction [1-9], three collections of aphorisms [10-29], sayings of Agur and Lemuel [30-31:9], and praise of the 'eishit chayil/ideal wife [31:10-31]), select themes, challenging verses, and problematic interpretations are elaborated in analysis and commentary. Additional notes add to the context and meaning of the commentary. Fear of the Lord (Prov 1:7, 31:30), apt description of the proverbial man and woman, who chooses wisdom over folly. This lesson is adroitly argued in Wilson's research and guide to living faith.—**Zev Garber**

Christianity

Dictionaries and Encyclopedias

696.   Encyclopedia of Christianity in the Global South. Lamport, Mark A., ed. Lanham, Md., Rowman & Littlefield, 2018. 2v. illus. maps. index. $250.00/set; $237.50 (e-book). ISBN 13: 978-1-4422-7156-2; 978-1-4422-7157-9 (e-book).

Christianity and the South are almost like two peas in a pod. Of course the volumes before are about the international reach of Christianity in the global South, not just the southern part of the United States. But the South as a region and Christianity as a religion have almost become hand-in-glove, no matter how much fun others may make of them. The gothic Southern writer Flannery O'Connor reveals this in all of her works, but especially *Wise Blood*. She captures the essence in a mere sentence: "It began to drizzle rain," she writes, "and he turned on the windshield wipers; they made a great clatter like two idiots clapping in church."

Christianity has been far more successful in the global South than it has in the regional South, if for no other reason than the global South appears to take the matter more seriously. From Latin America, to Africa, to South Asia to the Caribbean, Christianity is a conflagration of intensity compared to the balefire it barely remains in more northern climes. The preface tries to capture reasons for this, but the two volumes speak more directly to its overarching influence.

Continent and countries are arranged alphabetically in the two volumes, from Africa to Zimbabwe. Entries provide a quick overview with specific challenges that Christianity faced. More than anything, the entries remind readers that Christianity is no longer exclusively a western phenomenon. Each entry gives readers an excellent introduction to this religion in whatever the country. Volume two tackles short histories of Christianity in its various global southern regions. The contributors take on Christianity in Africa, East Asia, South Asia, Latin America, the Middle East, Oceania, and much, much more. The hopes, dreams, challenges, successes, and failures are brought out in these various brief summaries. These are excellent volumes for any size library and should find many users seeking their insights.—**Mark Y. Herring**

697.   Thorsen, Don. Pocket Dictionary of Christian Spirituality. Downers Grove, Ill., InterVarsity Press, 2018. 143p. $10.00pa. ISBN 13: 978-0-8308-4967-3.

How can devout Christians orient the whole of their lives around their faith? Don Thorsen, professor of theology at Azusa Pacific, provides the reader of IVP's *Pocket Dictionary of Christian Spirituality* with definitions for the many spiritual disciplines that Christians past and present have cultivated to bring them closer to God this side of heaven. Christians develop their spirituality through practices including: reading scripture; hearing testimony; affirming belief and faith; conversion; baptism; prayer; fasting; hospitality; sacrifice; silence; worship; and others. Though personally committed to the Wesleyan branch of theology, Don Thorsen's definitions reach outside of related practices, ideas, movements, and theology. Yet the coverage is not as uniform as one might wish, and the student should be ready to use the dictionary as a springboard into further spiritual study. New converts and beginning students will find the dictionary accessible and succinct; terms are defined "simply not simplistically."

This installment of The IVP Pocket Reference Series fills a gap in the recent publishing of Christian spirituality reference works, which has been very rare in recent years. Although the cover of the Pocket Dictionary claims to define over 300 terms, the actual number is much greater. The terms are arranged alphabetically in bold face on 128 pages. Some definitions capture a full page of text (see "sacrament") while others require just 1-2 sentences (see "adoration"). Within definitions an asterisk indicates that the next word has also been defined in the dictionary, acting as a cross-reference. Where scripture references appear in parenthesis, these act as scripture roots—not proofs. The "pocketbook" title is appropriate given the small size of the volume and its very affordable price. Recommended for high school, college, and public libraries reference sections serving Christian communities or with undergraduate courses in Christianity.—**Amy Koehler**

Handbooks and Yearbooks

698.   Kaatz, Kevin W. **Documents of the Rise of Christianity.** Santa Barbara, Calif., ABC-CLIO, 2019. 246p. index. (Eyewitness to History). $94.00. ISBN 13: 978-1-4408-5430-9; 978-1-4408-5431-6 (e-book).

This book provides access to a number of primary source documents from the first five centuries of Christianity. Many of them were written in Greek, Aramaic, and Coptic; some were translated into Latin, but many of them have been translated from their original languages for this volume. There is a very nice section on evaluating and interpreting primary source documents prior to the content, and while each translated text is provided with an introduction for context, the editors have chosen to let the texts speak for themselves with a minimal amount of additional comment. A very nice chronology of the history of the early Christian Church is provided from its beginnings to the 5th century. Some of the texts include Josephus's *Jewish Wars,* Irenaeus's *Against Heresies,* Alexander of Lycopolis's *Against the Manichaeans,* a number of letters and writings by Ambrose and Augustine, and a number of letters from Leo the Great. An excellent addition to any theology or religion collection related to Christian primary source studies.—**Bradford Lee Eden**

699.   Wagner, John A. **Documents of the Reformation.** Santa Barbara, Calif., ABC-CLIO, 2019. 263p. index. (Eyewitness to History series). $94.00. ISBN 13: 978-1-4408-6082-9; 978-1-4408-6083-6 (e-book).

This volume provides excerpts of primary source documents related to the 16th-century European Reformation. Sixty document excerpts are divided into 12 chapter sections, from "The Late Medieval Church and its Discontent," "Martin Luther," "The Peasants' War," "John Calvin," and the "Catholic Reformation," to name a few. The documents include a wide range of speeches, letters, polemics, council decrees, journal entries, and statutes, while each chapter section includes an introduction and bibliography. Appendixes include a comparison of Catholic and Protestant positions on key doctrines, and a listing of 16th-century monarchs and popes. This book is an excellent collection of first-hand historical information related to the Reformation, and is another addition to the Eyewitness to History series from ABC-CLIO. This title, and the whole series, is highly recommended.—**Bradford Lee Eden**

Islam

Handbooks and Yearbooks

700.   Considine, Craig. **Muslims in America: Examining the Facts.** Santa Barbara, Calif., ABC-CLIO, 2018. 227p. index. (Contemporary Debates). $63.00. ISBN 13: 978-1-4408-6053-9; 978-1-4408-6054-6 (e-book).

Like other volumes in the Contemporary Debates series, this volume uses a question and answer format to explore the place, role, and contributions of Muslims in the United States. Thirty-one questions are asked in five sections: history of Muslims on American soil, demographics and diversity, politics, Islamophobia, and American national identity. Each question has a two-part text: "Answer" (a single paragraph) and "The Facts" (an elaborated discussion, usually four or five pages). Most of the questions, and answers, demonstrate how inaccurate and how harmful many stereotypes about Muslims in the United States are. Each question also has a "Further Reading" section which lists up to forty items for further information on the topic discussed. Some are print references and some are internet sites.

The book states that it "is intended for use by high school and undergraduate students as well as members of the general public." (p. ix) That clearly indicates that many libraries should consider either the print or e-book version of this title. With a straightforward format, and numerous leads to other useful information on the subject, this book will benefit many sorts of readers.—**Mark Schumacher**

701.   **Handbook of Islamic Education.** Holger Daun and Reza Arjmand, eds. New York, Springer Publishing, 2018. 952p. illus. index. (International Handbooks of Religion and Education 7). $449.99. ISBN 13: 978-3-319-64682-4; 978-3-319-64683-1 (e-book).

This handbook aims to provide readers with a general understanding of Islamic education and its international varieties. More specifically, it strives to introduce the origins and foundations of Islamic education, the ways in which Islamic education adapted from colonial times to the present, and the interactions between the state and Islamic education. The discussion of Islamic education focuses on twenty-five countries selected because they meet one or more of the following criteria: they have a large Muslim population, they have large Muslim groups compared to overall population, or they conform to specific patterns of interaction between the state and schools (public or Islamic). Country studies include Iran, Egypt, Turkey, Saudi Arabia, Morocco, Afghanistan, Tajikistan, India, Pakistan, Morocco, South Africa, Malaysia, Indonesia, the Philippines, France, England, the Netherlands, Russia, and the United States. There are also chapters on Latin America, Eastern Europe, the Nordic Countries, and West, East, and Central Africa. The country studies are formulaic, describing the relationship between Islamic and Western education, the degree of state involvement in educational arrangements, and the degree to which curriculum includes Islamic elements. Material is presented in three parts: Islamic Education: Historical Perspective, Origin, and Foundation; Islam and Education in the Modern Era: Social, Cultural, Political, and Economic Changes and Responses; and Islamic Education Around the World: Commonalities and Varieties. An extensive index rounds out the work. The work is thorough, complex, broad-based, well-researched, and reliable. It has obvious value for schools of education and religion and would be useful to scholars in other disciplines. Highly recommended for large academic libraries.—**ARBA Staff Reviewer**

Judaism

Atlases

702. Wodzinski, Marcin, and Waldemar Spallek (cartographer). **Historical Atlas of Hasidism.** Princeton, N.J., Princeton University Press, 2018. 265p. illus. maps. index. $75.00. ISBN 13: 978-0-691-17401-3.

Hasidism, a branch of Orthodox Judaism that embraces ecstatic, mystical song and prayer, began in 18th-century Poland. It spread across Eastern Europe and now has adherents around the world. This atlas created by a Polish professor of Jewish studies and a cartographer is a valuable new resource that offers fresh insights into the history of this movement.

The introduction provides an overview, placing Hasidism within the larger realm of Judaism. The nine chapters that follow include well-documented essays on history as well as colorful maps charting the path of the movement, tables, illustrations, and photographs. Marginal notes offer references. The essays provide sociological and economic analysis that broadens the scope of this specialized work. The Hebrew and Yiddish words used are transliterated and defined when they appear for the first time. Place names, which may have many variants, often appear in brackets. The index includes the major alternative forms. An extensive bibliography of sources in many languages offers material for further research.

This is a very important resource for scholars in Judaic studies, history, and religion. General readers who are interested in the topic will find it accessible as well.—**Barbara M. Bibel**

Handbooks and Yearbooks

703. **Early Jewish Literature: An Anthology.** Brad Embry, Ronald Herms, and Archie T. Wright, eds. Grand Rapids, Mich., William B. Eerdmans, 2018. 2v. index. $125.00/set. ISBN 13: 978-0-8028-6669-1.

This two-volume work compiles literature from the Second Temple period of Jewish history, from 516/515 B.C.E. to 70 C.E. Thus, these are prerabbinic materials from the era before the codification of Rabbinic Judaism. Because this period of literature was prolific and highly varied, students of such literature might face difficulties of scale in identifying and consulting appropriate versions and translations of each individual work.

Early Jewish Literature resolves these potential challenges by compiling an authoritative array of primary source materials and providing a critical introduction to each selected text. Each introduction includes: a narrative description; author and provenance information; context on the date and occasion; bibliographical information on the text, language, sources, and transmission; relevant theology; and sometimes contemporary reception, further reading, and advanced reading.

Full or representative excerpts of texts are pulled from scripture and other holy/religious texts like psalms and prayers, narratives of a historical, romantic, or testamentary nature, legal and wisdom literature, and so forth. Selected titles include Susanna, Jewish Antiquities, the Melchizedek Scroll, Wiles of the Wicked Woman, the Qumran Messianic Texts, The Testament of Abraham, and so on. In all, the volumes cover an extensive variety, accurately reflecting the robust literary landscape of the Second Temple period.

Glossaries of biographical names and terms, as well as indexes for subjects and the titles of ancient literature, make this lengthy two-volume anthology more accessible and reference friendly. In all, especially given the inclusion of primary source materials, this would serve as an excellent reference work for anyone interested in particular Second Temple period texts, as well as a vigorous general survey for those seeking a wide knowledge of the whole period.—**Autumn Faulkner**

Part IV
SCIENCE AND TECHNOLOGY

29 Science and Technology in General

General Works

Dictionaries and Encyclopedias

704.   **Encyclopedia of Engineering Geology.** Peter T. Bobrowsky and Brian Marker, eds. New York, Springer Publishing, 2018. 978p. illus. index. $549.00. ISBN 13: 978-3-319-73566-5; 978-3-319-73568-9 (e-book).

This encyclopedia aims to provide undergraduate and graduate students in engineering geology with technical definitions of the terms, phrases, concepts, issues, and principles necessary for this field that (though not new) is experiencing new interest. The encyclopedia covers both engineering and geology and the places where they overlap. As the preface points out, engineering geology incorporates a wide range of topics, so it is a must for students to have access to clear and concise explanations that make clear the relationships between topics. Users can consult the table of contents and/or the subject index to jump to a particular subject. Altogether there are nearly 300 entries; each is written and signed by one of the 200 specialists listed in the front matter and each is reviewed by an editorial team member. Entries vary in length, but all are written in a straightforward, accessible style. Shorter entries (anywhere from a few paragraphs to approximately one page) cover such things as Poisson's ratio, concrete, Hooke's law, aquitard, and blasting. Hooke's law, for example, is two paragraphs long with cross-references and references. Other articles are a few pages long (e.g., chemical weathering, erosion, field testing, sea level, and collapsible soils). The entry on sea level (at almost 4 pages) contains a definition, three subheadings, four figures, and references. The longest entries can take more than ten pages to adequately explain such things as climate change, landfill, compression, and soil laboratory tests. In addition to a subject index, the encyclopedia provides an author index. Highly recommended to academic libraries.—**ARBA Staff Reviewer**

Digital Resources

705.   **Dimensions. https://www.dimensions.ai/.** [Website] Free. Date reviewed: 2018.

Dimensions is a digital research hub where users can access over ninety million scientific publications covering topics related to such fields as public health, genetics, applied economics, materials engineering, geophysics, agricultural biotechnology, and clinical sciences. The site further links these publications to relevant patents, grants, and clinical trials, offers metrics related to document usability, and more, helping to create a more complete research picture. Users initially select the Access Free App button on the right side of the homepage, and can then conduct a key word search with the addition of filters including Publication Year, Researcher, Fields of Research, Publication Type, Source Title, Journal List, and Open Access. Users can sort publications by publication date, relevance, citations, and other filters. Publications are listed by title, author, and publication date. Each document includes references and citations, and may also include links to related publications, funding sources, and more. An Attention Score alerts users to the way people have been discussing the selected publication (e.g., social media). Most publications can be opened directly as a PDF, or there will be links to full texts at a publisher's site. Users who register with Dimensions (free) gain the further ability to save documents into their own library, save searches, export, sync to other devices, and to perform other tasks. Institutional subscriptions allow simultaneous data searches on the selected research subject. The vast quantity of publications, coupled with the excellent array of tools and features, enable users to open up diverse channels of information to meet a wide variety of research needs.—**ARBA Staff Reviewer**

Handbooks and Yearbooks

706.   **Principles of Scientific Research.** Hackensack, N.J., Salem Press, 2017. 400p. illus. index. (Principles of series). $165.00. ISBN 13: 978-1-68217-609-2; 978-1-68217-610-8 (e-book).

This volume, one in a series of introductory science texts, offers a straightforward presentation of information regarding general scientific research—its major discoveries, approaches, and figures.

One hundred five alphabetical entries cover concepts such as Cross-Sectional Sampling, Hypothesis Testing, and Proofs, in addition to notable figures of scientific research such as Mary Leakey, Albert Einstein, and Stephen Hawking. Concept entries generally include an abstract paragraph to define the concept, principal terms, a list of related fields of study, a concise essay, and a list of further readings. Entries may also include an illustration or some other conceptual visualization as well as a sample problem.

Entries covering Notable Figures in Scientific Research will generally include a brief biographical sketch, a description of the individual's research focus, key discoveries, and further reading. For example, the entry on Austrian botanist Gregor Mendel discusses his impoverished upbringing, his work in heredity (building on Darwin's evolutionary theory), the impact of Mendel's research on genetics and molecular biology, and a good description of his pivotal experiments with pea plants.

Several appendixes complete the volume and present a Timeline of Inventions and Scientific Advancements, a Glossary, a Bibliography, and a Subject Index. The volume, also available online, provides a solid introduction to scientific research and is recommended to school libraries looking for an introductory work in this field.—**ARBA Staff Reviewer**

30 Agricultural Sciences

Food Sciences and Technology

Dictionaries and Encyclopedias

707.   Ravindran, P.N. **The Encyclopedia of Herbs and Spices.** Boston, CABI, 2017. 2v. illus. $660.00/set. ISBN 13: 978-1-7806-4315-1.

This book is a scientific encyclopedia on herbs and spices written by P.N. Ravindran, who, among other positions, has served as National Coordinator for Spices Research under the Indian Council of Agricultural Research and the Director of the Centre for Medicinal Plants Research. Altogether there are 240 chapters on 260 spices. Each chapter follows the same format, starting with a black-and-white sketch of the plant from which the spice is derived and an introduction. For each entry, readers will find the following: taxonomy, botanical notes, chemical notes, functional properties, medicinal uses, culinary uses, safety issues, and references. The introduction is detailed, informative, and easy to read, even for a layperson. Several sections include definitions for spices, condiments, seasonings, and herbs; a history of the spice trade; the use of spices in beauty care products and cooking; the use of spices as preservatives; spices in traditional medicine and health care; and more. There are a number of tables in the introduction that provide interesting information and supplement the narrative. For example, there is one table on the important nutraceutical spices and the biological properties of their constituents. Overall, this is a reliable and comprehensive reference source and is recommended for academic and large public libraries.—**ARBA Staff Reviewer**

708.   **We Eat What? A Cultural Encyclopedia of Unusual Foods in the United States.** Jonathan Deutsch, ed. Santa Barbara, Calif., Greenwood Press/ABC-CLIO, 2018. 340p. illus. index. $94.00. ISBN 13: 978-1-4408-4111-8; 978-1-4408-4112-5 (e-book).

This book offers readers articles about 114 "unusual foods," provided by 45 contributors with a variety of backgrounds, most in academic settings. In fact, a small number of the entries seem to this reviewer rather "usual," like cherry pie, grits, and funnel cake, while others are quite curious: armadillo, muskrat, and akutaq (an Alaskan Native food). While sometimes the curiosity of an item is simply the creature from which it comes, other dishes are simply very localized and thus barely known outside a single city or county. One part of nearly every article is the history of the dish: an origin among 18th-century German immigrants, an invention in an Iowa restaurant, a "regional specialty" of a Virginia county, or a plant (taro) brought to Polynesia (Hawaii) 1,000 years ago from the Indo-Malaysian peninsula. Occasionally, an item, such as "hot dish," will have a several possible preparations, where ingredients can be chosen from a variety of meats, vegetables, and even spices. Although some of these foods are quite rare and not easily found, the text frequently provides a sociocultural look at the role of these American foods in a fascinating way. In so doing, the volume explores the foodways of these items.

There is a recipe editor for this work, and there are recipes for most of the entries, including muskrat, burgoo (a stew), and walrus flippers. (First step: "Wash the walrus flippers in fresh water.") Nearly all entries have a "Further Reading" section, listing from 2 to 19 items, while about 45 of the entries include a black-and-white photograph of the dish. This book should be of interest to institutions connected to the culinary arts and possibly to some public libraries.

(It should be noted that a few of the entries here (bear, poi, and others) are reprinted from an earlier book edited by Jonathan Deutsch: They Eat That? (see ARBA 2013, entry 1148), an examination of unusual foods eaten around the world. The introduction here repeats that of the earlier book.)—**Mark Schumacher**

Digital Resources

709.   **Equity at the Table https://equityatthetable.com.** [Website] Free. Date reviewed: 2019.

Equity at the Table (EATT) is designed as a way to support women of color and gender nonconforming individuals of color in the food industry. It functions as a directory of food industry professionals, covering a range of specialties including chef, distiller, farmer/grower, photographer, vintner, recipe tester, food stylist, and many others. Individual profiles may include photographs, occupation(s), general location, and other personal information, alongside social media or other contact information. The directory can be explored in a number of ways. Users can focus on any of the forty-three categories of Food Professionals, or arrange the directory by Resources for Food Professionals (e.g., language translator, literary agent, cookbook copy editor and/or indexer, publicist), Location and Identification, which emphasizes ethnicity, LGBTQ, and Individuals with Disability options. Users can also search the directory by name. EATT could be an excellent resource for these historically marginalized groups starting at the high school level, particularly as more high schools work to emphasize an inclusive educational atmosphere while reconsidering the benefits of vocational programming.—**ARBA Staff Reviewer**

710.   **Global Nutrient Database https://nutrition.healthdata.org/global-nutrient-database.** [Website] Free. Date reviewed: 2019.

The Global Nutrient Database shows general nutrition data for areas around the world, comparing nutrient availability over a thirty-year time span. Information is displayed via two simple data visualizations that users can customize according to selected nutrients, countries, or "Super Regions," which include High Income Countries; Latin America and the Caribbean; North Africa and the Middle East; Central Europe, Eastern Europe, and Central Asia; South Asia; Southeast Asia, East Asia and Oceania; and Sub-Saharan Africa.

The central map graphic displays countries colored according to nutrient availability, with blue-shaded areas seeing less availability and red areas seeing more. Users can apply nutrient, year, and Super Region filters depending on the information they seek, and can also click on the map to find information for individual countries. For this database, nutrients are considered to be alcohol, carbohydrates, energy, fats, fiber, folic acid, iron, MUFA (monounsaturated fatty acids), omega 3, protein, PUFA (polyunsaturated fatty acids), saturated fats, sugar, vitamin A , and zinc. The visualization below the map graphs nutrient availability over time. Users can examine all regions over time or isolate one country (for example, the graph shows that the availability of protein in the Democratic Republic of Congo has declined between 1980 and 2013). Additional information includes Nutrition Facts (similar to what is found on the side of a cereal box) related to a chosen region/country. A chart displays the daily allowance percentage of various nutrients, showing their relation to energy intake. Users can also click on the Data Sources link at the top of the page to access information on the myriad studies used in gathering the data. The Global Nutrient Database offers an easy and quick way to gather information on nutrition worldwide.—**ARBA Staff Reviewer**

Handbooks and Yearbooks

711.   Chevallier, Jim. **A History of the Food of Paris: From Roast Mammoth to Steak Frites.** Lanham, Md., Rowman & Littlefield, 2018. 254p. illus. index. (Big City Food Biographies Series). $38.00; $36.00 (e-book). ISBN 13: 978-1-4422-7282-8; 978-1-4422-7283-5 (e-book).

Part of the Big City Food Biographies series from Rowman & Littlefield, this volume focuses on the food of Paris, France. Written from a first-person perspective, the author takes the reader on a culinary exploration of this well-known and famous city. The first three chapters provide a history of food in Paris from its origins up to the present; the following four chapters discuss ways in which food was and is obtained or sold in chapters entitled "Selling Food: Markets, Fairs, Shops, and Supermarkets," "Selling Meals: Before the Restaurant," "Selling Meals: The Restaurant," and "Selling Meals: Moving toward Modernity." The final four chapters detail foreign and immigrant food, drinks, Paris cookbooks, and signature dishes. Sprinkled with black-and-white pictures and illustrations of Paris and its history in relation to food, this book is a wonderful guide for anyone visiting Paris and looking to experience its culinary history and modern restaurants.— **Bradford Lee Eden**

712.   Hunwick, Heather. **The Food and Drink of Sydney: A History.** Lanham, Md., Rowman & Littlefield, 2018. 240p. illus. index. (Big City Food Biographies Series). $38.00; $36.00 (e-book). ISBN 13: 978-1-4422-5203; 978-1-4422-5204-2 (e-book).

This book is one of the latest volumes in the publisher's Big City Food Biographies series, joining new volumes about Paris, Madrid, and Taipei, and older ones about Portland, Chicago, and New York. (Recently, the subtitle has changed from "Food Biography" to "History.") The series "focuses on those metropolises celebrated as culinary destinations, with their iconic dishes, ethnic neighborhoods, markets, restaurants and chefs." The book looks at the evolution of the food world in Sydney and the state of New South Wales, from the arrival of the "First Fleet" in the 1780s (bringing British convicts to Australia) to the present day, presented within a broad historical setting. In the early years of British presence, food was constantly inadequate, both for the convicts and for other members of the British colony. The author traces the evolution of farming in the area, as well as the early attempts to raise farm animals, cows and pigs, and more generally the broad evolution of food in the area. Some 40 or 50 restaurants are mentioned throughout the book, from a few in the 19th century to dozens of contemporary establishments offering a wide range of cuisines.

(As with some of the earlier volumes in this series, indexing is sometimes hit-and-miss. An individual may be indexed as appearing on one or two pages, but not on others, while some people, places, and landmarks are not included at all.) Given the setting of this book (in a city in Australia), library interest in the United States may be limited. It is, however, an interesting approach to presenting two centuries of life in an important urban area, and especially for institutions with programs related the culinary arts, or the history of Oceania, this volume could be useful.—**Mark Schumacher**

713.   Puckette, Madeline, and Justin Hammack. **Wine Folly: Magnum Edition. The Master Guide.** 2d ed. Garden City Park, N.Y., Avery Publishing, 2018. 320. illus. maps. index. $35.00. ISBN 13: 978-0-5255-3389-4.

This is the second edition of *Wine Folly,* co-authored by sommelier Madeline Puckette and Justin Hammack. In this master edition, users will find nearly twice the information provided in the first. The book begins with a brief introduction and basic information about wine (how it is made, how to store it, etc.) and moves on to information about wine classification, wine labeling, and wine traits (tannins, sweetness, etc). The third section on wine and grapes contains information about 100 wines that includes tasting notes, food pairings, serving recommendations, and regional distribution. For example, if a user flips to Bordeaux Blend (Red), she will learn that this variety pairs well with red meat and that it should be served in an oversized glass at room temperature after it has been decanted for 60 minutes. The regional section includes 35 wine maps that showcase what types of wine grow where. This section contains 15 more maps than the first edition of the book. The maps are high quality, as are the infographics and other illustrations that are used throughout the book. More information can be found at https://winefolly.com/, which can be accessed for free. This book is an obvious choice for the libraries of culinary schools and for anyone training to be a sommelier. Its accessibility makes it a good choice for individuals wanting to know more about wine.—**ARBA Staff Reviewer**

Veterinary Science

Handbooks and Yearbooks

714.   **CRC Handbook of Marine Mammal Medicine.** 3d ed. Frances M. D. Gulland, Leslie A. Dierauf, and Karyl L. Whitman, eds. Boca Raton, Fla., CRC Press, 2018. 1144p. illus. index. $169.95. ISBN 13: 978-1-4987-9687-3.

This is the first update in more than 16 years (the first edition published more than 27 years ago). The editors, a veterinarian specializing in marine mammals, a retired wildlife veterinarian, and a wildlife behavioral ecologist, pen a preface, which is followed by a list of the book's more than 100 contributors. The editors arrange the book in 8 sections: Global Marine Mammal Health Concerns, Anatomy and Physiology, Pathology, Infectious Diseases, Medicine, Anesthesia, and Surgery, Husbandry, Health Assessments, and Taxon Specific Medicine. Chapters within these sections are easy to read, even for the layperson, and include tables of contents, introductions, conclusions, and references. A number of color and black-and-white figures, graphs, and tables enhance the text. Chapters include information on oil spills and responses, ethics and animal welfare, anatomy, stress and marine mammals, harmful algae and toxins, pharmaceuticals and formularies, walrus medicine, and many other topics. Five appendixes follow these chapters: "Normal Hematology and Serum," "Chemistry Changes," "Taxon-Specific Blood References," "Literature Cited on Blood Parameters," "Conversions," and "International Stranding Networks." An index rounds out the work. Recommended for academic libraries.—**ARBA Staff Reviewer**

31 Biological Sciences

Biology

Dictionaries and Encyclopedias

715. **Salem Health: Genetics & Inherited Conditions, Second Edition.** 2d ed. Hackensack, N.J., Salem Press, 2017. 3v. illus. index. $395.00/set. ISBN 13: 978-1-68217-603-0; 978-1-68217-604-7 (e-book).

Public and college libraries would serve readers well by including this three-volume set (hard copy and online) in its reference section. Entries target the general reader. Whether a reader wants to understand the relevance of totipotent cells to cloning or consider the ethical issues surrounding cloning, these volumes provide a good starting point. Hundreds of common syndromes—from Aarskog to XYY are described in a standardized format that includes risk, symptoms, screening and diagnosis, prevention and outcomes, and further reading. The prevention sections in entries cluster around the recommendation to consult with a genetic counselor and that's representative of the tempered approach authors of entries take. Rightly fearing that eugenics is a tarnished term, one author recommends replacing it with the term euphenics, but the terms are not synonymous. Even so, the ethical difficulties proposed by genetic testing and response to tests must be considered and they are. Two photos of Hermann Boehm in three volumes, owing to entries with overlapping content, are two more than anyone wants to see, however. The reader gets access to basic information topics like the importance of Drosophila fruit flies in twentieth-century genetic studies and the structure of a bacteriophage. The reader also can weigh the difficulties of designing meaningful and ethical trials of gene therapies, tying criminality and genetics together, or elucidating the origin of altruism. Appendixes—biographies of geneticists, Nobel Prize winners in genetics, timeline of major development —are nice features, although opinion (value of CRISPER) and politics (value of presidents) creep into the timeline section. A glossary (minus the term euphenics), a bibliography, and a comprehensive index round out the text, which on the whole is carefully thought out and skillfully delivered.—**Diane M. Calabrese**

Digital Resources

716.   **Cell Image Library http://www.cellimagelibrary.org/home.** [Website] Free. Date reviewed: 2019.

This site from the Center for Research in Biological Systems contains thousands of high-quality still and moving images of cells from a wide range of organisms. The site can be explored in several ways. Users may first choose to examine the Featured Image or the Images of Note gallery. Alternatively, users can conduct a basic or advanced search or select from several category tabs at the top of the page (Cell Process, Cell Component, Cell Type, Organism). Within each category, users will find a gallery of representative image entries marked by the number of similar images in the gallery. The database, for example, includes over five thousand images of Cells by Organism, found within the Cell Type category. Under Cell Process, users can scroll through a gallery of over thirty images, each representing a distinct cell process. Users will find images of cell adhesion, cell death, DNA metabolism, immune system processes, nuclear organization, photosynthesis, signal transduction, and others. The Cell Component gallery images include, among other things, the chromosome, the Golgi apparatus, molecular machinery, neurons, plasma membrane, and vesicle. Cell Type offers a wide range of examples, including the blood cell, cardiac muscle cell, ectodermal cell, fibroblast, fat cell, and retinal cone cell. Users can also explore by organism, finding cell images in the context of the greater being (scientific name), such as amoeba, chlorella, fungia, paramecium caudatum, salmonella, and over two thousand images related to homo sapiens. A microbial category of cell images appears to be under development. Within all categories, users can select an image to access information such as its NCBI (National Center for Biotechnology Information) organism classification, description, technical details, biological sources, attribution and imaging information, and sample preparation. Users can examine the image here or in a detailed viewer, and/or select the Image Data Download Options tab. While certainly containing its share of advanced technical information on cells, the site is easy to navigate.—**ARBA Staff Reviewer**

717.   **U.S. Forest Service. National Lichens and Air Quality Database and Clearinghouse. http://gis.nacse.org/lichenair/.** [Website] Free. Date reviewed: 2018.

For over 25 years the U.S. Forest Service has studied lichens in their effort to understand the effects of air pollutants on the environment. This website presents data which looks at both the general presence of lichens across regional forest communities and the particulars of lichen composition through tissue analysis. Data has culminated in over 170,000 records on more than 15,000 lichen (mainly noncrustose) tissue samples. The homepage offers general information on how lichen surveys have been conducted. Within the Database Queries link on the left column of the page, users can explore four general data categories. The Lichen Plot tracks where surveys have been conducted with information on climate, environmental conditions, and more. Elemental Analysis looks at what elements have been measured (ash, arsenic, chlorine, etc.) in particular areas of lichen growth (considering elevation, precipitation, etc.). The Element Threshold covers Region 6 (Pacific Northwest) in terms of measuring the element percentages by lichen species and wilderness areas, and Lichen Species offers general information on types of observed lichens per area and their air quality tolerance. Within each query, users can easily access the USFS Region Map and Database Field Definitions covering elements and other technical terms. Helpful foundational information is also provided. The Element Analysis Threshold and Sensitivity Ratings link uses Region 6 to illustrate key data findings. A table outlines the regional base for percentage concentrations across roughly 25 elements and 10 lichen species, while a larger listing of over 200 North American lichen species notes their nitrogen requirement and sulfur dioxide sensitivity ratings (each species is a link to further information). There is also excellent information on air pollution effects on lichens, including links to information on nitrogen, sulfur, and acidic deposition, ozone, and more. Users can also access a host of reports, publications, and protocols and a generous collection of lichen images, including Illustrations, lichen structures, and photographs. Educators in particular would find the Fun with Lichens and Air Quality: Projects and Ideas link useful. While definitely technical, the data is nonetheless straightforward, and, with the accompanying resources, the site would appeal to a range of ecological professionals, educators, and students.—**ARBA Staff Reviewer**

Handbooks and Yearbooks

718.   **Genetics.** 2d ed. Edited by Paula Kepos/Kepos Media. Farmington Hills, Mich., Gale/Cengage Learning, 2018. 4v. illus. index. $630.00/set. ISBN 13: 978-1-4103-8079-1; 978-1-4103-8080-7 (e-book).

Genetics is a four-volume set that consists of 264 entries. There are 100 core entries selected from topics often found in middle and high school curriculum. The entries run from a page to four pages and are written to high-school-level reading comprehension. Individual entries consist of topics with helpful definitions printed alongside the text for words students may find unfamiliar. Each signed entry is followed by a *see also* section and a bibliography. The monograph contains good quality images and graphics that will help students writing reports. Each volume also contains an "Instructional Guide" for teachers. The guide maps sections of the set to Next Generation Science Standards (NGSS) and contains suggested questions and activities for students. Another helpful tool for students is the "Thematic Outline." Since the entire set is in alpha order the thematic outline will help students make connections between sections, more so than just the *see also* suggestions. The monographs are hardback and have sturdy binding; the text size is large and clear. Each volume concludes with a short glossary and the last volume contains a cumulative index. This is a highly recommended set for middle and high school media centers, as well as for public libraries serving a large population of students.—**Melissa M. Johnson**

719.   **Principles of Biotechnology.** Christina A. Crawford, ed. Hackensack, N.J., Salem Press, 2018. 466p. illus. index. (Principles of series). $165.00. ISBN 13: 978-1-68217-678-8; 978-1-68217-679-5 (e-book).

Principles of Biotechnology is a one-volume reference book, the ninth book in the Principles of series that includes titles on chemistry, physics, astronomy, computer science, physical science, biology, and scientific research. *Principles of Biotechnology* contains over 130 articles; 109 are alphabetical subject entries covering basic principles of biotechnology and 23 are biographical entries. The writing style is entry level, and coverage ranges from alternative energy sources to cloning, synthetic fuels, genetically modified organisms, DNA and genetics topics, and plant biotechnology.

Alphabetical subject entries include an abstract, followed by the entry text (including subheadings such as Basic Principles, Background, How It Works, Applications and Products, Social Contexts, and Future Prospects; entries conclude with a bibliography of sources for further reading. Biographical entries provide information on key researchers and scientists (entries may include headings titled Early Life, Life's Work, Impact, and Significance) and conclude with a bibliography of sources for further reading. All signed entries are 1-2 pages in length. Some entries have illustrations or black-and-white photographs. The volume concludes with a timeline of noted advances in biotechnology, a glossary of terms, a general bibliography, and a subject index.

Minor criticisms include older sources cited in the bibliography (for a source like this, current information sources are essential) and this reviewer would prefer clearer, higher-quality images and photos. The biographical entries could be eliminated in lieu of stronger, more substantial topical entries.

Principles of Biotechnology is a basic reference source for introductory information, history, and application of biotechnology. Most appropriate for high school and public library collections.—**Caroline L. Gilson**

720.   Smith, Rachelle M. **The Biology of Beauty: The Science behind Human Attractiveness.** Santa Barbara, Calif., Greenwood Press/ABC-CLIO, 2018. 265p. illus. index. $61.00. ISBN 13: 978-1-4408-4988-6; 978-1-4408-4989-3 (e-book).

In *The Biology of Beauty: The Science behind Human Attractiveness* Rachelle M. Smith presents an analysis of human conceptions of beauty as remnants of evolutionary advantages wrought through our biology and the perseverance of particular traits. The purpose of the book is to examine the many ways that biology affects notions of beauty as well as the ways beauty permeates our lives, whether through makeup and beauty routines or the ways people who are perceived to be beautiful are treated differently by society.

The book is written in two parts. The first part "Understanding Beauty" aims to explain the biological basis for beauty as well as the many facets of the human experience as it pertains to beauty including behavior, environmental influence, and psychological repercussions. The second part of the book "Beauty from Head to Toe" acts as an encyclopedia of a handful of common body parts that are subject to beauty standards. These include things like feet, teeth, and body shape. Throughout the second part of the book, there are boxes with extended information called "cultural sidebars" that examine other aspects of beauty in more detail in other cultures. Finally, the book includes a glossary, references and further reading, and an index.

The Biology of Beauty is written in a very accessible and easy-to-read style common to many reference books that introduce the reader to novel topics. However, there are a few issues with the content that are not helped by this writing style. The book takes largely a Eurocentric and heteronormative view of beauty without significantly addressing this bias. Presumably, the heteronormative view is due in large part to the blind spots of evolutionary psychology that underpin many of the assertions in the text. With regards to Eurocentrism, many statements are made in the book concerning the cross-cultural nature of beauty standards, but when mentioned by name, they include largely white societies or "African hunter-gatherer[s]" (p. 7). The "cultural sidebars" throughout the second part of the book serve to further "otherize" nonwhite cultures and persons by presenting them as outside of the norm of the beauty standards in the main text. All ten "cultural sidebars" feature nonwhite groups, and are the rare parts of the book that take a deeper look at cultural influences on beauty standards. These issues with the text would have been much improved by in-text citations in the main narrative. Although in-text citations are not typical in introductory reference works, not being able to follow the citation trail back to the research for some of the more potentially contentious assertions does a disservice to the reader. With the above caveats in mind, this book would be appropriate for libraries serving psychology departments that focus on evolutionary psychology as long as other texts that explore multicultural conceptions of beauty were provided.—**Carin Graves**

Botany

Dictionaries and Encyclopedias

721.   **Rodale's Ultimate Encyclopedia of Organic Gardening: The Indispensable Green Resource for Every Gardener.** Rev ed. Fern Marshall Bradley, Barbara W. Ellis, and Ellen Phillips, eds. Emmaus, Pa., Rodale Inc., 2017. 720p. illus. index. $27.99pa. ISBN 13: 978-1-63565-098-3.

This is a revised and updated version of the 1959 original that appeared in paperback in 2009. The book has been updated to reflect environmental concerns, plant preferences, and other interests and issues, but the goal of the volume remains the same—to provide a usable, comprehensive reference written by American gardeners for American gardeners. An introduction, usage guide, and list of entries begin the book. There are 314 entries in total, 28 of which the book describes as core entries. These core entries fall into 1 of 4 categories: Gardening Techniques (garden design, landscaping, planting, propagation, pruning and training, and seed starting and seed saving); Organic Garden Management (animal pests, beneficial insects, composts, cover crops, fertilizers, mulch, pests, crop diseases and disorders, pollinators, soil, water conservation, watering, and weeds); Food Crops (brambles, edible landscaping, fruit trees, herbs, nut trees, and vegetable gardening); and Ornamental Plants (annuals, biennials, bulbs, groundcovers, perennials, shrubs, and trees). The usage guide suggests reading these core entries first before looking at the information in the rest of the encyclopedia. The book is easy to use. Readers can consult a variety of finding aids—the table of contents, the index, or a quick reference that lists plants by type (annuals, perennials, vines, etc.). Cross-references are used throughout. Plants are given both a botanical name and a common name. The encyclopedia lists food names by common name and organizes ornamental plants by botanical name (the index provides the botanical name next to the common name). Entries vary in length, with the core entries being by far the longest. There are black-and-white photographs and illustrations. Entries also have textboxes with extra information (e.g., a list of annuals that do well in shade). In the back of the book, users will find a guide to diagnosing common plant problems, a glossary, resources, recommended readings, a list of contributors, the aforementioned quick reference guide, the USDA map of hardiness zone, and an index. Recommended for public libraries.—**ARBA Staff Reviewer**

Digital Resources

722.   **Calflora https://calflora.org//.** [Website] Free. Date reviewed: 2019.

The Calflora database is hosted on a nonprofit site led by a professional team listed under the About Calflora link on the homepage. The site offers several ways to identify California plants. Users can go directly to the search bar, or click on links for plants by their common, scientific, or family name. Searches can be refined by California county; duration (annual, perennial, biennial); status (native to California, not native, California Native Plant Society (CNPS) rare plants, invasive plants, affinity for serpentine soil); lifeform (grasslike, herb, shrub, tree, fern, vine); community (chaparral, Douglas fir forest, freshwater wetlands, etc.); category (dicot, algae, lichen, etc.); elevation; when it blooms; and order (family name, scientific name, rarity, etc.). Users can choose to view results with or without photos. Clicking on a plant name will produce a map, photographs, distribution information, location(s) most suitable to grow the plant, and more. Users can discover additional data by clicking on map pinpoints and by clicking on location suitability. Registered users have the opportunity to upload observation information to the site. This reliable, comprehensive, and free-to-use site is recommended.—**ARBA Staff Reviewer**

723.   **Mid-Atlantic Megalopolis https://www.mamdigitization.org/.** [Website] Free. Date reviewed: 2019.

This website gathers information from thirteen institutions to create a valuable examination of vascular plant life in urban centers within the mid-Atlantic region of the United States. The site hosts data on close to one million plant specimens which help users understand the relationships between plants and the urban centers in which they exist. The yellow MAM Data Portal tab at the top of the page accesses images, field notes, and other specimen records that users can approach in a variety of ways. Users can conduct a Taxon Search from the central field or select the Search tab to Search Collections or Map Search. Both options allow access to individual contributing institution collections. Users can select the Images tab to either Search Images or open the Image Browser. The Image Browser is further organized allowing users to Browse by Family, Genus, or Species, with choices alphabetized for easy reference. Available information for each specimen varies as contributing sources have different materials. It may include a series of related web links (e.g., Encyclopedia of Life, International Plant Names Index) in addition to catalog, taxon, family, collector name, collection date, locality, elevation, habitat, description, and more. Users can also examine the herbarium by specific location under the Mid-Atlantic Floras tab (this option is currently available for Maryland, New York, Pennsylvania, and Washington D.C., with the best example being the NYC EcoFlora, also available in a separate tab). Each herbarium contribution may be constructed differently, but will generally present a checklist of all documented local specimens, which may be listed for one or more locations throughout the state. The checklists can be filtered to display synonyms or images, and include common names, notes & vouchers, taxon authors, and other information. Clicking on a family or genus/species links to its account in the herbarium, which may include a variety of color photographs and brief description of leaves, flowers, fruit, habitat and ecology, and etymology. A small Games link may be included in a location checklist, leading to useful resources (flash card quizzes, name games, etc.) for the introductory student. Interactive Tools help users can find coordinates on the mid-Atlantic region map to build species lists.—**ARBA Staff Reviewer**

724.   **Orchids: Nature's Art https://www.si.edu/spotlight/orchids.** [Website] Free. Date reviewed: 2019.

This page from the Smithsonian Institution draws from several sources to create a digital gallery of orchid specimen photographs intermingled with orchid-centered artwork. The page also includes a link to a database where users can find general descriptive information on over 8,000 specimens of orchids. Users can scroll through the randomly mixed gallery of orchid specimen and artwork photographs, each of which is identified by collection (generally either the Smithsonian Gardens or the Cooper Hewitt Collection at the Smithsonian Design Museum), artwork name, or specimen name. Clicking on an item in the gallery accesses its individual photograph collection where users can examine the orchid from several angles. Photographs are generally of excellent quality—some so clear they capture petal texture—and may be accompanied by basic descriptive information such as plant parentage, provenance, topic, general taxonomy (group, class, subclass, superorder, order, family, genus), flower color, range, and more. Information accompanying artworks may include catalogue status, credit, medium, type, and object name. It is not clear how many items are in the gallery, though the selection gives an excellent idea of the range of flowers, including Dendrobium Lolita, Laeliocattleya, Santa Barbara Sunset "Peaches," Cymbidium Koushu Dream "Sweet Sugar," and Vanda Yarnisa Gold. Users can click on the Show More tab at the bottom of the page to display further selections. Selecting the 8,000 Specimens link navigates to the Orchid Smithsonian Garden page of the Collections Search Center, where users can implement several search options, create lists, and find thousands of orchid-related records. The merging of the Orchids: Nature's Art exhibit with the larger database is an excellent way to increase engagement options.—**ARBA Staff Reviewer**

Handbooks and Yearbooks

725.   Begley, Eva. **Plants of Northern California.** Guilford, Conn., Falcon Guides, 2018. 424p. illus. maps. index. $29.95pa. ISBN 13: 978-1-4930-3184-9.

This guide covers most of California north of San Francisco Bay and the Sacramento-San Joaquin River Delta and west of the Sierra Nevada mountain range. The book does not cover the Modoc Plateau, which is typically considered part of the Great Basin. This is an incredibly varied region that includes everything from coastline to high mountains. As the author readily admits, some groups are underrepresented (conifers, sedges, rushes ferns, grasses, etc.). The first part of the book includes approximately 11 pages on the life and structure of plants. This section contains easily understandable definitions and black-and-white illustrations. This is a great section for someone who is new to plant identification. For each plant, there is a high-quality color photograph. There is also data on the family to which the plant belongs, the scientific name, the height, the leaf description, the elevation where the plant grows or is typically found, habitat information, and comments. Comments vary depending on the species under discussion. Readers will learn, for example, that coast redwoods can live more than 2,000 years, among other information. The bulk of the book is devoted to flowering plants, some familiar and some less familiar. The book concludes with a glossary, lists of species by color (the main color of the flowers) with bold text indicating plants native to California, and a list of selected references subdivided by general, local floras, trees, weeds, and Native American uses of plants. An index rounds out this book that is recommended for public libraries—**ARBA Staff Reviewer**

726.   **How Plants Work: Form, Diversity, Survival.** Blackmore, Stephen, ed. Princeton, N.J., Princeton University Press, 2018. 368p. illus. index. $35.00. ISBN 13: 978-0-6911-7749-6.

Impressionistic and eclectic, this is not a straight-line reference book. Yet for the nonbotanist who relishes immersion in fascinating anecdotes and a basic, if diffuse, introduction to plant anatomy—with a bit of phylogeny and ecology added in—there's the satisfaction of learning something new on almost every page. For instance, blue rose seekers sanguine about genetically modifying organisms may soon find their coveted bloom thanks to gene transfer from delphinium. The juniper "berries" that flavor gin are actually fleshy female cones. And Goethe who gave us Faust also contributed to theory of plant morphology, especially the modular arrangement of shoots. With six authors writing separate sections, there is overlap among examples—e.g., corpse flower and arum spadix, as well as accounts—e.g., Rhynie Chert in Scotland. Oddly, the Goldilocks metaphor for water availability seems to be the only cross-referenced topic. Some terms likely familiar only to us who studied botany are used before being defined in later chapters. And there's plenty of a philosophical nature to quibble over, such as the designation of Earth as a singular planet and the decision to print the book in China even after decrying wood trafficking by that nation. A more robust glossary, a tougher editor, and more visible credit to the many photographers whose efforts, Shutterstock or not, make the visual presentation of plants and plant parts a truly lovely one would have added much.—**Diane M. Calabrese**

727.   Rittershausen, Brian, and Wilma Rittershausen. **Orchids: A Practical Guide for Gardeners.** Leicestershire, England, Lorenz Books, 2017. 256p. illus. index. $35.00. ISBN 13: 978-0-7548-3363-5.

This reference begins with several reasons for growing orchids, the long history of orchids, the different habitats in which the plants can be found, the botany of orchids, and the development of hybrids. The book offers valuable direction on how to grow orchids indoors or outdoors (in the ground or in a greenhouse). The book also provides advice on placement, growing temperature, light exposure, necessary tools and equipment, different composts, potting techniques, fertilizing, watering, and propagation. There are informative textboxes throughout these sections that help reinforce information. In the "Care and Cultivation" chapter, readers will find extra information, including a calendar of care and a table of common problems. The second half of the book showcases the wide range and beauty of orchids in a directory divided into popular orchids and specialist orchids. For each type of orchid, users will learn about where the orchid originated, best growing conditions, and more. Each entry is beautifully illustrated with high-quality, color photographs (there are hundreds of color photographs in the book). A glossary, lists of suppliers in the United Kingdom, the United States, and Australia, and an index complete the work. This well-priced book will encourage orchid growers and would-be orchid growers everywhere. Highly recommended for public libraries.—**ARBA Staff Reviewer**

728.   Smith, Welby R. **Sedges and Rushes of Minnesota.** Minneapolis, Minn., University of Minnesota Press, 2018. 696p. illus. index. $39.95pa. ISBN 13: 978-1-51790-275-9.

This hefty volume brings care and expertise to a regional plant species study. Surveying roughly 250 species of sedges (grass-like plants with triangular stems) and rushes (waterside plants with stem-like leaves) found within the state of Minnesota, the book presents basic information such as a plant's physical appearance, development, and habitat.

The book organizes the information alphabetically by Genus (with the large Genus Carex further organized by taxonomic section). Accounts are limited to one page, with a second devoted to color photographs of the plant either in close-up or habitat. Accounts include detailed scientific description including plant component measurements, shape, texture, size, and other characteristics. The page also includes a distribution map showing locations of plant habitats within Minnesota.

Beyond the individual species entries, readers can find supplemental information such as a Key to Genera of Sedges and Rushes in Minnesota, a glossary, a bibliography, and an index. The introduction to the volume provides general information regarding book structure and the state of Minnesota in relation to its vegetation zones, maps, and more.

The volume, though a bit heavy, would be useful for outdoor field excursions, as it offers accessible and detailed information about these particular plant species which would appeal to naturalists, botanists, regional educators, and students.—**ARBA Staff Reviewer**

Natural History

Digital Resources

729.   **Darwin Manuscripts Project. https://www.amnh.org/our-research/darwin-manuscripts-project/.** [Website] Free. Date reviewed: 2018.

This project out of the American Museum of Natural History has digitized and transcribed thousands of pages of research conducted by renowned 19th-century naturalist Charles Darwin. The organization of the manuscripts on the site is reflective of the development of Darwin's work so users can trace Darwin's evolution of thought. The site requires users to agree to basic terms and conditions before examining content. Users can then select from a series of links on the left side of the homepage to access materials. Edited Manuscripts are organized by Beagle Voyage, Darwin's Evolution Papers, Geology, and Darwin's Reading (which includes annotations and abstracts on the scientific literature in his personal library). Good contextual information may also be included as precursor to these sections; users can align Darwin's work on evolution with the Beagle Voyage, his London Years, and the Down House Years. Materials include notes, abstracts, portfolios, and more, all of which work as a foundation for his groundbreaking theory of evolution. Users can also navigate the materials along various themes via Catalogues. That is, users can examine materials based on their physical collection (e.g., Cambridge University Library, Edinburgh University Library, Karpeles Museum) or their general subject of study, which for this website include Beagle, Botany, Humans, German Books, and Pigeons. Pocket Diaries contain both scientific and personal reflections generally spanning the years 1838-1881. For most all of the manuscripts, users can click on a page number or title to access the digital image. Some, but not all materials have transcripts. Users can also keyword search the manuscripts from the homepage. Under the Featured Collections link, the site has gathered a delightful assortment of drawings and stories created by Darwin's family members adding a bit of personal perspective on the man. Information under the Content link at the bottom of the homepage helps to define the various forms of the

Darwin Manuscripts (such as drafts, abstracts, marginalia, etc.). Those seeking technical information can find it under the Symbols & Editing link.—**ARBA Staff Reviewer**

730.   **Darwin online. Http://darwin-online.org.uk/.** [Website] Free. Date reviewed: 2018.

Darwin Online is a definitive source for studying revered naturalist Charles Darwin and his abundant work in the life sciences. It offers general information on his life and times in addition to full digital editions of his private papers, manuscripts, and published works encompassing hundreds of thousands of individual pages. The site also includes supplementary information such as reviews of Darwin's books, obituaries, and reminiscences. As the site is so comprehensive, users should first click the About Us tab at the top of the page to access the helpful Introduction to Darwin Online and User Guide links. Users can then access materials in a variety of ways. Scrolling down through the homepage presents a series of links categorized as Darwin's Complete Publications, Darwin's Private Papers & Manuscripts, and Supplementary items (e.g., Works About Darwin), and more. Users can also conduct a basic or advanced search from the bar or, alternatively, select from the Publications, Manuscripts, or Biography tabs on the same menu bar for direct access to those materials. Under Publications, users can find Darwin's most famous work *On the Origin of the Species,* various editions of the meticulous *Journal of Researches* (Voyage of the Beagle), and many other books, pamphlets, or articles. Many of the larger publications are accompanied by good foundational material as well. Users can also search or browse an extensive list of lecture notes, itemizations of university expenses, photographs, sketches, diary entries, field notebooks, and other items under the Manuscripts tab. Users can view the digital original and transcribed text either separately or together on the screen, employ the zoom feature, translate the materials into several languages, or perform other functions. The Biography page presents a biographical sketch of the naturalist, a timeline, photographs, links to affiliated materials, and more.—**ARBA Staff Reviewer**

Handbooks and Yearbooks

731.   Randall, Jan A. **Endangered Species: A Reference Handbook.** Santa Barbara, Calif., Greenwood Press/ABC-CLIO, 2018. 396p. illus. index. 60.00. ISBN 13: 978-1-4408-4899-5; 978-1-4408-4900-8 (e-book).

Jan Randall, a former faculty member at Central Missouri State University and San Francisco State University, authors this work that is part of ABC-CLIO's Contemporary World Issues series on the Environment. Labeled a reference handbook, the main part of the book is divided into the following chapters: "Background and History"; "Problems, Controversies, and Solutions"; "Perspectives"; "Profiles" (on people and organizations); and "Data and Documents." Each chapter includes several essays on related topics, each running about one to five pages. References are provided after each chapter and can run several pages. Two additional chapters provide a bibliography to further reading—divided into books, articles, comments, and hearings, internet sources, and reports—and a chronology of important events related to endangered species. Overall, I found this work lacking. The author tried to connect too many topics to endangered species, and correspondingly the work lacks coherence. For example, in "Background and History," the author discusses events in the national forests, national wildlife refuges, national parks, etc., as precursors to the Endangered Species Act, but their relationships are not made very clear. The author would have done better by addressing fewer topics and making stronger connections between the ones included. This work seems like a hodgepodge of information, with none of it described in enough detail to leave you satisfied.—**Kevin McDonough**

Zoology

General Works

Handbooks and Yearbooks

732.   Ryder, Thomas J., ed. **State Wildlife Management and Conservation.** Baltimore, Md., Johns Hopkins University Press, 2018. 238p. illus. index. $75.00. ISBN 13: 978-1-4214-2446-0; 978-1-4214-2447-7 (e-book).

A first of its kind, this unique book details state wildlife agencies' contributions to wildlife conservation and management. Edited by Thomas Ryder, and authored by numerous wildlife professionals, this book examines the history and current structure of state wildlife agencies; issues involved with law enforcement, game management, and human-wildlife conflict; efforts to manage wildlife diseases; the role of field wildlife research in state wildlife management; future needs and challenges; and issues involved in balancing the needs of hunters, nonhunters, and animal right advocates. Each chapter varies in length from 15 to 20 pages, and the overall book has more of an academic tone and approach. Bibliographies of source material conclude most chapters, but are variable in length. Some have very few references, while others cover several pages. Some chapters include black-and-white photographs and figures, but most of the book is text based. Obviously, as this book is attempting to address state wildlife agencies as a whole, its approach is very broad. For example in "State Management of Big Game" and the separate chapter on furbearers, much of the discussion is on data collection techniques used to assess populations. In some instances, case studies are included to provide more specific, state-level examples. Overall, this is a useful book, particularly the chapters on the history and legal basis for state wildlife management agencies. The tone makes this work more suitable to academic than public libraries.—**Kevin McDonough**

733.   Sale, Richard, and Per Michelsen. **Wildlife of the Arctic.** Princeton, N.J., Princeton University Press, 2018. 336p. illus. maps. index. (Princeton Pocket Guides). $19.95pa. ISBN 13: 978-0-691-18054-0.

The narwhal got its name from Scandinavians who saw a resemblance between its skin and a human corpse. Such fascinating tidbits add to the concise descriptions of the wildlife living in the Arctic. The only rat-free region of the planet outside Antarctica, the Arctic is home to plenty of voles, lemmings, and lagomorphs. The beauty of the Arctic fox is rivaled by the butterflies that visit flowers as far north as 82 degrees latitude in summer. Birds, mammals, fish, marine animals, plants, fungi, and insects are all given their due herein with nugget descriptions and photos, as well as a general statement about distribution. An adder and the common lizard are the only reptiles that have been documented north of the Arctic Circle; the Siberian wood frog gets close but stays south of the demarcation. Photos of wildlife are good, and their placement facilitates comparing pictures and descriptions. Explanations of arctic phenomena, such as what accounts for aurora and parhelia, are models of clarity. So too are accounts of the interplay between sea water and fresh water and the richness of species to which ice melt pools contribute. There is an index arranged by common and scientific names. A distraction from the content stems from the font, which is too small and too gray-toned to not become a strain on eyes. The single map could be more intelligible. And the discussion of climate change and the Paris accord—including political considerations—loses its punch when the reader observes the book was printed in China. Actions to protect the environment must match words and that requires printing in a place where there are environmental safeguards.—**Diane M. Calabrese**

Birds

734.   **Birds of Chile.** Howell, Stephen N. G., and Fabrice Schmitt. Princeton, N.J., Princeton University Press, 2018. 240p. illus. maps. index. $29.95pa. ISBN 13: 978-0-69116-739-8.

Birds of Chile documents the many species of birds found in the South American country of Chile, which has become a significant birding center in recent years. This highly portable book offers over one thousand color photographs alongside brief but effective species accounts that help identify the diverse array of Chilean birds from the tiny Chilean Woodstar to the mighty King Penguin.

Birds are arranged in "field-friendly groupings" (not necessarily taxonomic) including Swimming Waterbirds, Flying Waterbirds, Walking Waterbirds, Gamebirds and Allies, Raptors and Owls, Larger Landbirds, Aerial Landbirds, and Songbirds.

Color photographs—several to a page—show birds in habitat or close-up on identifying features. Accompanying the photographs are brief species accounts which may include information such as feeding habits, sounds, range, physical features, and behavioral characteristics. Text boxes may overlay photographs and provide further distinguishing detail (e.g., the Chilean Tinamou is "distinctive in range; bushy crest often raised and lowered as birds walk"). Other text boxes may highlight notable physical features, gender distinction, and more.

An excellent Introduction (covering Geography, Habitat, Bird Distribution, Migration, etc.) employs maps, a list of terms and abbreviations, scenic photos, and other supporting information. There is also an appendix of rare and local species and an index of English names.

Birders, natural historians, biologists and others would appreciate this compact but rich guide to the *Birds of Chile.* Recommended .—**ARBA Staff Reviewer**

735. Buckley, P. A., Walter Sedwitz, William J. Norse, and John Kieran. **Urban Ornithology: 150 Years of Birds in New York City.** Ithaca, N.Y., Comstock Publishing Associates/Cornell University Press, 2018. 514p. maps. index. $75.00. ISBN 13: 978-1-5017-1961-5; 978-1-5017-1963-9 (e-book).

This historical analysis of birds in New York City's natural areas starts with 1872 and ends in 2016. Specifically, the Northwest Bronx and Van Cortlandt Park comprise the study area, and the authors tracked breeding species and include bird censuses from 1937 to 2015. The impacts of the loss of wetlands and other unique habitats on birdlife (breeding, wintering, and migratory), and which bird species have been lost or gained over the study timeframe are some of the interesting information this title contains. After an overview, species accounts follow. The various data is displayed through figures and tables, with appendixes, indexes, and a list of the literature cited completing the volume. Researchers and birders alike will find this resource a treasure trove of New York City avifauna details.—**Denise A. Garofalo**

736. Forshaw, Joseph M. Illustrated by Frank Knight. **Vanished and Vanishing Parrots: Profiling Extinct and Endangered Species.** Ithaca, N.Y., Comstock Publishing Associates/Cornell University Press, 2017. 323p. illus. maps. index. $95.00. ISBN 13: 978-1-5017-0469-7.

Parrots are one of the most endangered groups of birds, and one of the world's leading authorities on these birds authored this comprehensive title on extinct and threatened parrots. Content is arranged into geographic areas: Australasia, Afro-Asia, and Neotropical. A general introduction to parrots of a region includes threats that are endangering or that caused extinction, such as habit loss or the international live-bird trade, as well as conservation methods in place or suggested. This encyclopedic work has beautiful color plates, references, and index. Bird lovers and ornithology researchers will find this title a valuable reference.—**Denise A. Garofalo**

737. Hams, Fred. **The Practical Encyclopedia of Chicken Keeping.** Leicestershire, England, Lorenz Books, 2017. 256p. illus. $35.00. ISBN 13: 978-0-7548-3366-6.

This encyclopedia will prove a valuable guide for those interested in keeping chickens or for those who already own them. Though the focus is on chickens, the book provides basic (brief) information on ducks, geese, guinea fowl, and turkeys. The first half of the book covers a lot of ground from the history of chickens to how to choose the right breed to how to house and feed them to keeping them healthy and safe. Throughout this section, users will enjoy hundreds of color photographs of different breeds; there are approximately two dozen photographs that illustrate steps for those interested in building their own chicken enclosures. The second half of the book contains directories of foundational breeds like the Derbyshire Redcap, Friesian, Leghorn, and Java; true bantams; and manmade breeds. These are followed by a directory of ducks, geese, and turkeys. Entries vary in length from about half a page to two pages and contain a general description of the breed plus a textbox with essential characteristics like size, varieties, temperament, best environment, and egg yield. All are enhanced by a high-quality color photograph. The work concludes with a glossary and an index. It is worth noting that the encyclopedia is not specific to the United States, but it nevertheless contains information useful to anyone who wants to raise chickens. Highly recommended to public libraries.—**ARBA Staff Reviewer**

738.   Lindo, David. **How to Be an Urban Birder.** Princeton, N.J., Princeton University Press, 2018. 232p. illus. $18.95pa. ISBN 13: 978-0-691-17962-9.

Naturalist, writer, and educator David Lindo communicates his enthusiasm for urban birding in this title, which has a forward written by English chef and restaurateur Jamie Oliver. The book covers the urban (city) birding background, urban landscape, includes the best places to look for birds in urban locales, tips on how to attract birds to your yard or garden, plus suggestions on birding gear. The striking color photographs of birds in cities and towns enhance the information imparted. The tips and information can easily apply to any city locale, not just the author's British home. Novices to birding, especially city and urban dwellers, will find this book of particular interest.—**Denise A. Garofalo**

739.   Vallely, Andrew C., and Dale Dyer. **Birds of Central America: Belize, Guatemala, Honduras, El Salvador, Nicaragua, Costa Rica, and Panama.** Princeton, N.J., Princeton University Press, 2018. 584p. illus. maps. index. $49.50pa. ISBN 13: 978-0-961-13801-5; 978-0-691-13802-2 (e-book).

This book describes over 1,200 species of birds found in the 7 countries in the title. A 17-page introduction, with illustrations, tables, and maps, describes the environments in Central America and explains quite clearly how the entries for each of the birds are organized: identifying the appearance of the bird, where it is found, what kind of environment it lives in, and what calls it makes. Each of the entries also has a map indicating 4 categories of presence of the species: breeding resident, breeding visitor, winter resident, or transient. One gets a good sense of the detail provided in this book by the information provided for the two dozen species of hummingbirds found in the region.

The striking illustrations, done by Dyer, often show differences between immature and adult birds, breeding and nonbreeding birds, and males and females. Usefully, each plate indicates the scale of the birds depicted, from 10-13% of their actual size for hawks, herons, and other large birds, to 75% for hummingbirds and similar small birds. Geographical variations are sometimes shown and can be as detailed as the difference between a hummingbird's appearances in west Panama compared to east Panama!

Princeton University press is renowned for its many excellent volumes on birds around the world—such as those of New Guinea, Peru, New Jersey, and the West Indies. Any library with ornithologists, bird lovers, or bird watchers among their patrons should consider this book, so packed full of information on over 1,000 kinds of beautiful birds.—**Mark Schumacher**

740.   Wheeler, Brian K. **Birds of Prey of the East: A Field Guide.** Princeton, N.J., Princeton University Press, 2018. 296p. illus. maps. index. $27.95pa. ISBN 13: 978-0-691-11706-5.

This regional bird guide covers 27 species and 3 casual and accidental species that reside or migrate east of the Mississippi River. The introduction provides background about the author and his love of drawing birds, the organization of the guide, as well as the techniques he used to create the 72 plates illustrating the book. Names, common names, poses and plumage guides for age differences, how the birds look in flight, habitat, nesting, movements, and comparison with other species round out each entry. The plates' backgrounds are darker than most guides, and the poses of the birds are consistent from species to species, to aid in identification and comparison. Rounding out the title is a list of plates and an index, maps, and a bibliography. The use of less scientific vocabulary makes the content more user friendly for general birders, but both casual birders and scientists will find this title useful for identifying and studying eastern US birds of prey.—**Denise A. Garofalo**

741.   Wheeler, Brian K. **Birds of Prey of the West: A Field Guide.** Princeton, N.J., Princeton University Press, 2018. 359p. illus. maps. index. $27.95pa. ISBN 13: 978-0-691-11718-8.

Covering 33 species that reside or migrate west of the Mississippi, this regional bird guide uses less scientific vocabulary, which makes the content more accessible for the casual birder. Background about the author and his love of drawing birds, the organization of the guide, as well as the techniques he used to create the 85 plates illustrating the book is provided in the introduction. The guide content contains names, common names, poses and plumage guides for age differences, how the birds look in flight, habitat, nesting, movements, and comparison with other species. One noteworthy mention is the color of the plates' backgrounds; they are darker than most guides, to allow easier viewing and comparison of species. Also, the poses of the birds are consistent from species to species (the birds all face the same way from species to species), to aid in identification and comparison. The title also contains a list of plates and an index, maps, and a bibliography. Scientists as well as general birders will find this title useful for identifying and studying western US birds of prey.—**Denise A. Garofalo**

Canidae

742.   Castelló, José R. **Canids of the World: Wolves, Wild Dogs, Foxes, Jackals, Coyotes, and Their Relatives.** Princeton, N.J., Princeton University Press, 2018. 332p. illus. maps. index. $79.95. ISBN 13: 978-0-691-18372-5.

The canid mouse leap is familiar to most dog owners. It's one behavioral trait among many that ties beloved pets to their taxonomic family members. Domestic dogs probably diverged from the gray wolf. And wolves and hominids have a recorded association that may span 300,000 years. Like hominids, canids tend toward a high degree of social interaction. This excellent, streamlined path to identification is all the richer because it encompasses phylogeny, behavior, distribution, and diet of canids. Dentition and bone structure are figured and described with clarity. Pelage and morphs are illustrated with very good photos. Throughout, the reader gains a great appreciation of the adaptive capabilities of canids. The fennec fox, the smallest canid, can subsist without water. Many species (and subspecies), such as the Patagonian fox and the chilla fox, are not the predators but are instead the potential prey in an interaction with domestic dogs. And many species of canids simply take over abandoned burrows instead of digging their own. The too-placid Falkland Island wolf was declared extinct in 1876, having gone willingly to those who would cull it or take its coat. Today, many recognized canid subspecies are threatened with extinction because of hybridization and introgression, but that fact is also a reminder the dynamism of populations within the 13 genera of the family. From the arctic wolf that lives above 67 degrees latitude and eats musk oxen, caribou, seals, and arctic hare to the crab-eating foxes, canids are endlessly fascinating, even before we reflect upon their ties to bears. Superb illustrations coupled with crisp, clear, and concise text make this a volume as useful to a vertebrate biologist as it is to a weekend naturalist or just a dog lover.—**Diane M. Calabrese**

Fishes

743.   **Marine Fishes of Arctic Canada.** Brian W. Coad and James D. Reist, eds. Toronto, University of Toronto Press, 2018. 632p. illus. maps. index. $102.00. ISBN 13: 978-1-4426-4710-7.

Marine Fishes of Arctic Canada shines a light on over 200 species of fish that make the frigid waters of the Canadian arctic their home. Species accounts describe individuals and families alongside enlightening contextual information that brings environmental, historical, and cultural perspectives to the forefront. The book describes fish living in Baffin Bay, the Davis Strait, Beaufort Sea, and other areas whose expansive, remote, and treacherous waters have been difficult to assess.

A generous introduction offers extensive information with sections discussing habitats, climate, arctic fish, northern cultures, and traditional ecological knowledge, as well as basic information regarding scientific names, fish structure, and more. Tables, maps, and other visualizations within the introduction address surface currents and ice movements, biodiversity of arctic marine fishes, arctic water temperature and salinity profiles, and other factors. A checklist of species provides a quick reference to all accounted families of Canadian arctic marine species as well as extralimital species (anomalies) and brackish water species. A series of keys illustrate external fish characteristics (e.g., pectoral fin, spines, gill opening, etc.) with species examples.

The bulk of the book methodically details family and species accounts for 58 fish families from Notacanthidae (deep-sea spiny eels) to Stromateidae (butterfishes) and others. Brief essays touch on species distribution, physical description, habitat, migration, behavior, commercial appeal, and other topics. Particular paragraphs may address common names (English, French, and indigenous), taxonomy, biology, and more. A map highlights species distribution, and the account may also include a black-and-white illustration and/or a color photograph.

Marine Fishes of Arctic Canada also contains an extensive index, a list of data sources, a bibliography, and a generous glossary of geographic, biologic, and other relevant terms (hadal zone, head clasper, gill raker, hypersaline). The book would be an excellent reference for a range of academic studies. Highly recommended.—**ARBA Staff Reviewer**

Insects

744.   Cowles, Jilian. **Amazing Arachnids.** Princeton, N.J., Princeton University Press, 2018. 328p. illus. index. $45.00. ISBN 13: 978-0-637-17658-1.

Despite impressive defenses and an origin that dates back 400 million years, arachnids are not without predators. The grasshopper mouse, which weighs less than one ounce, preys on the venomous and potentially lethal bark scorpion; and a species of mantid is a brood parasite that deposits its eggs in those of spiders. Supported by abundant photos that focus on species of the U.S. Southwest, the text provides wide treatment of the physiology, morphology, phylogeny, ecology, and distribution of arachnids. Arrangement is by arachnid order. Many arachnid traits contribute to their antiquity. Among them are ability of some species to bear live offspring (through apoikogenic or katoikogenic development); versatile palps adapted for digging, insemination, sensory use; and venoms. The ability of spiders to produce silk, which is deployed in myriad ways, certainly gives them a competitive edge. The section on silk is the best in the book. From the vinegaroons that eject acetic acid to defend themselves to the harvestmen that aggregate for warmth, amazing is an apt descriptor for arachnids. The book covers so much territory that Maria Sibylla Merian's engraving of a South American tarantula eating a bird and the search for pharmaceuticals among venoms are two of the numerous points the author connects. Negatives include the use of terms babies, hands, finger, and rear end instead of the correct scientific terminology. There's also overreach for florid stories where the science suffices. And to adopt the affection the author has for the word paradox, it's a paradox the author laments the toll humans are extracting on arachnids and yet the book was printed in a nation lacking environmental regulations.—**Diane M. Calabrese**

Marine Animals

745.   Stevens, Guy, Daniel Fernanco, Marc Dando, and Giuseppe Notarbartolo di Sciara. **Guide to the Manta and Devil Rays of the World.** Princeton, N.J., Princeton University Press, 2018. 144p. illus. maps. index. $19.95pa. ISBN 13: 978-0-691-18332-9.

The good news is it may be the pectoral fin of a manta or devil ray breaking the surface of the water and not the dorsal fin of a shark. Belonging to a single family (Mobulidae) with a single genus, there are ten (possibly eleven) species of manta and devil rays. The eight devil ray species get their common name from rolled up cephalic fins reminiscent of horns. The gill structures that make mantas and devils successful filter feeders in their pelagic habitat now add to their vulnerability. In recent decades the gills have become coveted as components of natural remedies, particularly in China. The Manta Trust, a U.K.- and U.S.-registered charity, supports coordinated efforts to conserve mobulids about which a surprising amount is still not known. This guide to species enables divers, snorkelers, aquarium visitors, and fresh-catch marketgoers to make reliable identifications of species. Citizen scientists are encouraged to contribute information to the IDtheManta global database and protocols are provided. Individual mantas and devils can be identified by unique patterns of pigmented spots on their ventral side. Feeding formations, size range (think German shepherd to elephant), distribution (circumtropical species are weighty ones), associated species (e.g., Remoras), regenerative powers, live births (after egg hatches internally) give the reader much to ponder about the fascinating, flat, and diamond-shaped creatures. Muddled review of utility of DNA analysis, absence of a cladogram, frequent colloquialisms ("fishy") and asides ("body salon"), and no discussion of the tail merit attention in a second edition; and that edition should be printed in a country with high environmental standards.—**Diane M. Calabrese**

Reptiles and Amphibians

746.   Krysko, Kenneth L., Kevin M. Enge, and Paul E. Moler. **Amphibians and Reptiles of Florida.** Gainesville, Fla., University of Florida Press, 2019. 708p. illus. maps. index. $80.00. ISBN 13: 978-1-68340-044-8.

Amphibians and Reptiles of Florida is the first significant resource on herpetofauna in Florida. Previous works have been field guides, or comprehensive works on turtles and nonnative species. An introduction discusses the history of Florida herpetology, environmental characteristics of the state, sources of locality records, status of species, and more. Species accounts are provided for each of the 155 native and 64 established nonnative amphibians and reptiles in Florida, mostly written by authorities rather than the authors. Accounts are based on personal observations in the field and scientific literature, and grouped by order, suborder, and family. Each species description includes identification features, taxonomy, geographic distribution and habitat, reproduction and development, diet, behavior, conservation, and colored range maps. Range maps have circles indicating cataloged vouchered records of a species (e.g. collected specimens and photographs), triangles representing credible unvouchered records, and squares when only the county is known. Symbol colors represent records prior to or after a specific date. The book includes one or more colored images for each species, representing sex and adult/juvenile stages if dissimilar. Occasionally images of larval amphibians are included if distinct. Additional features include a 12-page glossary and approximately 90 pages of references.

Make no mistake, this is a guide for serious amateur or professional herpetologists. People interested in identifying amphibians or reptiles, and learning brief natural history information will find *A Field Guide to Snakes of Florida* (Gulf Publishing, 1997) and *A Field Guide to Florida Reptiles and Amphibians* (Gulf Publishing, 1998) more accessible. However, this source will be standard in all academic libraries and most public libraries. Highly recommended.—**Kevin McDonough**

32 Engineering

General Works

Dictionaries and Encyclopedias

747. **A Dictionary of Electronics and Electrical Engineering.** 5th ed. Andrew J. Butterfield and John Szymanski, eds. New York, Oxford University Press, 2018. 720p. $18.95pa. ISBN 13: 978-0-1987-2572-5; 978-0-1917-9271-7 (e-book).

This title first published in 1979 as the *Penguin Dictionary of Electronics.* Now in its 5th edition, the dictionary contains over 5,200 entries, 700 of which are new. Older entries have been completely revised and updated. The new entries reflect developments in the field concerning such subjects as robotics, nanotechnology, and image processing. Entries vary in length; some are references to other entries (e.g., EBD, *see* Electronic Brakeforce Distribution) while some are paragraphs long (e.g., radar). The editors also make use of *see also* references. Overall, the dictionary provides comprehensive coverage of topics using straightforward language that is suitable for nonmajors. Several helpful tables are included at the end of the book—Graphical Symbols, Colour Codes, Properties of Important Semiconductors; Electric and Magnetic Quantities; Base SI Units; Periodic Table of the Elements; Major Discoveries and Inventions in Electricity and Electronics, Abbreviations and Acronyms, and more. Recommended.—**ARBA Staff Reviewer**

Digital Resources

748. **National Science Foundation Science and Engineering State Profiles. https://www.nsf.gov/statistics/states/.** [Website] Free. Date reviewed: 2018.

This page from the greater National Science Foundation presents state-level information related to science and engineering program financing and employment (there is some information related to health sciences as well). Users can isolate information for any of the fifty U.S. states as well as Washington D.C. and Puerto Rico, or compare data for up to seven states at a time within a table listing sixteen data characteristics. The table also includes a listing of federal research and development obligations across major government agencies, including NASA and the Departments of Agriculture, Energy, Health & Human Services, and more. From this page, users can access the data by clicking on a state within the national map graphic. Collected data measures personal income per capita, number of science and engineering doctorates awarded, state research and development expenditures, amount of available academic research space, utility patents issued to state residents, and other information. For each characteristic, the table notes a state's national ranking and compares its totals with national figures. Above the map, several tabs provide access to supplemental information. General Notes provides foundational material on the data tool, sources, etc. Data Sources match particular data points with source links which include the U.S. Department of Commerce, the U.S. Department of Labor, the National Center for Science and Engineering Statistics, and other departments. Previous Profiles presents a list of links to full State Profiles going back to 2011 (profiles are also available going back as far as 2003 via the Publication Series Page link). The Schedule of Next Release Dates tab on the left column of the main page notes when data will next be updated.—**ARBA Staff Reviewer**

Environmental Engineering

749.   Spelling, Frank R. **Environmental Engineering Dictionary.** 5th ed. Lanham, Md., Bernan Press, 2018. 694p. $189.00. ISBN 13: 978-1-59888-970-3.

Following the first four editions by C.C. Lee, compiler Frank Spellman (Emeritus, Old Dominion University) provides an update to Lee's environmental engineering dictionary; however, he defines it as "both a dictionary and an encyclopedia." In his preface, Spellman identifies approximately 36 environmental topical areas that are addressed in the new edition. Spellman intends that users will include general readers, students, and industry allied professionals. The volume is organized alphabetically and terms are defined in an abbreviated fashion; in other words, many terms do not offer a thorough definition. The definitions of many key terms, however, turn into lengthy articles, and these articles are the strength of the volume. Surprisingly, for as complete as the work is intended to be, some basic terms and concepts used in environmental engineering were not found in the dictionary (e.g., natural attenuation, time of concentration, etc.). After 679 pages, the dictionary is followed by approximately 10 pages of helpful references and recommended readings.—**Jennifer Brooks Huffman**

Materials Science

750.   Arblaster, John W. **Selected Values of the Crystallographic Properties of the Elements.** Materials Park, Ohio, ASM International, 2018. 684p. index. $249.00. ISBN 13: 978-1-62708-154-2; 978-1-62708-155-9 (e-book).

A large compilation of data on the crystallographic properties of the elements, this volume attempts to bring all reasonable data values together in one location, building on substantial work in the 1970s (notably the work of Yeram Touloukian and colleagues) and adding in more focused research in the intervening years. Each element is covered in approximately 15 pages, including as many isotopes and allotropes as possible. Each chapter is supported with copious references. Text is large and readable, making the many charts and tables easy to reference, and this would be functional in a lab or library. The greatest problem with this resource is its format. The print copy, although attractive, is largely useless, and the ebook will still be cumbersome to access. In the present day, a more interactive platform is the obvious solution. In the meantime, until accurate scientific apps become practical and widespread, this should be useful to any collection dealing with the subject.—**Peter Larsen**

751.   **ASM Handbook, Volume 18: Friction, Lubrication, and Wear Technology.** Greg E. Totten, ed. Materials Park, Ohio, ASM International, 2017. 1108p. index. $297.00. ISBN 13: 978-1-62708-070-5; 978-1-62708-142-9 (e-book).

The earlier edition of *Friction, Lubrication and Wear Technology* was published in 1992, and since then better surface characterization techniques, and subsequent tribological test methods have been developed. As a result, this 2017 edition includes several new entries devoted to methods of lab testing and analysis, and entries that extend the reader's understanding and analysis of complex tribosystems involving thermal, mechanical, materials, and chemical influences. The most noticeable change is that the newer edition is reorganized; it has expanded its focus on lubrication (as new lubricants have been developed), and has entries that highlight the emergence of nanotribology and fine-scale phenomena. Overall, the new edition provides more recent updates, delves deeper into friction and wear fundamentals, and serves well as a multidisciplinary resource for not only the tribologist, but also broader engineering community.—**Muhammed Hassanali**

752.   **ASM Handbook, Volume 1A: Cast Iron Science and Technology.** Doru M. Stefanescu, ed. Materials Park, Ohio, ASM International, 2017. 772p. index. $297.00. ISBN 13: 978-1-62708-133-7; 978-1-62708-134-4 (e-book).

The *ASM Handbook* volume 1 was meant to be a comprehensive guide to compositions, properties, performance, and selection of cast irons, carbon and low-alloy steels, tool steels, stainless steels, and superalloys, providing readers with data for alloy designations, compositions, and mechanical and physical properties. With the advances in material science, cast iron has been split away from volume 1 into its own publication (volume 1A), devoted specifically to cast iron. As the level of specialization increases in the metal processing industry, it is anticipated that additional splits (as this one) will be needed to adequately cover the metals processing industrial space.

The work starts with sections on history and classifications of cast irons, and is followed by thermodynamics of pertinent transformations (both in the liquid phase, and when the metal undergoes solidification). The next section surveys processing techniques, largely focusing on preparing the liquid metal, the casting process, and heat treatments. Downstream processes (primarily metal joining, such as welding and brazing, machining, and coating) are also covered. Engineering properties and how processing changes them are discussed in the next section. The next five sections focus on specific classes of cast iron: grey castings, ductile castings, compacted graphite castings, high alloy castings, and malleable castings.

Each section consists of a collection of independent papers. As stand-alone papers, one would expect overlap among them, not only within a section, but also across different sections. As more work in the area of iron castings is done, additional material will require more judicious selection of papers in this volume. However, it is good to see a separate cast iron handbook which serves as the reference for industry.—**Muhammed Hassanali**

753.   **Hot Working Guide: A Compendium of Processing Maps.** 2d ed. Y.V.R.K. Prasad, K.P. Rao, and S. Sasidhara, eds. Materials Park, Ohio, ASM International, 2015. 628p. $265.00. ISBN 13: 978-1-62708-091-0; 978-1-62708-092-7 (e-book).

The first edition of the *Hot Working Guide* was published in 1997, and since then several new grades of metals and their alloys have become widely and commercially used. The second edition includes several new entries; some of the materials in the first edition (generally those that were produced through different processes) have been consolidated into one entry which considers only one production process. In other cases, certain alloys have been removed. The first edition had a separate section on zinc and its alloys; these have now moved to the Other Materials section, and four maps have been reduced to two.

The most noticeable change between the first and second edition is the absence of stress-strain curves in the second edition. The editors claim that these were of little value in the hot working process, and hence were removed to include the large number of materials added. Most products that are hot processed need to undergo some secondary machining process, often in the same place where it was hot formed. For these secondary operations, knowledge of the material's stress-strain behavior is an important consideration for downstream processes, and hence an important feature of the first edition. Overall, it is good to see new materials added, and consolidation of materials that are less commonly used, but sad to see the stress-strain curves go.—**Muhammed Hassanali**

33 Health Sciences

General Works

Almanacs

754. **Plunkett's Health Care Industry Almanac 2018.** Jack Plunkett, ed. Houston, Tex., Plunkett Research, 2017. 681p. index. $379.99pa. ISBN 13: 978-1-62831-455-7; 978-1-62831-795-4 (e-book).

This book is designed as a broad reference source for general readers. There is a usage guide in the front of the book that explains the volume's organization. The first section covers the health care industry as a whole and contains the following three chapters: "Major Trends Affecting the Health Care Industry"; "Health Care Industry Statistics," which has information on such things as Medicare, Medicaid, patients, hospitals, and more; and "Important Health Care Industry Contacts—Address, Telephone Numbers, Internet Sites." This last section is in alphabetic order, starting with Alzheimer's Disease and ending with U.S. Government Agencies. The second section provides information about THE HEALTHCARE 500, leading corporations in the health care industry. Most of the companies are based in the United States but many are global. This section includes an index of companies within industry groups, such as ambulance services, hospitals, dialysis centers, and pharmaceuticals and drug manufacturing. There is also an alphabetical index to companies, by state headquarters (if based in the United States) or by country if international. Users will also find individual profiles of each company, containing such things as information on brands, divisions, and affiliations, top officers, growth plans, and financials. Book data is well supported by the use of tables, graphs, and charts. The book also contains "A Short HealthCare Industry Glossary" and two additional indexes "Index of Firms Noted as 'Hot Spots for Advancement' for Women and Minorities" and "Index by Subsidiaries, Brand Names and Selected Affiliations." This is a good starting point for researchers looking into health care firms and/or basic information on the status of the health care industry. Recommended for large public libraries.—**ARBA Staff Reviewer**

Dictionaries and Encyclopedias

755. **Encyclopedia of Public Health.** Sally Kuykendall, ed. Santa Barbara, Calif., Greenwood Press/ABC-CLIO, 2018. 2v. illus. index. $198.00/set. ISBN 13: 978-1-61069-982-2; 978-1-61069-983-9 (e-book).

Public health covers a wide range of programs and disciplines. This encyclopedia provides an overview of the field for lay readers. The editor and contributors are academics and health professionals. The approximately 240 alphabetical signed entries range in length from two to eight pages. They include brief bibliographies. The book begins with an introduction covering the public health field and its goals. A chronology documents the history of the field from 1754 BCE to 2016.

The entries demonstrate the many facets of public health. They include diseases and health problems (addictions, environmental health, epidemics); government organizations (Centers for Disease Control and Prevention, Food and Drug Administration); laws and guidelines (Affordable Care Act, public health law); history of public health (Middle Ages, pandemic); people (Louis Pasteur, Margaret Sanger); principles (health literacy, cultural competence); professional organizations and resources (American Public Health Association, The Nation's Health); programs (family planning, Medicare); and areas of practice (health administration, nutrition, bioterrorism). Volume two includes a series of controversies in public health to encourage critical thinking about topics such as the regulation of drug prices and the right of parents to refuse vaccinations for their children. It also has a directory of organizations and a glossary.

This is a useful resource for public, academic, and consumer health libraries.— **Barbara M. Bibel**

756. **The Gale Encyclopedia of Diets: A Guide to Health and Nutrition.** 3d ed. Deirdre Hiam, ed. Farmington Hills, Mich., Gale/Cengage Learning, 2018. 2v. illus. index. $535.00/set. ISBN 13: 978-1-4103-8827-8.

Now in its third edition, this award-winning reference continues to provide "authoritative and balanced information" (xiii) on a wide array of diets, basic nutrition, diseases associated with nutrition, and vitamins and supplements. The more than 300 in-depth articles are written by a large team of medical writers and cover fad diets that promise quick weight loss (three-day diets), commercial weight loss programs (Weight Watchers), diets used as therapy (ketogenic), and diets that are more of a lifestyle choice (macrobiotic). This edition includes more than 20 new entries, including articles on hydration, sugar-sweetened beverages, and plant-based eating. Each diet is described in detail, its benefits and risks are addressed as is the question of whether there is any legitimate research supporting the diet's claims. Within each article key terms are defined and all key terms are assembled in one master glossary. The index is crucial for finding topics that do not have their own entry such as *The China Study,* a book about an important long-term health study. Despite the broad coverage there are three surprising omissions: the Flat Belly Diet, the Nutritarian Diet, and the MIND Diet. The text is uniformly well written and enhanced with color photos, tables, charts and diagrams, making this the go-to resource for comparative information on diets and nutrition. Libraries that do not own the second edition should acquire this easy-to-use, attractive resource, suitable for both ready reference and the general public. Highly recommended.—**Cynthia Knight**

Digital Resources

757.   **EWG's Guide to Sunscreens https://www.ewg.org/sunscreen.** [Website] Free. Date reviewed: 2019.

This annually updated guide from the Environmental Working Group offers expert sunscreen safety ratings that include generous information about such items as sunscreen efficacy, cost, and ingredients. Although it is important to note that all known brands may not appear in the database, users can nonetheless find information on many familiar brands and products. Users can search by particular brand or alternatively select from several category tabs, including Best Beach & Sport Sunscreens, Best Scoring Kids Sunscreens, and Best Moisturizers with SPF. Colorful graphics enhance a product profile which generally includes a chart showing the selected product's ranking against other products in same category, a Health Concerns scale, a UVA/UVB Balance scale, a Top Findings summary list, a detailed Ingredients list (noting concerns if any), and an EWG rating from one to ten with the lower number indicating the better product. Users may choose to get quickly to the information they seek via the FAQs, which address the most common questions about sunscreens and skin protection. They can also read the executive summary of the larger report, which is full of data infographics that touch on issues borne out of the annual sunscreen testing, noting things like the percentage rise in mineral-only sunscreens and vitamin A usage. The Read the Report tab leads to the full detailed and well-organized annual report, extensively referenced, with chapters such as "8 Little-Known Facts about Sunscreens," "The Problem with Vitamin A," and "Do Sunscreens Prevent Skin Damage?"—**ARBA Staff Reviewer**

758.   **Explore Health Careers. https://explorehealthcareers.org/.** [Website] Free. Date reviewed: 2018.

Explore Health Careers offers an abundance of information about the wide range of career options in the health care field. The easy-to-navigate site helps users get answers to important questions and is full of resources and descriptive information about myriad health care career paths. The key feature of the website is the gallery from which users can find information on specific health care specialties. Users can scroll down through the gallery and select from twenty-seven categories, including Sports Medicine, Veterinary Medicine, Optometry, Occupational Therapy, Mental Health, Forensic Science, and many others. Users will find clear information including average salary, required years of higher education, job outlook, and a generally brief but thorough description of tasks, academic requirements, working conditions, and more. There is also a list of applicable resources. Good foundational information can be found within the tabs running across the top of the homepage or via the buttons in the center of the page. The Career Explorer helps users consider the demands and characteristics of a health care career. It also offers general insight into types of health careers in relation to education, and an excellent Career Explorer search tool which works in relation to education and salary parameters. Paying for College and Your Education tabs offer an abundance of straightforward information about such topics as applying to college, planning your studies, enrichment programs, and more. Users can also conduct a scholarship search, with links to a database of millions of scholarships for which users can create a profile. Resources are generous and include links to self-assessment surveys and tools, links to information on health care policy and diversity in health care, educational resources, and links to organizations for health care students. The generous amount of information and resources, coupled with the site's ease of use, encourages the interest of a more diverse job seeker pool, crucial to meeting the world's changing health care needs. Explore Health Careers would appeal to high school and university students and educators across a variety of disciplines.—**ARBA Staff Reviewer**

759.   **Healthfinder https://healthfinder.gov.** [Website] Free. Date reviewed: 2019.
     Healthfinder (from the U.S. Department of Health and Human Services) offers basic information on an array of general health topics within an easy-to-navigate A-Z directory. Users will find generally brief, plain language summaries of over 120 topics in addition to special features designed to make healthcare conversations easier. Healthfinder does not provide comprehensive information, rather it focuses on prevention, screenings, preparation, general treatment options, and enhanced communication with medical professionals, offering a good foundation for further research. Slides on the homepage show accessible ways to consider several common health concerns, such as a Calcium Shopping List and Questions for the Doctor on Type 2 Diabetes. Users can also take a quiz on a number of health topics such as Parenting and Aging. The main feature of Healthfinder, however, is the A-Z directory of topics, including Nutrition, Medicare, Maternal Health, Substance Abuse, Skin Protection, Vaccines, Child Development, and many others. While the topics do not necessarily include particular conditions and diseases, they do cover general information regarding broader afflictions such as cancer, stroke, and the flu. Broader topics may also include subtopics. Under Children's Health, for example, users can find detail on protecting children from injury, helping children maintain a health weight, protecting families from lead, and more. Each entry is well organized and may include sections such an Overview, The Basics, Take Action, and Common Questions. Entries make good use of bullet points and may offer additional resources such as checklists, quick tips, and informational PDFs.—**ARBA Staff Reviewer**

Directories

760.   **The Complete Directory for Pediatric Disorders, 2017/2018.** 9th ed. Amenia, N.Y., Grey House Publishing, 2017. 1114p. index. $165.00. ISBN 13: 978-1-68217-360-2.
     The Complete Directory for Pediatric Disorders "provides current, understandable medical information, resources and support services for 213 pediatric disorders." This directory is arranged within four sections: I. Disorders, which contains 213 chapters on specific disorders; II. General Resources, a directory of 1,014 resources including government agencies, national associations, state agencies, and support groups; III. The Human Body, containing 14 detailed descriptions of body systems or medical categories; and IV. Indexes by Entry (Geography, Disorder, and Related Term). Additionally, the book offers the following: "Glossary: A Concise Guide to Medical Terminology"; "Glossary of Acronyms"; "Guidelines for Obtaining Additional Information and Resources"; "Disorders by Biologic System Affected"; and an essay by Johns Hopkins Bloomberg School of Public Health "Modest Increases in Kids' Physical Activity Could Avert Billions in Medical and Other Costs." Section I is arranged alphabetically by name of illness/disorder and

among those covered are: Asthma; Acute Gastrointestinal Infections; Autistic Disorder; Bipolar Disorder; Conjunctivitis; Cystic Fibrosis; HIV Infection; Otitis Media; Obsessive Compulsive Disorder; Prematurity; and Seizures. Each chapter contains name of disorder, description, related disorders that it covers plus a list of directory information broken into sections for Government Agencies, State Agencies and Support Groups, Research Centers, Audio and Video, Book Publishers, Web Sites, Magazines, Newsletters, Pamphlets, and Camps. Entries include name, address, phone, fax, website, stated purpose, and directors. *The Complete Directory for Pediatric Disorders* is a comprehensive, highly recommended resource for medical professionals and patients and those researching guides to resources for specific disorders. It is especially recommended for public and medical libraries.— **Lucy Heckman**

761. **The Complete Directory for People with Chronic Illness, 2017-18.** 13th ed. Amenia, N.Y., Grey House Publishing, 2017. 1200p. index. $165.00. ISBN 13: 978-1-68217-376-3.

The Complete Directory for People with Chronic Illness "offers a comprehensive overview of 90 specific chronic illnesses from Addison's to Wilson's Disease" and each chapter includes a description of the medical conditions and a list of resources. Additionally the directory provides three useful sections: a two-part table covering body systems and chronic illnesses; "Cognitive Behavioral Therapy Improves Functioning for People with Chronic Pain Study Shows," an essay; and "Next Steps after Your Diagnosis: finding Information and Support," presenting five basic steps to help cope with the chronic illness diagnosis. The bulk of the book is comprised of chapters on the 90 chronic illnesses: Down Syndrome, tuberculosis, brain tumors, hypertension, sleep disorders, skin disorders, hearing impairment, heart disease, and many more. New to this edition is a chapter on post-traumatic stress disorder. This edition also includes approximately 10,000 new and updated listings. In each chapter, resources listed are arranged within sections: National Agencies and Associations; State Agencies and Associations; Foundations; Research Centers: Support Groups and Hotlines; Books; Children's Books; Magazines; Newsletters; Pamphlets; Audio and Video; and Web Sites. Organizations listed contain information about name, address, website, telephones, officers, and a description of mission. Book entries include author, title, address of publisher, description, phone number, website, and ISBN number. *The Complete Directory for People with Chronic Illness* is highly recommended for public library collections. It brings together in one volume a wealth of information about specific chronic illnesses.—**Lucy Heckman**

Handbooks and Yearbooks

762. **Adolescent Health Sourcebook.** 4th ed. Siva Ganesh Maharaja, ed. Detroit, Omnigraphics, 2018. 756p. (Health Reference Series). $85.00. ISBN 13: 978-0-7808-1611-4; 978-0-7808-1612-1 (e-book).

This substantial hardcover book from Omnigraphics attempts to inform adolescents, who may participate in high-risk behaviors without being fully aware of the consequences, with reliable information. The book contains nine parts: An Overview of Adolescent Health; Staying Healthy during Adolescence; Puberty, Sexuality, and Reproductive Health;

Common Health Concerns of Teens and Their Parents; Emotional, Social, and Mental Health Concerns among Adolescents; Substance Abuse and Adolescents; Adolescent Safety Concerns; Violence against Adolescents; and Additional Help and Information. Prior knowledge is not necessary for understanding the content. Much of the material is based on publications issued by numerous government agencies. The appropriate bolding, bullet formats, and graphics and tables assist readers, enhance retention, and encourage continued reading. The editor presents much of the content in a clear and concise question-and-answer format. Furthermore, the book includes a directory of Adolescent Health Organizations and a glossary of terms about adolescent health. The *Adolescent Health Sourcebook* offers parents, teens, and caregivers basic information about growth, development, and related safety issues during adolescence and may help facilitate a positive step towards seeking professional help or reconsidering hasty decisions that lead to undesirable coming of age consequences. Like other volumes in Omnigraphics' Health Reference Series, this one is a welcome addition to library shelves. Recommended.— **Thomas E. Baker**

763. Blackwell, Amy Hackney. **Living Green: Your Questions Answered.** Santa Barbara, Calif., Greenwood Press/ABC-CLIO, 2018. 133p. index. (Q&A Health Guides). $39.00. ISBN 13: 978-1-4408-5982-3; 978-1-4408-5983-0 (e-book).

In this book, author Amy Hackney Blackwell discusses what it means to live a green lifestyle, addressing the topic in an engaging writing style that utilizes a question-and-answer format. The book first addresses basic questions about such topics as climate change and the ozone layer. The following portion of the book is divided into well-documented sections on power; transportation; waste reduction, reuse, and recycling; food; water; and other issues and concerns. Readers will learn about fossil fuels, ethanol, composting, how agriculture affects the environment, food sourcing, water use, and ecotourism, among many other topics. These are followed by a selection of five case studies that suggest ways ordinary people can contribute to green living. A glossary, a directory of resources, and an extensive index round out the work. *Living Green* will serve students in middle school, high school, and college. Recommended for school, academic, and public libraries.— **Thomas E. Baker**

764. Boslaugh, Sarah. **Transgender Health Issues.** Santa Barbara, Calif., Greenwood Press/ABC-CLIO, 2018. 206p. index. (Health and Medical Issues Today). $40.00. ISBN 13: 978-1-4408-5887-1; 978-1-4408-5888-8 (e-book).

Transgender Health Issues is a single-volume title and is part of the Health and Medical Issues series (approximately fourteen books in the series to date). The book's foreword describes books published in this series as a first step for students and lay people in obtaining a solid overview on controversial topics in health care for the 21st century. Past books in the series have addressed topics such as plastic surgery, cutting and self-harm, body size, bullying, suicide and metal health, and infertility.

Transgender Health Issues offers information about specific health concerns of transgender people, such as the gender transition process and the health risks associated with certain procedures. In the introduction, the author describes the goals of the book: supplying information to help everyone understand and accept transgender people, fostering appreciation of the complexity of transgender identity, and providing information to those actively seeking transgender issues information.

The book is organized in three sections: part one, Overview, contains background information and context (with chapters defining what it means to be transgender, historical context, transitioning, and physical and mental health issues); part two, Controversies and Issues, contains contemporary issues (including discrimination, access to health care, normative gender dichotomies, parenting and family issues, and research issues); and part three, Scenarios, contains case studies. The book contains narrative chapters within the three sections that are easy to read and nontechnical. Chapters have survey data and cited sources noted and woven into the narrative. The book concludes with a glossary, a timeline, sources for further information, and an index.

Transgender Health Issues provides a basic introduction to transgender health issues and topics; like any medical source, one should consult with a physician for complete medical advice and information. This is a balanced source, recommended for the circulating collection of a high school or a public library collection.—**Caroline L. Gilson**

765.   Davidson, Tish. **The Vaccine Debate.** Santa Barbara, Calif., Greenwood Press/ ABC-CLIO, 2019. 238p. index. (Health and Medical Issues Today). $40.00. ISBN 13: 978-1-4408-4353-2; 978-1-4408-4354-9 (e-book).

This volume follows the approach of earlier works in this series, which examined topics such as obesity, steroids, concussions, plastic surgery, and bullying. Like those books, it is divided into three sections: overview and background information, issues and controversies, and scenarios (case studies). The first section presents a great deal of science, discussing, for example, the roles of granulocytes, dendritic cells, and inactivated and polyvalent vaccines. A clear history of vaccination in the United Kingdom and the United States, along with a presentation of the evolution of opposition movements, conclude the section. The "Issues" chapters elaborate on the concerns of the anti-vaccination movement, including the claim that certain vaccines can cause autism. While solid medical research has repeatedly shown that vaccination is a safe and wise procedure, some groups continue to oppose it. Each of the five case studies has a narrative and an analysis, most involving problems encountered by children who had not had all their vaccinations or had not been vaccinated at all.

The final pages of the book include useful information: a timeline, a bibliography, a glossary, and a list of websites with views on both sides of the vaccine controversy. This book addresses an important issue and should be considered by all public, high school, and academic libraries.—**Mark Schumacher**

766.   Dimmick, Christine. **Detox Your Home: A Guide to Removing Toxins from Your Life and Bringing Health into Your Home.** Lanham, Md., Rowman & Littlefield, 2018. 204p. index. $32.00; $30.00 (e-book). ISBN 13: 978-1-4422-7720-5; 978-1-4422-7721-2 (e-book).

The author, founder of the Good Home Company, examines the many toxins at play in everyday life. Following an introduction that highlights the limits of regulating institutions like the FDA and the USDA and the ways in which labels mislead consumers are five parts comprised of 18 chapters. The first part, Detox Your Skin, looks at the toxins in several items: shampoos and conditioners, body creams, soaps, beauty products, and dental hygiene products. Part II highlights dangers in the kitchen and pantry, discussing meat, water, pesticides, cookware, and more. The third part focuses on cleaning agents used throughout the house. Part IV, Detox Your Wardrobe, discusses topics many people overlook when thinking about potentially harmful chemicals. The last part, Detox Your Stuff, focuses on such items as electronics, children's toys, and bedding. Chapters vary in length depending on subject. For instance, the chapter on face and body creams in the first part of the book details harmful chemicals, suggests ways to detox, notes impacts on health and the environment, and presents advice from experts (this includes two Q&As with beauty experts). On the other hand, the chapter on bees and pesticides is only two pages long. The book makes good use of black-and-white tables and figures. The chapter on toxins in children's toys, for example, has a two-page spreadsheet of the hazardous chemicals used in products designed for children. At the end of the book, readers will find a useful resources section that will direct them to further information and more healthy consumer products. A notes section and an index round out the book, which is recommended for the circulating collection of public libraries.—**ARBA Staff Reviewer**

767.   Galpar, Amy, and Christina Daigneault. **Plant-Based Beauty: The Essential Guide to Using Natural Ingredients for Health, Wellness & Personal Skincare with 50-Plus Recipes.** Dallas, Tex., BenBella Books, 2018. 256p. illus. index. $22.00. ISBN 13: 978-1-9446-4885-5.

This guide presents information in two parts to people who want to make their own natural skincare products. The first part, Natural Beauty Basics, instructs readers in how to read a label, how skincare works, essential oils, plant extracts, whole plant parts, how to infuse oils, and more. There are also beauty ingredient charts and a list of the kitchen tools necessary for making everything from body cream to hair serum. Part 2, Beauty Recipes, provides readers with detailed instructions for making facial masks, dry skin body cleansers, healthy hand-sanitizing gels, and other products. The end of the book includes resources for beauty blending ingredients, notes, a glossary, an index, a recipe index, and notes about the author. This is a great guide for those who want to know what goes in to what they put on their bodies. It is more detailed than a similar title, *Compassionate Chicks Guide to DIY Beauty,* (see ARBA 2018, entry 770). Recommended.—**ARBA Staff Reviewer**

768.   Haelle, Tara. **Vaccination Investigation: The History and Science of Vaccines.** Minneapolis, Minn., Twenty-First Century Books/Lerner Publishing Group, 2018. 120p. index. 37.32. ISBN 13: 978-1-5124-2530-7.

Students who wonder why the flu vaccine isn't more effective or question the value of the HVP vaccine for themselves will find answers in this instructive overview of the history, current use, and future of vaccines. Chapters document the pioneers in the field and their insights to the causes of diseases and their efforts to develop vaccines. Included are Edward Jenner's work to prevent smallpox, Maurice Hillman's teams' development of over 40 vaccines, and the two women responsible for the pertussis vaccine. Difficulties in developing, testing, and producing vaccines are described, including failures due to problems such as lax oversight and defective materials. Even when vaccines prove effective, a variety of reasons limit their use in the US as well as in the rest of the world, such as distrust of the government delivering the vaccines, and problems reaching rural areas. Researchers work with new techniques to try to eliminate old diseases such as AIDS and malaria as well as newer ones like Zika and Ebola. The chapter on vaccine basics features helpful illustrations to illuminate difficult concepts. The book includes additional resources, a glossary, and an index. Recommended.—**Anitra Gordon**

Medicine

General Works

Dictionaries and Encyclopedias

769.   **Infectious Diseases In Context.** 2d ed. Thomas Riggs, ed. Farmington Hills, Mich., Gale/Cengage Learning, 2018. 2v. illus. index. $379.00/set. ISBN 13: 978-1-4103-8128-6.

Infectious Diseases In Context is a two-volume encyclopedia for high school students or general readers wanting to understand key scientific facts, social and historical contexts, and political and ethical debates surrounding specific infectious diseases. The second edition (see ARBA 2008, entry 1229) has more than 260 entries and includes new entries on anellovirus, anti-cytokine antibody syndromes, enterovirus 71 infection, macrophage Activation Syndrome, microsporidiosis, Powassan virus, President Obama's initiative on combating antibiotic resistance, protozoan diseases, sepsis as a WHO priority, severe fever with thrombocytopenia syndrome, talaromycosis, tick-borne diseases, Venezuelan equine encephalitis virus, and Zika virus. Entries are arranged alphabetically, and most are about 3-5 pages in length. Each entry is broken into sections: introduction; a Words to Know sidebar; disease history, characteristics, and transmission; scope and distribution; treatment and prevention; impacts and issues; and a short bibliography of books, periodicals, and websites for further study. Colored maps and pictures are scattered throughout the two volumes, but the emphasis is on well-organized and displayed text. Other nice features include a 15-page glossary, which provides entries on the Words to Know sidebars, and a chronology of many of the most significant events in the history of infectious diseases. As this source is meant for students, there is a good introductory section on how to cite entries in different styles and an explanation on how to use primary sources. Highly recommended for high school and public libraries.—**Kevin McDonough**

770.   **Magill's Medical Guide.** 8th ed. Hackensack, N.J., Salem Press, 2018. 5v. illus. index. $495.00/set. ISBN 13: 978-1-68217-631-3; 978-1-61925-215-8 (e-book).

This encyclopedia set provides a vast amount of information regarding human anatomy, health, and hundreds of medical conditions ranging from abdominal disorders to "zoonoses." The contributing authors, medical editors, and publisher have produced a valuable and timely resource that is likely to complement a variety of libraries.

Each encyclopedia begins with a contents section with corresponding page numbers. This is followed by a complete list of contents for all 5 volumes with corresponding page numbers. The set is broken down as follows: Abdomen to Conception, Concussion to Hair Transplantation, Hammertoe Correction to Narcotics, Nasal Polyp Removal to Skin Grating, and Skin Lesion Removal to Zoonoses. Thousands of entries are presented throughout this set.

A majority of the content of volumes 1 through 5 includes various medical terms. The latter portions of volumes 1 through 4 include "Entries by Anatomy or System Affected" followed by "Entries by Specialties or Related Fields." The latter section of volume 5 includes a glossary, symptoms and warning signs, diseases and other medical conditions, a pharmaceutical list, types of health care providers, a general bibliography, and an index. Black-and-white illustrations, pictures, artwork, and tables are present throughout the 5-volume series. All are clear and easy to read. Colored images do not appear to be included.

A comprehensive and contemporary resource, users are also encouraged to consult with additional resources and experts prior to forming any final medical decisions. This guidance is included in the beginning of each volume in a "Note to Readers" paragraph. This encyclopedia series would likely complement a primary care provider's medical library, a professional library, such as a medical institution, or a personal library of an individual with interested in human anatomy, science, wellness, and/or healthcare. The publisher notes that this series is also available online and the back cover of each text includes a QR code.—**Paul M. Murphy, III**

771.　McCullough, Laurence B. **Historical Dictionary of Medical Ethics.** Lanham, Md., Rowman & Littlefield, 2018. 330p. (Historical Dictionaries of Religions, Philosophies, and Movements). $95.00; $90.00 (e-book). ISBN 13: 978-1-5381-1428-5; 978-1-5381-1429-2 (e-book).

McCullough, a medical educator and authority on medical ethics and its history and a leading advocate of emphasizing the practical rather than the theoretical nature of medical ethics, has written a concise dictionary that seeks to provide clear, consistent definitions related to the history and practice of professional medical ethics. The work includes short entries, averaging 200-500 words, defining core concepts, historical figures in the history of medical ethics, schools of thought, landmark cases and laws, controversies, terminology, and tools for ethical decision-making. The entries are primarily, but not exclusively, based on the history and philosophy of Western medical ethics. While the dictionary would be most useful for the medical practitioner, the definitions are written in nontechnical language, making it an accessible source of information for patients, policy makers, or even the general community. A chronology lists important eras and events from ancient times to the present, and an extensive introduction addresses the relationship of professional medical ethics to philosophy, theology, and bioethics. A bibliography follows the approximately 300 pages of alphabetical entries. There are extensive cross-references, using bold fonts for defined terms within entries as well as *see* and *see also* references. With its unique focus on medical ethics, this volume is a welcome addition to the Historical Dictionaries of Religions, Philosophies, and Movements series.—**Theresa Muraski**

Digital Resources

772.　**Florence Nightingale Digitization Project. http://archives.bu.edu/web/florence-nightingale/about.** [Website] Free. Date reviewed: 2018.

This site acts as a portal to a digitized collection of over 2,300 letters written by "The Lady with the Lamp," Florence Nightingale. With original documents distributed throughout 20 museums, universities, and other collections, this portal is a boon for researchers interested in the woman who helped revolutionize health care. Users can select the Search the Collaborative Database tab from the top of the page to initiate a search by collection or via a listing of Suggested Search Terms, such as Military Medicine, Rural Health Services, Workhouses, and more. Selecting the Search tab accesses the full database, listing individual letters by addressee, date, and contributing collection. Users can also find more specific search options on the left side of the database page, including Personal Entities (e.g., Ebeneezer Butler, William Farr), Corporate Entities (e.g., British Nursing Association, Oxford University), and over 500 additional subjects, such as India, Crimean War, Sanitation, Midwifery, Cholera, and many subtopics within the nursing profession. Selected letters will generally include a brief description, summary, date, location, and named entities. The accompanying letter image will vary depending on the collection source, but users may be able to examine thumbnails or larger versions of the letter. Some letters may be accompanied by a transcript. Considering Florence Nightingale's significant achievements in field medicine, nursing, and general health policy, this portal would appeal to a variety of researchers.—**ARBA Staff Reviewer**

Handbooks and Yearbooks

773.   **Congenital Disorders Sourcebook.** 4th ed. Greg Mullin, ed. Detroit, Omnigraphics, 2018. 645p. index. $85.00. ISBN 13: 978-0-7808-1613-8.

This is the 4th edition of the *Congenital Disorders Sourcebook* (see ARBA 2014, entry 1199), one of the informational reference books in the Health Reference Series. In addition to discussing recent advances in diagnosing and treating birth defects, the book includes broad analysis on subjects such as preventing birth defects and other prenatal issues. The book is divided into 4 major parts, and each part has a collection of chapters (there are 36 chapters in all). Chapters include questions about the topics and descriptions of diagnosis, treatments, and prognosis. Black-and-white illustrations and some statistical charts and figures are included. The chapters also include descriptive surgery procedures. Part one includes 12 chapters and is an overview covering prenatal issues and preventing birth defects. Part 2 is a collection of 7 chapters and focuses on birth complications and prematurity; this section covers such topics as multiple births and perinatal infections. The third part, the largest in this volume, includes 15 chapters and addresses structural abnormalities and functional impairments such as heart and brain defects. Part 4 consists of chapters, a glossary, and resources for additional information. There is an index at the back of the volume. The contact information for hospitals and national associations was compiled from reliable sources and verified for accuracy (as of December 2017). An online activation code is included at the back of the book for access to the Health Reference Series database, which requires users to have a paid subscription. The well-organized chapters are all-encompassing but not too lengthy. This reference is suitable for high school and college research. The extensive treatment of congenital disorders would also make it a substantial addition to any public, academic, or consumer health library.—**Amy B. Parsons**

Alternative Medicine

774.   **Complementary and Alternative Medicine Information for Teens: Health Tips about Diverse Medical and Wellness Systems.** 3d ed. John Tilly, ed. Detroit, Omnigraphics, 2018. 399p. index. (Teen Health Series). $69.00. ISBN 13: 978-0-7808-1617-6; 978-0-7808-1618-3 (e-book).

Complementary and Alternative Medicine Information for Teens addresses diverse alternative medications, practices, and products that are not generally defined as part of conventional treatment plans. The use of alternative medicines such as herbal products and so-called nutraceuticals has soared in popularity among American youth.

The book is divided into chapters and parts, a strategy that makes the material accessible. Parts are Introduction to Complementary and Alternative Medicine [CAM], Whole Medical Systems, Manipulative Practices and Movement Therapies, Mind-Body Medicine, Biologically Based Practices, Energy Medicine, Creative Arts Therapy, CAM Treatments for Cancer and Other Diseases and Conditions, and If You Need More Information. Within these parts, readers will find general information on CAM usage statistics, finding a CAM practitioner, homeopathy, chiropractic medicine, tai chi and yoga, specialized diets, reiki, music therapy, and much more. The last section provides data on CAM medical trials, further reading suggestions, and a directory of CAM-related organizations. The writing style and layout appeal to the target audience as does the question-and-answer format. Readers will also be able to trust the material in this well-vetted reference. Recommended for school libraries.—**Thomas E. Baker**

775.   **Herbs at a Glance https://nccih.nih.gov/health/herbsataglance.htm.** [Website] Free. Date reviewed: 2019.

The free website, Herbs at a Glance, offers an easy way to find basic information on fifty-two different herbs commonly used as natural remedies for a range of ailments and conditions. The page presents an alphabetical listing of herbs, such as butterbur, cinnamon, fenugreek, garlic, horse chestnut, red clover, milk thistle, tea tree oil, valerian, and others. Users can click on an herb to access well-organized and generally brief fact sheets which include the following sections: Background, How Much Do We Know, What Have We Learned, What Do We Know About Safety, Keep in Mind, For More Information, and Key References. Each fact sheet also includes a color photo. The Background section may include information regarding where the herb is grown, historical usage, commercial products, and more. Following sections refer to common usage in regards to health and note safety concerns, potential side effects, and other issues. The material additionally notes Common Name(s) and Latin Name, and may refer to relevant clinical studies. Herbs at a Glance, while not necessarily comprehensive, is a quick way to find information on some of the most common medicinal herbs.—**ARBA Staff Reviewer**

Psychiatry

776.   Vitelli, Romeo. **Self-Injury: Your Questions Answered.** Santa Barbara, Calif., Greenwood Press/ABC-CLIO, 2018. 115p. index. (Q&A Health Guides). $39.00. ISBN 13: 978-1-4408-5444-6; 978-1-4408-5445-3 (e-book).

Self-Injury: Your Questions Answered addresses one of many sensitive topics that are essential for counselors, teachers, parents, and young people to understand. Timely intervention is essential. Self-injury behaviors can rapidly release tension. However, the outcome is only a quick fix—similar to drugs and alcohol.

This book, part of the Q&A Health Guides series from Greenwood Press, begins with an introduction, a "Guide to Health Literacy," and clarification of common misconceptions about self-injury (e.g., the assumption that more girls self-harm than boys). The bulk of the book is divided into several sections that relay information in a question-and-answer format. The first section of general information provides answers to such questions as "What is self-harm," "Is it only teenagers who harm themselves," and "Can self-harming be addictive." The section on Causes and Risk Factors asks questions about the role of trauma, bullying, substance abuse, autism, sexual abuse, brain disorders, and more in relation to self-harm. The Culture, Media, and Self-Injury section includes answers to queries about online self-harm subcultures and the likelihood of military veterans inflicting self-injury. In the section on treatment and prevention readers will get answers to questions about the need for inpatient programs, the use of mindfulness therapy, and more. The final section presents five case studies; a glossary, resources section, and an index round out the work. This is a very readable book that will certainly appeal to teens but may also appeal to patrons in a public library or to an undergraduate audience. Recommended.—**Thomas E. Baker**

Specific Diseases and Conditions

AIDS

777.   **Encyclopedia of AIDS.** Thomas J. Hope, Douglas D. Richman, and Mario Stevenson, eds. New York, Springer Publishing, 2018. 3v. illus. index. $999.00/set. ISBN 13: 978-1-4939-7100-8; 978-1-4939-7101-5 (e-book).

This 3-volume set is designed as a place to find comprehensive information about HIV/AIDS. All contributors, the editors-in-chief, and the members of the editorial advisory board are international experts whose credentials can be found in the front matter. The front matter also contains a topical list of the set's contents, grouped into sections like Anatomic Compartments and Vaccines. The more than 280 entries are arranged in an A-to-Z format; guide words are included to facilitate searching. Thorough entries vary in length (approximately 5 pages to more than a dozen pages); all are signed by contributors and all are subdivided depending on the topic under discussion. Entries include cross-references and references. These reference sections can be quite extensive—e.g., there are nearly 10 pages of references at the end of the entry for Anatomic Compartments as a Barrier to HIV Care. Coverage is comprehensive and broad, including information about HIV/AIDS in Europe; Latin America; Africa, Central, East, South, and Southeast Asia; and North America. Hundreds of color and black-and-white figures and tables illustrate concepts and enhance the overall usefulness of the encyclopedia. The encyclopedia will be regularly updated (in electronic format) so that information remains current. This expertly curated title is highly recommended for academic libraries, especially those that support medical schools.—**ARBA Staff Reviewer**

Allergies

778.   **Allergy Information for Teens.** 3d ed. Siva Ganesh Maharaja, ed. Detroit, Omnigraphics, 2018. 356p. index. (Teen Health series). $69.00. ISBN 13: 978-0-7808-1593-3; 978-0-7808-1594-0 (e-book).

This 3d edition (see ARBA 2014, entry 1214) is a handy resource book that provides information in six sections: Allergy Overview; Allergy Symptoms and Complications; Food Allergies and Intolerances; Other Common Allergy Triggers; Managing Allergies in Daily Life; and If You Need More Information. The production team made a deliberate effort to address the visual requirements of young readers. Bold fonts, an age appropriate writing style, drawings, charts, and bullet formatting enhance accessibility and encourage readers. Additional benefits include highlighted information boxes, line spacing, and useful graphic images. The book also overflows with helpful suggestions and explanations. For example, a special section assists readers in their daily struggle to avoid triggers that initiate cycles of unpleasant symptoms and unfortunate disruptions and interferences. The book is ideal for school and public libraries. Recommended.—**Thomas E. Baker**

Alzheimer Disease

779.   **Alzheimer Disease Sourcebook.** 7th ed. Angela L. Williams, ed. Detroit, Omnigraphics, 2019. 544p. (Health Reference Series). $85.00. ISBN 13: 978-0-7808-1677-0; 978-0-7808-1678-7 (e-book).

This updated reference on a disease that affects approximately 5 million Americans includes the following parts: Facts about the Brain and Cognitive Decline; Alzheimer Disease: The Most Common Type of Dementia; Other Dementia Disorders; Recognizing, Diagnosing, and Treating Symptoms of Alzheimer Disease and Dementia; Living with Alzheimer Disease and Dementias; Caregiver Concerns; and Additional Help and Information. These chapters are divided into parts, which makes it easy for users to navigate directly to a topic from the table of contents. Within these informative chapters, users will find information about the basics of brain structure; the signs and symptoms of Alzheimer Disease and the genetics of Alzheimer Disease; related diseases, such as Parkinson disease; dementia caused by infections; Alzheimer medications; support for caregivers; nutrition and exercise; residential facilities; support organizations; and so much more. An extensive index rounds out the work. The information in this book is reliable and vetted by a medical advisory board. Recommended.—**ARBA Staff Reviewer**

Asthma

780.   **Asthma Sourcebook.** 5th ed. Detroit, Omnigraphics, 2018. 500p. illus. index. $85.00. ISBN 13: 978-0-7808-1652-7; 978-0-7808-1653-4 (e-book).

This edition follows the 4th edition, published 2 years earlier; it is arranged like the earlier edition, and presents information on many aspects of asthma. The sections include Asthma Basics, Recognizing and Diagnosing Asthma, Medications and Asthma Management, Living with Asthma, Pediatric Asthma, Asthma in Other Special Populations, and, finally, a glossary and a directory of asthma-related resources. The text, given its medical subject, is quite readable and clearly presented. Because the book is divided into 133 short sections, readers can easily locate the specific information they are seeking. Like other titles in the publisher's Health Reference Series, much of the information is excerpted verbatim from government documents; a list of 17 institutions is provided in the preface to the text of the book. It might be useful to include the web addresses of the documents mentioned, as many are available. For instance, the text of "How the Lungs Work" (Section 1.2) is word for word from www.nhlbi.nih.gov/health-topics/how-lungs-work. Chapters 5 and 8 here, on asthma prevalence and diagnosis, are similar. Having all this information gathered from diverse resources is helpful for those wanting to learn about an illness that affects 25 million Americans. It is well presented, in manageable sections usually of a few pages, with clear headings and bullet points. Public and academic libraries that do not own the 4th edition, should consider this volume.—**Mark Schumacher**

Brain Disorders

781. **Brain Disorders Sourcebook.** 5th ed. John Tilly, ed. Detroit, Omnigraphics, 2018. 652p. index. (Health Reference Series). $85.00. ISBN 13: 978-0-7808-1620-6.

This volume updates the 4th edition (see ARBA 2016, entry 812). The 5th edition addresses conditions and treatments in nine sections comprised of 58 chapters. Parts include Brain Basics, Diagnosing and Treating Brain Disorders, Genetic and Congenital Brain Disorders, Brain Infections, Acquired and Traumatic Brain Injuries, Brain Tumors, Degenerative Brain Disorders, and Seizures and Neurological Disorders of Sleep. The last part is Additional Help and Information.

The information is presented in such a way that readers can approach the book without background knowledge. The use of bold fonts, graphic images, bullet formatting, and accessible writing style all facilitate use as does a suitable font size and line spacing. Furthermore, the information is vetted by a team of qualified, senior medical professions. Readers will also find documents from government agencies and other trusted sources.

Recommended.—**Thomas E. Baker**

Cancer

782. **Cancer Information for Teens.** 4th ed. Greg Mullin, ed. Detroit, Omnigraphics, 2018. 457p. index. (Teen Health Series). $69.00. ISBN 13: 978-0-7808-1615-2; 978-0-7808-1616-9 (e-book).

Cancer is not common among teenagers, but accurate information is essential for both cancer patients and those in their support groups. This 4th edition (see ARBA 2014, entry 1215) provides teens with information about cancer symptoms, complications, and treatments in six parts: Cancer Facts and Risk Factors; Cancers of Most Concern to Teens and Young Adults; Cancer Awareness, Diagnosis, and Treatment; Cancer Survivorship; When a Loved One Has Cancer; and If You Need More Information. The text is age appropriate and uses bold fonts, drawings, charts, bullet formatting, and highlighted information boxes to enhance readability and motivate interest. The book is a fast read that overflows with helpful suggestions and explanations. The question-and-answer format facilitates understanding and rivets attention, while the extensive index system enhances speedy information retrieval. This practical reference contribution is recommended for school and public libraries.—**Thomas E. Baker**

Eating Disorders

783. **Eating Disorders: Understanding Causes, Controversies, and Treatment.** Justine J. Reel, ed. Santa Barbara, Calif., Greenwood Press/ABC-CLIO, 2018. 2v. index. $198.00/set. ISBN 13: 978-1-4408-5300-5; 978-1-4408-5301-2 (e-book).

This two-volume set provides an alphabetical listing of eating disorders and their descriptions. Each listing is written by one of twenty contributors, including the editor, having backgrounds working in and researching the fields of health and psychology. The first volume contains entries A-M, and the second volume has entries N-Z. Each volume includes a complete list of content in both volumes, and also includes acknowledgments, a chronology, and an introduction. Editor Justine J. Reel uses the introduction to discuss her personal background and inspiration for creating *Eating Disorders,* and to provide a brief explanation of the set's contents. Researchers may find the chronology of eating disorders interesting; it provides historical references to eating disorders from the 1300s.

Reel states in the introduction that *Eating Disorders* can be used by either professionals or the general public to better understand problems with body image and food. All entries maintain a similar formatting style, but length and content vary. Some entries are significantly longer and subdivided into sections, while a few also include illustrative interviews. These interviews are with industry professionals and persons affected by eating disorders and each offers unique insight into specific topics. However, they are not listed separately either in the index or anywhere else in the volumes. At the end of each entry is a list of related topics found within the volumes, as well as a bibliography of referenced materials.

This two-volume set provides an easy-to-use alphabetical listing of eating disorders with comprehensive explanations in fairly short form. A glossary, directory of resources, information about the contributors, and a complete index is found at the end of the second volume. The resource directory lists books, journals, organizations, and websites. *Eating Disorders* is an excellent book for readers and researchers who are in the beginning stages of understanding eating disorders, treatment therapies, and organizations that specialize in helping those affected.—**Cynthia Goode**

784.   Newton, David E. **Eating Disorders in America: A Reference Handbook.** Santa Barbara, Calif., ABC-CLIO, 2019. 348p. illus. index. (Contemporary World Issues). $60.00. ISBN 13: 978-1-4408-5859-8; 978-1-4408-5860-4 (e-book).

Part of the Contemporary World Issues series from ABC-CLIO, this reference handbook focuses on eating disorders in America. The first two chapters define and describe the various eating disorders, their histories, backgrounds, and features: anorexia nervosa, bulimia nervosa, binge eating, ruminant disorder, orthorexia, pica, other specified feeding or eating disorder (OSFED), and avoidant/restrictive food intake disorder (ARFID). Extensive citations are provided for each of these disorders. The rest of the handbook includes a number of essays and perspectives by experts and psychologists, a number of profiles of well-known individuals such as Karen Carpenter who had one of these disorders along with various researchers and organizations whose work has advanced knowledge in these areas, and a large section of data and documents with tables and political amendments on this topic. An excellent resource and research handbook for any high school and college/university library.—**Bradford Lee Eden**

785.   Reel, Justine J. **Eating Disorders: Your Questions Answered.** Santa Barbara, Calif., Greenwood Press/ABC-CLIO, 2018. 145p. index. (Q&A Health Guides). $39.00. ISBN 13: 978-1-4408-5304-3; 978-1-4408-5305-0 (e-book).

This volume follows the structure for the Q & A Health Guides, including the excellent essay on health literacy common to the series. The topics covered explore not just food-related issues, but problems connected to exercise addiction, the impact of social media on body image, interconnections with sexuality, and underlying psychological issues. Although the volume does include a glossary, some important terms, such as body dysmorphia and ketogenic, are not included. However, the index is extensive, and readers can find page numbers for sections where the terms appear in the text. The content of the volume would be of interest to middle school students, but most middle schoolers would find it difficult to navigate the text. High school students and undergraduates are the ideal audience for the volume. The directory of resources includes monographs, journals, and websites. Only two of the five case studies deal with young adults.—**Delilah R. Alexander**

Infertility

786. Arenofsky, Janice. **Infertility Treatments.** Santa Barbara, Calif., Greenwood Press/ABC-CLIO, 2018. 208p. index. (Health and Medical Issues Today). $40.00. ISBN 13: 978-1-4408-5885-7; 978-1-4408-5886-4 (e-book).

Infertility Treatments is a single volume title and is part of the Health and Medical Issues series (approximately fourteen books in the series to date). The book's foreword describes books published in this series as a first step for students and lay people in obtaining a solid overview on controversial topics in health care for the 21st century. Past books in the series have addressed topics such as plastic surgery, cutting and self-harm, body size, bullying, suicide and metal health, and birth control.

Infertility Treatments offers information about specific health concerns of infertility and AFT or assisted fertility treatments. Technology advances such as genome mapping have expanded reproductive treatments. Topics covered in this volume include male and female causes of infertility, financial and legal concerns, medical treatments for infertility, adoption and alternative fertility therapies, and religious and ethical issues.

The book is organized in three sections: part one, containing background information and context (with chapters defining assisted reproductive technology, historical context, economic and legal implications, and the health-related consequences of various fertility procedures); part two, containing contemporary issues (including infertility stigma, and religious and ethical issues); and part three, case studies. The book contains narrative chapters within the three sections that are easy to read and nontechnical. Chapters have survey data and cited sources noted and woven into the narrative. There are no images or illustrations. The book concludes with a glossary, a timeline, sources for further information, and an index.

Infertility Treatments provides a basic introduction to assisted reproductive technology; like any medical source, one should consult with a physician for complete medical advice and information. This is a good introductory source, recommended for the circulating collection of a high school or public library collection.—**Caroline L. Gilson**

Obesity

787. Kelly, Evelyn B. **Obesity.** 2d ed. Santa Barbara, Calif., Greenwood Press/ABC-CLIO, 2018. 258p. index. (Health & Medical Issues Today). $40.00. ISBN 13: 978-1-4408-5881-9; 978-1-4408-5882-6 (e-book).

This second edition (the previous volume published in 2006) provides readers with updated information, coverage of new topics, and a revised third part that includes case studies. This book follows the structure of other titles in the Health & Medical Issues Today series. A series forward is followed by a preface, an overview and background section, a section on issues and controversies, and case studies. A glossary, timeline, suggestions for further resources, an index, and information about the author round out the work. The tone and diction in the volume vary dramatically from section to section, with paragraphs on "I-don't-care-itis" followed thirty pages later by a detailed model of the structure of a triglyceride molecule. Another drawback to the text is the hectoring tone, which emphasizes personal responsibility for physical exercise and appropriate lifestyle choices. Portions of the text featuring detailed scientific vocabulary would be useful for high school and college students doing medical research into obesity. Interesting facts about the history of eating disorders also appear.—**Delilah R. Alexander**

Sexually Transmitted Diseases

788.   Newton, David E. **STDs in the United States: A Reference Handbook.** Santa Barbara, Calif., ABC-CLIO, 2018. 350p. illus. index. $60.00. ISBN 13: 978-1-4408-5857-4; 978-1-4408-5858-1 (e-book).

Easy to read and comprehend, this reference book offers readers broad coverage about sexually transmitted diseases (STDs). Teens will get a glimpse into the history of STDs not only in modern times, but in the ancient world and the Middle Ages, as well. Treatment and origin of individual transmittable diseases is discussed. Problems, controversies, and solutions involving a variety of diseases—including gonorrhea, chlamydia, and syphilis—and such emerging STDs as lymphogranuloma are discussed. Taking the topic a step forward, the author has included a section allowing others to give perspectives on this growing epidemic. Along with data and statistics to be used for comparison, users will gain perspectives from a variety of people who have contributed to the field and groups that work to fight against this epidemic. Plenty of additional print and web resources are offered to further student research. Tables of information will deepen the user's understanding, while black-and-white photographs help introduce each chapter and allow the reader to see that anyone can get STDs. If a library could have only one resource for STDs, this would be one to consider. The book includes a list of additional resources and an index. Recommended.—**Karen Alexander**

789.   Quinn, Paul. **Sexually Transmitted Diseases: Your Questions Answered.** Santa Barbara, Calif., Greenwood Press/ABC-CLIO, 2018. 155p. index. (Q&A Health Guides). $39.00. ISBN 13: 978-1-4408-5316-6; 978-1-4408-5317-3 (e-book).

This excellent book provides important information in an accessible yet highly detailed fashion. All the volumes in this series follow the same general outline, including an opening eight-page essay on health literacy. Each also contains a brief sketch of five common myths related to the subject, case studies, a glossary, and an index. Over half the material falls under the heading "Different Types of STDs," covering nineteen different afflictions with straightforward medical information that includes references to websites for further research. A Directory of Resources expands on these outside sources. Both medical terminology and common slang terms are included so that readers can easily navigate social contexts and health professional settings. The tone is informative rather than alarming. High school and college students are the natural audience for the book, but any young or older adult with questions about sexual health would find the book helpful.—**Delilah R. Alexander**

Sleep Disorders

790.   Barone, Daniel A., and Lawrence A. Armour. **Let's Talk about Sleep: A Guide to Understanding and Improving Your Slumber.** Lanham, Md., Rowman & Littlefield, 2018. 182p. index. $33.00; $31.00 (e-book). ISBN 13: 978-1-5381-0398-2; 978-1-5381-0399-9 (e-book).

Let's Talk About Sleep: A Guide to Understanding and Improving Your Slumber is an empathetic resource book for sleep deprivation sufferers, a problem that afflicts a huge number of Americans. National Institutes of Health (NIH) statistics show that 50-70 million Americans suffer from chronic sleep disorders.

In our fast-paced, stressful society, adequate sleep is essential to productivity, a feeling of well-being, intellectual pursuits, and overall health. A balanced lifestyle is often difficult to achieve. According to the NIH, 1 in 25 Americans take prescribed medication to help them sleep, while more than one-third of Americans do not get enough sleep on a regular basis. Moreover, sleep disorders account for an estimated 16 billion dollars in medical costs annually. Indirect costs include absenteeism, decreased productivity, and related factors.

Thirteen well-organized chapters include bulleted formatting that enhances understanding and encourages further reading. The authors intertwine scholarly research, case studies, and clinical experience. The writing is clear and concise, and the fonts are easy to read. The use of case studies, notes, a glossary, a bibliography, and additional resources enhance reader understanding and support observations. Chapter titles motivate readers to explore related topics. The appropriate use of bolding within chapters helps organize paragraphs.

Public, high school, middle school, and college libraries will benefit by including this book in their collection.—**Thomas E. Baker**

Sports Medicine

791.   **Careers in Sports Medicine & Training.** Hackensack, N.J., Salem Press, 2018. 344p. illus. index. $125.00. ISBN 13: 978-1-68217-923-9; 978-1-68217-940-6 (e-book).

This straightforward career guide provides users with valuable information on 24 careers (ordered alphabetically) related to sports medicine and training. Each career is treated in an individual chapter that ranges in length from 3,500 to 4,500 words. Each chapter is arranged using the same format: career snapshot; overview; occupational specialties; work environment; education, training, and advancement; earnings and advancement; employment and outlook; selected schools; and more information. This material is enhanced by the use of black-and-white photographs, charts and tables, fun facts, famous firsts, and conversations with real people working in a particular profession. The reader comes away with valuable information, delivered in an easy-to-read and engaging way.

If a reader turns to this book for advice on a career in physical therapy, for example, she will learn that it is in the health science career cluster; that the average salary is $86,850 per year; that physical therapists interact with patients daily; that work typically takes place in rehabilitation facilities, hospitals, nursing homes, therapy clinics, and schools; that it is important to have excellent communication skills; that physical therapists earn master's or doctoral degrees after graduation from college; that physical therapy emerged as a profession during World War I; and much more. From the "Conversation With… Aracelly Latino-Feliz," the Founder/Director of Physical Therapy at The Movement Institute in Dania Beach, Florida, readers learn, among other things, that there are many job opportunities in physical therapy, that physical therapists need to be compassionate and patient, and that those interested in physical therapy should consider spending a day shadowing someone working in the profession. The book concludes with two appendixes, "Holland Code" (designed to help people determine their preferred work environment) and "General Bibliography," followed by an index. Recommended for public, school, and academic libraries.—**ARBA Staff Reviewer**

34 Technology

General Works

Dictionaries and Encyclopedias

792. **The SAGE Encyclopedia of Surveillance, Security, and Privacy.** Bruce A. Arrigo, ed. Thousand Oaks, Calif., Sage, 2018. 4v. $385.00/set. ISBN 13: 978-1-4833-5994-6; 978-1-4833-5992-2 (e-book).

This four-volume encyclopedia from SAGE casts a wide net, covering digital technology and how it impacts society. The set is international and includes hundreds of entries of varying lengths, some of which are subdivided. Entries contain *see also* references when necessary, as well as suggestions for further reading. The encyclopedia is arranged in an A-to-Z format, but, helpfully, there is a reader's guide in the front matter that lists topics covered under twelve topical categories/themes: Digital Cultures, Cybercommunities, and Simulated Selves; Ethical Issues and Research Directions in Surveillance, Security, and Privacy; History and Philosophy of Surveillance Studies; Industries and Institutions of Surveillance and/or Security; Place, Space & the Body; Security, Civil Liberties & the Law; Security, Governance, and Democracy; Surveillance and Everyday Life; Surveillance, Identity, and Controlling Populations; Surveillance, Security, and Privacy around the World; Tools, Practices, and Decisions of Surveillance and Security Politics; and Trade in Surveillance, the Business of Security, and Strategies of Dissent. The topics covered include some that might be obvious, such as: data mining, Facebook, Apple, botnets, email, social media, cookies, texting, identity theft, and the FBI. But there are unexpected entries as well: Franz Kafka, Narcissism, culture of fear, global justice, concentration and internment camps, Mexico, eugenics industrial complex, and Tea Party, to name a few. The coverage mostly focuses on the period since the mid-to-late 20th century, but there are exceptions. For instance, one entry lists the first ten amendments that comprise the Bill of Rights. Another focuses on espionage in ancient Egypt. Nevertheless, it is made clear to users why particular topics are included in this reference. An index rounds out the work. Highly recommended to academic and public libraries.—**ARBA Staff Reviewer**

Digital Resources

793.   **Broadband Map https://broadbandmap.fcc.gov.** [Website] Free. Date reviewed: 2019.

This site from the Federal Communications Commission (FCC) allows users to examine Fixed Broadband Deployment across the national map. It additionally provides generous data on providers and the population they serve. The site considers various technologies (e.g., cable modem, fixed wireless, satellite, and others) broadband speeds, locations, and more as it presents information via its map and other data visualizations. The About tab offers essential context for understanding the interactive map, including the Overview of FCC Broadband Map video. Users can also access Service Provider deployment and subscription data in addition to several reports including the Internet Access Services Report, the Mobile Competition Report, and others. Users can either enter a specific address in the Search by Address field or select from several tabs to Explore the Data. The Location tab requests a specific address in the search field, or users can hover over a location on the map which is shaded to reflect the Number of Fixed Residential Broadband Providers. For a selected location, the summary notes the available technology, speed, and provider information (company name, technology, speed). The Area summary provides county-wide information, and includes graphs relating population make up with broadband use. An Area Comparison creates a table comparing the percentage of population with broadband service (no providers, one or more, etc.) across states, counties, congressional districts, etc. The Providers tab offers details on up to three providers at a time and displays provider coverage overlap and population coverage. Entering a provider name (a list is provided) shows service area(s) on the national map as well as a chart showing percentage of population covered by selected provider and percentage of each provider's broadband footprint with each speed based on applicable technology (cable, fiber, etc.). Users can examine both download and upload speeds. The Broadband Map helps researchers, consumers, policy makers, and others understand how information is distributed across the U.S.—**ARBA Staff Reviewer**

794.   **Prior Art Archive https://www.priorartarchive.org.** [Website] Free. Date reviewed: 2019.

The Prior Art Archive, a joint project of Cisco and Massachusetts Institute of Technology, gathers an array of IT design and operations materials into one database to facilitate access to key foundational information that continues to influence current IT development. Created with the intent to mitigate an overcomplicated patenting process and the issuance of bad patents on old or obvious technology, the site offers instruction manuals, reference materials, and more for key IT components and systems. Users enter a search term(s) in the central field to access the database. Once inside, the search results can be filtered by Date Range, File Type (PDF, web page), and File Source. Materials, which can be sorted by date or relevance, are presented by topic or document title, with a brief document excerpt, source, date uploaded, date originally published, and relevant Customs Procedure Codes (CPC). Users can find documents with titles such as Protocol Translator Configuration and Reference, Router Products Command Reference, Fast Ethernet Interface Processor Installation and Configuration, NetFlow Services Solutions Guide, and much more. While straightforward in design, the website requires that users have a general idea of what they are searching for to access the database as there are no basic browsing options. The site is not comprehensive—users (with registration) continue to contribute documents. Still, the expansive database would be a valuable resource for patent lawyers, engineers, designers, and others in the tech industry.—**ARBA Staff Reviewer**

Handbooks and Yearbooks

795.   Carrier, Mark. **From Smartphones to Social Media: How Technology Affects Our Brains and Behavior.** Santa Barbara, Calif., Greenwood Press/ABC-CLIO, 2018. 280p. $94.00. ISBN 13: 978-1-4408-5178-0; 978-1-4408-5179-7 (e-book).

Each of the ten chapters follows roughly the same outline, beginning with a case study and ending with a brief interview with a researcher from that particular area, such as social relationships, electronic aggression, and emotions. The focus is on compiling and analyzing research from the past decade in order to narrow down the enormous amount of research now available. However, some case studies are drawn from research in the 1990s, and the experts interviewed refer to older research. The first chapter contains a glossary, and a second, longer glossary with some overlap can be found following the last chapter. An extensive index and list of resources can help readers who want to concentrate on one issue, and the text itself includes helpful cross-references to other chapters where similar material is discussed. High school and college students will find the reference book easy to use.—**Delilah R. Alexander**

Computers

796.   **Computer History Museum. http://www.computerhistory.org/.** [Website] Free. Date reviewed: 2018.

The Computer History Museum is a vital repository of historical documents, objects, videos, and other materials which work to tell the story of computer technology. Users can learn about the museum archive and examine some items up close via the Collections tab on the homepage. The best way to access the database is through the Catalog Search. Once users enter a search term or phrase (e.g., Windows, floppy disk, video games), they are able to browse related museum holdings as organized by Physical Object, Text, Audio, Still Image, Moving Image, Software, or All. While the database remains an excellent inventory of the more than one hundred thousand items in the full museum collections, it is important to note that many items have not been digitized. Some items are accompanied by a thumbnail image (can be enlarged), a PDF, or video clip. Highlights from the digital archive include the signed motherboard which helped power the first of Facebook's open computer servers, an array of floppy disk drives, a Magnavox Odyssey Video Game System, some of the earliest ipods, a Pac Man tabletop game, and more. Other significant collections within the archive can be accessed via links on the left side of the homepage. The Fairchild Notebooks reference some of the earliest work on microelectronics which paved the way for significant breakthroughs in semiconductor development and manufacturing. Two hundred and sixty-four marketing brochures advertise data processing systems, printers, personal computers, software, and other items, reflecting the ephemera of the business side of computers. The Gwen Bell Collection is a compelling archive of the earliest calculating machines such as a proportional compass from 1680, the Burroughs Adding Machine from 1910, and a host of slide rules, integrators, encryption device parts, toy robots, typewriters, pocket watches, planimeters, and much more. Oral Histories provide transcripts and video interviews with individuals affiliated with the world of computers. Users can listen to Grace Hopper, naval officer and computer scientist; Mark Mothersbaugh, technopop musician; Pitch Johnson, Silicon Valley venture capitalist; and many others. Although the site would benefit from digitizing more of its collection, there is nonetheless ample material.—**ARBA Staff Reviewer**

797.   **Principles of Programming & Coding.** Hackensack, N.J., Salem Press, 2018. 362p. illus. index. $165.00. ISBN 13: 978-1-68217-676-4; 978-1-68217-677-1 (e-book).

This recent installment in Salem Press's Principles of series begins with an editor's introduction which explains the basics of programming and coding, provides an overview of the computer evolution, and outlines the contents of the book. A list of contributors precedes the approximately 140 entries arranged in alphabetic order. Most entries contain the following: fields of study, abstract, principal terms, and a bibliography. The text explains the background and significance of the topic to programming and coding and also describes the way a process works or how a procedure is related to writing effective code and programs. Topics include, among many others, autonomic computing, control systems, cowboy coding, data mining, drones, extreme programming, firewalls, interactive constructs, motherboards, network security, prototyping, rational choice theory, signal processing, test doubles, variables and values, and working memory. Entries are approximately one to three pages and are enhanced by black-and-white photos, sample problems, charts, and graphs. Not all entries focus on the scientific and technical facets of programming and coding. For instance, there are entries for crowdfunding and crowdsourcing, digital divide, digital native, e-learning, net neutrality, objectivity, and privacy rights. The book includes an annotated "Time Line of Inventions and Advancements in Programming and Coding," which starts in 1948 and runs to 2014, a glossary of terms, a bibliography, and an index. This book provides a solid introduction to the topic of programming and coding.—**ARBA Staff Reviewer**

Internet

798.   **Internet Abuses and Privacy Rights.** Bronx, N.Y., H. W. Wilson, 2017. 216p. illus. index. (The Reference Shelf, volume 89, number 2). $75.00pa. ISBN 13: 978-1-68217-452-4.

Like other books in this six-volume set, this work presents texts (thirty-one in this case) from a variety of sources that examine issues concerning privacy and safety on the internet. The sources include magazines, blogs, NPR and PBS programs, and website articles, from Slate.com and other sites. All were first published in 2016 or 2017. There are five sections, each with a brief introduction: Personal Cybersecurity, Net Neutrality and Government Surveillance, New Challenges to Privacy, Internet News and Accountability, and The Power and Influence of Technology. The articles run from two to fourteen pages. Considering the focus of this book, many of the pieces present the risks and dangers facing users of the internet, particularly the threats to the safety of individuals' personal information. While some passages presume some prior knowledge of the internet's functioning, many are accessible to the broad audience interested in or concerned about the issues presented here. From "fake news" and its effect on people's behavior and political decisions, to the various aspects of net neutrality, this selection of texts presents a number of topics worthy of the public's attention, particularly in the recent light of the Facebook revelations concerning personal information being used to affect the 2016 presidential election.

This text will be a useful addition to public, school and academic libraries, and they all should consider placing it in their collections. Unfortunately, the copyediting is at times mediocre: the four-page preface and other texts have several minor errors that become a distraction when reading. Curiously, the two-page "Index" has only proper names, including forty-four references to Donald Trump and twenty-six references to Hillary Clinton, but no mention of other names found in the text, or any reference to "network neutrality" or any other important subject terms related to this topic. This format for the index appears in all the Reference Shelf volumes.—**Mark Schumacher**

Medical Technology

799. **Health Technology Sourcebook.** Greg Mullin, ed. Detroit, Omnigraphics, 2018. 516p. index. (Health Reference Series). $85.00. ISBN 13: 978-0-7808-1591-9.

This volume in the comprehensive Health Reference Series provides up-to-date information about a range of healthcare technology related to such topics as preventative, diagnostic, and assistive treatments and research. The reference is designed to inform general readers, patients, nonprofessional caregivers, family members, and others about complex and rapidly advancing technologies in a clear and concise way.

The volume is organized into nine sections filled with a range of topical chapters. It begins with a good overview of healthcare technology in general (e.g., descriptions of Telehealth, general benefits of e-health, etc.) and then proceeds to address Technology and Preventative Healthcare, Diagnostic Technology, The Role of Technology in Treatment, Rehabilitation and Assistive Technologies, and Health Information Technology. Later sections discuss Legal and Ethical Concerns and the Future of Health Technology, while a closing section offers a glossary of terms and a directory of related agencies.

Individual chapters within each broader section are further segmented into specific topics. Chapters within the Diagnostic Technology section, for example, detail the latest technology behind such things as the Electrocardiogram, MRI, Mammogram, Nuclear Medicine, Virtual Colonoscopy, and Live Cell Imaging. Other topics examine Space Technologies in the Rehabilitation of Movement Disorders, Digital Health Records, Robotics, Health Information Technology Legislation and Regulations, and much more. Topic discussion may include definitions, pros and cons, trends, and examples of use.

The material is clear and concise and employs the generous use of short paragraphs, headers and subheaders, bullet points, and other tools for ease of navigation. While the information in the volume is copious, it is always targeted toward the general reader and thus never overwhelms. This first edition reference tackles a complex aspect of healthcare, providing current information in a straightforward way.—**ARBA Staff Reviewer**

Robotics

800.   Newton, David E. **Robots: A Reference Handbook.** Santa Barbara, Calif., ABC-CLIO, 2018. 340p. illus. index. (Contemporary World Issues). $60.00. ISBN 13: 978-1-4408-5861-1; 978-1-4408-5862-8 (e-book).

Dating back more than 2,000 years, automata/robots have had a place in cultures worldwide. The opening chapter of this book traces that history into the 21st century. The next chapter (some 67 pages) examines "Problems, Controversies, and Solutions," looking at topics including the impact of robots now and in the future on human employment and human life generally. The "Perspectives" section then presents 8 brief essays, by various authors, on the diverse places and roles of robotics in today's world. The "Profiles" text offers 24 entries on individuals and organizations of importance to the evolution and growth of robotics. Leonardo da Vinci and Heron, a figure from 1st-century Alexandria (Egypt), are among the earliest individuals discussed. A final section on "Data and Documents" contains 5 tables and 13 documents from the last 20 years, including legislation, legal cases, and various government reports. A 48-page bibliography ("Resources") and the reference lists from the first 2 chapters offer many resources, both print and online, for readers to explore the subject further.

Copy editing is regretfully disappointing; misspelled or misused words and incorrect subject/verb agreement are too frequent. That said, there is much fascinating and useful information about robots and robotics, past and present. Since this technology will grow in importance in the years to come, most academic, public, and school libraries should consider adding this book.—**Mark Schumacher**

35 Physical Sciences and Mathematics

Physical Sciences

General Works

801. **The Einstein Papers Project. http://www.einstein.caltech.edu/.** [Website] Free. Date reviewed: 2018.

The Einstein Papers Project consolidates a large collection of correspondence, diary entries, scientific writings, and more connected to renowned physicist Albert Einstein. Users can examine a volume series of organized and annotated transcriptions or explore a database of primary source materials. The database is accessible via the Resources tab on the menu bar or more directly via the Einstein Archives Online link on the left column of the homepage. It is highly recommended that users first read the Tips for Searching the Database Fields as users need to keyword search through eight fields (full text, title, persons, etc.) to access the records. Manuscripts, correspondence, lecture notes, speeches, newspaper clippings, and many other raw materials are cataloged with archival call number, relevant date(s), main author, language, document type, and other information. There may also be a listing of links to Similar Items. The Finding Aid link offers added contextual information in terms of exploring the database, such as Einstein's Biographical Timeline. While users are able to gather basic information on many artifacts, it is important to note that many items are not accompanied by digital images and permission must be requested to examine others. There is a link to the Gallery, offering a tour of collection highlights (ideal as finding artifacts with digital images is somewhat difficult). However, the link is, as of this review, blank. Examining the materials under both the Collected Papers of Albert Einstein and the Digital Einstein tab on the menu bar is perhaps a bit more satisfying experience. These links lead to the annotated full text of 400 writings of Einstein, over 3,000 letters to and from him, and over 2,500 abstracts. This collection is organized into 14 designated volumes in the original German, many with English translation supplements. Users can scroll through a gallery of volumes and click on a title to access a table of contents and the writings which span roughly 46 years. Users will find correspondence with colleagues and family, academic papers, research notes and much documentation on his groundbreaking scientific theories. The site as a whole is a good digital launching point into the story of one of the greatest minds of the 20th century. Although the Einstein Archive is somewhat cumbersome to use, the well-organized volumes within the Digital Einstein portion of the site are well worth examination.—**ARBA Staff Reviewer**

Earth and Planetary Sciences

Astronomy and Space Sciences

802. Dickinson, Terence. **Hubble's Universe: Greatest Discoveries and Latest Images.** 2d ed. New York, Firefly Books, 2017. 332p. illus. index. $35.00. ISBN 13: 978-1-77085-997-5.

This is an updated and expanded edition of a title that first published in 2012. The author, Terence Dickinson, has written 15 astronomy books, served as a former editor of *SkyNews,* and was staff astronomer at McLaughlin Planetarium at Royal Ontario Museum and Strasenburgh Planetarium in Rochester, New York. The book is comprised of hundreds of color, captioned photographs taken by Hubble since it launched in 1990, but there is also a good deal of astronomical information in the book's 11 chapters: "Hubble's Universe"; "Hubble's Top Science Accomplishments"; "Crucibles of Creation"; "Starry Tapestry"; "Blaze of Glory"; "Hubble's Invisible Universe"; "Empires of Stars"; "Neighbor Worlds: The Planets"; "Hubble's Strange Universe"; and "Hubble Update: 2012-2017." In these chapters, readers will learn about such things as the launch of Hubble, its mission, the replacement of equipment over the years, black hole discoveries, and the presence of dark matter. The book concludes with two pages on the James Webb Space Telescope that will replace Hubble when launched, a page of resources, and an index. Recommended for public libraries.—**ARBA Staff Reviewer**

Geology

803. Bryan, T. Scott. **Geysers of Yellowstone.** 5th ed. Louisville, Colo., University Press of Colorado, 2018. 590p. illus. maps. index. $24.95pa. ISBN 13: 978-1-60732-839-1; 978-1-60732-840-7 (e-book).

Following up on the first four, author T. Scott Bryan (Emeritus, Victor Valley Community College) provides an updated fifth edition to this important work documenting geyser location and activity through 2017 in Wyoming's Yellowstone National Park. The last edition published in 2008 (see ARBA 2009, entry 1322). In an appendix, supplementary information on other worldwide geyser fields is also provided. Organized in 13 chapters and 589 pages, the first chapter informs readers about basic geyser characteristics and behavior while chapter 2 provides background information specific to the geysers found within Yellowstone. Both chapters contain supporting figures. Chapters 3 through 12 provide specific information on geyser location and activity within the park; first organized by named geyser basin and then by named geyser group or complex within a basin. The final chapter follows up with descriptions and locations of 18 miscellaneous geyser areas within the park. Most of the geyser locational information is accompanied by maps and black-and-white photographs. Navigation through portions of the book may be difficult for some readers. All the geyser locational maps are numbered but are not accompanied with short descriptive texts linking them to the corresponding geyser group(s) descriptions. Additionally, black-and-white photographs are found throughout the work and are accompanied by short descriptive texts linking them to geysers and geyser groups; however, they are not numbered or cross-referenced in either the table of contents or the index. Thankfully, all of the tables provided are numbered and accompanied by a short descriptive text and are identified in the table of contents. Finally, although map numbers identify the location of the majority of the described geysers, maps showing some locations are not available for their corresponding geyser groups (e.g., Rabbit Creek Hot Springs, Imperial Group). A glossary and index are provided as well as a list of suggested readings.—**Jennifer Brooks Huffman**

804.   **Encyclopedia of Geochemistry: A Comprehensive Reference Source on the Chemistry of the Earth.** William M. White, ed. New York, Springer Publishing, 2018. 1557. illus. index. (Encyclopedia of Earth Science Series). $499.00. ISBN 13: 978-3-319-39311-7; 978-3-319-39312-1 (e-book).

Under the editorship of William M. White, 300 area experts (listed in the front matter along with their affiliations) cover more than 330 topics associated with the vast topic of geochemistry. Articles are arranged in an A-Z format (from Ab ignitio Calculations to Zirconium) and vary in length depending on the topic. For example, copper, Fick's Law, incompatible elements, lithophile elements, oil shale, silicon, and supergene are approximately 1-2 pages. Entries like mineralogy, halogens, krypton, and entropy are treated in approximately 4-6 pages, and coal, xenon isotopes, ozone and stratospheric chemistry, and atmospheric evolution get longer articles. Articles are subdivided depending on length and provide supplemental tables, figures, and equations. All entries are signed and include reference sources and cross-references. The encyclopedia concludes with an author index and a subject index. Recommended for academic libraries.—**ARBA Staff Reviewer**

Oceanography

805.   **Allen Coral Atlas http://allencoralatlas.org/.** [Website] Free. Date reviewed: 2019.

The Allen Coral Atlas allows a virtual exploration of five distinct coral reefs, displaying geomorphic and benthic features over a global satellite image map. Users can presently examine reefs at Heron Island (Australia), Mo'orea (central pacific), Karimunjawa (Indonesia), West Hawaii, Lighthouse Reef (western Caribbean), and Kayankerni reef (Sri Lanka). In the near future the site will incorporate data for all tropical shallow coral reefs. The FAQ tab links to the project timeline with the goal of complete coral reef mapping, an expanded glossary, and more by the fall of 2020. Users can access the map via the Explore the Atlas or Atlas tabs, then use the menu on the right side of the page to incorporate Data Layers. Colored markings reflect a Benthic Analysis of the selected reef, indicating reef composition such as rubble, sand, seagrass, and breaking waves. Colors also mark the Geomorphic Analysis of the reef region, describing features such as an open complex lagoon, reef rim, slope, land, and plateau. Users can click the Legend link to access the full listing of each of the Geomorphic Zones and Benthic classes incorporated into the atlas. Adding the Satellite Coral Reef Mosaic layer incorporates a more complete satellite view of the reef area while omitting it allows users to examine the selected reef in isolation. The Bathymetry tab indicates a surrounding ocean depth reading. A small icon next to the reef location name accesses its data particulars. These include selected, mapped, and filtered area of entire reef in square kilometers; relevant ocean depth in meters; and specific measurements and percentages for all applicable geomorphic zones and benthic classes. For example, Heron Island contains 3.73 square kilometers of deep lagoon, which is 5.83 percent of the total reef area measured, and 15.4 square kilometers of sand, which accounts for 24.06 percent of total area measured. As the Allen Coral Atlas continues to develop, it will be a useful tool for students and educators of environmental and marine sciences in addition to policy makers and conservationists around the globe.—**ARBA Staff Reviewer**

Paleontology

806.   Carlton, Robert L. Oleniacz, Brittany A., ed. **A Concise Dictionary of Paleontology.** New York, Springer Publishing, 2018. 322p. $249.00. ISBN 13: 978-3-319-73054-7; 978-3-319-73055-4 (e-book).

This dictionary is designed for beginning students in the field; thus, the author and technical editor took care to make the language as accessible as possible and to keep the theoretical concepts to a minimum. The author points out that this dictionary fills a gap in the field between books that are too specialized or too generalized to be considered comprehensive. This dictionary covers the most important paleontological terms, taxonomy, concepts, and localities. Entries vary in length from one sentence to several paragraphs. The use of *see* and *see also* references makes navigation an easy task. Entries include classification and other relationships first, then a physical description and information on collecting localities and chonostratigraphic position. Entries for descriptive terms include only terms used in the dictionary. A bibliography rounds out the work. Recommended for academic libraries.—**ARBA Staff Reviewer**

Mathematics

Handbooks & Yearbooks

807.   **The Best Writing on Mathematics 2018.** Mircea Pitici, ed. Princeton, N.J., Princeton University Press, 2018. 250p. illus. $24.95pa. ISBN 13: 978-0-691-18276-6.

Pitici, professor of advanced calculus at Syracuse University, outlined in the introduction to the ninth annual installment of *The Best Writing on Mathematics 2018* that the aim of this text is to reach a wide audience with articles—18 total—from authors of diverse backgrounds.

Though the title implies content heavy in mathematical theories, such is not the case. While there is a collection of articles that delve deep into game theory, numeration, the mischievousness of chance, and other paradoxes, there is also an engaging discussion on disciplinary disagreements on probability and the challenge of being a writing mathematician.

The text opens with a refreshing reflection on mathematics' contribution to humanity by Frances Su, past President of the Mathematical Association of America. Pitici then balances the arrangement of articles so that the middle of the text is deeper in mathematical concepts than the beginning or end, easing the reader in and then out, ending on a light note while never sacrificing the mathematical import of each article.

True to Pitici's interdisciplinary approach, other articles cover modeling, the essentials of problem solving, and active learning strategies. For mathematicians who are also cloaked as historians, Pitici includes writings that feed their passion, too—from a contextual reflection on Eugene P. Wigner, to the intersection between physics and mathematics, an examination of mathematic writings by Ancient Babylonians, and the mathematics of World War II.

As in the previous editions, Pitici closes with a bibliography of notable writings and more, also from 2017.—**Heather Freas Adair**

36 Resource Sciences

Energy

Handbooks and Yearbooks

808. **Careers in Green Energy.** Hackensack, N.J., Salem Press, 2018. 362p. illus. index. $125.99. ISBN 13: 978-1-68217-922-2; 978-1-68217-936-9 (e-book).

The U.S. Department of Energy (DOE) reports annual increases in energy employment positions. Moreover, approximately 6.4 million Americans work in the energy sector. Career options are diverse and include numerous interesting fields: computers, engineering, architecture, construction, and urban planning. This title has 23 alphabetically arranged chapters on green energy careers that that range in length from 3,500 to 4,500 words. Chapters include: Snapshot, Sphere of Work, Work Environment, Duties and Responsibilities, Occupational Specialties, Physical Environment, Employment Outlook, Conversations With (interviews with professionals in the career), Education, and more. Some of the careers included are civil engineer, energy engineer, industrial engineer, meteorologist, renewable energy technician, solar energy system installer, wind energy engineer, and heating and cooling technician. There are "Fun Facts" throughout (e.g., in the mining and geological engineer section, readers learn that cell phones contain more than 35 minerals). Creative design layouts, easy-to-read fonts, charts, tables, and bullet formatting peak interest and hook readers. Additionally, the subject index assists readers in their examination of concepts, technologies, terms, and specific occupations. There are two appendixes: "Holland Code," designed to help students choose the right career, and "General Bibliography." *Careers in Green Energy* supports positive career exploration journeys. Well-versed library acquisitions decision-makers understand the importance of books about encourage youthful inquiries and interactive involvement. This book is specifically for high school and undergraduate students. Recommended.—**Thomas E. Baker**

809. **Handbook of Energy Politics.** Jennifer I. Considine and Paik Keun-Wook, eds. Northampton, Mass., Edward Elgar, 2018. 496p. index. $260.00. ISBN 13: 978-1-78471-229-7; 978-1-78471-230-3 (e-book).

This book offers advanced analyses of the many aspects of the geopolitics of energy. Worldwide in scope, the studies range from environmental issues affecting natural gas development in British Columbia and energy security in the Republic of Korea to Sino-Russian natural gas cooperation and economic development led by the natural resources in Sub-Saharan Africa. This breadth of coverage is mirrored by the fact that the authors work in twelve different countries, from Canada to Singapore. The text is arranged in five parts. The first two examine aspects of the demand and supply sides of the energy industry. Part three studies "influences in geopolitics," while sections four and five look at financial markets in the energy industry and environmental issues. Documentation of the research presented is incredibly substantial. One chapter has more than 150 items in its bibliography, mostly government documents, while another has 149 notes and more than 120 items in the bibliography. As one would expect, many items are internet-accessible items. (A note: There are hundreds of abbreviations throughout the volume: "The accounting standards are promulgated by IIRC, IRRC, SASB, CIMA, ICAEW, CDSB." (p. 311) Many of them are not explained or spelled out. Occasionally the reader finds an explanation elsewhere, but a separate list would be quite helpful.) The back cover of the book states that it is "invaluable for upper-level graduates and postgraduates of public policy and environmental politics," presumably using British terms. The text also mentions that policy-makers will benefit. In the American setting, universities with programs in these fields or special libraries devoted to energy or public policy will find it useful. Background knowledge will be helpful for understanding the more detailed aspects of this research.—**Mark Schumacher**

810.   **The Oxford Handbook of Energy and Society.** Debra J. Davidson and Matthias Gross, eds. New York, Oxford University Press, 2018. 600p. index. $150.00. ISBN 13: 978-0-19-063385-1.

This installment in the Oxford Handbooks series was produced under the guidance of editors Debra J. Davidson, professor of Environmental Sociology in the department of Resource Economics and Environmental Sociology at the University of Alberta, and Matthias Gross, professor of Environmental Sociology at Helmholtz Centre for Environmental Research in Leipzig and at the University of Jena, Germany. Following information about the editors and academic contributors is an introductory chapter "A Time of Change, A Time for Change: Energy-Society Relations in the Twenty-First Century." This introductory material discusses such big topics as the continually increasing hunger for energy in the world, the politics of climate change, and attitudes about the transition to renewable energy sources. It also explains the rationale of the organization of the book into seven parts: Key Contemporary Dynamics and Theoretical Contributions; The Persistent Material and Geopolitical Relevance of Fossil Fuels; Consumption Dynamics; Perspectives on Energy Equity and Energy Poverty; Energy and Publics; Energy (Re)takes Center Stage in Politics; and Emerging Trends in the Energy-Society Relationship. The volume valuably provides international coverage (though skewed toward Western societies) in chapters that include "Energy, Climate Change, and Global Governance: The 2015 Paris Agreement in Perspective"; "Energy Markets and Trading"; "Shifts in Energy Consumption Driven by Urbanization"; "Industrializing Countries as the New Energy Consumers"; and "Are We on the Cusp of a Global Renewable Energy Transition?" Chapters include works cited and suggestions for further reading. This volume is also available in Oxford Handbooks Online. Recommended for academic libraries.—**ARBA Staff Reviewer**

Environmental Science

Biography

811.   **American Environmental Leaders: From Colonial Times to the Present.** 3d ed. Anne Becher and Joseph Richey, eds. Amenia, N.Y., Grey House Publishing, 2018. 2v. illus. index. $255.00/set. ISBN 13: 978-1-68217-731-0; 978-1-68217-732-7 (e-book).

This third edition (see ARBA 2009, entry 1331) is comprised of 2 substantial volumes that paint a comprehensive portrait of environmental efforts since the colonial era. Moreover, the comprehensive collection takes an interdisciplinary approach. Inside the 2 volumes, users will find biographies of 499 men and women (scientists, advocates, businessmen, musicians, and many others). Entries range in length (1-4 pages) and include life dates and bibliographies. Volume 1 has an introduction and list of contributors (there are 47 in total, 6 of whom are new), and volume 2 appendixes include: "Table of Contents," "Introduction to Key Documents," a "Timeline of American Environmentalism," and an "Index." Both the timeline and index are updated. The set makes generous use of photograph images—a bonus for readers. The verso (left page) and recto (right side) are of the same size, aspect ratio, and appropriately centered—basic units of excellent book design. The margins and fonts are both practical and aesthetically pleasing. *American Environmental Leaders: From Colonial Times to the Present* serves the needs of a broad readership and is highly recommended for public, school, and academic libraries.—**Thomas E. Baker**

Dictionaries and Encyclopedias

812.   **Environmental Health in the 21st Century: From Air Pollution to Zoonotic Diseases.** Richard Crume, ed. Santa Barbara, Calif., Greenwood Press/ABC-CLIO, 2018. 2v. illus. index. $198.00/set. ISBN 13: 978-1-4408-4364-8; 978-1-4408-4365-5 (e-book).

Environmental disasters are common, and the current relaxation of regulations will increase them. This new encyclopedia examines current environmental health issues in an accessible format. The editor and contributors are professionals working in various aspects of environmental science. The alphabetical entries cover a wide range of such topics as: environmental pollution (aviation emissions, drinking water quality, and regulation); health sciences (allergens in the environment, respiratory disease, and air pollution); energy and climate (carbon dioxide and the carbon cycle, ocean acidification); waste management (biodegradable materials, health benefits of, recycling); and built environment (ambient air quality, sick building syndrome). An appendix offers steps to reducing your environmental exposure, and a glossary and directory of resources provide further information for research. Alphabetical and topical lists of entries and a derailed index make it easy to locate material. With information on topics ranging from antibiotic resistance to zoonotic diseases, this easy-to-use resource is very useful for public and school libraries.—**Barbara M. Bibel**

813.   **The Gale Encyclopedia of Environmental Health.** 2d ed. Jacqueline L. Longe, ed. Farmington Hills, Mich., Gale/Cengage Learning, 2019. 2v. illus. index. $535.00/set. ISBN 13: 978-1-4103-8823-0; 978-1-4103-8826-1 (e-book).

Hurricanes, chemical spills, antibiotic resistance, and contaminated foods are among the issues considered when discussing environmental health. The 2d edition of this encyclopedia from Gale contains 283 articles covering this important topic. Thirty of them are new. The alphabetical entries provide information on historic, natural, and manmade environmental health events. The articles are written by health professionals, academics, and science writers. They include color photographs, textboxes with definitions of key terms, interesting historical information, and questions to ask physicians as well as resource lists of online and print information and organizations. Topics covered include environmental health crises (acid rain, drought), organizations and legislation (UNICEF, Occupational Health and Safety Act), and diseases and conditions (ammonia exposure, emergent diseases). Among the new entries are those on Ebola virus disease, Stockholm planetary boundaries, water scarcity, Nipah virus disease, and Zika virus disease. The entries are comprehensive, ranging in length from 1 to 12 pages. The articles on environmental crises and diseases include a definition, description, demographics, causes and symptoms, common diseases and disorders, treatment, public health role and response, prognosis, and prevention. Those on organizations and legislation include a definition, purpose, demographics, description, results, research and general acceptance, interactions, complications, aftercare, and parental concerns. The book begins with a chronology of major environmental health events from 165 to 2018. It ends with a list of organizations, a glossary, and a comprehensive index.

With articles on contemporary issues such as climate change, food safety, and traveler's health as well as fracking and Gulf War Syndrome, this will be a useful resource for students with assignments as well as anyone interested in the environment or public health.—**Barbara M. Bibel**

Digital Resources

814.   **Green Living Online https://www.greenlivingonline.com.** [Website] Free. Date reviewed: 2019.

Green Living Online brings important concepts of social and environmental responsibility to consumers, showing them practical ways to incorporate these ideas into their everyday lives. The site offers content related to numerous topics in addition to a variety of blogs that reflect the latest information on a range of sustainable living ideas. Green Living Online is designed for browsing, with its ample use of color photos and large selection of topics from which to choose, including Food, Home & Garden, Fashion & Gear, Health & Beauty, Transport & Travel, and Natural Resources. Users simply select from the tab relevant to their interest, or, alternatively, conduct a search from the bar in the top right corner of the homepage. Food primarily offers a selection of healthy and easy-to-prepare recipes focused on fresh fruits and vegetables, such as an enoki mushroom salad. Home & Garden offers landscape tips in mind of sustainability (e.g., drought and wildlife consideration), with posts such as "Eco responsible landscaping tips" and "Guide to natural spring cleaning." Fashion & Gear features articles such as "Healthy skin care," "Eco-chic fashion," and "Back to school the greener way." Health & Beauty offers

"Aromatherapy for healthy skin," "Grow your own healing herbs," and "Keeping drugs out of our drinking water." Transport & Travel featured pieces such as "Going carless" and "7 easy ways to green your commute" while Natural Resources offers information on "Greener home computing," "Ten ways to use the sun's energy," and more. Some of the content applies regionally to the Ontario region of Canada; however, many articles would appeal to consumers worldwide. While topics focus mainly on advice for everyday living, larger issues are addressed as well (albeit in a more cursory way) from energy independence and energy efficiency to climate change and global food security.—**ARBA Staff Reviewer**

815.   **Project Toxic Docs https://www.toxicdocs.org.** [Website] Free. Date reviewed: 2019.

Project Toxic Docs allows access to millions of pages of previously hidden corporate documents about toxic contaminants, with the goal of corporate accountability and consumer education. The project has unearthed and digitized meeting notes, internal memos, emails, board minutes, expert witness testimony, and more related to corporations such as Monsanto, Dow Chemical, Mobil Oil, Alcoa, and DuPont in particular regards to their treatment of asbestos, polyvinyl chloride, benzene, silica, and lead.

Users can conduct a general search from the prominent bar or can incorporate information regarding Year Range, Toxic Substance, Firm, or Special Collection information into an advanced search. The Special Collection designation refers to particular issues such as Asbestos and Railroads, South Africa, New PCB files, and Poison Papers. The Advanced Search option is recommended to narrow the display options within the millions of pages.

Documents are presented as a straightforward gallery with little if any contextual information. Users can scroll down through the gallery, and for each document, side scroll through its pages in a thumbnail view. Users can alternatively view documents in a reader, download, or favorite for future reference. Users will encounter a range of documents including, but not limited to, reports on resident relocations due to area contaminants, letters between the Environmental Protection Agency and various offenders, whistleblower letters exposing violations, and cover-ups.

Project Toxic Docs helps bring corporate accountability and the environmental and social impact of industry—a crucial issue today—to light.—**ARBA Staff Reviewer**

816.   **Threatened Island Biodiversity Database http://tib.islandconservation.org/.** [Website] Free. Date reviewed: 2019.

The Threatened Island Biodiversity Database tracks islands and island groups around the world where biodiversity is at risk, presenting information on island-breeding vertebrate animal species that are considered either critically endangered or endangered on the International Union for Conservation of Nature (IUCN) Red List, a definitive gauge of species preservation. The database also includes several species listed as Extinct in the Wild and local seabirds of vulnerable status. From the homepage, users can select the Explore Map tab to access the interactive map database. Users can search the database by geographic location (region, country, or island), threatened species, or invasive species. A threatened species search can be filtered by type, order, family, Red List status, and/or scientific or common name, while invasive species parameters include type and/or scientific or common name. Alternatively, users can select a dot on the map to find a particular island or archipelago before selecting the Island Details tab on the right side of the map. Available information includes location Name, Coordinates, Region, Country, Archipelago, (number of) Threatened Species, Invasive Species, Eradication, and Human Population range. Users can click on species types to find more detail, including current Red List status for Threatened Species. A thumbnail gallery contains links to further information and images for select species. The database contains information for the Macaroni Penguin of the South Shetland Islands, the Turks & Caicos Ground Iguana, the Vancouver Island Marmot, the Canary Islands shrew, and many others. For more explanation of database terms, users can find definitions related to animal groups and their present and historic breeding status under the More Info link at the top of the map. This easy-to-navigate database would be a valuable resource for educators and students.—**ARBA Staff Reviewer**

817. **Urban Mine Platform www.urbanmineplatform.eu/.** [Website] Free. Date reviewed: 2019.

This website publishes data on vehicles, batteries, and electrical and electronic equipment (EEE) for twenty-eight members of the European Union (EU) plus Switzerland and Norway. In particular, the platform examines composition, stores, and waste flows of these products. Users can consider a number of parameters when viewing and/or utilizing data. The site is generally easy to navigate, with users able to select from a menu on the left side of the page or from the clearly marked tabs in the center. Essentially, for each type (Vehicles, Batteries, EEE) of product, users can find data regarding their movement from market to stock to waste (Urban Mine), specified material elements (Compositions), and Waste Flows (including some recycling data). Users can learn broad information about the industries or hone in on a particular EU nation's data. Colorful bar charts tally a range of information, including the number of battery cells put on the market (broken down into types such as lithium-based, rechargeable lithium, nickel-cadmium, and lead-based acid); the amount of waste generated in kilotons for cables, magnetrons, refrigerants, thermostats, specified solar cells, and other items; the percentage of vehicles including diesel, petrol, hybrid electric, natural gas, and others that are leaving the stock; and much more. Charts may encompass some twenty years of data, and may also include projected data. Charts may also include explanations, and users can access extensive metadata and information on base surveys and other source documents via the More Information button in the lower right corner of each chart page. Also at the bottom of the page, users can access the Final Report—the ProSUM project—and a short glossary. The data on the Urban Mine Platform may be most useful for college-level coursework, but could also be useful information for upper-level high school students. Members of the general public will also find the material reliable and informative.—**ARBA Staff Reviewer**

Directories

818. **Woody Plants of the Northern Forest.** Jenkins, Jerry. Ithaca, N.Y., Comstock Publishing Associates/Cornell University Press, 2018. 61p. illus. maps. index. $16.95pa. ISBN 13: 978-1-5017-1968-4.

The majority of the 265 woody plants present in the Northern Forest region (the oak forests of the eastern United States and the boreal forests of eastern Canada) are illustrated in *Woody Plants of the Northern Forest*. High-resolution studio photos are annotated with detailed identification markers and notes. Content is divided into two general guides—one guide is to buds and twigs, and one is to leaves. The systematic section is arranged into five areas: evergreens, opposite buds, alternate buds, opposite leaves, and alternate leaves. The title includes a visual glossary, a gallery, two separate maps (winter and summer), and an index. Anyone interested in forests and their stewardship will find this title of use.—**Denise A. Garofalo**

Handbooks and Yearbooks

819. Claudino-Sales, Vanda. **Coastal World Heritage Sites.** New York, Springer Publishing, 2019. 602p. illus. maps. index. $139.00. ISBN 13: 978-94-024-1526-7; 978-94-024-1528-4 (e-book).

In this volume of the Coastal Research Library series, readers will find 84 World Coastal Heritage sites. Sites are located on all continents except Antarctica and occur as islands, gulfs, and barrier reefs in all oceans. In the preface, the author explains that as of January, 2018, there were 1,073 sites in 167 countries on UNESCO's World Heritage List (832 are cultural, 206 are natural, and 35 are mixed). This book focuses on the natural and mixed UNESCO World Heritage List sites that are coastal. Specifically, this book conveys information about the natural setting, biodiversity, and conservation challenges in all 84 sites in 48 countries. As the author points out, each of these sites is vulnerable to decay, is subject to social and economic conditions, and is endangered by the degradation and destruction associated with climate change and with rising sea levels resulting from global warming. The author hopes this resource can give "the coastal community of researchers and scientists elements to deal with the knowledge of the World Coastal Heritage, with the goal of finding means to think, participate, and contribute in its preservation." Each entry comprises several pages and includes an abstract, introduction, map, references, and a color photograph. The first 7 parts cover World Coastal Heritage sites on the continental coasts of Africa, Asia, Central America, Europe, North America, Oceania, and South America. The next 11 parts cover World Coastal Heritage sites in the islands, gulfs, and reefs of the Arctic Ocean, Atlantic Ocean, Indian Ocean, Pacific Ocean, Southern Ocean, Caribbean Sea, China Sea, Mediterranean Sea, North Sea, Red Sea, and East Indian Archipelago. Sites include such places as the Whale Sanctuary of El Viscaino, Mexico; Olympic National Park, USA; the Wet Tropics of Queensland, Australia; Gros Morne National Park, Canada; Aldabara Atoll, Seychelles; and the Giant's Causeway and Causeway Coast in the United Kingdom of Great Britain & Northern Ireland. Highly recommended.—**ARBA Staff Reviewer**

820. Duram, Leslie A. **Environmental Geography: People and the Environment.** Santa Barbara, Calif., ABC-CLIO, 2018. 320p. illus. maps. index. $94.00. ISBN 13: 978-1-4408-5610-5; 978-1-4408-5611-2 (e-book).

With complete candor, and sometimes humor, author Leslie A. Duram (Southern Illinois University, Carbondale) provides an updated look at the complicated relationship between people and the environment. Throughout her book, Duram describes numerous environmental problems, identifies what human actions (or inactions) caused these situations, and presents ideas that may increase public awareness and ultimately lead to mitigation of the conditions. The work is organized in three major sections focused on the following themes: how people affect the environment, how the environment affects people, and how natural resources can be sustainably managed. In each section, Duram introduces several complex environmental issues related to the theme and then supports the reader's understanding with case studies of real-world examples. Following the case studies, she includes descriptions of related environmental key terms and concepts. As an underlying global environmental issue, readers will find that the topic of climate change is examined throughout the book. Figures and black-and-white photographs support the text; however, they are not numbered or cross-referenced in the table of contents. A glossary, bibliography, and index are provided along with a list of suggested readings.—**Jennifer Brooks Huffman**

821.   **The Environmental Debate: A Documentary History with Timeline, Glossary, and Appendices.** 3d ed. Peninah Neimark and Peter Rhoades Mott, eds. Hackensack, N.J., Salem Press, 2017. 348p. index. $165.00. ISBN 13: 978-1-68217-551-4.

Containing excerpted sections of primary source documents ranging from the Genesis creation account up to the United States' withdraw from the Paris Climate Accord, *The Environmental Debate* ambitiously attempts to bring together texts that have shaped and influenced American environmental thought. The third edition of *The Environmental Debate* provides an updated list of documents related to environmental issues in the United States. Building on the previous edition, published in 2011, the third edition includes 185 documents, 17 of which are new to this edition, divided into 8 chronological sections. The documents address environmental issues related to population, land use and property rights, water availability and quality, energy, air quality and climate change, waste management, toxic and radioactive waste, wilderness and wildlife, and fisheries, oceans, and aquatic life. The newly added documents come with a focus on recent controversies and polarization surrounding environmental discourse, but with notable omissions. In particular, trends like the local agriculture movement and major ongoing news events like the danger of failing infrastructure in general and the Flint water crisis specifically seem worthy of inclusion. Even so, the breadth of coverage is impressive and *The Environmental Debate* provides a useful overview of environmental thought and action in the United States.—**Eric Tans**

822.   Issitt, Micah L. **The Environment.** Amenia, N.Y., Grey House Publishing, 2019. (Opinions Throughout History). $195.00. ISBN 13: 978-1-62817-593-6.

This title is the fifth volume in Gray House Publishing's Opinions Throughout History series. The author is Micah L. Issitt, an independent scholar whose other contributions to the series include *National Security vs. Civil and Privacy Rights* (see ARBA 2019, entry 263), *Immigration* (see ARBA 2019, entry 179), and *Drug Use & Abuse* (see ARBA 2019, entry 462). The title contains 28 chapters, each beginning with an introduction, followed by a list of topics covered, historical overview, the text of the document(s), conclusion, discussion questions, and bibliographic citations. Supplementary materials include a chronology, glossary, historical snapshots, and bibliography. Notable is the inclusion of copious black-and-white illustrations.

At the heart of this work are the documents that the respective chapters are built around, and they represent an eclectic mix. Some can be easily located in other sources, such as the excerpt from John Muir's *Our National Parks* or President Ronald Reagan's

Statement on Signing the Montreal Protocol on Ozone-Depleting Substances. Others seem an odd fit. For example, the first chapter "Pre-American Ecology: Environmental Alteration is Addressed (1100-1854)" is ostensibly about the relationship between American Indian peoples and the environment, yet the document that is utilized in the chapter is a 1985 article entitled "Thus Spoke Chief Seattle: The Story of an Undocumented Speech." This work conveniently packages a variety of primary source documents, including some that focus on particularly salient topics like climate change, and thus would prove useful for school libraries.—**John R. Burch Jr.**

823. **The Palgrave Handbook of Sustainability: Case Studies and Practical Solutions.** Robert Brinkman and Sandra J. Garren, eds. New York, Palgrave Macmillan, 2018. 871p. illus. index. $349.99; $269.00 (e-book). ISBN 13: 978-3-319-71389-2; 978-3-319-71388-5 (e-book).

This handbook is divided into four parts: Environment, Equity, Economy, and Regional and Local Examples. All efforts were made to create a comprehensive reference, though the editors acknowledge that this is a nearly impossible task to achieve. Part 1, Environment, reviews several topics related to environmental sustainability, examining situations around the world where this is challenging in such chapters as "Policy Design for Sustainability at Multiple Scales: The Case of Transboundary Haze in Southeast Asia" and "America's Path to Drinking Water Infrastructure Inequality and Environmental Injustice: The Case of Flint, Michigan." In the second part, Equity, articles reflect on social equity and what people are doing to address inequality. Taken together, they demonstrate the differences individuals can make as well as the importance of leadership from governments, nonprofits, and community groups. Chapters include "Methods for Integrated Sustainability Assessment: The Case of Small Holder Farming in Karnataka, South Africa" and "Japanese Women and Antinuclear Activism after the Fukushima Accident." The articles in the Economy section address the tension between economic growth and the pursuit of economic sustainability. Among the eleven chapters in the section are "Economic Development and Sustainability: A Case Study from Long Island, New York" and "We'd Like Our Clothes Back Please: Partnering with Consumers to Achieve Sustainability Goals." Case studies in the final section are drawn from examples worldwide, some of which have been successful and some of which have not yet achieved sustainability goals. Articles are authored by experts in the field and include notes and suggestions for further reading. An index rounds out the work. Highly recommended for academic libraries.—**ARBA Staff Reviewer**

824. **Principles of Sustainability.** Hackensack, N.J., Salem Press, 2017. 400p. (Principles of series). $165.00. ISBN 13: 978-1-68217-607-8; 978-1-68217-608-5 (e-book).

This volume is an excellent foundational resource for students and educators across many fields who are interested in the concept of sustainability. As part of the Principles of series, it offers nearly 150 alphabetical entries providing information on the basics of sustainability alongside related legislation, organizations, and events pertaining to it.

Entries generally include a brief summary definition, a list of related fields of study, a concise but instructive essay, and a bibliography. Entries may also include an illustration or other conceptual visualization (map, graph, etc.). The entry on hazardous waste, for example, includes a discussion on environmental problems, methods for handling waste, and U.S. legislation. It also lists such relevant fields of study as government, international relations, ecology, and environmentalism. An entry for Pandemics displays the Pandemic

Severity Index in addition to information on the spread of infectious diseases, the environment and pandemic disease, and other topics. Other entries in the volume address beach erosion, controlled burning, Earth Day, glacial melting, land-use policy, renewable energy, superfund legislation, water conservation, and more.

Several appendixes follow the entries and include the "U.S. Federal Laws Concerning the Environment" (e.g., Endangered Species Act of 1973), a "Directory of U.S. National Parks, Major World National Parks and Protected Areas," "Environmental Organizations" (e.g., the Environmental Defense Fund), a "Sustainability Timeline," and a listing of "Key Figures in Sustainability" (e.g., Edward Abbey, Jacques Cousteau, Rachel Carson). The volume also includes an extensive bibliography. Recommended for school libraries.—**ARBA Staff Reviewer**

Water

Handbooks and Yearbooks

825.   **The Oxford Handbook of Water Politics and Policy.** Ken Conca and Erika Weinthal, eds. New York, Oxford University Press, 2018. 712p. index. $150.00. ISBN 13: 978-0-19-933508-4.

There are approximately 332.5 million cubic miles of water on Earth. Of that amount, roughly 96.5 percent is saline water found primarily in oceans and seas. Only 2.5 percent is freshwater, but more than two-thirds of that is inaccessible due to being stored in glaciers or ice caps. The freshwater that is available is not evenly distributed, thus there is intense competition within and between countries to secure the water resources that are required. Ken Conca, Professor of International Relations at American University, and Erika Weinthal, Professor of Environmental Policy at Duke University, are joined by 49 scholars from around the world, whose specialties lie in such diverse fields as agriculture, environmental studies, geography, hydrology, political science, and sociology, in producing an impressive handbook that explores the varying ways that water politics manifests itself globally. It contains 27 essays organized in 7 sections: Introduction; Poverty, Rights, and Ethics; Food, Energy, and Water; Water and the Politics of Scale; Law, Economics, and Water Management; The Politics of Transboundary Waters; and The Politics of Water Knowledge. Each essay concludes with an extensive list of references. There are separate author and subject indexes that facilitate access to the contents of this work. This valuable interdisciplinary reference tool is a must-purchase for academic libraries.—**John R. Burch Jr.**

37 Transportation

General Works

826. **Handbook of International Trade and Transportation.** Bruce A. Blonigen and Wesley W. Wilson, eds. Northampton, Mass., Edward Elgar, 2018. 704p. index. $350.00. ISBN 13: 978-1-78536-614-7; 978-1-78536-615-4 (e-book).

The editors of this handbook argue that little has been published at the intersection of transport—the movement of goods—and international trade—the costs associated with those goods. This volume attempts to address that gap, and is designed for scholars who may be quite familiar with one area but not the other, as well as advanced undergraduate and graduate students seeking introductions to the combined fields. Fifty authors, from nearly twenty different countries and NGOs, contributed to twenty-three chapters, divided into six parts. These parts investigate data and modeling techniques regarding global trade patterns; costs associated with trade and international borders; agents of trade, particularly in importing and exporting; logistics, bureaucracy, and their costs; infrastructure, ports, and vessels; and trade and transportation networks, especially focusing on pricing, alliances, and cartels. The writing is quite technical, occasionally incorporating complex equations regarding costs and trade efficiencies. All chapters have extensive references, and the volume identifies important prior work and areas needing future research. Researchers and reference librarians trying to find specific trade data will most appreciate chapter 3, which describes several major trade data sources, and highlights the variations that lead to errors and incompatibilities when comparing data drawn from these various sources. The volume will be most useful in specialized collections around economics, transportation, trade, and international relations; its cost will likely preclude its addition to more general collections.—**Peter H. McCracken**

Ground

827. Cagle, Gregory A. **Scenes from an Automotive Wonderland: Remarkable Cars Spotted in Postwar Europe.** Jefferson, N.C., McFarland, 2018. 231p. illus. index. $39.95pa. ISBN 13: 978-1-4766-7178-9; 978-1-4766-3053-3 (e-book).

Author Gregory Cagle grew up the son of a diplomat in Europe in the 1950s and he loved cars. He acquired a camera and began taking pictures of unusual cars as they traveled around the continent. This book is a collection of his photographs with extremely informative descriptions and a history of each car. Many of the cars photographed "in the wild" (meaning not in a museum, but on the streets being used) are very rare today, and some were rare then. All are European cars, mostly German and Italian, save for three cars from the United States.

The book is divided into sections with whimsical names such as Lilliputia (microcars), Mundania (average cars), and Built for Speed (racing cars). Each car gets one or two black-and-white photographs on the right-hand page with some description of where and when the photo was taken. The left-hand page has a few paragraphs explaining the history of the car, and perhaps the history of the automaker as well. The writing is very personable and engaging. The book is very well researched and has quite an extensive bibliography and a useful index. There are a dozen color photos in the center of the book. Recommended for public libraries.—**Robert M. Lindsey**

828.   Garratt, Colin. **An Illustrated Encyclopedia of Locomotives: A Guide to the Golden Age of Train Engines from 1830 to 2000.** Leicestershire, England, Lorenz Books, 2018. 256. illus. index. $25.00. ISBN 13: 978-0-7548-3439-7.

Prolific author Colin Garratt, whose many works include *The World Encyclopedia of Locomotives* and *The Complete Book of Locomotives,* relays nearly two centuries of locomotive history, illustrated by seven hundred photographs. The coverage is international, with locomotives from Asia, North America, Europe and the United Kingdom, and Australia. The long coverage timeframe means that the book traces the evolution in locomotives from steam power to diesel and electric, from the very first locomotives to today's Eurostar and the Japanese bullet train. Textboxes provide specifics for more than one hundred locomotive designs. This book is a great value at $25.00. With its reliable information and high-quality photographs, it is recommended to the circulating collection of public libraries.—**ARBA Staff Reviewer**

829.   **Seattle's Freeway Revolt: A Directory of Historical Resources http://cdm16118. contentdm.oclc.org/cdm/singleitem/collection/p15015coll6/id/8732.**   [Website]   Date reviewed: 2019.

Seattle's Freeway Revolt: A Directory of Historical Resources gathers information on many years of civic wrangling over the development of freeways through the city of Seattle, Washington. Users can print, download, or explore the PDF directory online, finding copious information on the planning, legislation, activism, and more related to the Pacific Northwest community's response to the mass consumption of the automobile and the infrastructure it demanded. The directory serves as a gateway to key information in books, news articles, maps, photographs, plans, and other documents that provide insight on the long battle between freeway planners and a range of activist groups, culminating in business and home preservation, a heightened regard for public transit, and drastically reduced freeway development. While not offering direct access to primary documents, the directory makes it easy to know where they are and how to access them, and provides valuable context to the documents and the story of the revolt. A table of contents, to which users can return from any page in the PDF, organizes the directory into nine sections beginning with a Historical Overview that describes a backdrop of late 1960s social activism and presents a quick Timeline of Key Events. Key Resources offers an annotated bibliography of a range of transportation-focused primary publications, such as research reports, monographs, in-depth articles (e.g., the ten part Freeway Revolt series published in the *Christian Science Monitor*), and more. Key Planning Reports offers a chronological listing of freeway network proposals and related national legislation such as the Seattle Planning Commission Comprehensive Plan (1956) and the Federal Aid Highway Act of 1956. Newspaper and Periodical Articles lists cited articles chronologically and include date, publication, page, headline, author, and other information. The section also includes tips for locating articles. Primary Resources lists and describes original collections from a wide range of archives. These repositories (such as the Seattle Municipal Archives or the Rainier Valley Historical Society) host photographs, maps, audio recordings, videos, and other materials. Users can discover navigation tips and tools alongside contextual information like dates, material types, and archive contact information. An excellent Narrative Timeline provides generous detail as it organizes events into Early Milestones; Route Refinements, Funding, and Early Resistance; Hearings, Rallies, Media and More, etc. Organizations Involved in the Revolt displays a lengthy list of Community Associations, Environmental Groups, Civic Groups, and others, showing how both prominent and grassroots organizations/individuals connected with the freeway revolt. Information in this section generally includes operating years, key persons, and mission. The directory is an excellent tool to use in finding information on the historical, geographical, political, and other facets of this successful revolt in Seattle.—**ARBA Staff Reviewer**

Water

830.   **Dutch East India Shipping between Netherlands and Asia 1595-1795 https://resources.huygens.knaw.nl.das.** [Website] Free. Date reviewed: 2019.

Setting sail at the dawn of the 17th century, the Dutch East India Company (VOC in original Dutch) made thousands of voyages to Asia as it dominated trade in this region. This site offers data and contextual information regarding two centuries worth of Dutch East India Company shipping voyages to various ports in Asia. The original site uses the Dutch language, but some key information can be translated to English. The homepage offers general background and site navigation information, as well as a link to a general VOC glossary with definitions of terms found throughout the project. Users can search terms in the original Dutch, or download a one hundred page PDF, also in Dutch (It does not appear that the glossary can be translated). Under the Resources header, users can access data tables from the To Travel link on the left side of the page. Tables display numbered voyages (1–8194) alongside Name of Ship, Master, Date/Place of Departure, Arrival at/Departure from Cape, and Date of/Place of Arrival. Users can click on the Details field to view the full voyage profile, which may also include numbers on board, tonnage, and other particulars (e.g., "The AMSTERDAM was set on fire near Bawean 11-01-1597"). Users can conduct an advanced Search or Search all Resources from the homepage as well. The Digital Publications link accesses the full digital book *Dutch-Asiatic Shipping in the 17th and 18th Centuries,* which supplies the narrative from which the tables are derived. The book can be examined as a PDF or in other formats, and an English translation is accessible on the left side of the page. From here, users can click on any chapter title link to navigate. The book is rich with detail and explores topics such as "The Cape of Good Hope" and "The Seaway to Asia: Route, Duration and Risks." It contains several appendixes, a generous bibliography, and four indexes listing ship, personal, and geographical names as well as subjects.—**ARBA Staff Reviewer**

Author/Title Index

Reference is to entry number.

Subject Index

Reference is to entry number.

Relevant lib, 344

Shaping the campus conversation on
    student learning & experience, 279

Transforming libs to serve graduate
    students, 280

COLLEGE SPORTS
Playing grounds of college football, 436

COMIC BOOKS. *See also* **GRAPHIC
NOVELS; MANGA**
Critical survey of graphic novels: heroes
    & superheroes, 2d ed, 641
Critical survey of graphic novels: manga,
    2d ed, 642

COMMUNICABLE DISEASES
Infectious diseases in context, 2d ed, 769

COMMUNICATION
Careers in media & communication, 493
Careers in social media, 491
Emoji dict [Website], 484
Emojipedia [Website], 485
Oxford ency of intergroup
    communication, 486

COMPUTER PROGRAMMING
Principles of programming & coding, 797

COMPUTERS
Computer History Museum [Website], 796

**CONSOLIDATION AND MERGER
OF CORPORATIONS**
Mergers & acquisitions from A to Z, 4th
    ed, 58

CONSTITUTIONAL LAW
American values & freedoms, 226
Bill of Rights, 2d ed, 232
Equal protection, 234
Mapping first amendment conflicts
    [Website], 233

CONSUMER BEHAVIOR
SAGE hndbk of consumer culture, 17

CONSUMER GUIDES
Weiss Ratings consumer box set, 67
Weiss Ratings investment research gd to
    bond & money market mutual funds, 63

Weiss Ratings investment research gd to
    exchange-traded funds, 64
Weiss Ratings investment research gd to
    stock mutual funds, 65
Weiss Ratings investment research gd to
    stocks, 66

CONSUMPTION (ECONOMICS)
SAGE hndbk of consumer culture, 17

COPYRIGHT
Licensing digital content, 3d ed, 316

CORAL REEFS
Allen coral atlas [Website], 805

CORPORATION LAW
Research hndbk on the hist of corporate &
    company law, 236
Research hndbk on the regulation of
    mutual funds, 237

CORPORATIONS
Project toxic docs [Website], 815
Thomas register [Website], 78

CORRECTIONAL INSTITUTIONS
American prisons & jails, 240

COSMETICS
Plant-based beauty, 767

COUNTERCULTURE
Woodstock archive [Website], 168

CRAFTS
Quilt index [Website], 512

CRIME
American violence [Website], 245
Encyclopedia of rape & sexual violence,
    241
Gangland, 242
Gun violence & mass shootings, 255
Handy forensics answer bk, 251
InSight crime [Website], 248
K-12 school shooting database [Website],
    249
Lexis Nexis community crime map
    [Website], 250
Mass shootings in America, 243
Medieval murder map [Website], 195

Encyclopedia of unaired tv pilots, 1945-
2018, 657
Glamour girls of sixties Hollywood, 651
Single season sitcoms of the 1990s, 669
Television series of the 1990s, 677
Television series of the 2000s, 678
Twilight Zone ency, 656
Whedonverse catalog, 670

TENNIS
Wimbledon archive [Website], 442

TERRORISM
Defining documents in American hist: the
legacy of 9/11, 172
Palgrave hndbk of criminal & terrorism
financing law, 253
Terrorism, 256
Terrorism worldwide, 2016, 238
Terrorism worldwide, 2017, 239

TEXAS
Handy Tex. Answer bk, 30

TEXTILE STUDIES
Handbook of textile culture, 515

THEATER
Complete bk of 1930s Broadway
musicals, 681
Decades of modern American drama, 684
Historical dict of African American
theater, 2d ed, 682
Shakespeare's Globe archive [Website],
683

THEISM
Theism & atheism, 687

TOLSTOY, LEO (1828-1910)
Critical insights: Leo Tolstoy, 614

TOURISM INDUSTRY
Handbook of Human Resource mgmt in
the tourism & hospitality industries, 86
SAGE hndbk of tourism mgmt, 80

TRANSGENDER PEOPLE . *See also*
SEXUAL MINORITIES
Documents of the LGBT movement, 458
Transgender, 454

**TRANSGENDER PEOPLE - HEALTH
AND HYGIENE**
Transgender health issues, 764

TRANSNATIONAL CRIME
Transnational crime & global security, 257

TRANSPORTATION
Handbook of intl trade & transportation,
826
Seattle's freeway revolt [Website], 829

TRAVEL
Amsterdam, 11th ed, 144
Central Asia, 7th ed, 138
China, 6th ed, 139
Essential Italy, 140
Essential Switzerland, 141
Fast talk Latin American Spanish, 2d ed,
550
Fast talk Spanish, 4th ed, 551
Fordor's Barcelona with highlights of
Catalonia, 6th ed, 142
Gold panning Colo., 441
Manhattan nobody knows, 143
Michelin gd: Chicago, 145
Michelin gd: main cities of Europe, 146
Russia, 147
USA, 10th ed, 148

TRINIDAD & TOBAGO
Historical dict of Trinidad & Tobago, 41

TURKEY
Historical dict of Turkey, 4th ed, 39

TYPOGRAPHY
Fonts in use [Website], 537

UNIDENTIFIED FLYING OBJECTS
UFO ency, 3d ed, 422

UNITED KINGDOM
Portable antiquities scheme [Website], 150

UNITED NATIONS
UN digital lib [Website], 380

UNITED STATES
America & its rivals, 19